EAT UP
NEW ZEALAND
THE BACH EDITION

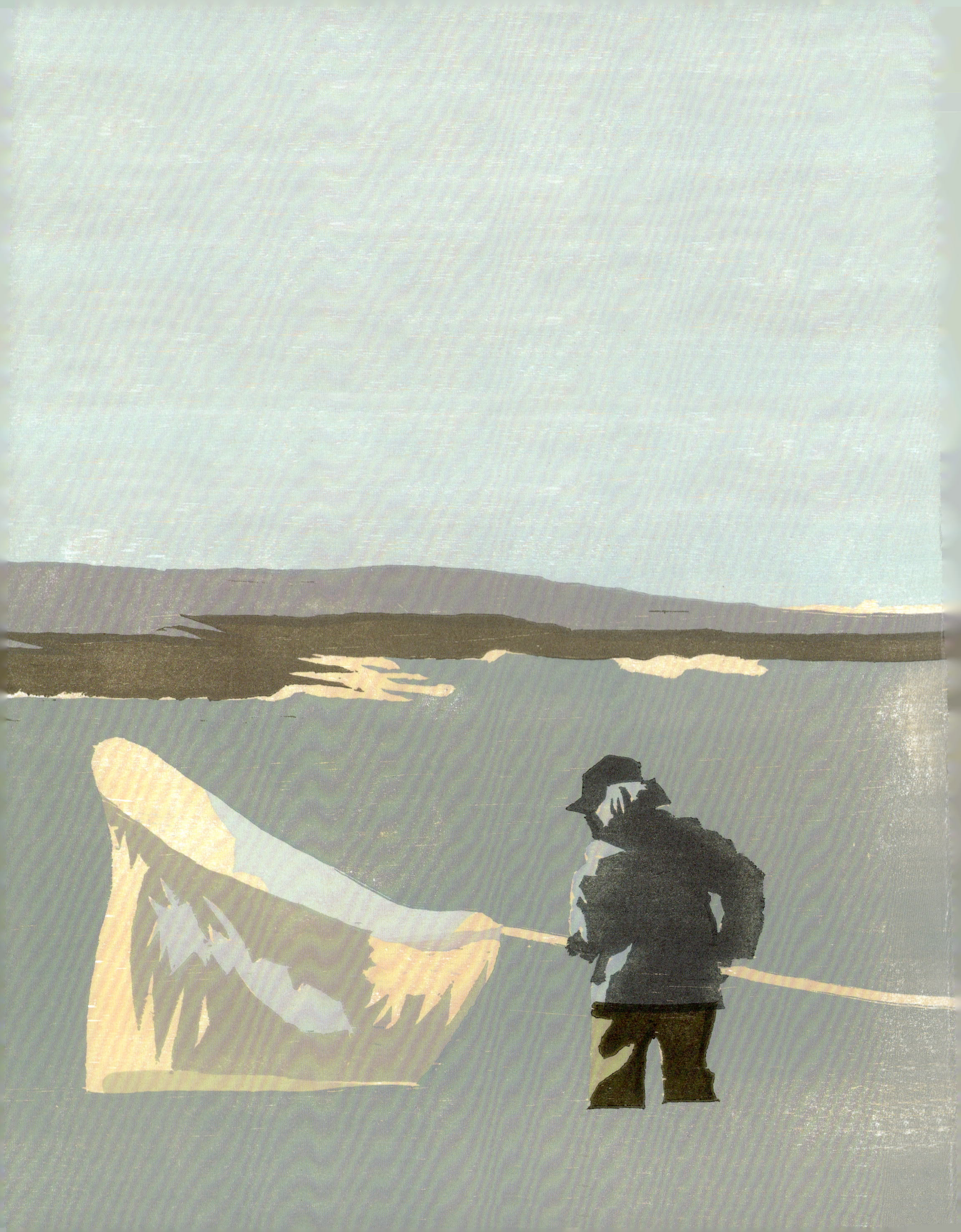

AL BROWN
EAT UP
NEW ZEALAND
THE BACH EDITION

RECIPES BY AL BROWN WITH HAYDEN SCOTT

PHOTOGRAPHY BY JOSH GRIGGS

ALLEN&UNWIN
SYDNEY・MELBOURNE・AUCKLAND・LONDON

First published in 2017
This revised edition published in 2023

Recipes and text © Al Brown 2017, 2023
Photographs (unless otherwise credited on page 458) © Josh Griggs 2017, 2023

All rights reserved. No part of this book may be reproduced or transmitted in any form or by any means, electronic or mechanical, including photocopying, recording or by any information storage and retrieval system, without prior permission in writing from the publisher.

Allen & Unwin
Level 2, 10 College Hill, Freemans Bay
Auckland 1011, New Zealand
Phone: (64 9) 377 3800
Email: auckland@allenandunwin.com
Web: www.allenandunwin.co.nz

83 Alexander Street
Crows Nest NSW 2065, Australia
Phone: (61 2) 8425 0100

A catalogue record for this book is available from the National Library of New Zealand.

ISBN 978 1 99100 645 5

Design by The Gas Project
Artwork on page 2 by Geoffrey Notman

Typeset in Tiempos and Brandon Grotesque
Printed by C&C Offset Printing Co. Ltd, China

10 9 8 7 6 5 4 3 2 1

TO MY DAUGHTERS, ALICE AND CONNIE—

MAY GOOD FOOD AND GREAT COMPANY ALWAYS BE CLOSE AT HAND!

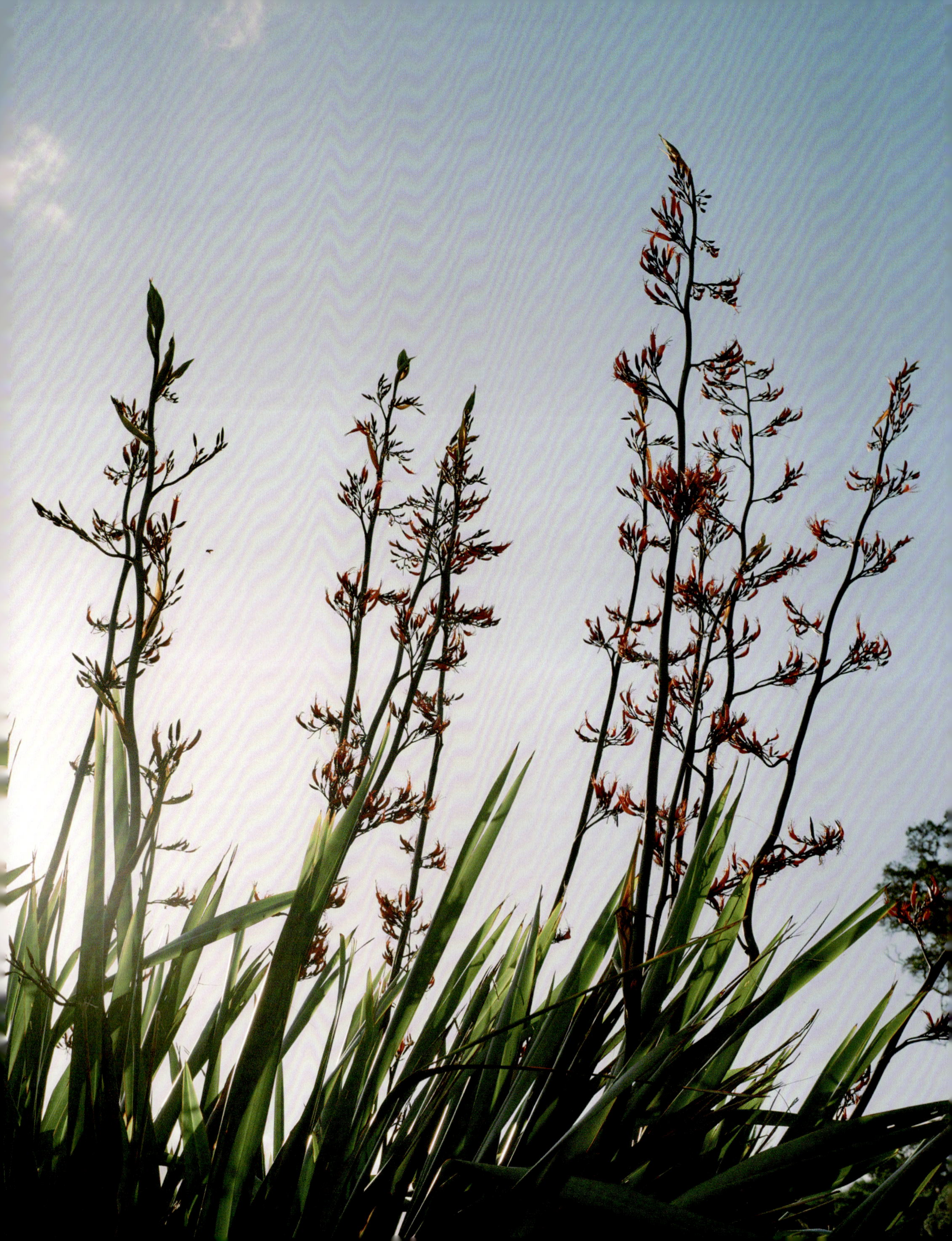

Contents

Introduction
Kupu whakataki—p.11

Seafood
Kaimoana—p.35

Bird
Manu—p.143

Animal
Mīti—p.191

Vege
Huawhenua—p.267

Pudding
Purini—p.313

Whipped cream
Kirīmi pāhukahuka—p.341

Baked
Ō tunu—p.363

Preserves
Kai whakapounamu—p.403

Go-tos and garnishes
Hokihokinga me ngā kīnaki—p.437

Index
Kuputohu—p.452

Let us give thanks
He mihi—p.462

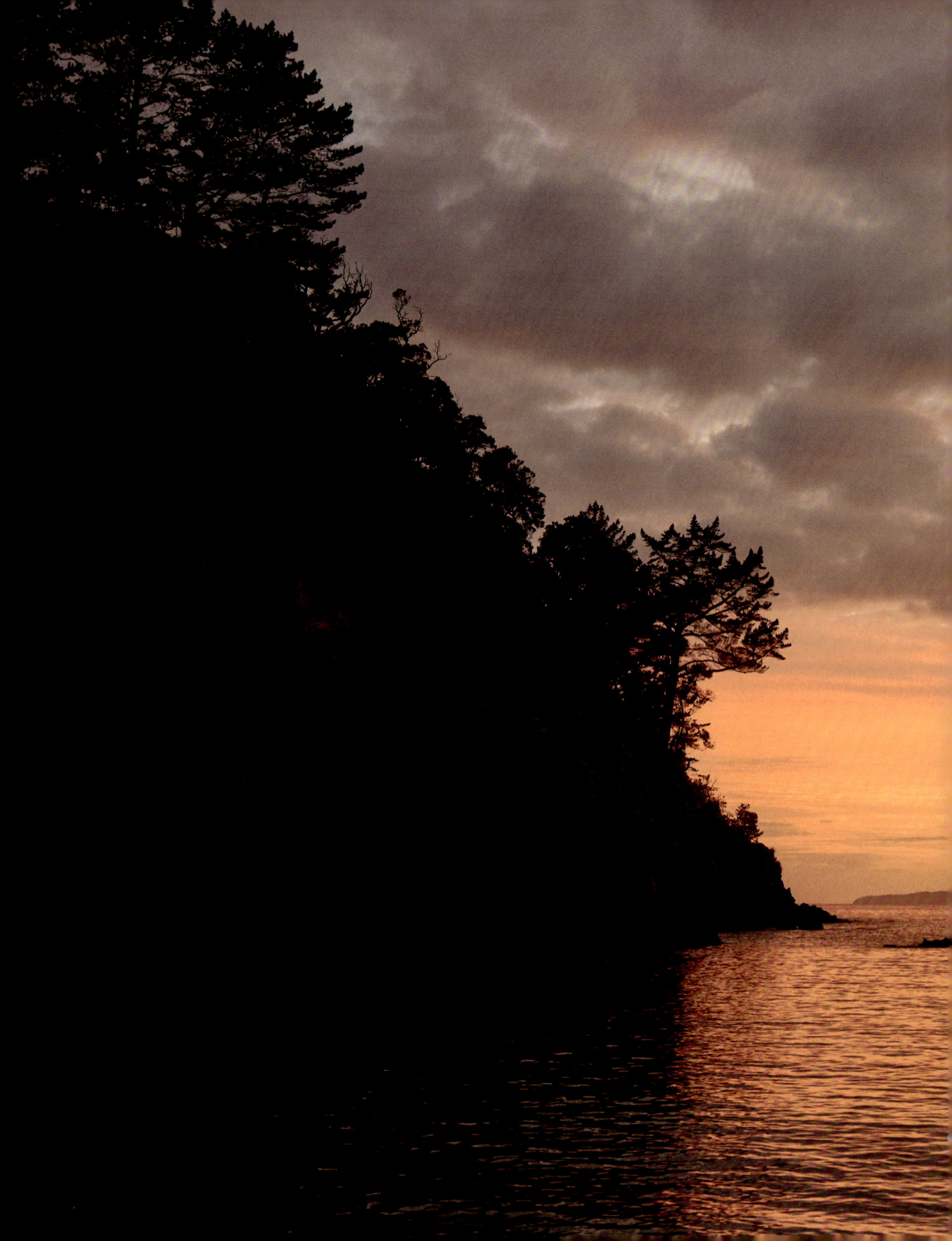

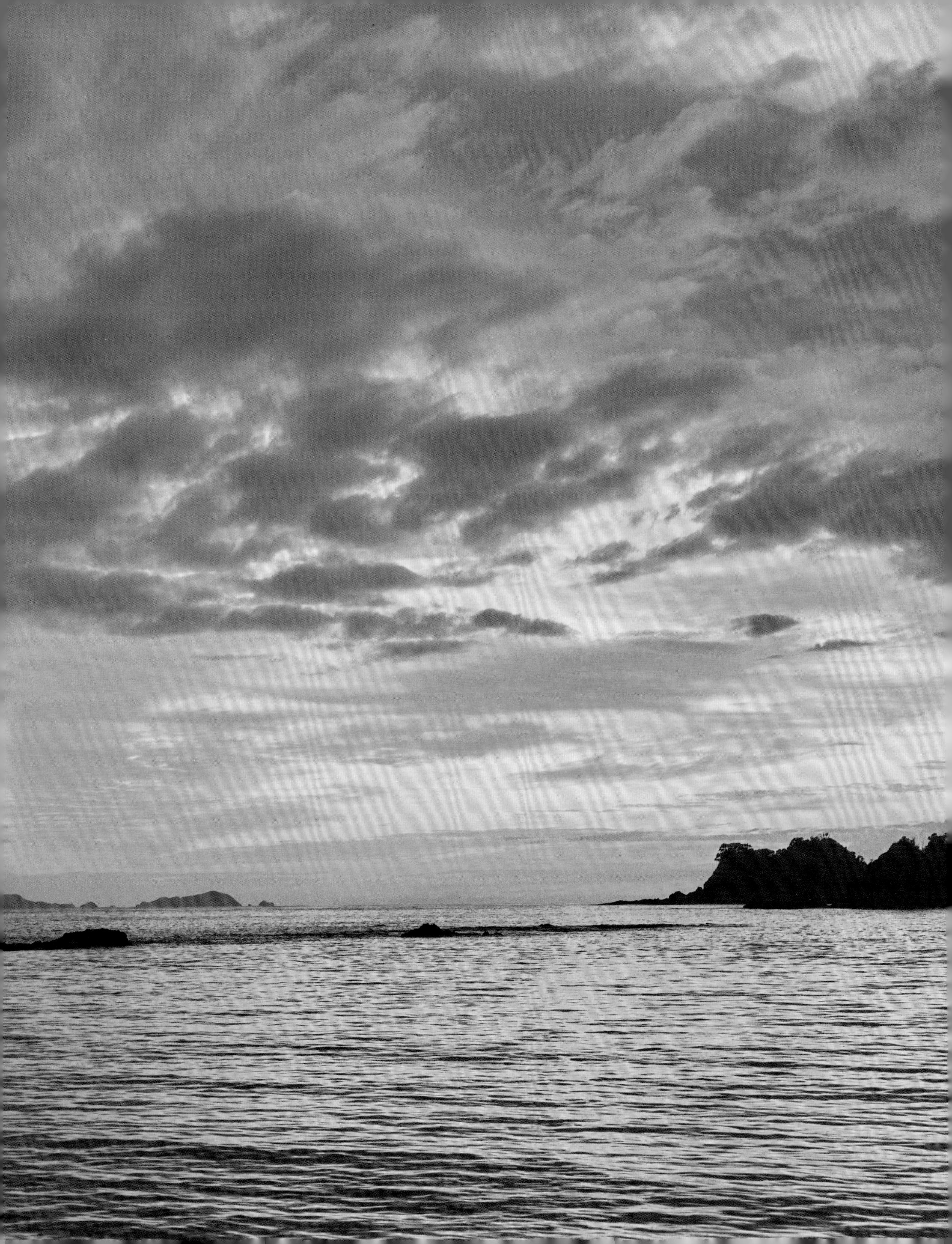

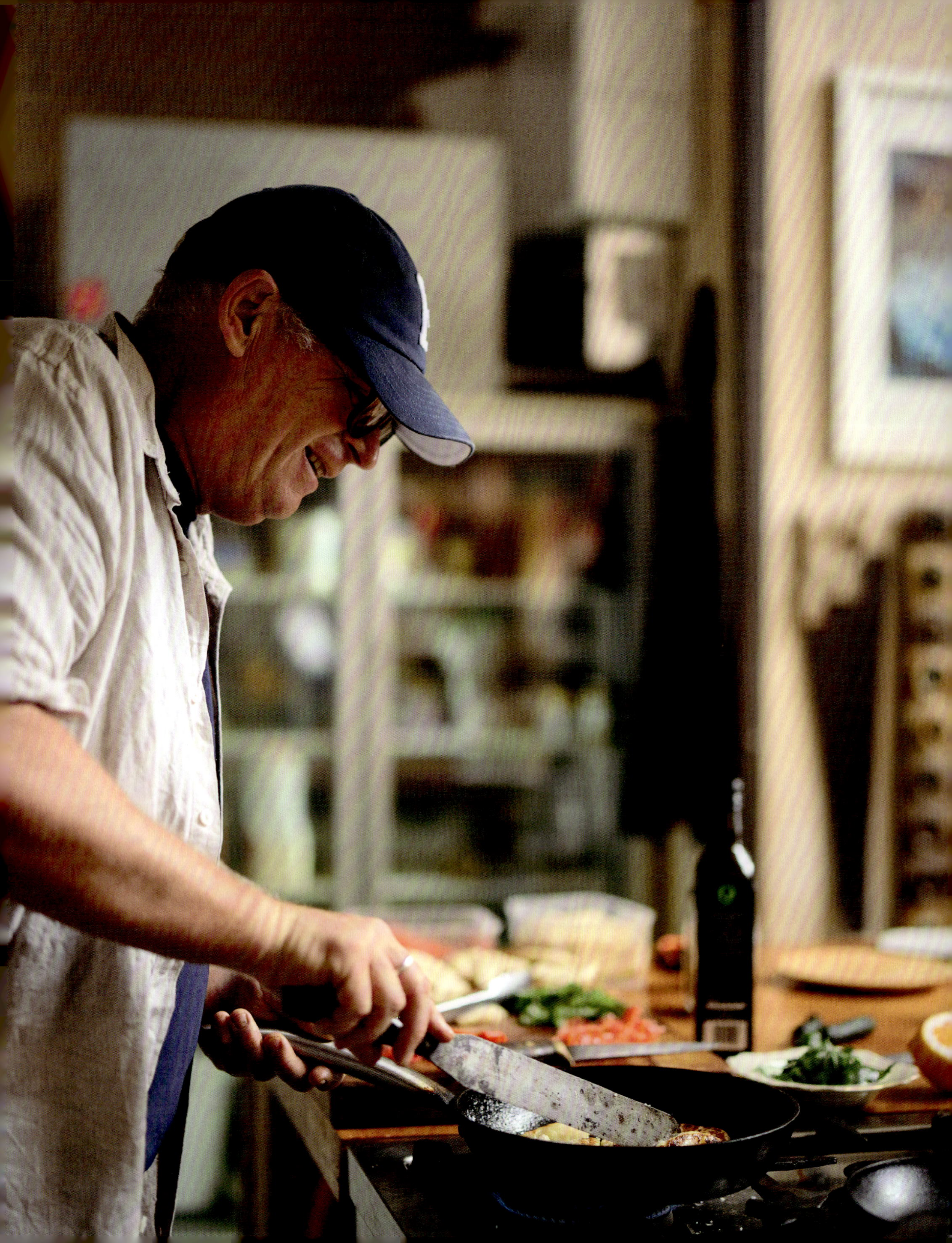

Introduction / Kupu whakataki

In Baches We Believe

The word 'bach' is such an evocative word. When I hear it or see it written in any form, a wave of joy always washes over me. It's a funny old word, as it doesn't really look the way that it is actually pronounced.

There are two schools of thought on where the word 'bach' originated from. The first is that it's shortened from the words 'bachelor pad', which is okay, but it doesn't fit the narrative in my head of what a bach represents.

'Bachelor pad' feels a little lonely, sad and disingenuous, and feels more like the opposite of the vision I get in my mind when I hear the word 'bach'. The other theory, and the one that I prefer, is that it is derived from a Welsh word meaning small or little. The early Welsh immigrant miners used the term 'ty bach', which means a small house or outbuilding.

Both work, so I guess just go with whatever theory suits you. You may of course have another idea of where the word came from. And for all you folks from the deep south of Aotearoa, please don't be too put out, just substitute the word 'bach' with your favoured term of 'crib' (which I also dig) wherever you see fit. 'Kōpuha' is the reo name for bach, and that has got a beautiful ring to it too.

As it turns out, I'm actually writing this at my bach up north. It's not quite considered the 'far north', but it's a little north of Whangārei with east coast pōhutukawa-tree vibes.

I spend as much time up here as I possibly can. All of January and any holiday periods see a steady procession of family, friends and whānau come and go. The dynamic changes with each new bunch of arrivals. A week of my two daughters and their friends sees me become camp dad, hanging out with a posse of twenty-somethings: feeding, watering, continuously telling them to put their shit away or yelling 'KEEP IT DOWN' as my tolerance batteries begin to run low. Next it might be a few close friends in for a spell, which is super easy as these kind of folks know what is required to keep bach life floating on easy street with everyone pitching in.

It is a special time of the year when fun and good times reign supreme. I wouldn't have it any other way, exhausting as it is sometimes. The rest of the year, while friends and

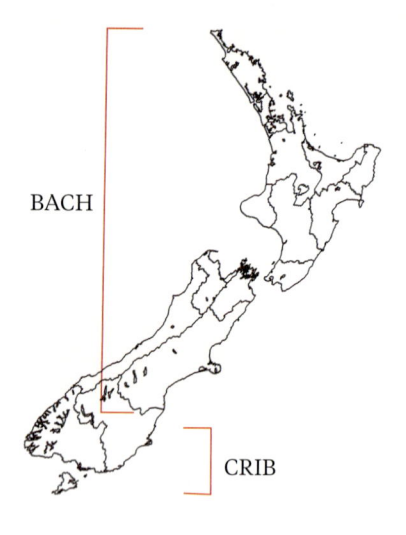

It is said that the dividing line between the terms 'bach' and 'crib' is the Waitaki River, but the word you use may also depend on your heritage—or your vintage.

family come and go, I actually spend a lot of time up here just by myself. I rent a small apartment in downtown Auckland, so I consider my bach my actual home. The juxtaposition couldn't be more pronounced. While I love city living, I need to balance the sirens, late-night screams and rubbish trucks with solitude, nature and sunsets. It's critical for my mental game to get away from the masses, with the silence and the tranquillity giving me peace of mind.

When I was young, our holidays were spent at the Castlepoint campground, in an old wooden caravan nick-named 'The Pie-Cart'. We had a bunch of friends who also had baches out at Castlepoint, so I would have been three or four years old when I was first introduced to these special dwellings that have had an indelible and enduring effect on me for as long as I can remember.

Recollections and memories from that long ago are sketchy at the best, but I swear I can still close my eyes now and recall in quite a bit of detail the Falloons', the Maxwells' and the Whites' baches dotted along the foreshore of this extraordinary location on the east coast of Wairarapa. These three, along with the other 100-odd baches there, are still standing in that beautiful salty wind-blown weathered environment. No two baches are the same. Most are devoid of maintained gardens, with just the odd shrub or native tree, their front and back yards all covered with thick spongy kikuyu grass that feels like you are walking on nature's duvet.

The once-bright colours from the original paintwork are now all washed-out blues, greens, reds, yellows and oranges, with the old nail-heads bleeding that deep golden rust colour down the weatherboards, linking them all together like a coastal badge of honour.

I find baches such sensory dwellings . . . from every angle their individual unique character is evident. And not just from the outside, but also from the inside looking out. Small paint-chipped windowsills, often hard to open, frame the views that have been etched into your mind since you first looked out as a child.

The layouts inside are each original in their simple and humble form. Small modest bedrooms, narrow hallways, cramped bathrooms with paltry washbasins and inadequate shelves for storage are all signs of a bygone era that we still fondly think of with nostalgia.

Living rooms with mismatched old armchairs and couches that are not particularly generous in size and are always ranked from least comfortable to most comfortable. If you are lucky enough to find yourself in the family favourite, you won't be surprised to find it occupied after you pop out of the room for a second or two. Over the years I have witnessed many a squabble in that arena, along with fights over the favourite pillow, favourite mug, best beach towel . . .

Bookshelves with old encyclopaedias, reference books on native fauna and wildlife, stacks of old *National Geographic* mags and an abundance of well-worn paperbacks with swollen pages from inadvertently having had a cup of 'instant' spilled on them.

There are often old dressers, too good to discard and perfectly adequate for the bach, their hard-to-open drawers filled with a plethora of boardgames with missing components, jigsaw puzzles with missing pieces, multiple packs of cards with missing jokers etc., and notepads with faded 500 scores and doodles from years ago. Time capsules of summers and winters past.

It won't come as too much of a surprise, but the room that inspires the most affection for me is, of course, the kitchen.

The kitchen is the space in any abode (old or new) that embodies and welcomes all the senses.

The familiar sight of a faded Formica kitchen table anchoring the room, the whistle of the old kettle, the sweet smell of fresh baking escaping from the worn-out seals of an old Shacklock electric oven, the feel of that favourite teacup clasped between your hands first thing in the morning; and, of course, the taste of some sort of fritter fresh from the skillet or being passed about with the first round of G&Ts in the late afternoon.

I often speak of the importance of people and place and how those two simple ingredients—who you are with and where you are physically located—play such a significant role in our most vivid and influential food memories. Bach kitchens evoke that narrative. The kitchen of course is the heart and the hub of the bach: from a pre-dawn early morning cuppa to those welcome impromptu visits throughout the day, as friends drop in unannounced.

I love the way we forgo our regular lives of formality and structure: lunch often gets eaten mid-afternoon, which then pushes out dinner well into the night. Once the dishes are washed, dried and put away, the kitchen table then hosts the obligatory late-night card game or some version of Scrabble. The whisky bottle will usually make an appearance, along with half a packet of chocolate biscuits or the last few pieces of ginger crunch, which—while still tasty—by now have unfortunately lost their 'crunch'!

And that's the thing: baches seem to bring a liberating sense of freedom, where life's regular timing is simply ignored or paid no mind. The somewhat rigidity of formal everyday life, with its protocols and established ways, is replaced with a spirit of generosity, nourishing hospitality, and tolerance for bouts of harmless lawlessness.

I think it's the mis-fitness and informality of baches that seems to strike a chord in our collective character as a country. There is a sense of letting go, and a comfort that comes with familiarity and simplicity.

There is something almost sacred that most baches embody, which I believe stems from the original family or whānau who built or moved the dwelling to its location. As the decades pass, each new generation and the descendants of these original families continue to add layer upon layer of that spiritual DNA to each humble residence.

'If these walls could talk' is the line that always comes to my mind when I'm lucky enough to be staying in a classic bach.

It has been fun updating and re-releasing *Eat Up* as the 'Bach Edition'. I get another bite of the cherry as it were. I have always been super proud of the 'original', and, even though it was released in 2017, the recipes still ring true to me. The vision was always to celebrate where we had come from with our food, and where we are currently.

I have penned five cookbooks over the past fifteen years or so. I recently got them all out and spent an afternoon reading some of the text, looking at the photos and going over many of the recipes. I found it cathartic, as well as reassuring. My philosophy around how I like to cook and serve hasn't changed much at all in the past twenty years. I have never really been swayed by trends that become popular for a time, then come and go over the years.

I am always inspired by clever food, no matter where it originates from. But I believe there is a fine line between clever food and overly worked pretentious food, which I think is more about the personal ego of the chef who created the dish. As in 'Look at me, I am so clever' rather than looking at it from the diners' perspective: Is it tasty? Is it generous? Is there textural contrast in the components? Are the layers of flavour balanced? Was it a satisfying plate of food that left you feeling *I would, or I could, order that again?*

To be totally honest, I don't believe I'm an overly talented chef. What I do know is that I understand the fundamentals of a well-executed dish. I am relatively confident in my ability to cook a lot of decent-tasting food, and I also think I have a good handle on, or understanding of, what people enjoy—and why.

The two main drivers when I am cooking are generosity and fun. They are kind of like insurance policies around how the dish will be perceived. Both of these components are at the basis of my thinking with every dish that I think up and work on. I like to trust there is some creativity in there too, but being generous and having fun is what I think eating is all about.

Bach food is all about that . . . it is not complicated, it doesn't require a trip to a speciality food store or taking out a second mortgage to purchase a bloody sous vide machine, etc. It is about feeding loved ones who are famished with food that is simple, fresh, delicious and, thank goodness, sometimes a little down and dirty.

I have added another fifteen or so new recipes that I wrote in the bach up north, mostly over the past six months. They are all approachable, doable and deliciously edible, as are all the originals. I like to make a bunch of pre-holiday preps to have on hand to save time and make things a little easier.

That way, when push comes to shove you have things like vinaigrettes, mayos, spice mixes and crunchy garnishes to add texture to salads and the like, and chutneys and relishes at hand to help smooth the way and make you look like you know what you are doing, even when you are two gins and a chardonnay into it!

Josh Griggs, our crazy talented photographer, has added some more beautiful pics; Gary Stewart has tweaked the original design and added some cool bach-centric fluff; while my wingman, Haydo Scott, has ridden shotgun, testing recipes and organising photo shoots, etc.

Anyway, I hope you love it, share it, use and abuse it. Always keep in mind that nothing pleases a cookbook author more than a wine-splashed, sauce-splattered and oil-stained cover!

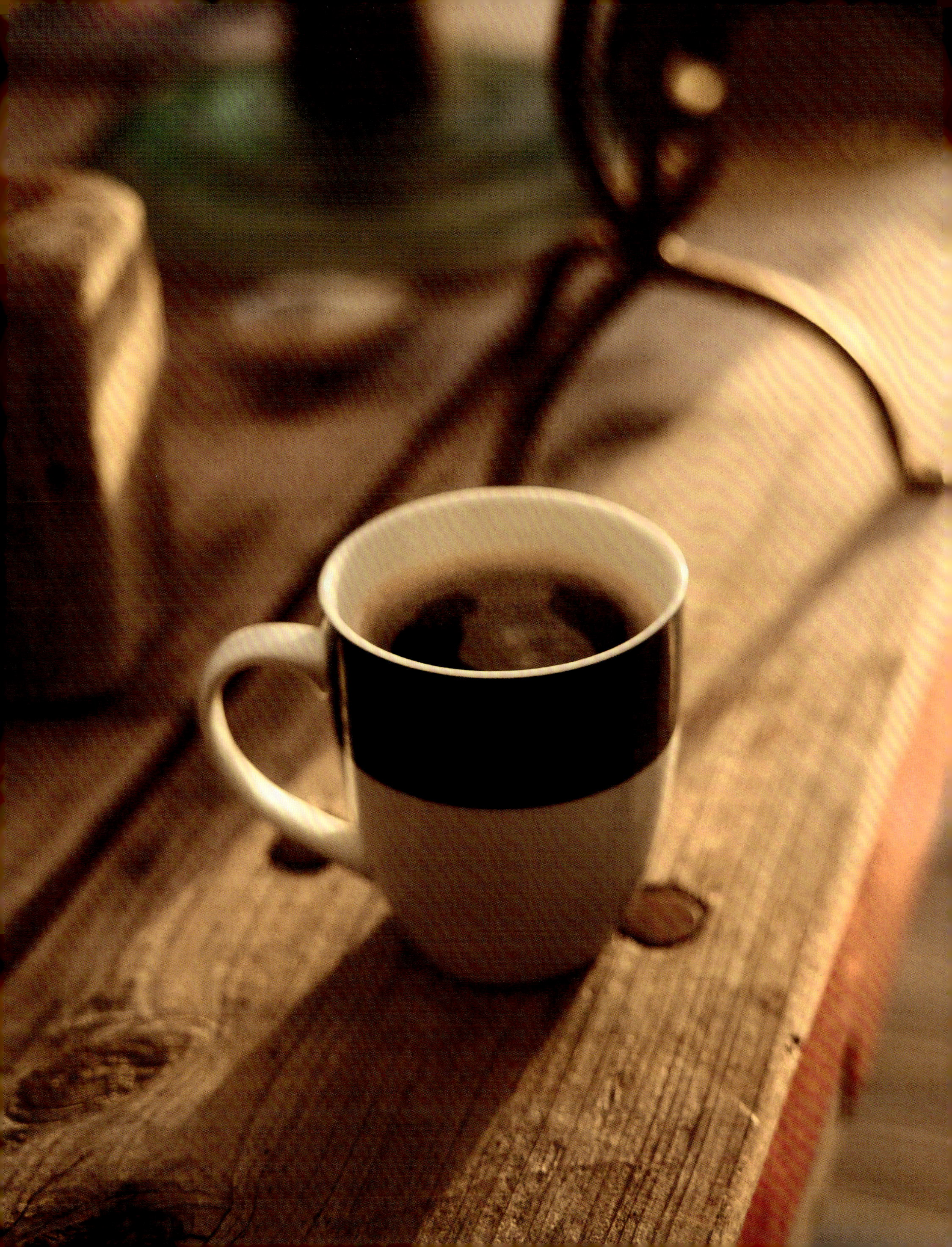

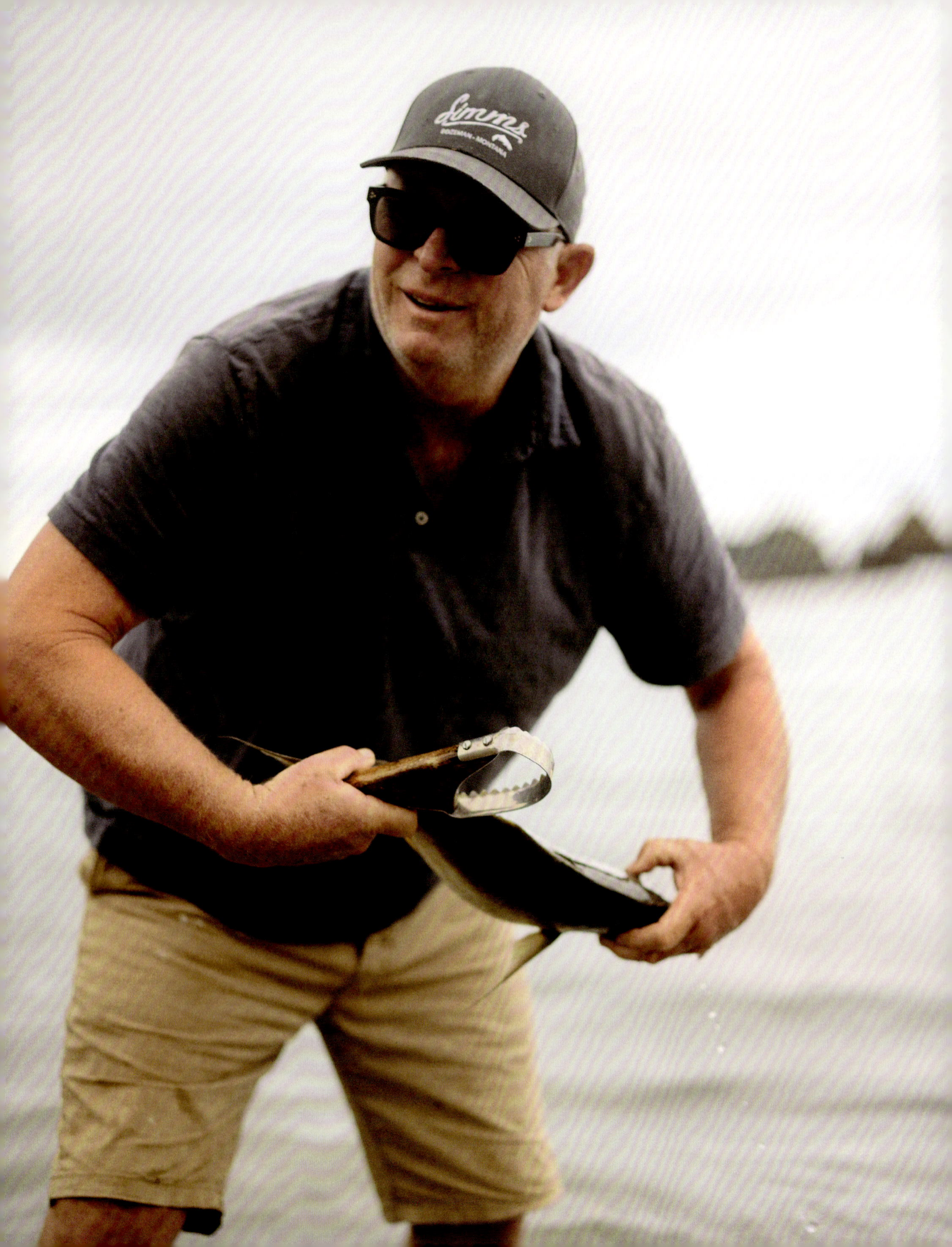
Simms

Is There Such a Thing as Kiwi Cuisine?

I am often asked what the cuisine of our country is, and I still don't really have a succinct answer. What I do know is that, having made cooking my career, I feel very fortunate to have been part of New Zealand's extraordinary culinary adventure for more than 30 years, during which time our food culture has evolved dramatically with the influence of cuisines from all over the world.

I'm sure that our strong desire to travel, and our adventurous spirit and keenness to explore every corner of the globe, have played a substantial part in shaping where we are today, food-wise. So many young people in our country go on an OE (overseas experience) or gap year, and I have always felt this must be partly responsible for the remarkable change that has occurred in a very short space of time. Travel opens our minds and exposes us to so many possibilities—we've learned a lot along the way. If we can grow grapes, surely we can grow olives? Tick. If we can grow olives, what about pine nuts? Tick. Saffron? Tick. Truffles? Tick. Wasabi? Tick. Oysters? Tick. 'Light bulb' moments. If it crosses our minds, there is a better than average chance that it can probably be realised. The riches that we now produce in this little country of ours at the bottom of the world are becoming almost embarrassing.

Travel, the internet and all the other platforms available have opened up every conceivable style of cooking, old and new, for our talented cooks and chefs to explore. Because of this, I doubt we will ever have a 'New Zealand cuisine' as such—and I don't actually think that's a bad thing. Old World countries created their own styles of food and cuisine because for centuries people didn't have the ability to travel and explore, and they were relatively closed off from the rest of the world. Being a New World country, and not bound by tradition, gives us a real sense of freedom with our cooking. We can essentially 'magpie' from everywhere. I think our trump card in the world's culinary deck, though, has to be our proximity to an abundance of products and produce. The fact that we are a small country is a massive advantage with regard to the volume of flavour we can get into our cooking, because it takes very little time to get fresh produce from the land or sea into our pans and pots and onto our plates.

It has never been lost on me how fortunate I am to have grown up in New Zealand and also to have chosen to cook for a career. I grew up on a sheep and cattle farm northeast of Masterton in rural Wairarapa. Although I would describe my mother as a pretty bog-standard cook, I still have a bunch of terrific food memories truly etched into my eating DNA. My love of 'well' cooked lamb with dark, rich gravy made from dripping, flour, pan scrapings and second-hand water from the boiled vege, along with roasted root vegetables, homemade mint sauce and crab-apple jelly is still as vividly strong today as it was when I was a child. Mum's baking repertoire was not that varied or expansive, but she could make a half-decent banana cake, and her ginger crunch is still the best I've ever tasted. Mum also produced her share of preserves each year. Her pickled beetroot was spot on, and I remember her stewed peaches, which we ate like a summer treat in winter. The memory of Mum's peach chutney, slathered on quarter-inch-thick slices of cold mutton and stuck between slices of white bread, will be with me forever.

I think I have a duty here to touch on the subject of pavlova, because it seems that, over the generations, home cooks up and down the country have been judged on their ability to make the perfect example of New Zealand's favourite and most famous celebratory dessert. I will confess that Mum's pav was a 'fingers crossed' affair from year to year: some were magnificent examples of exactly what a pavlova should be, while others needed quite a lot of whipped cream and fruit to give them the pass mark. Looking back, I learned a lot from each of Mum's pav attempts, and those cooking lessons are still relevant today—sometimes (maybe often) food doesn't turn out how you want it to, or how you thought it was meant to.

My interest in cooking started when I was probably seven or eight years old. I was hardly obsessed, but certainly it was a hobby for me, and I gave it a nudge every couple of weeks.
I am still not certain whether it was the creative process that I was drawn to, or the fact that I had a sweet tooth. I've always had that sweet tooth and, with no dairy or sweet store down the road, my sugar fix became a DIY situation via the *Edmonds Cookery Book*, New Zealand's most iconic and bestselling recipe book. I always thought I was a bit of a dab hand at pikelets, pancakes and the like, but the pages that had the most spills on them were from the Sweets section at the back. Chocolate fudge, toffee, coconut ice and hokey pokey were all good friends of mine.

I have previously described New Zealand's food scene of the past—say, 40- or 50-odd years ago—as a bit of a culinary wasteland. There is some truth in that, but on reflection I think I was being a bit harsh. From the mid-nineteenth century, European food culture arrived with the first European settlers. I'm pretty sure the British would be the first to admit that their culinary heritage of the past couple of centuries has not garnered much of an international reputation—to be brutally honest, it has been the subject of ridicule for as long as I can remember. (Unfairly so these days, I might add, with serious hero chefs of mine such as Marco Pierre White, Fergus and Margot Henderson, Rick Stein, Jamie Oliver and, of course, food magician Heston Blumenthal well and truly burying those myths and mistruths decades ago.) Here in New Zealand, whether we enjoyed them or not, the following were staples for most of us: shepherd's pie and cottage pie, roast beef and Yorkshire pudding, devilled kidneys, beef olives and onion gravy, Scotch eggs, bubble and squeak, toad-in-the-hole, and puddings like spotted dick, tapioca, and stuffed baked apples with custard.

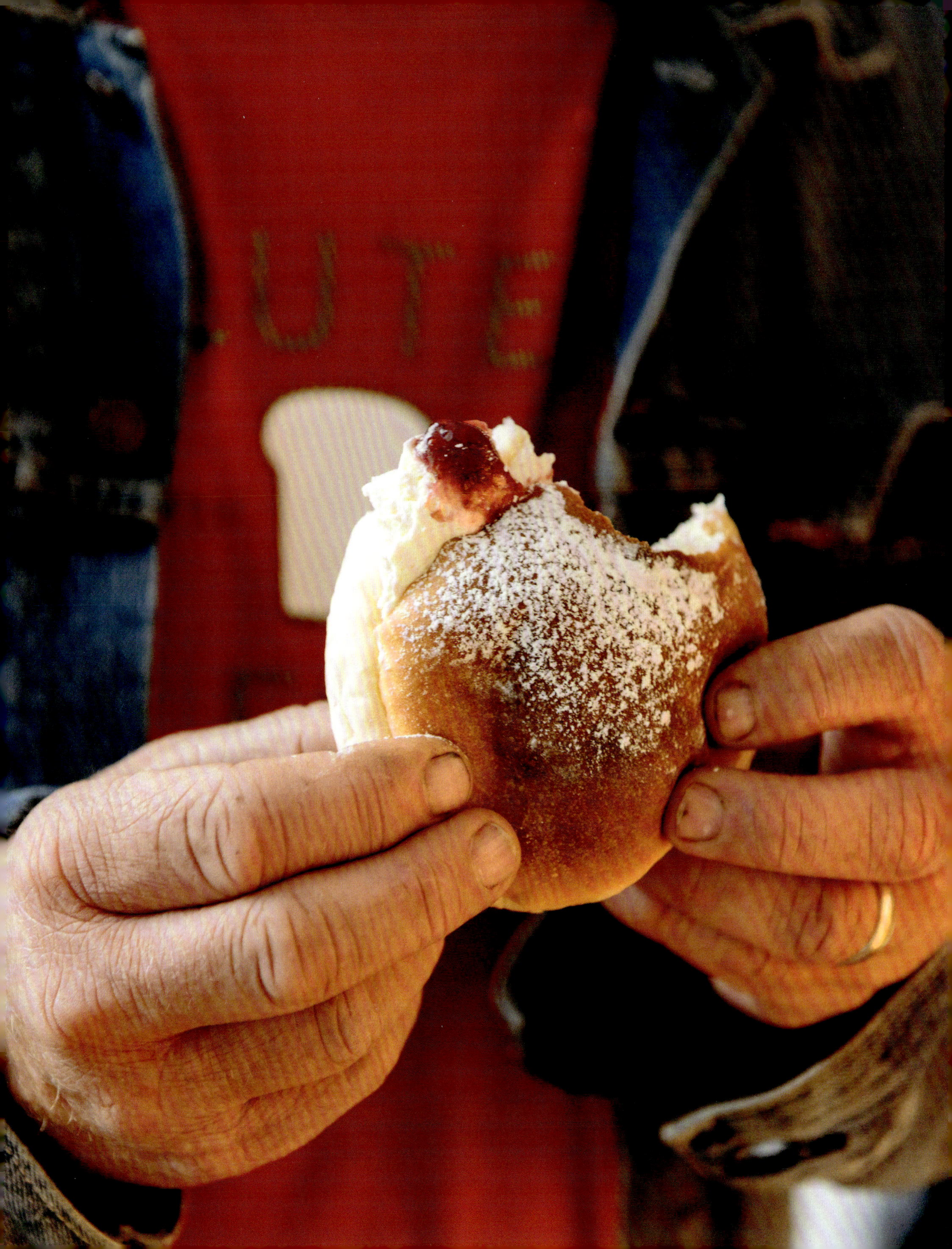

Don't get me wrong, there is a lot of good eating in those dishes. Take a well-made cottage pie, for instance: savoury mince cooked down slowly with vegetables and rich stock, counterbalanced with a layer of soft, creamy whipped potato, all covered in a bubbling blanket of melted cheese, where pieces of cheddar have crept up the corners to become dark brown, salty and crisp. To most of us, cottage pie will never sound as exotic or fascinating as dishes like bouillabaisse, paella or rabbit pappardelle. That doesn't matter. Food is not, and never will be, a competition. We might wax on about a duck confit we ate years ago in a small bistro in Paris, but I can guarantee you that there will be folk from France who have travelled to our fair shores and recall in detail something called 'tuatua fritters', which they ate in a beachside bach somewhere in a province they still can't pronounce even vaguely correctly. A perfectly executed example of any dish, whether it's from here or somewhere more exotic, will always be delicious. I for one will continue to cook, devour and cherish the old-country heritage dishes that helped to shape my upbringing.

We are all blessed to live here in New Zealand, and I say this even though I am not a particularly religious man. As I often mumble to anyone who cares to listen, 'If you live in this country, you have essentially won Lotto Division One.' That we live in paradise is not by any stretch an overstatement. Sure, we can all find things to moan and grizzle about, but mostly they are just First World problems, which, in the scheme of things, pale when you look around at where we live and what is on offer right on our doorsteps.

It's not hard to appreciate things like the extraordinarily diverse natural landscape that we call home. A coastline so stunning it never fails to take my breath away. Imposing mountains and volcanoes. Then there's our beautiful rivers and lakes—

although they might still look in relatively good shape, we'd only get a C– at best for the way we're caring for them, in my view. It goes without saying that they need to be treasured and cared for by every New Zealander; we need to understand how darn precious they are to all of us. I truly believe that they are the veins and the vital organs of our country. Our exquisite farmland is also in need of a serious care stocktake. Enough dairy, I say— and before you hard-working cockies get your hackles up, yes I do understand the significant contribution that dairy makes to keeping this country afloat. But tourism is banging on that door with a loud and forceful knock. If we can work out the infrastructure and the most desirable way to show off this utopia of ours to the rest of the world, while letting Mother Nature be the headmistress, things will work out for the best.

The growing diversity of people in this country is also cause for celebration. Those from other countries and cultures who are lucky enough to call New Zealand home add wonderful layers of interest and goodness, and that ultimately makes our country a far more stimulating and interesting place to live. As I've said, I'm very proud to be cooking wonderful, nostalgic Kiwi-centric dishes, but it's the almost exhaustive explosion of new products grown here in New Zealand that really blows my mind. Our cuisine is a mix of old favourites combined with new, exciting flavours and ideas from elsewhere. We have the freedom to use influences from all over the globe, and this, coupled with our amazing fresh produce, is creating unique new food, fresh and full of flavour.

Despite my love for our food culture, there's not a whole lot that I actually enjoy about writing cookbooks. I could be wrong, but I have a hunch that most cookbook authors feel the same degree of overwhelming angst at what lies ahead when they take on such a sizable project. It is quite the undertaking, and

I take my hat off to anyone hitting the keyboard late into the night or very (very) early in the morning, as in my case.

Writing any sort of book is always a very personal affair, and it's often a roller-coaster of emotions with a degree of soul-searching at times. There are several factors involved in bringing a cookbook to fruition. What weighs the heaviest on my mind is the thought of creating, testing and then writing 100-plus recipes. Each one has to be written in such a precise instructional style, which I often think seems somewhat counterintuitive to the creative process and freedom of expression that comes with the actual cooking of food.

Having said that, I do really love cookbooks. I don't have a massive cookbook library, but I add about a half dozen or so to my collection each year. I am quite particular about them, and I usually buy only those that give me more than just a bunch of glossy photos, instructions and measurements. The minute I pick up a cookbook, I need to connect with it. Things like design, look and feel are important to me, as these things offer up the first glimpse of the personality behind the words. However, it is the writing and the words that ultimately draw me in. A quick read of a few recipe introductions will give me a starting point from which I can begin to understand the philosophy, reasoning and convictions behind the author's food. I have always felt it is such a private endeavour, sharing not just recipes, but also the author's thoughts and considerations around how the food between the pages came to be. It's only then that the recipes will begin to come alive, enlightening, inspiring and, in many cases, influencing the way I view food and cooking. That is what I admire the most about great cookbooks, and that is what I try to keep front of mind when I am tasked with writing another one myself.

Over the years I have read a swag of books written by successful chefs. These great chefs have often published dozens of recipe books throughout their careers. I have a number of them taking up space on various bookshelves at work and at home, and they're great if I'm trying to reference something or to get a bit of inspiration when I'm creating a menu for one thing or another. More interesting to me, though, is getting a read on the person behind the food. I enjoy discovering what their influences have been, why they opened their respective restaurants, and their general philosophy on life.

Many of these chefs start by painting a vivid picture of what was often an idyllic culinary upbringing. I sometimes feel a bit insecure when these wonderful chefs and cooks look back and reflect on their cooking and food memories from their formative years. Stories of helping their papa make fresh pesto from the bushels of the brightest green basil leaves that grew between the rows of sun-warmed, vine-ripened tomatoes, or kneeling on the high chair to help their grandmother press slices of perfectly ripe pear into crisp, golden pie shells filled with homemade frangipane always sounded so wonderfully exotic. I used to wonder how I could possibly become a successful chef if I hadn't grown up surrounded by generations of family members preparing, cooking and passing down the hundreds of years of experience from their particular cultures and cuisines.

But, while I may not have grown up with memories like the scent of Mama's minestrone wafting down the driveway in greeting as I hopped off the rural school bus, I do have great food and cooking recollections. While they may not be as romantic as those of the chefs who I have admired for as long as I can remember, what I do now understand is that, no matter what culture or country you grow up in, your food memories play an important role in your life.

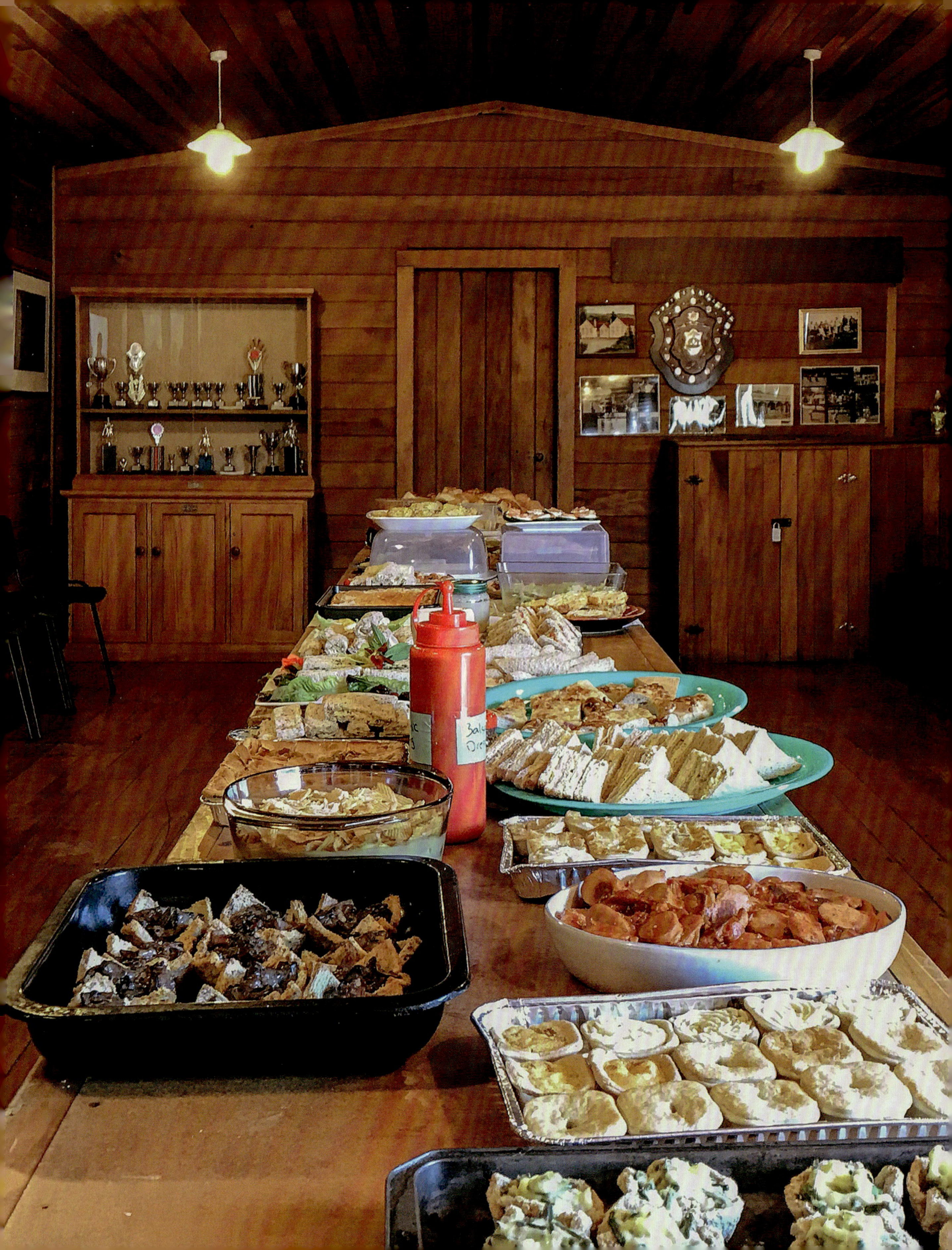

In the pages of this book I have attempted to acknowledge and celebrate where we in New Zealand have come from and where we are now. It's kind of 'Old Testament, New Testament'. It's about honouring the classic dishes that have for many years anchored the tables in our homes, our rural halls, our woolsheds, rest areas and picnic spots. They are classics for a number of reasons, but mainly because they were made and made again, improved, honed and refined for decades. They help recall memories, flood us with nostalgia and generally make us feel good. The other dishes in this book are my personal take on where we are today, using the remarkable amount of new products and produce available to us.

I would describe my cooking as relatively pared back; some would possibly say laid-back. I like to draw inspiration from anywhere and everywhere and never want to be put in a box. Some recipes are a bit posh and take a few steps. Others are down and dirty, where I have channelled my inner bogan. I have included recipes that have been shared with me over the years, and I even hunted down an old girlfriend's mother for her bran muffin recipe.

This is definitely a cookbook that you can use every day, and I encourage you to give a few of the recipes a nudge. Even if you're someone who sees kitchens as mystical places where food magically appears, please read, reminisce and take in the beautiful photography that I trust has captured New Zealand's character, personality and grace, using our delicious food as a means of this expression.

There is much to celebrate.

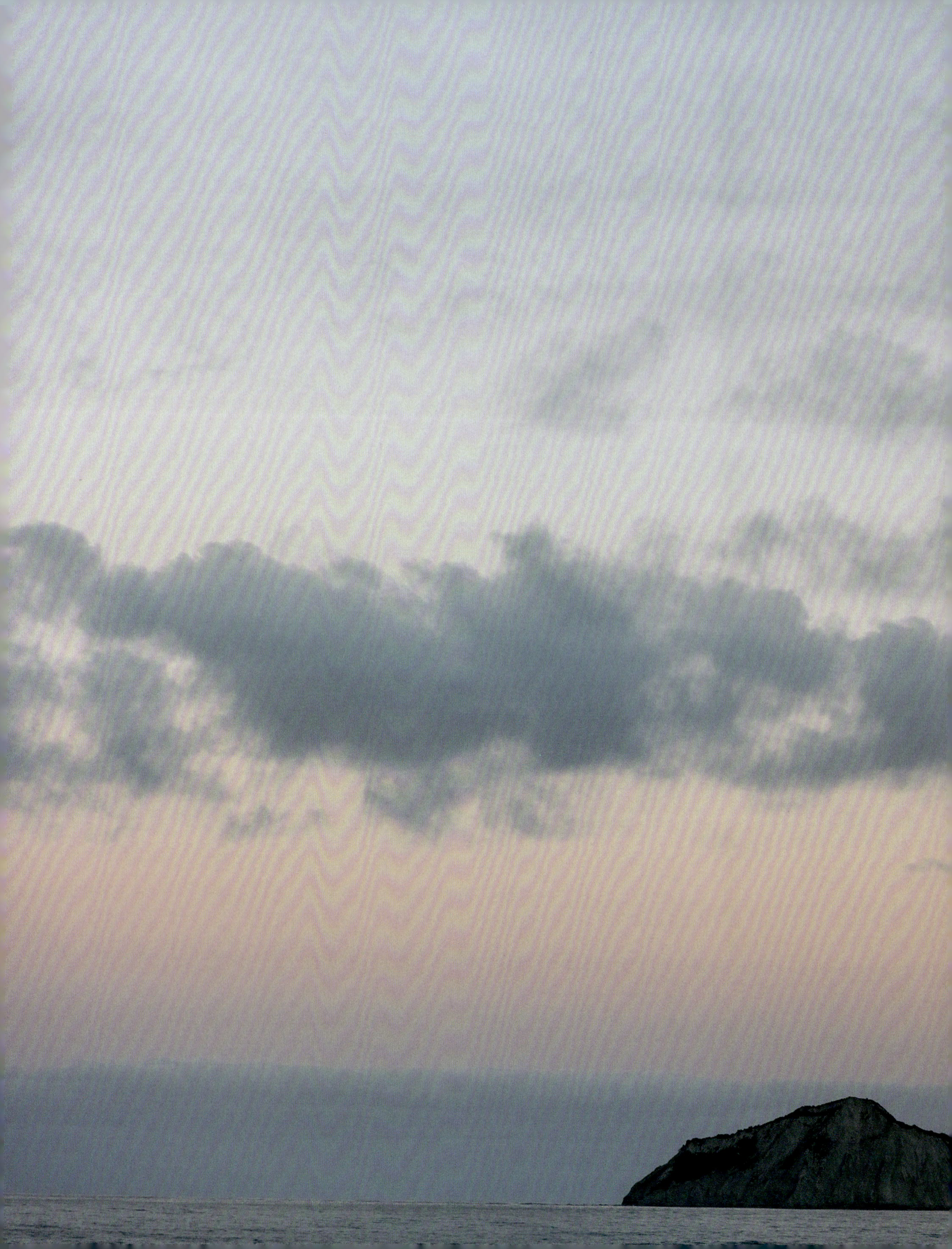

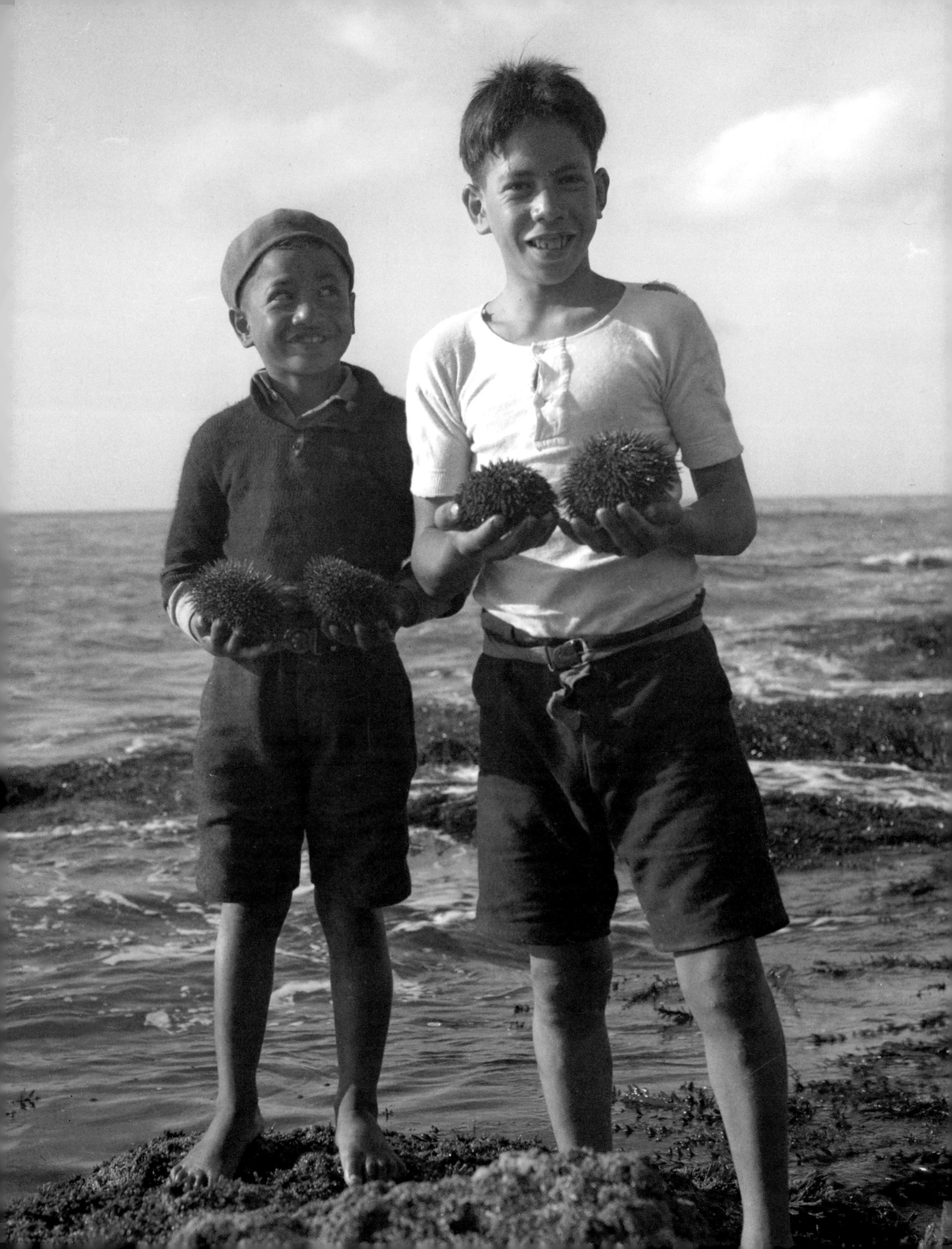

SEAFOOD

KAIMOANA

36 EAT UP NEW ZEALAND: THE BACH EDITION

Trevally sashimi with ponzu and truffle oil

Trevally is my favourite fish to eat raw. It also eats beautifully simply cooked and smoked. I have made this ponzu recipe for more than 25 years. It comes from the Duane Park Café in New York City, where I used to work. There, ponzu was served with crisp skate wing, and this was one of the restaurant's signature dishes. The addition of serving the sauce with a few drops of truffle oil comes from good friend and great chef Hamish Brown, who has been involved in a couple of extraordinarily good Japanese-inspired restaurants in London, Roka and Zuma. I would never have thought to combine ponzu and truffle, but trust me, it is a delicious combination.

Serves 8–10 platter styles, or 6 as a starter

PONZU SAUCE
½ cup (125 ml/4 fl oz) rice wine vinegar
½ cup (125 ml/4 fl oz) soy sauce
¼ cup (60 ml/2 fl oz) red wine
1½ tablespoons dried bonito flakes
2 pickled plums (available at most Asian stores)
1 lime, quartered

TO SERVE
600 g (1 lb 5 oz) fresh trevally fillets, thinly sliced
½ avocado, destoned and flesh diced
1 spring onion, thinly sliced
½ red chilli, thinly sliced
½ tablespoon sesame seeds, toasted
few drops truffle oil
1–2 limes, cut into wedges

To make the ponzu sauce, place all the ingredients in a small saucepan and place over medium-low heat. Bring up to a very slight simmer, then simmer for 15 minutes to let the flavours infuse. Remove from the heat and strain through a fine sieve or, better still, a sieve lined with muslin (cheesecloth). Cool to room temperature, then refrigerate.

When ready to serve, line a platter with the thinly sliced trevally. Spoon over liberal amounts of the ponzu sauce; the trevally should be basically soaking in it. Scatter about small cubes of avocado, followed by the spring onion and chilli. Finish with a sprinkle of toasted sesame seeds and a few drops of truffle oil here and there. Serve with lime wedges for squeezing.

Salmon crudo with apple and fennel

'Crudo' is an Italian raw-fish preparation. Essentially, it's the same as Japanese sashimi. However, it's much more subtle and delicate. With no wasabi or soy to accompany it, crudo is more about the good-quality olive oil and what that brings to the flavour of the fresh fish. I have used my lemon and fennel olive oil with this raw salmon, producing a really pared-back and subtle result.

Serves 6 as a starter

300 g (10½ oz) fresh salmon fillet, pin bones removed
zest of 1 orange
⅓ cup (80 ml/2½ fl oz) Al Brown & Co Lemon and Fennel Infused Olive Oil or extra-virgin olive oil
1 Granny Smith apple, cut into matchsticks
fennel fronds or dill sprigs, to serve
tart apple syrup (available at most supermarkets), to serve
flaky sea salt and freshly ground black pepper

Prepare the salmon. With your sharpest knife, cut the salmon into slices as fine as possible. If your knife skills leave a little to be desired, place your fillet in the freezer for 20 or 30 minutes to firm up, which will make the slicing much easier.

Place the slices in a small container, and once you have a layer of salmon slices covering the bottom, using a microplane or a fine grater, finely grate over some of the orange zest. Repeat with more layers of salmon and orange zest. Finally, pour over the olive oil and move the container about a bit so the oil gets in between the layers. Cover with clingfilm and refrigerate for a few hours or preferably overnight.

When ready to serve, carefully lay out the marinated salmon on a large platter. Scatter about the apple matchsticks, followed by the fennel fronds or dill. Drizzle over some apple syrup, then finish by seasoning with flaky sea salt and freshly ground black pepper. Serve with a bunch of forks to let people help themselves.

SEAFOOD 39

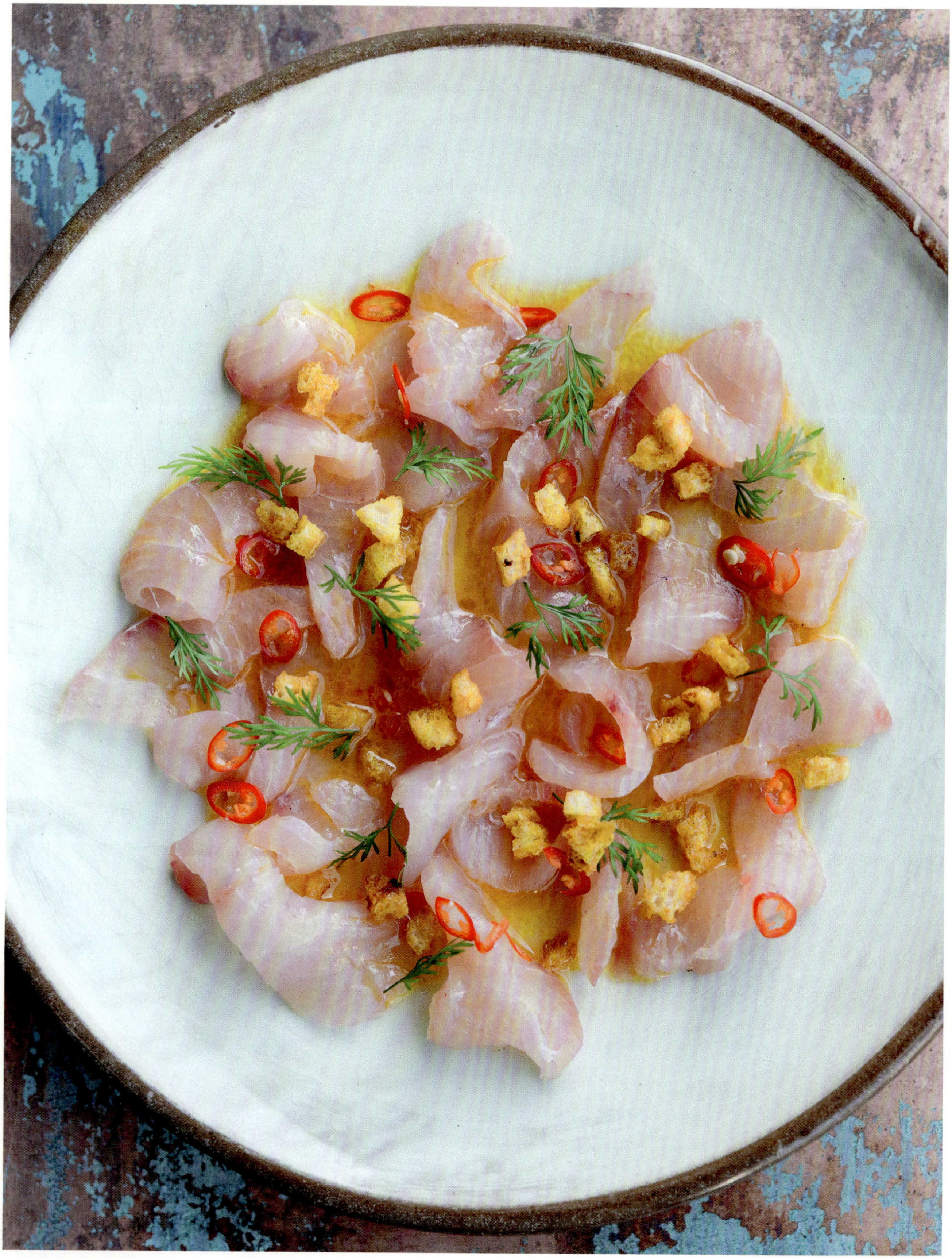

Kingfish sashimi with mandarin and dill

Fresh, beautifully prepared raw fish is all about the texture. The fish is essentially the vehicle for other flavours and textures to ride alongside and enhance. This dish is a little cracker. I have upped the relatively mild acidity from the mandarin juice with some really good-quality chardonnay vinegar. Sliced fresh chilli adds a little heat, the dill brings a fresh, subtle herby note, while the tiny, crisp mandarin croutons give a delicious crunch to the dish.

Serves 6 as a starter

MANDARIN CROUTONS
¼ baguette, crust removed
finely grated zest of 2 mandarins
1 tablespoon mandarin juice
1½ tablespoons olive oil

KINGFISH MARINADE
½ cup (125 ml/4 fl oz) mandarin juice
¼ cup (60 ml/2 fl oz) chardonnay vinegar or white wine vinegar
⅓ cup (80 ml/2½ fl oz) Al Brown & Co Orange and Chilli Infused Olive Oil or extra-virgin olive oil
flaky sea salt
600 g (1 lb 5 oz) kingfish
dill sprigs, to serve
red chilli, finely sliced, to serve

Preheat your oven to 180°C (350°F).

To make the mandarin croutons, take the crust-less baguette and cut into 5 mm (¼ in) or smaller squares. (You should have about 1 cupful.) Place the bread squares in a small mixing bowl with the mandarin zest and juice and olive oil. With clean hands, gently mix together so the mandarin zest and juice get absorbed into the bread.

Spread out the croutons onto a large baking tray and bake for 5 minutes or so, until golden and crunchy. Remove from the oven, then cool and store in an airtight container until required.

For the kingfish marinade, whisk the mandarin juice and vinegar in a small mixing bowl, add the oil, then season with a generous amount of salt. Refrigerate until required.

To serve, slice the kingfish as thinly as possible and arrange on a platter or individual plates. Spoon over liberal amounts of the chilled marinade. Pick small dill sprigs and arrange randomly over the fish and scatter with the chilli. Finish by sprinkling the little crisp mandarin croutons about. Eat now.

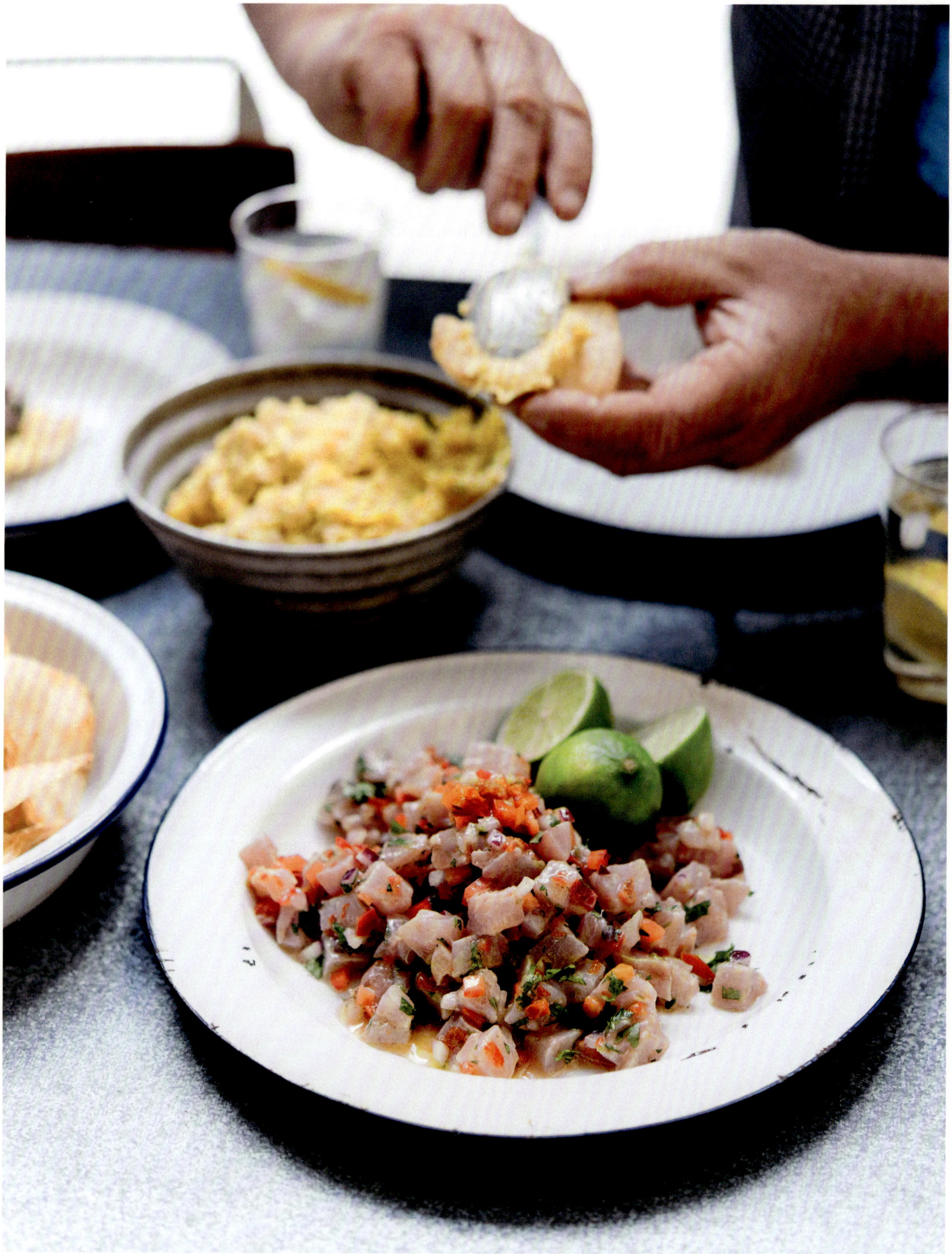

Kahawai ceviche with spiced creamed corn

Most folks who know me know that I have a real soft spot for kahawai. As far as varieties of fish go, it ticks all the boxes—still relatively plentiful, pretty easy to catch, is a great 'scrapper' and eats beautifully. Only the uneducated believe this wonderful fish is only good for the smoker. While I agree that it does smoke up beautifully, it also eats just as well freshly cooked and of course raw. I never usually use a recipe for ceviche. As long as there is an acid component (like citrus juice or vinegar, which essentially 'cooks' the fish), heat of some sort (in the form of hot sauce or fresh chillies) and some good oil as a starting point, the rest is up to you. Think herbs and crunchy raw vegetables. This ceviche goes down the Mexican path, with the master stroke being the creamed corn infused with the heat of pickled jalapeños. A bottle of decent tequila directly from the freezer would make perfect sense in this situation!

Serves 10–12 platter styles

SPICED CREAMED CORN
5 corncobs
sea salt
1–2 tablespoons pickled jalapeño (page 420), or store-bought jalapeño
1 teaspoon roasted, ground cumin seeds
1 tablespoon lime juice

CEVICHE
500 g (1 lb 2 oz) fresh kahawai, cut into 1 cm (½ in) dice
⅓ cup red onion, finely diced
8 jarred whole sweet piquanté peppers (such as Peppadew), finely diced
1 cup finely diced red capsicum
finely grated zest of 2 limes
2–3 tablespoons lime juice
½ cup (125 ml/4 fl oz) Al Brown & Co Lemon and Fennel Infused Olive Oil or extra virgin olive oil
½ cup (15 g/½ oz) roughly chopped coriander leaves
pinch sugar
4–5 glugs hot sauce
flaky sea salt and freshly ground black pepper

TO SERVE
home-made (page 442) or store-bought fried flour tortilla chips
lime wedges

To make the creamed corn, place the corncobs in a large saucepan, cover with cold water and add a liberal pinch or two of salt. Place over high heat, bring up to the boil, then lower the heat. Simmer on a rolling boil for 10 minutes. Remove from the heat, drain and let cool before cutting the corn kernels off the cobs. You need approximately 2 cups (400 g/14 oz) of corn kernels.

Place the corn in the food processor, along with as much pickled jalapeño as you desire, the cumin and the lime juice. Process for a minute. Tip into a small bowl, taste and season accordingly. Refrigerate until required.

For the ceviche, combine the fish, onion, peppers, capsicum, lime zest and juice, olive oil, coriander and sugar in a small bowl. Mix thoroughly, then add the amount of hot sauce that suits your style. Season with salt and pepper. Chill in the fridge to marinate for 30 minutes or so.

When ready to serve, if you're making your own fried tortilla chips, make a batch of flour tortillas (page 442), then cut them into your desired shape and deep-fry or shallow-fry them for a minute or so until golden.

Plate up the ceviche, and have the spiced creamed corn and tortillas on the side. It's a help-yourself situation, in this order: tortilla chip, creamed corn, ceviche, squeeze of lime and a coriander leaf or two.

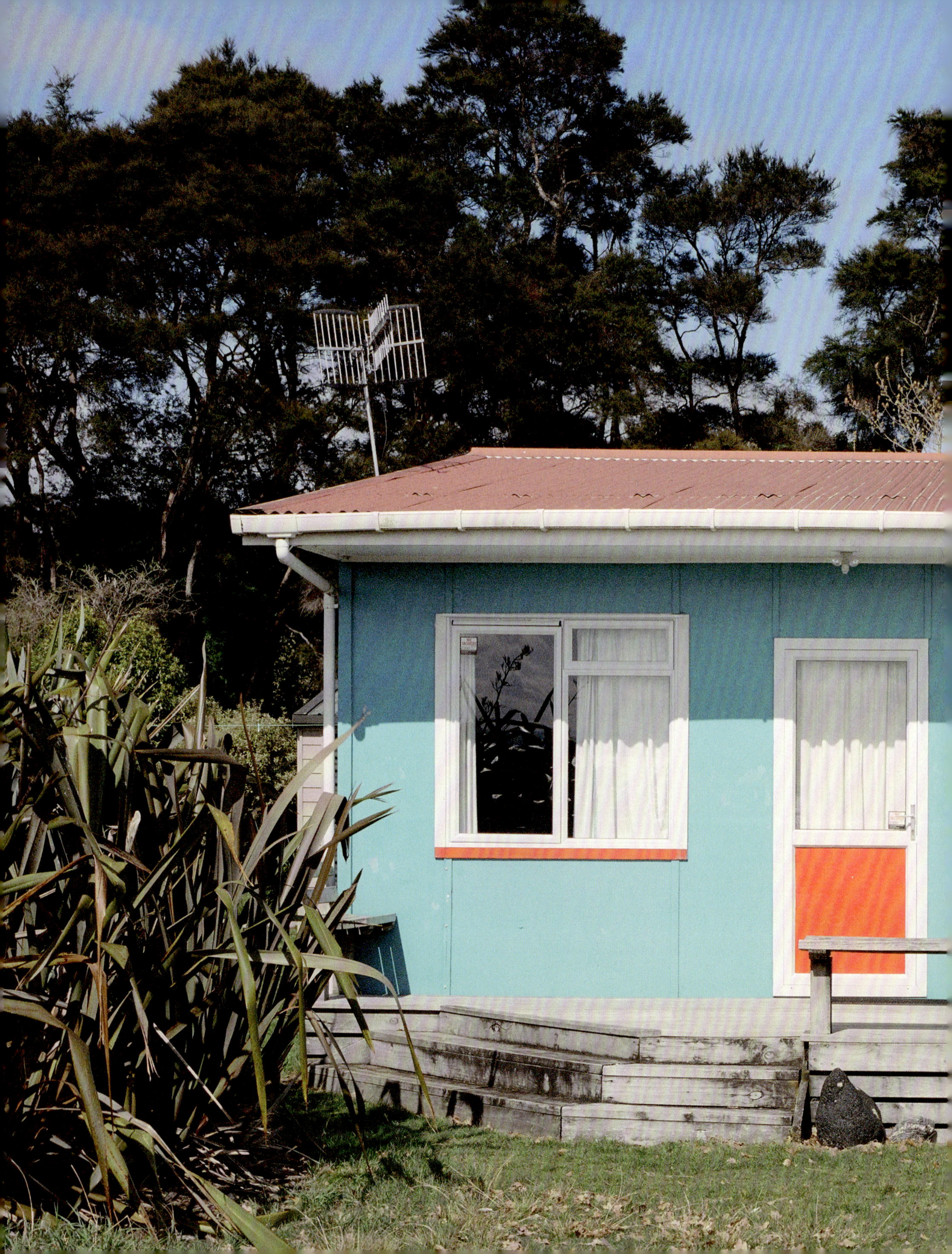

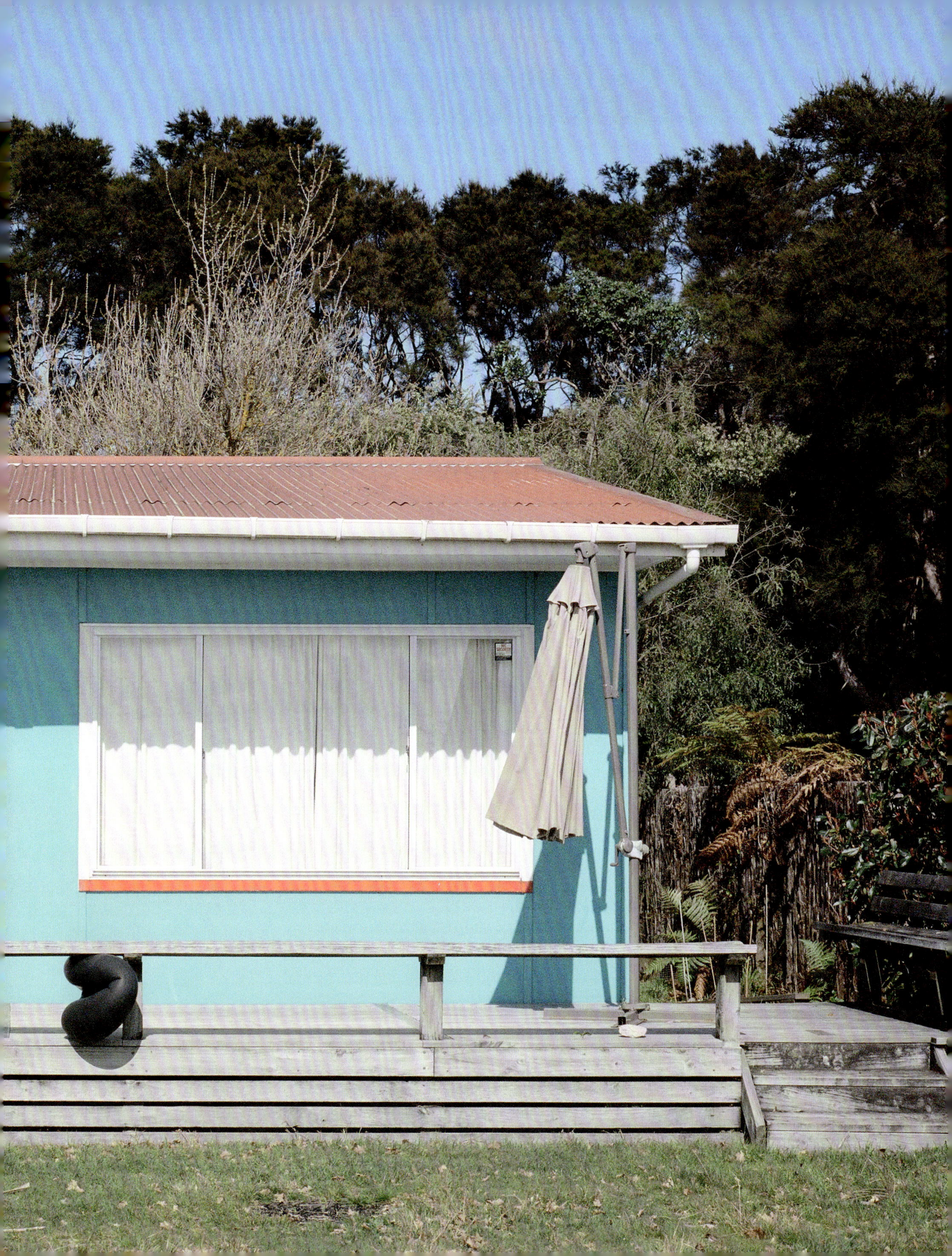

Trevally sashimi with soy syrup, wasabi peas and Kewpie mayo

This has become a staple on the Depot menu for a while now. I developed it up at the bach a few years back, when I had some fresh trevally but not a lot of other ingredients. So I whipped up the soy syrup, then went foraging in my pantry for other ingredients to add. Turns out it's a bit of a winner of a dish. Everyone seems to rave about it, which I always find a bit embarrassing because this recipe is essentially just two ingredients. I prepare a jar of the sweet, salty syrup each summer and make this dish often. It works with any fresh raw fish.

Serves 6

SOY SYRUP
1 cup (250 ml/9 fl oz) soy sauce
1 cup (220 g/7¾ oz) sugar

TO ASSEMBLE AND SERVE
600 g (1 lb 5 oz) super fresh trevally (or whatever fresh fish you have scored)
Kewpie Spicy Mayonnaise (any Kewpie or mayo will work)
¼ cup (25 g/1 oz) wasabi peas, crushed
micro basil or regular basil, finely chopped
toasted sesame seeds (optional)
fresh chilli, thinly sliced (optional)

Chill your platter.
    To make the soy syrup, place the soy and sugar into a small saucepan over medium-high heat. Keeping a watchful eye on it, bring it up to the boil, then lower the temperature to a simmer. Reduce for 10 minutes or so. When any syrup is hot it will be a lot runnier than when it cools, so what I like to do is place a saucer in the fridge and after 10 minutes I put a couple of drops on the cold plate to see how syrupy it is. You don't want to over-reduce it as it will be too thick.

Take the sharpest knife you have, give it a couple of passes on the steel, then slice the fish into smallish pieces, as thinly as possible. Arrange them on the chilled platter.
    Take the Kewpie mayo and squeeze a small amount onto each piece of fish. Scatter over the crushed wasabi peas. Drizzle the soy syrup over it all—less is more, as you can always add a bit extra. Scatter over some basil if you have it. For a couple of optional extras, you can sprinkle over a few sesame seeds or add chilli slices if you want to turn up the temp a little more. Serve now.

SEAFOOD

48   EAT UP NEW ZEALAND: THE BACH EDITION

Raw mullet with cream of horseradish, apple and dill

When it comes to sashimi or similar, there are so many species of fish that seem to get overlooked in favour of their more expensive and posh cousins, such as tuna, salmon and kingfish. Fresh mullet is definitely one that is hardly ever considered when it comes to eating fish in the raw. But the golden rule I keep in mind is that if it's an oily fish it's generally going to do well in uncooked applications—so mullet works!

This is such a wonderful, clean and refreshing dish. If you can score a jar of Mandys Horseradish (produced down in Canterbury) to use in the recipe, even better. I have included a recipe for apple syrup, but you can also purchase this in organic stores, some supermarkets and good delis.

Serves 6

CREAM OF HORSERADISH WITH FRESH DILL
½ cup (125 g/4½ oz) sour cream
½ cup (120 g/4¼ oz) mayonnaise
½ cup (120 g/4¼ oz) horseradish sauce
¼ cup (15 g/½ oz) fresh dill, finely chopped
1 tablespoon cider vinegar
flaky sea salt and freshly ground black pepper

APPLE SYRUP
1 litre (35 fl oz) apple juice
½ cup (110 g/3¾ oz) sugar
½ cup (125 ml/4 fl oz) cider vinegar
juice of 1 lemon

TO ASSEMBLE AND SERVE
600 g (1 lb 5 oz) fresh mullet fillet, cut into small cubes
1 Granny Smith apple, cut into matchsticks
fresh dill tips
lemon fennel or lemon olive oil
1 lemon, for squeezing
flaky sea salt and freshly ground black pepper

To make the cream of horseradish, place all the ingredients except for the salt and pepper in a small bowl. Mix together. Taste, then season accordingly with salt and pepper. Refrigerate until required.

For the apple syrup, place all the ingredients in a suitable-sized saucepan over medium-low heat. Reduce until you have around 1 cup. Test that it's ready by placing a couple of drops on a saucer in the fridge for a minute or two. The syrup will always be thicker when it cools. Keep the syrup in a jar in the fridge; it will last forever.

To serve, put ten or so liberal dots of the cream of horseradish on each of six side plates. Top each dot with a piece of the fresh mullet.

Add two or three matchsticks of apple on and around each piece of mullet, followed by a few tips of fresh dill. Now add a few dots of apple syrup and olive oil, and finish with a squeeze of lemon juice and a little salt and pepper.

Snapper tartare

You can make a tartare out of practically any species of fish. It's a classic dish that can be made from all the offcuts and scrapings from the fish frames, much like ceviche. There are no real rules when it comes to making a fish tartare. You will need a citrus juice or an acid of some sort, plus seasoning and some sort of oil to give the fish some depth and richness. Then it's up to you.

The snapper skin crackling (see page 446) is worth the work, but by all means serve this with something else like lavosh or simple water crackers.

Serves 6 as a starter

400 g (14 oz) snapper fillet, cut into small dice
½ cup radish, small dice
¾ cup Granny Smith apple, small dice
1 lime, fine zest and diced segments
1 tablespoon lime juice
2 teaspoon hot sauce
¾ cup (185 ml/6 fl oz) Al Brown & Co Lemon and Fennel Oil or extra-virgin olive oil
⅓ cup (20 g/¾ oz) finely chopped dill
2 tablespoons apple syrup
flaky sea salt and freshly ground black pepper
snapper skin crackling (optional) (page 446), to serve

Place all the ingredients except the seasoning and the crackling into a suitable-sized bowl and gently mix through. Taste, then season accordingly. Refrigerate for 5–10 minutes before serving.

To serve, divvy up the tartare between individual plates. Use a round cookie cutter if you want a neat circle of tartare, otherwise just spoon it on and go rustic styles. Serve with the snapper skin crackling, if using, on the side.

SEAFOOD 51

Fried kina on toast

This simple dish could be considered slightly controversial, as I believe most kina eaters would think it was sacrilege to consume kina in any other state than raw. Don't get me wrong, I love raw kina and will always pick up a dozen or so when going for a dive. The thing is, I want more Kiwis (especially Pākehā) to start understanding how delicious they are, and by serving them this way I see it as the gateway to discovering how darn tasty sea urchin (kina) can be.

There is also another motive running alongside what I've said in this intro: in parts of New Zealand we have created what are now called 'kina barrens', where the kina have taken over and consumed much of the kelp forests, creating an imbalance in our delicate and precious ocean ecosystem. This has come about due to the overfishing of kina predators, such as snapper and rock lobster. So let's eat more kina, helping the kelp re-establish and in turn getting our fisheries back in balance and abundance.

Serves . . . up to you

kina tongues
plain flour (start with 1 cup; increase for a larger batch)
ground cumin (start with 2 tablespoons; increase for a larger batch)
flaky sea salt and freshly ground black pepper

Vogel's bread (I prefer Very Thin slices)
flaky sea salt and freshly ground black pepper
canola oil, for frying
butter, for frying
a lemon or two, for squeezing

To best extract the delicate kina tongues, crack the kina open and turn the shell upside down to drain for a few minutes. This helps the dark, ugly-looking membrane dislodge itself from the tongue.

Run a spoon up and under each kina tongue, gently placing the tongues in a bowl until you complete the task. Refrigerate until required.

Mix the flour and cumin together thoroughly in a bowl (use a ratio of 1 cup of flour to 2 tablespoons cumin).

Place a skillet or frying pan over medium heat. Start toasting your Vogel's bread.

Take the kina tongues and carefully place them on some kitchen paper. Put another piece of kitchen paper on top to get the kina tongues as dry as possible. Season with salt and pepper.

Once your skillet is hot, place a dozen or so kina tongues in a dry sieve and spoon over liberal amounts of the cumin flour. Lightly shake the sieve so the excess flour mix falls through into a bowl; you can use this again for the next batch. The tongues will have taken on a light dusting of the flour mix and should be separated from each other.

Add a small amount of canola oil to the hot pan, then carefully add the kina tongues, along with a teaspoon or so of butter. Cook the kina for no more than a minute either side. They will caramelise quickly, and the trick is to not overcook them as you want them still soft in the centre.

Spoon the cooked kina tongues onto buttered Vogel's toast, squeeze over some lemon juice, tuck in, and feel your eyes roll back in your head—you won't believe how good these are.

P.S. You could always top these with a fried egg . . . just saying.

SEAFOOD 53

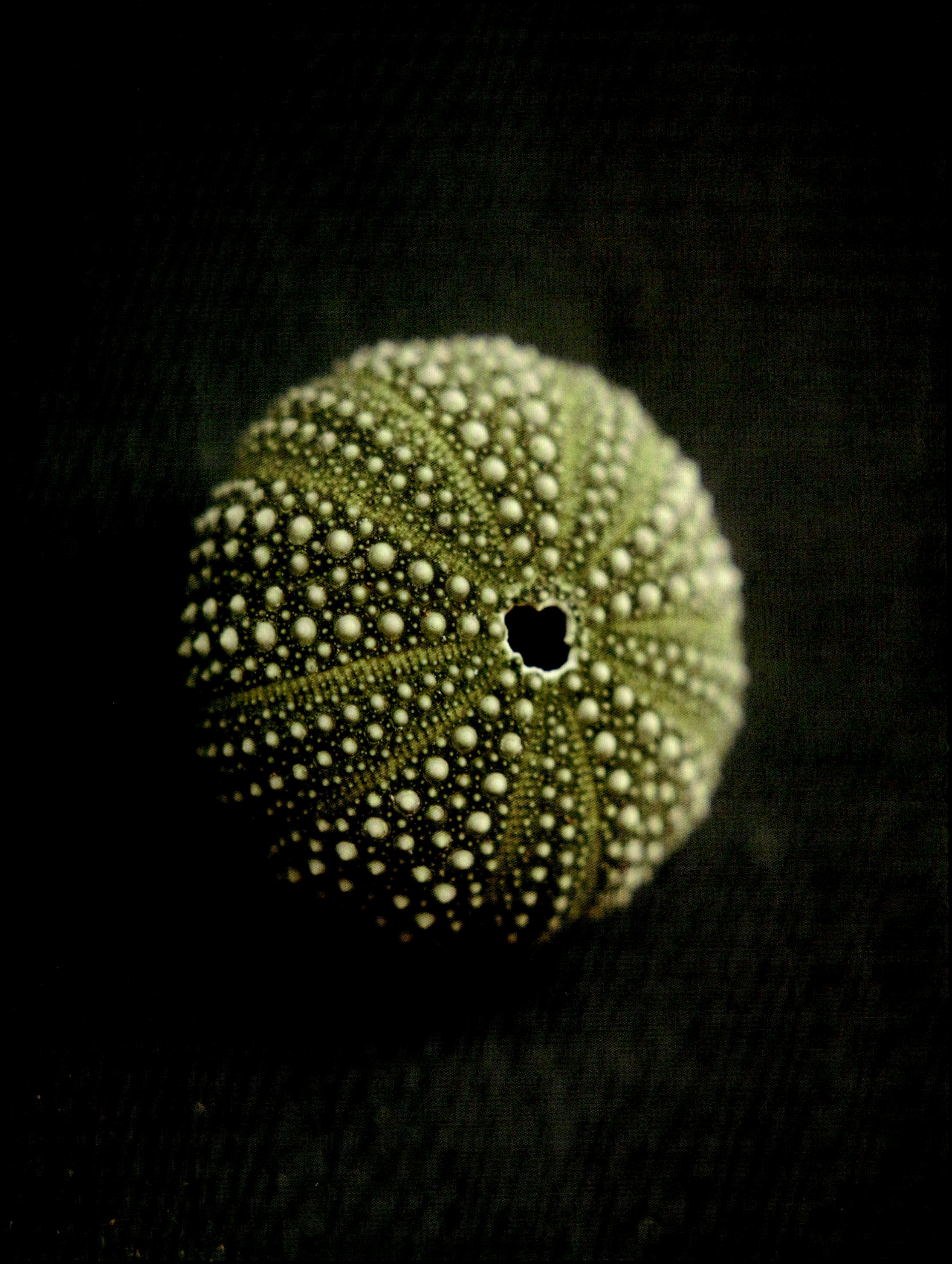

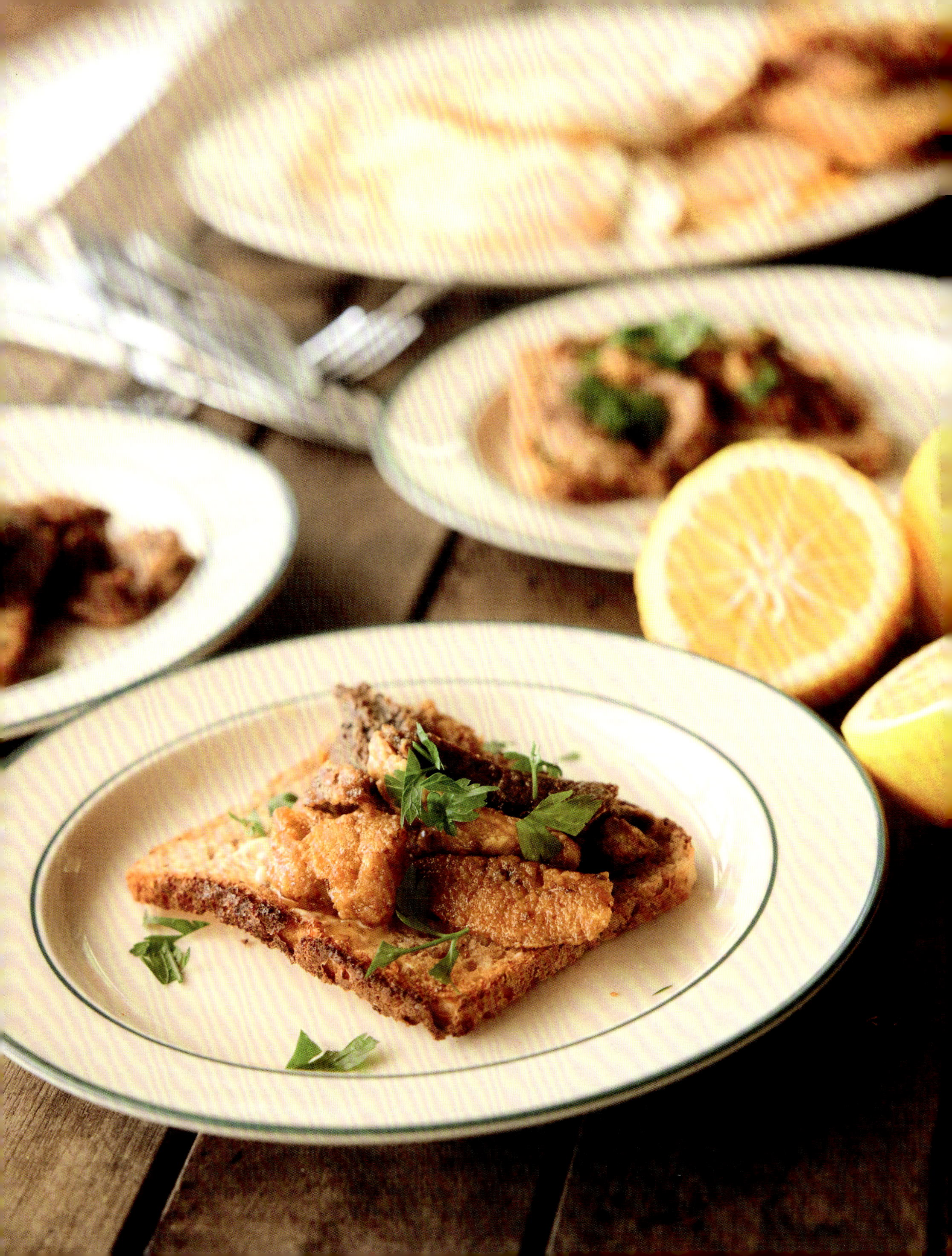

Spiced roasted snapper wings with ranch dressing

Technically these guys are probably 'snapper throats', but with a couple of their fins still attached we have always called them 'wings'. Hand on heart they contain the tastiest and sweetest flesh of practically any fish species. As is often the case it's all about being close to the bone. It's a messy job eating these delicious morsels; there are no small bones to contend with, just beautiful little nooks and crannies to extract these edible treasures from. A little tip . . . it pays to thoroughly scale the whole fish first before removing the fillets then the throats (wings), as it's a real pain to scale the individual throats. You should do this anyway, as it's way easier to fillet a fish that has been scaled, and snapper tastes so much better cooked with the skin on!

The spice mix will make enough for 1–1.5 kg of wings in total, so just make it up and use a liberal amount, depending on how many wings you have. Store any leftover spice mix in an airtight container.

3 tablespoons roasted, ground cumin seeds
1½ tablespoons sweet smoked paprika
3 tablespoons sumac
snapper wings (however many you've got!)
finely grated lemon zest
olive oil
flaky sea salt and freshly ground black pepper
ranch dressing, to serve
lemon wedges, to serve

Place the cumin seeds, paprika and sumac in a bowl and mix to combine. Set aside until required.

Heat up your barbecue, or preheat your oven to 180°C (350°F).

Take the snapper wings and, with a sharp knife, split them down the centre to create what I call two wings. It you have some kitchen shears handy, cut off and discard any large fins.

Place the wings in a large mixing bowl. Add the lemon zest, douse in some olive oil, then add liberal amounts of the spice mix followed by some sea salt and pepper. Use your hands to rub the ingredients together until fully incorporated.

Either cook on the barbecue or place in a roasting dish and cook for 15–20 minutes in the oven. Serve with the ranch dressing for dipping, lemon wedges and plenty of kitchen paper or napkins for wiping up!

SEAFOOD

58   EAT UP NEW ZEALAND: THE BACH EDITION

Tempura scallop butties with preserved lemon mayo

If the penny hasn't dropped by now, I'm sure it will have by the end of this book: I'm a bit of a fan of basic white bread. There was no Vogel's or wholegrain when I was growing up; bread was soft, white and delicious, as it still is today. I'm glad that there's a whole bunch of bread choices out there, and although I don't eat a lot of white bread any more I still love to use it in my cooking. Other than it being near texturally perfect, it also reinforces the nostalgia of the past, which is important to me. These battered scallop butties are fantastic. I've made them with oysters and different types of fritter too. Like a well-made club sandwich, everyone loves a little white bread now and then.

Makes 24

PRESERVED LEMON MAYO
½ cup (125 g/4½ oz) mayonnaise
1 preserved lemon, zest only, finely diced
1 tablespoon lemon juice

TEMPURA BATTER
2 egg yolks
½ cup (125 ml/4 fl oz) canola oil
1½ cups (375 ml/13 fl oz) soda water
1 cup (150 g/5½ oz) self-raising flour

TO COOK AND SERVE
12 slices white bread
watercress, to serve
cooking oil, for deep-frying
24 scallops
½ lemon, for squeezing

To make the preserved lemon mayo, combine the ingredients in a small bowl, then refrigerate until required.

Make the batter. In a bowl, whisk the egg yolks and oil together. Stir through the soda water. Using a fork, gently stir in the flour, making sure to not over-mix. Refrigerate until required.

Take a small cookie cutter that gives you four rounds of bread from each slice of bread; you should have 48 rounds. Lay the bread rounds out on a clean work surface. Schmear a little preserved lemon mayo on each round, then top just half of the rounds with a sprig of watercress.

Heat the oil in your deep-fryer or add a decent amount of cooking oil to a heavy-bottomed saucepan. You want to cook the battered scallops at 180°C (350°F). To get a gauge on the temperature of the oil, drop a cube of bread into it when you think it's near 180°C. It should turn golden in around 60 seconds.

Once the oil is hot, dip the scallops into the tempura batter, letting most of the batter drip off. Add a six or eight scallops at a time to the pan, and cook for about a minute to a minute and a half, until the batter has just begun to turn golden. Repeat with the remaining scallops.

To serve, place the cooked battered scallops on the 24 bread rounds with just the lemon mayo on them. Give them a squeeze of lemon juice, then place the watercress-lined lids on top, spear together with a toothpick and place on a plate or platter to serve.

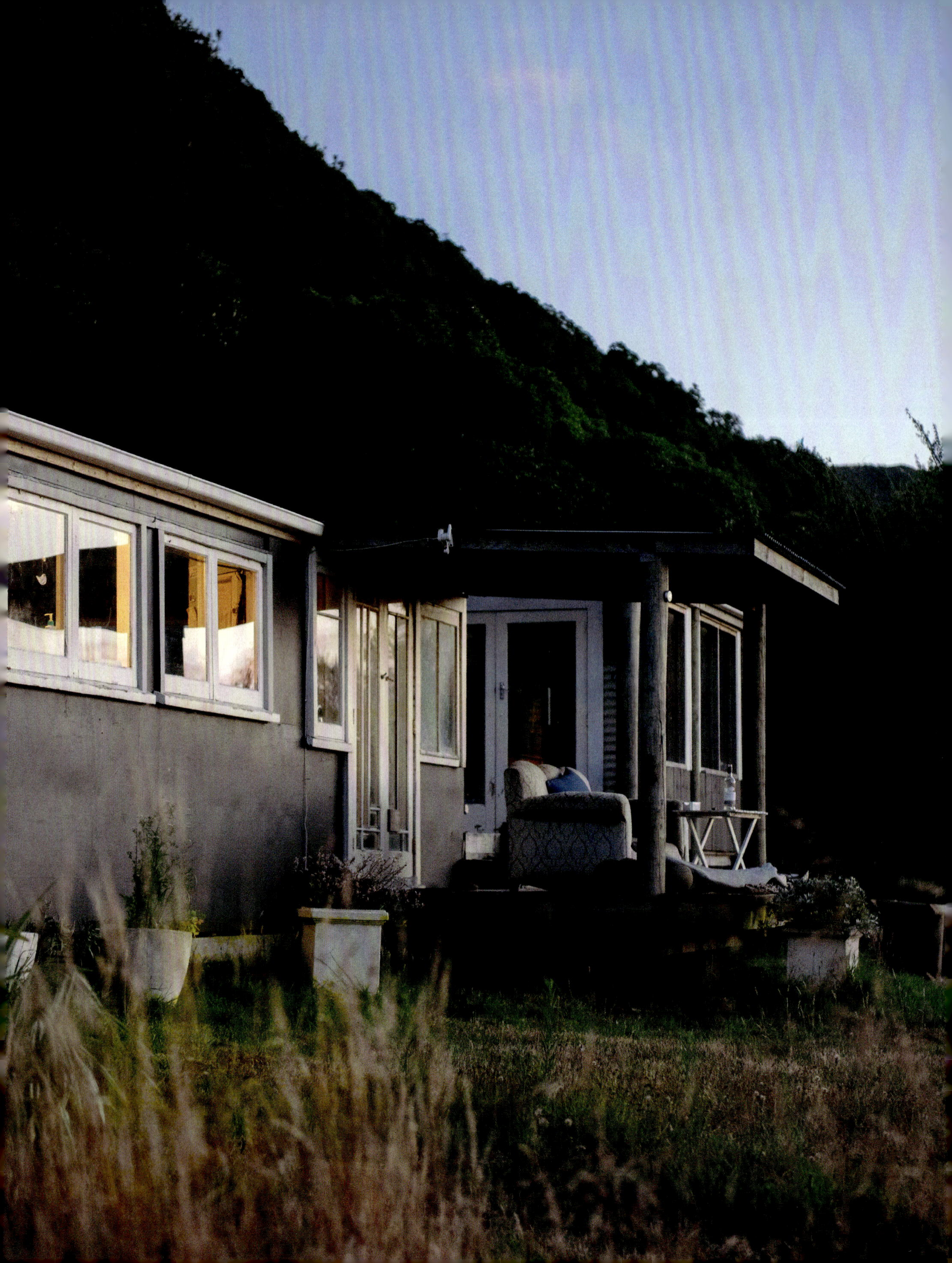

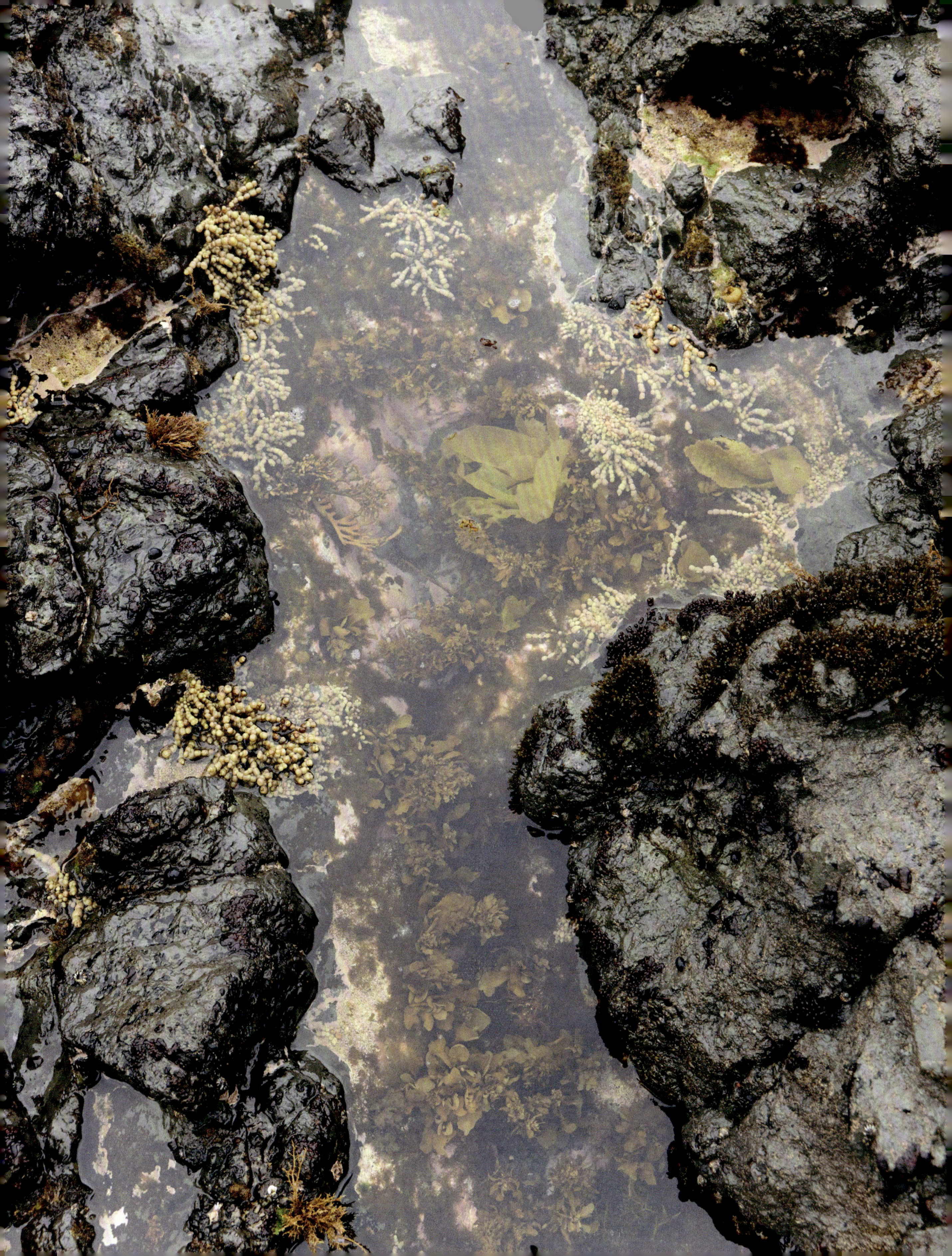

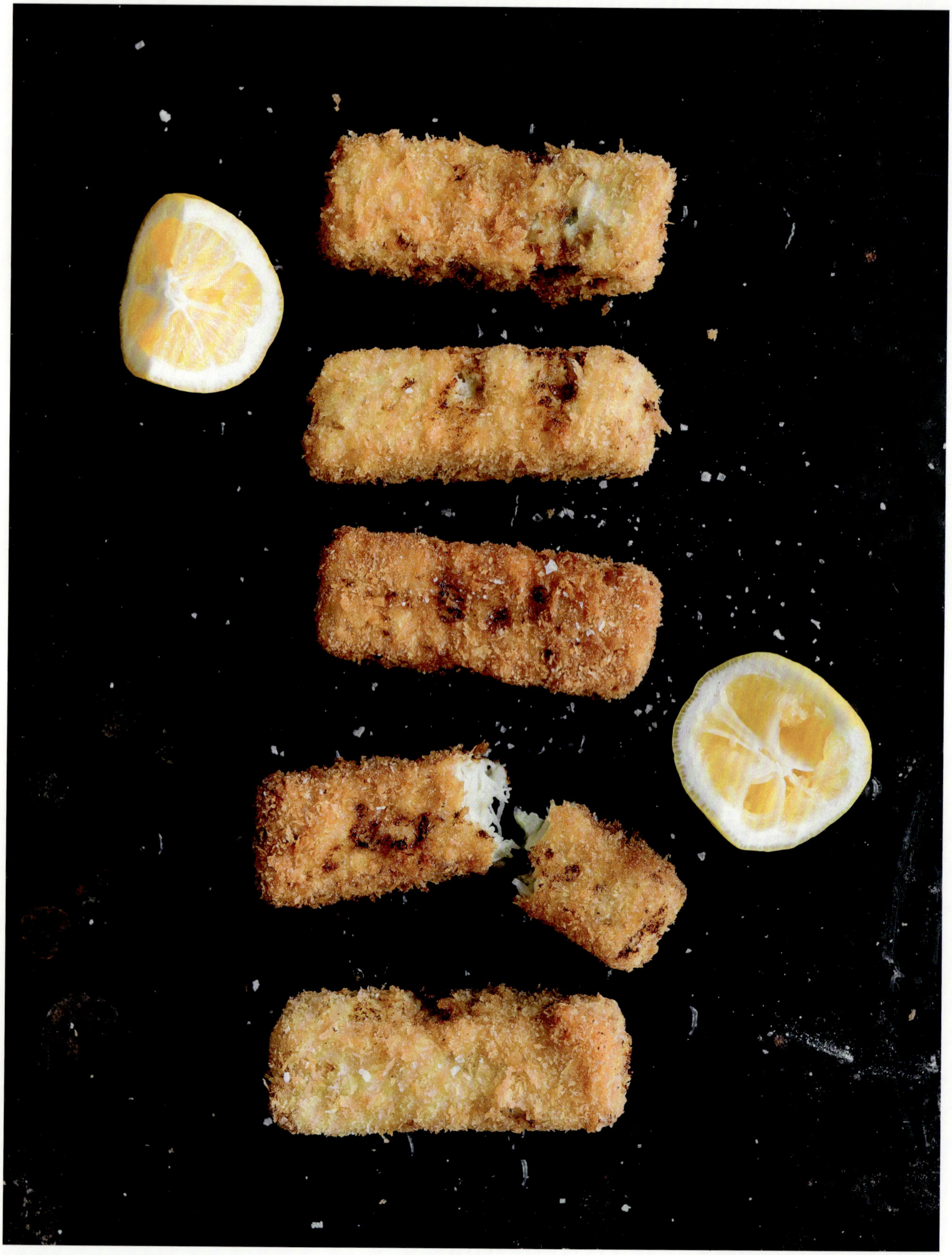

Paddle crab fish fingers

Paddle crabs are another underutilised delicacy that are prolific around most sandy beaches of New Zealand. I really enjoy the pastime of setting a few crab pots at low tide, then checking and emptying them every twenty minutes or so. It's a really cheap way to gather a seriously good eating crustacean.

Crabs are a little bit of work when it comes to removing the meat once cooked, but that's all part of the fun. Alternatively, you can of course purchase frozen crabmeat at most good fishmongers or delis. Cooked crayfish would also work here as a great substitute for the crab—just chop it up nice and fine.

Makes 18 fingers

50 g (1¾ oz) butter
1 cup (150 g/5½ oz) finely diced shallots
⅓ cup (45 g/1½ oz) finely diced celery
finely grated zest and juice of 1 lemon
500 g (1 lb 2 oz) picked crabmeat
2 tablespoons plain flour
1 cup (250 ml/9 fl oz) milk
1 cup (250 ml/9 fl oz) cream

1 tablespoon finely chopped tarragon
pinch cayenne pepper
flaky sea salt and freshly ground black pepper
1 cup (150 g/5½ oz) plain flour
3 eggs, beaten
2 cups (160 g/5½ oz) breadcrumbs
cooking oil, for shallow-frying
lemon halves, to serve

Melt 25 g (1 oz) butter in a suitable-sized saucepan over low heat, and add the shallots and celery along with the lemon zest. Sweat for 20 minutes, stirring occasionally, until soft and translucent. Fold in the crabmeat, then remove from the heat. Set aside.

Melt the remaining butter in a separate pan over medium-low heat. Add the 2 tablespoons flour, stir to create a roux, cook for a minute or two, then whisk in the milk and cream. Cook for a further 3–4 minutes, until the mixture thickens. Pour this over the crab mixture, add the tarragon and cayenne pepper and stir through. To finish the mix, add the juice from the zested lemon and season to taste with salt and pepper.

Line a small tray or container with clingfilm, then pour in the crab mixture. Spread it about so the layer is about 1.5 cm (½ in) thick. Place in the freezer for a couple of hours to firm up.

Remove the crab mixture from the freezer and let it soften a little. Set up your breading station: flour in one container, beaten eggs in another, then the breadcrumbs in a third. Once the crab mixture has softened a little, cut into rectangles. Dip each crab portion in the flour, then the beaten eggs, then cover liberally with the breadcrumbs. Handle with care and place on a tray and refrigerate until ready to cook.

Preheat your oven to 100°C (200°F). Place a frying pan over medium-high heat and add enough cooking oil to shallow-fry.

Cook the crab fish fingers in batches until golden on both sides, keeping the first lot warm in the oven while you finish cooking the remaining fingers. Serve hot with lemon halves for squeezing.

Oyster fritters

A lot less hassle than battered and deep-fried, these oyster fritters are super easy and very quick to put together. Even the raw oyster naysayers are happy to down a number of these delicious mouthfuls. I generally shuck live oysters for whatever preparation I'm undertaking. However, there are plenty of fresh oysters on the half shell or, if you must, pre-shucked in a pottle that will work perfectly well for this simple recipe.

Makes 24 fritters

1 whole egg
2 eggs, separated
2 tablespoons cream
⅓ cup (50 g/1¾ oz) plain flour
flaky sea salt and freshly ground black pepper
24 oysters
canola oil, for frying
butter, for frying
lemon halves, to serve

To make the batter, place the egg, 2 egg yolks and cream in a bowl, and whisk to combine. Sift in the flour, whisking all the time to make a smooth and silky batter. Season with salt and pepper.

Place the 2 egg whites in a bowl and whisk to soft peaks. Fold gently into the fritter batter, then fold in the oysters.

Place a cast-iron pan or other heavy-bottomed pan on the stovetop and bring up to medium heat. Add a little cooking oil and, using tongs or a spoon, add the batter-covered oysters one at a time to the pan Cook the oysters in batches for a minute or so on the first side until just golden on the edges, then flip to cook for a further minute on the other side. Add a knob of butter to the pan just prior to removing the fritters. Keep the fritters warm while you repeat the process with the remaining battered oysters.

Serve immediately with a pinch of flaky sea salt and lemon halves for squeezing over.

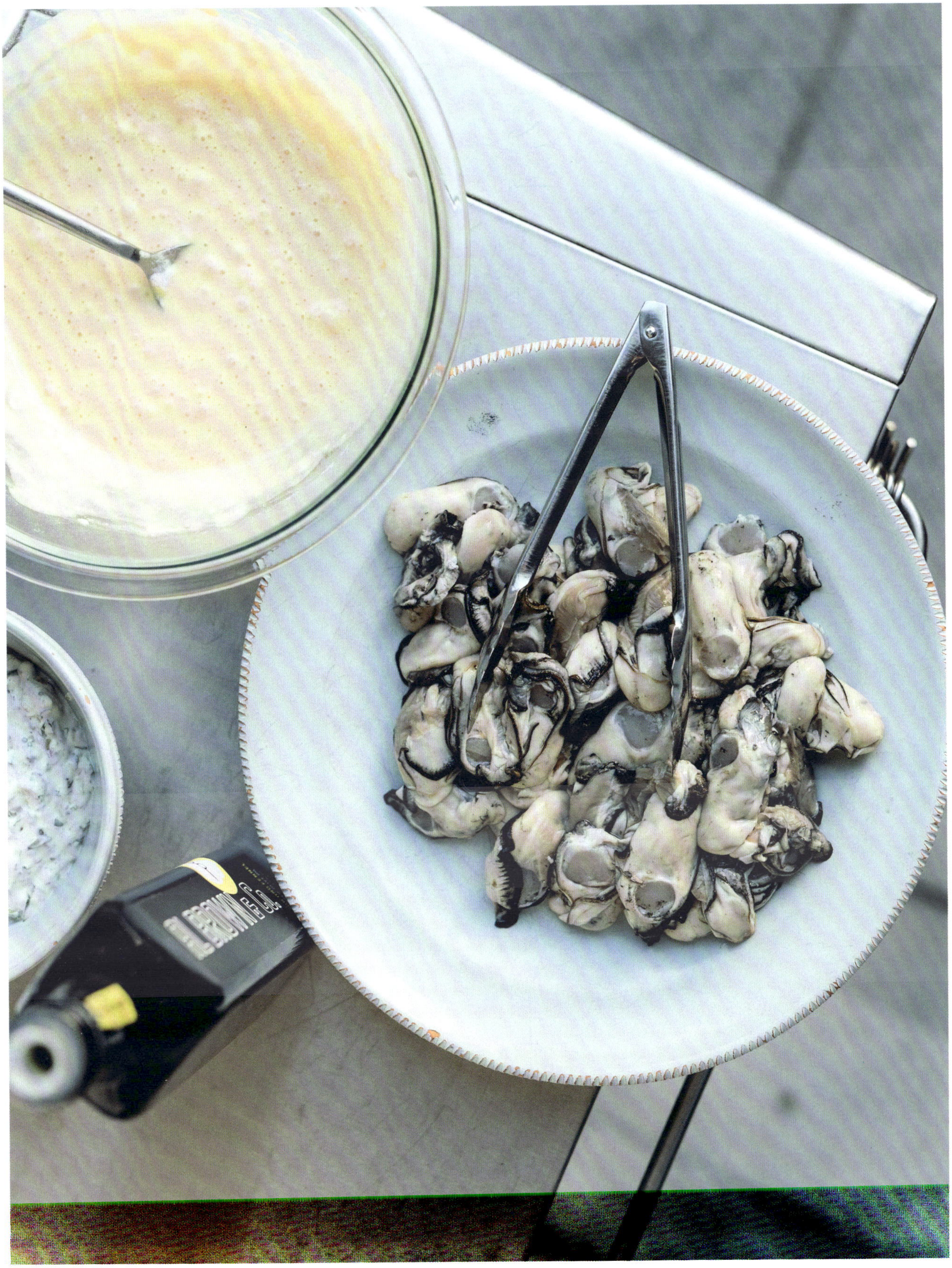

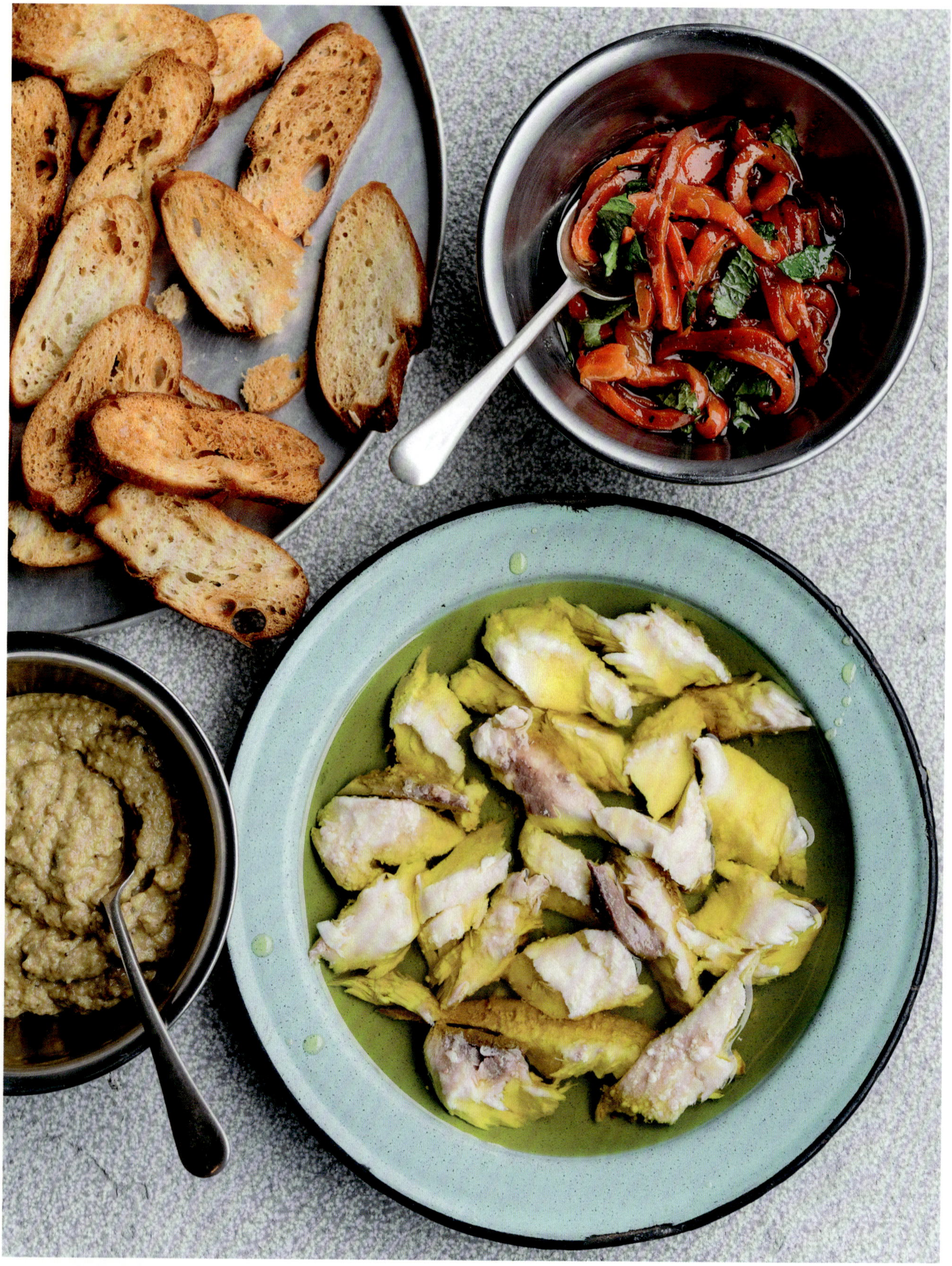

Olive oil poached trevally with baba ganoush, roasted capsicum and mint

Trevally is one of my favourite fish for sure. I stopped serving commercially caught tuna years ago. Fish like trevally are, amongst others like mackerel, kingfish and kahawai, a 'go-to' fish where traditionally many would use tuna. Fresh and served raw, it is extraordinarily good. It smokes up beautifully as well. And, cooked and served as it is in this recipe, I believe you may begin to think differently about our humble trevally.

Serves 6

BABA GANOUSH
4 eggplants
½ cup (125 ml/4 fl oz) olive oil
1 teaspoon smoked paprika
1 tablespoon ground cumin
1 tablespoon ground coriander
1 teaspoon ground cinnamon
½ teaspoon ground ginger
½ teaspoon ground turmeric
1 tablespoon flaky sea salt
juice of 1 lemon
1 tablespoon tahini
½ teaspoon sugar

ROASTED CAPSICUM AND MINT
3 roasted or chargrilled whole red capsicums
½ cup (125 ml/4 fl oz) olive oil
2 tablespoons sherry vinegar
1 cup (20 g/¾ oz) mint leaves
1 teaspoon sugar

TO COOK AND SERVE
600 g (1 lb 5 oz) trevally fillets
flaky sea salt and fresh black pepper
2 cups (500 ml/2 fl oz) extra-virgin olive oil
bruschetta, to serve (optional)

Preheat your oven to 200°C (400°F).

To make the baba ganoush, halve each of the eggplants lengthways. With a sharp paring knife, score the flesh in a 2 cm (¾ in) criss-cross fashion. Brush the scored flesh with the olive oil.

Mix together the spices and salt in a small bowl, then sprinkle liberally over the scored eggplant flesh. Place on a roasting tray, scored sides up, and place in the oven. Cook for approximately 30–40 minutes, until the eggplant is soft and collapsing.

Remove from the oven, let cool for a few minutes, then carefully scrape the cooked flesh away from the skin and place in a food processor. You can discard the skin. Add the lemon juice, tahini and sugar, and blitz to a rustic purée. Taste to check the seasoning and adjust accordingly.

For the roasted capsicum and mint, peel the capsicums, removing and discarding the core and seeds. Cut the flesh into 5 mm (¼ in) wide strips. Place in a medium-sized bowl. Pour over the olive oil and vinegar. Rough chop the mint, then add along with the sugar to the bowl. Season to taste and refrigerate until required.

Preheat your oven to 130°C (250°F).

Lay the fish fillets in a snug-fitting oven tray with highish sides. Season with salt, then pour over the olive oil to cover the fish. Place the tray over medium-high heat. When the oil just begins to bubble at the sides, place the tray in the oven and cook for 3–4 minutes,

Recipe continued overleaf...

or until the fish has turned opaque. Remove and let the fish finish cooking in the hot oil. If white beads of what looks like milk appear on the fish, remove immediately from the oil, let the oil cool a little, then return the fish to the oil. You want the trevally to be just cooked through and no more. Refrigerate until required.

You can serve this dish like a salad, with the baba ganoush spread on a plate, topped with roughly torn pieces of the poached trevally on top, then the capsicum and mint to finish. Alternatively, if it's a help-yourself informal affair, just serve the three components in dishes next to each other with a pile of bruschetta on the side for people to make up their own small bites.

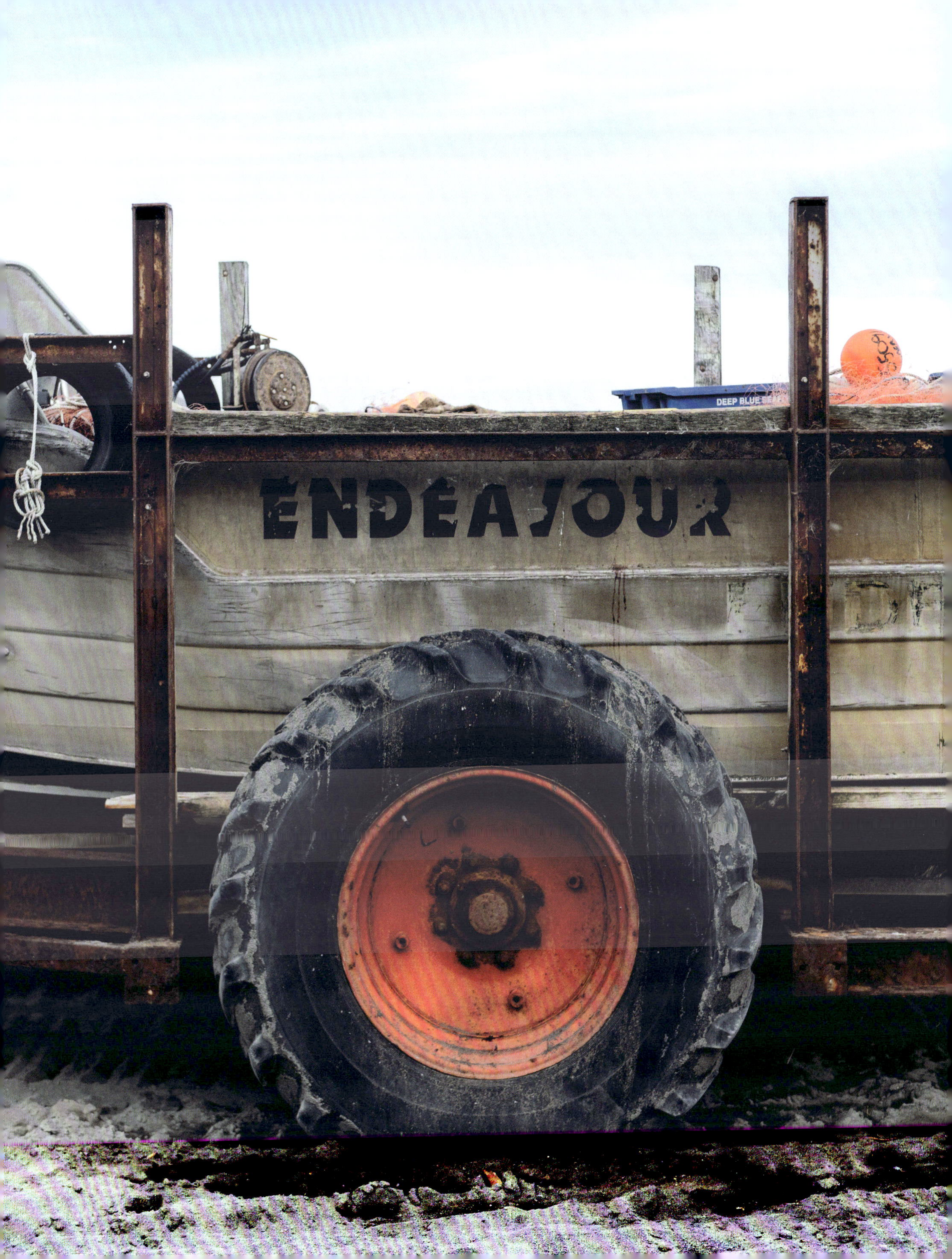
ENDEAVOUR

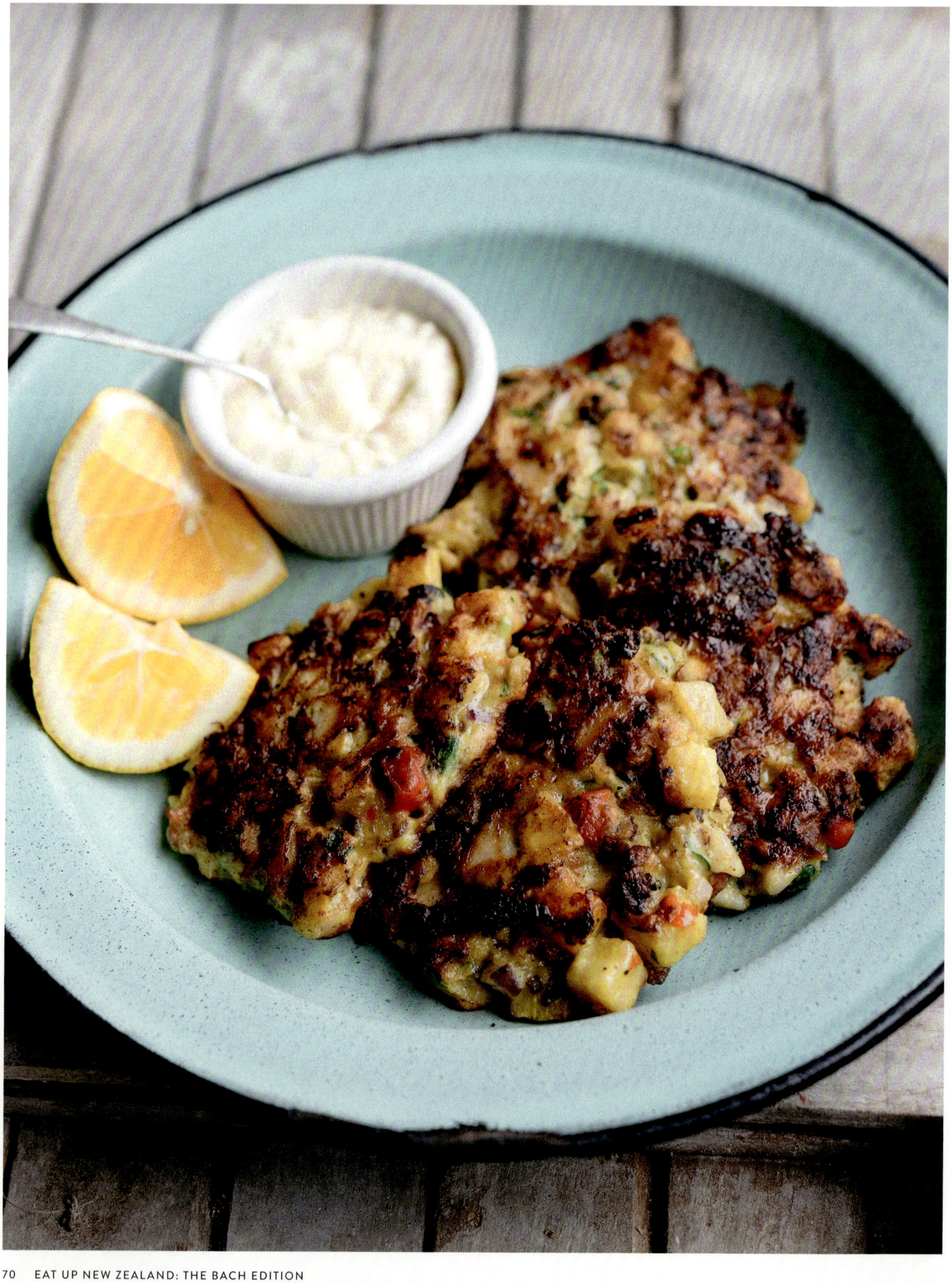

Tuatua and kūmara fritters with egg, gherkin and caper mayonnaise

These fritters would come close, for me personally, to a dish that encapsulates New Zealand cuisine almost perfectly. A fritter is such an informal but delicious thing to cook and eat. You can substitute different shellfish in this recipe, like mussels, pipi or cockles. The kūmara is an inherently Kiwi vege, helping to bulk out the recipe if you are short on the kaimoana, and of course it adds a subtle sweetness to the equation.

Makes 12 large or 24 small fritters

EGG, GHERKIN AND CAPER MAYO
1 cup (250 g/9 oz) mayonnaise
2 hard-boiled eggs, peeled and rough chopped
⅓ cup gherkins, finely diced
¼ cup capers, rinsed and finely chopped
finely grated zest and juice of 1 lemon
¼ cup (7 g/¼ oz) finely chopped parsley

FRITTERS
650 g (1 lb 7 oz) tuatua meat
350 g (12 oz) kūmara, cut into 1 cm (½ in) dice
½ cup (80 g/2¾ oz) finely diced red onion
¼ cup (60 ml/2 fl oz) sweet chilli sauce
⅓ cup (15 g/½ oz) basil leaves, finely chopped
1½ tablespoons lemon juice
3 eggs
¾ cup (110 g/3¾ oz) plain flour
flaky sea salt and freshly ground black pepper
cooking oil, for frying
lemon halves, to serve

To make the egg, gherkin and caper mayo, place all the ingredients in a bowl, mix together then refrigerate until required.

Take the tuatua and place in a colander to drain. Now roughly chop and place in a medium-sized bowl.

For the kūmara, place in a small saucepan, cover with salted cold water, then place over high heat. Bring to the boil and cook for 2–3 minutes, until just soft through. Drain, spread on a tray and let cool.

Add the kūmara to the bowl with the tuatua, followed by the onion, chilli sauce, basil and lemon juice. Mix through.

With a stick blender, blitz the eggs and flour together in a bowl to create a thick batter. Add to the tuatua mixture and mix through. Take the stick blender and blitz about a cup of the mix, then fold this back in (this will help bind the fritter and hold it together when cooking). Season with salt and pepper, and refrigerate until required.

Place a cast-iron pan or similar heavy-bottomed pan over medium heat. Once hot, add a splash of oil and cook off one small fritter to check and adjust the seasoning if necessary.

Cook the fritters to your desired size, until golden and cooked through. They should take a couple of minutes on each side.

Serve with the egg, gherkin and caper mayo, and lemon halves on the side. Eat now.

Pāua pies

I stumbled across pāua pies in the last 12 months at a pretty nondescript bakery on the main street of Kawakawa in our beloved Far North. They were definitely a bit down and dirty and pretty lean on actual pāua. However, I loved the idea of a pāua pie so I set about creating a recipe. I have also cheated a little bit, by using half pāua and half frozen squid tubes. Squid has a very similar texture to pāua, so this way you stretch that 'black gold'. This recipe makes regular-sized typical Kiwi oval-shaped pies (we use 12 cm x 15 cm moulds), but you could always make mini pies, which would be a groovy little pass-around. (See page 167 for the steps to make individual pies.) You're going to enjoy these—they are bloody delicious and worth the effort!

Makes 6 pies

PIE FILLING
350 g (12½ oz) minced pāua
350 g (12½ oz) minced squid tubes
⅓ cup (80 ml/2½ fl oz) cooking oil
3 cups (465 g/1 lb) finely chopped onion
1 cup (140 g/5 oz) finely chopped celery
1½ tablespoons finely chopped garlic
1½ tablespoons finely chopped tarragon
pinch dried chilli flakes
30 g (1 oz) butter
30 g (1 oz) plain flour, plus extra for dusting
2 cups (500 ml/17 fl oz) milk
½ cup (125 ml/4 fl oz) cream
2 teaspoons squid ink (optional)
2 tablespoons lemon juice
flaky sea salt and freshly ground black pepper

TO ASSEMBLE
1 quantity Eve's mum's pastry (page 442)
1 egg, beaten

Take the pāua and squid and place them in your food processor. Process for 30 seconds to a minute until the pāua takes on a creamier texture.

Place a frying pan over medium-low heat. Add the oil followed by the onion, celery, garlic, tarragon and chilli flakes. Sweat, stirring occasionally, over low heat for about 20 minutes, until the vegetables are soft and translucent. Turn the heat up to medium and add the creamed pāua and squid mixture. Cook for 15 minutes or so, until all the moisture has concentrated and cooked out. Take off the heat and set aside.

Melt the butter in a small saucepan over medium-low heat. Add the flour and stir to create a roux. Now, cook for 1–2 minutes, then whisk in the milk and cream. Cook until the mixture thickens, then continue to cook for another couple of minutes. Pour over the pāua and onion mixture. Place back on the heat and bring up to a simmer. Add the squid ink, if using, and lemon juice. Taste, then season accordingly with salt and pepper. Take off the heat and let cool. Refrigerate until completely cold before making the pies.

When you're ready to make the pies, preheat your oven to 200°C (400°F).

Take the pastry and cut into two portions. Dust your clean work surface with flour, then roll out both pastry portions to about 3 cm (1¼ in) thick. Use your pie moulds to cut out six pie tops (if using the traditional oval-shaped moulds), then set aside. Gather all the remaining pastry, including offcuts, press together then roll out again to the same thickness. This time, cut around the moulds but add 1–2 cm (½ –¾ in) around the circumference to allow for the depth in the pie mould.

Grease your pie moulds with butter or oil, then line with the larger oval-shaped pastry bases. Spoon in the cold filling, dividing it evenly between the six pies. Brush the edges of the pastry bases with the beaten egg, then place the tops on top. Pinch together, cut away any excess pastry, then fold the two layers of pastry around the edges. Brush the tops of the pies with the remaining beaten egg, then make a small hole in the centre of the pie lids.

Bake in the preheated oven for 30–40 minutes, until the pies are golden on the top and, more importantly, the bottom.

Remove from the oven and let the pies cool for at least 15 minutes before consuming. I like to serve these old-school in a paper bag.

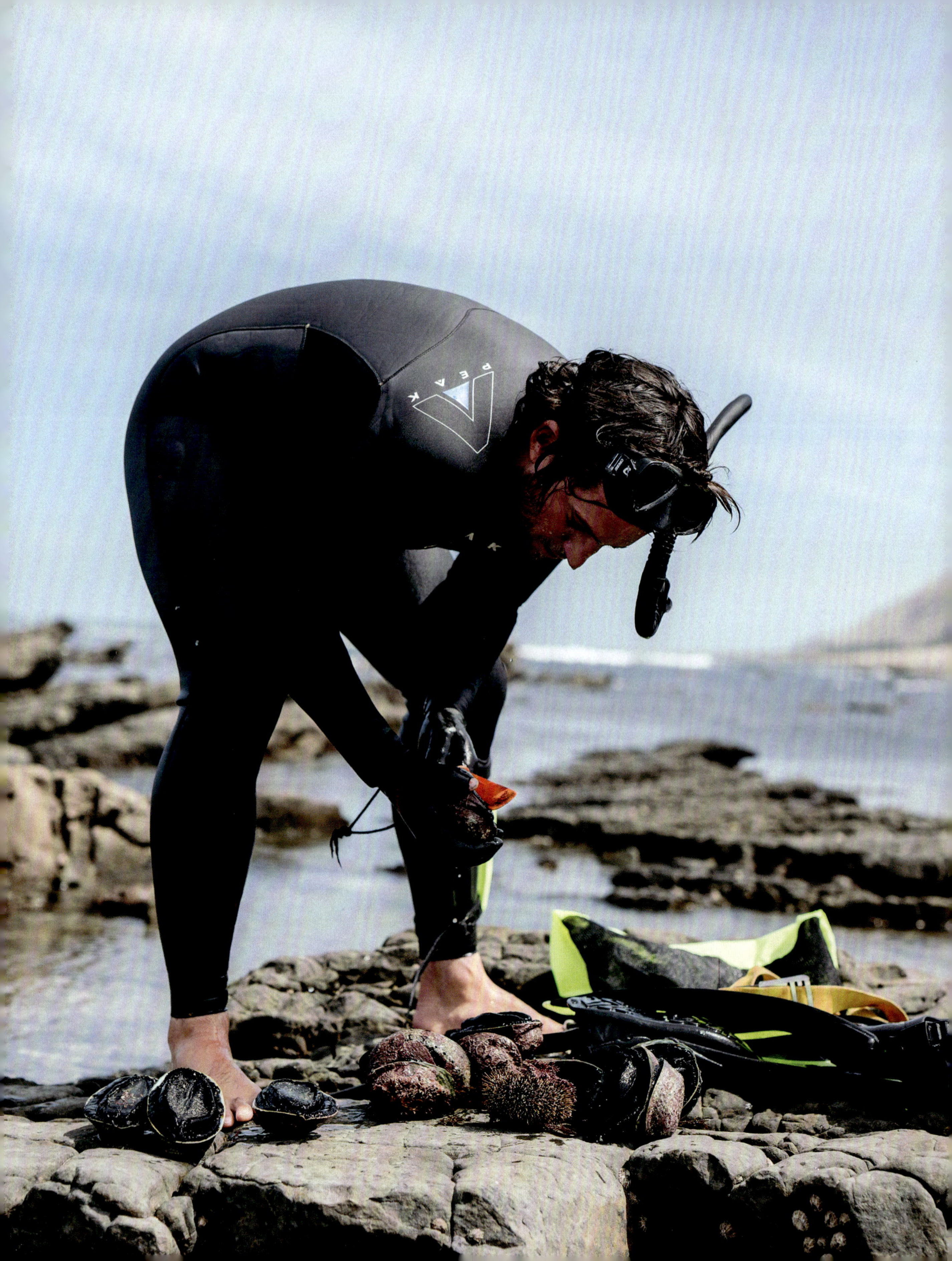
PEAK

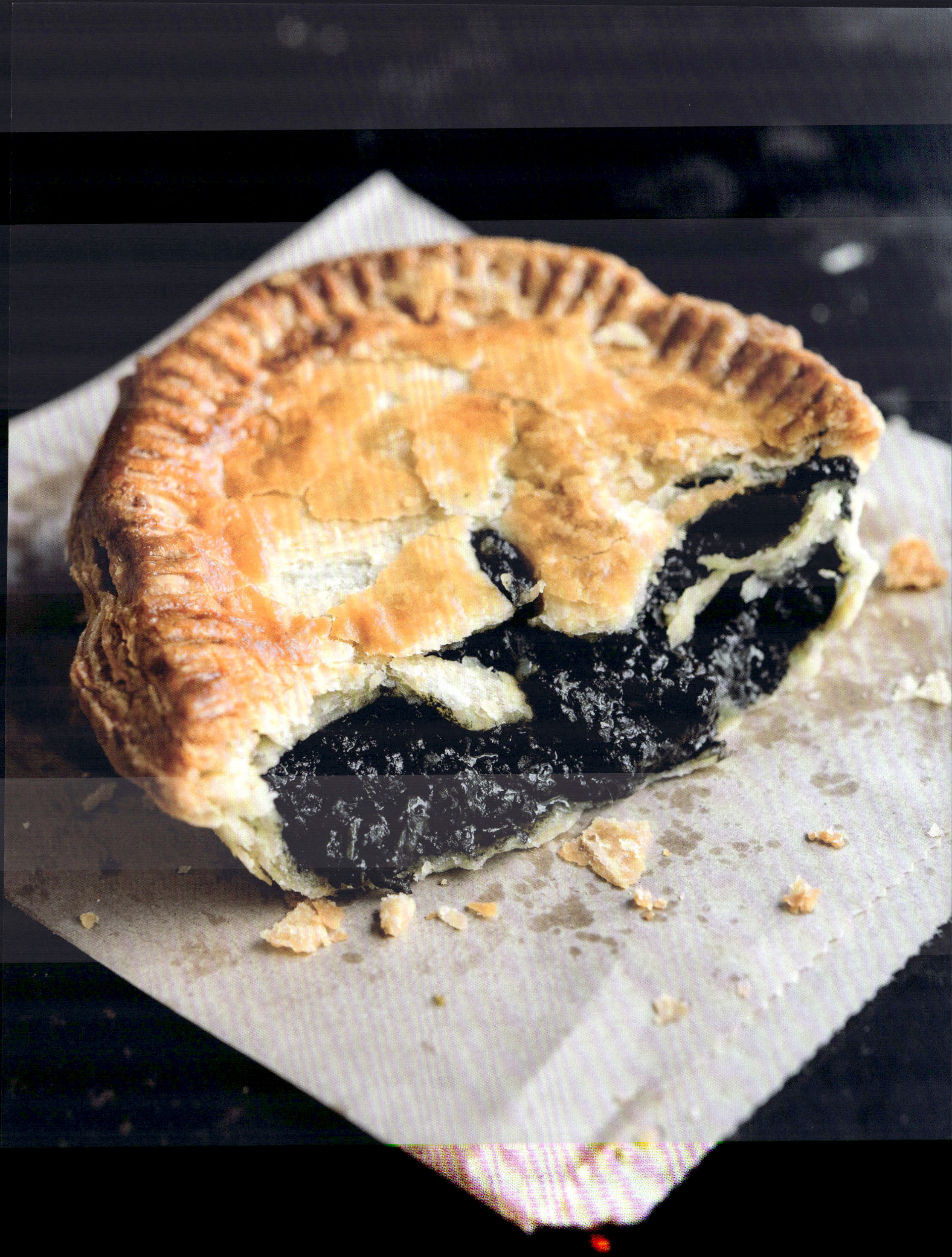

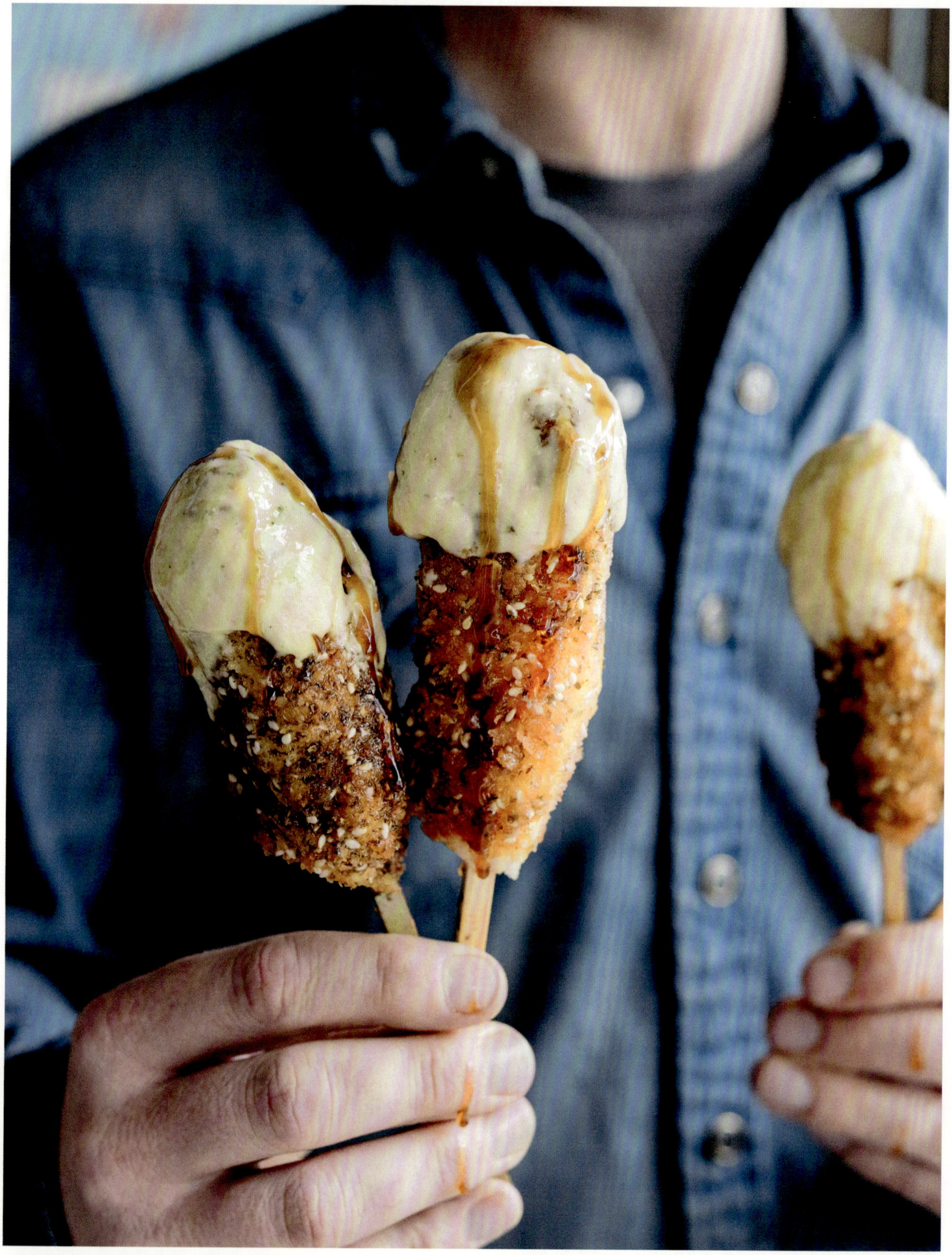

Craydog with wasabi mayo and ginger lime syrup

Every once in a while, you come up with an idea that turns out to be a real doozy. We made and served these craydogs for a relatively upmarket chefs' dinner a while back and they were a huge hit. They are sort of a down-and-dirty corndog but made with a half crayfish tail that you would normally only experience in a fine dining gaff. Fun, delicious and slightly outrageous. You'll need six hotdog sticks or bamboo skewers (if using hotdog sticks, sharpen to a point on one end).

Serves 6

CRAYDOGS
3 crayfish
1 cup (150 g/5½ oz) plain flour
3 eggs, beaten
2 cups (200 g/7 oz) dried breadcrumbs, such as panko
¼ cup (40 g/1½ oz) sesame seeds
½ cup dried seaweed flakes
flaky sea salt and freshly ground black pepper
canola oil, for frying
3 limes, cut into wedges, to serve

WASABI MAYO
1½ cups (375 g/13 oz) mayonnaise
1 tablespoon grated fresh wasabi or 1½ tablespoons processed green wasabi
2 teaspoons soy sauce

GINGER LIME SYRUP
⅓ cup (80 ml/2½ fl oz) soy sauce
200 ml (7 fl oz) rice wine vinegar
100 ml (3½ fl oz) white wine vinegar
¼ cup (60 ml/2 fl oz) lime juice
240 g (8½ oz) rock sugar, smashed up (available from Asian supermarkets)
1 thumb (8 g) ginger, cut in matchsticks

To prepare the crayfish, place in the freezer for 30 minutes. Remove and thaw out. Just that little bit of freezing makes it possible to remove the crayfish meat from the shell as a whole piece. Halve the tails lengthways, remove the poo tube and gently peel away the shell. Refrigerate until required.

For the wasabi mayo, combine the ingredients in a mixing bowl. Refrigerate until required.

Next, make the ginger lime syrup. In a suitable-sized saucepan, place the ingredients over medium-low heat. Boil, lower the heat, then simmer and reduce until it becomes a little syrupy. It will thicken when it cools. Remove from the heat, let cool, then refrigerate until required.

Now take three bowls. In the first place the flour, in the second the beaten eggs, and in the third combine the breadcrumbs, sesame seeds and seaweed flakes. Season the halved crayfish tails with salt and pepper. Place in the flour, pat off any excess, dip into the egg, then roll in the breadcrumb mixture. Carefully insert the hotdog stick or bamboo skewer into each portion, forming the crayfish into a sausage-like shape with your hand as you do so. Refrigerate until required.

Preheat your oven to 200°C (400°F).

Place a frying pan over medium heat. Add a generous amount of canola oil, and once hot, sauté the craydogs for 1–2 minutes, until golden brown all over. Be vigilant; they will brown quickly. Remove from the pan and place on a baking tray. Bake for a further 2–4 minutes, until the craydogs are firm to the touch and cooked through.

Simply serve the craydogs with a dollop of wasabi mayo, some ginger lime syrup drizzled over and lime wedges.

Battered kahawai 'Mumbai tacos' with curry lime mayo and carrot mango chutney

My personal thinking on the humble kahawai is that it's time we treasured this extraordinary fish that inhabits much of the coastline around Aotearoa. Kahawai were aptly named 'the people's fish' a long time ago, and that I believe was likely due to them being one of our most abundant native species, as well as an extremely important and treasured food source for Māori. Sadly, that is not the case these days, as they have been fished hard commercially since the eighties—and, infuriatingly, mainly for fishmeal and bait. Luckily for us they still do school off the coast, but in much smaller numbers. The sighting of a kahawai boil-up these days still gets my heart racing.

I like to target them on a fly rod. You can do battle with a large one for a good ten minutes, as pound for pound they are such great scrappers. There are two fish fables that have dogged the kahawai for as long as I can remember. One is that you have to bleed kahawai. No matter how you bleed it, the blood line down the fillet next to the skin will remain. Yes, you can remove it, but I really like this stronger part of the fish. The second piece of lore that I would like to put an end to is that kahawai is only good for smoking. Yes, it smokes well, but it also eats beautifully raw, and—as we can attest to at Depot—it grills brilliantly. The golden rule with cooking oily fish is that if you overcook it, it tends to dry out. So just keep this in mind and you will start to regard the amazing kahawai as a very valuable culinary treasure of Aotearoa.

Serves 6 (2–3 tortillas per person)

CURRY LIME MAYO
1 cup (235 g/8½ oz) mayonnaise
2 tablespoons store-bought lime pickle, finely diced
½ tablespoon curry powder
1 teaspoon ground cumin
½ teaspoon ground turmeric
¼ cup (7 g/¼ oz) roughly chopped coriander leaves
flaky sea salt and freshly ground black pepper

CARROT MANGO CHUTNEY
⅓ cup (80 ml/2½ fl oz) cooking oil
30–40 curry leaves
½ tablespoon cumin seeds
1 tablespoon black mustard seeds
pinch chilli flakes
2 tablespoons finely chopped ginger
3 garlic cloves, finely chopped
500 g (1 lb 2 oz) carrots, shoestring cut
1 teaspoon ground turmeric
juice of 2 lemons
¾ cup (210 g/7½ oz) store-bought mango chutney
flaky sea salt and freshly ground black pepper
½ cup (15 g/½ oz) roughly chopped coriander leaves, plus extra to serve

TEMPURA BATTER
2 egg yolks
½ cup (125 ml/4 fl oz) canola oil
1½ cups (375 ml/13 fl oz) soda water
1 cup (150 g/5½ oz) self-raising flour
¼ cup (25 g/1 oz) cumin seeds

TO COOK AND SERVE
2 litres (70 fl oz) cooking oil, for deep-frying
2 kg (4 lb 8 oz) kahawai fillets
flaky sea salt and freshly ground black pepper
flour, for dusting
12–18 flour tortillas (page 442) or store-bought tortillas
½ head iceberg lettuce, shredded
lime or lemon wedges

Recipe continued overleaf...

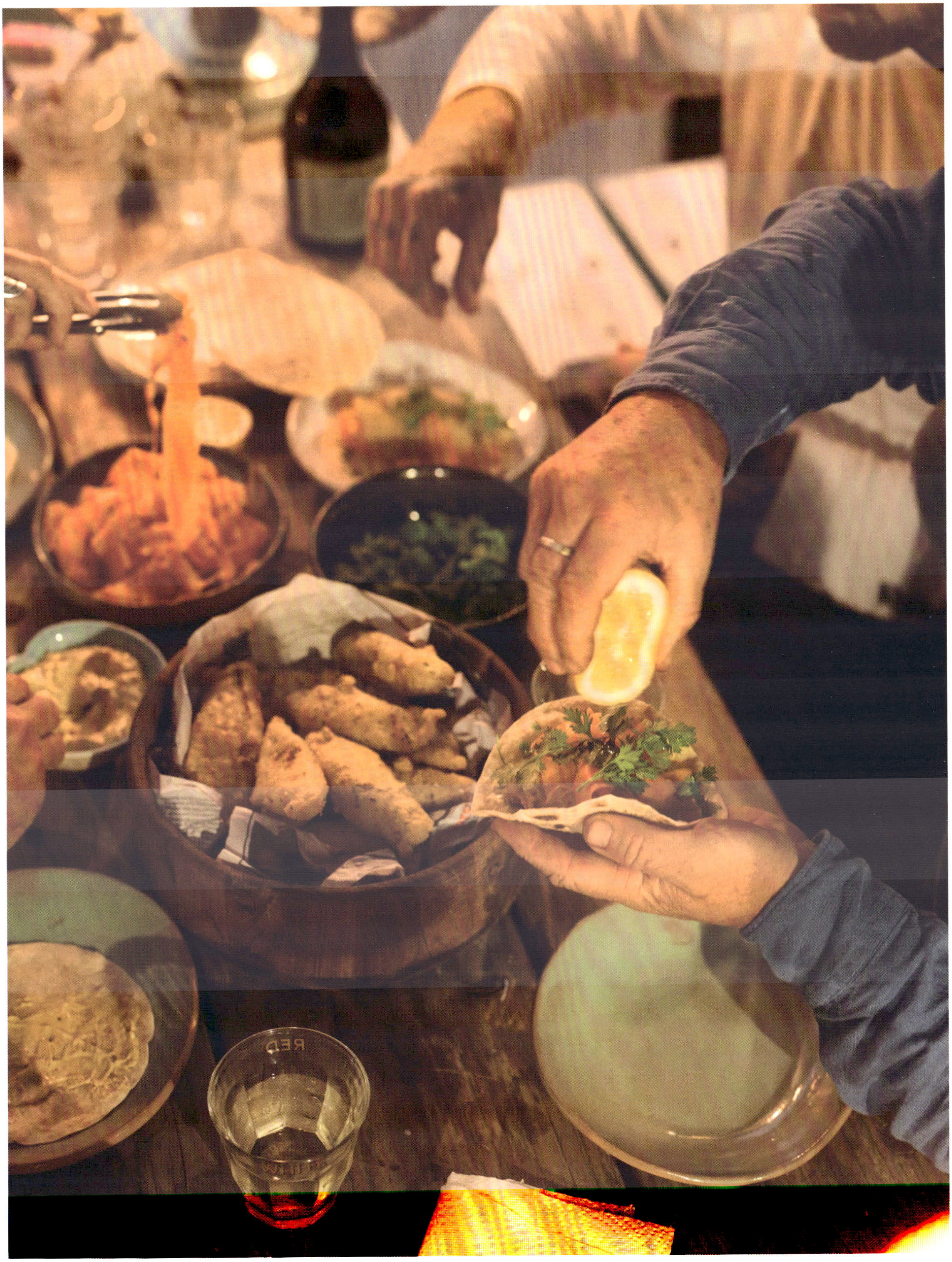

To make the curry lime mayo, empty the mayonnaise into a suitable-sized bowl. Fold in all the ingredients except for the salt and pepper. Taste, then season accordingly. It won't need too much salt as the lime pickle dials up the saltiness.

To make the carrot mango chutney, place a large heavy-bottomed saucepan or skillet over medium heat. Once hot, add the oil, followed by the curry leaves, cumin seeds, black mustard seeds and chilli flakes. Cook for a couple of minutes, stirring with a wooden spoon.

Add the ginger and garlic. Stir and cook for another minute or so, then add the carrots and turmeric. Cook for about 10 minutes, stirring. Once the carrot has wilted but still has a little resistance to the bite, add the lemon juice, then remove from the heat. Let the mixture cool a little before stirring through the mango chutney. Season with salt and pepper. Place in an airtight container and refrigerate until required (you'll add the coriander just before serving).

For the tempura batter, in a bowl, whisk the egg yolks and oil together. Stir through the soda water, then use a fork to stir in the flour, making sure not to overmix. Stir in the cumin seeds. Refrigerate until required.

Now, this is how I cook my fish tortillas: I cook the fish component twice. The first time for a minute or so, just until the batter has set on the outside but the fish is still basically raw in the centre. Then the second time just before serving. That way you can get all the messy side of flouring and battering out of the way, so that when it's time to cook and serve the fish tortillas it's really fast and easy, as everything is basically ready to go.

Place the oil in your deep-fryer or heavy-bottomed saucepan and bring up to 180°C (350°F). You can gauge this by adding a piece of bread to the oil; if it's at around 180°C (350°F), it will take about a minute for the bread to turn golden and crisp. Also remember you can use the oil at least half a dozen times. Just cool, strain and then funnel back into the oil bottles that housed the oil.

Cut your kahawai fillets into pieces just a bit bigger that an adult middle finger. Season with salt and pepper.

Dust five to six pieces with flour, then dip them into the batter. With a set of tongs, working quickly and carefully, place the battered kahawai into the oil. Cook for a minute or so, then remove and place on some kitchen paper. Repeat in batches until you've completed the task. You can do this part a day before: just cover and refrigerate the half-cooked kahawai until required.

When ready to serve, preheat your oven to 160°C (315°F). Bring your oil back up to 180°C (350°F).

Split your tortillas into two piles. Wrap the tortillas in tinfoil and place in the oven for 15 minutes or so to heat through.

Stir the coriander through the carrot mango chutney.

Re-fry your battered kahawai portions in batches for 3 minutes or so, until golden and crisp. Keep warm.

Once all the fish is done and the tortillas are hot, get everyone to serve themselves. Build your tortillas starting with curry lime mayo, then lettuce, then fish, and top with some carrot mango chutney. Garnish with extra coriander and serve with lime or lemon wedges for squeezing over. Eat and repeat.

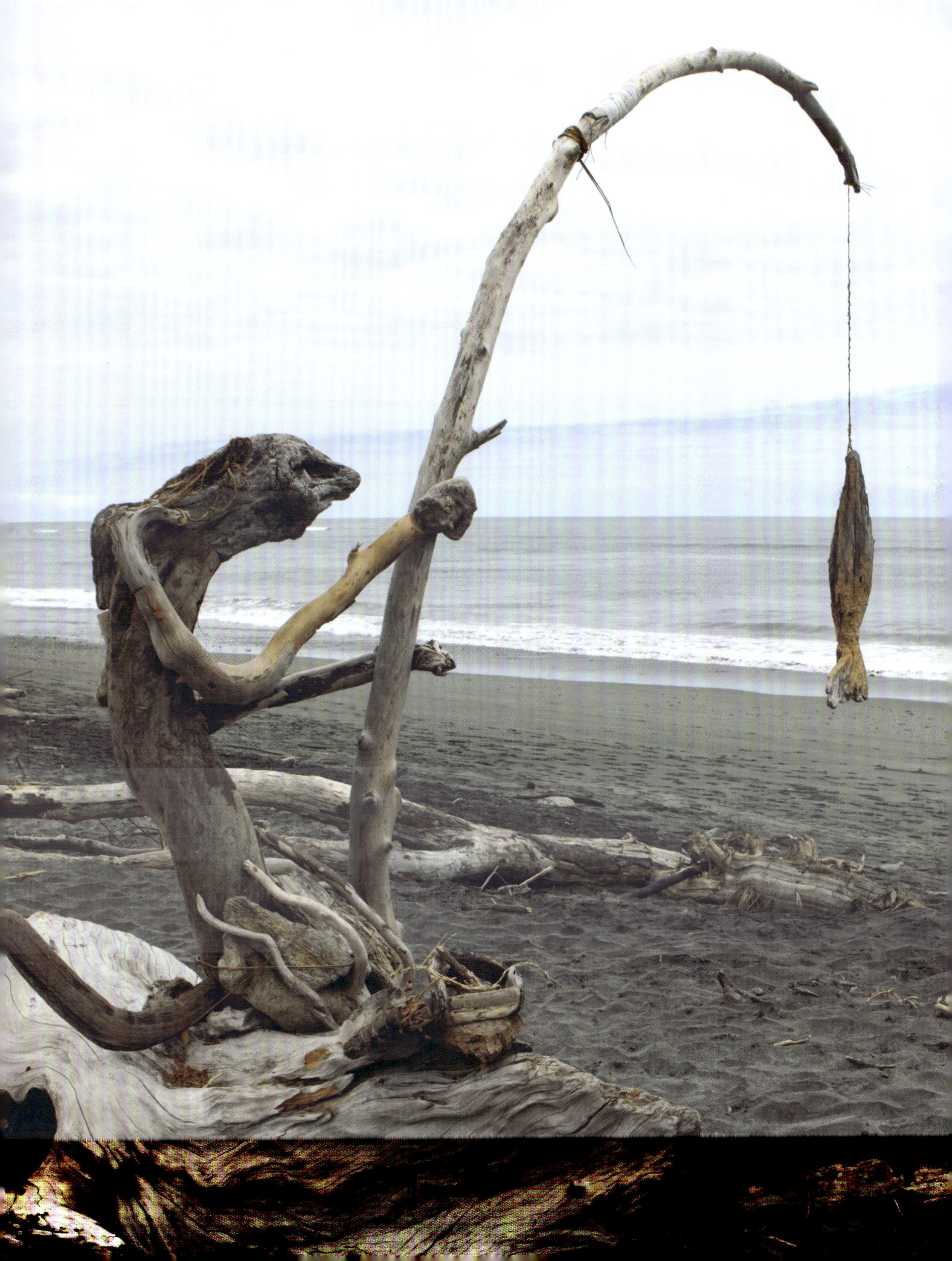

82 EAT UP NEW ZEALAND: THE BACH EDITION

Crayfish rolls with thousand island sauce and pickled cucumber

Lobster rolls have been a staple on menus up and down the northeastern seaboard of America for decades. It seems to have taken a while for the rest of the world to catch on to how simple and delicious it is to consume one of the world's tastiest crustaceans this way. There is nothing too complicated about the filling in a lobster or crayfish roll. Usually, there is some iceberg lettuce for crunch and some creamy, mayonnaise-y dressing to bind the cooked crayfish, but what makes a great crayfish or lobster roll is just that—the roll. It's all about the style, and the 'love' you give that super-soft white roll. Good-quality soft hotdog rolls are the go, and the only real secret here is you butter and toast the outside of the rolls on a flat top or in a skillet. Haydo came up with this easy pickled cucumber condiment, which does a great job cutting through the richness of the other ingredients and adds a mere hint of posh to this delicious sandwich.

Makes 12 rolls

THOUSAND ISLAND SAUCE
1½ cups (375 g/13 oz) mayonnaise
2½ tablespoons ketchup
2 teaspoons lemon juice
¼ teaspoon smoked paprika
few drops hot sauce
flaky sea salt and freshly ground black pepper

PICKLED CUCUMBER RIBBONS
1 telegraph cucumber
1½ cups (375 ml/13 fl oz) white wine vinegar
¾ cup (185 ml/6 fl oz) water
¾ cup (170 g/6 oz) caster sugar
2 teaspoons flaky sea salt

TO SERVE
2 x 700 g (1 lb 9 oz) cooked crayfish
butter, at room temperature
12 hotdog rolls, split
½ head iceberg lettuce, finely sliced
2 lemons, halved, to serve

To make the thousand island sauce, combine the mayonnaise, ketchup, lemon juice and paprika in a small bowl. Season to taste with the hot sauce, salt and pepper. Refrigerate until required.

For the pickled cucumber ribbons, cut the cucumber in half. With a decent vegetable peeler, peel ribbons of the cucumber into a bowl until you hit the inner core of seeds. Discard the seeds and core. Repeat with the remaining cucumber half. Place the vinegar, water, sugar and salt in a saucepan over medium heat. Simmer for 10 minutes, until sugar and salt have dissolved. Remove from the heat and let cool completely.

Recipe continued overleaf...

Pour the cooled brine over the cucumber ribbons and refrigerate until required.

Pick all the meat out of the whole cooked crayfish and place in a bowl. Remember, there is nearly a third of the crayfish meat in the body and the legs of the crayfish—it's not just about the tail! Chop up all the crayfish meat, leaving some good-sized chunks. Stir through as much of the thousand island sauce as you like. Taste and adjust seasoning if necessary. Set aside.

Lightly butter the outsides of the hotdog buns.

Place a large frying pan over medium-low heat. Once hot, toast the buns in the pan until golden all over and steaming but soft in the centre. They will only need 20 or 30 seconds on each side to turn golden, so keep an eye on them. Keep warm while you repeat with the remaining rolls.

To finish, open up the warm toasted rolls a little, then place a little of the finely sliced iceberg lettuce in between. Top with the dressed crayfish, then add a ribbon or two of the pickled cucumber. A squeeze of lemon juice and they are ready to serve. Eat now.

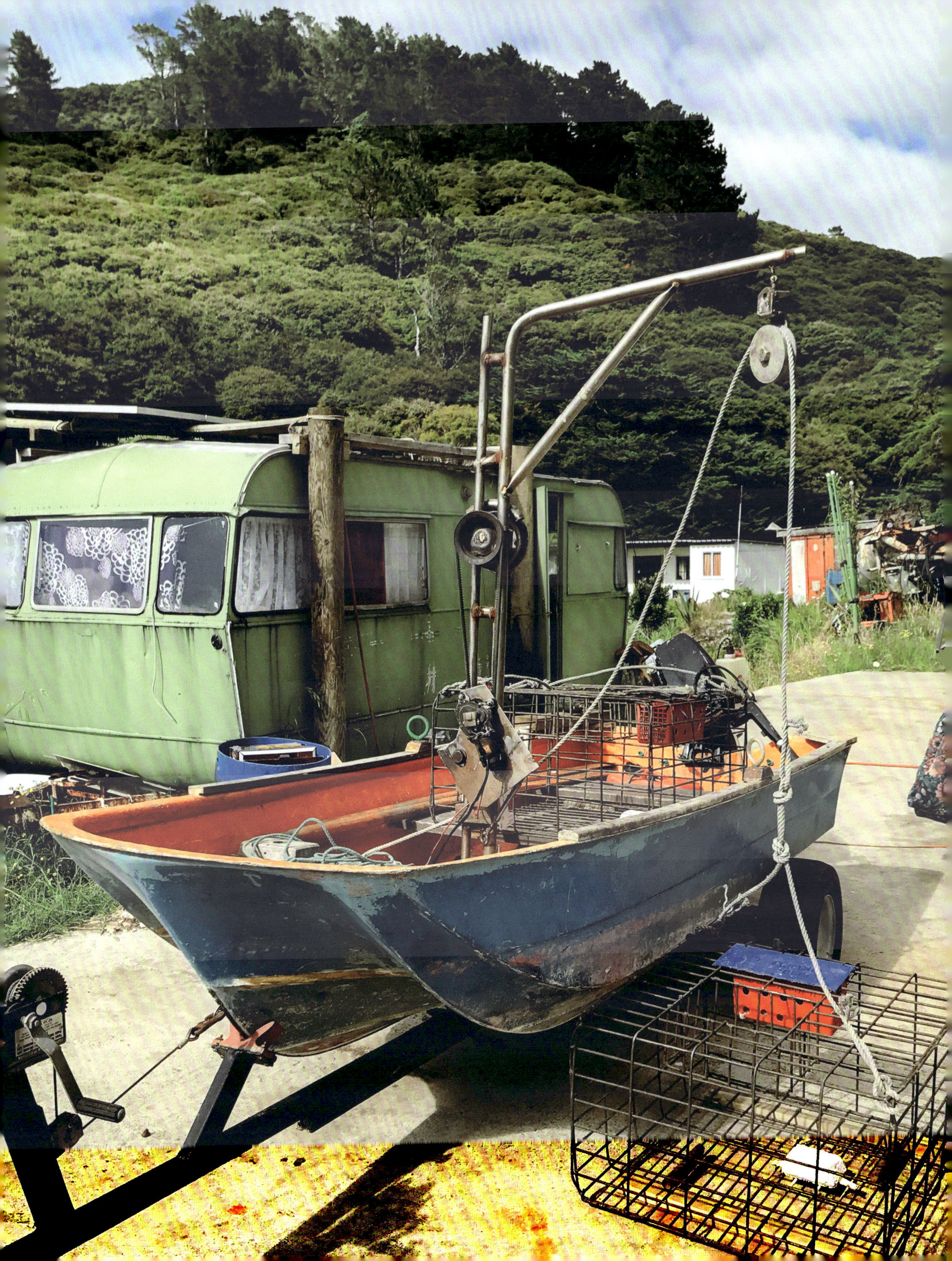

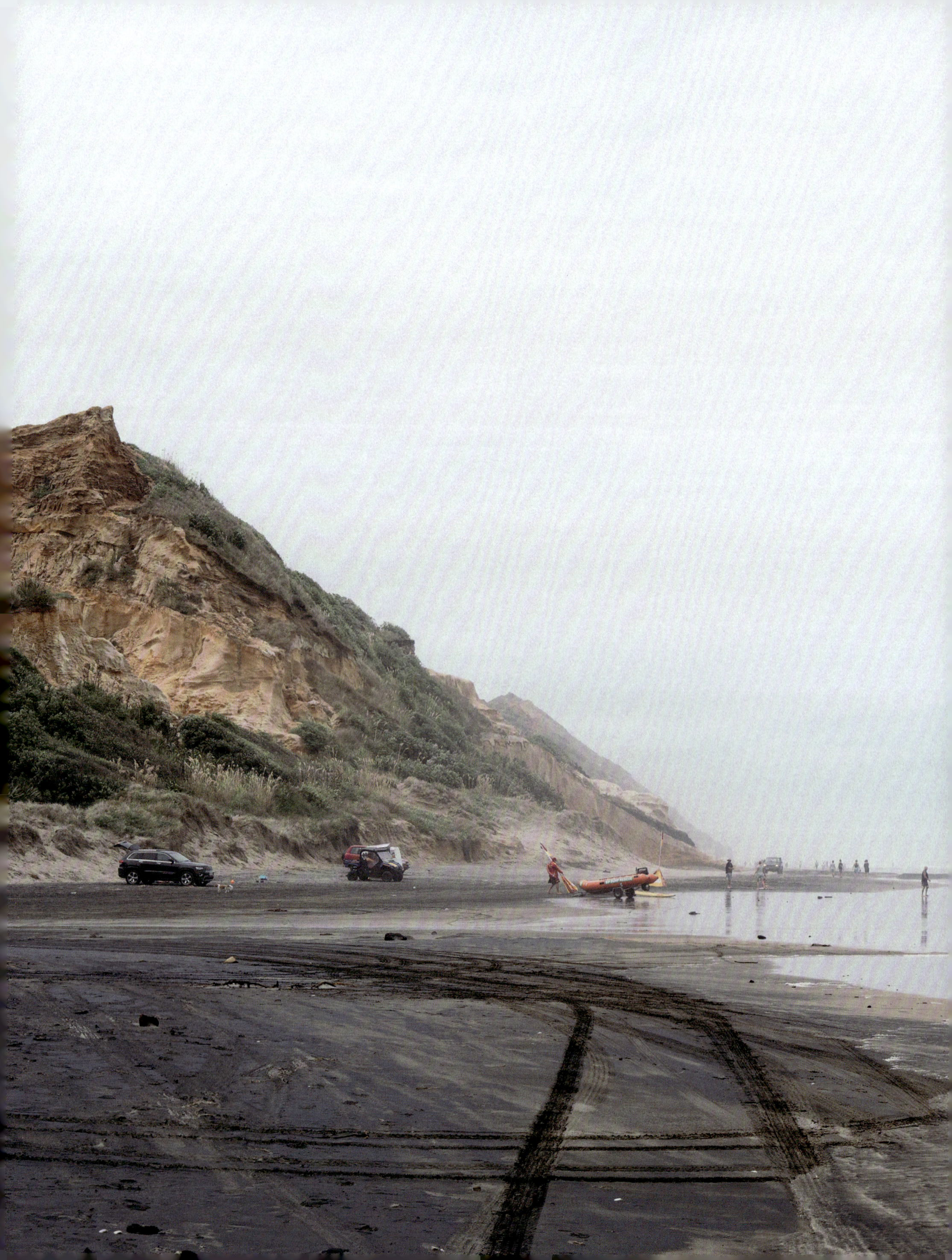

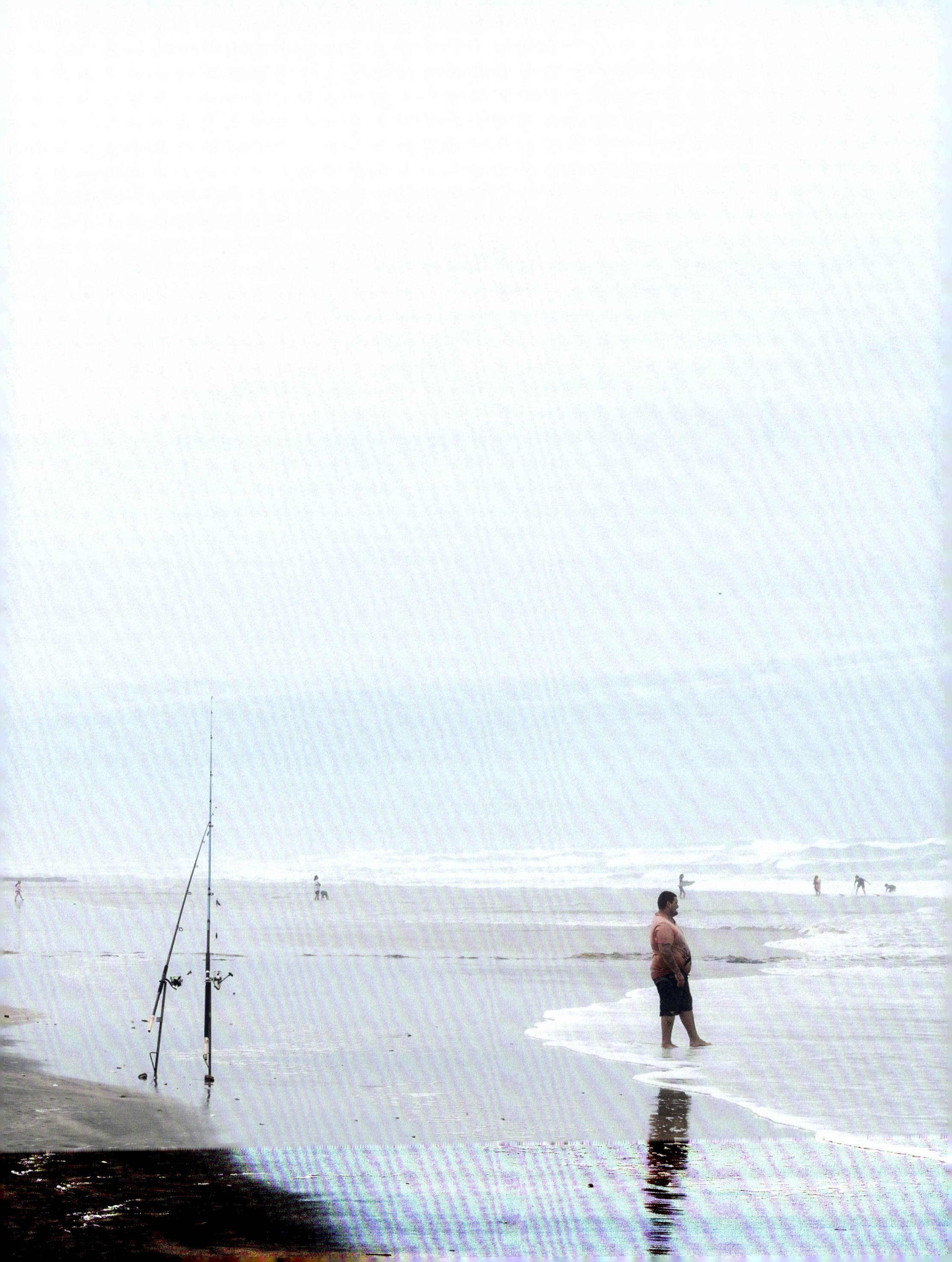

88　EAT UP NEW ZEALAND: THE BACH EDITION

Grilled mussels with Café de Paris butter

Café de Paris butter was developed in the 1940s at a restaurant in Geneva called Café de Paris (there's a surprise!). I'm not sure who the chef was who came up with this crazy-good butter with a list of ingredients as long as your arm; however, I am sure glad he or she did. Traditionally served with steak, I have found that this delicious butter can be served, within reason, with practically anything savoury. Don't be put off by the long list of ingredients, as once you assemble them all it's actually really easy to make. Go with me on this—it's worth the effort, and this recipe makes a good amount, so you can divide it up after you have made it and freeze the rest.

Serves 6–8 as a starter

CAFÉ DE PARIS BUTTER
1 cup (250 g/9 oz) unsalted butter, diced, plus 2½ tablespoons
¼ cup (40 g/1½ oz) finely diced shallots
1 tablespoon finely chopped garlic
2 teaspoons curry powder
¼ cup (60 ml/2 fl oz) white wine
2 tablespoons Worcestershire sauce
1½ tablespoons Dijon mustard
1½ tablespoons wholegrain mustard
pinch cayenne pepper
1 tablespoon lemon juice
2 anchovies, finely diced
2 tablespoons capers, rinsed and finely diced
½ tablespoon finely chopped thyme
1 tablespoon each finely chopped dill, parsley, tarragon and chives
flaky sea salt and freshly ground black pepper

MUSSELS
24–36 greenshell mussels
½ cup (125 ml/4 fl oz) white wine
½ cup (125 ml/4 fl oz) water
lemon halves, for squeezing
lemon and herb croutons (page 446), to serve

To make the Café de Paris butter, place a small pan over medium-low heat. Add the 2½ tablespoons butter, along with the shallots, garlic and curry powder. Sweat for 5 minutes, then pour in the wine and add the Worcestershire sauce. Cook for a further 5 minutes or so, until the liquid has reduced. Take the pan off the heat and let cool to room temperature.

Place the shallot mixture in a bowl along with the remaining ingredients. Using clean hands, work all the ingredients together until combined. Taste and season liberally with salt and pepper. Spoon out in two lots onto clingfilm and shape into two logs. Carefully wrap and twist the ends like a sausage. Freeze one log of the butter and refrigerate the other until required.

Prepare the mussels. Debeard and place in a large saucepan over high heat. Pour over the white wine and water. Give the saucepan a shake after 5 minutes, then remove the mussels one at a time as they open up. Discard any that haven't opened. Let the mussels cool, then remove the top half of the shell and discard. Detach the mussel, then lay it back in the half shell. Refrigerate until required.

Preheat the grill. Arrange the mussels (in their half shell) on a baking tray. Slice small discs of the Café de Paris butter and place one on top of each mussel. Place under the grill for 1–2 minutes, or until the butter has melted and the mussels have begun to caramelise. Remove from the grill. Let cool for a couple of minutes before placing on a platter. Top with a few lemon croutons on each. Serve with the lemon halves on the side and a big pile of kitchen paper or napkins to catch the juices. Eat now.

Tempura cauliflower with smoked kahawai cream

The more I cook, taste and eat, the more I find pleasure in simplicity, where dishes are completely pared back to a couple of components that produce a harmony rarely experienced in more complex dishes. This dish is so very humble but offers up such a delightful eating experience. I have used my sentimental favourite, smoked kahawai, but of course you can change that out for any smoked fish you may be lucky enough to have in your refrigerator.

Serves 6 as a starter, or more as a pass-around

SMOKED KAHAWAI CREAM
250 g (9 oz) smoked kahawai, torn into pieces
½ cup (125 g/4½ oz) sour cream
¼ cup (60 ml/2 fl oz) cream (optional)
1–2 tablespoons lemon juice
flaky sea salt and freshly ground black pepper

TEMPURA CAULIFLOWER
½ head cauliflower
1 cup tempura flour (available from most supermarkets)
1 cup water
flaky sea salt and freshly ground black pepper
8 cups (2 litres/68 fl oz) canola oil, for deep-frying
Al Brown and Co Lemon and Fennel Infused Olive Oil or extra-virgin olive oil
finely grated zest of 1–2 lemons
fried red chillies, to serve (optional) (page 445)

To make the smoked kahawai cream, place the fish and sour cream in a bowl. Using a stick blender, blitz for a couple of minutes to create a smooth paste. Pass through a sieve into a clean bowl. If the consistency is quite stiff, fold through some of the cream. Add the lemon juice, season to taste with salt and a generous grind of pepper.

For the cauliflower, use a sharp knife to break down the cauliflower into florets no bigger than the size of a chestnut. Place in a bowl.

Whisk the tempura flour with the water in a separate bowl. The tempura batter should be quite thin and runny. Pour just enough of the batter over the cauliflower pieces to lightly coat. Season with salt and pepper. Discard the rest of the batter.

Heat the oil in your deep-fryer or a suitable-sized saucepan to 180°C (350°F). You can gauge this by adding a piece of bread to the oil; if it's at around 180°C, it will take about a minute for the bread to turn golden and crisp.

Deep-fry the cauliflower in batches for approximately 2–3 minutes, until golden brown. Turn out onto kitchen paper to drain as you continue to cook the remaining cauliflower.

To serve, spread the smoked kahawai cream either on individual plates or a larger platter. Top with the warm, crisp tempura cauliflower and some extra-virgin olive oil. To finish, finely grate over the lemon zest, sprinkle over the fried chillies, if using, and season with salt and pepper. Eat now.

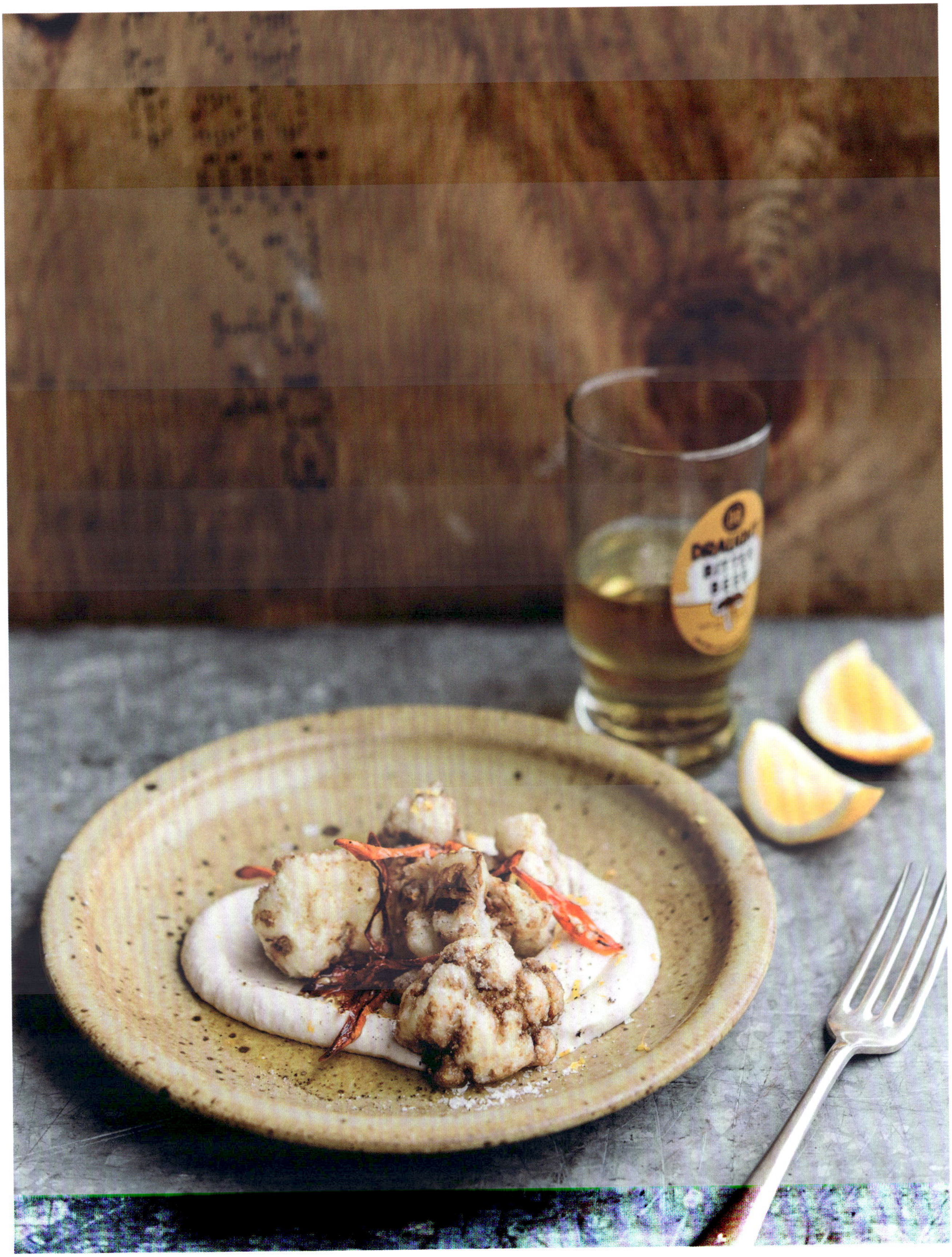

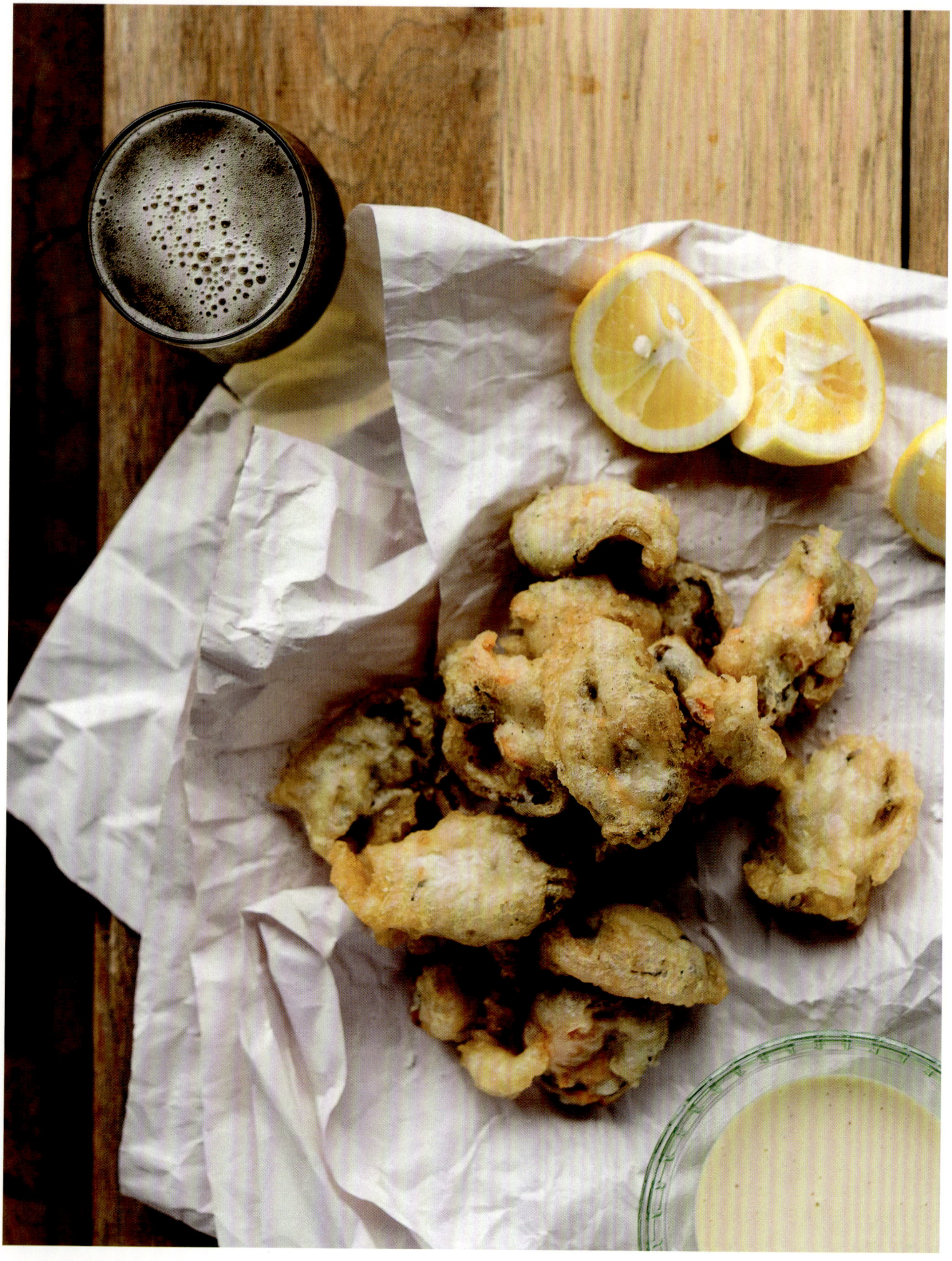

Battered mussels with malt vinegar mayo

A good friend of mine, Rob Pooley, introduced me to the glorious world of deep-fried mussels a number of years back when he and I cooked at a large event on the banks of Lake Wakatipu. If you like fried oysters, well, this is the poor man's version. But I swear if you close your eyes, you'll be convinced that you are actually eating fried oysters. No joking, I swear!

Makes 24

MALT VINEGAR MAYO
4 egg yolks
½ tablespoon Dijon mustard
75 ml (2½ fl oz) malt vinegar
2 teaspoons sugar
1½ cups (375 ml/13 fl oz) canola oil
flaky sea salt and freshly ground black pepper

BATTERED MUSSELS
2 egg yolks
½ cup (125 ml/4 fl oz) canola oil, plus 2 litres (68 fl oz/8 cups) for deep-frying
1½ cups (375 ml/13 fl oz) soda water
1 cup (150 g/5½ oz) self-raising flour
24 freshly shucked mussels
lemon halves, to serve

To make the malt vinegar mayo, place the egg yolks, mustard, vinegar and sugar in a jar or jug. Using a stick blender, blitz for 10 seconds, then slowly drizzle in the oil, blitzing all the time, to form an emulsion. Taste, season with flaky salt and pepper, and refrigerate until required.

For the batter, in a clean bowl lightly whisk the egg yolks and canola oil together. Stir through the soda water. Using a fork, gently stir in the flour until just incorporated—be careful not to over-mix. Refrigerate for 20–30 minutes.

Heat the remaining oil in your deep-fryer to 180°C (350°F). Alternatively, heat the oil in a heavy-bottomed saucepan. You can gauge this by adding a piece of bread to the oil; if it's at around 180°C, it will take about a minute for the bread to turn golden and crisp.

Working in batches, dip the mussels into the tempura batter then carefully place in the hot oil. Cook for a couple of minutes, until golden all over. Remove with a slotted spoon and drain on kitchen towels. Keep warm while you finish cooking the rest of the mussels.

To serve, season with salt and pepper. Place the deep-fried mussels on a platter with the malt vinegar mayo on the side and bunch of lemon halves for squeezing. Eat now.

Mussels mornay

As a child, I would have been lucky to go to a restaurant once a year. However, what I do remember from those simple family restaurants like Cobb & Co. is that, on those special occasions that we were lucky enough to go, I think you could pretty much guarantee there would always be a mornay dish on the menu somewhere. Just hearing the word 'mornay' conjures up images of bubbling molten cheese enveloping delicious morsels of seafood, bathing in a glorious, rich, silky white sauce. I have used fresh mussels here as they are such good value, and they also make a terrific stock during the cooking process. And let's face it, anything covered in what I just described is going to taste fab. Keep your crayfish and scallops for a simpler application.

Serves 6

MUSSELS
3 kg (6 lb 10 oz) greenshell mussels
1 cup (250 ml/9 fl oz) Sauvignon Blanc

MORNAY SAUCE
80 g (2¾ oz) butter
2 tablespoons cooking oil
2 cups (300 g/10½ oz) finely diced onion
1 cup (140 g/5 oz) finely diced celery
⅓ cup (55 g/2 oz) plain flour
2 cups (500 ml/17 fl oz) milk

1½ cups (375 ml/13 fl oz) cream
2 teaspoons Dijon mustard
2 teaspoons hot sauce
juice of 1 lemon
120 g (4¼ oz) Gruyère cheese, grated
flaky sea salt and freshly ground black pepper
120 g (4¼ oz) tasty cheese, grated

TO SERVE
grated tasty cheese
crusty bread and crisp green salad leaves (optional)

Debeard your mussels, and place in a large saucepan. Pour in a cup or so of the Sav Blanc, pop the lid on and place the pan over high heat. After 5 minutes or so, carefully give the pan a shake (this helps the mussels open up). Once the shells start to open, use tongs to remove the individual mussels as they open, and let cool. Bear in mind that the longer the mussels stay in the pan once they open, the dryer they will become. Discard any mussels that failed to open. Strain the cooking liquid through a fine sieve and reserve.

Once the mussels are cool enough to handle, remove and discard the shells, along with any remaining beards. Chop each mussel into thirds, place in a bowl and refrigerate until required.

For the mornay sauce, melt 25 g (¾ oz) butter in a small saucepan over low heat. Add the oil, onion and celery and sweat for about 30 minutes, until the vegetables are translucent and softened. Take off the heat and set aside.

Next, place a large saucepan over medium-low heat. Add the remaining 55 g (2 oz) butter and, once melted, whisk in the flour. Cook out the roux for a couple of minutes, then gradually whisk in the mussel-cooking liquid, milk and cream, a little at a time to eliminate lumps, until silky and smooth. Whisk in the mustard, hot sauce and lemon juice, then fold in the Gruyère cheese. Finally, add the cooked onions, celery and chopped mussels. Stir through, taste and season accordingly. Remove from the heat and divvy up into individual bowls or one large ovenproof dish. Let cool, then refrigerate until required.

Preheat your oven to 150°C (300°F).

Take the mussel mornay and divvy up the grated cheese on top. Place in the oven and cook until hot though and the cheese is bubbling and beginning to caramelise. If you want the cheese to golden up a bit more, place under the grill for a couple of minutes. Let the mussel mornay cool for a bit before serving. Crusty bread and a green salad work a treat next to this deliciously rich dish.

Dredge Oyster
Silver Warehou
Elephant Fish
Ling
Greenshell Mussels
Black Oreo Dory
Rig
Red Cod
Blue Warehou
John Dory
Jack Mackerel
Monkfish
Smooth Oreo Dory
Orange Roughy
Hake
New Zealand Sole
Barracuda
Blue Mackerel
Skate
Tarakihi
Red Gurnard
Arrow Squid
Hoki
Southern Blue Whiting
Sand Flounder
School Shark
Trumpeter
Mirror Dory
Tuatua
Bluenose
Snapper
Kahawai
Blue Shark
Lemon Sole
Octopus
Gemfish
Swimming Crab
Sea Perch
Groper
Scallop
Spiny Dogfish
Brill
Venus Clam
Ghost Shark
Blue Moki
Grey Mullet
Southern Spider Crab
Frostfish
Southern Bluefin Tuna
Paua
Ray's Bream
Grenadiers
Alfonsino
Skipjack Tuna
Red Pearl Fish
Quinnat Salmon
Ribaldo
Conger Eel
Cockle
Albacore Tuna
Pilchard
Sea Cucumber
Freshwater Eel
Spiny Rock Lobster
Cardinal Fish
Yellowbelly Flounder
Scampi
Yellowtail Kingfish
Trevally
Leatherjacket
Blue Cod
Pacific Oyster
Kina
Yellow Fin Tuna
Turbot
Whitebait
Yellow-eyed Mullet
Pipi
Illustration by Jenny Sahng

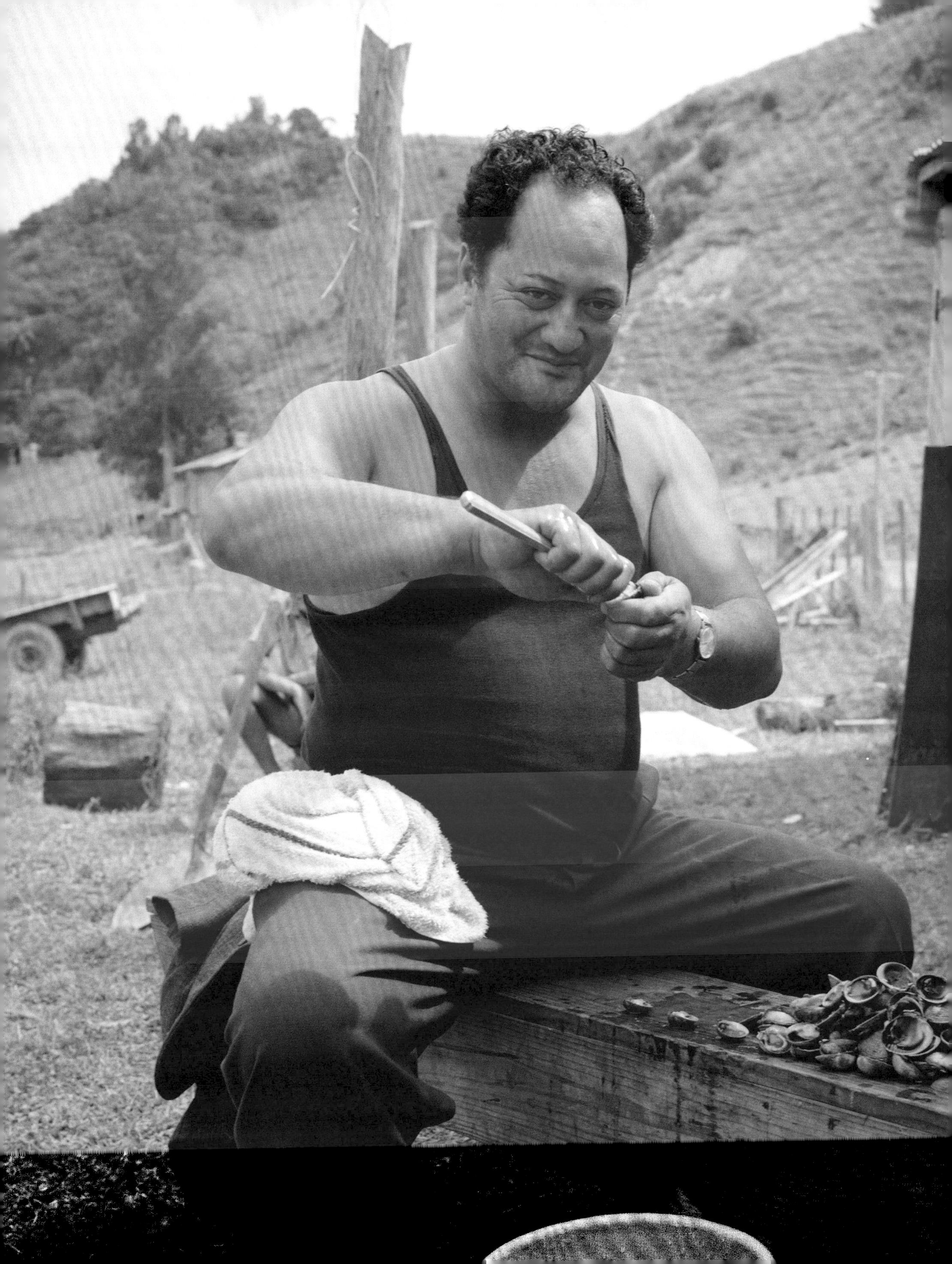

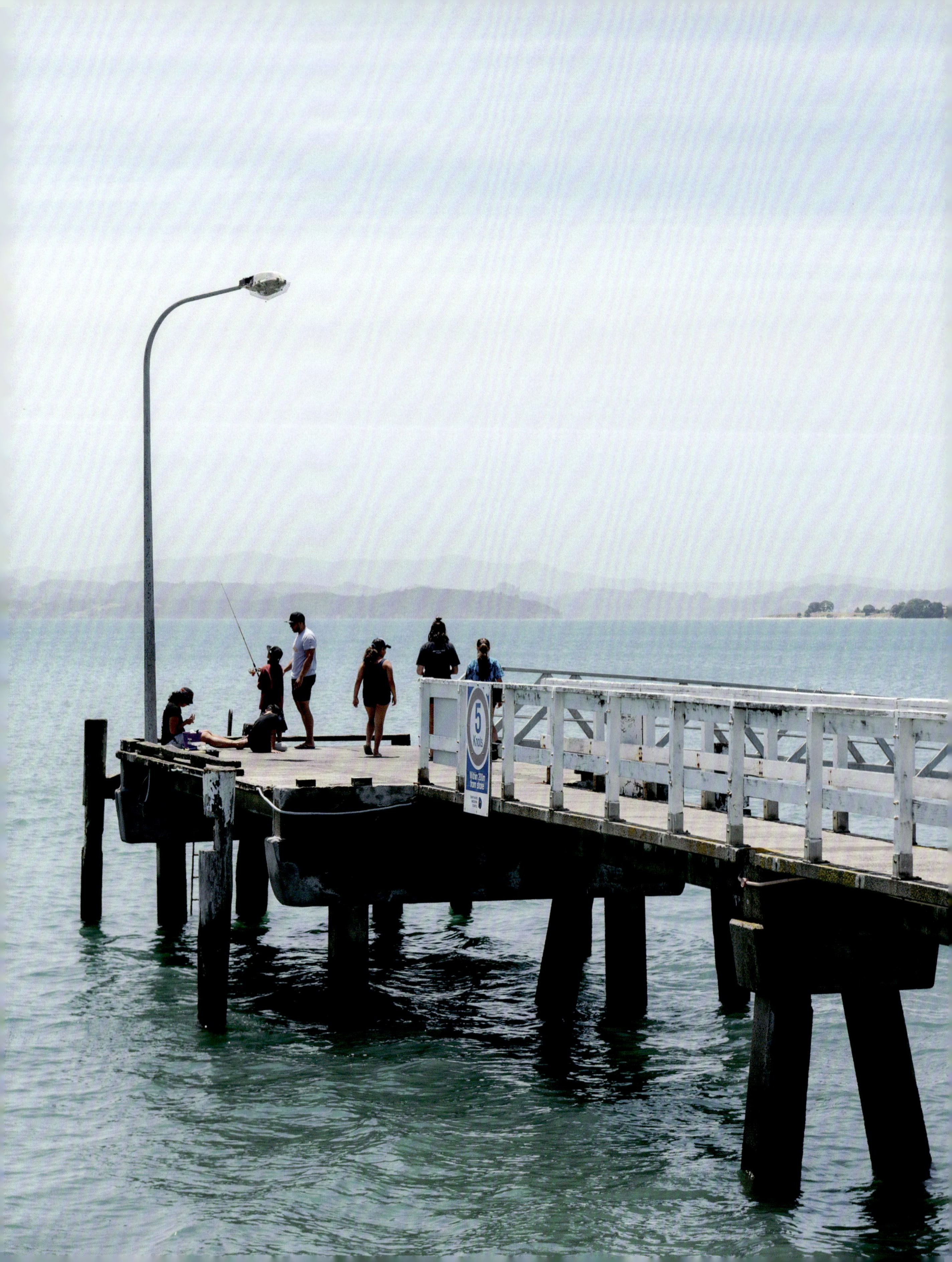

Our Precious Ocean

I am often asked a couple of particular questions: 'What is your favourite food to cook?' and 'What is your favourite food to eat?' I expect it's the same for most chefs or people who cook for a living. These questions used to annoy me, for a number of reasons.

On reflection, I think I was just tired of being asked the same thing all the time, and I thought of it as a kind of 'small-talk' question that seemed a bit silly—sort of like asking an artist what their favourite colour is.

The answer really depends on the day, the circumstance and my mood at the time. But, honestly, I think it mostly bothered me because I didn't have a consistent answer.

However, while I found it hard to narrow it down, the answer that most often comes to mind is without a doubt 'seafood'. Freshly shucked oysters have always been near the top of the list, but then there's also pāua, sautéed scallops, whitebait fritters, hāpuka belly, raw tuatua, poached crayfish, trevally sashimi and so on . . . This is probably why I rarely have the same answer to those questions, and why I still find it impossible to choose.

It's a big statement, but I think we must have close to the greatest selection and variety of fish and shellfish of anywhere in the world. I have no data to back that up; it is more of a hunch, based on my travels and what I have witnessed during my 50-plus years. Sure, there are amazing fish markets dotted all around the world's great coastlines, but the thing I notice whenever I walk the aisles of these markets is that a good percentage of the fish or shellfish on offer arrived by plane, not by boat! Thanks to our geographical position, we have something unique and exceptional in New Zealand. There is one word in my mind that describes and defines it the best, and that simple word is 'precious'.

I care deeply about all of New Zealand, but I guess it's due to my love of fishing that it's the waterways, lakes, rivers and our coastlines and oceans that I hold in the highest regard and cherish more than anything else. I published my first big cookbook, *Go Fish*, in 2009, and (I guess a bit like your first 'big' anything) I treasure that book just a little more than any of the others I've been lucky enough to publish over the years. I still pick it up from time to time—generally to refresh my memory regarding one recipe or another—but when I was first putting *Eat Up* together I sat down and read some of the longer pieces I wrote about my love of fish and shellfish, fishing and gathering, and my concerns for our oceans with their finite resource. That was 2009—in the scheme of things, not really a long time ago—but my worries and concerns about the state of our resource are even more urgent today.

The state of our oceans really polarises people and they get very passionate about it. But this is a good thing, because it clearly shows that people care very deeply about our oceans. It is a very high-octane subject for anyone, whether you are involved recreationally, commercially, scientifically or spiritually with our water. There does now seem to be more resolve on the part of everyone concerned to find an outcome that can somehow appease all parties. Collectively, we have to get past the pointing of fingers and the blame game. What is done is done; we can't turn back the clock. What we can do, though, is acknowledge and learn from the past, and make damn sure, with all the technology and history at our fingertips, that we understand the gravity of the situation. It is getting serious now, and we all need to be tolerant and patient, and listen to each other with respect and understanding.

I'm the first to say I don't have all the answers. What I do know is that we have a better opportunity in New Zealand than in most other countries because of our global position and distance from major centres of population. As a chef and as a recreational fisherman, I have a foot in both camps. I have relationships with the commercial sector, whereby I purchase fish and shellfish for my restaurant customers, but my biggest other love (besides my family) and my favourite thing to do is to go fishing. I also know that as a chef I have options and I have a voice. I feel I have a responsibility to persuade and sometimes even influence people. My restaurants give me the perfect opportunity to serve seafood that many people will never have tried or even thought to try.

As a recreational fisher myself, nearly everything comes down to making thoughtful choices. The question that I ask myself before I head out for a fish is basically the same question that I ask when I go to my fishmonger to buy some fish: 'How much fish do I need?' If I have a bunch of people coming around for dinner, I'll work out how much I need for that. If I've borrowed the neighbour's chainsaw recently, it would be nice to give him a feed of fish. However, if it's just me at home for a few days, then I don't need a lot of fish at all. I take these things into consideration and fish accordingly.

What I choose to take home is not going to have any real bearing on the enjoyment factor of my day's fishing. Like most people who go out fishing, I want to catch lots of fish, and if you look after these precious and fragile creatures you can catch them all day. The difference, of course, is that you only keep what you need and carefully release the others to swim for another day. Releasing fish back into their environment is still unfathomable to many anglers. It was to me for a long time, but now—and I say this hand on heart—releasing them is without question one of the things I love most about fishing. Just because the fish are on the bite and you are catching them doesn't mean that you need to kill them all. I know almost everyone has a freezer at home, but these are for bread, mince and ice cream. I bet that when you buy fish you never decide to grab an extra kilo or two to take home and put in the freezer. And, in truth, what comes out of the freezer is nothing like what you put in there. I beg you not to freeze fish!

I also believe it is time that the wonderful and passionate fish-eaters of this country got a little more adventurous. It's tough to break old habits, but it's also very liberating—and, in this case, it is rewarding on so many levels. We Kiwis can be a parochial bunch. If you live in the top of 'the North' I'm guessing your favourite fish is probably snapper; if you're at the bottom of 'the South' it's probably going to be blue cod. It's only natural when we all grow up in different regions, hearing our parents and grandparents extol the virtues of our local varieties. These fish—whether blue cod, snapper, hāpuka, tarakihi or gurnard—are unquestionably delicious eating fish, and I'm not for a moment suggesting that you stop eating them. I'm just reminding you that there are dozens of other fish swimming in our waters that are equally delicious, and I encourage you to give the not-so-popular varieties a go. Make it a bit of a game. When you're buying fish, ask the server to add a little piece of something that you haven't tried before. Likewise when you're fishing: if you catch a variety that you would normally put back, iki it, ice it down and give it a whirl. There is so much information out there on how to prepare, cook and eat practically every kind of fish. You can learn which ones eat well raw or marinated, which suit being cooked in a wet situation like a stew or curry, and which simply need to be cooked in a frying pan with a knob of butter and a squeeze of lemon juice to finish.

There's a bunch of mistruths out there that need to be exposed for the fibs they are. An example of this is the idea that kahawai are only good for smoking. That's a load of hogwash. I eat kahawai raw, I marinate it, I give it the batter treatment . . . and yes, it does smoke wonderfully well, but what most people don't realise is that kahawai is a delicious fish simply pan-fried. Likewise, many folk think fish like trevally, mackerel, yellow-eyed mullet and piper are all only good for bait. I agree, they do make great bait; however, they are also all terrific eating fish.

I feel that we have had it too good for too long. Most of us have grown up eating skinless, boneless, pearly white fillets of what we consider to be premium fish. Eating the smaller species and cooking fish whole is a different kind of eating experience.

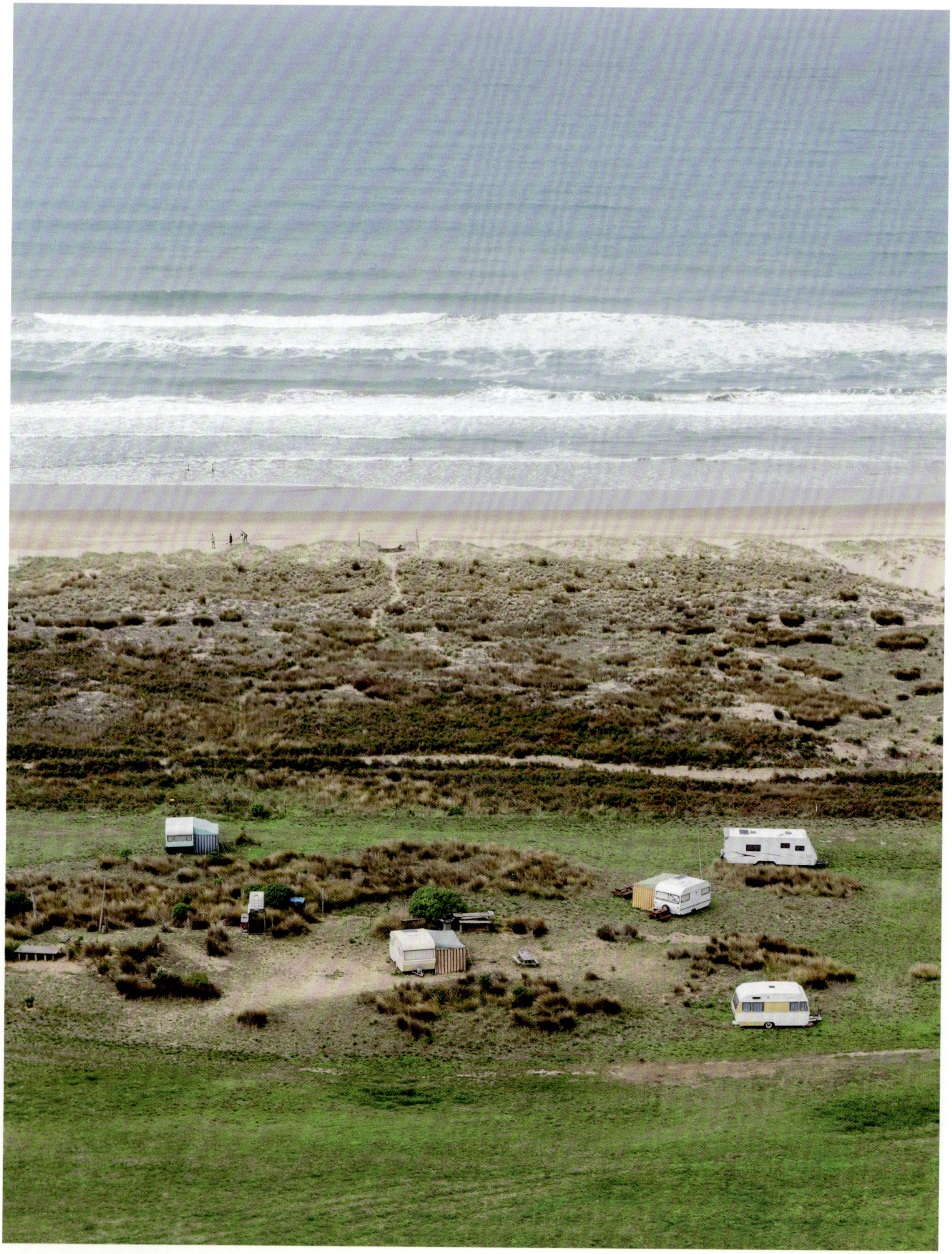

It's a bit slower, as you take your time extracting the cooked fish away from the frame. But, just like when you pick the leg meat from crayfish or crabs, your patience will always be rewarded, because cooking fish on the bone gives a much more intense volume of flavour. Slowing down in general is something that I believe we should all be trying to do, and this style of cooking lends itself perfectly to more time around the table. This means more conversation, more laughter, more wine and generally more good times.

When you catch fish, along with looking after them as the extremely precious resource that they are, you need to waste as little as possible. Recreationally and commercially, waste is definitely a big issue. We have got to get away from whipping off the fillets and throwing away a third of the fish. The crazy thing is that the third that we throw away is what many people around the world consider the best, tastiest parts: the belly, the wings, the skin, the head and the frames. Eating a variety of fish and not wasting anything is just common sense. It takes the pressure off the 'premium' species, and it certainly takes the pressure off your wallet.

There is no question that the commercial sector is investing money and time into research on better and more sustainable methods of fishing, and they should be applauded for that. After all, if they don't do it, they won't have a business. And as for the recreational fishers out there, there is also a small movement that is slowly making an impact on the Kiwis who love to fish. We need to be mindful of the role each of us plays individually in doing our part to make sure that the generations that follow get to enjoy and reap the rewards of living in this extraordinary country of ours, which is surrounded by some of the most beautiful, pure and still relatively abundant ocean in the world.

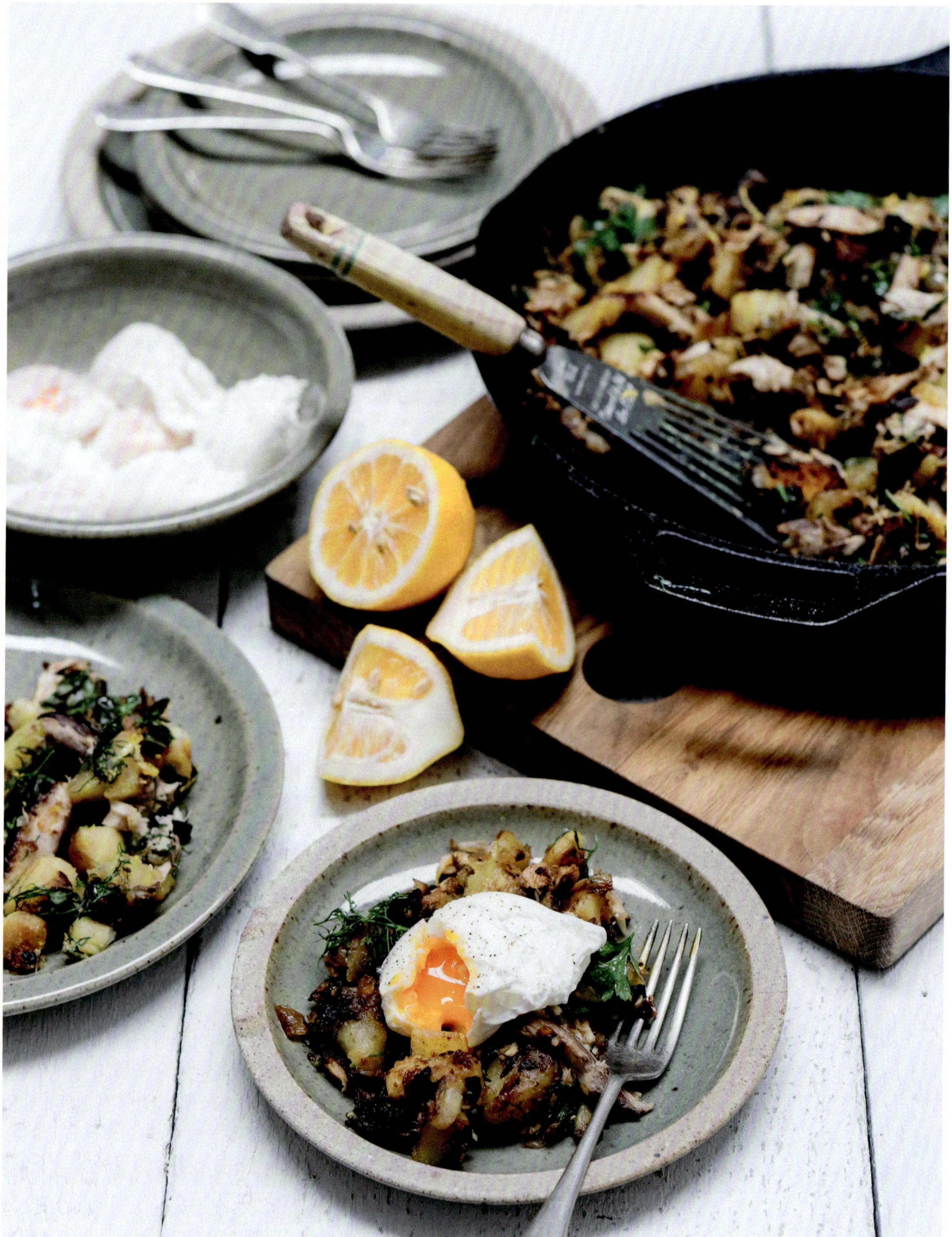

Smoked kahawai mishmash

We serve a similar version of this at 'The Fed' Delicatessen. It's hands-down my favourite breakfast. I love the name 'mishmash', the Jewish term for a type of potato-based hash where there are no rules when it comes to what you throw in. It may seem like there's a lot of fresh herbs in this recipe, but trust me it's this combination that lightens up the dish with so much freshness. As far as accompaniments go, this dish is begging for poached eggs, and plenty of lemon halves for squeezing.

Serves 6 as a brunch dish

⅓ cup (80 ml/2½ fl oz) canola oil
3 cups (465 g/1 lb) diced onion
1 kg (2 lb 3 oz) cooked potato, roughly chopped
500 g (1 lb 2 oz) smoked kahawai, shredded
¼ cup (7 g/¼ oz) roughly chopped tarragon
½ cup (30 g/1 oz) roughly chopped dill
½ cup (15 g/½ oz) roughly chopped parsley
½ cup (30 g/1 oz) roughly chopped basil
finely grated zest and juice of 2 lemons
flaky sea salt and freshly ground black pepper
poached eggs, to serve
lemon halves, to serve

Place a large frying pan over medium-low heat. Once hot, add the oil along with the onion. Cook for 10–15 minutes, stirring occasionally, until the onion is golden and caramelised.

Add the potato, along with the smoked kahawai. Mix through and don't stir for at least 5–6 minutes as you want a nice crispy layer to form on the bottom. Use a metal spatula to flip the mishmash and cook until golden on the other side.

Mix through the freshly chopped herbs, followed by the lemon zest and juice. Season with salt and pepper. Keep warm.

Divvy up the mishmash between warm plates, adding a poached egg and a lemon half for squeezing to each one. You're going to love this. Eat now.

Poached hāpuka with battered pumpkin, pickled red onion rings and Kalamata olive mayo

As a country we typically don't eat a lot of chilled, poached fish. Salmon has a great oil content so stays wonderfully moist when eaten cold. The critical trick with serving ocean-going 'whitefish' in a chilled, poached fashion is that you don't overcook the fish, as it tends to dry out and become a little stringy. Don't be put off by this—just be a little more vigilant than normal when poaching the hāpuka.

Serves 6 as a starter

PICKLED RED ONION RINGS
2 red onions, sliced into fine rings
½ cup (125 ml/4 fl oz) red wine vinegar
½ cup (110 g/3¾ oz) sugar
1 cup (250 ml/9 fl oz) water
2 cinnamon sticks
2 star anise
6 cardamom pods
½ teaspoon fennel seeds
pinch dried chilli flakes
1 teaspoon sea salt

KALAMATA OLIVE MAYO
½ cup (60 g/2¼ oz) pitted kalamata olives
1 cup (250 g/9 oz) mayonnaise

HĀPUKA SALAD
600 g (1 lb 5 oz) hāpuka fillets, cut into 1.5 cm thick pieces
1 lemon, sliced
2 bay leaves
2–3 parsley sprigs

TO COOK AND SERVE
4 cups (1 litre/35 fl oz) canola oil, for deep-frying
400 g (14 oz) peeled pumpkin
1 cup (125 g/4½ oz) tempura flour
¾ cup (185 ml/6 fl oz) sparkling water
1 bunch watercress
flaky sea salt and freshly ground black pepper
extra-virgin olive oil, to drizzle
lemon wedges, to serve (optional)

To make the pickled red onion rings, place the onion slices in a small mixing bowl. Heat the remaining ingredients in a small saucepan over medium-low heat. Bring up to a simmer, stir to dissolve the sugar, then pour over the onion. Cover and refrigerate for a couple of hours or preferably overnight.

For the Kalamata olive mayo, place the olives and mayonnaise in a jar or similar. Using a stick blender, blitz until smooth. Refrigerate until required.

Preheat your oven to 180°C (350°F).

Place the fish in an ovenproof dish so the pieces fit snugly. Top with the lemon slices and add the bay leaves and parsley. Boil the kettle and pour over enough hot water to cover the fish. Wrap the dish in tinfoil and place in the oven for 6 minutes. After this time, check at regular 2-minute intervals until the fish is just opaque. If the fillet is thicker, it will take a little longer to poach. Remove from the poaching liquid once just cooked. Let cool, then return the fish to the liquid and refrigerate until required.

Heat the oil in your deep-fryer or a suitable-sized saucepan to 180°C. You can gauge this by adding a piece of bread to the oil; if it's at around 180°C, it will take about a minute for the bread to turn golden and crisp.

Take the pumpkin and cut into pieces that are no thicker than 5 mm (¼ in). Place in a small bowl.

Make the tempura batter by whisking the tempura flour and sparkling water together—the batter should be quite runny. Pour over just enough of the batter to very lightly coat the pumpkin pieces. Discard the leftover batter.

In batches, fry the battered pumpkin pieces for about 3–4 minutes, until golden and cooked through. Remove with a slotted spoon and let cool slightly on kitchen towels.

To plate, spoon out and spread some of the kalamata mayo on to each serving plate. Add pieces of poached fish and scatter with the tempura pumpkin. To finish, place the watercress and some of the pickled onion rings in a bowl and toss to combine. Top the fish and pumpkin with the watercress and pickled red onions. Season with salt and pepper, and drizzle with a little extra-virgin olive oil. Serve with lemon wedges, if you like.

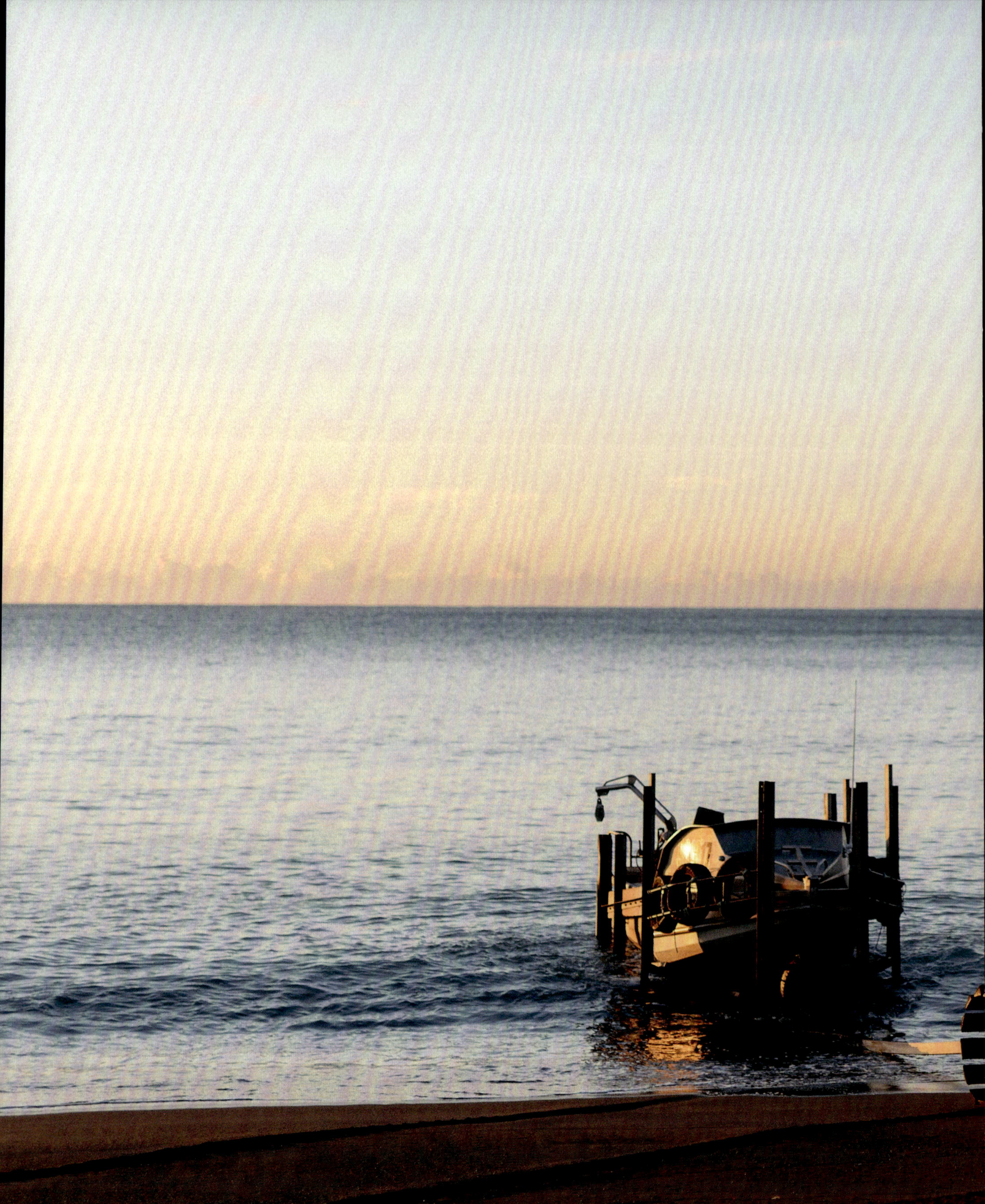

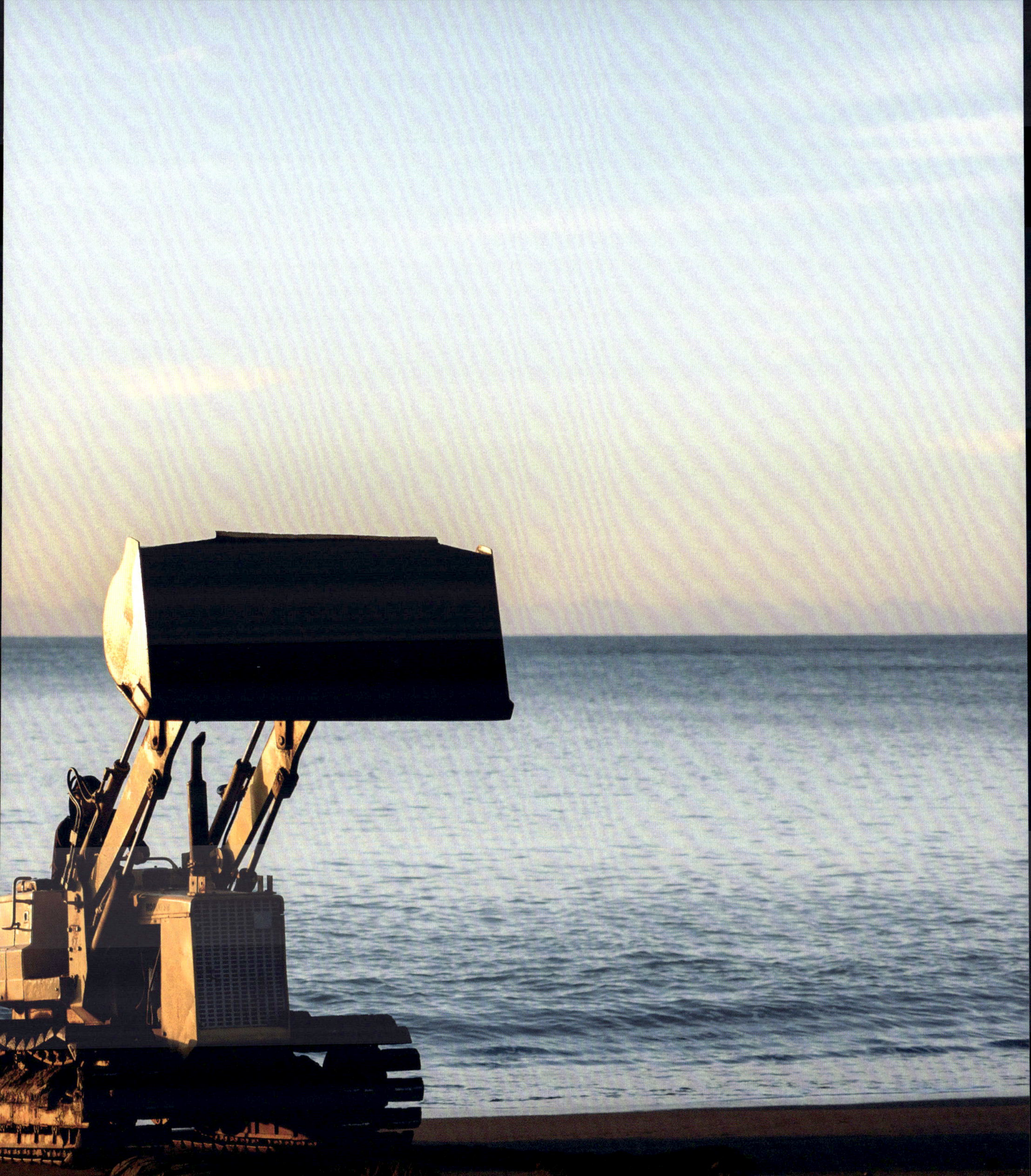

Breakfast of kings: whitebait on toast with tartare and fried egg

This is probably my favourite dish in this book. It just speaks volumes to me of New Zealand on many levels. It's a dish made with one of our most precious seasonal delicacies, but served in such a humble, no-fuss sort of manner. A similar version of this dish would have been eaten hundreds of thousands of times on the riverside or in whitebait baches and cribs up and down the country, ever since we figured out how to catch these slippery, mysterious little fish.

Serves 6

TARTARE SAUCE
1 cup (250 g/9 oz) mayonnaise
¼ cup finely diced red onion
¼ cup roughly chopped capers
⅓ cup finely diced gherkins
⅓ cup finely chopped parsley
finely grated zest of 1 lemon, plus 1 tablespoon juice
flaky sea salt and freshly ground black pepper

TO COOK AND SERVE
cooking oil, for frying
butter, for frying
6 eggs
500 g (1 lb 2 oz) fresh whitebait
plain flour, to dust
flaky sea salt and freshly ground black pepper
6 pieces toast-slice bread
lemon wedges, to serve

To make the tartare sauce, mix all the ingredients except the salt and pepper together in a bowl. Taste and season accordingly with salt and pepper. Refrigerate until required.

Turn on your warming drawer or preheat your oven to 90°C (100°F).
  Place a large frying pan over medium-high heat. Once hot, add a little oil and a knob of butter and fry your eggs. Remove and place on a tray lined with kitchen paper, and keep warm in the oven or warming drawer.
  Wipe clean the pan, then place back over medium-high heat and add a liberal amount of oil. Pat your whitebait dry with kitchen paper. Place a large sieve over a large bowl. Add a handful of whitebait to the sieve, then cover with a liberal amount of flour. Shake the sieve and, with clean hands, toss the whitebait until the excess flour falls through the sieve and there is just a micro covering of flour on the individual whitebait.
  Sprinkle the flour-dusted whitebait over the bottom of the pan and season with salt and pepper. Let the whitebait cook for at least a minute, so it starts to caramelise, before turning. Add a knob of butter and continue cooking for a further minute or so. Place the cooked whitebait on a tray lined with kitchen paper, and place in the oven to keep warm while you repeat the process with the remaining whitebait.
  Toast and butter your bread.

To plate, place a piece of toast in the centre of each plate. Schmear over a liberal amount of tartare sauce, divvy up the cooked whitebait, then top each with a fried egg. Lemon on the side and you're good to go. Eat now!

SEAFOOD

Whitebait fritters

Everyone seems to have their own take on how you make the ultimate whitebait fritter with this wonderful delicacy of ours that we are so fortunate to eat occasionally. My only thing is really that, if you are making whitebait fritters, they should be loaded with whitebait like they cook them on the Coast—West, that is!

Makes about 18 large fritters

1 kg (2 lb 3 oz) whitebait
3 eggs, separated
2 tablespoons plain flour
flaky sea salt and freshly ground black pepper
canola oil, for frying
butter, for frying
lemon wedges, for squeezing

Preheat your oven to 110°C (225°F).
    Rinse and pat dry your whitebait. In a medium-sized mixing bowl, add the egg yolks along with the flour. Whisk together until smooth, then fold through your whitebait and season with salt and pepper.
    In a large mixing bowl, with a clean whisk, whip the egg whites to medium stiffness. Carefully fold the whisked egg whites into the whitebait mixture a little at a time until incorporated.
    Heat a cast-iron pan or other heavy-bottomed pan over medium-low heat. Once up to heat, add a little oil. Using a large serving spoon, add five or six fritters to the pan. Cook the fritters for a couple of minutes either side, until golden. I like to finish them with a little knob of butter just before removing from the pan. Repeat with the remaining mixture while you keep the cooked fritters warm on a tray in the oven.
    Serve on a platter with a couple of lemon wedges for squeezing. Eat now.

SEAFOOD 115

Seared scallops with chorizo and citrus potato purée

This is a real doozy. It's pretty simple and eats wonderfully well. It's hard to go wrong with fresh scallops, good-quality chorizo sausage and a super-creamy citrus potato purée. I say 'good-quality' chorizo, and what I mean by that is there needs to be plenty of fat in the sausage. The fat from the chorizo renders, providing the flavoursome oil that you cook the scallops in. For texture I've added some thin bruschetta pieces that I have brushed with a squid ink butter before cooking.

Serves 6 as a starter

CITRUS POTATO PURÉE
500 g (1 lb 2 oz) Agria potatoes, peeled and cut into large dice
100 g (3½ oz) butter, cubed
1 cup (250 ml/9 fl oz) cream
¼ cup (60 ml/2 fl oz) lemon juice
flaky sea salt and freshly ground black pepper

SQUID INK BRUSCHETTA
30 g (1 oz) butter, at room temperature
1 tablespoon squid ink
¼ baguette, sliced as thinly as possible

TO COOK AND SERVE
cooking oil, for frying
150 g (5½ oz) good-quality chorizo sausage, cut into thinnish slices
500 g (1 lb 2 oz) scallops
1 cup (150 g/5 oz) cherry tomatoes, halved
½ cup (15 g/½ oz) basil leaves, torn

To make the citrus potato purée, put the potato in a suitable-sized saucepan, cover with salted cold water and place over high heat. Bring up to the boil, then simmer for around 20 minutes until the potato is soft and falling apart. Drain. Put the boiled potato through a ricer (or use a potato masher), add the cubes of butter then mix together.

Pour the cream into a small saucepan, then place over medium-low heat. Bring up to a simmer and, once hot, using a spatula, slowly fold in the buttery mashed potato. Now add the lemon juice, taste and season accordingly with salt and pepper. Refrigerate until required.

Preheat your oven to 180°C (350°F).

For the squid ink bruschetta, take the butter and place it in a small mixing bowl. Add the squid ink, then mix through until combined. Brush the slices of baguette with the squid ink butter on both sides. Place on a baking tray and cook for 7–10 minutes, until crisp. Remove, let cool and store in an airtight container until required.

When ready to serve, heat the citrus potato purée in a small saucepan slowly over low heat, stirring as you go, or alternatively heat up in the microwave.

Place a cast-iron pan or heavy-bottomed pan over medium-high heat. Once hot, add a little splash of oil, then cook the sliced chorizo, in batches, until golden on each side. Season the scallops, then add to the pan. Fry for no more than a minute on either side. Finish by tossing in the cherry tomatoes and torn-up basil leaves.

To serve, place a liberal amount of citrus potato purée in the centre of each plate. Divvy up the chorizo and scallops on top, then finish by breaking up a few of the squid ink bruschetta and scattering on the top for texture. Serve now.

SEAFOOD 117

Sautéed squid with arrabbiata sauce and basil

In the middle of winter on clear, still nights in and around Auckland, and I presume in other harbours up and down the country, there is quite the community of 'night crawlers' tossing squid jigs into the darkness, off rocky outcrops, jetties and wharves. It's a community that I've joined over the past few years and I've quickly found there is something quite addictive about fishing for these mystical creatures in the pitch black of night. I don't believe there is a more beautiful creature to be found in the ocean than squid. The colours and patterns that the individual species exhibit when they come out of the water are truly extraordinary. The other thing, and the reason why so many of us are prepared to leave our log fires and heat pumps and venture out into the chilly abyss, is that fresh squid is simply off the scale when it comes to the eating. I've also used squid ink in this recipe because I love the flavour and the jet-black colour, but it's totally optional. You can purchase this interesting ingredient at most good delis or markets that have a fishmonger as part of their offering. Use what you require, then refrigerate or freeze the rest.

Serves 6

ARRABBIATA SAUCE
⅓ cup (80 ml/2½ fl oz) olive oil
2 tablespoons finely minced garlic
½ teaspoon dried chilli flakes
½ cup (125 ml/4 fl oz) port
½ cup (125 ml/4 fl oz) red wine
2 x 400 g tins whole peeled tomatoes, blitzed to a purée
2 tablespoons tomato paste
1 tablespoon sugar
25 g (1 oz) butter
flaky sea salt and freshly ground black pepper

TO COOK AND SERVE
2–3 prepared squid
flaky sea salt and freshly ground black pepper
1 teaspoon squid ink (optional)
canola oil, for frying
1 cup basil leaves, roughly chopped
finely grated zest and juice of 2 lemons
extra-virgin olive oil, to drizzle
crusty bread, to serve

To make the arrabbiata sauce, heat the olive oil in a heavy-bottomed saucepan over medium heat. Add the garlic and chilli flakes, stir continuously with a wooden spoon and watch the garlic start to change colour. Once the garlic takes on a nice dark-golden colour, immediately pour in the port and red wine. Be mindful that as you add the alcohol, it will spit and bubble for a few seconds. Cook down for a few minutes then add the blitzed tomatoes, tomato paste and sugar. Turn down the heat to low and cook for a further 15–20 minutes, until nice and thick. Remove from the heat, whisk in the butter, then taste and season accordingly with salt and pepper. Let cool to room temperature, then refrigerate until required. It will keep in the fridge for a week.

When ready to serve, pour the arrabbiata sauce into a saucepan and heat over medium-low heat, stirring occasionally.

In a bowl, add the prepared squid. Season liberally with salt and pepper. Add a teaspoon of squid ink if you have scored some, and mix through.

Place a large cast-iron pan or heavy-bottomed pan over medium-high heat. Once hot, add a little oil, then add half of the squid. Cook for 3–4 minutes, turning the pieces of squid halfway through the cooking process. Finish by sprinkling over a liberal amount of the fresh basil, just prior to removing the cooked squid from the pan. Keep warm, while you repeat the process with the remaining squid.

To serve, spoon out some of the hot arrabbiata sauce into the centre of warm plates. Top with the cooked squid, then finish with the lemon zest, a squeeze of the juice and then a splash of extra-virgin olive oil. Crusty bread on the side would be the go! Eat now.

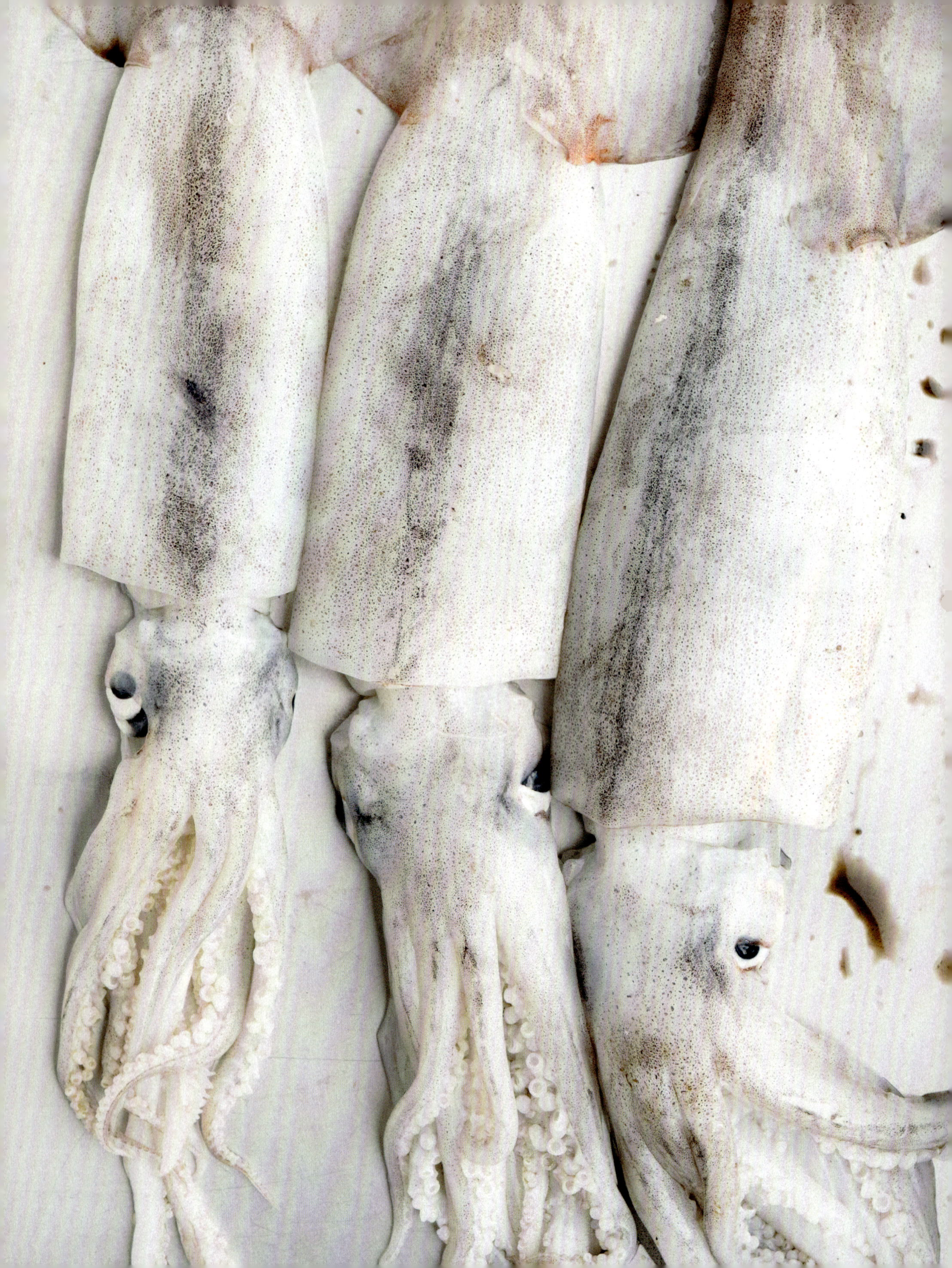

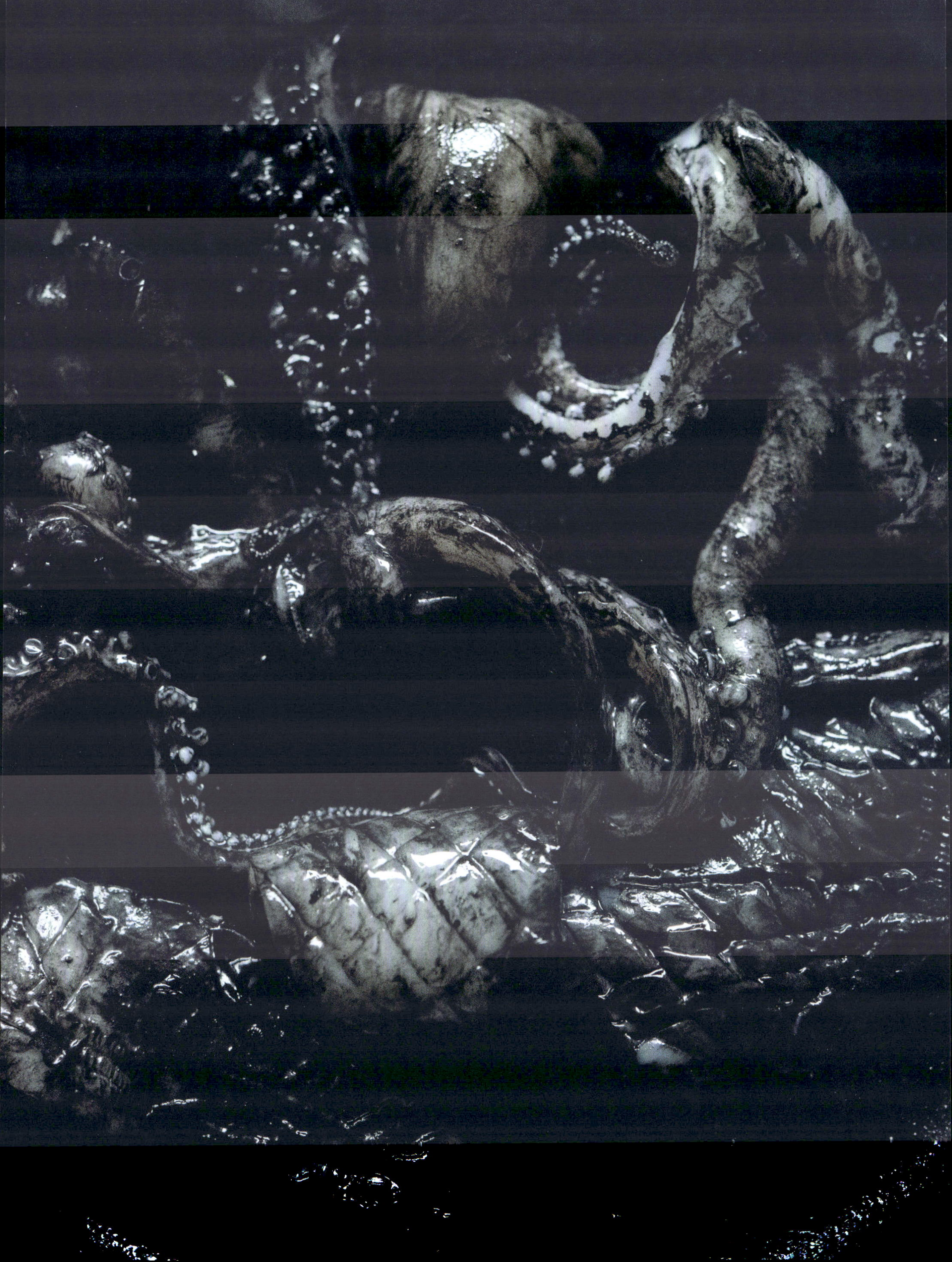

Smoked fish and curried cauliflower Yorkshire puddings

Like most New Zealanders, my introduction to the British staple Yorkshire puddings saw them sitting next to roast beef with a decent pan gravy somewhere close by. Yorkshire puddings (originally called 'dripping puddings') were traditionally served with gravy, prior to the roast being served. Back in the 1800s, this was evidently an attempt at cost-saving, so the diner, after consuming a cheap and filling dish, would eat less of the expensive roast beef on offer. I have used Yorkshire puddings in all sorts of guises for a long time. Here is one of my latest, and I'm thrilled with the way it eats. The flavours are those borrowed from an adopted British classic that I adore: kedgeree. I like to top this dish off with a poached egg. It's a dish that lends itself to a brunch situation, or a satisfying casual Sunday night dinner.

You have a bunch of options when it comes to Yorkshire pudding moulds. Large muffin trays work, but you can make one large pudding using a regular ovenproof dish. I happen to have a bunch of small 12 cm (4¾ oz) cast-iron pans that work a treat.

Serves 6

FISH AND CAULIFLOWER
⅓ cup (80 ml/2½ fl oz) cooking oil
2 cups (310 g/5½ oz) finely diced onion
¾ cup (100 g/3½ oz) finely diced celery
2 tablespoons curry powder
1 tablespoon ground cumin
½ teaspoon ground turmeric
25 g (1 oz) butter
25 g (1 oz) plain flour
3 cups (750 ml/26 fl oz) milk
1 cup (250 ml/9 fl oz) cream
½ head cauliflower, cut into florets
400 g (14 oz) smoked trevally or similar, torn into pieces
1 cup cooked lentils
finely grated zest of 1 lemon, plus 2 tablespoons lemon juice
flaky sea salt and freshly ground black pepper

YORKSHIRE PUDDINGS
2 eggs
⅔ cup (170 ml/5½ fl oz) milk
½ cup (125 ml/4 fl oz) water
¾ cup (185 ml/6 fl oz) canola oil, plus extra for the moulds
1 cup (150 g/5½ oz) plain flour
½ teaspoon flaky sea salt

TO SERVE
6 poached eggs
parsley, roughly chopped, to serve
lemon wedges, to serve

Place a large, heavy-bottomed saucepan over medium-low heat. Once hot, add the oil, followed by the onion and celery. Sweat, stirring occasionally, for 15 minutes then add the curry powder, cumin and turmeric. Let the spices cook out with the vegetables for 5 minutes. Now add the butter and, once melted through, sprinkle over the flour. It will immediately thicken into a paste. Now add around 1 cup (250 ml/9 fl oz) of the milk. Briskly whisk as the sauce thickens, then continue to add the remaining milk and the cream.

Add the cauliflower florets and cook over low heat, stirring occasionally, for 20 minutes or so until the cauliflower is cooked through. To finish, add in the smoked fish and cooked lentils. Stir through the lemon zest and juice, and season to taste with salt and pepper. Remove from the heat and, if not using immediately, let the mixture cool and refrigerate until required.

Preheat your oven to 200°C (400°F).

To make the Yorkshire puddings, blitz the eggs in a blender, add the milk, water and oil and blitz again to combine. Now add the flour and salt, and process to form a silky-smooth batter. Pour into a jug and let the batter rest for 20 minutes or so.

Place your chosen Yorkshire pudding moulds onto a baking tray—this will catch any excess oil during the cooking process. Pour a liberal amount of oil into the bottom of the moulds—the oil should come up at least 1 cm (½ in). Place the moulds in the oven for 5 minutes or so to heat up. (You want the oil to be very hot but not smoking.)

Once the oil is hot, carefully remove the tray of moulds from the oven and pour the Yorkshire batter a little over halfway up the sides of the moulds. Place immediately back in the oven and bake for 15–20 minutes, until the puddings are puffed, golden and crisp. Remove from the oven and, using tongs, carefully lift them out of the moulds and place on a wire rack to cool.

Turn the oven down to 180°C (350°F).

Place the smoked fish and curried cauliflower mix in a saucepan and bring up to a simmer, stirring occasionally.

Put the Yorkshire puddings on an oven tray and place in the oven for a few minutes to crisp up.

To serve, place a Yorkshire pudding in the centre of each warm plate. Spoon generous amounts of the smoked fish and cauliflower into the puddings. Top each with a poached egg. Hit each plate with a little chopped parsley, and a wedge of lemon for squeezing. **Serve now.**

Grilled octopus with chorizo, fried potatoes and rouille

I have been besotted with octopus since I had my first taste of this delicacy in Greece years ago on my OE. It's taken a while for Kiwis to embrace these molluscs, which I believe is probably due to our lack of understanding of how to cook these somewhat mystical creatures. It's true that there is a bit of technique involved in getting octopus really tender, and I for one have had varied success at times. The thing is, though, even if the octopus has a little resistance in the bite, I still get immense pleasure from it. A bit of chew when it comes to eating has never put me off. Anyhow, the following method is how we cook 'em, and the result is always delicious. Rouille, by the way, is kind of a creamy mayonnaise flavoured with goodies such as roasted red capsicum, garlic and anchovies. It's traditionally served with bouillabaisse (a traditional Provençal fish stew), but also works a treat in this situation. I like to cook my octopus over charcoal or hardwood to garner tons of flavour. If you have the time, I encourage you to do the same; however, the result is nearly as good using the method here.

Serves 6

STOCK
2 cups (310 g/11 oz) roughly chopped onion
2 cups (310 g/11 oz) roughly chopped carrot
2 cups (310 g/11 oz) celery, roughly chopped
4 garlic cloves, roughly chopped
finely grated zest of 1 lemon
3 star anise
3 bay leaves
1 tablespoon sea salt
1 cup (250 ml/9 fl oz) red wine
8 cups (2 litres/68 fl oz) water
1 x 3 kg (6 lb 12 oz) cleaned and prepared octopus (beak, eyes and gut removed)

ROUILLE
1 cup (250 g/9 oz) mayonnaise
1 whole roasted capsicum, peeled and deseeded
6 garlic cloves
2–4 anchovies
2½ tablespoons tomato paste
½ tablespoon smoked sweet paprika
⅓ cup breadcrumbs
1½ tablespoons lemon juice
pinch sugar
Tabasco sauce, to taste
flaky sea salt and freshly ground black pepper

TO COOK AND SERVE
canola oil, for frying
300 g (10½ oz) good-quality chorizo sausages, roughly chopped
1 kg (2 lb 4 oz) baby new potatoes, cooked and quartered
1 teaspoon smoked sweet paprika
flaky sea salt and freshly ground black pepper
2 spring onions, thinly sliced
Al Brown & Co Orange and Chilli Infused Olive Oil or extra-virgin olive oil
lemon wedges, to serve

Take a large stockpot and three-quarters fill with well-salted water (it should taste like the sea). Place over the heat and bring up to the boil.

In a separate large saucepan, add all the stock ingredients, except the octopus. Bring up to the boil, then lower the heat to a simmer.

Once the water in the stockpot is rapidly boiling, blanch the octopus by carefully lowering it, using a slotted spoon, into the boiling water for 10 seconds or so. Remove the octopus, return the water to the boil, and repeat this process twice more. The octopus will turn pink and begin to shrink and curl up. Now add the blanched octopus to the simmering pan with the vegetables, wine and spices.

Weigh the octopus down with a cast-iron lid or similar and simmer for 45 minutes.

Check tenderness of the octopus after 45 minutes by slicing off a tentacle at the thick end, then cutting a sliver off to try. If you think it needs longer, cook for a further 15 minutes, then check again. Once cooked, remove the octopus from the stock, peel and discard some of the more obvious slimy skin from the back of the tentacles. I like to leave the suction cups on as they look great and eat well. Place the cooked octopus in a bowl. Cover with clingfilm and refrigerate until required. This step can be done a few days ahead.

To make the rouille, place all the ingredients except the Tabasco and salt and pepper, into a food processor. Blitz until combined. Pour into a bowl, then finish by seasoning with the Tabasco, salt and pepper. Refrigerate until required.

Remove the octopus from the refrigerator and slice into manageable pieces.

Place a large cast-iron pan over medium-high heat. Once hot, add a splash of canola oil, followed by the chorizo. Cook until the chorizo is golden and plenty of fat has rendered. With a slotted spoon, remove the cooked chorizo to a plate and keep warm, leaving behind that delicious, spicy fat.

Now add the cooked potato quarters. Fry over medium heat until beginning to colour and crisp on the edges. Sprinkle over the paprika and stir. Once golden all over, remove and add to the warm chorizo.

Finally, turn up the heat and add the octopus. Cook for 2–3 minutes until golden and crisp on the edges. Toss the octopus with the cooked chorizo and potatoes, and season. Divvy up onto warm plates and add a generous spoonful of rouille to each plate. Sprinkle over some spring onions and finish with a generous pour of the olive oil. Add a lemon wedge and serve!

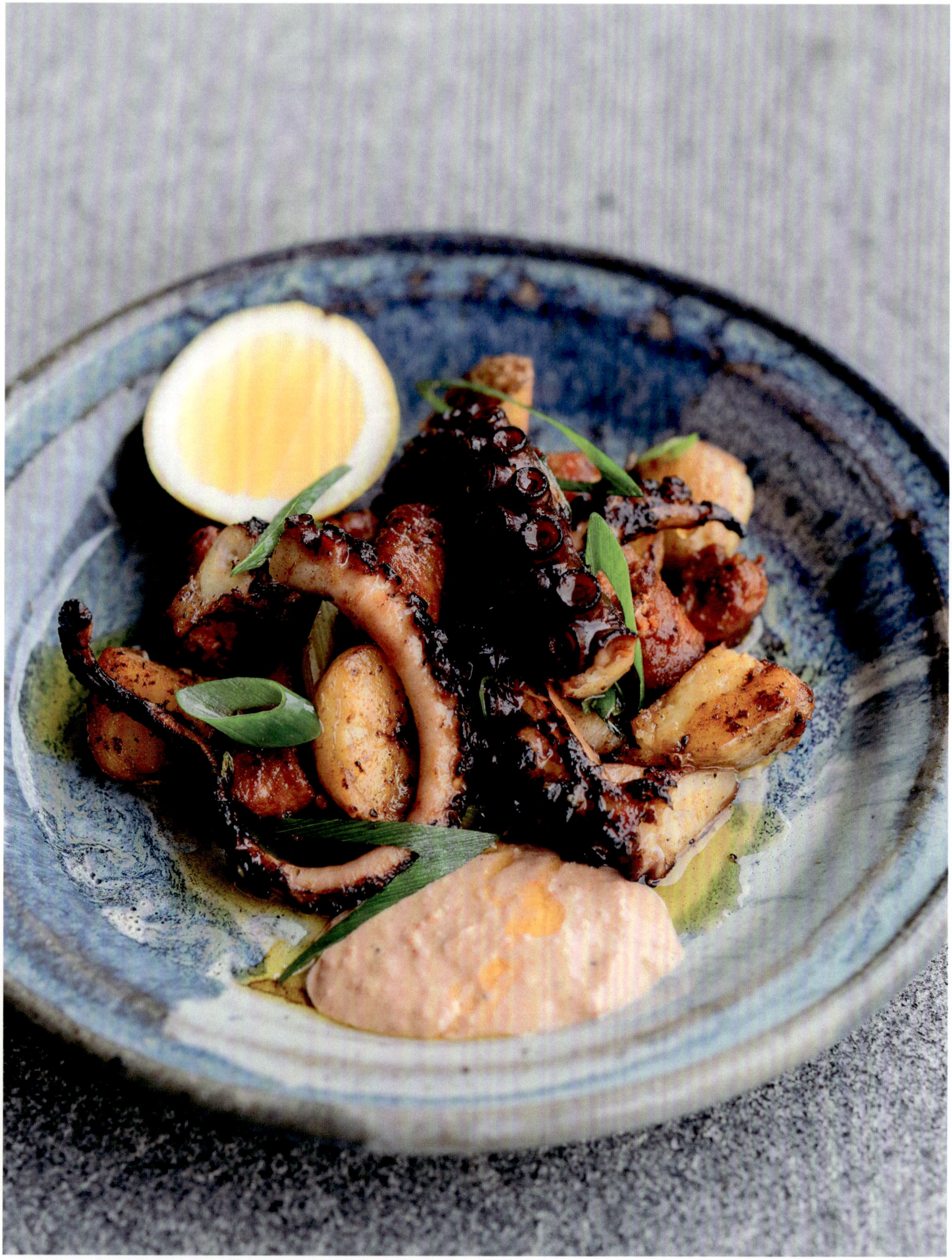

SEAFOOD 127

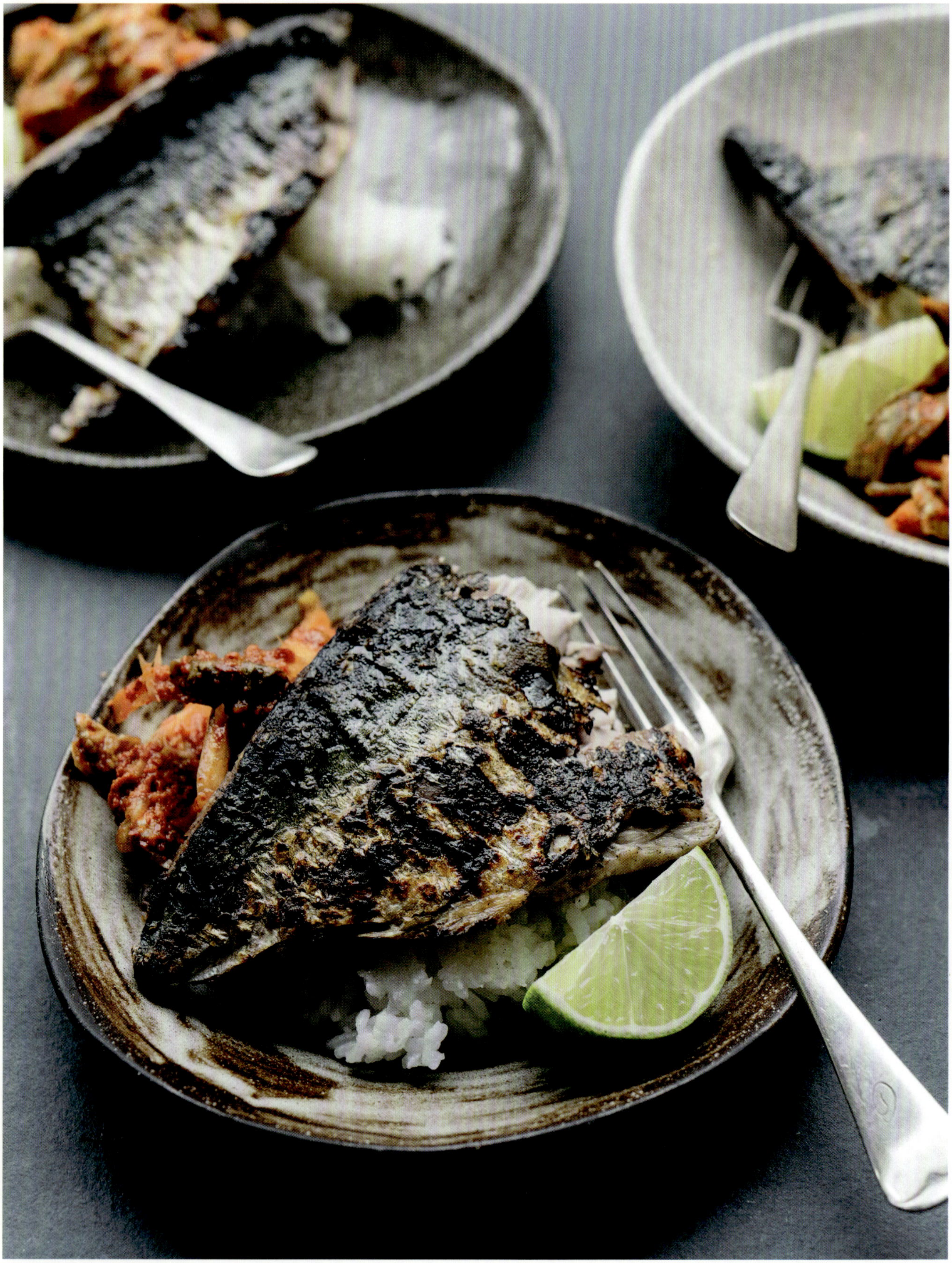

Grilled blue mackerel, sticky rice and kimchi

I had my first trip to Japan not long before I wrote this book and, as I suspect it would be for most chefs who visit this country, it kind of felt like a 'pilgrimage of respect', paying homage to their extraordinary, unique and masterful cuisine. I delighted in every mouthful. I love the simplicity, confidence and precision in the way the Japanese prepare and cook their food. I'm not a Michelin-star sort of guy, but I know that there are some extremely impressive high-end joints not just in Tokyo but scattered throughout the country. I struggle with the 'value proposition' of many of these experiences. My interest lies in sniffing out the more humble local joints that serve mind-blowing food but without all the fanfare associated with the famous gaffs.

Grilled mackerel is a bit of a staple in Japan, simply salted and often dipped in sake, or so-called 'saba shio'. I know kimchi is not Japanese (it's Korean); however, I ate a very similar dish to the recipe below on the side of a street down an alley with the roar of the subway overhead. Simple, value for money and perfectly satisfying—all the things that I adhere to. On a side note, if you catch or spot fresh mackerel at your fishmonger, give it a go. It's delicious raw and wonderful prepared like this, cooked all the way through with blistered skin.

Serves 6

STICKY RICE
2 cups (440 g/15½ oz) medium-grain rice
4 cups (1 litre/35 fl oz) cold water
2 tablespoons rice wine vinegar
1 tablespoon mirin
½ teaspoon sesame oil

TO COOK AND SERVE
6 x 160 g (5¾ oz) blue mackerel fillets, skin on
flaky sea salt
cooking oil
kimchi (page 430)
shallot crunchies (page 445) or use store-bought (optional)
lime wedges, to serve

To make the sticky rice, place the rice in a saucepan and cover with the cold water. Stir thoroughly. Place over high heat and bring up to the boil. Once boiling, reduce heat to low, cover the pan with a lid and allow to cook gently for 20 minutes. Take off the heat and stir through the rice wine vinegar, mirin and sesame oil. Keep warm.

Preheat your chargrill pan or a cast-iron pan over medium-high heat.

Season the fish liberally with the salt and bring up to room temperature.

Once your pan is hot, liberally brush the fillets with oil. Place skin side down and leave them as is for 3–4 minutes, or long as needed to get the skin blistering. Flip over and cook on the other side to finish.

Simply serve the grilled mackerel in a bowl with a heaped spoonful of the sticky rice and a liberal amount of kimchi on the side. Garnish with the shallot crunchies, if using, and lime wedges for squeezing.

Crayfish and clam linguine

I have always enjoyed putting combinations together that are kind of yin and yang price-wise. It's a way of serving something special while not blowing the budget, as the cheaper main ingredient helps stretch the more expensive product. Truth be known, while clams are considered by many as a little way down the sliding seafood scale, I will always go in to bat for these delicious molluscs, which not only offer up a great little chew but make their own incredible stock for a dish. By all means, instead of crayfish try other seafood with the clams such as prawns, scampi or lovely chunks of fresh sautéed fish. My advice is to get everything prepped and ready to go before you begin, as it needs to all comes together pretty quickly.

Serves 8

1 x 454 g packet dried linguine
⅓ cup (80 ml/2½ fl oz) extra-virgin olive oil, plus extra to drizzle
2 tablespoons finely diced garlic
2 chillies, finely sliced, or a pinch of dried chilli flakes
2 tablespoons finely chopped preserved lemon rind
⅓ cup roughly chopped capers
36 littleneck clams (cockles or similar)
½ cup (125 ml/4 fl oz) white wine
2 cooked crayfish, meat picked and roughly chopped
½ cup (15 g/½ oz) chopped flat-leaf parsley
25 g (1 oz) butter
freshly ground black pepper
warm crusty bread, to serve
lemon halves, to serve

Fill your largest saucepan with salted water and place over high heat. Bring up to the boil. Add a splash of olive oil to the water, along with the pasta. Stir to begin with to prevent the pasta from sticking together.

Place another large saucepan over medium-low heat. Once hot, add the olive oil, garlic, chillies, preserved lemon and capers. Cook for 2 minutes, then add the clams, along with the white wine. Place the lid on the pan, allow to simmer for 2–3 minutes, then give the pan a shake. Once the clams begin to open, turn off the heat, but keep the lid on.

Once the pasta is cooked, drain and add to the clams. Stir though to combine. Now stir in the crayfish, parsley and butter.

Divvy up into warm bowls, pouring some of the cooking liquid over each bowl. Finish with a liberal grind of fresh black pepper and a glug of olive oil.

Serve with warm crusty bread and lemons on the side for squeezing. Eat now.

SEAFOOD 131

132   EAT UP NEW ZEALAND: THE BACH EDITION

Pan-fried flounder with seaweed butter

Eating whole fried flounder is one of my favourite and fondest memories growing up. I guess we would have them maybe half a dozen times a year. They were and still seem to be relatively plentiful, and I find it hard to go past them when they are sitting there super fresh in their shiny, contrasting colour-toned skins. I think it wasn't just the sweet taste of flounder that I loved, but it was how wonderful a whole cooked fish looked on the plate, and the enjoyment that comes from eating the entire fish off the bone. This seaweed butter melted over the cooked flounder is a revelation. I use a bunch of different seaweed products available through good-quality food markets and Japanese stores, where they often have quite a range of different seaweed pastes and dried products. I urge you to try different combinations.

Serves 6

SEAWEED BUTTER
250 g (9 oz) good-quality butter, at room temperature
100 g (3½ oz) jar seasoned seaweed paste
100 g (3½ oz) wakame, roughly chopped
2 sheets nori, torn into small pieces
1 teaspoon wasabi paste

TO COOK AND SERVE
2 cups (300 g/10½ oz) plain flour
flaky sea salt and freshly ground black pepper
6 whole flounder or sole, head and top skin removed
canola oil, for frying
lemon wedges, to serve

To make the seaweed butter, place the butter in a stand mixer fitted with the paddle attachment, or use a handheld electric whisk. Whip the butter until light and airy. Remove and place in a bowl along with the seaweed paste, wakame, nori and wasabi. Mix through until combined. Keep as is or form into a log shape and wrap in clingfilm. Refrigerate until required, but always serve the butter at room temperature so it melts over the cooked fish.

Preheat your oven or warming drawer to 90°C (200°F).
    Place a cast-iron pan or heavy-bottomed pan over medium heat. Season a couple of cups of flour with salt and pepper, then dip the flounder into the seasoned flour a couple of times, dusting off any excess.
    Add a liberal dash of canola oil to the hot pan, then carefully add the flounder, flesh side down. Fry for 3–4 minutes, then turn and repeat on the other side until cooked through. Place on an ovenproof tray and keep warm in the oven or warming drawer while you fry the remaining flounder.

To serve, place a flounder on each warm plate, and spoon over a liberal amount of the seaweed butter. Serve immediately with a wedge of lemon, and if it happens to be breakfast, a side of fried eggs is always going to be a winner.

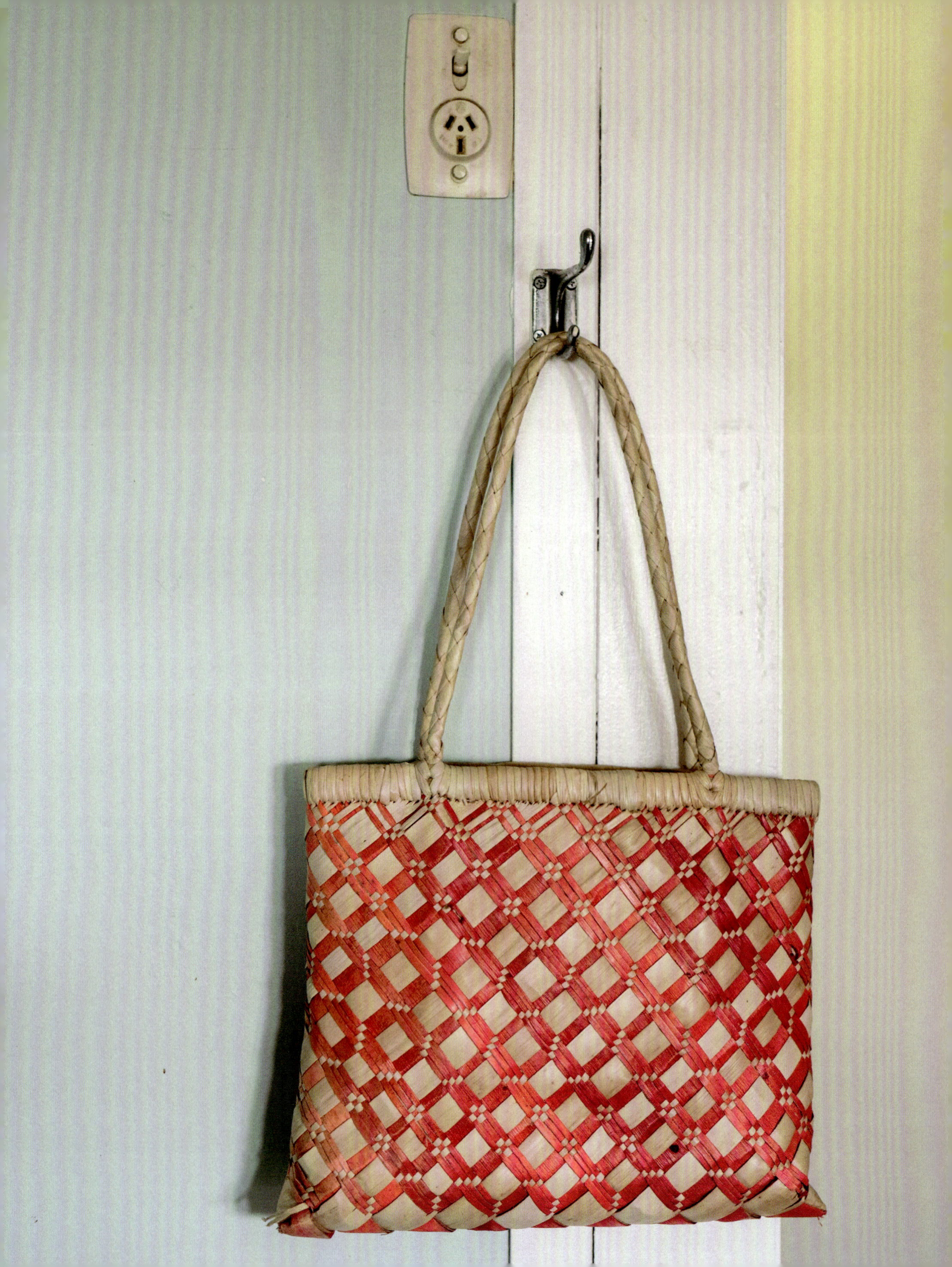

Overhand Knot	Figure Eight Knot	Stevedore Knot
Alpine Butterfly	Ashley Stopper Knot	Alpine Butterfly Bend
Square (Reef) Knot	Granny Knot	Sheet Knot
Two Half Hitches	Bowline	Slipknot

Hāpuka steaks with roasted fennel and lemon

Most of the time it's these sorts of dishes that I love to eat. There are essentially just two ingredients: fish and fennel. It couldn't be easier to prepare, and is wonderful to eat.

Serves 6

4 fennel bulbs
2–3 red chillies, roughly chopped
2–3 lemons, quartered
⅓ cup (80 ml/2½ fl oz) extra-virgin olive oil
flaky sea salt and freshly ground black pepper
6 hāpuka steaks
cooking oil, for frying
mayonnaise, to serve (optional)

Preheat your oven to 180°C (350°F).
    Take the fennel bulbs and cut them into quarters. Cut off as much of the tough inner core as possible. Place in a bowl with the chillies, lemon quarters and olive oil, and season liberally with salt and pepper.
    Line a deepish oven tray with baking paper and tip in the fennel and lemon. Roast for 25–35 minutes, or until the fennel is soft and golden. Remove and keep warm.
    Place a large cast-iron or heavy-bottomed pan over medium-high heat.
    Season the fish steaks. Once the pan is hot, add some cooking oil and place the steaks in the pan (but make sure you don't overcrowd the pan). Depending on how big or thick the steaks are, turn once they are lovely and golden on one side. Repeat on the other side until they are just cooked through. Keep the steaks warm while you cook the remaining ones.

Serve the hāpuka steaks with a pile of the roasted fennel and lemon on the side. Some mayonnaise would be a nice touch also. Eat now.

SEAFOOD 137

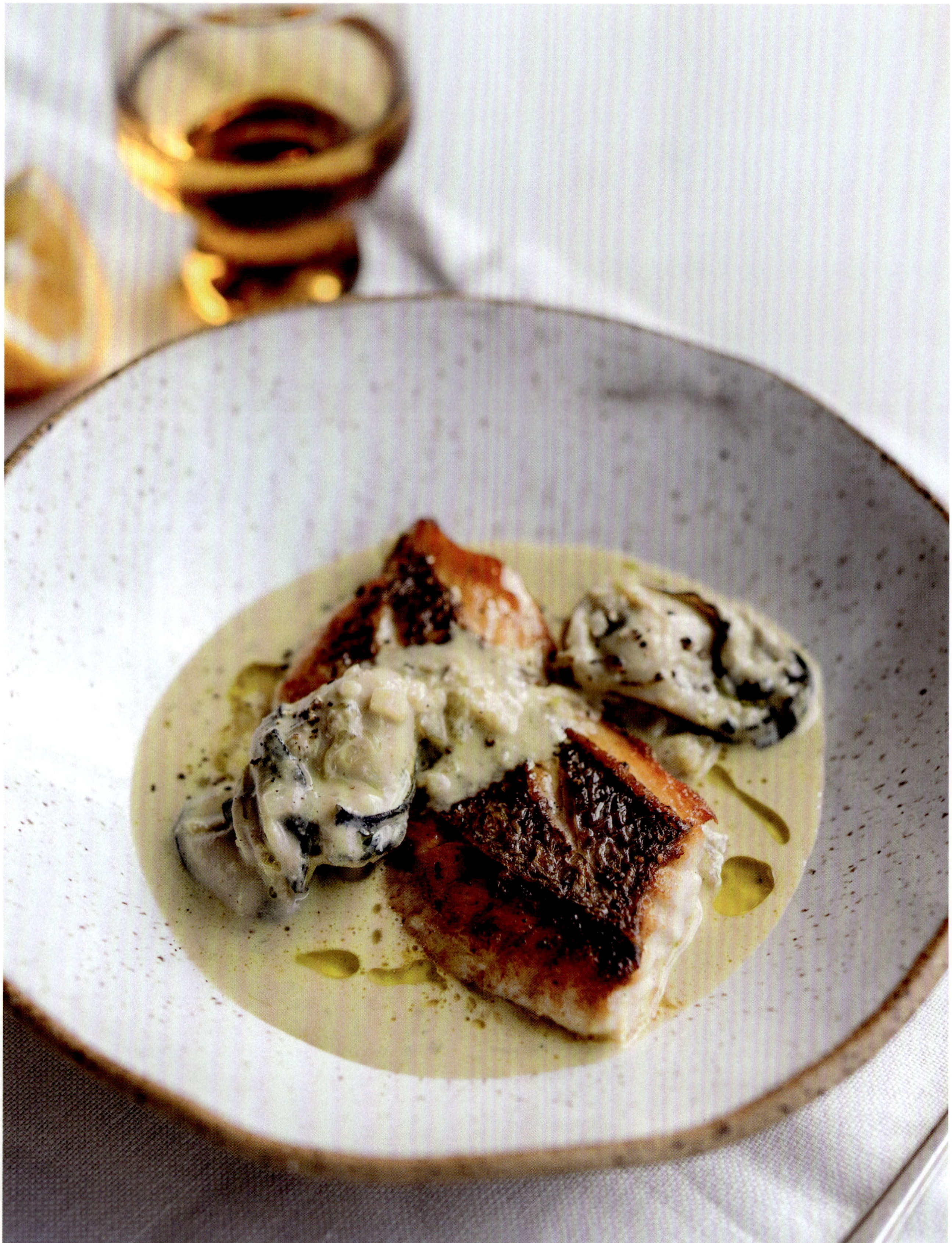

Crispy-skin snapper with oyster stew

This is a wickedly rich and decadent dish. I roll this one out only occasionally, and it's normally in the middle of winter when the oysters are plump and in great nick and the snapper have put on plenty of weight, with a wonderful layer of fat between the crisp skin and the fillet of fish.

Serves 6

OYSTER STEW
50 g (1¾ oz) butter
1 cup (150 g/5½ oz) finely diced shallots
½ cup (70 g/2½ oz) finely diced celery
½ cup (125 ml/4 fl oz) sweet sherry
36 freshly shucked oysters, plus liquor
1 cup (250 ml/9 fl oz) chicken stock
2 cups (500 ml/17 fl oz) cream
Tabasco sauce, to taste

TO COOK AND SERVE
6 x 100 g (3½ oz) snapper fillets, skin on and scored
flaky sea salt and freshly ground black pepper
cooking oil, for frying
Al Brown & Co Lemon and Fennel Infused Olive Oil or extra-virgin olive oil
lemon wedges, to serve

Take a heavy-bottomed saucepan and place over medium-low heat. Add the butter, along with the shallots and celery. Sweat for 20 minutes, until the vegetables are soft and translucent.

Turn the heat up a little. Pour in the sherry, let it bubble and reduce for a couple of minutes, then strain off the liquor from the oysters and add that to the sherry. Bring back up to the boil and pour in the chicken stock. Simmer and reduce for 10 minutes, stir in the cream and cook for a further 5 minutes or so.

Now add 12 of the shucked oysters to the pan (refrigerate the remainder until serving). Cook the oysters for 1–2 minutes, remove the plump, cooked oysters with a slotted spoon, along with about 1 cup (250 ml/9 fl oz) of the liquid, and place in a bowl. Using a stick blender, process the oysters and reserved liquid until smooth, then return to the pan.

Add the Tabasco to taste, then cool and refrigerate until required.

Pour the oyster stew into a saucepan and place over medium heat. Bring up to a simmer.

Place a cast-iron pan or heavy-bottomed pan over high heat. Season the snapper skin liberally with salt and a little pepper. Once the pan is hot, add a little oil then place the snapper portions, skin side down, in the pan. Fry for 3–4 minutes until the edges are golden and the skin becomes crisp. Turn the fish and cook, depending on how thick the fillets are, for a further minute or so. Once the fish is just cooked through, remove from the pan and keep warm.

When the oyster stew is simmering, drop in the remaining shucked oysters. Let them plump up for a couple of minutes.

To serve, ladle the oyster stew into warm bowls then top with a piece of snapper, skin side up. Spoon over a little olive oil and serve with the lemon wedges on the side. Eat now.

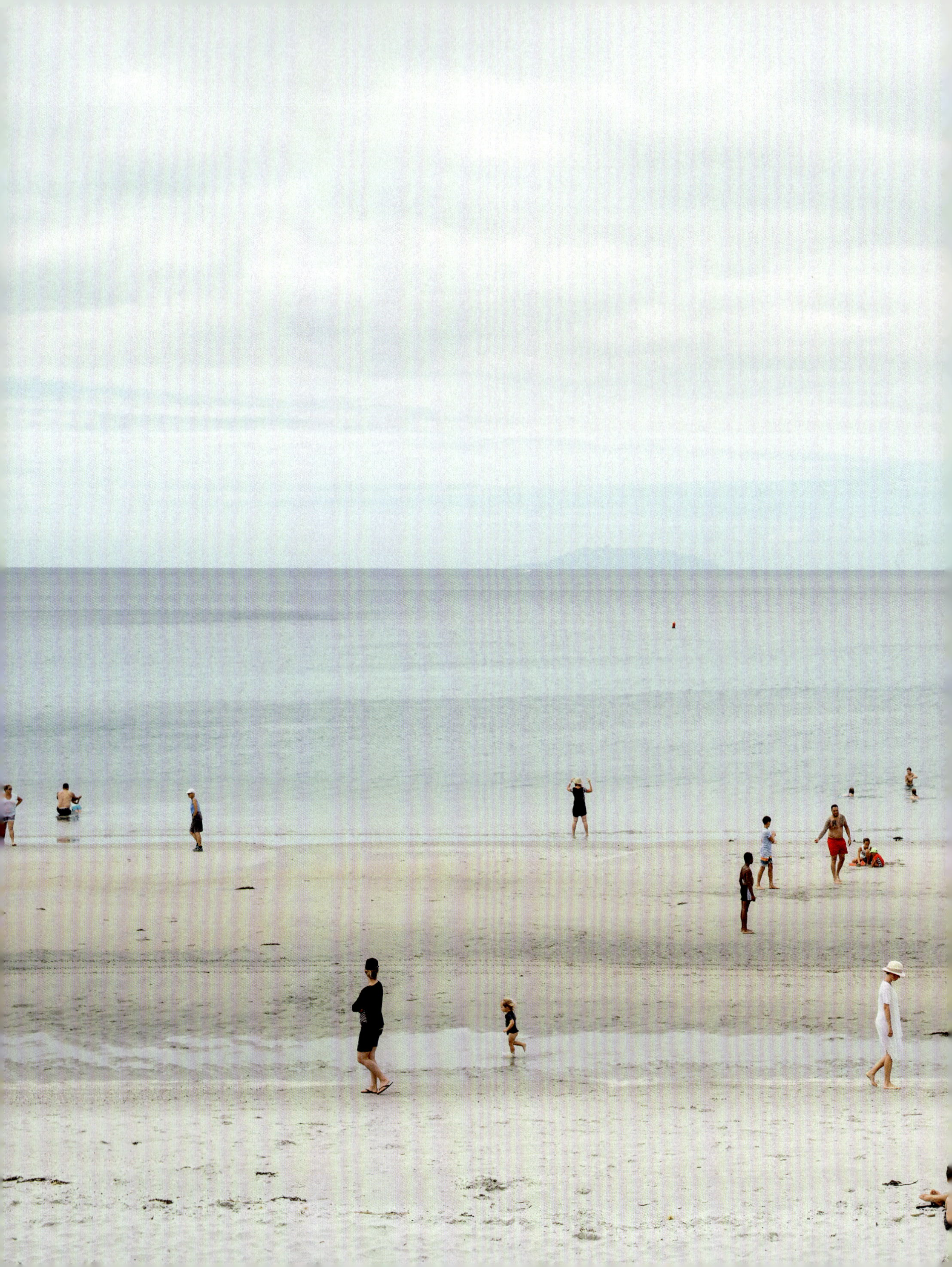

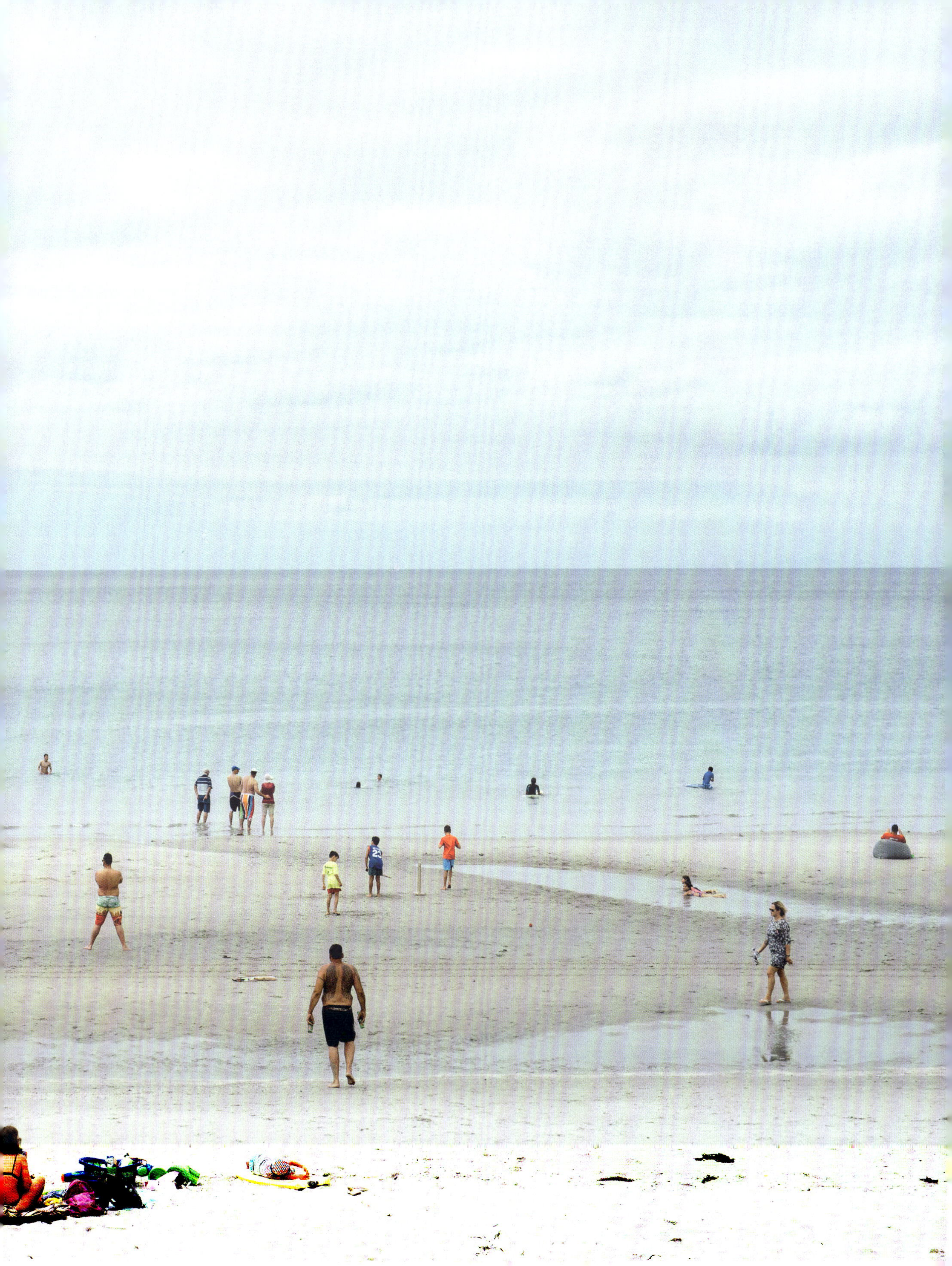

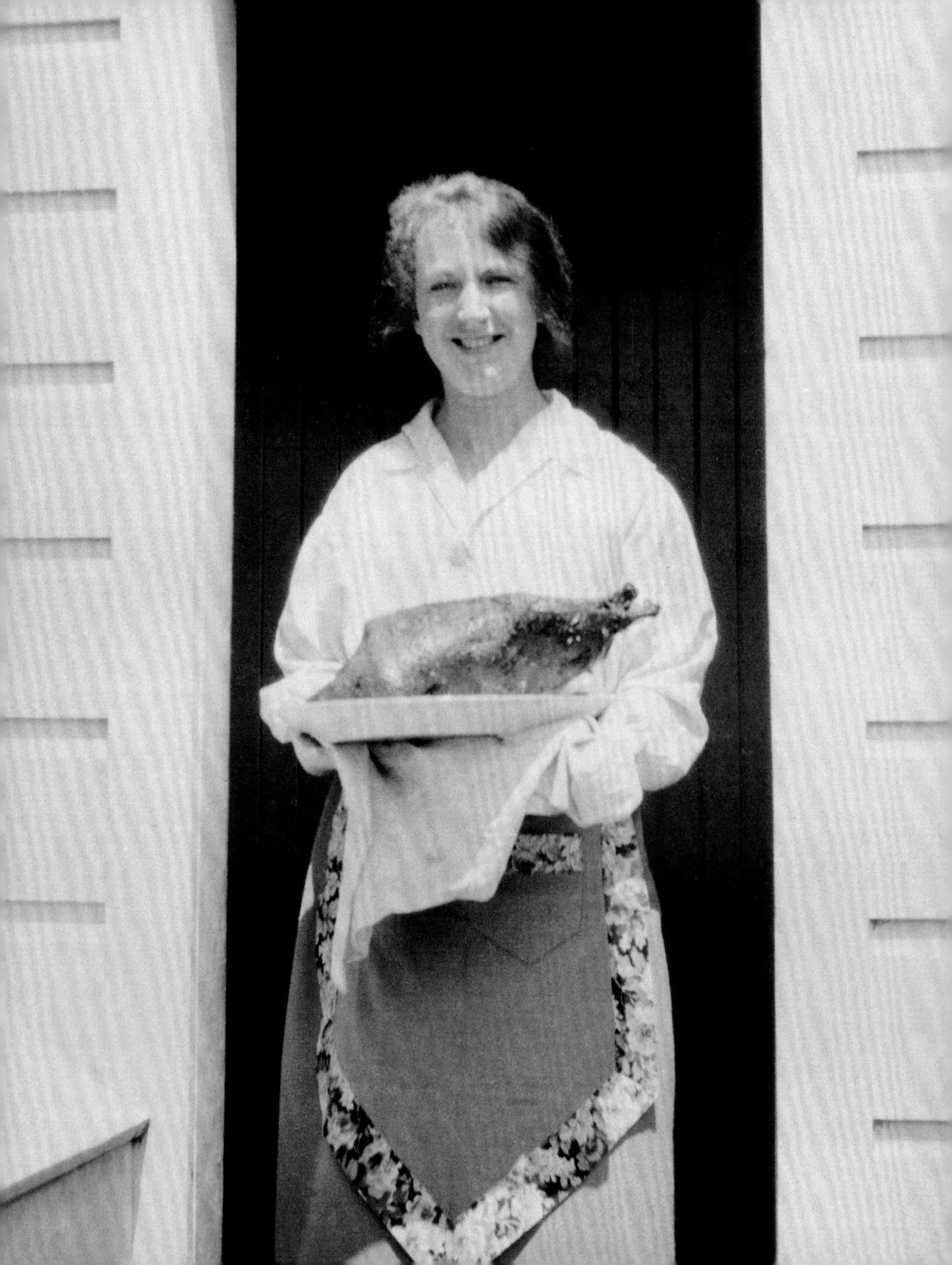

BIRD
MANU

Curried eggs

I've always had a bit of a soft spot for curried eggs. Mum used to make them as a 'pre' for dinner parties. They were a bit of a mainstay, along with 'devils on horseback', tinned-asparagus rolls and exotic edible works of art like whole pineapples with a bunch of cheese- and cherry-loaded toothpicks anchoring the spread. Traditional curried egg recipes were pretty standard: egg, curry powder, mayo and maybe a bit of curly parsley for colour. As you'll see below, I've attempted to take them up a notch or two on the culinary ladder.

Makes 24

CURRIED EGGS
12 hard-boiled eggs, peeled
3 tablespoons canola oil
½ cup (80 g/2¾ oz) finely diced shallots
1 tablespoon finely chopped ginger
1 teaspoon finely chopped garlic
1 teaspoon garam masala
2 teaspoons ground cumin
2 teaspoons curry powder
½ teaspoon ground turmeric
1½ teaspoons hot sauce, such as Kaitaia Fire
1 cup (250 g/9 oz) mayonnaise
1 tablespoon lemon juice
flaky sea salt and freshly ground black pepper

TO SERVE (OPTIONAL)
fried red chillies (page 445)
fried curry leaves (page 445)
dukkah (page 444)
handful coriander leaves

Take a sharp knife and cut the hard-boiled eggs in half lengthways. Carefully remove the yolks and place in a small bowl. Keep the egg-white halves on a tray in the fridge until required.

Place a small saucepan over medium-low heat. Once hot, add the oil, along with the shallots, ginger and garlic. Stirring occasionally with a wooden spoon, sweat the mix for 10–15 minutes, until soft and translucent. Add the spices, stir through and cook out for a couple of minutes before adding the contents of the pan to the cooked egg yolks. Let cool. Add the hot sauce, mayo and lemon juice to the egg yolk and spice mixture. Season to taste. Combine with a fork or wooden spoon until soft and creamy.

Place the curried egg mixture into a piping bag. Take the egg-white halves from the fridge and pipe the curried egg mix into the centres. Place in the fridge to keep cool prior to serving.

You'll see I have put a bunch of 'to serve' garnish options, all of which are optional. It's up to you. I have used all of these and, other than the extra layers of taste that they bring, it's actually the textural contrast that really adds to the eating enjoyment.

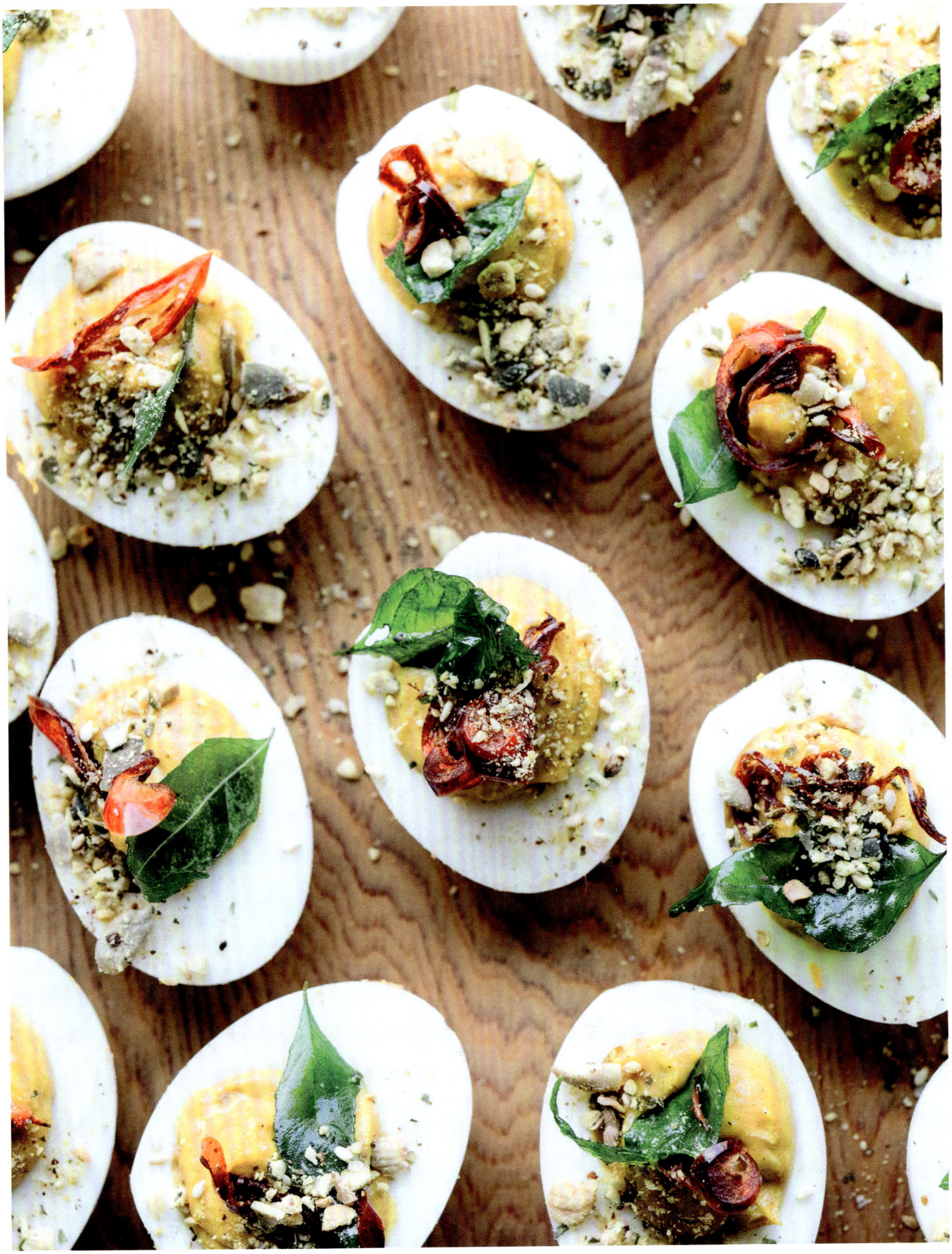

Chicken liver parfait with pear liqueur jelly and fried bread

This chicken liver parfait recipe has been with me for more than 30 years. I learnt it from a chef named Dave Marshall at a great restaurant called Paradiso that was in Courtenay Place in Wellington. It's been in my go-to repertoire since, and is an absolute beauty. Rich, decadent and silky smooth, it's about as close to fresh foie gras as you'll get without eating the real thing. I've topped the parfait with a layer of poire Williams (pear brandy) jelly, which makes it a bit posh, however the humble fried bread keeps that in check. By the way, duck livers work just as well.

Makes 1 x regular loaf

CHICKEN LIVER PARFAIT
300 ml (10½ fl oz) port
3 thyme stems
250 g (9 oz) chicken livers, obvious sinews removed
2 juniper berries
2 whole eggs, plus 4 egg yolks
1 cup (250 ml/9 fl oz) clarified butter, melted
1½ teaspoons flaky sea salt
pinch finely ground black pepper

PEAR LIQUEUR JELLY
1 cup (250 ml/9 fl oz) Poire Williams (or something similar, like pear schnapps)
3½ gelatine leaves

FRIED BREAD
2 cups (300 g/10½ oz) plain flour, plus extra for dusting
2 teaspoons baking powder
1 teaspoon salt
1 cup (250 ml/9 fl oz) milk
canola oil, for shallow-frying
flaky sea salt and freshly ground black pepper

Preheat your oven 120°C (235°F).

To make the chicken liver parfait, pour the port into a small saucepan and add the thyme. Place over medium heat, bring to a simmer and reduce the port down until thick and syrupy, about 50 ml (1¾ fl oz). Remove from the heat, let cool, then discard the thyme.

Place the chicken livers, reduced port and juniper berries in a blender or food processor. Blitz the livers and, with the motor running, slowly add the whole eggs, yolks and clarified butter. Finish by adding flaky sea salt and finely ground black pepper.

Take the runny liver mixture and pass through a fine sieve, to get rid of any lumps. Tip into a regular loaf tin. Place the loaf tin into a high-sided roasting dish. Boil the jug, then pour the boiling water into the roasting dish so it comes three-quarters of the way up the sides of the loaf tin. Cover the lot tightly with tinfoil, then place in the centre of your preheated oven. Check after 20–25 minutes or so—the parfait is cooked if it has just set but is still just slightly nervous in the centre. If not, cover again tightly and check every 5–10 minutes. Once cooked, remove from the water bath and let the parfait cool on a rack before refrigerating.

For the pear liqueur jelly topping, heat the liqueur in a small saucepan over low heat. Once hot, remove from the heat and set aside. Soak the gelatine leaves in cold water for 2–3 minutes, until soft and pliable. Drain the gelatine leaves and add to the warm liqueur. Stir through until dissolved. Allow to cool a little more, but while still warm pour over the cold chicken liver parfait and refrigerate again so the jelly sets.

To make the fried bread, place the flour, baking powder and salt into a large bowl. Mix in the milk to form a dough. Do not knead or overwork. Turn the dough out onto a floured bench and pat down to a 1 cm (½ in) thickness. Cut portions of dough into even-sized squares.

In a frying pan or heavy-bottom saucepan, add enough oil to shallow-fry, about 1 cm (½ in) deep, and place over medium heat. Give the oil 4–5 minutes to heat up, then test the heat with a piece of the dough. It should turn golden on one side after a minute of frying, then turn with tongs and repeat the frying on the other side. Fry the dough in batches, until puffed and golden brown. Remove from the oil and drain on kitchen paper. Season with salt.

Serve the fried bread alongside the parfait and let everyone help themselves. Have a pinch of flaky sea salt and a grind of fresh black pepper on hand.

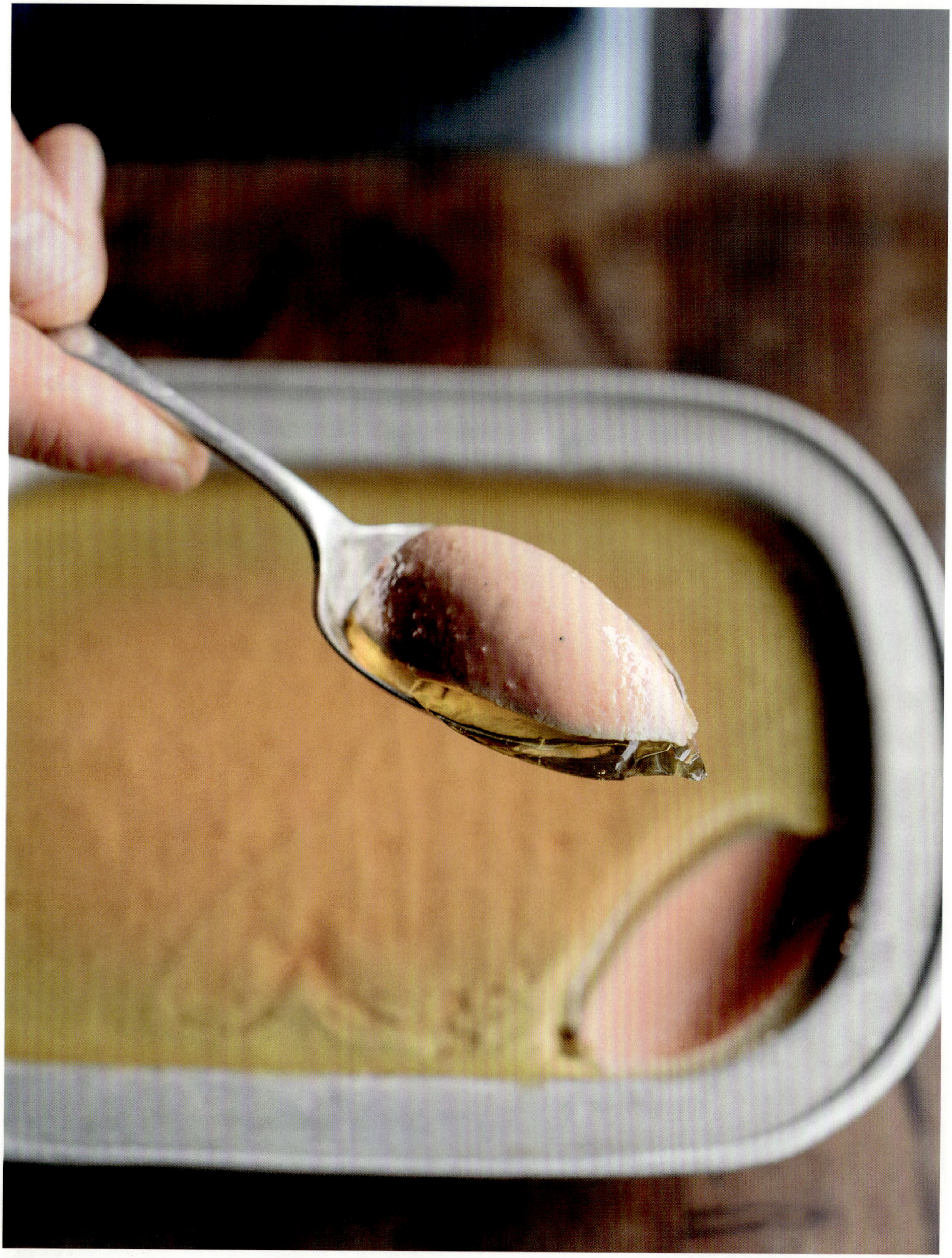

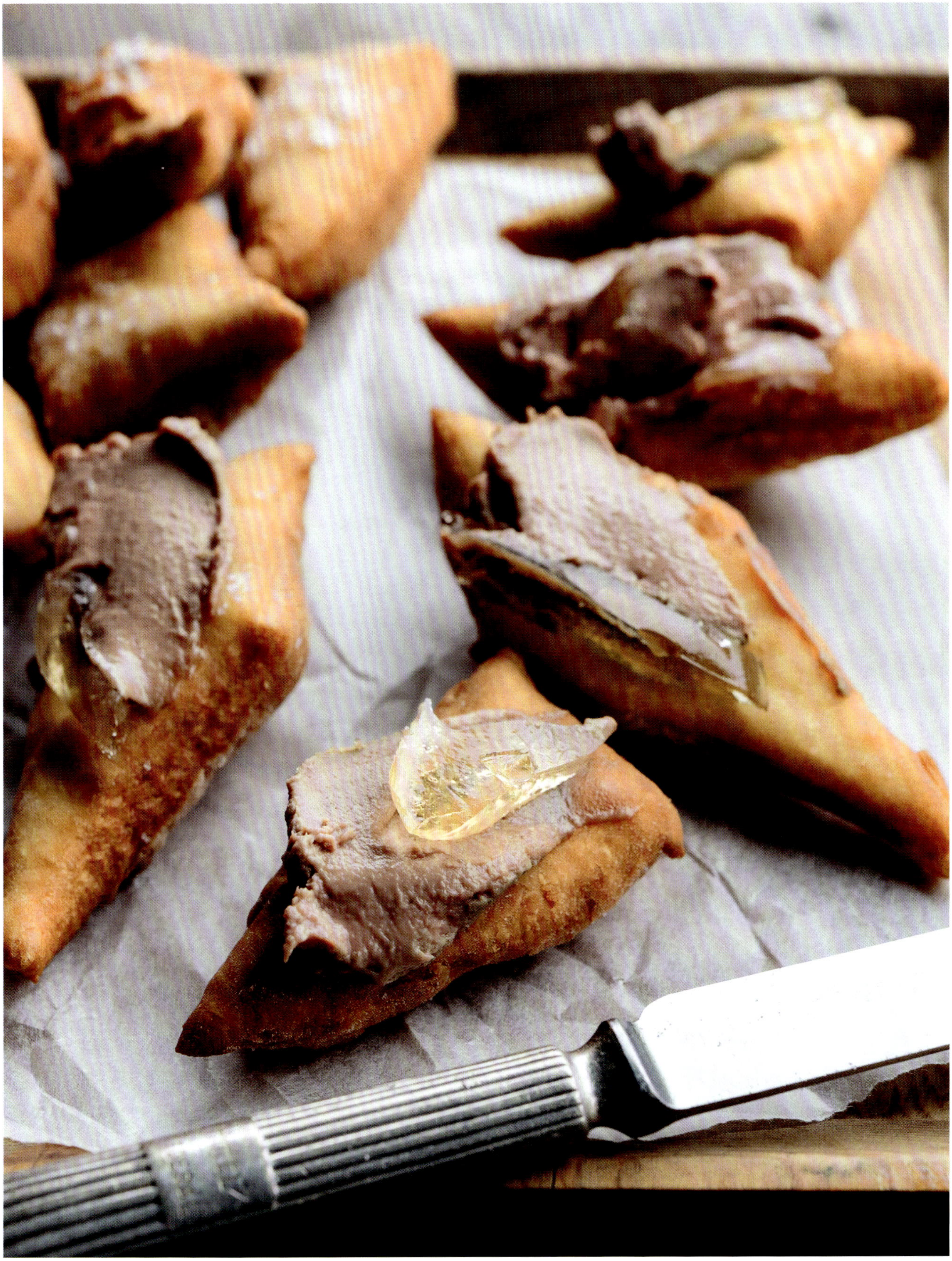

150 EAT UP NEW ZEALAND: THE BACH EDITION

Duck breast and fig salad on macadamia romesco

This is quite a special salad with very decadent ingredients. I love the interplay of flavours and textures. The duck brings richness, the salad leaves bitterness, the macadamia nut romesco adds a creamy, nutty texture, and the sweetness from the fig vino cotto ties it all together. I've written instructions for brining the duck breasts; this is optional, but I always brine mine for two reasons: flavour and tenderness.

Serves 6 as a starter

DUCK AND BRINE
6 duck breasts
3 tablespoons flaky sea salt
2 tablespoons sugar
12 black peppercorns
2 bay leaves
2 cups (500 ml/17 fl oz) water

MACADAMIA ROMESCO
2 cups torn-up stale bread
250 ml (9 fl oz/1 cup) milk
120 g (4¼ oz/¾ cup) roasted macadamia nuts
1½ tablespoons white wine vinegar
1 tablespoon Dijon mustard
1 teaspoon sugar
250 ml (9 fl oz/1 cup) walnut oil (or peanut oil), plus extra to dress
flaky sea salt and freshly ground black pepper

TO COOK AND SERVE
9 fresh figs, quartered
1 witloof, sliced
½ radicchio, leaves separated and torn
½ bunch watercress
12 flat-leaf parsley stalks, leaves picked
½ cup yellow celery leaves, torn
½ small red onion, finely sliced
½ cup (80 g/2¾ oz) roasted macadamia nuts, halved
fig vino cotto (available at any decent deli or food speciality store), to dress

Trim any excess fat off the duck breasts, but leave a full covering over the breast meat. With a sharp knife, score the fat with a fine criss-cross pattern. Place the breasts in a bowl.

For the brine, place the salt, sugar, peppercorns and bay leaves in a small saucepan along with the water. Place over medium-low heat and stir until the salt and sugar have dissolved. Remove the pan from the heat and let the brine cool completely before pouring over the duck breasts. Place in the refrigerator to brine for at least 6 hours, preferably overnight.

To make the macadamia romesco, place the ripped-up stale bread, along with the milk, macadamia nuts, vinegar, mustard and sugar, in a food processor. Process for a minute, then slowly drizzle in the walnut oil until thick and emulsified. Season to taste, and refrigerate.

Place a frying pan over low heat. After a minute or so, place the duck breasts in the pan, skin side down. For the next 10 minutes, render the fat from the skin. As the fat liquefies in the pan, pour it off every few minutes, and set aside to use for cooking later. Now increase the heat to medium, and fry the duck breasts until the skin on the fat side is nicely golden and crisp. Turn over and fry for a further 3–4 minutes, until cooked through. Remove from the pan and rest in a warm place for at least 5 minutes.

    For the salad, place the figs in a bowl along with the witloof, radicchio, watercress, parsley, celery leaves, red onion and macadamia nuts. Slice the rested duck breasts, and add to the salad. Dress the salad with the fig vino cotto and walnut oil, and season.

To serve, spoon the macadamia romesco onto plates, then top with the duck and fig salad. Serve now.

NATIVE BIRDS OF NEW ZEALAND.

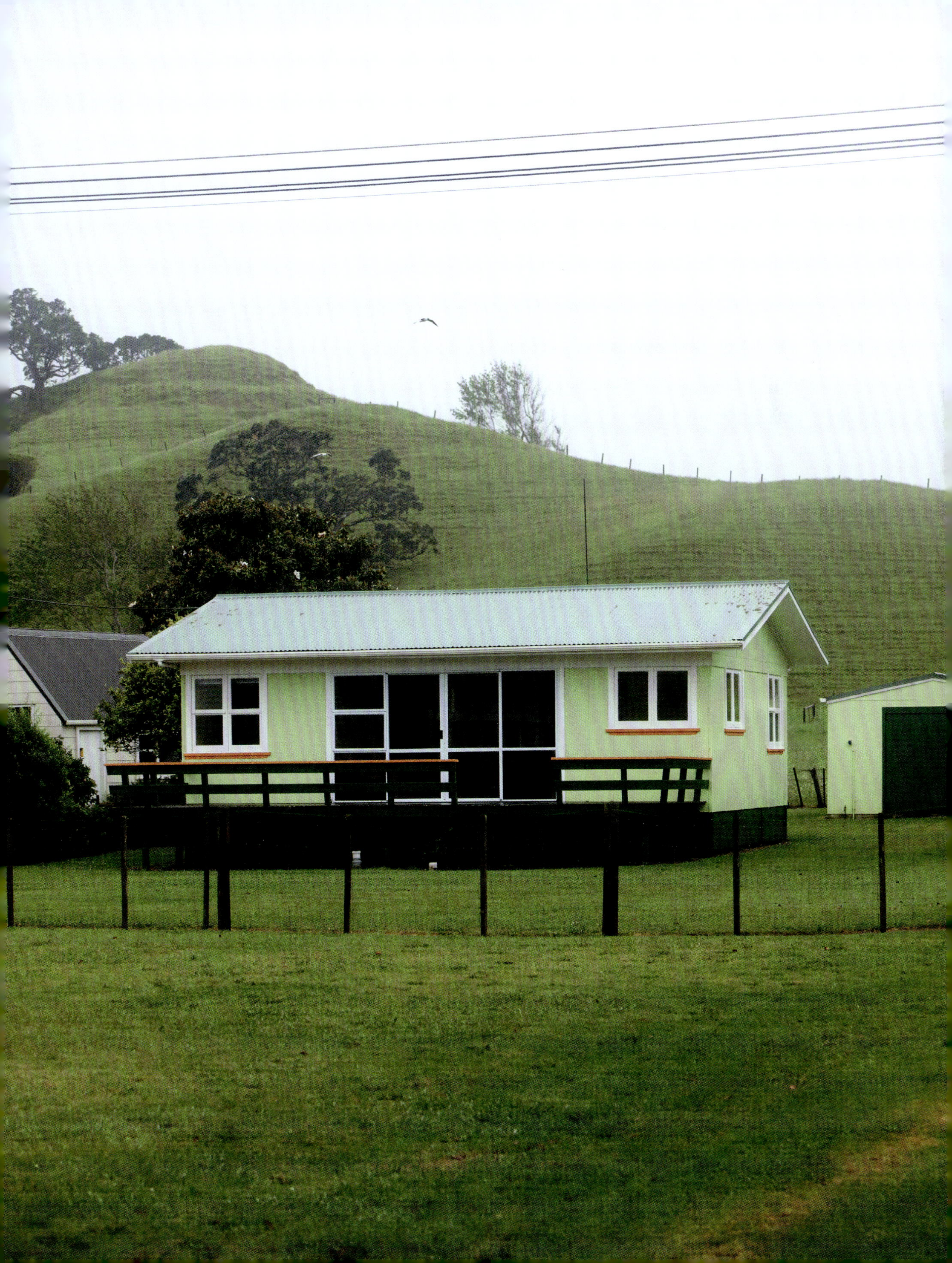

Duck shepherd's pie

Here's a bit of a new spin on an old classic. There is a fair bit of work in this recipe, but it's definitely one that can be prepared over three days or more. If you want to use wild duck, by all means do so. I'd use, say, four wild birds in place of two domestic farmed ducks.

Serves 6 to 8

ROASTED DUCK STEW
2 whole ducks
cooking oil, for frying
3 cups onion, diced
1½ cups carrot, diced
1 cup celery stalks, diced
6 garlic cloves, crushed
30 g (1 oz) ginger, roughly chopped
4 star anise
1 cinnamon stick
2 teaspoons fennel seeds, toasted and crushed
pinch dried chilli flakes
zest and juice of 2 oranges
1 cup (250 ml/9 fl oz) port
2 cups (500 ml/17 fl oz) chicken stock
2 cups (500 ml/17 fl oz) beef stock
90 g (3¼ oz) butter
90 g (3¼ oz) plain flour

KŪMARA MASH
1 kg (2 lb 4oz) golden kūmara, peeled and cut into small dice
50 g (1¾ oz) butter
250 ml (9 fl oz/1 cup) cream or full-cream milk
flaky sea salt and freshly ground black pepper

TO COOK AND SERVE
⅓ baguette, crust removed, diced
60 g (2¼ oz/1 cup) panko breadcrumbs
finely grated zest and juice of 1 orange
1 tablespoon brown sugar
50 g (1¾ oz) butter, melted
1 tablespoon finely chopped thyme
2 tablespoons chopped parsley
flaky sea salt and freshly ground black pepper

Preheat your oven to 160°C (325°F).

First, prepare the duck stew. Take the whole ducks, cut off the fat from around the necks and discard. With a sharp knife or kitchen shears, butterfly the duck by chopping down the backbone and gently splitting open the breast plate of the bird—essentially the whole duck should lie flat. Season both the butterflied birds with salt and pepper.

Take two roasting pans or heavy-bottomed ovenproof pans and place over medium-high heat. Once hot, add some cooking oil to each pan, then carefully place each duck, skin side down. Brown for 5 minutes to caramelise the skin. Remove the ducks once golden and set aside. Add the onion, carrot, celery, garlic, ginger, star anise, cinnamon, fennel and chilli flakes to the two pans. Cook for 10 minutes or so, stirring occasionally until the vegetables begin to caramelise.

Take a potato peeler and peel the zest from the oranges. Add the zest, along with the juice, to the vegetables. Now pour in the port and both stocks. Make sure you have an even amount of vegetables and liquid in the bottom of each roasting pan. Now nestle a duck into each. Cover both roasting pans with tinfoil and place in the oven. Cook for 2 hours, until the ducks are cooked.

Remove from the oven and discard the tinfoil. Let the ducks cool for 30 minutes before picking all the duck meat from the bones. Reserve the picked meat, then strain off all the braising liquid from the vegetables. Keep the braising liquid and discard the cooked vegetables.

Melt the butter in a saucepan and add the flour to form a roux. Cook this out for a minute or two. Using a whisk, slowly pour in the reserved duck braising liquid until incorporated and a thickish gravy develops. Remove from the heat and add the cooked duck meat. Tip the duck mixture into the bottom of a high-sided ovenproof pie dish.

For the kūmara mash topping, place the diced kūmara in a suitable-sized saucepan and cover with cold salted water. Place over medium-high heat, bring up to the boil, then lower the heat to a simmer. Cook for 5–10 minutes until the kūmara is soft. Drain and put the kūmara back into the pan along with the butter and cream. Mash the kūmara until silky smooth. Taste then season accordingly. While still warm, spoon the mash over the cooked duck, smoothing with a rubber spatula to form an even layer. Set aside while you make the crunchy topping.

In a bowl add the diced baguette, breadcrumbs, orange zest and juice and sugar. With clean hands, mix until combined, then pour in the melted butter and mix again. Finally, fold through the chopped thyme and parsley and season. Scatter this mixture over the top of the kūmara mash.

Preheat your oven to 160°C (325°F).

Place the pie in the centre of the oven and cook for 45 minutes to 1 hour, or until the topping is golden and crisp and the pie is piping hot in the middle. Remove from the oven and let it sit for 15 minutes before serving. Green salad and a good-quality loaf of hot crusty bread would work well in this particular situation.

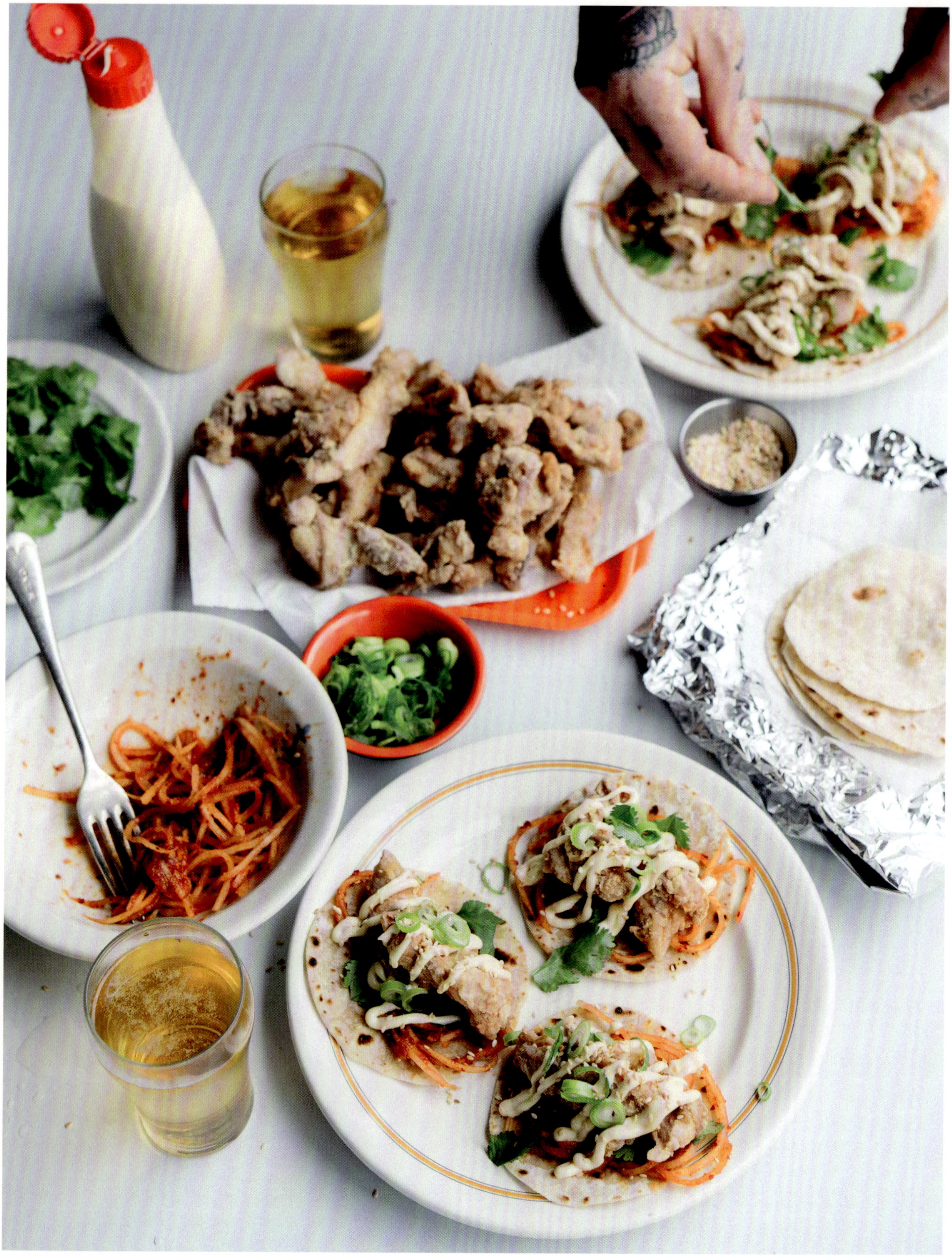

Chicken karaage tacos with fresh daikon kimchi and Kewpie

If you love food, Japan should be near the top of your must-visit list. Having recently made the pilgrimage with my family, I can confirm that what you've undoubtedly heard is true: the food is simply extraordinary in whichever direction you turn. We had two teenage girls on board who were not particularly into eating all the intrepid bits, but they definitely became huge fans of karaage chicken, sampling different versions as we travelled through various destinations. As far as fried chicken goes, this style, like so much of Japanese food, seems cleaner, has a more pronounced flavour and is less greasy than traditional fried chicken. I have added kimchi to the equation, which although not Japanese is the darling of the condiment world right now. Along with some Kewpie mayo, it makes this taco a little firecracker.

Makes 18 small tacos

CHICKEN KARAAGE
1 kg (2 lb 4 oz) boneless chicken thighs
1 tablespoon finely minced ginger
1½ tablespoons finely minced garlic
¼ cup (60 ml/2 fl oz) soy sauce

DAIKON KIMCHI
½ daikon radish, peeled
2–3 tablespoons kimchi paste (page 430)

TO COOK AND SERVE
18 flour tortillas (page 442)
canola oil, for deep-frying
2 cups (350 g/12 oz) rice flour
Kewpie mayonnaise, to serve
coriander leaves, to serve
sliced spring onion, to serve
toasted sesame seeds, to serve

To prepare the chicken, cut the chicken thighs into finger-sized strips and place in a bowl. Add the ginger, garlic and soy sauce, and mix thoroughly to coat. Cover and refrigerate until required. I like to marinate the chicken overnight.

For the daikon kimchi, use a sharp knife to cut your daikon into thin slices, then cut again into matchstick-thin strips. Soak the strips in a bowl of iced water for 30 minutes to crisp the daikon, then strain off the water and dry the daikon with a clean tea towel. Place in a bowl and mix through enough kimchi paste to lightly cover. Refrigerate until required.

Preheat your oven to 130°C (250°F).

Wrap your tortillas in tinfoil and place in the oven to heat through for 15–20 minutes.

Heat the oil in your deep-fryer to 180°C (350°F). Alternatively, heat a decent amount of oil in a heavy-bottomed saucepan and bring the oil up to 180 °C. You can gauge this by adding a piece of bread to the oil; if it's at around 180°C, it will take about a minute for the bread to turn golden and crisp.

Drain the marinated chicken, then dust with the rice flour, just prior to deep-frying in the hot oil. Cook the strips of chicken in batches for approximately 3 minutes, until golden and cooked through. Keep warm.

With this sort of set up, let everyone serve themselves . . . tortilla down, fresh daikon kimchi next, followed by the chicken karaage, Kewpie mayo to top, then coriander, spring onions and sesame seeds to finish. Consume, then go again.

Muttonbird and kūmara cakes with hot sauce mayo

Only occasionally am I lucky enough to get to eat muttonbird. Some would say it's an acquired taste. I, on the other hand, totally understand why it is held in such high regard and considered a delicacy by Māori. I have a couple of sources that I can occasionally score one or two tītī from, and I believe not having at least one muttonbird recipe in this book would be quite remiss. These are delicious, by the way, and the hot sauce mayo rides wonderfully well next to the gutsy flavour of the birds.

Serves 6

MUTTONBIRD AND KŪMARA CAKES
3 muttonbirds
⅓ cup (80 ml/2½ fl oz) cooking oil, plus extra for frying
3 cups (465 g/1 lb) finely diced onion
1 cup (140 g/5 oz) finely diced celery
1½ cups (235 g/8½ oz) finely diced green capsicum
1 tablespoon finely diced garlic
500 g (1 lb 2 oz) cooked kūmara, cut into 1 cm (½ in) dice
½ cup (125 g/4½ oz) mayonnaise
flaky sea salt and freshly ground black pepper
2 cups (120 g/4¼ oz) panko breadcrumbs

HOT SAUCE MAYO
1 cup (250 g/9 oz) mayonnaise
1 tablespoon hot sauce, such as Kaitaia Fire

Place the muttonbirds in a large saucepan and cover with warm water. Place over high heat and bring up to the boil, then lower the heat to a simmer. Cook for 25 minutes or so, then drain off the water and refill with fresh water. Repeat this process two more times. The birds are ready when the meat comes away from the bone with ease. Remove and, once cool enough to handle, pick the meat from the bones, discarding the fat and carcasses. Roughly chop the cooked muttonbird meat, and refrigerate until required.

Heat the oil in a saucepan over medium-low heat. Add the onion, celery, capsicum and garlic. Sweat for 20 minutes, stirring occasionally until the vegetables are soft and translucent. Remove and transfer to a bowl to cool.

Once the cooked vegetables are cooled, add the muttonbird meat along with the cooked kūmara and mayonnaise. Mix through until combined. Taste and season accordingly; the mixture will probably not need much salt.

Form the muttonbird mixture into cakes/patties, then toss in the breadcrumbs and shape. Refrigerate until required.

For the hot sauce mayo, combine the mayonnaise and hot sauce together in a small bowl. Refrigerate until required.

Preheat your oven to 160°C (325°F).

Place a frying pan over medium-low heat. Once hot, add some cooking oil then add half of the muttonbird cakes. Cook for a couple of minutes on each side, until golden, then place on an oven tray and keep warm in the oven while you fry the remaining cakes. Serve with a liberal lick of the hot sauce mayo. Eat now.

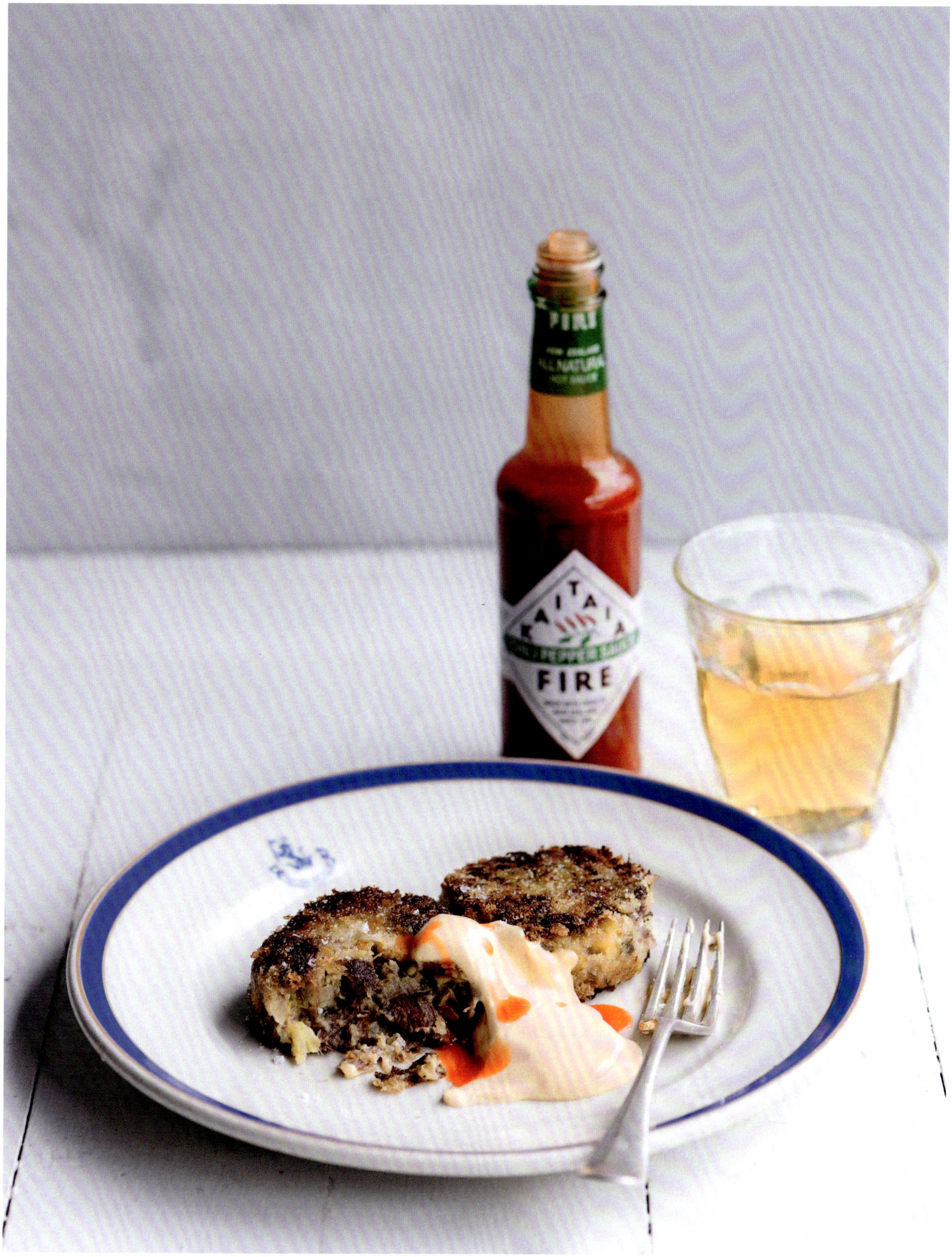
FIRE
KAITAIA
FIRE

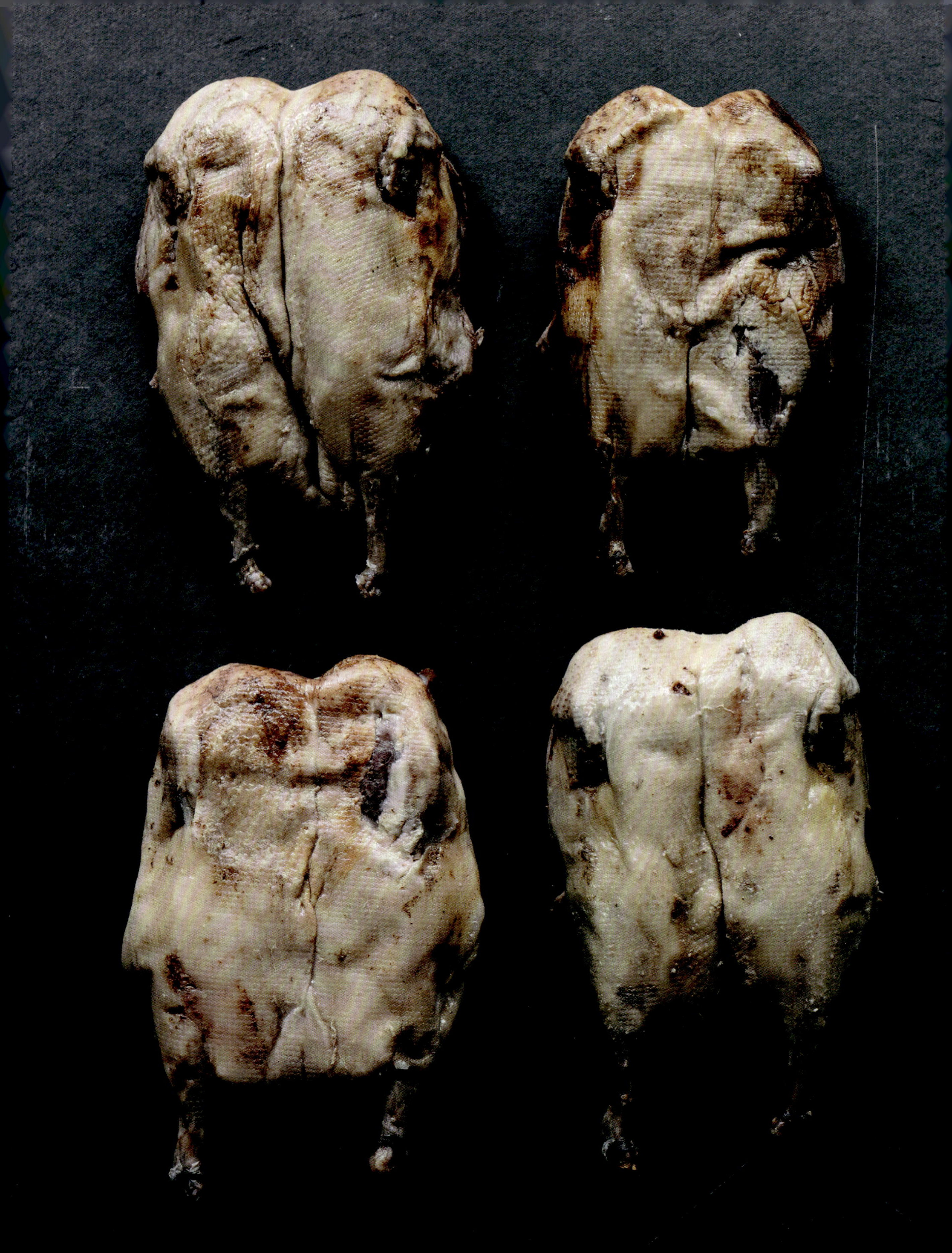

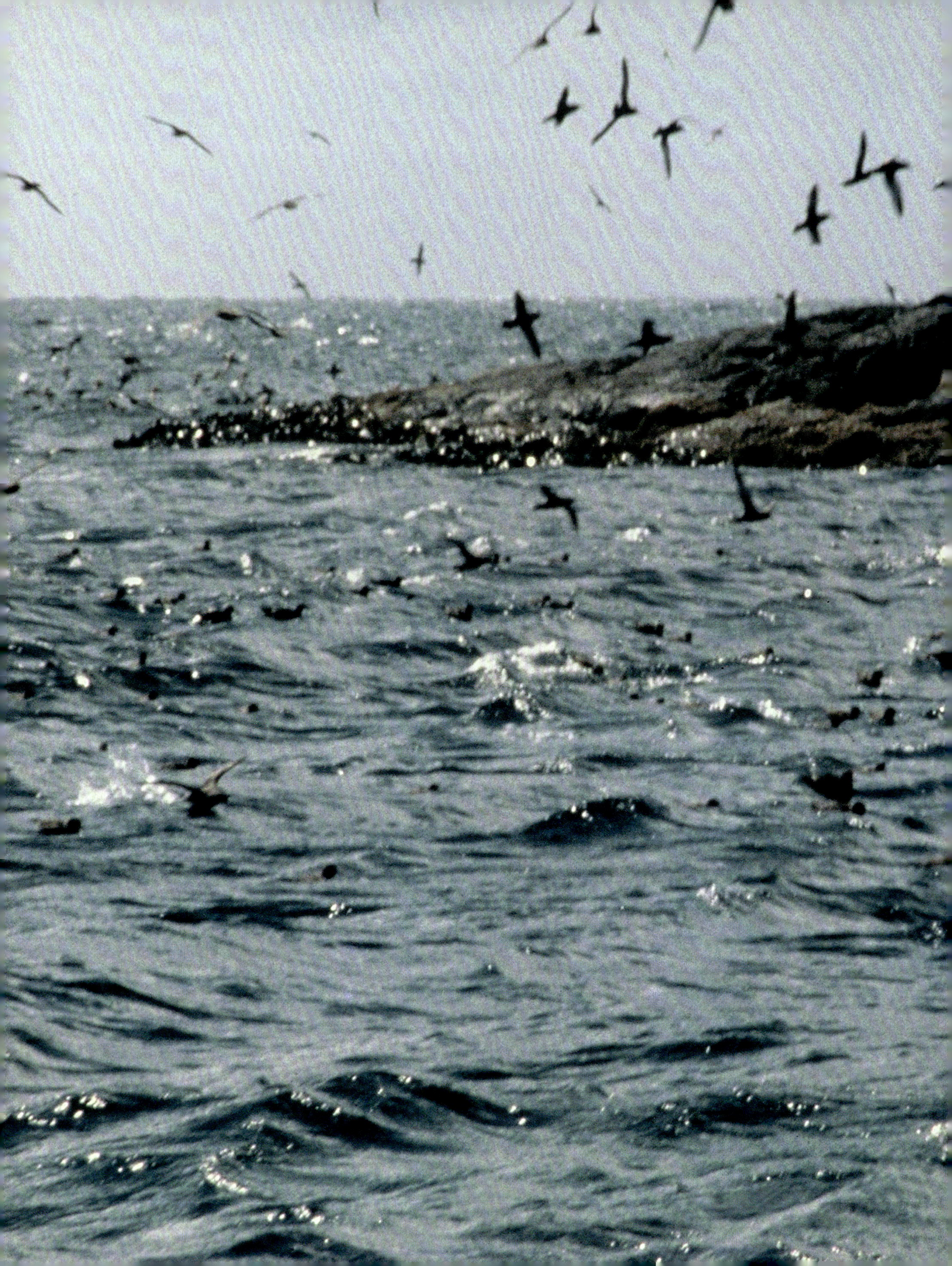

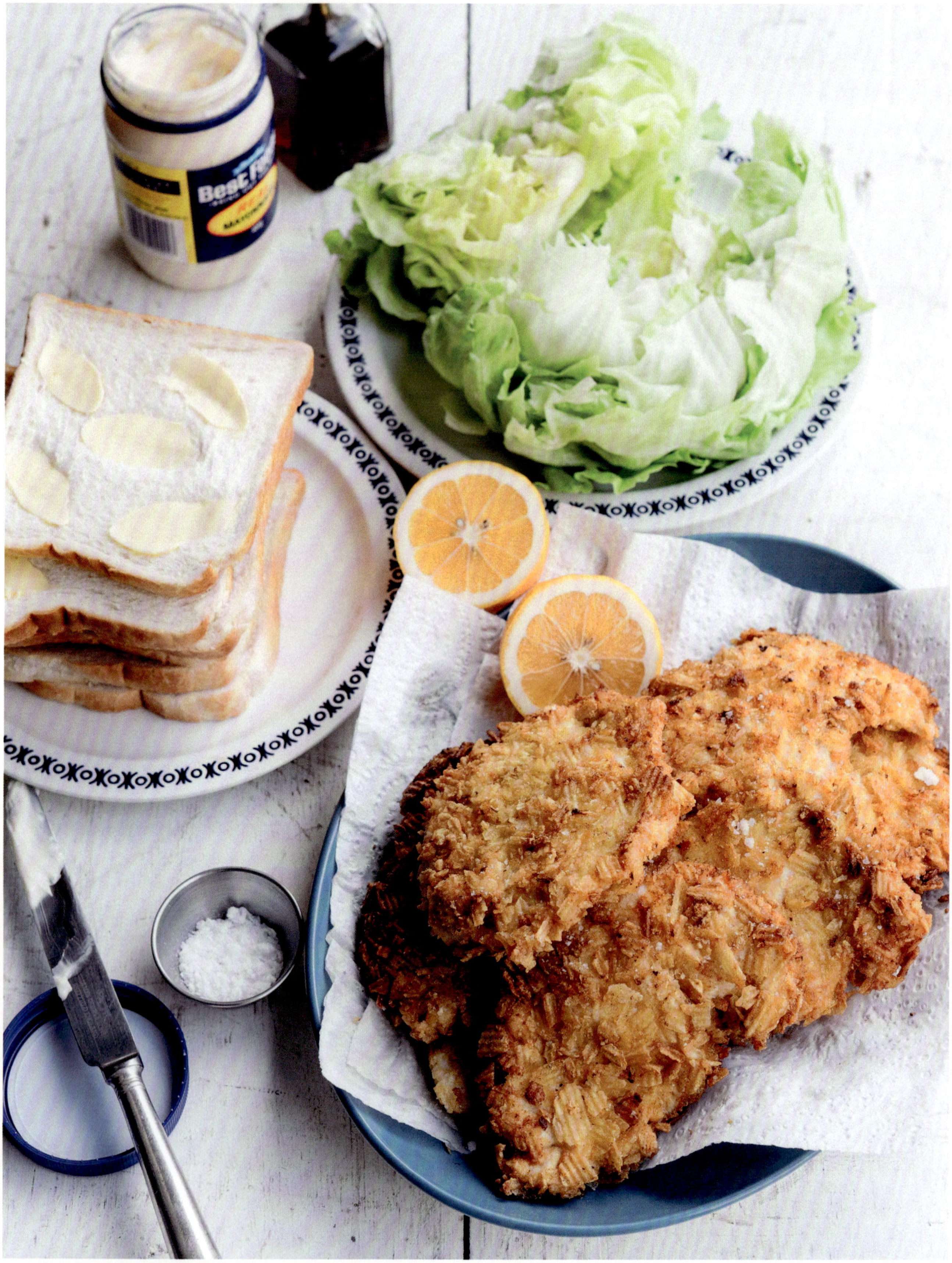

Salt and vinegar chip chicken schnitzel sandwiches

This recipe is a bit of fun, and the kids will go nuts for them. Basically, a schnitzel is just a vehicle to take on any kind of crumb you can think of. Breakfast cereals, crushed wasabi peas or dukkah can all take the place of breadcrumbs.

Makes 6 sandwiches

SCHNITZEL
3 large chicken breasts
1 cup (150 g/5½ oz) plain flour
3 eggs, beaten
150 g (5½ oz) packet salt and vinegar chips, crushed to rough crumbs

TO COOK AND SERVE
cooking oil, for shallow-frying
12 slices buttered white toast-slice bread
mayonnaise, for spreading
few drops malt vinegar
8–12 iceberg lettuce leaves

To make the schnitzel, take the chicken breasts and slice them in half on the diagonal so each piece is similar in size and weight. One at a time, place each piece of chicken between two pieces of clingfilm. With a meat cleaver or rolling pin, gently tap the chicken out into a flat schnitzel about 5 mm (¼ in) thick. (Don't fret if you create a couple of holes here and there in them.)

Once they are all flattened, set up your breading station. Flour in the first bowl, beaten eggs in the next and finally your crushed salt and vinegar chips in the last bowl.

Dip the schnitzels into the flour first, followed by the eggs, then finally press firmly into the crushed chips to get a good covering. Repeat until all the schnitzels are completed.

Place a large frying pan over medium heat. Add enough oil to shallow-fry, about 1 cm (½ in) deep. Once the oil is hot, using tongs, carefully add one or two schnitzels at a time. Cook for a minute or two on either side, until cooked through, golden and crisp. Lower the heat slightly if the chicken is browning too fast or crank up the heat if it's taking too long. Remove with a slotted spoon, drain on kitchen paper and keep warm while you finish the rest.

To put the sandwiches together, lay six pieces of the buttered bread down on a clean chopping board. Spread over a little mayo, then top each slice with a crispy chip schnitzel. Sprinkle the schnitzel with a few drops of vinegar, add a leaf or two of lettuce then complete the sandwich by adding the top layer of mayo-spread bread. Squish down gently, then cut in half or eat 'em whole.

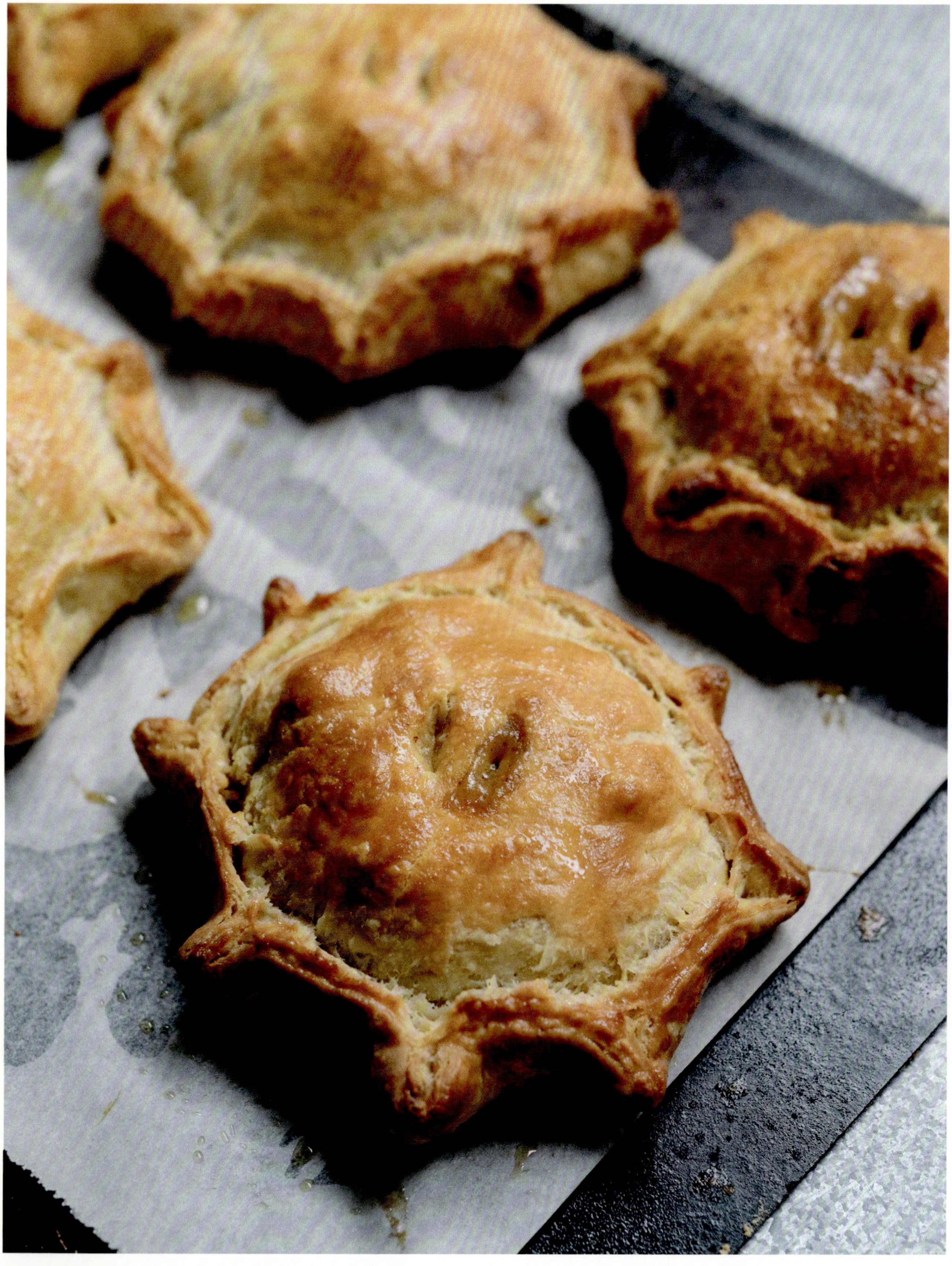

Chicken and chorizo pies

Chicken and chorizo is a cracker filling for a pie, as it has tons of flavour. It's worth keeping this in mind when making any sort of pie. When you wrap something in a blanket of delicious pastry it will always 'dumb down' the flavour of the filling (exactly the same thing that happens when adding two slices of bread to a sandwich filling). These pies have quite a Spanish–Mexican taste to them, so would equally make a bunch of tasty wee individual empanadas.

Makes 10 individual small pies or 2 large pies

CHICKEN AND CHORIZO PIES
⅓ cup (80 ml/2½ fl oz) cooking oil
1 cup diced good-quality chorizo sausages
2 cups (310 g/11 oz) diced onion
1 cup (140 g/5 oz) diced celery
3 tablespoons finely diced garlic
⅓ cup (50 g/1¾ oz) dried currants
1½ tablespoons cumin seeds, roasted and ground
1 tablespoon fennel seeds, roasted and ground
1 teaspoon smoked sweet paprika
700 g (1 lb 9 oz) chicken thighs, diced
1½ cups (375 ml/13 fl oz) chicken stock
3 cups golden kūmara, cut into 1 cm (½ in) dice
1 cup (250 ml/9 fl oz) cream
2 cups corn kernels
1 tablespoon butter
1 tablespoon plain flour, plus extra for dusting
flaky sea salt and freshly ground black pepper

CUMIN SOUR CREAM
1½ tablespoons cumin seeds, roasted and ground
250 g (9 oz) sour cream
finely grated zest of 1 lemon, plus 1½ tablespoons lemon juice

TO ASSEMBLE
1 batch Eve's mum's pastry (page 442)
2 eggs, beaten, for brushing
coriander leaves, to serve

Take a large heavy-bottomed saucepan and place over medium-high heat. Once hot, add the oil along with the chorizo. Allow to caramelise for 5 minutes, then add the onion, celery, garlic and currants. Turn the heat down to low and sweat for 10 minutes before adding the ground roasted spices and paprika. Cook gently for a further 10 minutes, stirring occasionally to prevent the spices from catching.

Now add the chicken, turn the heat up to medium and fry until cooked through. Add the stock, along with the kūmara. Bring up to a slow boil, stirring occasionally for 5 minutes before adding the cream and the corn kernels.

In a bowl, and with your fingers, work the butter into the flour until combined. Bring the chicken mixture up to the boil. While stirring with a wooden spoon, drop in bits of the combined flour and butter; this will thicken the mix. Cook for a further 5 minutes or so, taste and season liberally with salt and pepper. Remove from the heat and let cool. Refrigerate until cold.

To make the cumin sour cream, place all the ingredients in a small bowl. Whisk until combined. Refrigerate until required.

Preheat your oven to 180°C (350°F).

Dust a clean, dry, smooth work surface with flour. Roll out the pastry to around 3 mm (1/12 in) thick. Take two circular plates or similar, one that is approximately 12 cm (4¾ in) in diameter, the other around 10 cm (4 in). From the first rolling of the pastry,

Recipe continued overleaf . . .

cut the 10 smaller circles, which will be your tops of the pies. Dust with flour and set aside. Now cut 10 larger circles, rerolling the offcuts to make your bases to the pies.

Lay out the bases on the floured surface and spoon into the centre of each pastry base around ¾ cup of the chicken and chorizo mix. Make sure there is about 1.5 cm (½ in) of pastry visible around the circumference of the base. Brush this circular strip of pastry with the beaten egg.

Place the smaller circles of pastry over the filling, then bring up the egg-brushed sides of the bases and carefully pinch together with the top pastry circles. Refrigerate the pies for 10 minutes to cool and firm the pastry.

Line a baking tray with baking paper and arrange the pies on top. Place in the oven. Check after 30 minutes, then check at 5-minute intervals. The pies are cooked when they are crisp and golden brown all over. Remove from the oven and let the pies sit for 2 minutes before serving with the cumin sour cream and some fresh coriander leaves on the side. You will love these pies. Big effort equals tasty results!

BIRD 167

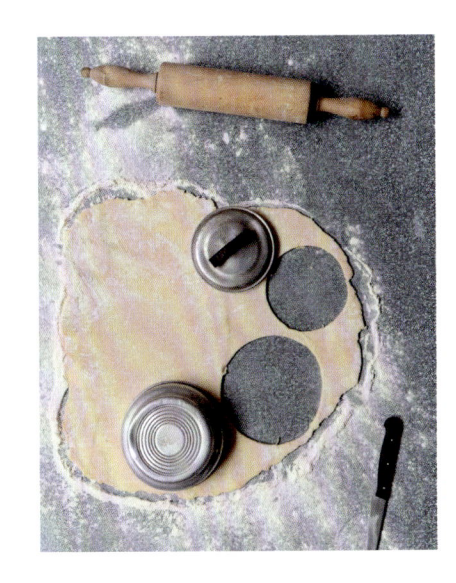

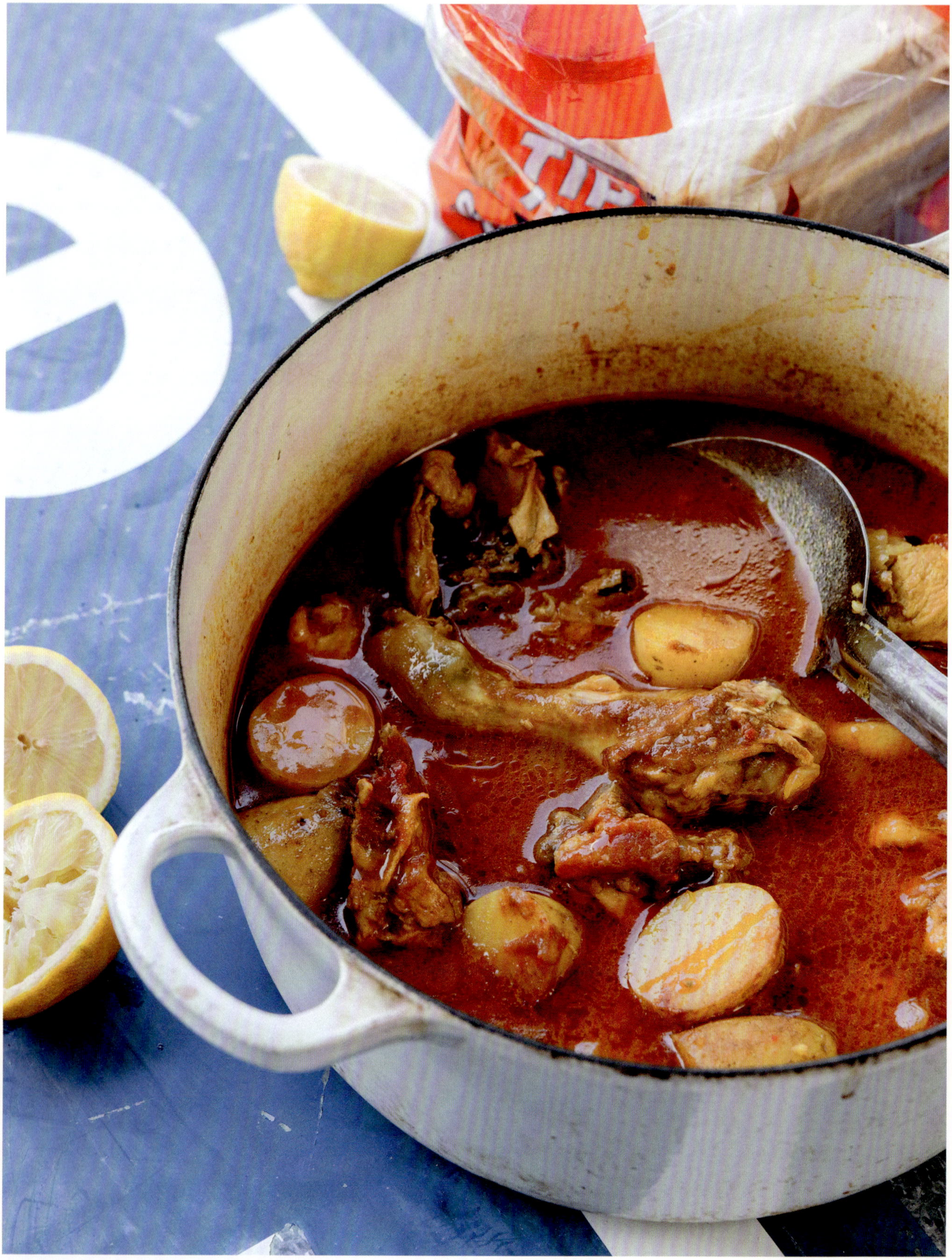
TIP

Puspa's chicken curry

I have published this chicken curry recipe in a previous book, but I wanted to include it in here as well—I have eaten this particular dish too many times to count and it holds a special place in my culinary heart. Puspa is the mother of a terrific friend of mine, Sanjay Dayal. Puspa used to make a big batch of this curry once a week for her family, then the generous amount of leftovers would be brought into their shop Cuba Fruit Supply in Wellington to be consumed for lunch the following day. I have always felt it was a real privilege to share this humble curry with Sanjay, his sister Joshna and the rest of the Cuba Fruit crew once a week, sitting out the back amongst the crates and banana boxes, the only accompaniments being thickly sliced, toasted white bread and lemon halves. Thanks again, Puspa.

Serves 6

2 tablespoons canola oil
8 whole cloves
1 cinnamon stick
6 cardamom pods
1½ cups (235 g/8½ oz) diced onion
2 tablespoons finely chopped ginger
2 tablespoons finely chopped chilli
2 teaspoons finely chopped garlic
2 teaspoons garam masala
4 teaspoons ground coriander

4 teaspoons ground cumin
1 teaspoon ground turmeric
1–2 teaspoons chilli powder
1 x whole chicken, cut into chunky pieces, bone in
250 ml (9 fl oz/1 cup) chicken stock
400 g tin whole peeled tomatoes
6 gourmet potatoes, unpeeled and halved
flaky sea salt

Place a large saucepan over medium heat. Add the oil, cloves, cinnamon stick and cardamom pods and fry for 1 minute. Reduce the heat to low and add the onion. Cook for a few minutes until translucent. Stir in the ginger, chilli, garlic and ground spices, and cook for about 2 minutes. Add the chicken pieces, stock, tomatoes and their juice and potatoes, then stir together. Bring up to a gentle simmer, cover and cook for 40 minutes over low heat, stirring occasionally.

Remove curry from the heat and cool. Season to taste.

Serve with rice if you please, or go Cuba Fruit styles and enjoy with toasted slices of thick white bread and some lemon halves for squeezing.

Turkey meatloaf with whipped potato, gravy and cherry relish

I'm a massive fan of any sort of meatloaf. Humble to a fault, but so nourishing and comforting. This is an old recipe I picked up in the States when I was working there many years ago. Turkey is a lean meat but with a really distinctive flavour that takes on herbs and spices, giving great results. Add a silky-smooth and decadent whipped potato, a good pan gravy and a fruit-driven relish or chutney and you have an incredibly satisfying dish. A green salad on the side makes perfect sense to balance and cut through the richness. If you can't find turkey mince, by all means use chicken mince instead. And don't freak out about the amount of butter and cream in the potato. You can cut it back if you feel you must, but keep in mind you don't have whipped potatoes everyday!

Serves 6

TURKEY MEATLOAF
¾ cup (185 ml/6 fl oz) canola oil
1 cup (155 g/5½ oz) diced onion
1 cup (140 g/5 oz) finely diced celery
2 garlic cloves, finely chopped
500 g (1 lb 2 oz) turkey mince
1 egg, beaten
1 cup (60 g/2¼ oz) panko breadcrumbs
½ cup dried cranberries
1 teaspoon fennel seeds, toasted and ground
1 teaspoon dried oregano
⅓ cup (10 g/¼ oz) finely chopped parsley
pinch dried chilli flakes
1 teaspoon flaky sea salt
freshly ground black pepper

WHIPPED POTATO
1 kg (2 lb 4 oz) Agria potatoes, peeled and cut into large dice
150 g (5½ oz) salted butter, at room temperature
2 cups (500 ml/17 fl oz) cream
flaky sea salt and freshly ground black pepper

TO SERVE
roast chicken gravy (page 443) or cheat it out with a couple of packets of Maggi
cherry relish (page 429)

Preheat your oven to 180°C (350°F).

Place a suitable-sized saucepan over low heat and add the oil, onion, celery and garlic. Sweat for 20 minutes, stirring occasionally until the vegetables are softened but without allowing too much colour. Remove from the heat and let cool.

Place the turkey mince, beaten egg, breadcrumbs, cranberries, cooled vegetable mixture, ground fennel, oregano, parsley, chilli flakes and salt and pepper into a large bowl and mix thoroughly to combine. The mixture should be sticky to the touch.

Grease a regular loaf tin and fill with the meatloaf mixture. Bake for 50 minutes, until golden on top and firm to the touch. Remove from the oven and allow to cool in the tin for 15–20 minutes before slicing (it will hold together better once it has cooled down a bit).

For the whipped potatoes, place the potatoes in a large saucepan and cover with cold salted water. Bring up to a boil then simmer for 20 minutes until cooked through. Drain, then place the potatoes in a colander in the pan and allow to steam-dry for 5 minutes.

Mash the potatoes and butter together in the pan. In a separate saucepan, heat the cream then gradually whip into the potato, a little at a time. Whipped potatoes should have a loose, silky-smooth consistency. Season to taste.

To serve, put a liberal spoon of the whipped potato onto warm plates. Add a generous slice of the turkey meatloaf, pour over gravy and finish with a spoonful of cherry relish. Serve with a simple green salad dressed with lemon and olive oil. Eat now.

BIRD 171

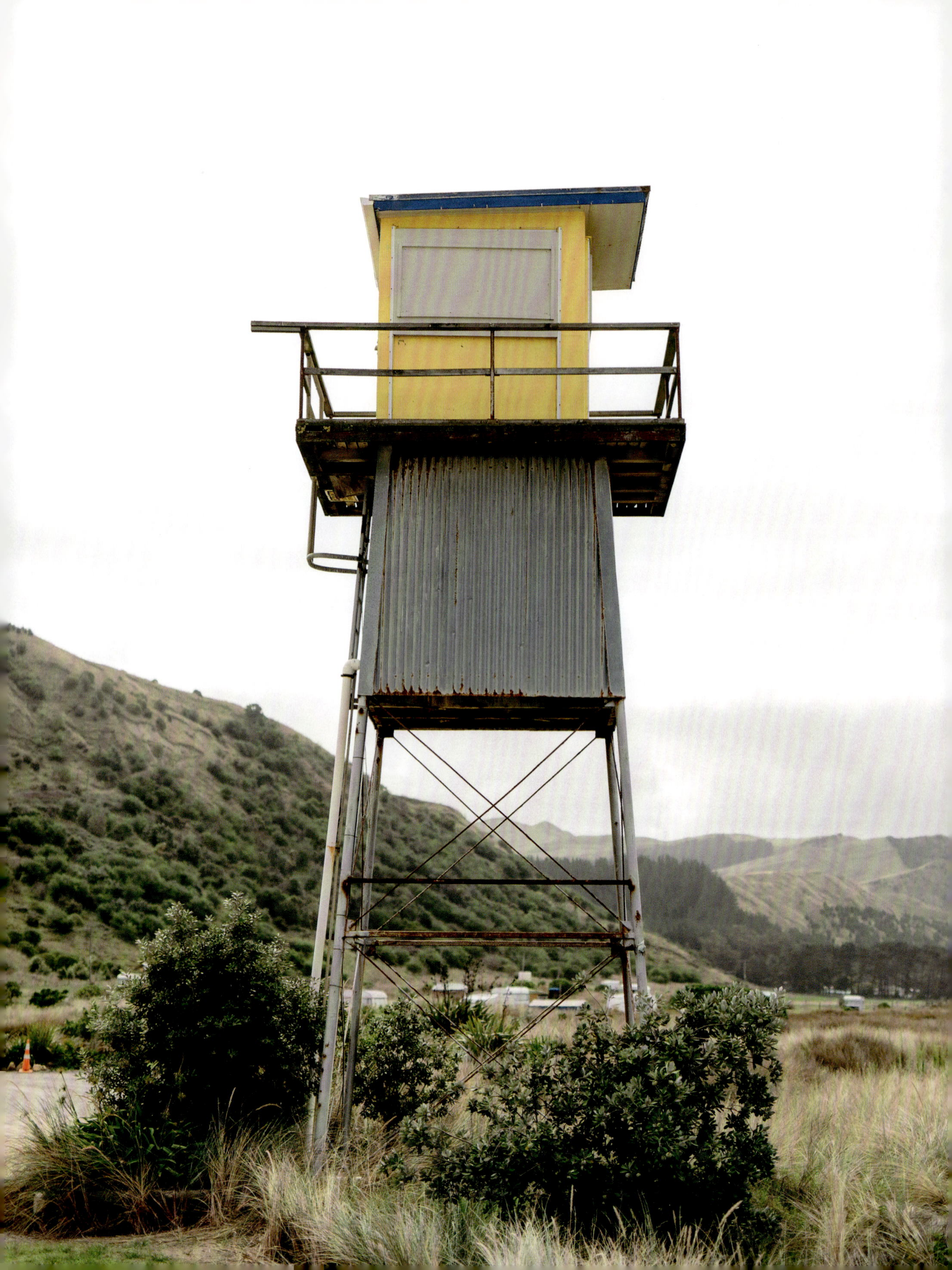

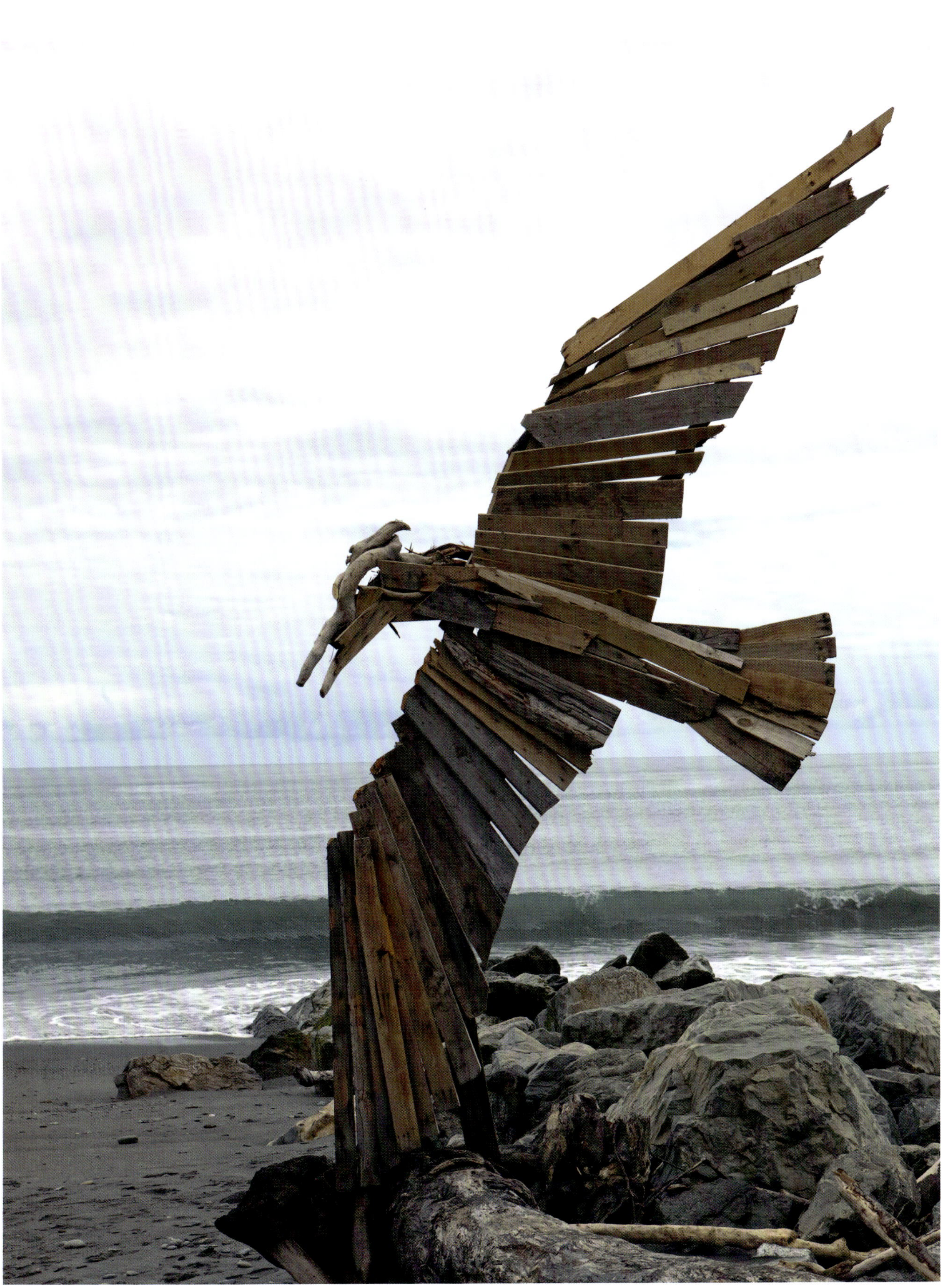

Charcoal roadside Mexican chicken tacos with black beans and tomatillo salsa

I was fortunate enough a few years back to have a terrific family holiday driving a rental car across the Yucatán in Mexico. We drove mainly secondary roads to experience as much of 'real' rural Mexico as possible. Nearly every village we drove through had one or two smoky charcoal roadside barbecues selling fresh chargrilled chicken that was marinated in lime and, among other things, annatto seed paste (also known as achiote). Annatto seed is naturally bright red, and besides the deep colour it also offers up a slightly sweet, peppery flavour with a hint of nutmeg. You can purchase annatto seed paste at Mexican supply stores and good delis. It's a useful condiment to have in the fridge—combined with a little lemon or lime juice, it can be used for a super-fast and tasty marinade for chicken, pork and lamb.

Serves 6

MEXICAN SPICED CHICKEN
1 whole chicken
1 tablespoon achiote paste
1 tablespoon cumin seeds, toasted and ground
1 teaspoon dried oregano
½ tablespoon finely minced garlic
finely grated zest of 1–2 limes
2 teaspoons white vinegar
2 teaspoons hot sauce
2 teaspoons flaky sea salt
¼ cup (60 ml/2 fl oz) cooking oil

REFRIED BLACK BEANS
1½ cups (300 g/10½ oz) dried black beans
4 cups (1 litre/35 fl oz) boiling water
1 teaspoon salt
⅓ cup (80 ml/2½ fl oz) oil
2 tablespoons finely chopped garlic
1 cup (155 g/5½ oz) finely diced onion
½ cup (15 g/½ oz) finely chopped coriander leaves and stalks

1½ tablespoons cumin seeds, toasted and ground
1 chipotle chilli, finely minced
flaky sea salt and freshly ground black pepper

TOMATILLO SALSA
2 cups tomatillo or tomatoes, cut into small dice
½ cup (80 g/2¾ oz) finely diced red onion
½ red chilli, finely minced
½ cup (15 g/½ oz) roughly chopped coriander leaves
½ teaspoon sugar
⅓ cup (80 ml/2½ fl oz) olive oil
juice of 1–2 limes
flaky sea salt and freshly ground black pepper

TO COOK AND SERVE
18 flour tortillas (page 442)
sour cream
extra lemons or limes, for squeezing

Take the bird and, with a sharp knife, split it down the centre of the backbone (the underside of the chicken, opposite side to the breasts). Open up the chicken and cut the breast plate just a little, but not all the way through, so that it opens up flat. Place the butterflied chicken in a large bowl and refrigerate.

Take a small bowl and add the chicken marinade ingredients. With clean hands or a wooden spoon, mix everything into a wet paste. Pour over the chicken, and leave to marinate in the refrigerator for a least a day (2–3 days is even better).

For the refried black beans, place the dried beans in a bowl, cover with the boiling water and add the salt. Cover the bowl and let the beans soak for an hour.

Place a saucepan over medium-low heat. Add the oil, then once hot add the garlic, onion, coriander, cumin and chilli. Sweat for 15 minutes, stirring occasionally to prevent sticking. Now add the beans along with the water they have been soaking in. Bring up to the boil over high heat, then reduce the heat to a simmer and cook for approximately 1 hour, or until the beans are relatively soft. If they look a bit dry, just add a bit more water.

Once soft, using a potato masher or similar, smash up the beans to a texture you are happy with. Taste and season accordingly. Refrigerate until required.

To make the tomatillo salsa, add all the ingredients to a bowl and season to taste with salt and pepper. Refrigerate until required.

You can cook the chicken on any style of barbecue. Even just roast it in the oven for a great result. However, if you can cook the chicken over charcoal the resulting smoke and flavour that is imparted is going to take this bird to a nirvana sort of situation. Cook the chicken for at least 40 minutes, making sure it is cooked all the way through (the juices should run clear when a skewer is inserted into the thickest part of the bird). Allow the chicken to rest for a further 10 minutes.

Gather all your elements before serving. Cook your tortillas over the grill or in a pan, then wrap in tinfoil to keep warm. Reheat the black beans. If they have thickened and become too gluggy, add a little chicken stock or water to thin out. Keep warm.

Break up or carve the chicken into pieces and serve alongside the warm tortillas, refried black beans, tomatillo salsa and sour cream. Have lemons or limes close by for squeezing. Get everyone to help themselves.

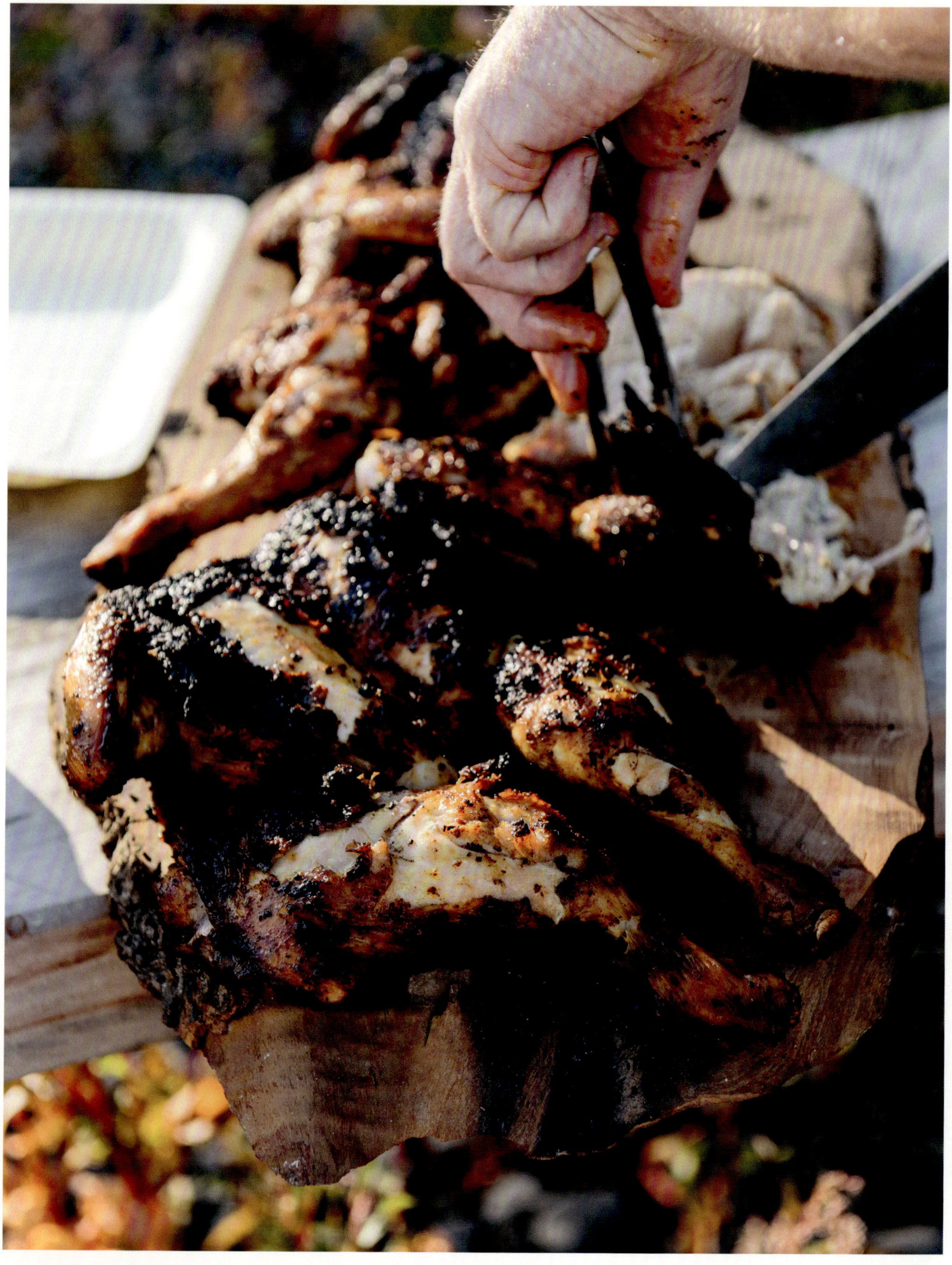

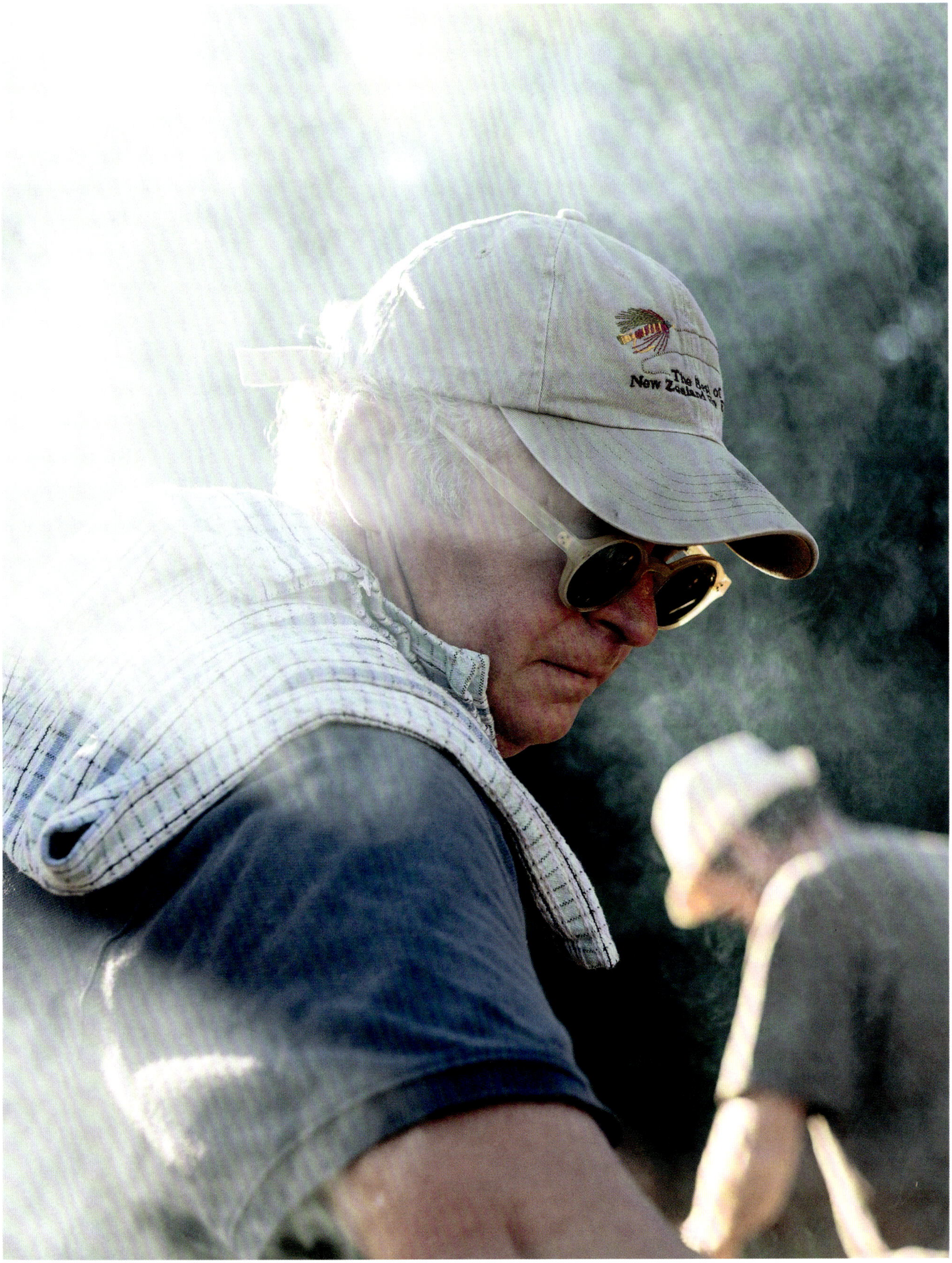
The Best of
New Zealand

Fried chicken bhaji with fresh coriander labneh

This is a bit of a riff on the classic Indian dish onion bhaji. Essentially it's crispy fried chicken but with Indian flavours, served with a fresh coriander labneh. Labneh is basically really thick yoghurt. We make it in the restaurant just by straining the whey out of plain yoghurt through a muslin cloth, which sits in a sieve set over a bowl in the fridge overnight. If you can't be bothered with that sort of faffing around, just use as thick a natural yoghurt as you can find.

Bonus points: this recipe is gluten-free. Vegan . . . not so much!

Serves 6 (100 g/3½ oz portions)

CHICKEN BHAJI
600 g (1 lb 5 oz) chicken thighs, cut into smallish pieces
2–3 teaspoons chilli paste (store-bought is all good)
2 tablespoons minced or grated ginger
2 tablespoons finely chopped garlic
¼ cup (60 ml/2 fl oz) lemon juice
2 tablespoons ground cumin
½ tablespoon cumin seeds
1 teaspoon ground turmeric
2 teaspoons ground coriander
2 teaspoons mustard seeds

1 cup (260 g/9¼ oz) thick natural yoghurt
1 cup (120 g/4¼ oz) chickpea flour
½ cup (60 g/2¼ oz) cornflour
2 teaspoons flaky sea salt
1 teaspoon freshly ground black pepper

FRESH CORIANDER LABNEH
⅔ cup (15 g/½ oz) coriander leaves
1½ cups (390 g/13¾ oz) strained natural yoghurt

TO COOK AND SERVE
2 litres (70 fl oz) canola oil or similar cooking oil
1½ cups (180 g/6½ oz) cornflour
lemon or lime wedges
coriander leaves
fried red chillies (optional) (page 445)
fried curry leaves (page 445)

Place the chicken pieces in a suitable-sized mixing bowl, then add the chilli paste, ginger, garlic and lemon juice. Mix thoroughly with a wooden spoon. Now add the spices and yoghurt and mix through. Add the chickpea flour and cornflour, season with salt and pepper, and mix everything together. The chicken will be covered in quite a thick paste. Refrigerate until required.

To make the labneh, take a stick blender or similar. Place the coriander in the bottom of a jar that the blender can fit into. Add a couple of tablespoons of the yoghurt on top of the coriander leaves, then blitz into a paste. Take the paste and fold it through the rest of the yoghurt. Refrigerate until required.

I like to cook the chicken in batches, and to make sure the chicken pieces are cooked through we are going to cook them twice. You can do the first cook ahead, then the second cook prior to serving. All the messy part has been done, so serving is a dream from that point.

Heat the oil in your deep-fryer or a heavy-bottomed saucepan and bring up to 160°C (315°F). Line a plate with kitchen paper.

Working with batches of six to eight pieces at a time, dip your chicken pieces into the cornflour, then carefully add them to your hot oil. Cook for around 3 minutes, then remove and place on the prepared plate. Continue until you have finished the first cook of all the chicken pieces. You can refrigerate these until you are ready to serve.

Now bring the oil up to 180°C (350°F). You can gauge this by adding a piece of bread to the oil; if it's at around 180°C (350°F), it will take about a minute for the bread to turn golden and crisp. In a couple of batches, cook the chicken pieces for another 2 minutes, until golden and super crisp.

To serve, use either individual plates or a platter. Spoon down some of the coriander labneh, top with the crisp chicken bhaji, then garnish with a wedge of lemon or lime, coriander leaves, fried chilli and curry leaves. Tuck in—these are delicious.

'The Fed' chicken salad sandwich

I can't remember a sandwich I didn't like. When they are made with fresh ingredients, they are just so darn delicious. From the humble club sandwich (which gets smashed at any event) to big toasted sourdough doorstoppers, there seems to be an occasion for them all.

I opened the Federal Deli in Auckland in 2013, based on my love of the Jewish delis that I frequented and loved so much when I lived and worked in Montréal and New York City way back when. We serve a bunch of sandwiches at The Fed, but two out-sell the others by a country mile: the Reuben and this one, our chicken salad sandwich. What takes this sandwich to a higher level of popularity is the crunchy chicken skin (crackling), which adds a super textural element. And the delicious rye bread that our friends at Loaf bakery make for us each day. Don't be shy to give this one the toastie treatment!

Serves 6

FED CHICKEN MIX
1 x whole roasted chicken, cold
¾ cup (185 g/6½ oz) mayonnaise
⅓ cup (50 g/1¾ oz) finely diced red onion
⅓ cup (50 g/1¾ oz) finely diced dill pickle
1 tablespoon finely chopped dill
flaky sea salt and freshly ground black pepper

TO ASSEMBLE AND SERVE
fresh bread* (see below)
butter
shredded iceberg lettuce ('Big Mac cut')
chicken skin crackling (page 446)

To make the Fed chicken mix, pull all the chicken meat, including the skin, from a cold roasted chook. Chop it up nice and fine, and place it in a suitable-sized bowl.

Fold in the rest of the ingredients except for the salt and pepper. Taste the mix, then season accordingly. Refrigerate until required.

Butter your fresh bread, place shredded iceberg on one slice, then top with a good amount of the chicken mix, followed by a decent amount of chicken skin crackling. Top with another slice of buttered bread.

If you're giving your sandwiches the toastie action, assemble them first, then butter the bread on the outsides. Bring a skillet or similar up to medium heat, and toast both sides of the sandwich until golden. Cut in half and serve now.

Fancy some gravy on the side? Just-add-water packet gravy will do the trick.

* If you want the real deal, drop in to The Fed and buy a loaf of caraway-seed-filled rye bread.

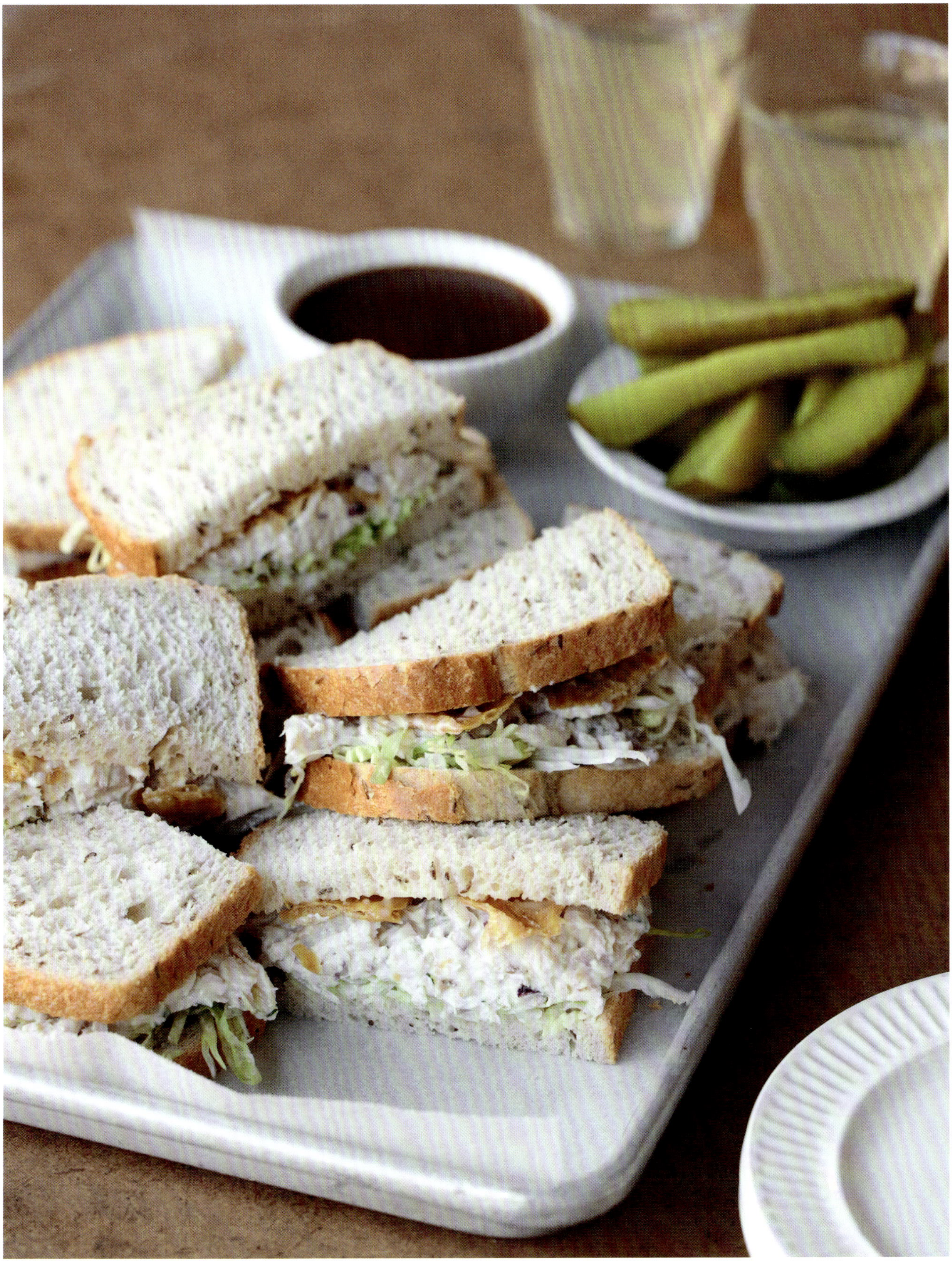

Chef 24/Automatic

left front — left rear — right rear — right front

Turning Up the Flavour Dial

Over the past 30 or so years, I have been lucky enough to have been invited to speak and cook at many events, both nationally and internationally. I feel very fortunate and proud to have been able to represent New Zealand on the culinary world stage, and to have had the privilege of hosting and entertaining numerous food writers, winemakers and international chefs.

There is a common thread that runs through all of these events and occasions. Whether I'm speaking or cooking, it's always the 'jewels' of the Kiwi food and wine scene that are front and centre. New Zealand lamb, venison, beef, greenshell mussels and salmon, along with our Sauvignon Blanc and Pinot Noir: these are still our culinary celebs, and deservedly so. All of these New Zealand products have now been in the international marketplace for quite some time, and that hasn't been an easy feat by any stretch! Our producers are constantly working to overcome hurdles of distance to the marketplace, the setting up of relationships, establishing distribution channels, and competition from all quarters.

In terms of taste, the products proudly speak for themselves, but that alone is never enough to secure a presence or hold pole position on the global stage. We should acknowledge and feel really grateful for the extraordinary amount of effort, time and money that many Kiwis have put into establishing these superstar products in the world market. It's dogged determination and persistence, coupled with great storytelling and genuine Kiwi hospitality, that has put these hero products from our small and remote country into the best hotels, food halls and restaurants around the world.

I'm a massive fan of all of the New Zealand hero products, and I have genuine admiration and respect for all of the growers, producers and companies who, over the decades, have done the hard yards, effectively paving the way for the next wave of exciting wares and products to leave our shores. What gives me the biggest buzz these days is the sheer variety of the 'little guys' tagging along, riding shotgun with the established heavyweights. While the majority of these products are not yet hitting the shelves in foreign markets, they are slowly but surely starting to be noticed. When I speak about or cook with these products, it's often the case that I'm met with a genuine look of surprise or bewilderment that they are actually grown or produced in New Zealand.

Olive oil, nut oil, oysters, wild surf clams, pine nuts, fresh wasabi, saffron, truffles, chocolate, numerous varieties of honey—it's almost embarrassing what this country of ours has up its sleeve. And that's literally just scratching the surface. The other point to note is that it's not just that we can grow, farm and harvest such an extensive variety of products; it's that most of them are truly world class when it comes to taste and usability.

I still get shudders down my spine when I recall many of those events—the stress and anxiety involved in cooking in foreign kitchens with cooks and chefs you have never worked with before or standing up on stage and speaking to hundreds of people is always nerve-wracking, but it's also addictive, with quite a high following all that trepidation and angst. Back in 2013, in San Francisco, when we had a crack at lifting the America's Cup—and let's not dwell on that most cruel of results—Haydo and I were cooking some of New Zealand's finest culinary products at various events around that great city. San Francisco is held in high regard as one of North America's top culinary destinations, and quite rightly so. I have eaten well on many occasions in this fun city.

We put on a number of lunches and dinners, but probably the biggest and most difficult we participated in was a two-day event we were invited to cook at that showcased 150 San Francisco restaurants, eateries and chefs. Over the two days, we were serving something like six or seven individual dishes, of around three or four hundred portions each. We were prepping everything out of a large and quite famous historic hotel that shall remain unnamed, situated in downtown San Fran. The hotel kitchen was massive, but also decrepit and looked as though it hadn't had a cent spent on it in what looked like more than half a century. It was simply archaic. The novelty of its sheer size and location wore off after about 30 minutes.

We were allocated a bunch of supposedly in-house hotel chefs to help with the extraordinary amount of preparation required to deal with all the gigs we were presenting at. It didn't take long to discover that we were working with a crew of people who had absolutely zero enthusiasm and not a single ounce of passion, and who were completely devoid of even basic cookery skills. They were certainly not chefs. In fact, they were not even cooks. They were, at best, what you would describe as 'reheaters'! It was a sad, depressing and hugely negative environment in which to spend a week working our damn butts off. But I've found in the past that tough conditions like that can actually make you very determined, and somehow Haydo and I managed to pull it all off, working hard from very early in the morning to way past bedtime, for days on end.

For the big 'chef/restaurant' event, we were serving tasting dishes that had four or five components. For example, one dish was a braised piece of New Zealand lamb shoulder on a cauliflower purée, with eggplant kasundi and a crisp curry leaf and toasted almond garnish. Having read all the other participants' menus on offer before the event, then watching the dishes being plated from the setups near us, I distinctly remember a wave of self-doubt washing over me and I whispered to Haydo that I thought we might be somewhat out of our depth. It's pretty natural in those sorts of high-octane—and at times stressful—circumstances to be somewhat intimidated. I think that most chefs have self-esteem issues, but that's another story altogether. Anyhow, there was nothing we could do but crack on as thousands of food- and wine-loving San Franciscans began streaming through the doors.

We began having queues like everyone else, but it quickly became apparent that we had quite a noticeable percentage of returning customers. You can't get a better endorsement than people making the effort to stand in line again for another helping. The returning folks had obviously enjoyed what that they had eaten, but there was a common theme to what they were all saying: they all kept going on about the depth of flavour. It wasn't so much about the dishes themselves, but the individual hero components. 'I've never tasted salmon with such intense flavour anywhere.' 'Who ever knew lamb had such a distinct and unique flavour?' And it went on and on—the flavour of the oysters, the flavour of the raw kingfish, the flavour of the clams, the wasabi, the olive oil and so on.

At the end of each session, and just before the change-over to another 50 restaurants, Haydo and I would scoot out, heading in different directions to bring back great-looking plates of goodies to share and greedily scoff before it was time to knuckle down and do it all again. Having worked alongside Haydo for nearly a decade by then, I could tell by the look on his face that we were thinking the same thing. There was a huge disconnect between how the food looked and how it actually tasted. I never like being critical, and some of the food we ate was bloody delicious, but to be completely honest a large percentage of the dishes we were tasting were pretty disappointing.

As I have mentioned, many of the other guys' and gals' dishes looked terrific, and in fact some were quite spectacular. The dilemma was that when we sampled a new dish there was often a pang of disappointment. It all tasted okay, but that is

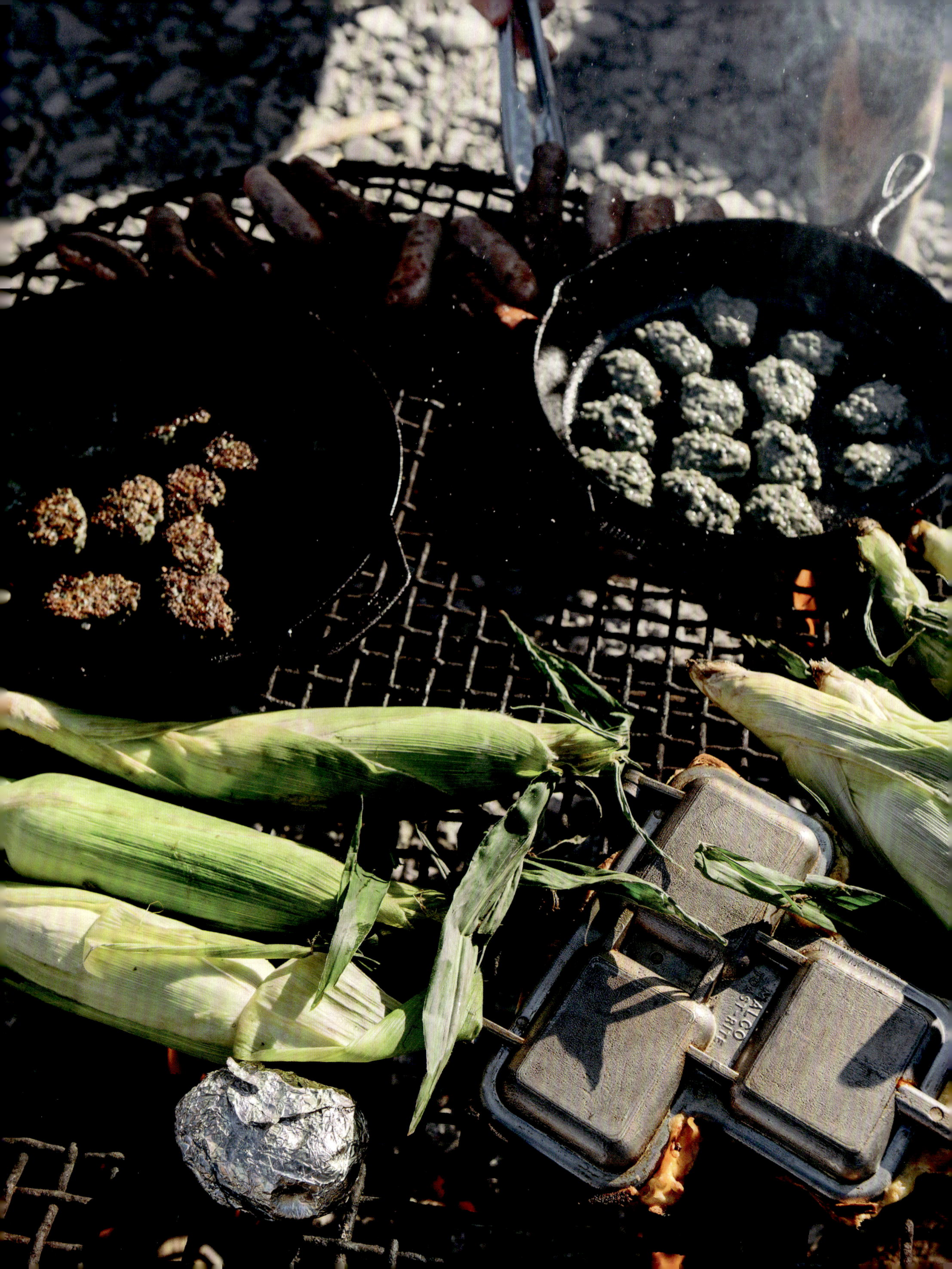

exactly the point: you can eat 'okay' anywhere. Unfortunately, the words that we kept bandying about were ones like 'bland', 'weak', 'dull', 'thin', 'tame' and 'mild'.

There was no question that the dishes were seasoned correctly and had good balance and texture. It was just that the heroes of the dishes lacked what I would describe as a punch of flavour. I recall saying to Haydo, 'It's as if they have turned the flavour dial down.' It is a phrase that has stuck with both of us, and is now part of our cooking and eating vocabulary, when we are either creating recipes or tasting something for the first time. We are constantly saying things like 'We need to turn up the volume of flavour' or—as is the case sometimes—'turn the flavour volume down'. I think it's good practice to think about what you are experiencing when you are eating something.

For example, take a cob of corn that you have picked up from a roadside stand. If you eat that corn the same evening, you know how extraordinarily good that corn is going to taste: sweet, crunchy and literally dripping with flavour. It's the same with a hand-picked strawberry, a ripe peach plucked from a tree, or freshly dug new potatoes, washed and cooked the same day. The closer to the source, the higher the volume on the flavour dial.

I firmly believe that this is our country's ace card in terms of our culinary prowess in the world. It's not just the massive variety of produce and product on offer; it's also our proximity to where that produce is grown or harvested, and the speed with which it reaches the plate, that gives us the edge in taste over most other countries.

But, back to that event—it was actually terrific, and by the end of the last day, although we were exhausted, we were enjoying the buzz of achievement, with a sense of pride and some relief that we had got through relatively unscathed.

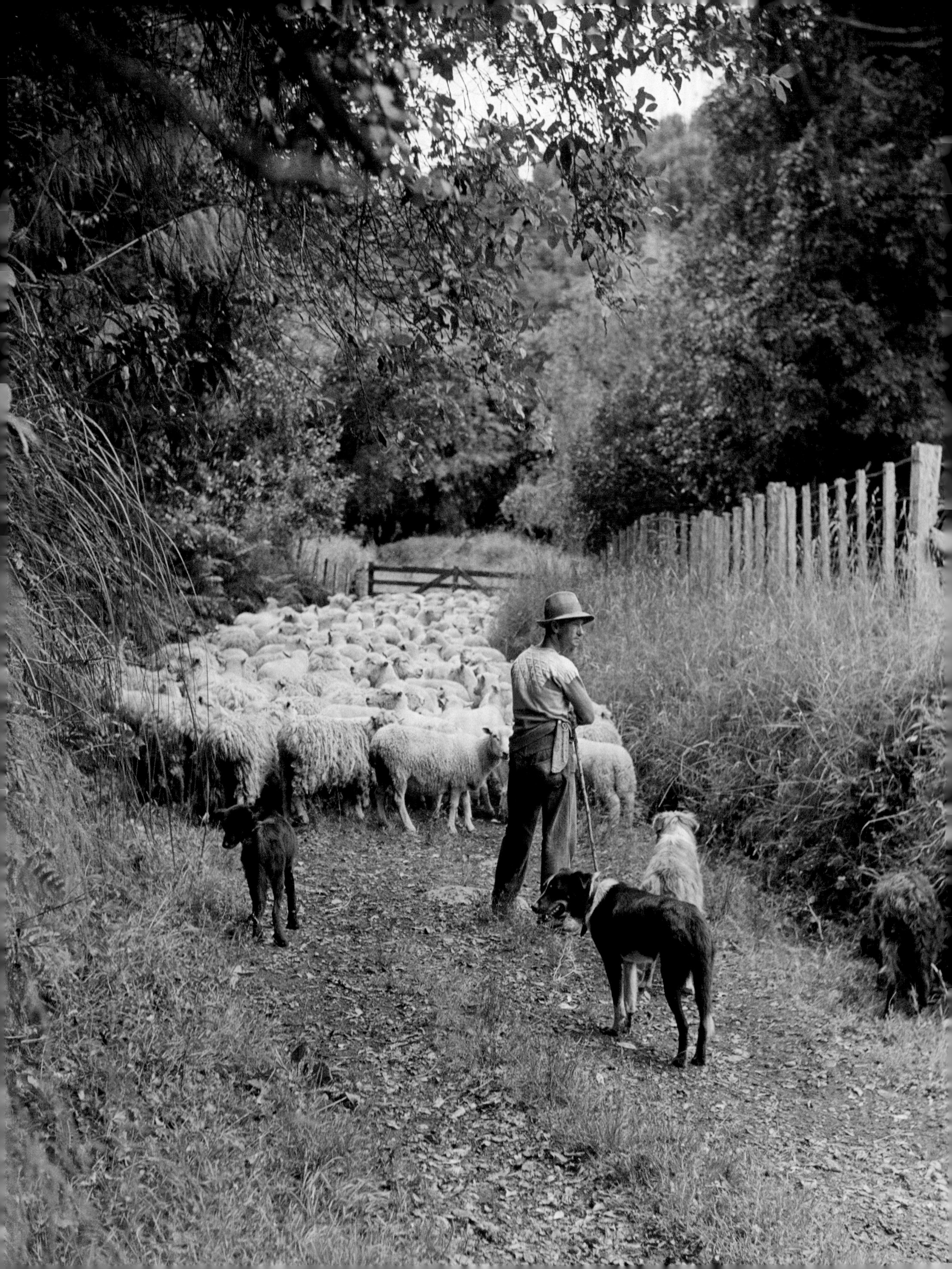

ANIMAL
MĪTI

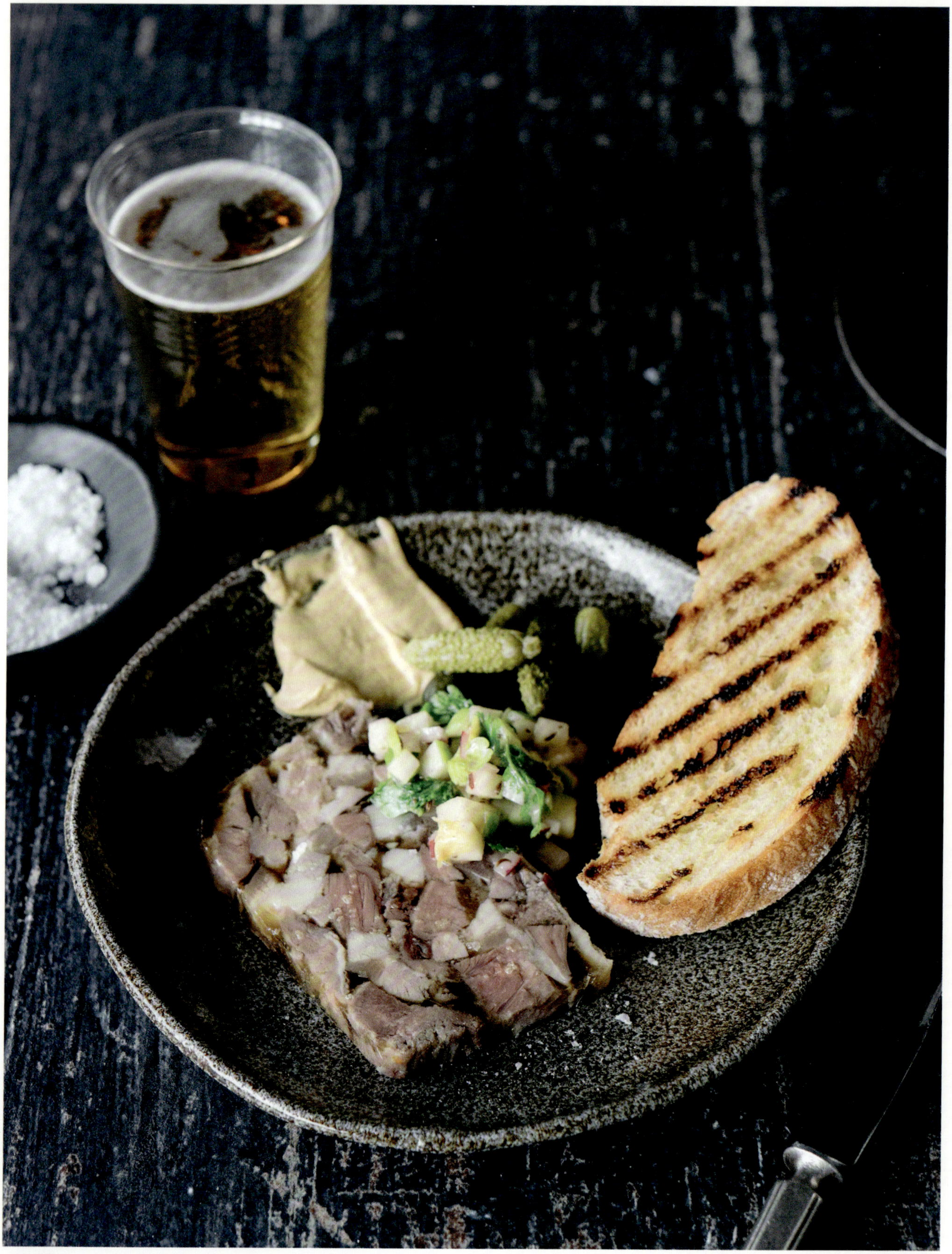

Pork brawn with apple and caraway salsa

I've always loved pork brawn. I was lucky enough to be introduced to it by way of pork brawn sandwiches, which I had on one day every year growing up, and that was the opening day of duck shooting. We had a bunch of great butchers who would shoot the dams on our farm every opening weekend, and I would meet up with them for lunch. Pork brawn always seemed, in a humble way, very exotic. Here's my version, served with a really fresh and tangy apple and caraway salsa.

Makes 1 x regular loaf

PORK BRAWN
1 x 4 kg (8 lb 13 oz) pig's head
4 pig's trotters
6 litres cold water
3 cups (465 g/1 lb) chopped onion
3 cups (465 g/1 lb) chopped carrot
3 cups (420 g/15 oz) chopped celery
4 thyme sprigs
2 rosemary sprigs
2 sage sprigs
10 black peppercorns
3 tablespoons flaky sea salt

APPLE AND CARAWAY SALSA
1 Granny Smith apple, diced
1 red chilli, finely chopped
⅓ cup (50 g/1¾ oz) chopped red onion
¼ cup (30 g/1¼ oz) roughly chopped yellow inner celery leaves
¼ cup (7 g/¼ oz) roughly chopped flat-leaf parsley
½ teaspoon celery seeds
1 teaspoon caraway seeds
¼ cup (60 ml/2 fl oz) cider vinegar
1 teaspoon Dijon mustard
2 tablespoons apple syrup
½ cup (125 ml/4 fl oz) canola oil
flaky sea salt and freshly ground black pepper

TO SERVE
cornichons
toasted ciabatta or similar
Dijon mustard

To make the pork brawn, firstly remove any obvious hair from the pig's head with a sharp knife or razor. Rinse the head and trotters under cold running water for 5 minutes.

Place all the ingredients for the brawn in a stockpot, making sure the pig's head is submerged in water. Place over high heat and bring up to a boil, then reduce the heat to low and cover with a lid. Cook gently on a low simmer for up to 4 hours, or until the meat is falling off the bones. Take the stockpot off the heat and let cool to room temperature. Remove the pig's head and trotters from the stock and set aside.

Pick all the meat off the bones and discard any excess fat. Rough chop the meat, along with some of the skin, and set aside.

Strain the stock through a fine sieve, back into the pot. You should have roughly 4 litres (135 fl oz) of liquid. Place over medium heat, bring up to a boil and reduce the stock for about 1 hour, skimming off any white froth that forms on the top. Remove the stock from the heat when it has reduced by about three-quarters, leaving you with 1 litre (35 fl oz) of stock. Taste and adjust the seasoning with salt and pepper.

Line a regular loaf tin with a double layer of clingfilm, then fill loosely to the top with the cooked chopped pork meat. Pour the hot stock over the meat to come up to the top. Place in the refrigerator and chill overnight until fully set.

Recipe continued overleaf...

To make the apple and caraway salsa, add the apple, along with the chilli, red onion, celery leaves, parsley, celery seeds and caraway seeds, to a mixing bowl. Mix through and set aside.

For the dressing, place the vinegar, mustard and apple syrup in a small saucepan and place over medium heat. Bring up to the boil, stir and reduce for a minute or so. Remove and pour into a container. Using a stick blender, add the oil in a slow, steady stream until emulsified. Let cool.

To finish the salsa, pour the dressing over the ingredients, season with salt and pepper, and refrigerate until required.

To serve, slice the pork brawn into 1 cm (½ in) thick slices, arrange on a platter or plate with the apple and caraway salsa, cornichons and some mustard on the side. Serve with toasted ciabatta.

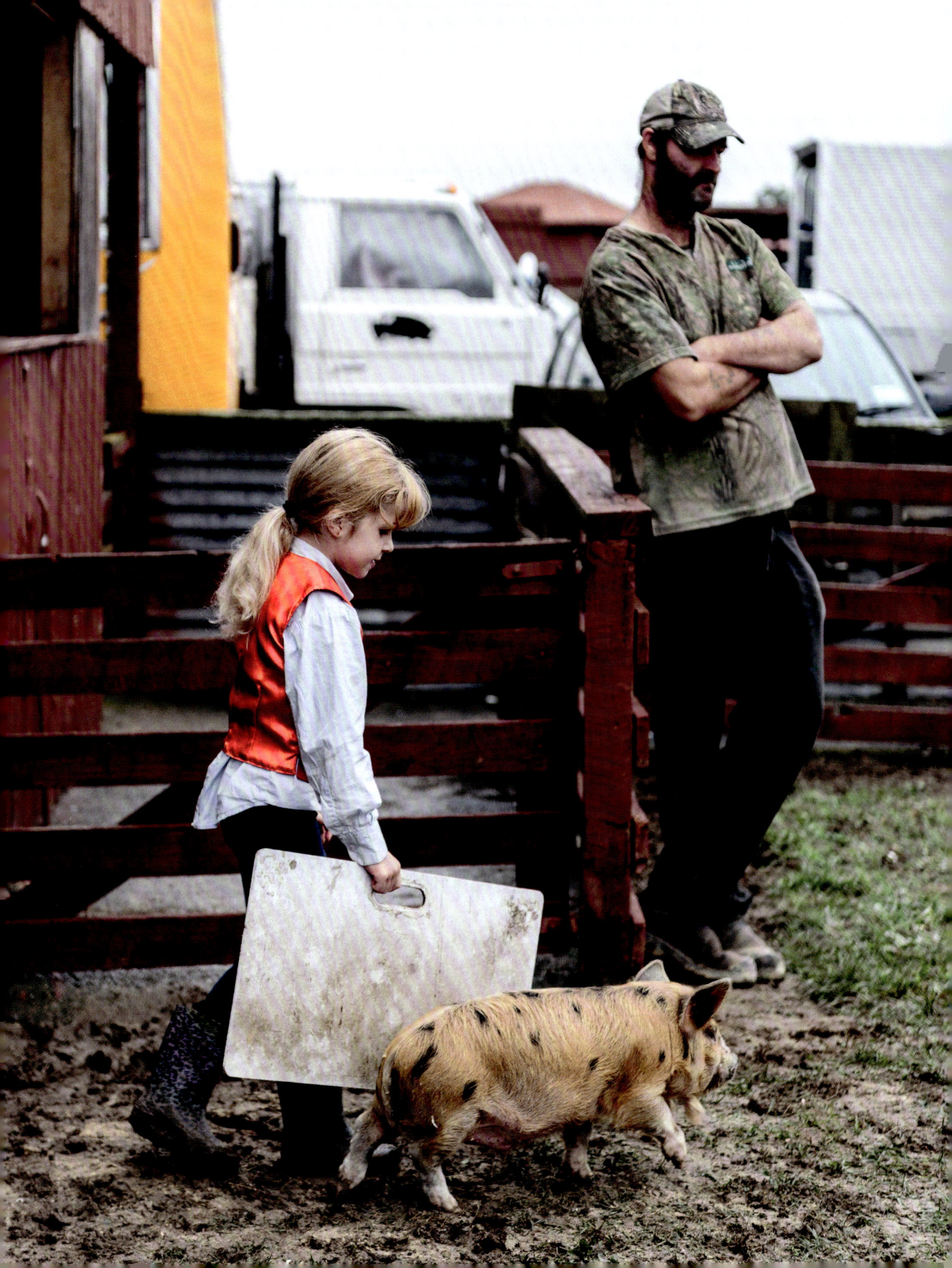

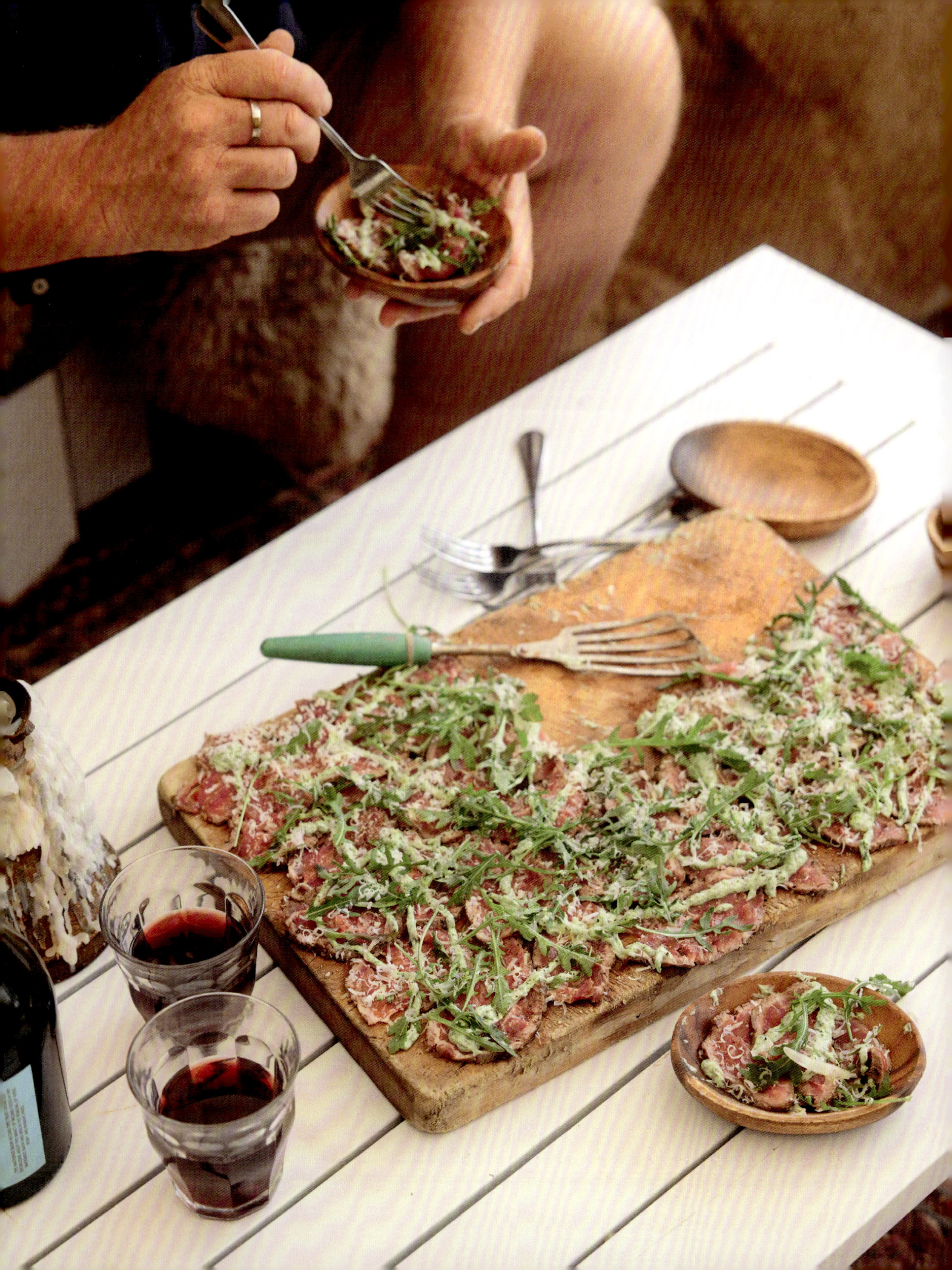

Rustic beef carpaccio with tarragon mayo, Parmesan and rocket

I say rustic, as this is a real bach version of carpaccio. Most restaurants sear their beef fillet then freeze it; when orders come through they slice it on a bacon slicer while it's still frozen so they can get it incredibly thin—this also helps retain its deep red colour. For this version we don't faff around. We sear the beef fillet, let it cool in the fridge for a bit, then just slice it as thin as we can. I actually prefer it, as it's far more generous served this way.

Serves 6

BEEF FILLET
1 kg (2 lb 4 oz) beef fillet
flaky sea salt and fresh coarsely ground black pepper
cooking oil

TARRAGON MAYO
¼ cup (7 g/¼ oz) tarragon leaves
¼ cup (7 g/¼ oz) flat-leaf parsley leaves
1 cup (235 g/8½ oz) mayonnaise
flaky sea salt and freshly ground black pepper

TO ASSEMBLE AND SERVE
1 handful rocket leaves
Parmesan cheese (use a fresh block if possible)
flaky sea salt and freshly ground black pepper

Using a sharp knife, trim any silver skin off the beef. Cut the beef into manageable rounds, about 4 cm (1½ in) in circumference. Liberally season the pieces with salt and pepper.

Place a frying pan or skillet over high heat. Add a dash of oil to the pan, then sear each piece as quickly as you can to caramelise the outsides.

Cool, then wrap the pieces nice and tightly in clingfilm and refrigerate for a couple of hours to help the beef set up.

To make the tarragon mayo, take a stick blender and a jar. Place the herbs in the bottom of the jar, along with a couple of tablespoons of mayonnaise. Blend this into a green paste. Now fold the paste back into the rest of the mayo, mix well and season with salt and pepper. Spoon into a squeezy bottle or a piping bag with a small hole. Refrigerate until required.

Place it on a platter in the fridge to get it nice and cold.

To serve, take your sharpest knife and slice the beef as thinly as possible. Lay out the pieces on the platter. Grab the tarragon mayo and do a liberal zig-zag pattern across the beef. Sprinkle with some rocket leaves, then grate the Parmesan cheese over the top. Serve now.

Spiced lamb tongue with hummus, feta, green olive and orange

I don't believe I'm going out on a limb here by saying that most Kiwis have an affinity with nearly all cuts of lamb. We love our roasts, our racks, our shoulders and our shanks, but when it comes to lamb offal most people take a pass. I usually can't go past any dishes on menus that mention things such as kidneys, lamb's fry or sweetbreads. However, the one part of the animal that hardly gets an airing anywhere these days is the lamb's tongue. To me, it's like the foie gras of the sheep world. Okay, that's a bit of a stretch, but what I'm trying to do here is emphasise how damn good they are to eat. If you are keen to try this recipe (and it really is well worth a try), my advice would be to drop by your local butcher and get him or her to order you a kilo or two to try. The tongue exhibits a wonderful lamb flavour, but it's the texture that I think is truly special and worth all the effort of cooking.

Serves 6

LAMB TONGUE
1 kg (2 lb 4 oz) lamb's tongues
1 cup (155 g/5½ oz) roughly chopped onion
1 cup (155 g/5½ oz) roughly chopped carrot
1 cup (140 g/5 oz) roughly chopped celery
4 garlic cloves
2 bay leaves
¼ cup (45 g/1½ oz) brown sugar
¼ cup (60 ml/2 fl oz) malt vinegar
6 cups (1.5 litres/52 fl oz) water

HUMMUS
2 x 400 g tins chickpeas, drained and rinsed
2 tablespoons tahini
1 tablespoon finely minced garlic
⅓ cup (80 ml/2½ fl oz) lemon juice
½ cup (125 ml/4 fl oz) extra-virgin olive oil

FETA, GREEN OLIVE AND ORANGE
100 g (3½ oz) feta cheese, roughly crumbled
12 green olives, pitted and cut in slivers
finely grated zest and juice of ½ orange
½ cup (125 ml/4 fl oz) Al Brown & Co Orange and Chilli Infused Olive Oil or good-quality extra-virgin olive oil

TO COOK AND SERVE
2 tablespoons ground sumac
1 tablespoon cumin seeds, toasted and ground
½ teaspoon smoked paprika
½ teaspoon ground cinnamon
flaky sea salt and freshly ground black pepper
canola oil, for frying

Prepare the lamb's tongue. Place the tongues, onion, carrot, celery, garlic, bay leaves, sugar and vinegar in a saucepan, then pour over the water. Place on the stovetop and bring up to the boil, then lower the heat and simmer the tongues for 2 hours.

Remove from the heat, drain the tongues and discard the cooking liquid along with the vegetables. When the lamb's tongues are cool enough to handle, peel the tough skin/membrane on the outer layer and discard. Refrigerate the tongues until required.

To make the hummus, place all the ingredients in a food processor. Pulse and blend to your preferred consistency. Taste and season with salt and pepper accordingly. Refrigerate until required.

In a small bowl, add the feta along with the green olives, orange zest and juice, and the oil. Gently fold it all together. Refrigerate until required.

Now mix the sumac, cumin, paprika and cinnamon together in a small bowl.

Cut the lamb's tongues in half lengthways. Season with salt and pepper, then dip the tongue halves in the rub to cover.

Place a frying pan over medium-low heat. Once hot, add a little canola oil, then cook the tongue halves for a couple of minutes on either side, until golden and crisp around the edges.

To serve, spoon some hummus into the centre of each plate, top with two or three sautéed lamb's tongue halves, then spoon over the feta and olive mix. Eat now.

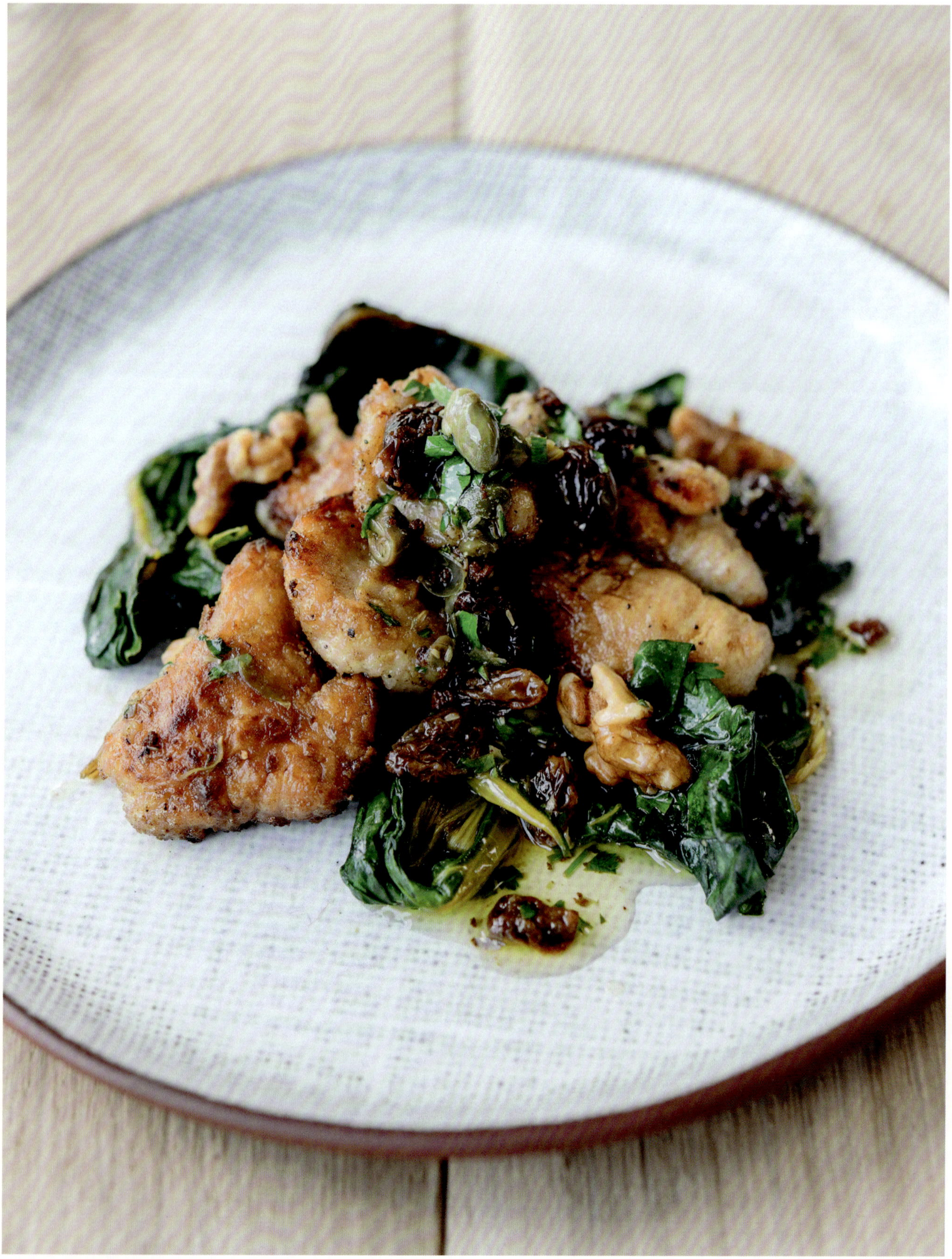

Lamb sweetbreads with silverbeet, raisins and caper burnt butter

This is a lovely little rich, wintery dish. The silverbeet makes a great foil to the sautéed sweetbreads. You'll see I remove the stalks from the silverbeet leaves, slice them up finely, then cook them down in a bit of butter until they caramelise, taking on a delicious nutty flavour. I then cook down the leaves until they are basically just wilted. The burnt butter, capers and raisins bring more nuttiness, saltiness and sweetness to the dish.

Serves 6 as a starter

SWEETBREADS
600 g (1 lb 5 oz) lamb sweetbreads
500 g (1 lb 2 oz) silverbeet
30 g (1 oz) butter
flaky sea salt and freshly ground black pepper

RAISIN AND CAPER BURNT BUTTER
200 g (7 oz) butter
1½ tablespoons lemon juice
2 tablespoons capers, roughly chopped
2 tablespoons raisins
¼ cup (7 g / ¼ oz) finely chopped flat-leaf parsley

TO COOK AND SERVE
½ cup (70 g/2½ oz) plain flour
cooking oil, for frying
⅓ cup (35 g/1¼ oz) toasted walnuts

To prepare the lamb sweetbreads, fill a saucepan with salted water and place over high heat. Once boiling, add the sweetbreads. Once it comes up to the boil again, cook for a minute or so, then, use a sieve or slotted spoon to remove the sweetbreads, transferring to a bowl or sink of iced water to cool down quickly.

Once cold, remove the sweetbreads and pat dry with kitchen paper. With clean hands, peel and discard as much of the skin-like membrane that covers the sweetbreads as possible. Refrigerate the blanched sweetbreads until required.

Take the silverbeet and, with a sharp knife, remove the stalks from the leaves. Slice the stalks into thin pieces. Place a large saucepan over medium-low heat, add the butter and, once melted, add the sliced silverbeet stalks. Sweat over low heat for about 20 minutes, stirring occasionally until the stalks become caramelised and soft.

Now take the leaves of the silverbeet and roughly chop. Stir through the caramelised stalks, and continue to cook for a couple of minutes until wilted. Taste, and when you're happy with the texture, season with a little salt and pepper. Set aside.

For the raisin and caper burnt butter, melt the butter in a small saucepan over medium-low heat. Allow the butter to cook for 3–5 more minutes, stirring, at which point the butter will begin to bubble and froth as the milk solids begin to caramelise. Once the butter starts to take on a golden colour, remove from the heat and add the lemon juice,

Recipe continued overleaf...

capers and raisins. Be mindful that when you add these, the butter will rise and froth and then go back down. Stir right to the bottom, removing as much of the caramelised milk solids from the base of the pan as possible—these brown bits add a lovely nutty flavour to the sauce. Take off the heat and let cool slightly. Stir through the chopped parsley and keep the sauce warm.

Season the blanched sweetbreads with a little salt and pepper, then dust in the flour, patting off any excess.

Place a frying pan over medium heat. Once hot, add a little oil, the floured sweetbreads and cook for 2–3 minutes on both sides, until golden all over.

To plate, divvy up the silverbeet in the centre of each plate, top with the sweetbreads, then spoon over the raisin and caper burnt butter sauce. Finish by adding a few toasted walnuts to each dish. Serve now.

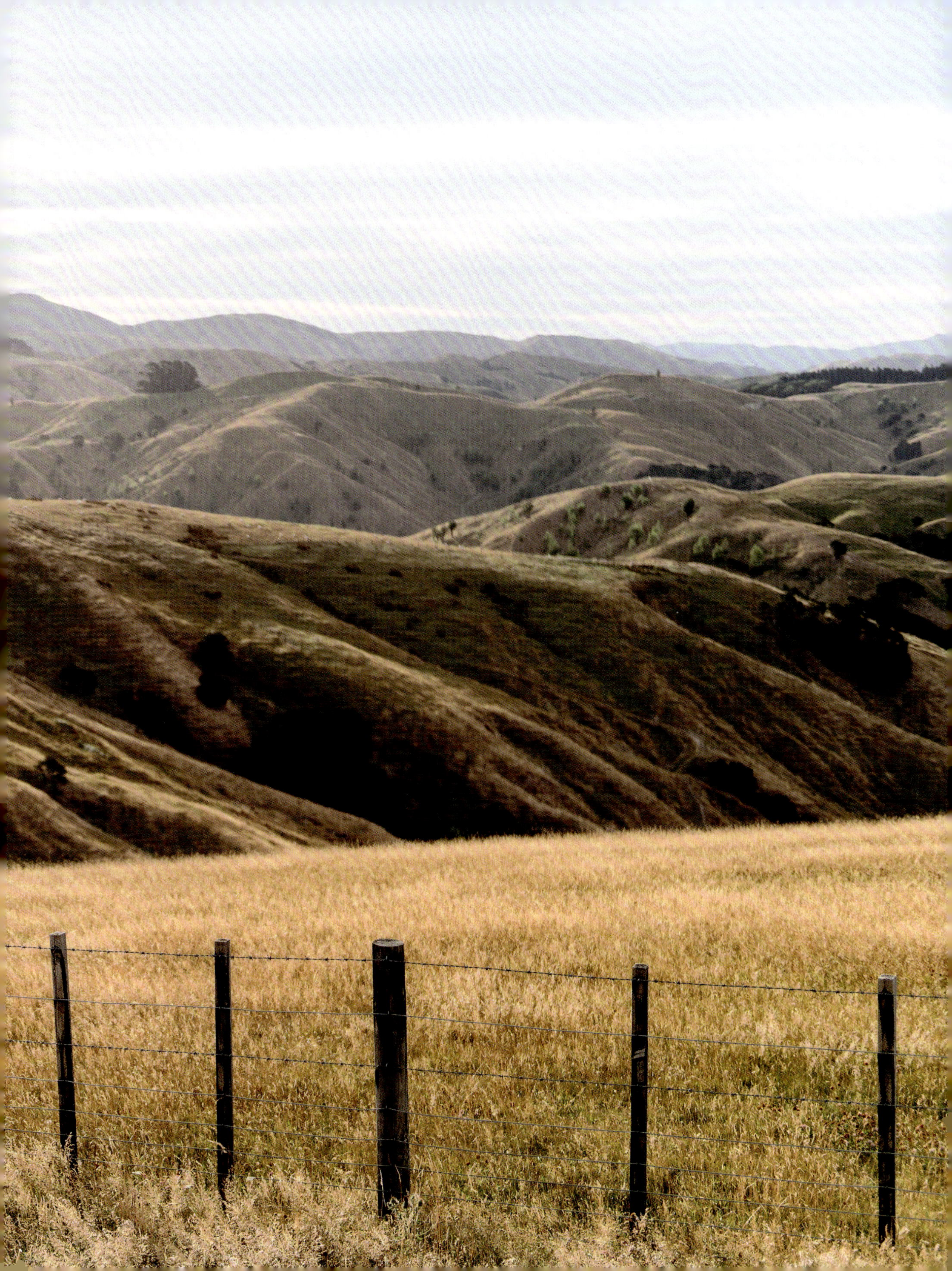

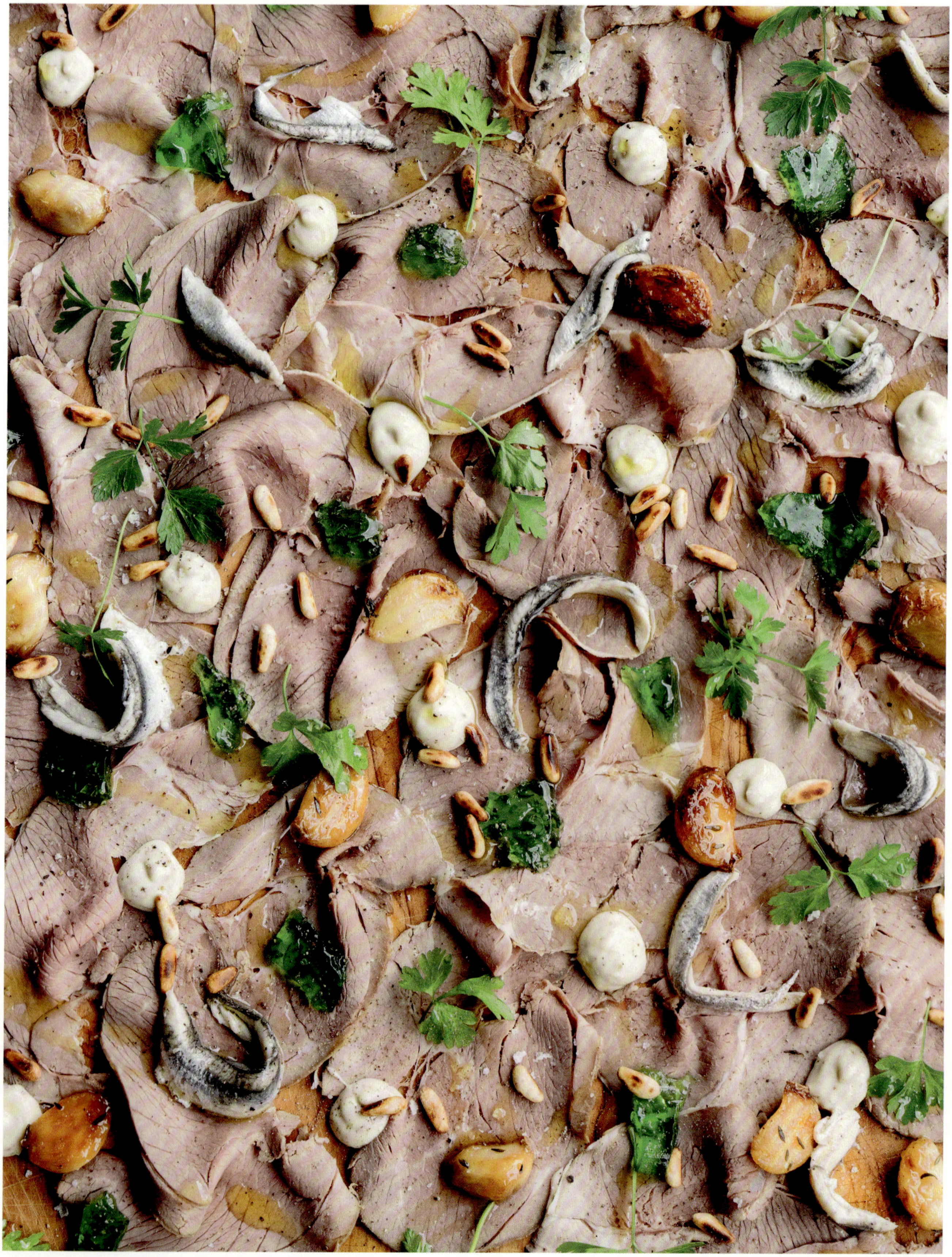

Shaved lamb with white anchovies, roasted garlic and mint jelly

I have always been a massive fan of what we Kiwis so eloquently call 'cold meat'! The leftovers from roasts of mutton, lamb, beef and occasionally pork all take on a different role when served cold; thick slices with a lick of mustard and chutney or relish make terrific sandwich fodder. Cold meat with a simple salad of iceberg lettuce, tomato, cucumber, pickled beetroot and warm minted new potatoes with the obligatory condensed milk mayonnaise was one of my favourite weekend lunches growing up.
I have had a bit of a play-around with the components, and this recipe is a nod of respect to the past, while serving it in a slightly more modern way with the introduction of white anchovies and roasted garlic.

Serves 6–8

ROASTED GARLIC
½ cup whole garlic cloves
2 tablespoons cooking oil
2 thyme sprigs
1 tablespoon water
olive oil

WHITE ANCHOVY MAYO
½ cup (125 g/4½ oz) mayonnaise
8 white anchovies

TO COOK AND SERVE
600 g cold roasted lamb
toasted pine nuts
16 white anchovies
mint jelly (page 430)
micro herbs (optional)
extra-virgin olive oil, to drizzle (optional)
flaky sea salt and freshly ground black pepper

Preheat your oven to 180°C (350°F).
　Place the garlic cloves in tinfoil and add a couple of tablespoons of cooking oil followed by the thyme sprigs and the water. Wrap the tinfoil into a parcel, place on an oven tray or roasting dish and roast for 20–25 minutes, until the garlic is soft through. Remove from the oven, discard the thyme and let cool. Transfer the roasted garlic cloves to a small jar and cover with olive oil. Set aside until required.

For the white anchovy mayo, place the ingredients in a food processor (or use a stick blender) and blitz together until smooth and incorporated. Refrigerate until required.

Slice the lamb as thinly as possible, either with a sharp knife or on a meat slicer.
　Spread out the sliced lamb on a large platter or individual plates. Dot about some of the white anchovy mayonnaise and likewise randomly place the mint jelly, roasted garlic cloves, extra white anchovies, pine nuts and micro herbs, if using. Finish with a drizzle of extra-virgin olive oil (if you want) and a liberal seasoning of flaky sea salt and freshly ground black pepper. Serve with a bunch of forks for everyone to help themselves.

Spiced braised pork, buttermilk pancakes, smoked chipotle butter and maple syrup

This recipe is modelled on a dish that I had in one of my all-time favourite restaurants, Joe Beef in Montréal. The two chefs who own it are super talented, cooking their style of no-nonsense food. They don't play by anyone's rules or follow any trends. They cook the classics beautifully, but also have a ton of fun, freestyling in any direction they see fit! They always have one breakfast item on the dinner menu, and the one they are pretty famous for is sautéed fresh foie gras, Canadian bacon and fried egg all stuffed inside a toasted English muffin with maple syrup and mustard. Yip, it's as wicked as it sounds. Anyway, the following, while not foie gras, is still a pretty naughty dish that is my nod of respect to Frédéric and David of Joe Beef.

Serves 6

SPICED BRAISED PORK
2 teaspoons salt
½ teaspoon freshly ground black pepper
2 teaspoons brown sugar
1 teaspoon ground ginger
1 teaspoon garlic powder
1 teaspoon smoked paprika
1 tablespoon cumin seeds, toasted and ground
1.5 kg (1 lb 5 oz) pork scotch fillet
¼ cup (60 ml/2 fl oz) canola oil or similar cooking oil
1 cup (250 ml/9 fl oz) chicken stock

SMOKED CHIPOTLE BUTTER
250 g (9 oz) salted butter, softened
1 tablespoon brown sugar
4 teaspoons finely chopped tinned chipotle peppers (available from delis and good supermarkets)
finely grated zest of 1 orange, plus 2 tablespoons orange juice
1½ teaspoons cumin seeds, toasted and ground
1 teaspoon smoked paprika
1½ teaspoons flaky sea salt
pinch freshly ground black pepper

BUTTERMILK PANCAKES
3 eggs
600 ml (21 fl oz) buttermilk
1 teaspoon baking soda
3¼ cups (485 g/1 lb 1 oz) plain flour
2 teaspoons baking powder
1 teaspoon flaky sea salt
¼ cup (55 g/2 oz) sugar
80 g butter, melted

TO COOK AND SERVE
butter, for frying
maple syrup

Preheat your oven to 150°C (300°F).

To make the pork, combine the salt, pepper, brown sugar, ginger, garlic powder, smoked paprika and cumin in a small bowl to create the rub. Massage onto the fillet of pork.

Place a frying pan over medium-high heat. Once hot, add the oil, followed by the pork. Sear until golden all over, then place in a roasting dish and add the chicken stock. Cover with tinfoil, then place over medium heat on the stovetop for 4–5 minutes, before placing in the preheated oven. Cook for 2½ hours, until the pork is super soft and tender.

Remove from the oven. Let cool for at least 30 minutes, but while still warm, pull the pork apart into manageable-sized pieces. Pour the cooking liquid over the pulled pork and refrigerate until required.

For the smoked chipotle butter, combine all the ingredients in a bowl until fully incorporated. Refrigerate until required.

Make the pancakes. To a stand mixer fitted with a whisk attachment, add the eggs, buttermilk and baking soda. Whisk for 20 seconds, until combined.

In a bowl, sift the flour and baking powder together.

With a spatula, stir the flour, baking powder, salt and sugar into the egg and buttermilk mixture. Once partially combined, place back on the stand mixer and whisk the batter until lump-free. Drizzle in the melted butter while the motor is running, until fully incorporated. Turn off the mixer and let the batter rest for 30 minutes.

Preheat your oven to 90°C (200°F).

Place the spiced braised pork in a saucepan over medium-low heat and slowly warm, stirring occasionally.

Place a non-stick frying pan over medium-low heat. Add a little butter and, once melted, ladle in the pancake batter. Cook, in batches, for 2–3 minutes on each side, until golden. Keep each batch warm in the oven while you finish making the rest of the pancakes.

To serve, place a pancake in the centre of a warm plate, top with some braised pork, add a dollop of the chipotle butter, then top with another pancake. Finish with another lump of butter then smother the whole thing with maple syrup. Eat now.

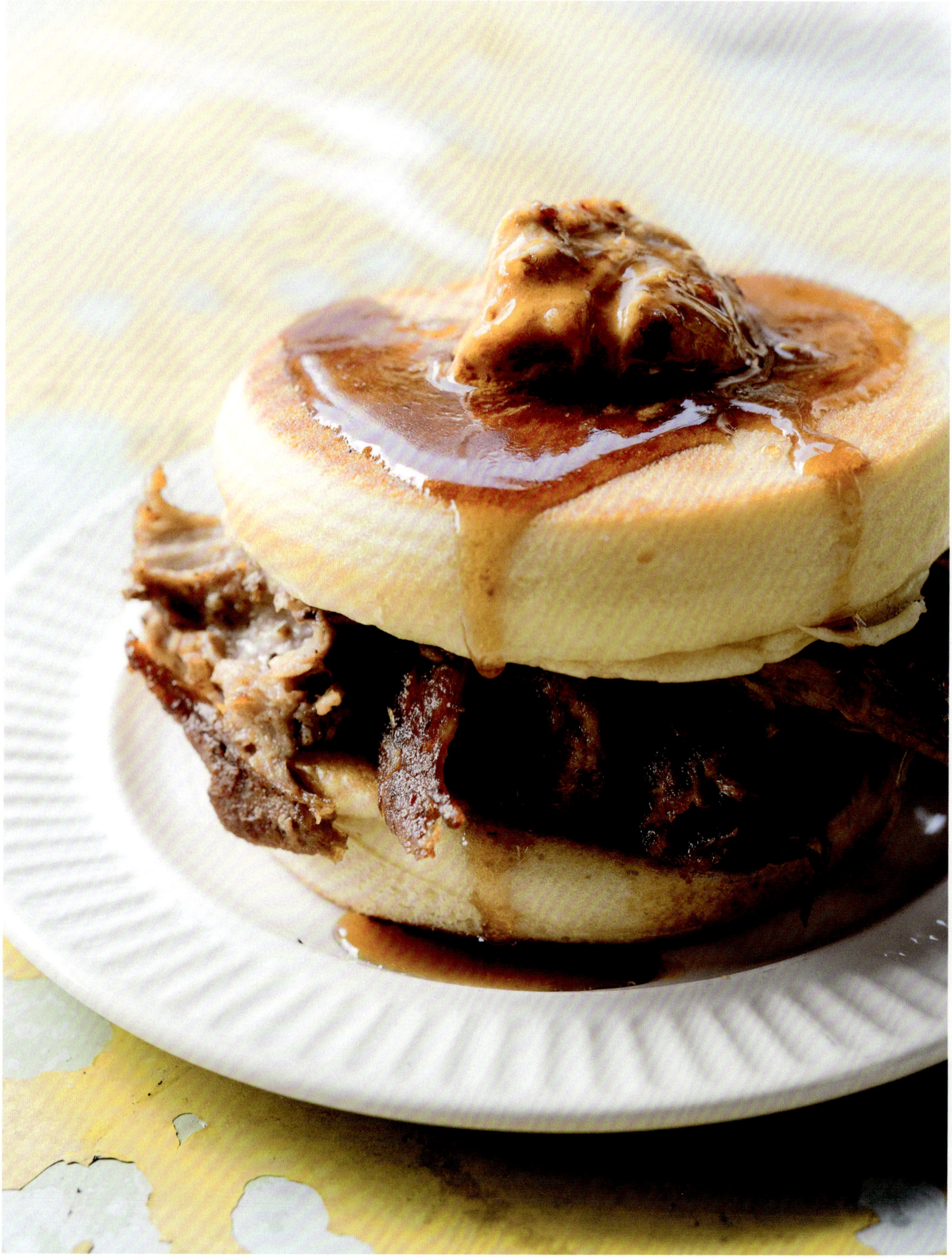

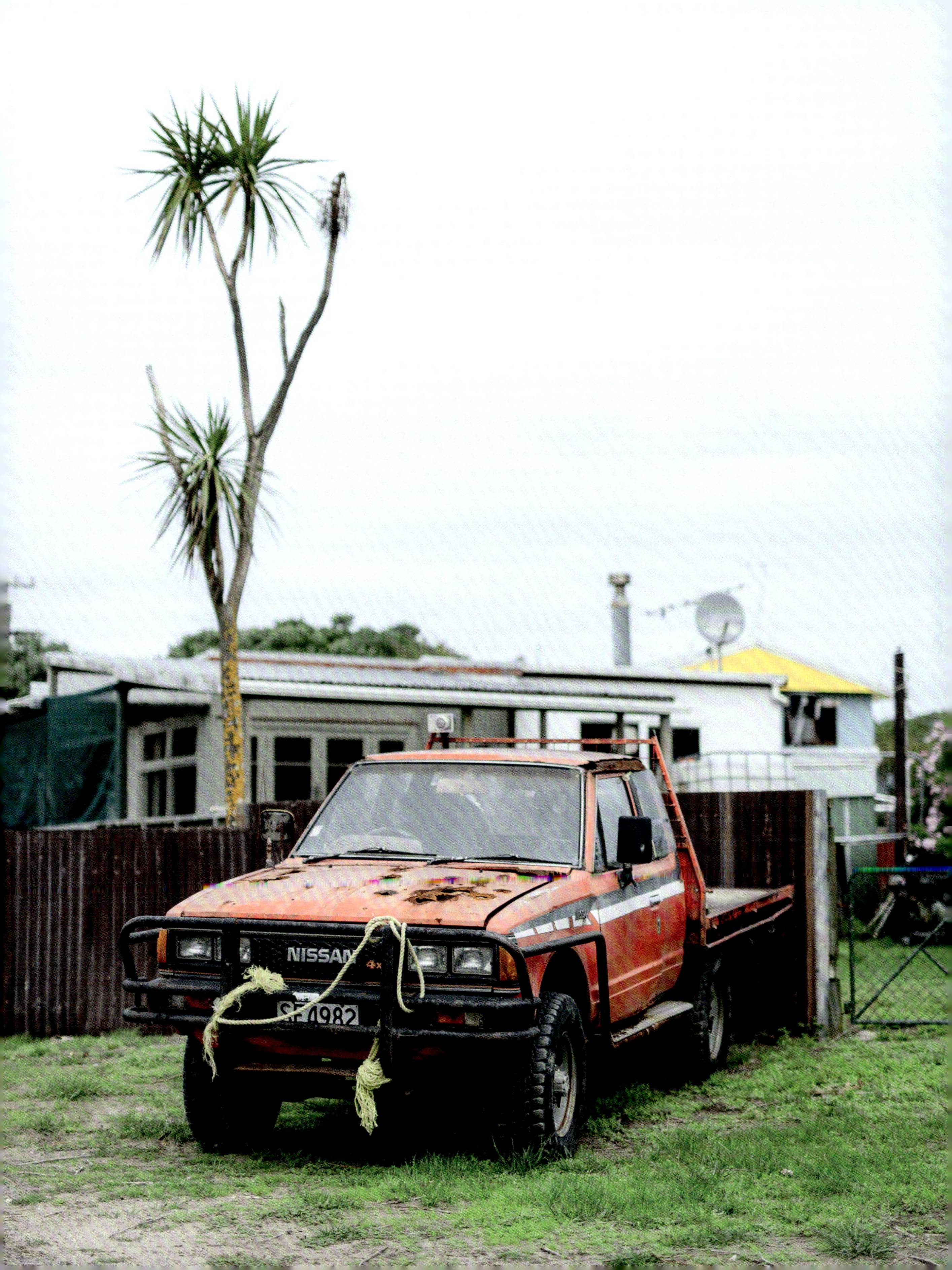
NISSAN

Meatballs with spiced tomato lentils

This is my current go-to winter brunch dish. I had something similar when visiting Melbourne a while back. It certainly doesn't scream Australia, but like New Zealand they have that melding of cultures and cuisines brought about by positive immigration policies, with one of the big ups being the introduction of new flavours and food ideas.

Serves 12

SPICED TOMATO RAGOUT
½ cup (125 ml/4 fl oz) canola oil or similar cooking oil
1 tablespoon yellow mustard seeds
1 tablespoon black mustard seeds
1 tablespoon cumin seeds, toasted and ground
1 tablespoon coriander seeds, toasted and ground
12 cardamom pods
1 teaspoon ground turmeric
½ teaspoon dried chilli flakes
6 stems curry leaves
500 g (1 lb 2 oz) onion, finely diced
300 g (10½ oz) ginger, finely chopped
300 g (10½ oz) garlic cloves, finely chopped
4 x 400 g tins whole peeled tomatoes, blitzed to a purée
1 cup (250 ml/9 fl oz) chicken stock
⅓ cup (90 g/3¼ oz) tomato paste
1½ tablespoons sugar

LENTILS
1½ cups (250 g/9 oz/11) green lentils, such as Puy lentils
2 cups (1 litre/35 fl oz) chicken stock
1 teaspoon flaky sea salt

MEATBALLS
500 g (1 lb 2 oz) lamb mince
500 g (1 lb 2 oz) beef mince
500 g (1 lb 2 oz) pork mince
250 g (9 oz) onion, finely chopped
1 tablespoon finely chopped garlic
⅓ cup (10 g/¼ oz) finely chopped parsley
⅓ cup (10 g/¼ oz) finely chopped coriander leaves
1 egg, beaten
½ cup (30 g/1 oz) panko breadcrumbs or other dried breadcrumbs
1 tablespoon flaky sea salt
1 teaspoon freshly ground black pepper

TO COOK AND SERVE
canola oil, for frying
12 eggs
thick natural yoghurt
coriander leaves
turmeric oil (page 443) (optional)
fried curry leaves (page 445) (optional)
shallot crunchies (page 445) (optional)
roasted slivered almonds (optional)
toast bread, flat bread or roti

First, make the ragout. Place a large, preferably heavy-bottomed saucepan over medium-low heat. Pour in the oil and, once hot, add all the spices, including the curry leaves. With a wooden spoon, stir about for a minute or two, then add the onion, ginger and garlic. Sweat gently over low heat for 10 minutes, stirring all the time to prevent the spices from sticking. Add the tomatoes, stock, tomato paste and sugar. Turn up the heat, bring up to the boil then lower the heat to a simmer and cook for 30 minutes, stirring occasionally. Season to taste with salt and pepper. Remove from the heat and let cool before refrigerating until required.

Place the lentils in a saucepan with the stock and the salt. Bring up to a boil over high heat, then drop the heat down to a rolling boil. Check the lentils after 20 or so minutes. They are ready when they are soft through but not mushy and falling apart. Once you are happy with them, drain and let cool. Add the lentils to the spiced tomato ragout.

To make the meatballs, place all the ingredients in a bowl and mix thoroughly with clean hands until combined. Roll into the size meatball that you prefer. If you roll them to about 25 g (1 oz) each you'll end up with approximately 60 small meatballs. Refrigerate what you think you'll require and freeze the rest.

Preheat your oven to 180°C (350°F).

Place a large ovenproof frying pan over medium-high heat. Once hot, pour in a little canola oil, then add the meatballs. Cook for 2 minutes on either side until caramelised. Now spoon in and around the meatballs liberal amounts of the spiced tomato ragout. Crack the eggs onto the top of the ragout, then place the pan into the preheated oven and cook for about 6–7 minutes, until the eggs are just cooked but the yolks still runny.

Remove from the oven and let cool slightly. Add dollops of natural yoghurt and sprinkle about the coriander leaves. For texture and flavour, add any combination of the optional garnishes listed. Serve with a pile of toast, flat bread or roti.

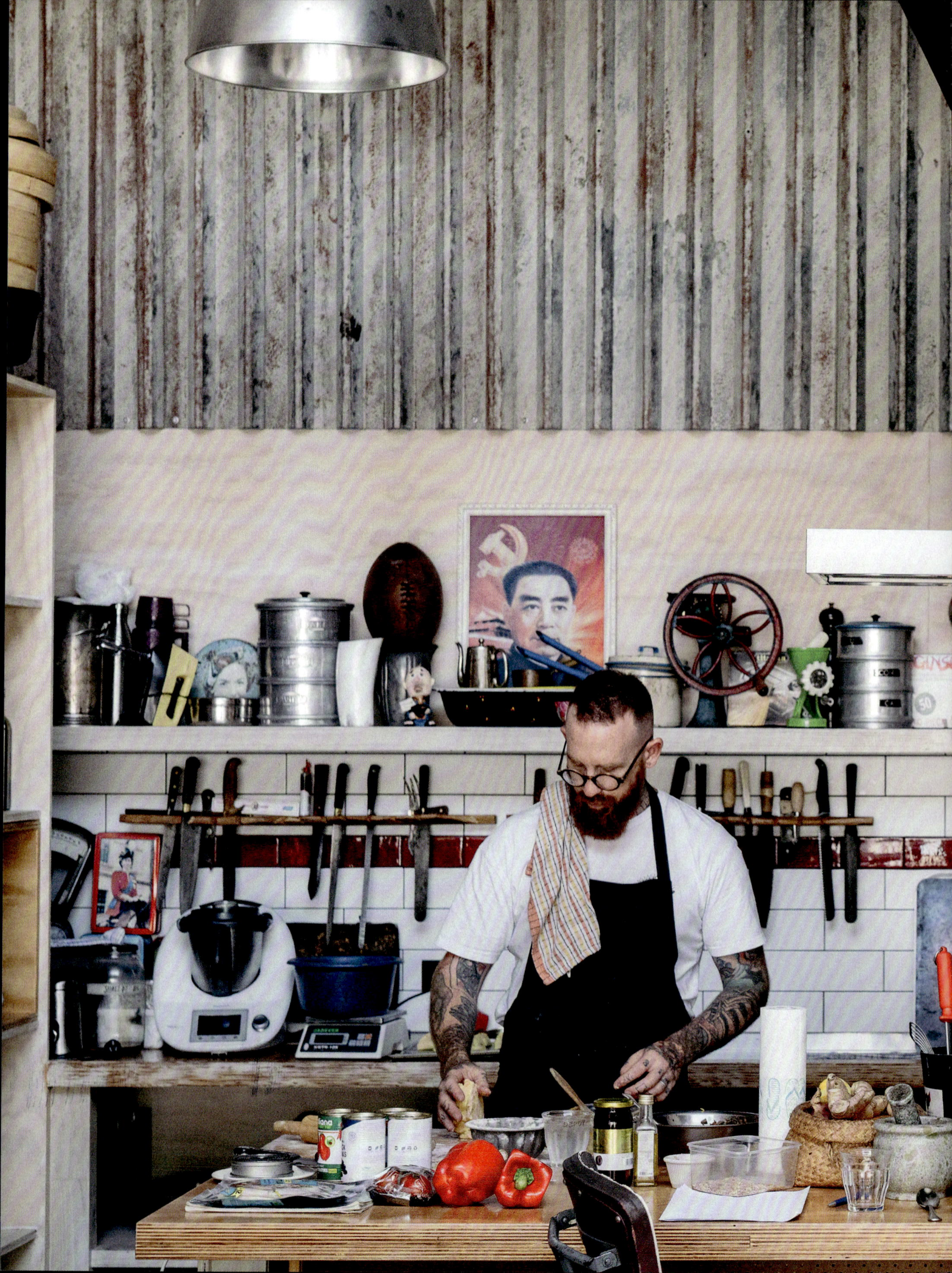

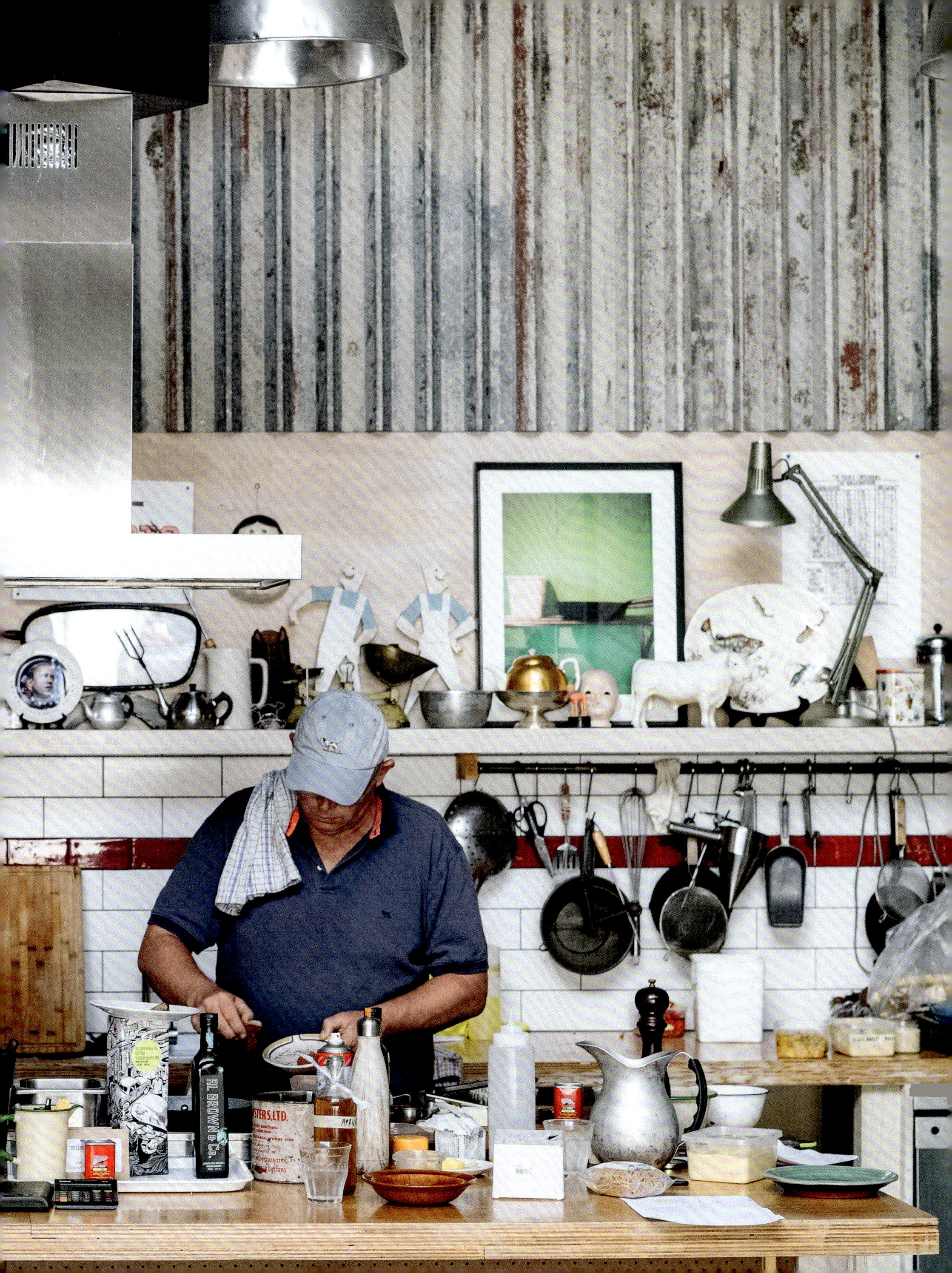
RL BROWN & Co.

Lamb shank empanadas with spiced yoghurt

These little half-moon shaped pies are commonly known as empanadas in Spain and Latin America. They are like little Cornish pasties except the filling is cooked before being wrapped in pastry. These guys also have a little more spice in them than a regular pasty. You can make these any size you like. Just like the sausage roll, with its blanket of golden pastry, any time you bring these out, they're not going to hang around long.

Makes 40–50

LAMB EMPANADAS
6 lamb shanks
flaky sea salt and freshly ground black pepper
½ cup (120 ml/4 fl oz) cooking oil
1 cup (250 ml/9 fl oz) chicken stock
1 cup (250 ml/9 fl oz) beef stock
1 cup (250 ml/9 fl oz) red wine
3 cups potatoes, cut into 1 cm (½ in) cubes
2 cups (310 g/11 oz) finely diced onion
1 cup (140 g/5 oz) finely chopped celery
1 cup (155 g/5½ oz) finely diced carrot
6 garlic cloves, finely chopped
¾ cup (110 g/3¾ oz) currants
½ teaspoon dried chilli flakes
1 teaspoon ground cinnamon
1½ tablespoons fennel seeds, toasted and ground
1½ tablespoons cumin seeds, toasted and ground
plain flour, for dusting
1 quantity Eve's mum's pastry (page 442)
2 eggs, separated
1 teaspoon water

SPICED YOGHURT
2 cups (500 g/1 lb 2 oz) thick natural yoghurt
¼ cup (60 ml/2 fl oz) cooking oil
25 g (1 oz) ginger, finely grated
50 g (1¾ oz) shallots, finely diced
1 tablespoon finely chopped garlic
pinch dried chilli flakes
1½ teaspoons ground ginger
1½ teaspoons cumin seeds, toasted and ground, plus extra to sprinkle
olive oil, to drizzle
1 red chilli, finely sliced, to serve
parsley or mint leaves, roughly chopped, to serve

Preheat your oven to 170°C (325°F).

Make the lamb filling. Place a large frying pan over high heat. Season the lamb shanks liberally with salt and pepper. Once the pan is hot, add ¼ cup oil, then sear the lamb shanks all over until golden brown. Place in a roasting dish and pour over the stocks, along with the red wine. Cover with tinfoil, then braise in the oven for 2–2½ hours, until the lamb is falling away from the bones. Remove, let cool, then strain the stock off the shanks. Keep the stock in the fridge for another day, then pick the lamb from the bones. Roughly chop the lamb meat, then place in a bowl.

Place the potatoes in a large saucepan and cover with cold water. Place over medium-high heat and bring up to the boil. Turn the heat down to a simmer and keep an eye on them—once they reach the boil they will be cooked through in around 6–7 minutes. Remove from the heat, drain and let cool. Add the cooled potatoes to the roughly chopped lamb shank meat.

Place a large frying pan over medium-low heat. Add the remaining oil, followed by the onion, celery, carrot, garlic and currants. Cook for 15 minutes, stirring occasionally until the vegetables are translucent and soft. Stir in the chilli flakes, cinnamon, fennel and cumin.

Now add this to the lamb and potato mix, stir through, taste, then season accordingly. Chill until required.

On a clean, lightly floured bench, roll out the pastry to 2 millimetres ($\frac{1}{12}$ in) thick. Using a round cookie cutter that is 8–10 cm (3¼–4 in) across, cut out pastry circles.

To make the individual lamb empanadas, take a cut-out circle of pastry and with a pastry brush, brush a little beaten egg white halfway around the edge of the pastry. Spoon on some of the lamb mix, then fold over and pinch the pastry edges together. Repeat until finished. Remember, you can re-roll the offcuts of pastry to create more pastry circles.

Refrigerate the empanadas until required.

To make the spiced yoghurt, pour the yoghurt into a bowl. Place a frying pan over medium-low heat. Once hot, add the oil, ginger, shallots and garlic, and cook for 10 minutes, stirring occasionally, until beginning to caramelise. Next, add the chilli flakes, ground ginger and cumin seeds. Stir through, cook for a further minute, then pour into the yoghurt and mix through. Allow to cool, then refrigerate until required.

Preheat your oven to 170°C (325°F).

Place the egg yolks in a small bowl, add the teaspoon of water, then mix through. Brush the empanadas with a little of the egg-yolk wash.

Brush an oven tray with a little cooking oil, then add the empanadas. Bake for approximately 20 minutes, until golden. Remove and cool slightly prior to serving.

Pour the spiced yoghurt into a shallow dish, then garnish with olive oil, ground cumin, slivers of fresh chilli and roughly chopped parsley or mint. Serve alongside the delicious empanadas. Eat now.

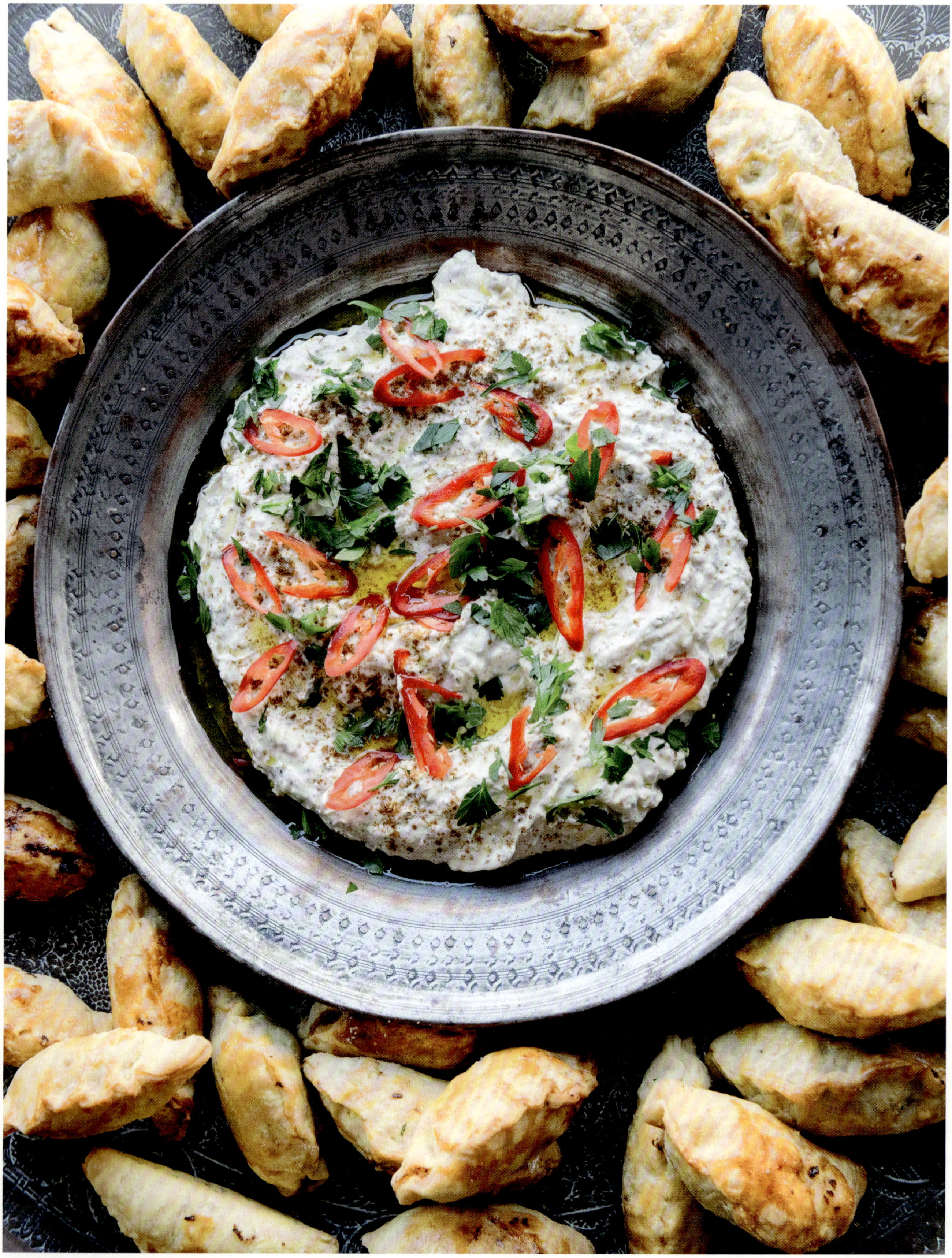

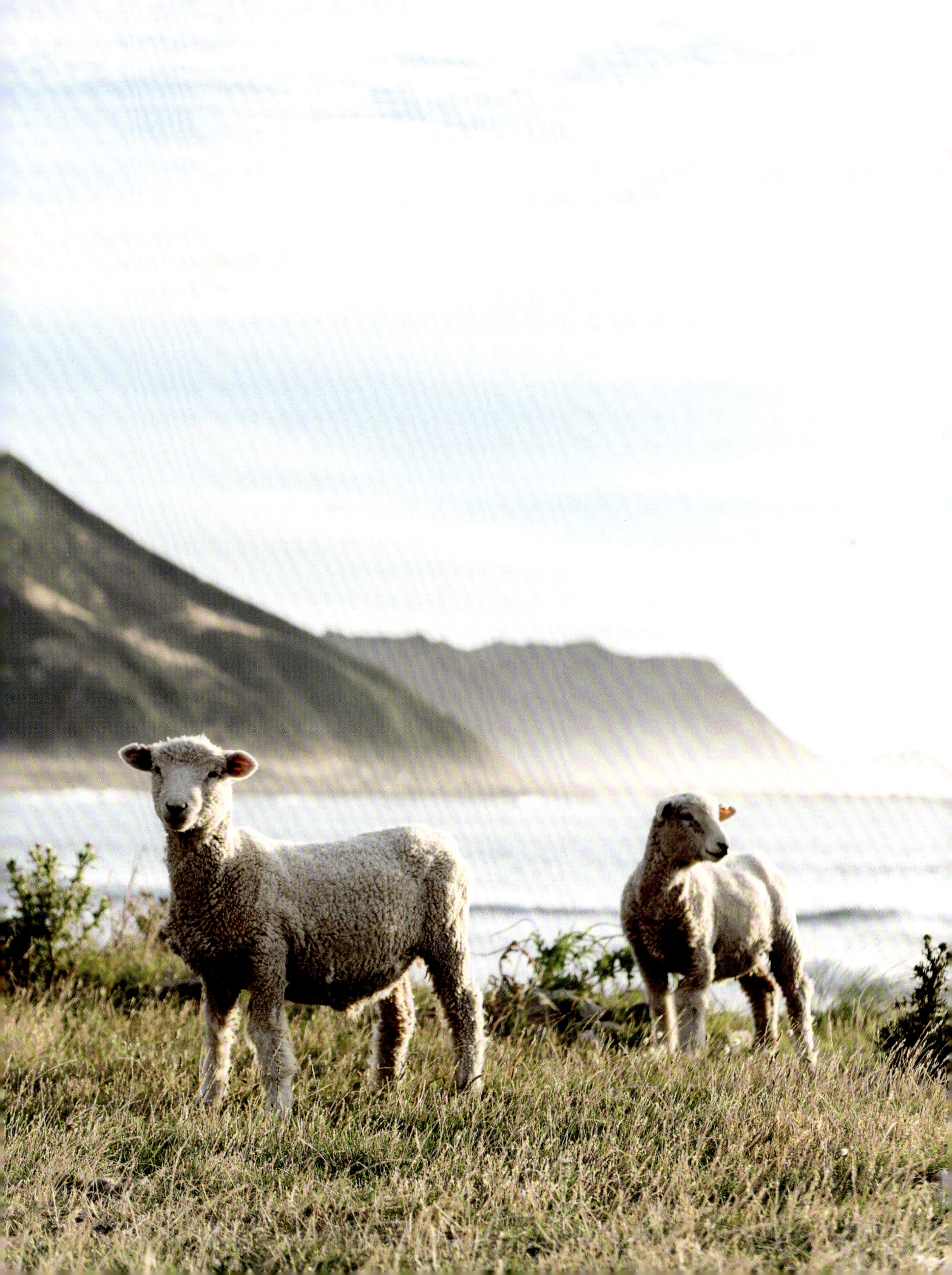

218 EAT UP NEW ZEALAND: THE BACH EDITION

Beef short ribs with pumpkin, maple and paprika purée

Beef short ribs are another secondary cut that always over-delivers when cooked low and slow. I never tire of this sort of dish. It's all about the simplicity of the two components and is comforting on many levels: falling-apart rib meat, lacquered with a reduced sauce, sitting on a silky-smooth roasted pumpkin purée that has hints of smoke and subtle sweetness from the maple syrup, finished with fried chilli and orange breadcrumbs, which creates a super-simple textural contrast to the dish. Look for beef ribs that have been cut through the middle of the bone, giving you slabs of short ribs that are easy to handle.

Serves 6

BEEF SHORT RIBS
2.5 kg (5 lb 8 oz) beef short ribs
flaky sea salt and freshly ground black pepper
cooking oil, for frying
2 cups (155 g/5½ oz) roughly chopped onion
2 cups (140 g/5 oz) roughly chopped celery
2 cups (155 g/5½ oz) roughly chopped carrot
4 garlic cloves, roughly chopped
2 thyme sprigs
2 bay leaves
¼ cup (60 g/2¼ oz) tomato paste
2 cups (500 ml/17 fl oz) red wine
2 cups (500 ml/17 fl oz) chicken stock
2 cups (500 ml/17 fl oz) beef stock

PUMPKIN, MAPLE AND PAPRIKA PURÉE
600 g (1 lb 5 oz) pumpkin, peeled and roughly chopped
¼ cup (60 ml/2 fl oz) cooking oil
1 teaspoon smoked paprika
flaky sea salt and freshly ground black pepper
¼ cup (60 ml/2 fl oz) maple syrup
250 ml (9 fl oz) cream

FRIED CHILLI AND ORANGE BREADCRUMBS
4 tablespoons canola oil or similar
1 cup (60 g/2¼ oz) panko breadcrumbs
finely grated zest and juice of 1 orange
2 red chillies, sliced super fine
¼ cup (7 g/¼ oz) finely chopped flat-leaf parsley

Preheat your oven to 150°C (300°F).

Place a large cast-iron pan over high heat. Season the slabs of beef ribs with liberal amounts of salt and pepper. Once the pan is hot, add a little cooking oil and sear the beef ribs on both sides, until dark and golden. Remove and place the slabs of ribs in a large roasting dish.

Place the pan back over the heat, and add a little more oil. Once up to heat again, add the onion, celery, carrot and garlic. Cook until the vegetables get plenty of colour, then toss in the thyme sprigs and bay leaves, followed by the tomato paste, red wine and stocks. Bring up to the boil, scraping any crusty bits off the bottom of the pan, then pour all over the beef ribs in the roasting dish. Cover with tinfoil, then place in the oven and cook for 3–4 hours, checking the ribs after 3 hours. The ribs are ready when the meat is soft and pulls off the bone easily.

Remove from the oven and let the ribs cool in the stock completely before carefully removing and refrigerating. Heat up the cooking liquid in a saucepan, strain and discard the vegetables and solids. Refrigerate the stock until required.

Recipe continued overleaf...

To make the pumpkin purée, preheat your oven to 200°C (400°F).

Place the pumpkin in a bowl with the cooking oil and smoked paprika, then season with salt and pepper. Toss together. Tip the ingredients into a roasting dish and roast for 40 minutes, until the pumpkin is caramel in colour and softened through. Pour over the maple syrup, and cook for a further 5 minutes.

Remove from the oven, and scrape the contents of the dish into a large saucepan. Place over medium-low heat, then add the cream. Simmer for 10 minutes or so, then use a stick blender to purée until silky smooth. If it's a little dry or thick, add a bit more cream or a little water. Taste and add more seasoning if necessary. Refrigerate until required.

To make the fried chilli and orange breadcrumbs, place a medium-large frying pan over medium-low heat. Once hot, add 2 tablespoons of oil, followed by the breadcrumbs and orange zest and juice. Toss and stir the breadcrumbs until they turn a lovely golden colour. Remove the pan immediately and spread out on a tray to stop the cooking.

Place the pan over high heat. Add the remaining oil and, once hot, add the chilli. Fry for 1–2 minutes, or until the chilli begins to turn golden brown around the edges. Remove with a slotted spoon and place the crispy fried chillies on kitchen paper to drain and let cool. Combine the fried chilli with the orange breadcrumbs and toss through the finely chopped parsley. Season and set aside.

Preheat your oven to 165°C (340°F).

Place the short rib stock in a saucepan and place over medium heat. Bring up to the boil, then turn down to a simmer. Allow to reduce to sauce consistency.

Take the slabs of ribs and, while cold, slice between the bones to create individual ribs. Place these in a roasting dish, pour over the reduced sauce, cover with tinfoil and place in the oven for 30 minutes, until the short ribs are hot through.

Heat up the pumpkin purée in a saucepan over low heat, stirring as you go, or microwave until hot.

To serve, divvy up the purée onto warm plates, add a rib plus some of the sauce, then finish with a liberal sprinkle of fried orange and chilli breadcrumbs. A green salad or simply cooked green vegetables would make a great bed partner. Eat now.

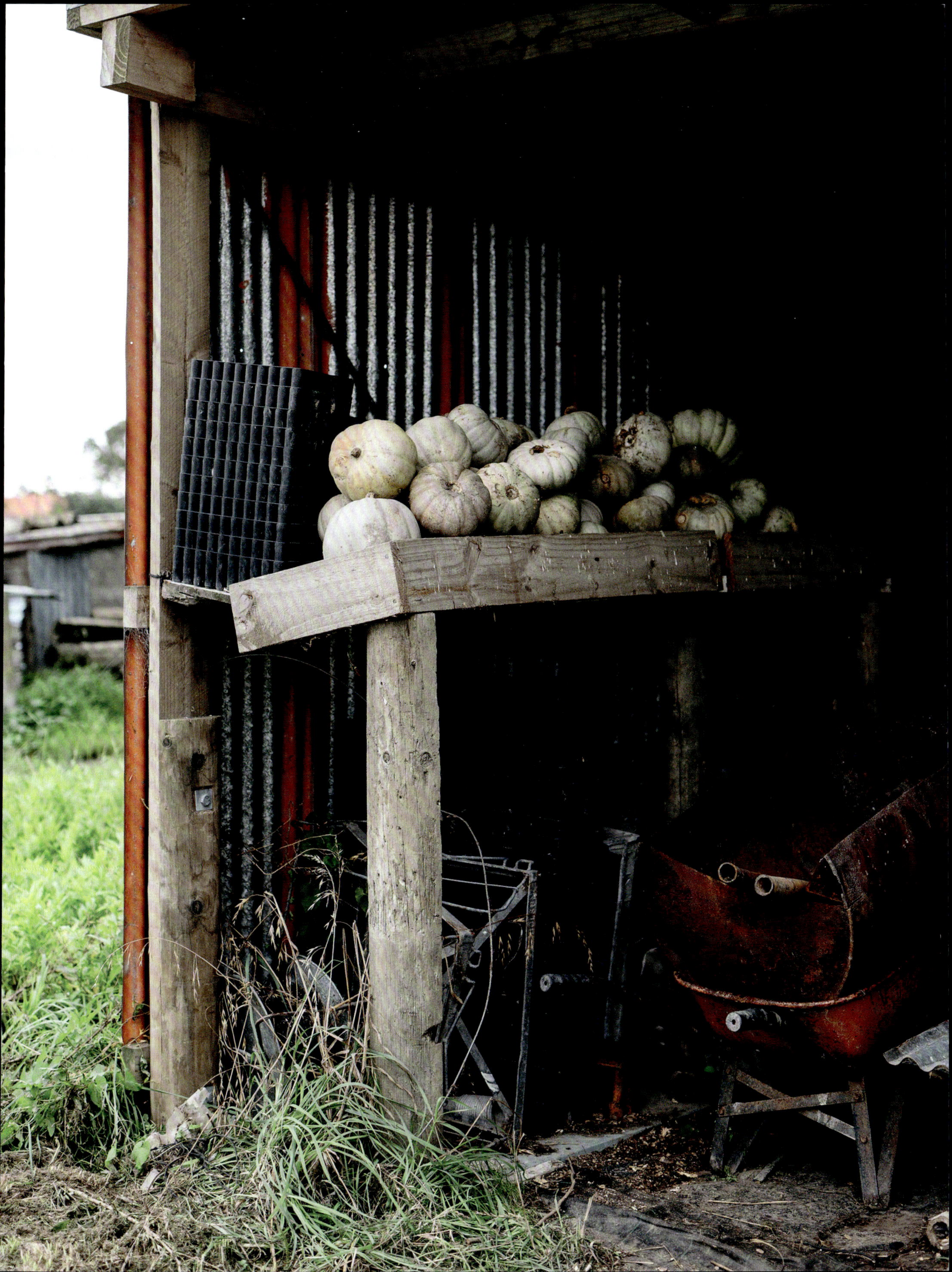

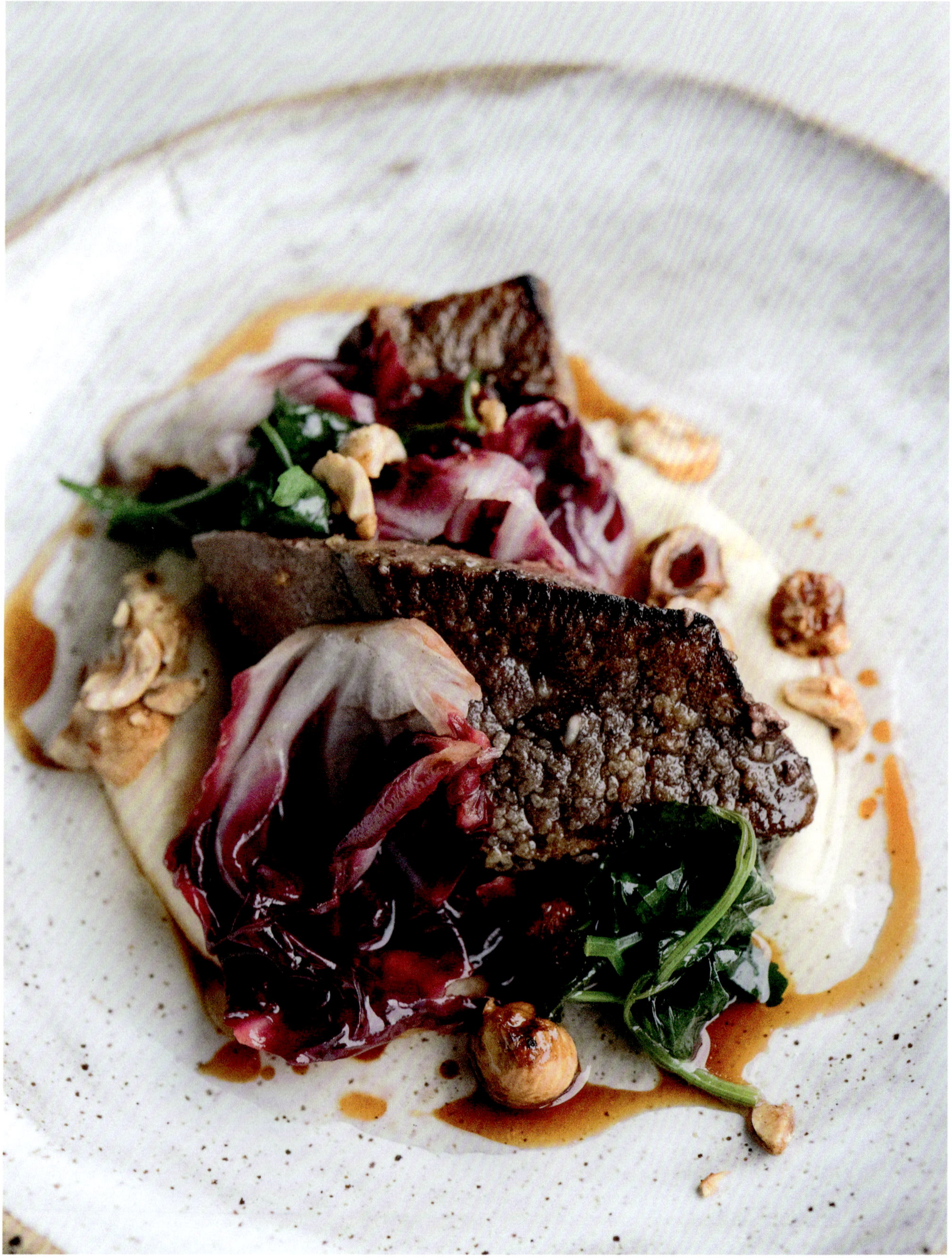

Lamb's fry with celeriac purée, radicchio and candied hazelnuts

There is a scattering of offal dishes throughout this chapter. I grew up eating offal often, and I feel it plays quite a role in our eating heritage. It's also now making a bit of a comeback in popularity, with a proliferation of talented chefs out there educating people on how to cook these wonderful but often misunderstood parts of the animal. I love this recipe. It takes the traditional lamb's fry away from its usual bed partners of bacon, caramelised onion and gravy. Here, I have added some bitterness to the savoury flavour of the lamb's fry, some richness in the form of a creamy celeriac purée, then candied hazelnuts for texture and a little sweetness. Try it. It's a delicious dish!

Serves 6 as a starter

CELERIAC PURÉE
1 kg (2 lb 4 oz) peeled celeriac, roughly chopped
2½ cups (625 ml/21½ fl oz) cream
flaky sea salt and freshly ground black pepper

TO COOK AND SERVE
1.2 kg (2 lb 10 oz) lamb's liver
flaky sea salt and freshly ground black pepper
plain flour, for dredging

canola oil, for frying
1 large radicchio, ripped into medium-sized pieces
60 ml (2 fl oz/¼ cup) sherry vinegar
2 tablespoons butter
1 cup (30 g/1 oz) flat-leaf parsley leaves
candied hazelnuts, roughly chopped (page 447)
walnut oil, to drizzle
sweet apple syrup, to drizzle

To make the celeriac purée, place the celeriac in a suitable-sized saucepan and cover with cold water. Place over high heat, and bring up to the boil, then simmer for 20 minutes, until softened. Take off the heat, drain the celeriac, put back into the pan and add the cream. Place the pan over medium-low heat, and reduce the cream by about half. Pour into a food processor or blender and purée until silky smooth. Season. If the celeriac is a little woody, pass the purée through a fine sieve to get rid of any tough pieces. Refrigerate until required.

Preheat your oven to 100°C (200°F).
　　Place the celeriac purée in a small saucepan and heat up over low heat, stirring occasionally. Once hot, remove and keep warm until required.
　　For the lamb's fry, take the liver and, with clean hands, remove the fine membrane that covers the livers. Once you get it started, it peels off easily. Portion the livers into 1.5 cm (½ in) thick slices. Season, then dredge in flour, patting off any excess flour.
　　Place a frying pan over medium-high heat. Add a little oil and, once hot, carefully add a few pieces of liver at a time, being careful not to overcrowd the pan. Cook the liver for no more than 20–30 seconds on either side; it should be medium or pink in the centre. Remove and keep warm while you repeat the process of cooking the rest of the liver.
　　Once the liver is cooked, wipe out the frying pan that it was cooked in. Place it back over medium-high heat. Once hot, add the ripped-up pieces of radicchio, followed by the vinegar and butter. Stir for a minute or so, until the radicchio has wilted. Season, then remove from the heat and mix through the parsley.

To serve, place some warm celeriac purée in the centre of each plate. Add a portion of lamb's fry, top with wilted radicchio and parsley, then spoon over chopped candied hazelnuts. Drizzle over some walnut oil and a few liberal drops of the sweet apple syrup. Eat now.

Beef cheeks with truffled swede

The popularity of beef cheeks is deserved. This wonderful secondary cut looks like a tough piece of sinewy meat in the shape of an oyster, but put it on the heat low and slow and it turns into a delicious, gelatinous, fork-tender cut fit for royalty. I've paired the cheeks with one of our country's most humble of vegetables, swede, cooked down in butter and laced with good truffle oil and a shaving of grated Parmesan. Rich, earthy and screaming for a 'Big Red' to be served alongside.

Serves 6

BEEF CHEEKS
3 beef cheeks
flaky sea salt and freshly ground black pepper
canola oil, for frying
1 large onion, diced
1 large carrot, diced
1½ celery stalks, diced
4 garlic cloves, chopped
4 thyme sprigs
2 bay leaves
2 tablespoons tomato paste
½ cup (125 ml/4 fl oz) red wine
½ cup (125 ml/4 fl oz) port
4 cups (1 litre/35 fl oz) chicken or beef stock

TRUFFLED SWEDE
1.5 kg (3 lb 5 oz) swede, peeled
100 g (3½ oz) butter
12 large sage leaves
flaky sea salt and freshly ground black pepper
few drops truffle oil, plus extra to serve if desired

TO SERVE
Parmesan cheese
wilted silverbeet (optional)

Preheat your oven to 150°C (300°F).

Using a sharp knife, trim any visible skin and fat from the cheeks. Season liberally with salt and pepper. Place a cast-iron casserole dish or similar on the stovetop and bring up to high heat. Once hot, add some oil, followed by the seasoned cheeks. Brown and caramelise the cheeks all over then remove and set aside. Add a little more oil, followed by the onion, carrot, celery, garlic, thyme sprigs and bay leaves. Cook for 10 minutes, stirring occasionally, until the vegetables are golden and caramelised. Add the tomato paste, stir to coat the vegetables, and cook to intensify the flavour for a further 2 minutes. Pour in the red wine and port to deglaze the saucepan.

Now add the stock, and place the cheeks back into the pan. Bring up to the boil, place the lid on the dish, then place the whole thing in the oven.

Check after 3 hours. The cheeks should come apart easily with a little downward pressure. Leave the cheeks to cool in the cooking liquid in the pan, then refrigerate until required.

For the swede, I know it's a bit of a pain, but grate the swede with a cheese grater.

Place a heavy-bottomed saucepan over medium-low heat. Add the butter, along with the grated swede and the sage leaves. Cook down for 30–40 minutes, stirring occasionally, being mindful that it doesn't catch on the bottom of the pan. Remove and discard the sage leaves. Season and add a few drops of truffle oil at a time, tasting as you go. Truffle oil is quite aggressive, and lucky for you (as it is expensive) a little goes a long way. Reserve and keep warm.

Preheat your oven to 150°C (300°F).

Place a casserole dish on the stovetop and bring up to a simmer. With a slotted spoon, carefully remove the cheeks and place in a small ovenproof dish. Spoon over about ½ cup (125 ml) of the cooking liquid. Cover with tinfoil and place the cheeks in the oven to reheat.

Take the rest of the cooking liquid, strain off the vegetables then put the cooking liquid back in a small saucepan. Place over medium-low heat, bring to a simmer and reduce to sauce consistency.

To serve, spoon out some of the truffled swede onto warm plates. Take the beef cheeks and, using either a knife or tongs, split the cheeks in half and place on or next to the truffled swede. Spoon over the reduced sauce, grate over a liberal amount of Parmesan and add a couple more drops of truffle oil per plate, if desired. I sometimes wilt a little silverbeet to ride alongside. Eat now.

Spiced lamb shoulder chops with labneh, honey and dukkah

Growing up on a farm where 'home kill' was the norm, we ate more lamb, hogget and mutton than any other protein. I never tire of sheep meat—in fact, if I have been overseas for a bit, when I arrive home it's usually a simple lamb chop that I look forward to eating the most. Racks of lamb and loin chops are normally the most tender; however, I have a real fondness for lamb shoulder chops. With their irregular bone and cartilage formations, shoulder chops offer up a far more interesting eat than the others. Some of the pockets of meat are super tender, others have a little more chew, and that is what I like about them. Chops are finger food; it's a messy job at times, but that's the appeal. The following recipe works wonderfully well, with spice, char, sour, sweet and nutty all hangin' out together. I like to let these chops marinate in the fridge for a couple of days prior to cooking.

Serves 6

LAMB AND MARINADE
1.5 kg (3 lb 5 oz) lamb shoulder chops
2 tablespoons ground sumac
1 tablespoon smoked paprika
1 tablespoon coriander seeds, toasted and ground
1½ tablespoons cumin seeds, toasted and ground
1 tablespoon flaky sea salt
½ teaspoon freshly ground black pepper
1½ tablespoons finely chopped garlic
1–2 red chillies, finely chopped
finely grated zest and juice of 2 lemons
½ cup (125 ml/4 fl oz) olive oil

TO SERVE
2 cups (500 g/1 lb 2 oz) labneh or thick natural yoghurt
⅓ cup (115 g/4 oz) runny honey
handful mint leaves
seeds of 1 pomegranate (optional)
dukkah (page 444)
2 lemons, cut into wedges

Place the lamb chops in a large bowl with all of the 444 ingredients. With clean hands, massage all the spices into the chops. Leave to marinate in the fridge for at least 2 days. The longer you marinate them, the better the result.

Preheat your chargrill, barbecue or oven grill to high.

Cook the shoulder chops all the way through, letting them get a decent amount of char and caramelisation on them. Remove and let rest for 5 minutes.

To serve, spread the labneh or yoghurt on a platter or plates. Top with the charred chops, then finish by drizzling over the runny honey, picked mint leaves, pomegranate seeds and dukkah. Serve with lemon quarters on the side for squeezing. Eat now.

ANIMAL 227

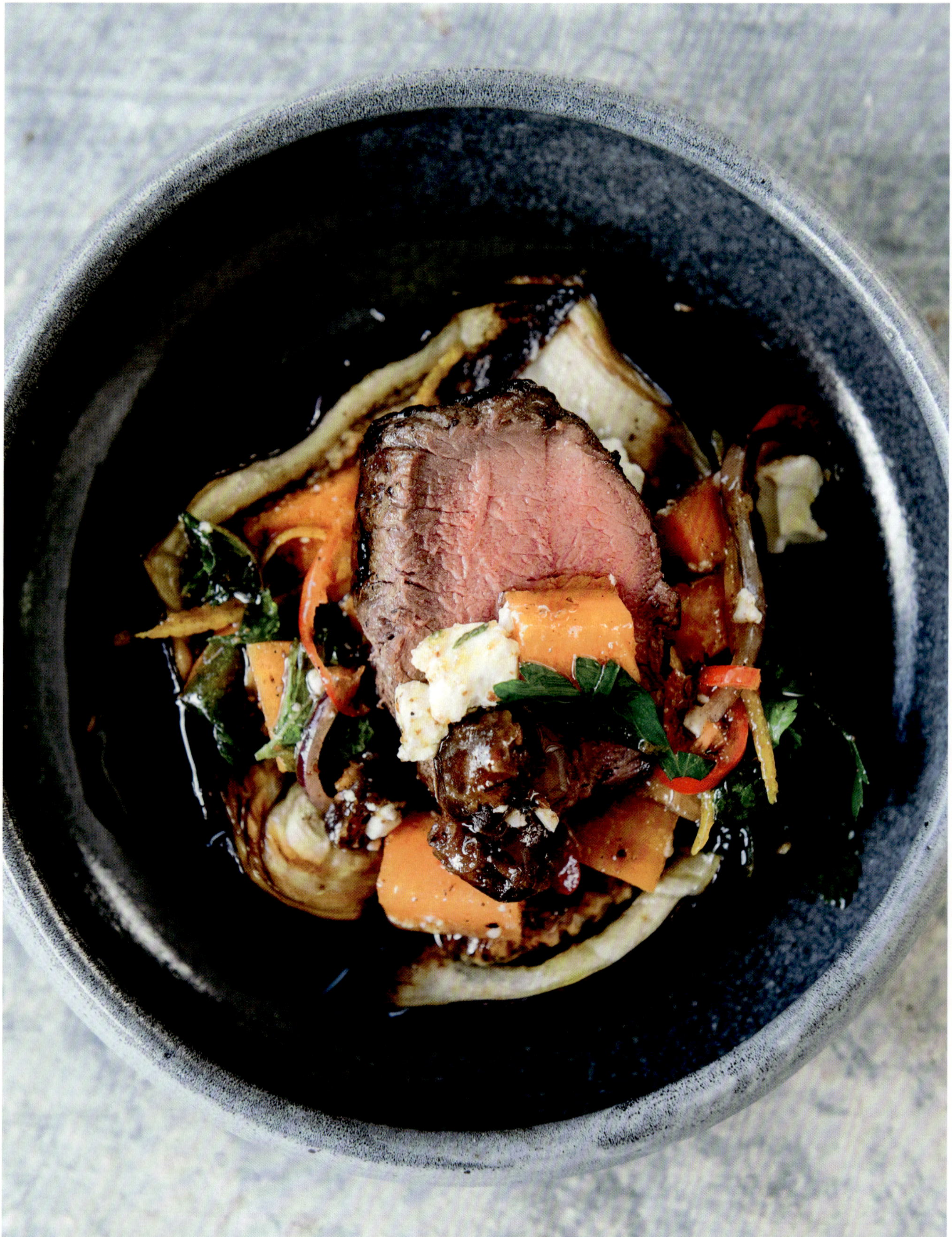

Venison back strap with roasted eggplant and a burnt carrot, feta and date relish

For a long time, I have for some reason looked upon venison as a protein suited more to the cooler months of the year. I enjoy slow-cooked venison stews, and have often cooked the fillets or back straps medium-rare and served them with a rich gravy, a fricassee of mushrooms and cherry relish. The following recipe is designed for summer eating. The eggplant and the burnt carrot relish can be made hours before, so once the venison is cooked, the meal comes together in a snap.

Serves 6–8

ROASTED EGGPLANT
2 large eggplant
cooking oil, for brushing and frying
flaky sea salt and freshly ground black pepper

BURNT CARROT, FETA AND DATE RELISH
4 carrots, cut into 1 cm (½ in) slices
flaky sea salt and freshly ground black pepper
cooking oil
½ small red onion, thinly sliced
1 red chilli, thinly sliced
½ cup (90 g/3¼ oz) pitted dates, roughly chopped
1 orange
¼ cup (7 g/¼ oz) roughly chopped flat-leaf parsley
¼ cup (10 g/¼ oz) roughly chopped mint leaves
¼ cup (7 g/¼ oz) roughly chopped coriander leaves
1 teaspoon cumin seeds, toasted and ground
1 teaspoon ground sumac
½ cup (75 g/2¾ oz) crumbled feta cheese
½ cup (125 ml/4 fl oz) Al Brown & Co Orange and Chilli Infused Olive Oil or extra-virgin olive oil

TO COOK AND SERVE
1.2 kg (2 lb 10 oz) venison back strap
flaky sea salt and freshly ground black pepper
cooking oil

Preheat your oven to 180°C (350°F).

Quarter the eggplant lengthways, then cut each quarter into six long triangular slices. You should have 24 slices in total. Brush the sides of the eggplant slices with oil and place on a roasting dish or oven tray lined with baking paper. Season liberally with salt and pepper. Roast for 25 minutes, or until golden and soft. Remove and set aside to cool.

For the burnt carrots, toss the carrot slices in a liberal amount of oil in a bowl, then season. Place a frying pan over medium heat. Once hot, add enough carrot slices to cover the base of the hot pan. Let the carrots cook until they get slightly charred, then turn and repeat on the other side. Remove and allow to cool.

Cut the burnt carrots into large dice and place in a suitable-sized mixing bowl. Now add the rest of the ingredients, gently mix through, taste and season accordingly.

If you're planning to serve in a couple of hours, keep the carrot relish at room temperature, otherwise refrigerate until required.

Recipe continued overleaf...

Preheat your oven to 180°C (350°F).

Cut your back strap in half, so you have a thick piece and a narrower, thinner piece. Season liberally with salt and pepper. Place a cast-iron casserole dish or heavy-bottomed ovenproof pan over medium-high heat. Once hot, pour in a little cooking oil and carefully add the pieces of venison. Caramelise on all sides until golden, then place in the oven. Remove the smaller piece after a couple of minutes, then the larger piece 2 minutes after that. The venison should still be relatively soft to the touch. Allow the venison to rest, uncovered, for at least 5–6 minutes.

To serve, place a few pieces of the roasted eggplant on each plate. Slice the venison into smallish medallions and rest up against the eggplant. To finish, spoon over liberal amounts of the burnt carrot, feta and date relish. Serve now.

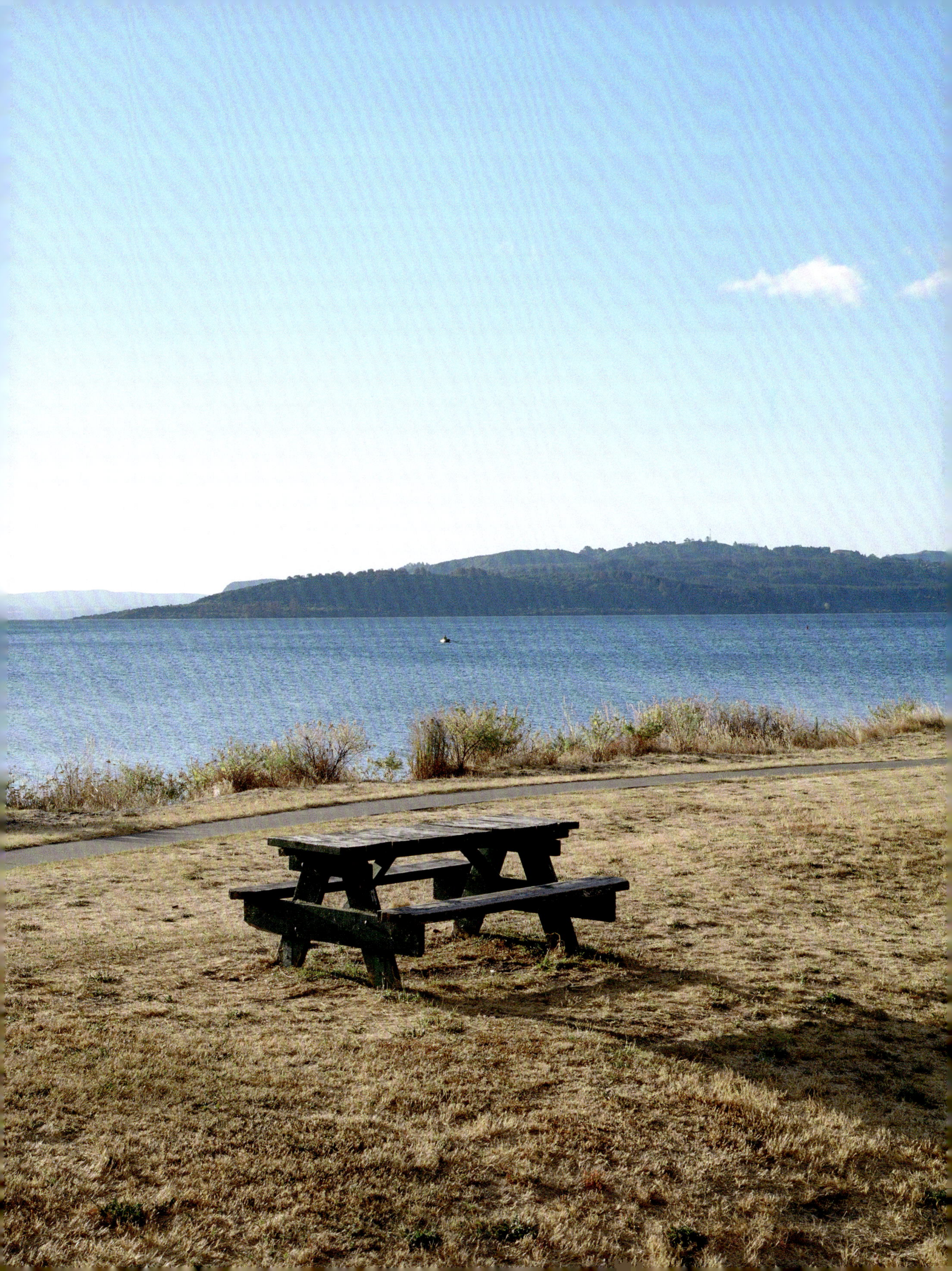

Braised rabbit with fresh pappardelle, broad beans and golden raisins

For the life of me I can't understand why, in a country where rabbits roam freely in nearly every corner, we don't eat more of these delicious pests. I have always felt that rabbit has many similarities to our feathered friend the chicken. Its lean white meat is not really gamey, but more subtly savoury in flavour. I like this dish a lot—it's the sort of recipe that you'd make on a weekend afternoon in the middle of winter, where all the preparation is taken care of over two or three hours, making the actual serving-up part a bit of a doddle. You can, of course, use store-bought pasta (practically any shape will do). I'm more of a dried-pasta sort of guy than fresh, due to convenience more than anything else. However, when I have time to go to the effort of making my own, I'm reminded why Italian cuisine is so universally adored.

Serves 6

BRAISED RABBIT
1 whole rabbit (approx. 800 g to 1 kg)
flaky sea salt and freshly ground black pepper
canola oil, for frying
1 large carrot, finely chopped
2 celery stalks, finely chopped
1 large onion, finely chopped
6 garlic cloves, rough chopped
1 rosemary sprig
2 thyme sprigs
2 sage sprigs
2 bay leaves
1 cup (250 ml/9 fl oz) white or rosé wine
4 cups (1 litre/35 fl oz) chicken stock

FRESH PAPPARDELLE
1⅔ cups (250 g/9 oz) '00' flour
1⅔ cups (250 g/9 oz) plain flour, plus extra for dusting
5 large eggs

TO COOK AND SERVE
¼ cup (60 ml/2 fl oz) canola oil
¾ cup (115 g/4 oz) finely sliced shallots
2 garlic cloves, finely chopped
1½ tablespoons finely chopped thyme leaves
1½ tablespoons finely chopped sage leaves
pinch dried chilli flakes
½ cup (60 g/2¼ oz) golden raisins
olive oil
1½ cups cooked and deshelled broad beans
½ cup (10 g/¼ oz) flat-leaf parsley leaves
1 tablespoon butter
flaky sea salt and freshly ground black pepper
Parmesan cheese, to serve

Preheat your oven to 160°C (325°F).

Take the rabbit and remove both the back and the front legs. With a cleaver or a heavy-duty knife, cut the torso into two halves.

Place a large frying pan over high heat. Season the rabbit portions with salt and pepper. Once the pan is hot, add a splash of oil, then sear the pieces of rabbit until golden on all sides. Place the rabbit in a large casserole dish or heavy-bottomed ovenproof pan.

Bring the pan back up to high heat. Add a bit more oil, then toss in the carrot, celery, onion and garlic, along with the herbs. Cook until the vegetables caramelise, about 10–15 minutes. Pour in the wine and deglaze the pan, scrapping any of the rabbit or vegetable bits that have stuck to the base of the pan. Add to the browned rabbit portions, then pour over the stock. Put the lid on the casserole dish, then place over high heat for 5 minutes. Transfer to the oven.

Check after 1½ hours. The meat should pull away easily from the bone. If it's still a little tight, return to the oven for a further 30 minutes or so.

Once the rabbit is cooked, remove from the oven. With tongs, carefully take out the rabbit portions and let them cool on a tray for 15 minutes. Take the vegetables and cooking liquid and strain through a fine sieve into a saucepan. Discard the braising vegetables and herb sprigs. Depending on how much liquid you have, place the cooking liquid over medium-low heat and reduce the stock down to about 1½ cups. Take off the heat, let cool, then refrigerate until required.

After the rabbit has cooled a bit, with clean hands, strip away all the braised meat from the rabbit frames. Refrigerate the rabbit meat and discard the bones.

To make the pasta, place both flours in a food processor and, with the motor running, add the eggs one at a time. Turn the rough dough out onto a clean surface and knead for 10–15 minutes, until the dough springs back when you make a finger indent. Wrap in clingfilm, and refrigerate for 30 minutes to let the dough relax.

Cut the dough into manageable pieces, then either using a pasta press or rolling pin, roll out the dough as thin as possible. Dry the pasta for 10 minutes by draping it over a towel rack or wooden spoon handle. With a sharp knife, cut the pasta into ribbons 3.5 cm (1½ in) wide. Toss the ribbons through a little flour or semolina to prevent the pasta from sticking together. Cover with a tea towel and set aside.

Three-quarters fill a large saucepan with salted water and place over high heat. Bring up to the boil, then lower to a simmer.

Take another large, heavy-bottom saucepan and place over medium-low heat. Once hot, add the oil, shallots, garlic, thyme, sage, chilli flakes and raisins. Cook, stirring occasionally, until the shallots have started to caramelise and turn golden. Add the rabbit meat along with the reduced braising stock.

Bring the salted water for the pasta up to a rolling boil, add a glug of olive oil, then stir in your pappardelle. The pasta should only need 2 minutes maximum to cook.

While the pasta is cooking, add the broad beans and parsley leaves to the pan with the rabbit and stir through for a couple of minutes. Drain the pasta and toss through the rabbit. Finally, add the butter, taste then season accordingly.

Serve up into warm bowls then finish with a liberal dusting of freshly grated Parmesan cheese. A simple green salad and a crusty warm baguette would be the go with this dish. Eat now.

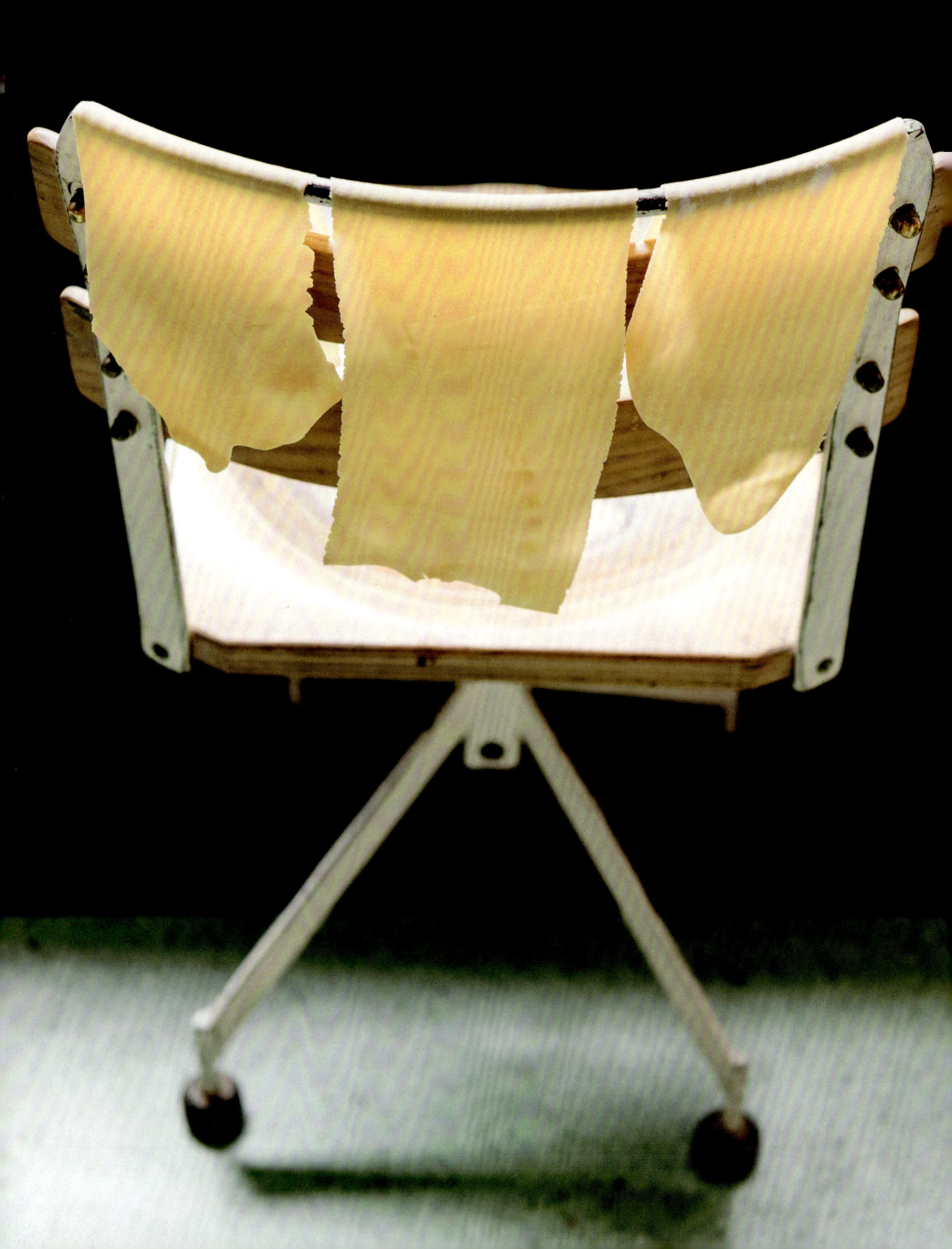

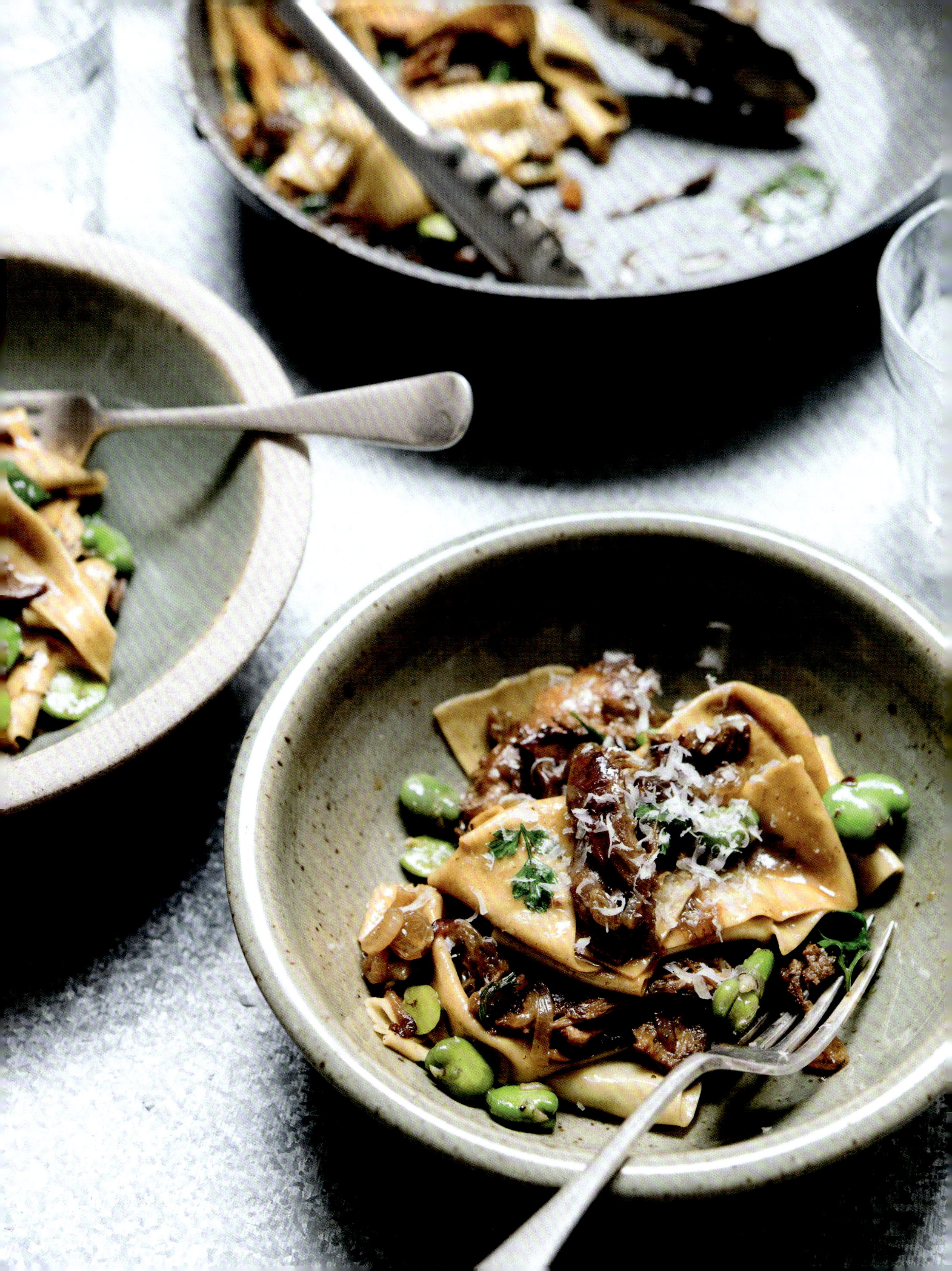

236   EAT UP NEW ZEALAND: THE BACH EDITION

Veal schnitzel with creamed celeriac and bitter green apple slaw

I think a schnitzel of any variety must be somewhere near the top of most people's ultimate comfort-food list. Texturally, schnitzels offer up so much with that pure golden crunch from the crumbed outer layer. They beg to be paired with a mash or purée of some sort, and I'm a big fan of a puddle of gravy sitting nearby. We have lightened this version up a bit by adding a silky-smooth celeriac purée and a slightly bitter (in a good way) apple slaw to bring some 'cut through' and freshness to the plate.

Serves 6 generously

SCHNITZEL
6 x 150 g (5½ oz) veal schnitzels
flaky sea salt and freshly ground black pepper
plain flour, for dusting
2–3 cups (120–180 g/4¼–6½ oz) panko breadcrumbs
3 eggs, beaten

CREAMED CELERIAC
1 kg (2 lb 4 oz) celeriac, peeled and diced
2½ cups (625 ml/21½ fl oz) cream
flaky sea salt and freshly ground black pepper

TO COOK AND SERVE
cooking oil, for frying
bitter green apple slaw (page 303), to serve

For the veal, season the individual schnitzels with salt and pepper. Set up your breading station. Place the flour and breadcrumbs on two separate plates, and the eggs in a bowl. Flour the schnitzels first, dusting off any excess prior to dipping in the beaten eggs, then finally pat them down in the breadcrumbs. Refrigerate until required.

In a saucepan, add the celeriac and cover with cold salted water. Place over high heat, bring up to the boil, then lower the heat to a simmer. Cook for approximately 20 minutes, until the celeriac is softened. Drain, add the cream, then place back in the pan over low heat. Cook for a further 10 minutes to reduce and thicken the cream.

Transfer the contents of the pan to a food processor (or use a stick blender) and blitz until smooth. Taste and season. Refrigerate until required.

Preheat your oven to 110°C (225°F).

Place a frying pan over medium-high heat. Once hot, add a liberal amount of oil and cook the schnitzels in batches for 2 minutes on either side, until golden and crisp. Place the cooked schnitzels on an oven tray, lined with kitchen paper, and keep warm in the oven until you have finished cooking all of the schnitzel. (I clean out my pan between each batch so there are no burnt breadcrumbs attached to the next batch of schnitzels.)

Heat up the celeriac purée slowly in a saucepan or the microwave.

To plate, add a veal schnitzel to each plate, add a liberal amount of the celeriac purée, then finish with a pile of the bitter green apple slaw. Eat now.

Steak and kidney pie

There are all sorts of pie recipes scattered throughout this book. We are a nation that simply adores any sort of pie, be it savoury or sweet. Latest stats confirm that per head of population we each consume 17 single-serve pies every year . . . that's 68 million consumed annually. Oh, my Lord! Hands down my favourite combo has always been steak and kidney. I love the intense savoury flavour that kidneys bring to a gravy situation. This is a cracking pie, where I use a 50:50 combination of steak to kidney. The plum sauce on page 424 loves this pie.

Serves 6–8

¼ cup (60 ml/2 fl oz) cooking oil
300 g (10½ oz) bacon, diced
1 kg (2 lb 4 oz) lamb kidneys
flaky sea salt and freshly ground black pepper
1 kg (2 lb 4 oz) blade steak
⅓ cup (50 g/1¾ oz) plain flour
1 cup (250 ml/9 fl oz) red wine
⅓ cup (80 ml/2½ fl oz) cooking oil
4 cups (620 g/1 lb 6 oz) finely diced onion

2 cups (280 g/10 oz) finely diced celery
4 cups (620 g/1 lb 6 oz) finely diced carrot
2 tablespoons fresh thyme, finely chopped
2–3 bay leaves
2 cups (500 ml/17 fl oz) chicken stock
2 cups (500 ml/17 fl oz) beef stock
2 tablespoons tomato paste
1 quantity Eve's mum's pastry (page 442)

Take a large cast-iron pan or heavy-bottomed pan and place over medium-high heat. Once hot, add the oil, followed by the bacon. Cook the bacon for 5 minutes, until golden. With a slotted spoon, spoon out the bacon into a large casserole dish. Keep the rendered bacon fat in the skillet.

With a sharp knife, cut the lamb kidneys lengthways and remove any obvious white gristle. Then cut the two halves in half again. Cut the blade steak into regular, bite-sized pieces. Place the prepared kidney and blade steak in a bowl, season liberally with salt and pepper, then add the flour and toss to coat.

Place the pan with the rendered bacon fat back on the heat. Once hot again, cook the kidney and pieces of steak in batches until golden brown, then add these to the casserole dish with the bacon.

Once all the meat is seared, add the wine to deglaze the pan, making sure to scrape the bottom of the pan to lift off all the caramelised bits and pieces. Pour this over the steak and kidney mix. Place the pan back over medium-low heat, add the oil, onion, celery, carrot, thyme and bay leaves. Cook for 15 minutes, stirring occasionally, until the onion is translucent or beginning to turn golden. Tip all of the vegetables and herbs into the casserole dish. Now add the stocks and tomato paste, stirring through until all is combined.

Place the casserole dish over medium-low heat and cover with a lid. Check after 10 minutes and, once the mix is beginning to bubble, turn the heat down to low. Continue to cook, covered, for 1½ hours, stirring occasionally to prevent sticking. Test the tenderness of the steak. Once soft through, the mix is ready. If it seems too loose and runny for a pie filling, leave the lid off and reduce for a bit until it thickens up. Remove from the heat, let cool, then refrigerate until required.

Preheat oven to 170°C (325°F).

You'll need a pie tin that is around 28 cm (11 in) in circumference and 3.5 cm (1½ in) high. Split the pastry dough in two and, on a clean and floured bench, roll both halves out to about 3–4 mm (⅛–³⁄₁₆ in) thick. Pick up the prepared pastry base by rolling it up onto your rolling pin, then gently unroll it over your tin. Carefully work the pastry into the base of the tin and up the sides. Leave a little extra around the circumference then cut off and discard or freeze any of the excess pastry.

Now fill the pastry-lined base with the cold steak and kidney mix. Roll the prepared pastry top onto the rolling pin as before, then unroll over the top of the pie. Again, cut away any excess then pinch the top and the base pastries together.

Use the tip of a knife to cut a couple of holes in the top of the pie, place in the centre of the oven and bake for about 45 minutes, or until the pastry is golden and crisp. Remove from the oven and let cool for 20 minutes before dishing up.

Corned beef with pea and spinach croquettes and mustard sauce

I have had a soft spot for corned beef for as long as I can remember. When I was growing up, we would eat corned beef at least once a month. It's one of the cheaper and more humble dishes, which I always think offers up a way more satisfying and pleasing result than it has any right to. I have modernised the dish that follows slightly by adding some texture in the form of a croquette, but the essence of what corned beef is to most people is, I think, still truly intact.

Serves 6–8

PEA AND SPINACH CROQUETTES
⅓ cup (90 g/3 oz) butter
1½ cups (400 g/14 oz) finely diced onion
2 cups (500 ml/17 fl oz) chicken stock
1 kg (2 lb 7 oz) frozen peas, thawed
200 g (7 oz) spinach leaves
flaky sea salt and freshly ground black pepper
½ cup (75 g/2½ oz) plain flour
4 eggs, beaten
2 cups (120 g/4¼ oz) panko breadcrumbs

CORNED BEEF
1.5 kg (3 lb 5 oz) brined corned beef
1 onion, roughly chopped
1 carrot, roughly chopped
1 celery stalk, roughly chopped
2 bay leaves

8 black peppercorns
8 cloves
⅓ cup (60 g/2¼ oz) brown sugar
⅓ cup (80 ml/2½ fl oz) malt vinegar

MUSTARD SAUCE
2 tablespoons butter
2 tablespoons plain flour
2 cups (500 ml/17 fl oz) milk
1 bay leaf
1 teaspoon sugar
2 teaspoon hot English mustard
2 tablespoons mild American mustard

TO COOK AND SERVE
canola oil, for shallow-frying
pecorino or Parmesan cheese, to serve

To make the croquettes, place a saucepan over low heat. Add the butter and the onions and sweat, stirring occasionally, for 10 minutes until the onions are softened. Now pour in the stock and turn up the heat. Reduce the stock by half, then add the peas and spinach. Bring up to the boil, then remove from the heat. Strain off the stock and discard.

    Place the peas and spinach in a food processor and blitz to a rough purée. Season to taste with salt and pepper, then spread out on a tray and place in the refrigerator to cool as quickly as possible. (This helps keep the mushed peas and spinach a vibrant green.)

    Once cold, shape the purée into croquette-sized shapes of your choice. I make a classic small cylinder shape of about 50 g (1¾ oz) each, which gives you around 20 croquettes.

    Crumb the croquettes in the usual manner, by dusting in flour, dipping into the eggs, then finally cover liberally with breadcrumbs. Refrigerate until required.

Prepare the corned beef. In a large saucepan, add the corned beef along with the remaining ingredients. Pour over enough cold water to cover the beef by about 2 cm (¾ in). Place over high heat and bring up to the boil, then drop the heat down to a rolling simmer. Keep an eye on it, and cook for 2 hours and 20 minutes. Leave to steep in the cooking liquid until you're ready to serve or refrigerate in the same way if you are going to eat this the following day.

For the mustard sauce, in a small saucepan, melt the butter. Add the flour to form a roux, whisking for a minute or two to cook out the flour. Slowly add the milk and toss in the bay leaf while continuing to whisk to form a silky smooth white sauce. Add the sugar and both mustards. Mix thoroughly, season and keep warm until required.

Preheat your oven to 100°C (200°F).

To fry the croquettes, place a large frying pan over medium heat. Add enough oil to come 5 mm (¼ in) up the side of the pan, and bring up to 180°C (350°F). You can gauge this by adding a piece of bread to the oil; if it's at around 180°C, it will take about a minute for the bread to turn golden and crisp. Shallow-fry the croquettes, in batches, until golden all over. Remove with a slotted spoon and place on kitchen paper to drain. Transfer the cooked croquettes to the oven to keep warm while you cook the remaining ones.

To serve, either slice the corned beef thinly and divide up between warm plates, or cut whole steak-like pieces for each plate, which is the way I love to serve it.

Add two or three croquettes to each plate, then a liberally pour over the mustard sauce. To finish, grate the pecorino or Parmesan over the top. Eat now.

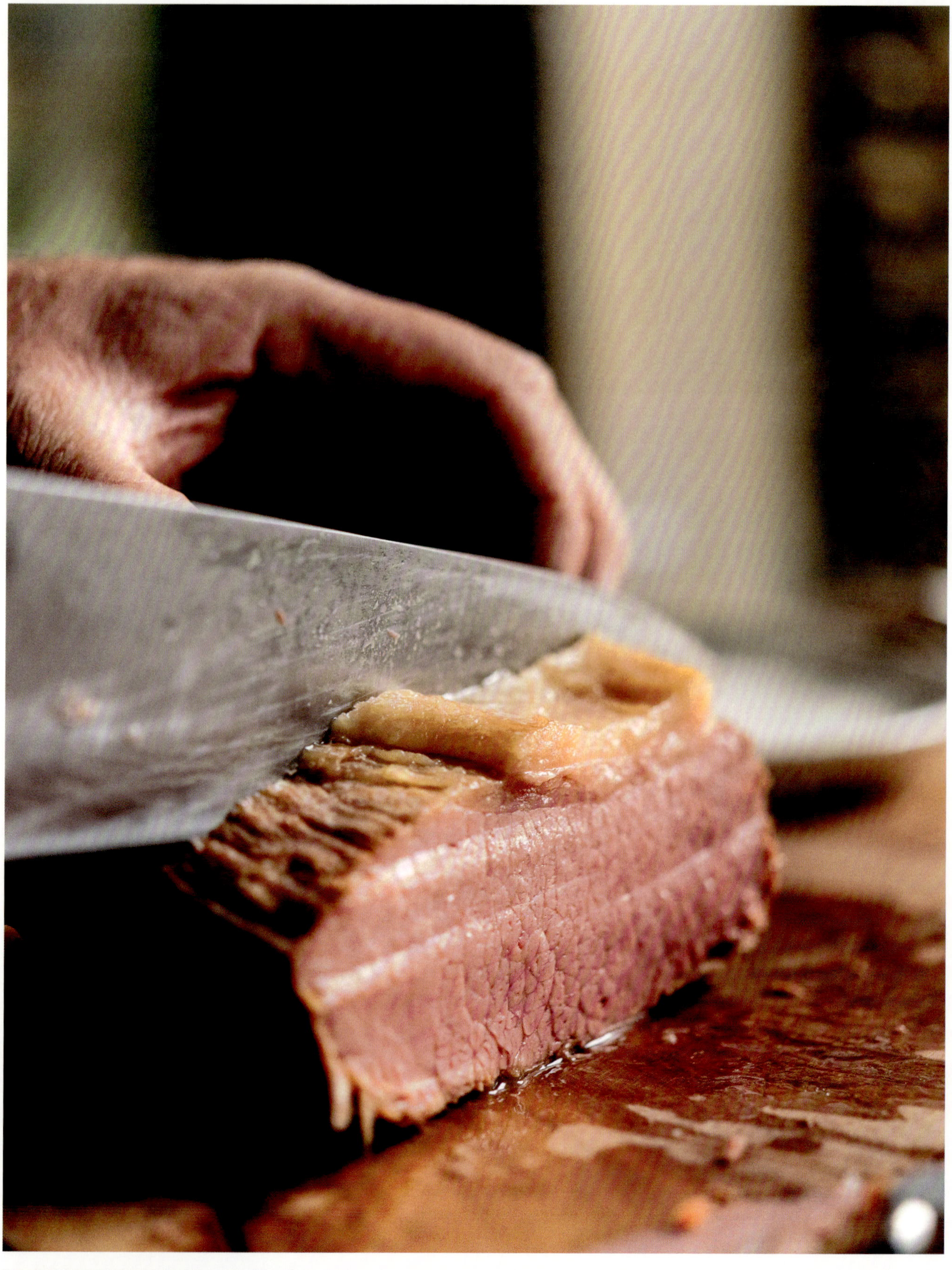

ANIMAL 243

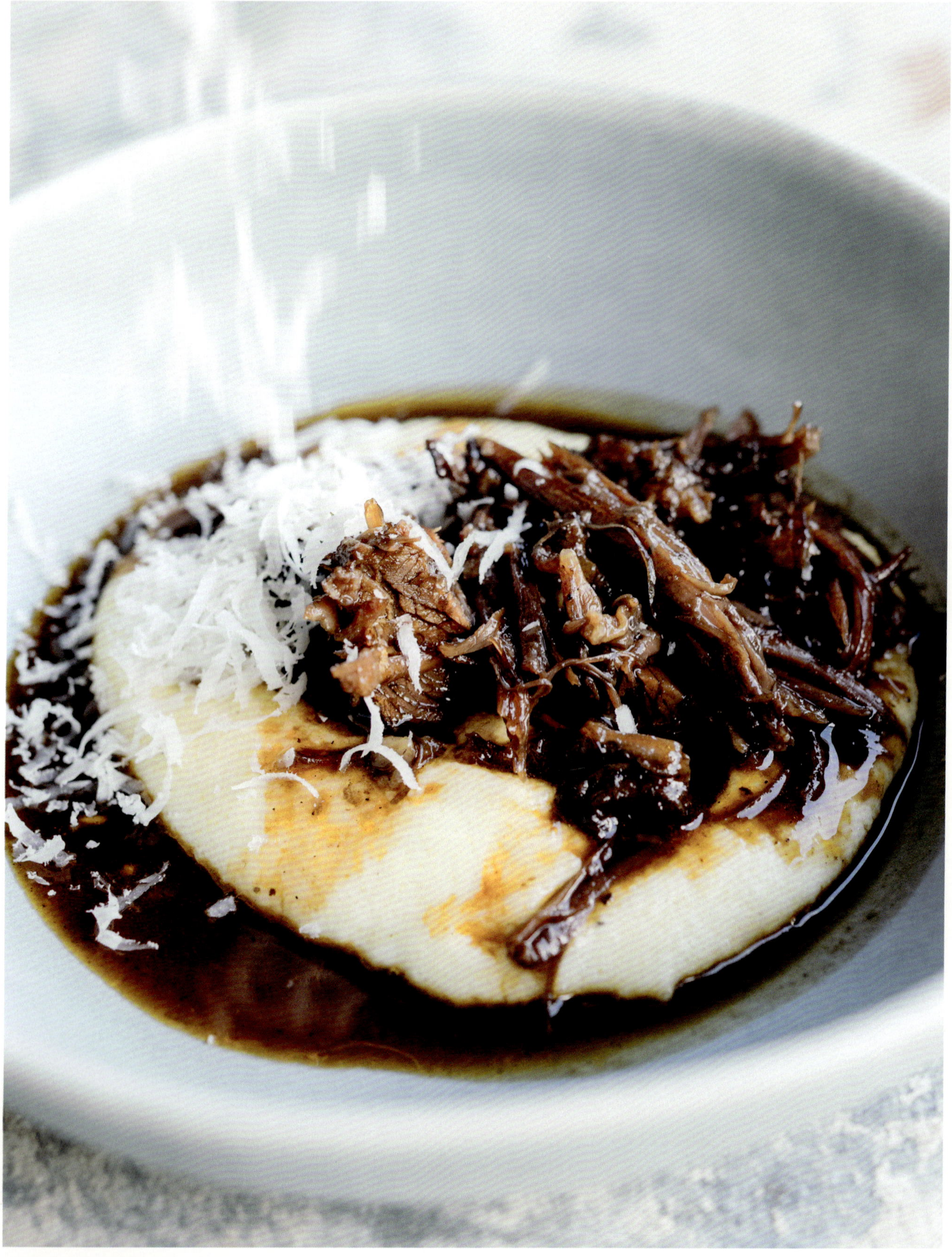

Pulled oxtail with soft Parmesan polenta

I believe the meat from an oxtail when cooked long and slow is the most favourable cut from the whole animal. I know that cuts like beef cheek, beef shin and brisket seem to be the popular guys on the block these days, but I urge you to give oxtail a try. Served here on velvety smooth polenta, finished with a grating of Parmesan, this dish is the king of comfort and just begging for a good-quality red alongside.

Serves 6

BRAISED OXTAIL
2 kg (4 lb 8 oz) oxtail
flaky sea salt and freshly ground black pepper
⅓ cup (80 ml/2½ fl oz) cooking oil
2 onions, roughly chopped
2 carrots, roughly chopped
2 celery stalks, roughly chopped
6 garlic cloves, roughly chopped
1 rosemary sprig
2 thyme sprigs
2 cups (500 ml/17 fl oz) red wine
2 cups (500 ml/17 fl oz) chicken stock
2 cups (500 ml/17 fl oz) beef stock
2 tablespoons tomato paste

PARMESAN POLENTA
3 cups (750 ml/26 fl oz) milk
1 cup (250 ml/9 fl oz) cream
125 g (4½ oz) instant fine polenta
½ cup (50 g/1¾ oz) finely grated Parmesan cheese, plus extra to serve
knob butter

Preheat your oven to 150°C (300°F).

Place a cast-iron pan or similar heavy-bottomed pan over medium-high heat. Season the oxtail with salt and pepper, add some of the oil to the skillet, then sear the pieces of oxtail until golden all over. Remove and place in a large casserole dish.

Leave the pan over the heat and add a bit more oil, followed by the onions, carrots, celery, garlic, rosemary and thyme. Brown the vegetables, then add to the dish with the oxtail. Next, pour the red wine and both stocks into the pan, add the tomato paste and place over high heat. Bring up to the boil, then pour this over the oxtail and vegetables. Cover the casserole dish with a lid or tinfoil, then place in the oven and cook for 3½ hours, or until the meat falls away from the bone.

Remove from the oven. Let the oxtail cool down enough to handle, then pick the meat from the bones. Discard the bones, then strain the cooking liquid through a sieve, discarding the vegetables and herbs. Pour the cooking liquid into a saucepan, place over medium-high heat and simmer to reduce by about half. Pour over the pulled meat and refrigerate until required.

To make the creamy polenta, place a saucepan over medium heat and add the milk and cream. Bring up to a simmer. While whisking continuously, add the polenta in a fine stream into the simmering liquid. Turn the heat down to low while you continue to whisk. As the polenta thickens, swap the whisk for a wooden spoon. Cook for 5–10 minutes.

Remove from the heat, then fold in the grated Parmesan and the butter. Season and keep warm.

Place the pulled braised oxtail in a saucepan and bring up to heat, stirring occasionally. To plate up, spoon out some creamy polenta into warm bowls. Top with the braised oxtail, then grate over liberal amounts of Parmesan. Serve now.

Roasted lamb shoulder with parsnip carrot hash and mint chimichurri

Roasted lamb with vegetables, peas, carrots, gravy and mint sauce will forever be near the top of the list when it comes to evoking wonderful eating memories of growing up. Mum's repertoire of evening meals was, like most 50 years ago, pretty stock standard. Hands down, roast was my favourite dinner. Served at least once a week, I never grew tired of eating it. The taste and texture of a good roast are its trump cards, but the delicious scent that permeates through the house as it cooks is also a thing of beauty. This recipe pays tribute to the past, but feels more like a nod to the future. I like that it remains relatively old-school in the sense that it is still a roast, but it's much lighter: gone are the gravy and the dripping-roasted vegetables. Instead, the lamb is flavoured with a spice rub, and a mint chimichurri offers up a depth of flavour and wonderfully cuts through the richness of the lamb. The carrots and parsnips are boiled, then mashed, then the hash is cooked in a skillet to caramelise and add the texture that traditional roasted vegetables bring to the table. I love the simplicity of this dish.

Serves 6

LAMB SHOULDER
1 lamb shoulder, bone in
¼ cup (60 ml/2 fl oz) canola oil, plus 2 tablespoons
2 tablespoons fennel seeds, roughly ground
2 tablespoons ground sumac
1 tablespoon flaky sea salt
1 teaspoon ground black pepper

MINT CHIMICHURRI
1½ cups (30 g/1 oz) mint leaves
1 cup (30 g/1 oz) parsley leaves
⅓ cup (25 g/1 oz) oregano
2 garlic cloves
1 tablespoon cumin seeds, toasted and ground
pinch dried chilli flakes
100 ml (3½ fl oz) olive oil
50 ml (1¾ fl oz) red wine vinegar
1½ teaspoons sugar
flaky sea salt and freshly ground black pepper

PARSNIP CARROT HASH
1 kg (2 lb 4 oz) parsnips, peeled and sliced
1 kg (2 lb 4 oz) carrots, peeled and sliced
⅓ cup (80 ml/2½ fl oz) canola oil
80 g (2¾ oz) butter

Preheat your oven to 180°C (350°F).
    Take the lamb shoulder and coat with the 2 tablespoons of canola oil. Mix the ground fennel seeds, sumac, salt and pepper together in a small bowl. Now rub this spice mix into and all over the lamb shoulder.
    Pour the remaining canola oil into a roasting pan or oven tray, then add the lamb shoulder. Roast for 1 hour, then drop the temperature down to 160°C (315°F) and cook for a further 2 hours. Remove and let the lamb rest for at least 20 minutes.

To make the mint chimichurri, place all the ingredients in a food processor or blender and blitz to a wet paste consistency. Refrigerate until required.

Preheat your oven to 150°C (300°F).
    Add the parsnips and carrots to a saucepan, cover with water and season with salt. Place over high heat, bring up to the boil, then lower to a simmer and cook for about 25 minutes, until softened. Remove from the heat, drain, and spread out on an oven tray.

Place in the oven for 10 minutes to dry out the cooked vegetables.
    Remove the parsnips and carrots from the oven, and while still hot, roughly mash together. Season liberally with salt and pepper. If not using immediately, keep refrigerated.

To make the hash, place a large frying pan over medium-low heat. Once hot, add half the oil and half the butter. Spread out the mashed parsnip and carrot in the hot skillet and cook for 10–15 minutes, until crisp on the bottom. Prior to flipping the vegetables to crisp the other side of the hash, drizzle over the rest of the oil and dot with the remaining butter. Turn with a spatula and cook for a further 10 minutes. The hash should be golden and slightly crisp. Keep warm.

Carve and divvy out the lamb, along with the parsnip and carrot hash. Spoon over liberal amounts of the chimichurri. Serve just as is or with a simply dressed crisp green salad on the side.

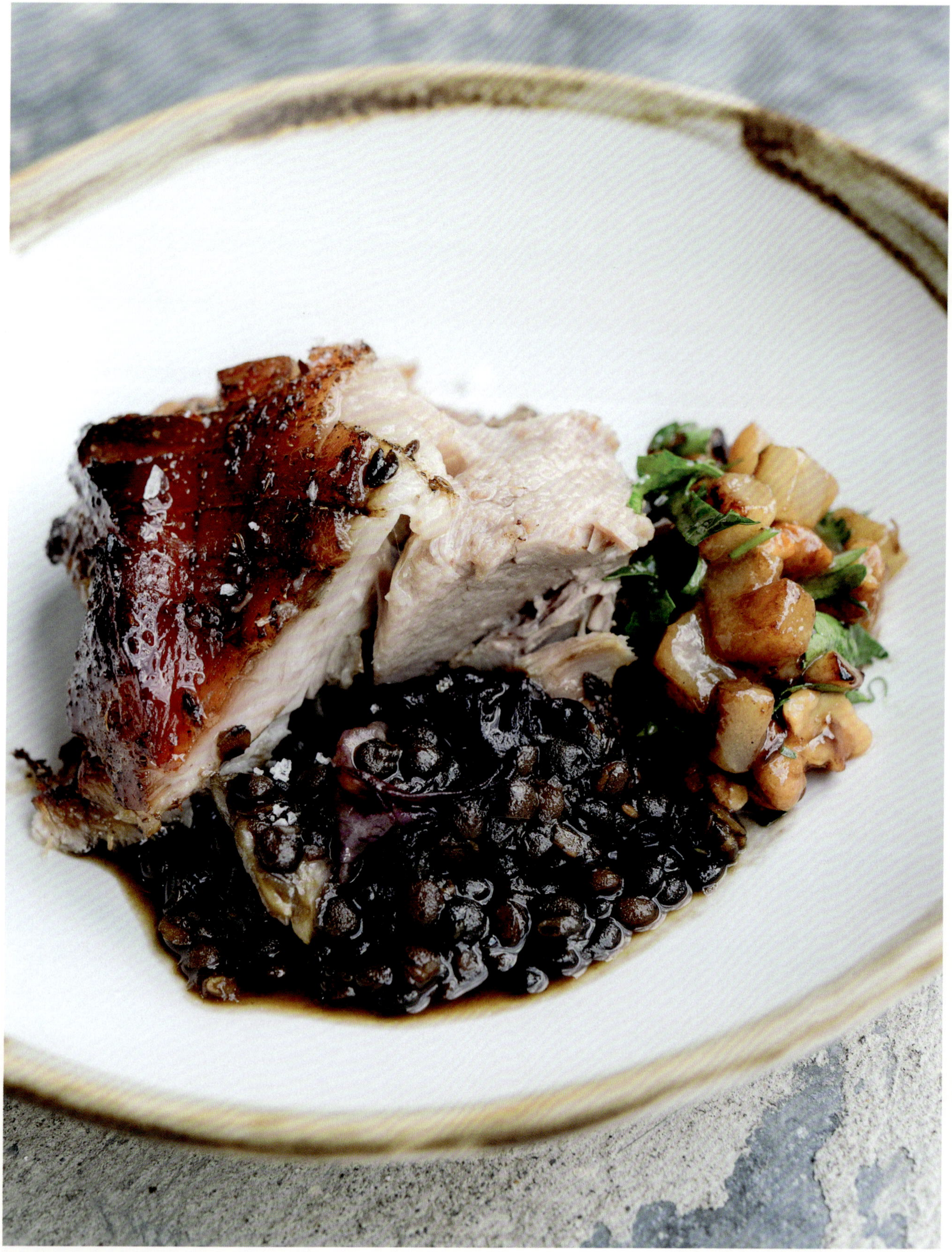

Braised pork shoulder with radicchio lentils, caramelised pear and walnut relish

In my mind, this is a winter Saturday- or Sunday-night dish. I say that as this is the kind of recipe that people who love to cook will get immense pleasure from. It's about spending the afternoon taking the time to enjoy the wonderful process of cooking something low and slow, when the most delicious of scents permeate the kitchen and intensify as the afternoon lengthens.

Prepare the radicchio lentils and the caramelised pear and walnut relish while the pork is cooking. Radicchio brings bitterness to the dish, which is balanced by the fresh pear and walnut relish. This fare deserves good-quality red wine, crusty bread and a simple green salad to round out the meal!

Serves 6

PORK SHOULDER
1 x 2.5 kg (5 lb 8 oz) boneless pork shoulder
1 tablespoon cumin seeds, toasted and ground
1 tablespoon fennel seeds, toasted and ground
½ teaspoon dried chilli flakes
1 tablespoon flaky sea salt
½ teaspoon freshly ground black pepper
finely grated zest of 2 lemons
¼ cup (60 ml/2 fl oz) cooking oil
1 cup (125 g/4½ oz) roughly chopped celery
1 cup (115 g/4 oz) roughly chopped carrot
2 cups (310 g/11 oz) roughly chopped onion
2 tablespoons picked and chopped thyme leaves
1½ cups (375 ml/13 fl oz) apple juice
3 cups (750 ml/6 fl oz) chicken stock
1 cup (250 ml/9 fl oz) beef stock
¼ cup (60 ml/2 fl oz) cider vinegar
¼ cup (60 ml/2 fl oz) runny honey

CARAMELISED PEAR AND WALNUT RELISH
⅓ cup (80 ml/2½ fl oz) sherry vinegar
2 tablespoons runny honey
1 teaspoon Dijon mustard
⅔ cup (170 ml/5½ fl oz) walnut oil (or half olive and half canola oil)
2 tablespoons cooking oil
3 firm, ripe pears, peeled and cut into 1 cm (½ in) dice
½ cup (50 g/1¾ oz) toasted walnuts, roughly chopped
¼ cup (7 g/¼ oz) roughly chopped flat-leaf parsley

RADICCHIO LENTILS
1½ cups (325 g/11½ oz) green lentils
6 cups (1.5 litres/52 fl oz) chicken stock
1 head radicchio, torn into pieces
flaky sea salt and freshly ground black pepper

Preheat your oven to 200°C (400°F).

Take the pork shoulder and score the skin in a criss-cross fashion with a sharp knife. (I keep a Stanley knife in my kitchen drawer for this exact purpose.) Place the pork in a large bowl, then add the cumin, fennel, chilli flakes, salt, pepper and lemon zest. Massage the ingredients all over the pork. Set aside.

Place a large cast-iron casserole dish or heavy-bottomed ovenproof pan over medium-high heat. Once hot, add the oil, along with the celery, carrot, onion and thyme. Cook the vegetables for 10 minutes or so, stirring occasionally, until dark and caramelised.

Now add the apple juice, stocks, cider vinegar and honey. Stir through, then top with the pork shoulder, skin side up. Place in the oven and cook, uncovered, for 30 minutes until the pork skin has started to caramelise. Now place the lid on the dish and turn the

Recipe continued overleaf...

oven down to 160°C (315°F). Continue to cook for 2½–3 hours. The pork shoulder is ready when it is tender and falls away when prodded.

Let cool for a bit, then carefully take the pork out of the cooking liquid. Cover with tinfoil to keep warm.

Strain off the cooking liquid from the vegetables. Reserve both.

To make the caramelised pear and walnut relish, place the vinegar, honey and mustard in a small saucepan over medium-high heat. Bring up to the boil and reduce for 2 minutes. Pour into a container, then take a stick blender and blitz while slowly drizzling in the walnut oil to form a thick and emulsified mixture. Set aside.

Place a non-stick frying pan over medium-high heat. Once hot, add the cooking oil, followed by the pears. Cook for about 5 minutes until the pears begin to caramelise. Remove and tip into a bowl. Let cool.

Add the toasted walnuts and parsley to the pears. Fold in just enough of the vinaigrette to dress the pear and walnut mixture. (Keep the rest for another day.) Leave the relish at room temperature or refrigerate until required.

To make the radicchio lentils, wash the lentils in a sieve, then place in a large saucepan. Add the reserved braising liquid from the pork, along with half the stock. Place over medium heat, bring up to the boil, then lower the heat to a rolling simmer. As the lentils absorb the stock, keep adding more until the lentils are soft to the bite but not falling apart, about 30–40 minutes.

Once you are happy with the texture, add a little more stock so it works as a loose sauce. Now add the radicchio and cook for a couple of minutes, until nicely wilted. Stir through the reserved pork-braised vegetables, then season to taste.

Bring the lentils up to heat, then ladle into warmed bowls. Carve or break up the pork shoulder into pieces, then place on top of the lentils. To finish off, spoon over the caramelised pear and walnut relish. Serve now.

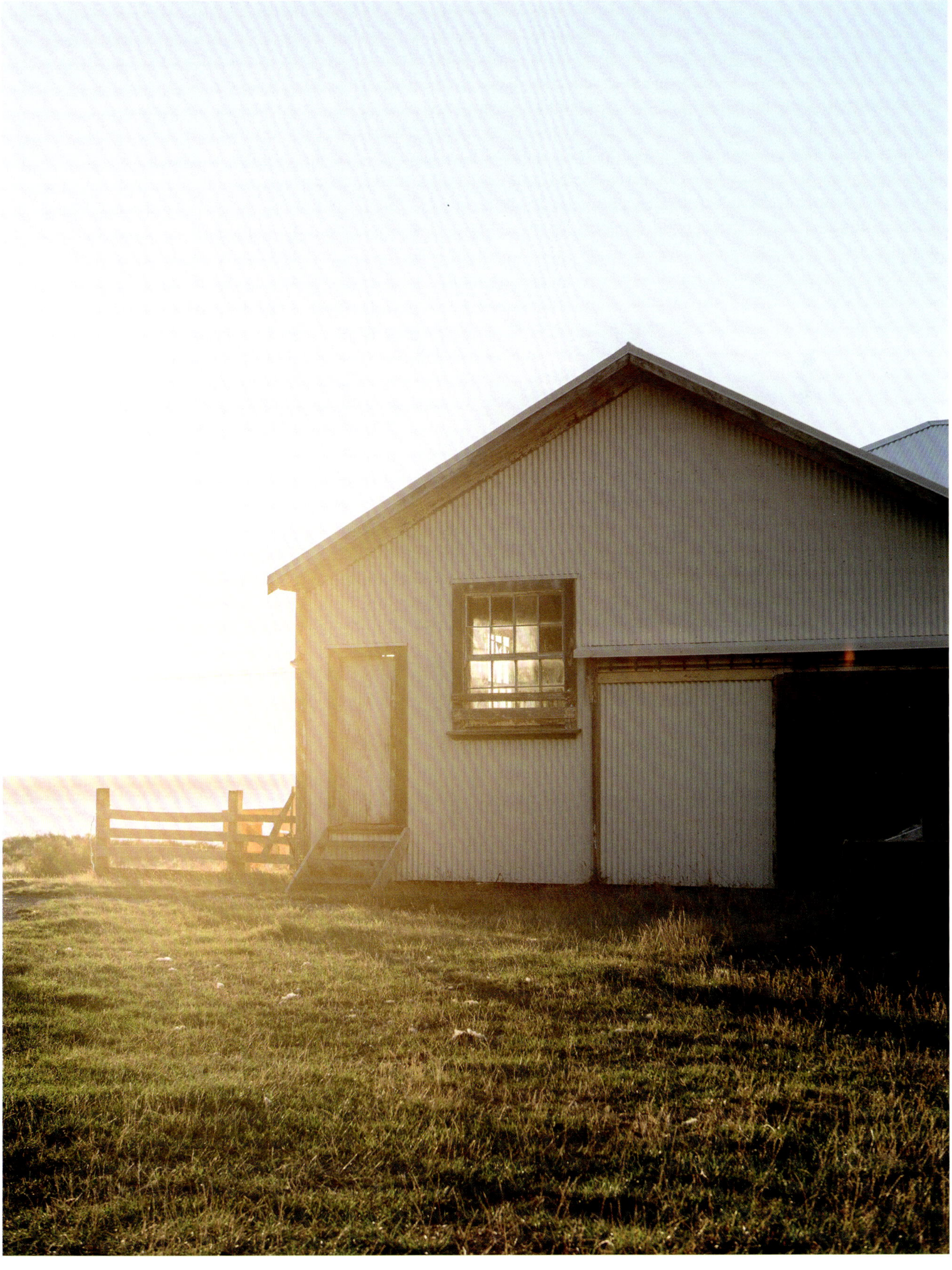

Roast leg of lamb with caramelised Brussels sprouts and crab-apple jelly

This is essentially the roast that I grew up on as a child, the only difference being that in winter I now roast Brussels sprouts as a side because I really enjoy the way they bring a slightly bitter, nutty and savoury component to the dish.

Serves 6 generously

LEG OF LAMB
2 onions, halved
2 celery stalks, halved
2 carrots, halved
⅓ cup (80 ml/2½ fl oz) dripping or cooking oil
3 tablespoons plain flour
1 x lamb leg, bone in
flaky sea salt and freshly ground black pepper

ROAST VEGE
2 parsnips, roughly chopped
¼ pumpkin, peeled and roughly chopped
2 medium kūmara, roughly chopped
4 medium carrots, roughly chopped
cooking oil

ROAST POTATOES
1 cup (250 ml/9 fl oz) canola oil
2 kg (4 lb 8 oz) Agria potatoes, peeled and halved or quartered if large

BRUSSELS SPROUTS
1 kg (2 lb 4 oz) Brussels sprouts
¼ cup (60 ml/2 fl oz) canola oil
flaky sea salt and freshly ground black pepper

GRAVY
3 tablespoons flour
⅓ cup (80 ml/2½ fl oz) red wine or port
1 tablespoon crab-apple jelly (page 431), plus extra to serve
1 cup (250 ml/9 fl oz) chicken stock or hot water
flaky sea salt and freshly ground black pepper
mint sauce or mint jelly (page 430), to serve

Preheat your oven to 200°C (400°F).
    Take a decent-sized roasting tray and spread the onions, celery and carrots on the base. Pour in the dripping or oil, sprinkle over 3 tablespoons of flour and place the leg of lamb on top. Season liberally with salt and pepper. Place in the oven and cook for 40 minutes, then turn your oven down to 160°C (315°F) and continue to cook for 2 hours. Remove from the oven and let the lamb rest on a chopping board for at least 20 minutes while you make the gravy.

Preheat your oven to 160°C (315°F).

For the roast vege, peel the vegetables and chop into your preferred size. Place the vegetables in a bowl. Pour over a little oil then season liberally with salt and pepper. Place a frying pan over medium-high heat. Add a few vegetables at a time, allowing them to caramelise before placing in an oiled dish. Roast in the oven for an hour, turning occasionally.

Now roast your potatoes. They turn out golden and crisp on the outside, and fluffy and light on the inside. Place the potatoes into a large saucepan and cover with cold salted water. Bring up to the boil, then simmer for about 8 minutes. They should be just getting soft around the outers of the potatoes. Remove and drain in a colander.

Place a roasting dish with 1 cup (250 ml/9 fl oz) canola oil in the oven for 5 minutes to get hot. Remove the dish, then carefully add the potatoes. Roast the potatoes for 45 minutes to an hour. Turn the potatoes with tongs a couple of times during the roasting period; they are ready when they are golden and crisp all over.

Start the Brussels sprouts when the roast vege are around halfway done. Preheat your oven to 180°C (350°F).

Take the Brussels sprouts and cut off the tough bottoms. With a sharp knife, score the bottoms by making a criss-cross in the stalk. Place in a bowl, add the canola oil and then toss with the salt and pepper.

Place a roasting dish in the oven for 5 minutes to heat up. Once hot, add the Brussels sprouts. Roast for 20–25 minutes, until golden and cooked through.

For the gravy, scoop out and discard all the well-cooked onions, celery and carrots from the lamb roasting tray. There will be heavily caramelised bits stuck to the bottom, which is all good. Pour off any excess oil or dripping, leaving around ¼ cup in the roasting tray. Place directly on the stovetop over low heat. Sprinkle in the flour and whisk to form a roux. Add the wine or port, crab-apple jelly and stock or water. Whisk continually to remove any of the roasted bits sticking to the bottom of the pan. Add more stock or water as you go, depending on the gravy consistency you like. Finally, strain through a sieve, taste and season accordingly, then pour into a jug and keep warm.

Personally, I like to serve a roast like this family-style with a bunch of platters and bowls and with everyone helping themselves. Make sure you warm the serving dishes and the plates. My only other go-to here would be a bowl of boiled peas with fresh mint, mint sauce or jelly, seasoning and a lick of butter.

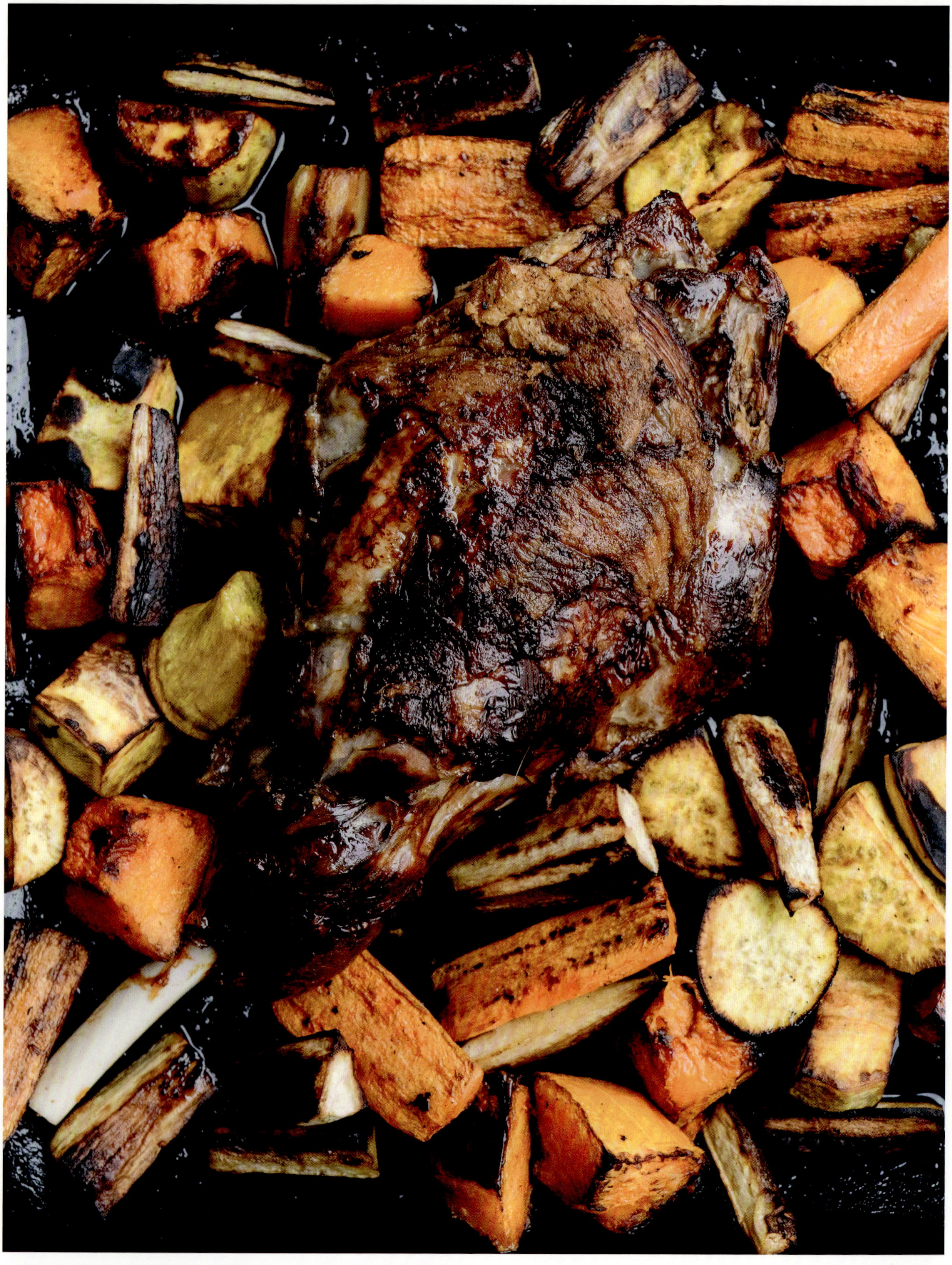

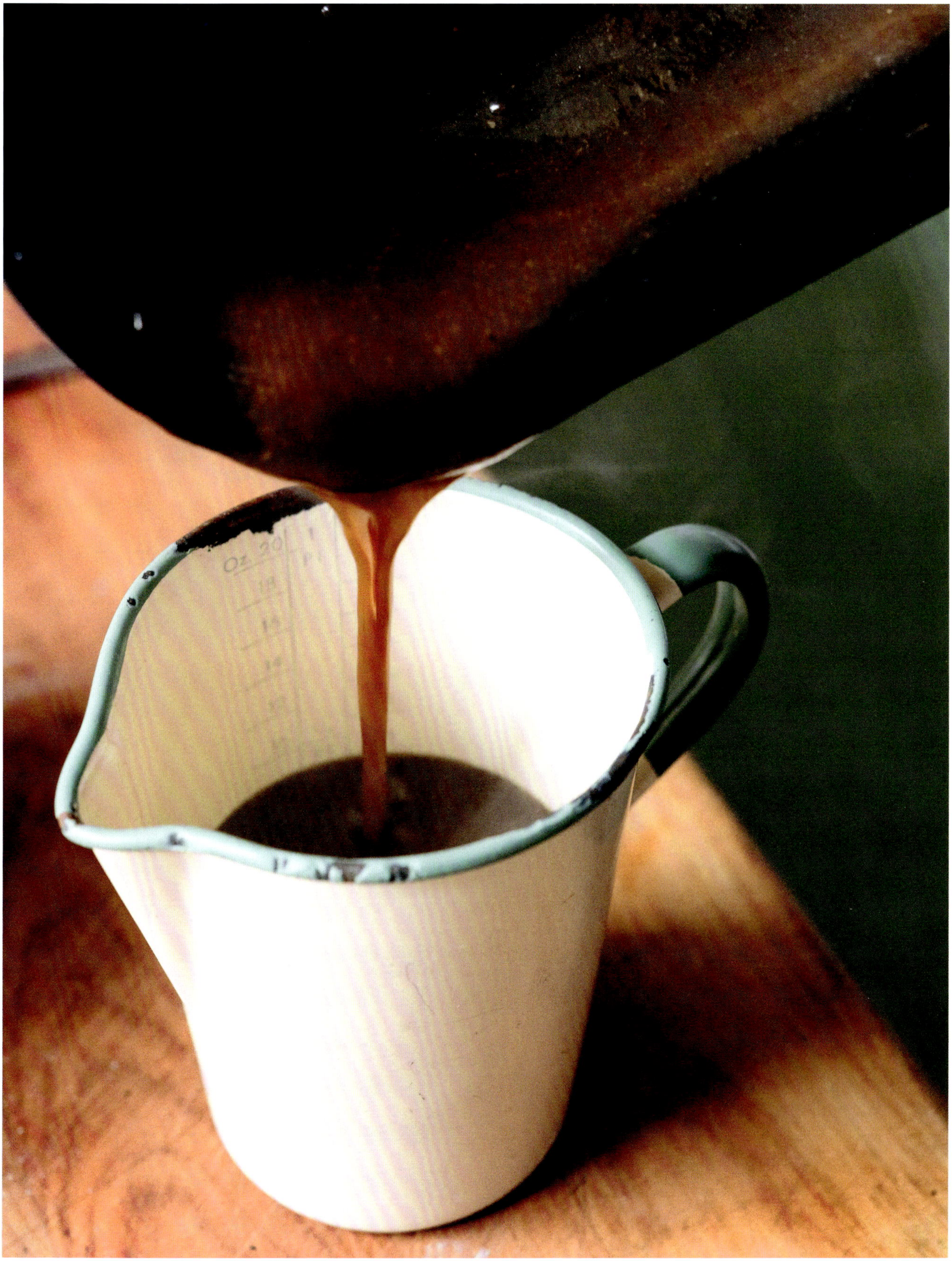

256   EAT UP NEW ZEALAND: THE BACH EDITION

Roasted pork knuckle with cream of caraway cabbage and caramelised apple

I adore these sorts of dishes: humble ingredients that offer up an eating pleasure often as delicious and even more satisfying than that of the expensive and popular. Ask your butcher for the front hocks from the pig, as they have a better meat-to-bone ratio and are even better value. You also might want to consider purchasing a Stanley knife for your culinary gadget drawer—they are perfect for scoring through tough pig skin when you want to create some legendary crackling action!

Serves 6

PORK KNUCKLE
3 x front shoulder pork hocks
flaky sea salt and freshly ground black pepper
cooking oil

CREAM OF CARAWAY CABBAGE
150 g (5½ oz) butter
3 cups (465 g/1 lb) finely diced onion
3 tablespoons whole caraway seeds
750 g (1 lb 10 oz) savoy cabbage (about ½ cabbage), finely sliced
⅓ cup (80 ml/2½ fl oz) chicken stock
1 cup (250 ml/9 fl oz) cream
200 g (7 oz) spinach, roughly chopped
flaky sea salt and freshly ground black pepper

CARAMELISED APPLE
3 Granny Smith apples, peeled
3 tablespoons sugar

TO SERVE
1 cup (250 ml/9 fl oz) gravy or jus (optional)

Preheat your oven to 200°C (400°F).

Take a sharp knife and score the thin pork skin that covers the hocks. Rub liberal amounts of salt and pepper into the cracks and all over the hocks. In a roasting dish, add a little cooking oil and about ½ cup (125 ml/4 fl oz) water.

Place the hocks in the oven and roast for 20–30 minutes, until the skin begins to bubble and crackle. Turn the oven temperature down to around 150°C (300°F). Cook for a couple of hours. The hocks are done when they are golden all over and the meat pulls away from the bone with little or no resistance.

Recipe continued overleaf...

To make the cream of caraway cabbage, place a large saucepan over low heat. Add the butter, onion and caraway seeds. Sweat gently for at least 20 minutes, stirring occasionally. You don't want any colour on the onion; it should just be translucent and soft. Turn the heat up to high and add the cabbage. Mix through with the onion, then add the stock. Keep stirring as the cabbage cooks down for 10–15 minutes. Again, you want the cabbage to soften and cook without any colour. Next, add the cream and the spinach. Once the spinach is wilted through, remove from the heat and ladle into a food processor or blender. Blitz until smooth, then pour back into the pan and season to taste. If not using immediately, refrigerate until required.

For the caramelised apple, place a frying pan over medium-high heat. Take the peeled apples and cut them into eighths. Place in a bowl with the sugar, then toss to combine.
    Add a little oil to the hot pan, add the pieces of apple and cook each side until golden and beginning to soften. Remove and keep warm.

If necessary, heat up the cream of caraway cabbage in a saucepan over low heat or in the microwave. Likewise, heat up the gravy or jus if using.
    Pull the pork hock meat and crackling away from the bone.
    Spoon a liberal amount of the cream of caraway cabbage onto warm plates, then top with pieces of the pork and crackling. Finish by adding the apple and, if using, pouring a little gravy or jus on and around. Eat now.

ANIMAL 259

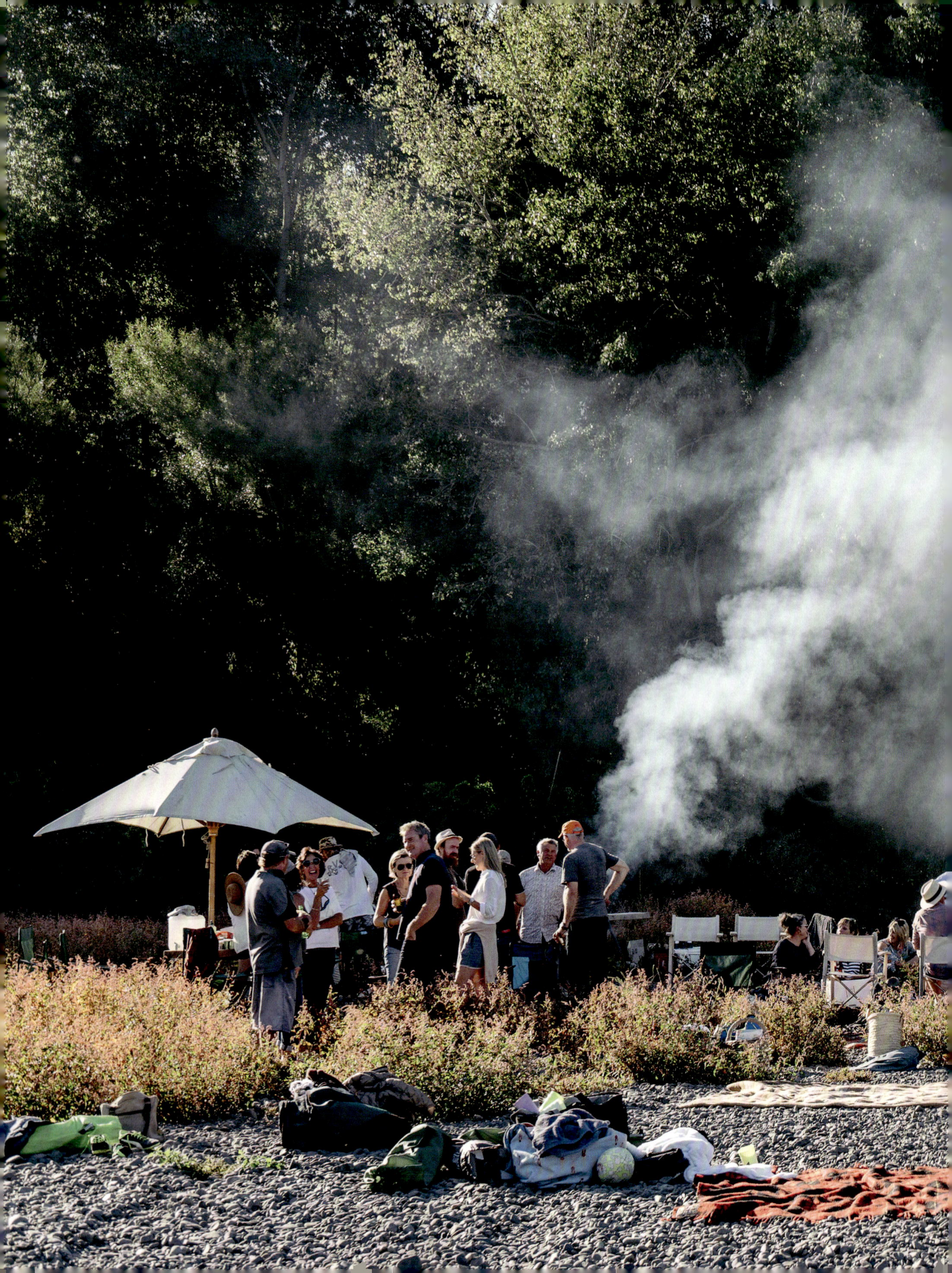

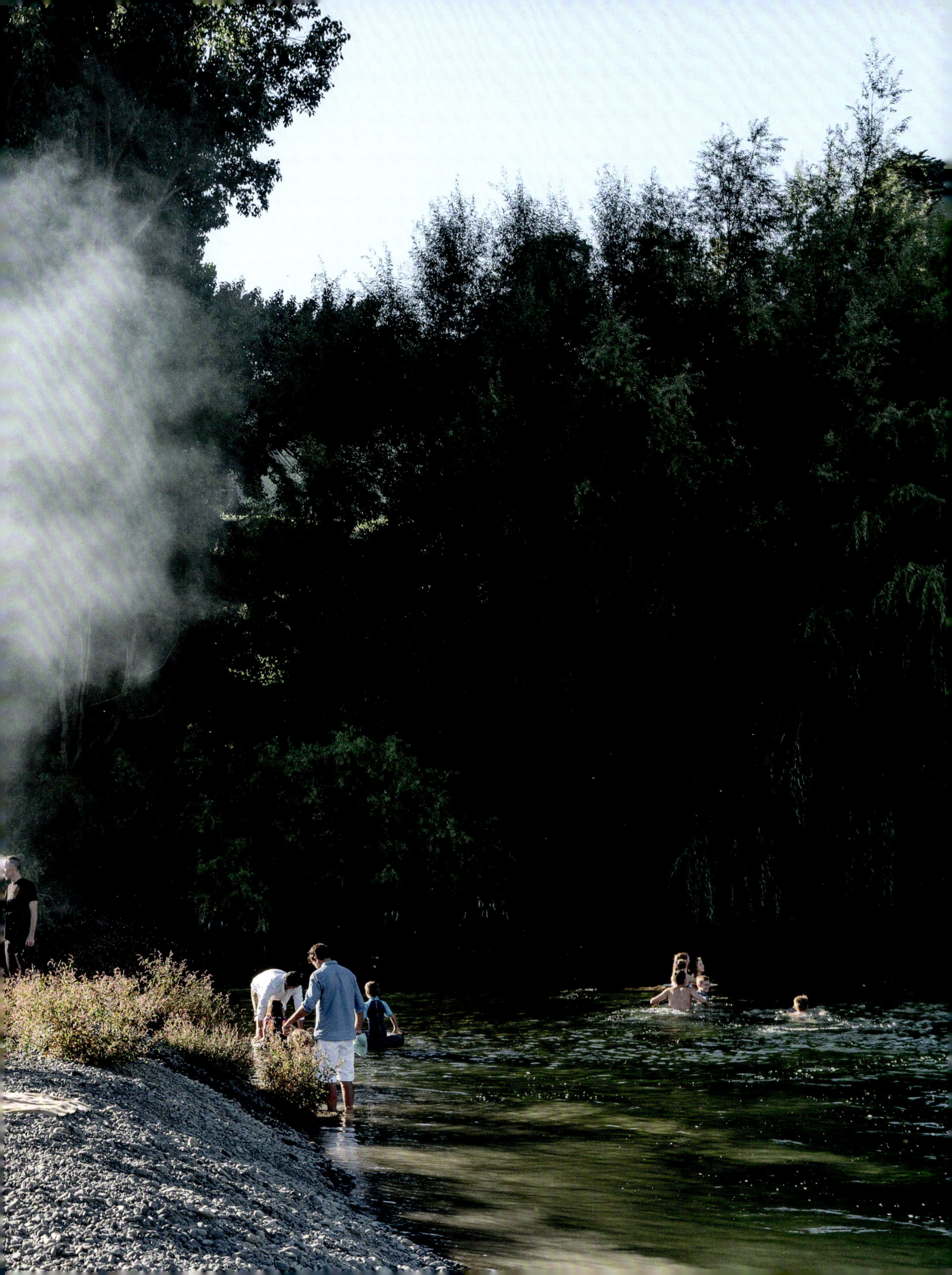

Smoked ham hock with mustard panna cotta and pickle vinaigrette

Ham and mustard are, for me, one of life's amazing culinary combos. Even as the weeks stretch into January, I never seem to tire of slowly working through the last of the champagne ham that got its first outing on 25 December. We are using smoked ham hock for this recipe, but I thought I'd mention Christmas ham as an option that would work equally well.

The mustard custard is a cracker; it's something I came up with years ago when I was engaged in developing menus for a certain airline out of Asia. You can use it as a separate component any time, or as a condiment for things like charcuterie, pâté and sausage, etc.

Makes 1 large or 6 small individual panna cotta

MUSTARD PANNA COTTA
1½ cups (375 ml/13 fl oz) cream
¼ cup (60 ml/2 fl oz) milk
¼ cup (60 g/2¼ oz) Al Brown Old Yella Habanero Mustard or Dijon mustard
1 teaspoon mustard powder
½ tablespoon sugar
1¾ gelatine leaves
1½ tablespoons lemon juice
flaky sea salt and freshly ground black pepper

SMOKED HAM HOCK
2 smoked ham hocks
1 carrot, roughly chopped
1 onion, roughly chopped
2 celery sticks, roughly chopped
2 bay leaves
8 peppercorns

PICKLE VINAIGRETTE
½ large green capsicum, finely diced
½ cup (70 g/2½ oz) finely diced gherkins
¼ cup (40 g/1½ oz) finely diced red onion
¼ cup (60 ml/2 fl oz) pickle juice
¼ cup (60 ml/2 fl oz) white vinegar
2 tablespoons sugar
¼ cup (60 g/2¼ oz) Al Brown Old Yella Habanero Mustard or Dijon mustard
¼ cup (60 g/2¼ oz) wholegrain mustard
1 cup (250ml/9 fl oz) canola oil
flaky sea salt and freshly ground black pepper

TO COOK AND SERVE
canola oil
flaky sea salt and freshly ground black pepper
fresh baguette or sourdough

To make the panna cotta, add the cream, milk, mustard, mustard powder and sugar to a suitable-sized saucepan and place over medium-low heat. Stir and bring up to a simmer, then remove from the heat.

Bloom the gelatine leaves in cold water, then stir through the mustard cream.

Set up an ice bath in a large bowl. Pour the mustard cream into a suitable-sized bowl and place it over the ice bath. Stir until it cools down to around room temperature. Now stir in the lemon juice and season with salt and pepper.

Divide the mixture into six dariole moulds, six small ramekins or one large ramekin (or similar). Place in the refrigerator to set for at least a couple of hours, or preferably overnight.

Place the ham hocks in a large saucepan. Add the carrot, onion, celery, bay leaves and peppercorns. Cover the ham hocks with cold water and place over high heat.

Once the ham hocks come up to the boil, turn down to a simmer, place the lid on the saucepan and cook for 2 hours or more. The hocks are ready when the meat pulls away from the bone with little resistance. Remove from the heat and strain off the vegetables, keeping the stock for soup or similar.

Once the hocks have cooled down enough to handle, with clean hands remove and discard the skin. Pull all the meat away from the bone. Place in a container and refrigerate until required.

To make the vinaigrette, place all the ingredients except the oil and the salt and pepper in a bowl. Mix together. Take a whisk and slowly drizzle in the oil, whisking continuously until all the oil is incorporated and emulsified. Taste and season accordingly with salt and pepper. Refrigerate until required.

If you've made six individual panna cotta, use a thin-bladed knife and run it around the inside edge of the moulds, letting air in so they release onto the centre of your serving plates. If you've made one large panna cotta you can either do the same or serve it in the ramekin.

Place a frying pan over medium-high heat and, once hot, add a little of the canola oil, followed by the pulled ham hock meat. Season with salt and pepper. Sauté for a minute or two to get some golden colour on the ham. Divide between the plates.

Finish by spooning some of the pickle vinaigrette over the warm ham, and serve with fresh or toasted bread. Eat now.

264　EAT UP NEW ZEALAND: THE BACH EDITION

ANIMAL 265

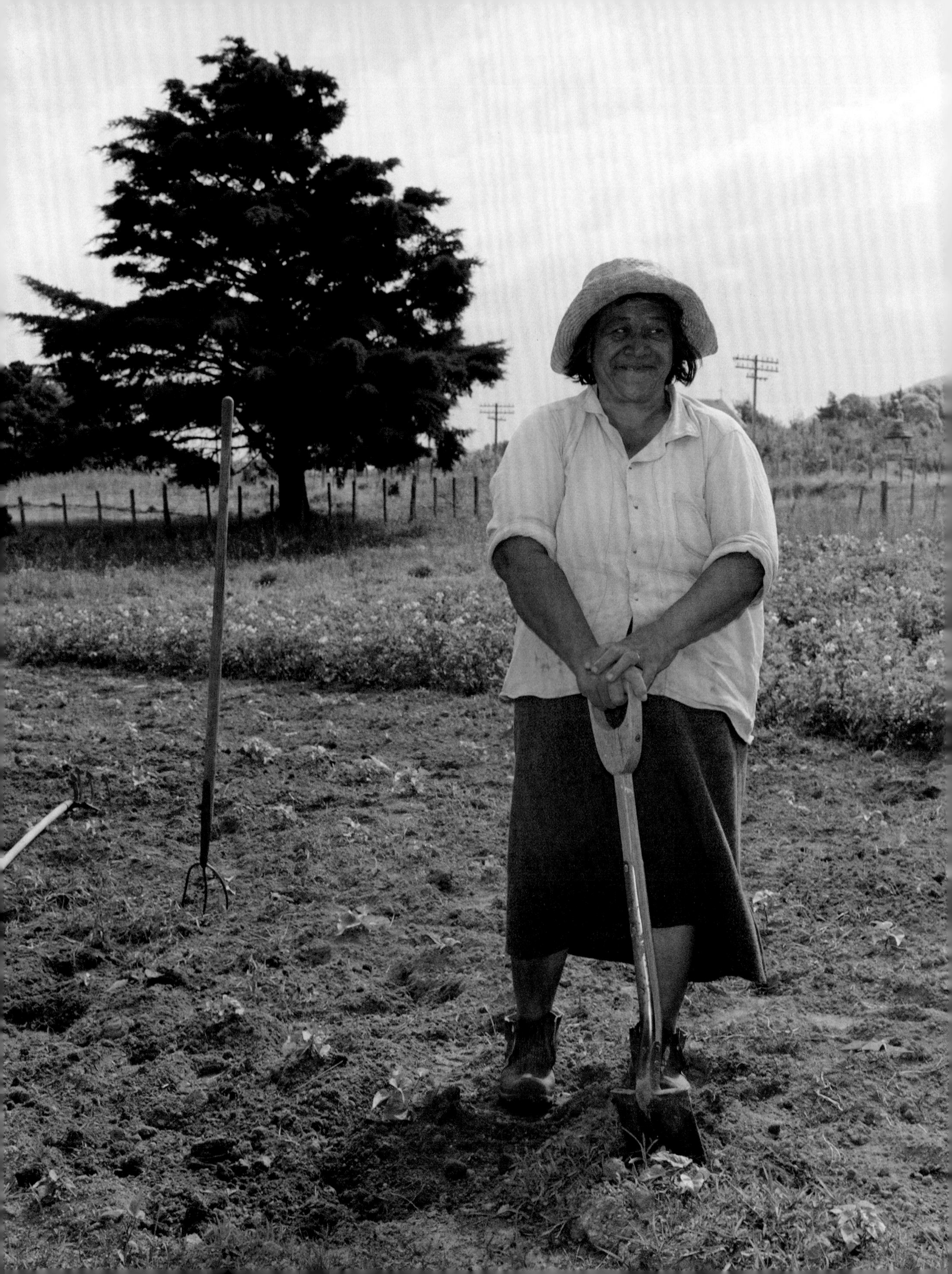

VEGE
HUAWHENUA

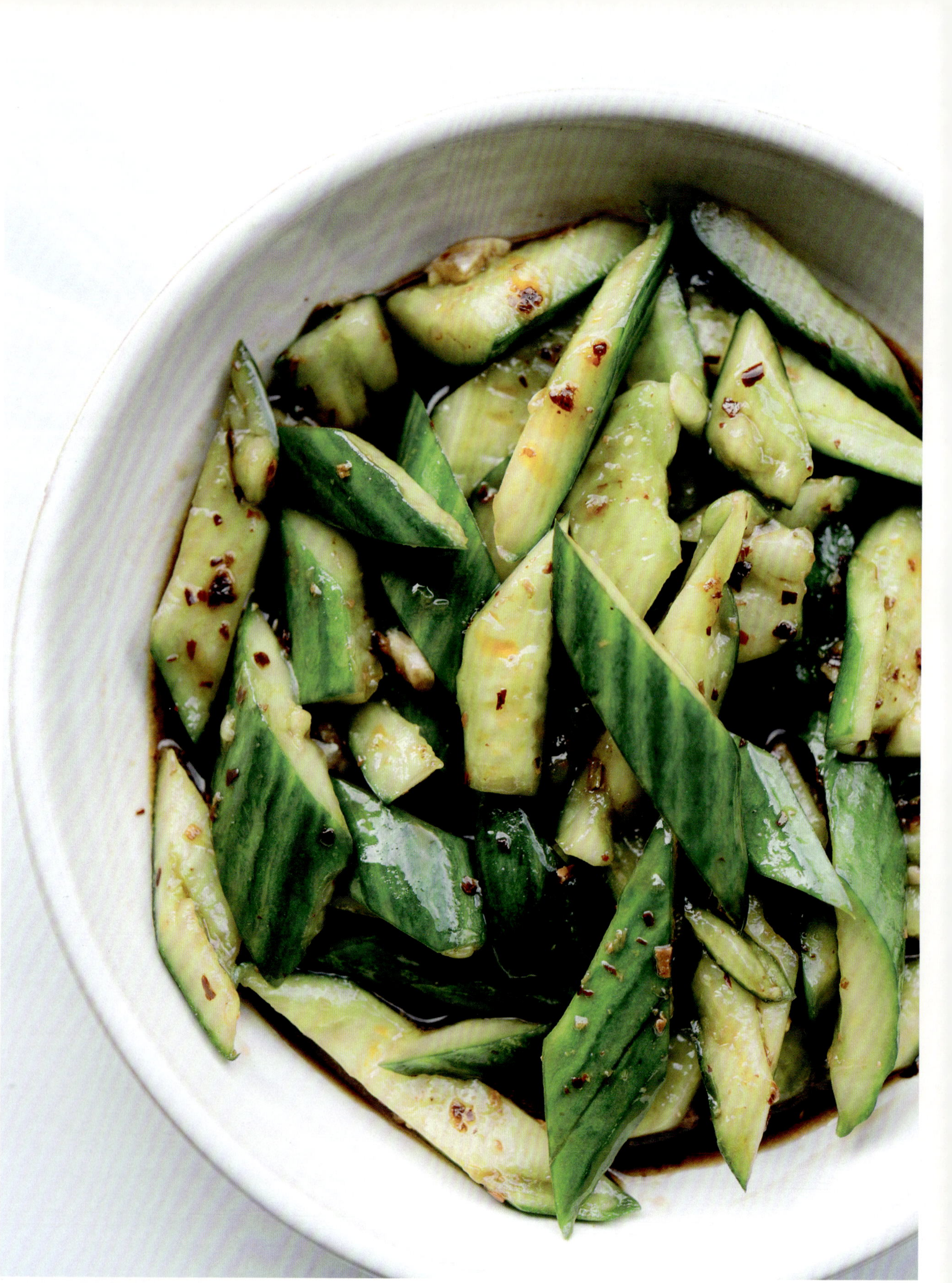

Smashed soy and chilli cucumber

This is a little starter dish that you often get variations of in restaurants in parts of China. It's such a fresh way to start a dinner, and great to dip into throughout the meal when the dishes start getting rich and complex. Do try it. It's simple to make and super crunchy and fresh.

Serves 6 as a side dish

600 g (1 lb 5 oz) cucumber (about 1½ telegraph cucumbers)
1 tablespoon flaky sea salt
1½ tablespoons sesame oil
2 tablespoons black vinegar or balsamic vinegar
2 tablespoons hot soy bean chilli paste
3 garlic cloves, finely chopped
1 teaspoon sugar
2 tablespoons soy sauce

Take the cucumbers and cut into thirds. Grab a large chef's knife and, using the flat of the blade, push down on the cucumbers. They will generally crack and split into three or four lengths. Scrap out the seeds and discard. Chop the cucumbers on an angle into bite-sized pieces. Place in a bowl with the remaining ingredients, and toss to combine. Refrigerate for 30 minutes.

Serve in a deep bowl with a bunch of chopsticks (or forks) on the side. Everyone loves smashed soy and chilli cucumber!

Oven-roasted kale with almond cream and dates

Kale seems to be the darling of the brassica world at present. It's a tough old green and, when boiling or steaming, it needs a decent amount of cooking time to render it soft enough to eat. For this relatively simple recipe, I have roasted it so it's cooked through but crunchy around the edges. The almond cream and chopped dates bring a decent richness to a vege once considered only winter cattle fodder!

Serves 6 as a starter

ALMOND CREAM
½ cup (45 g/1½ oz) blanched whole almonds, lightly toasted
1½ cups roughly chopped baguette, crust removed
1¼ cups (310 ml/10¾ fl oz) milk
1 garlic clove, finely chopped
1 teaspoon sherry vinegar
¼ cup (60 ml/2 fl oz) olive oil
pinch sugar
flaky sea salt and freshly ground black pepper

TO COOK AND SERVE
250 g (9 oz) kale
¼ cup (60 ml/2 fl oz) olive oil
flaky sea salt and freshly ground black pepper
1 cup (160 g/5½ oz) chopped dates
1 cup (155 g/5½ oz) paprika roasted almonds (page 446), roughly chopped
Al Brown & Co Orange and Chilli Infused Olive Oil or good-quality extra-virgin olive oil

To make the almond cream, soak the toasted almonds and bread in the milk for at least a couple of hours, preferably overnight.

Place the almond, bread and milk mixture into a food processor or blender. Add the garlic and vinegar, and blitz for a minute or two. Slowly add the olive oil, in a steady stream, until emulsified. Pass the almond cream through a fine sieve and discard any lumps. Season with the sugar, salt and pepper, and refrigerate until required.

Preheat your oven to 180°C (350°F).

Rip the kale leaves off the stalks and tear into largish pieces. Discard the stalks. Place the kale in a bowl, add the olive oil and toss, along with some seasoning. Spread out the kale on a roasting tray and place in the oven. Cook for approximately 10 minutes, until the kale is golden brown and crisp around the edges. Remove and let cool slightly.

To plate up, spread some of the almond cream on individual plates or one large platter. Spread the roasted kale over the almond cream. Finish by tossing over the chopped dates, paprika almonds and a good glug or two of olive oil. Eat now.

VEGE 271

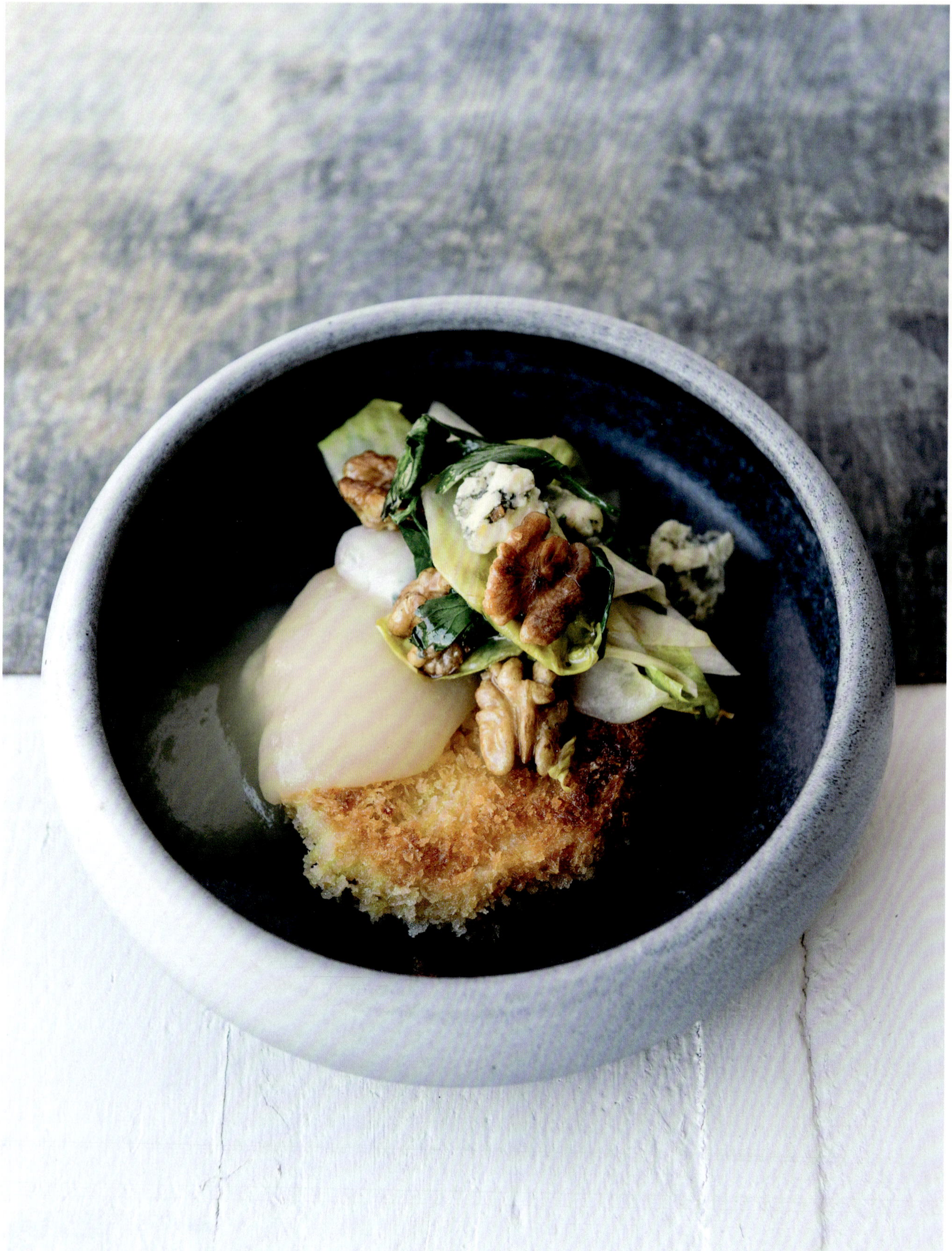

Crumbed celeriac with witloof, walnuts, blue cheese and apple sauce

This dish came out an absolute beauty. As it happens, often the image and taste of an idea in your head turns out to be disappointing in reality, but when we tested and ate this dish it actually delivered way more than we expected. Texturally, it's off the hook, but the layers of flavour seem to harmonise perfectly. The celeriac is soft in the centre but has the wonderful crunch from the panko crumb, the witloof and herbs bring a bitterness and freshness, the walnuts add a savoury nutty note, the blue cheese a richness, and the apple sauce brings sweetness and acidity to balance the whole dish.

Serves 6 as a side dish

APPLE SAUCE
3 Granny Smith apples, peeled, cored and diced
juice of 1 lemon
1 tablespoons sugar
1 cup (250 ml/9 fl oz) water

TO COOK AND SERVE
2 large celeriac
¼ cup (60 ml/2 fl oz) canola oil or other cooking oil, plus extra to brush
flaky sea salt
1 cup (250 ml/9 fl oz) water
1 cup (150 g/5½ oz) plain flour
2–3 eggs, beaten
2 cups (120 g/4¼ oz) panko breadcrumbs
¼ cup (60 ml/2 fl oz) extra-virgin olive oil
⅓ cup (40 g/1½ oz) walnuts
2 garlic cloves, finely chopped
2 witloof, core removed, cut into large slices
3 tablespoons cider vinegar
⅓ cup (10 g/¼ oz) chopped flat-leaf parsley
¼ cup yellow inner celery leaves
100 g (3½ oz) crumbled blue cheese

To make the apple sauce, place the ingredients into a small saucepan over medium-low heat, stirring occasionally, and cook for 20–30 minutes, until the apples are soft.

Remove from the heat and, using a stick blender or food processor, blitz to a smooth purée. Refrigerate until required.

Preheat your oven to 200°C (400°F).

Take the celeriac and cut off the tops and the gnarly bases, then peel. With a sharp knife, slice the celeriac into 1.5 cm (½ in) rounds. Brush with the canola oil and season liberally with salt. Place in a roasting tray, then add the water. Cover with tinfoil and

Recipe continued overleaf...

cook for approximately 40 minutes, until the celeriac is soft through and all the liquid has been absorbed. Remove and let cool.

Bread the rounds. Set up your crumbing station with the flour, egg and breadcrumbs in separate bowls. Dredge the rounds in the flour first, followed by the eggs and lastly coat with breadcrumbs. Place on a tray and refrigerate until required.

Preheat your oven to 100°C (200°F).

Place a frying pan over medium heat. Once hot, add enough cooking oil to shallow-fry the crumbed celeriac rounds. Cook for a minute or two on either side until golden. Remove and drain on a roasting tray lined with kitchen paper and place in the oven to keep warm.

Now place a non-stick frying pan over medium-low heat. Once hot, add the olive oil, followed by the walnuts. Move the walnuts around the pan until they take on a little colour, then add the garlic. As soon as the garlic begins to caramelise, add the witloof. Pour in the vinegar and toss to incorporate, then add the parsley and inner celery leaves. Toss again, remove from the heat and add the crumbled blue cheese.

To plate, place down a circle of the crisp celeriac, add a dollop of cold apple sauce, then top with some of the witloof, walnuts and blue cheese. Eat now.

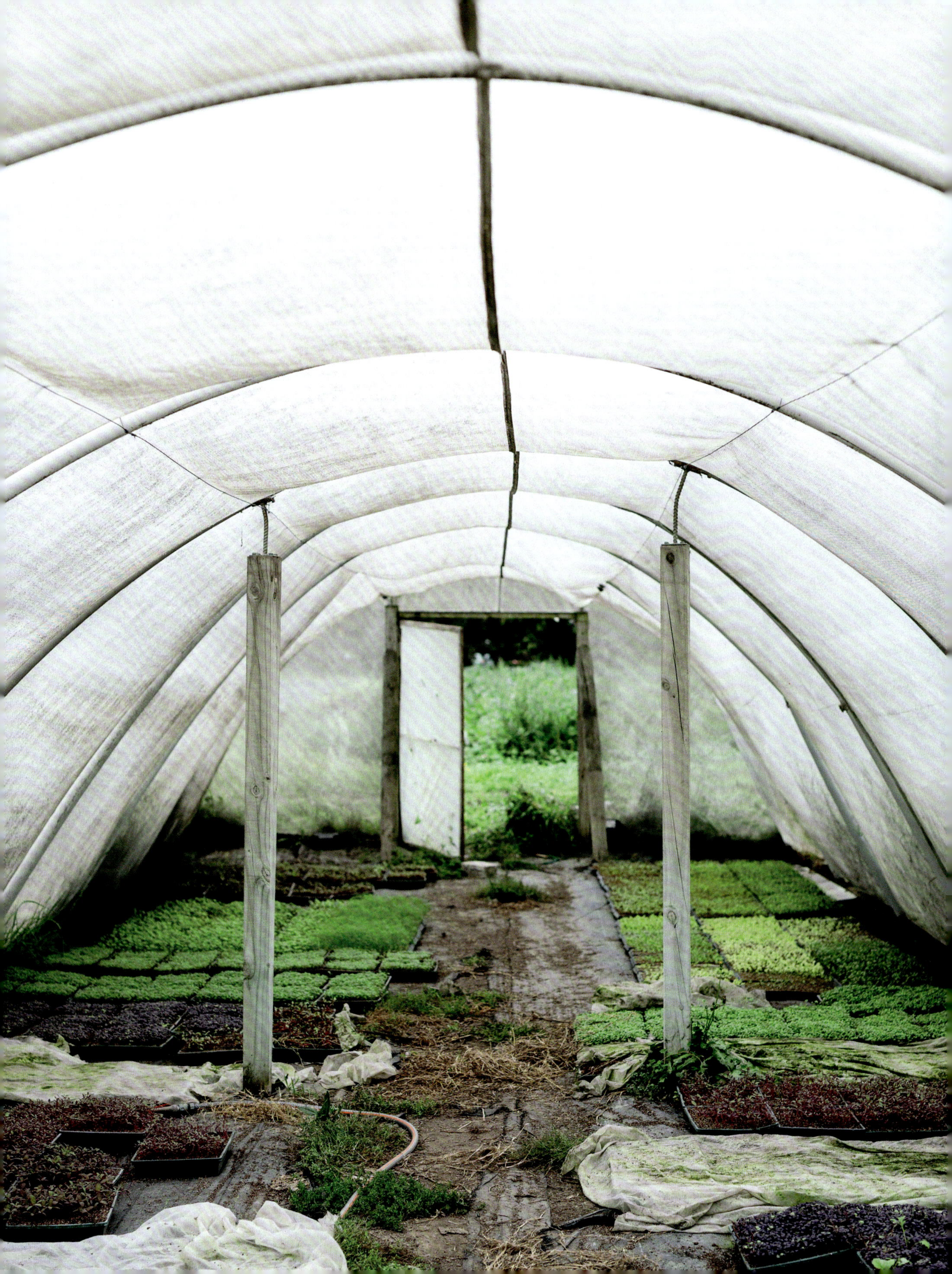

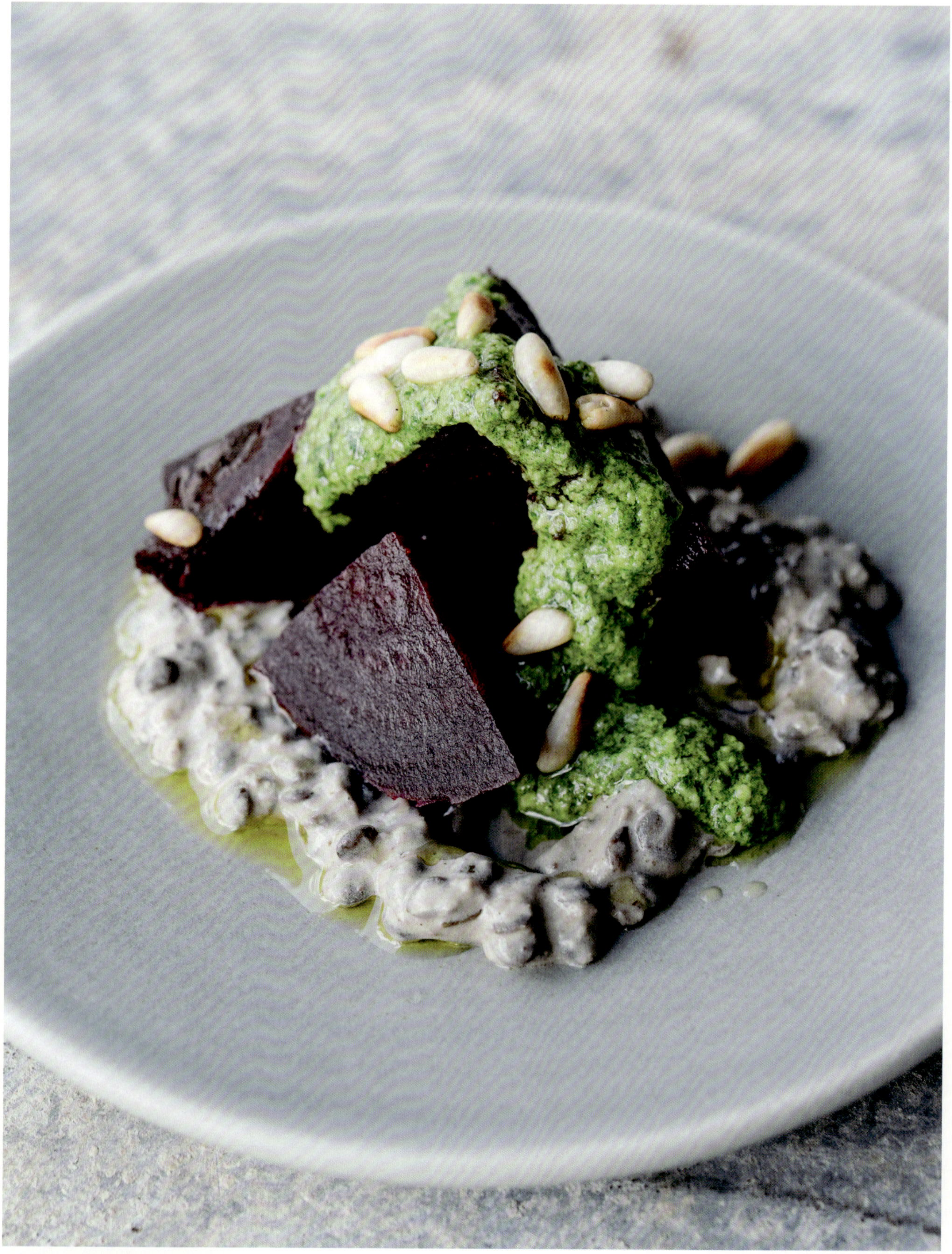

Beetroot and pesto on spiced yoghurt lentils

This is a terrific little salad or side dish. Basil and beetroot are a great combo, and the creamed lentils made with yoghurt and a bit of spice offer up a fragrant earthiness that complements the sweetness of the beetroot and the freshness of the pesto beautifully.

Serves 6 as a side dish

BEETROOT
1 kg (2 lb 4 oz) beetroot
½ cup (125 ml/4 fl oz) water
¼ cup (60 ml/2 fl oz) cooking oil
flaky sea salt and freshly ground black pepper

BASIL PESTO
1½ cups (75 g/2¾ oz) picked basil leaves
⅓ cup (50 g/1¾ oz) toasted pine nuts
⅓ cup (35 g/1¼ oz) grated Parmesan cheese
2 garlic cloves, finely chopped
2 teaspoons sugar
3 tablespoons lemon juice
½ cup (125 ml/4 fl oz) olive oil
flaky sea salt and freshly ground black pepper

CREAMED LENTILS
1½ cups (280 g/10 oz) dried green lentils
flaky sea salt
1 cup (250 g/9 oz) plain natural yoghurt
1 teaspoon toasted and ground cumin seeds
1 teaspoon toasted and ground fennel seeds
1½ tablespoons lemon juice
⅓ cup (80 ml/2½ fl oz) olive oil
freshly ground black pepper

TO SERVE
¼ cup (40 g/1½ oz) toasted pine nuts
extra-virgin olive oil, to drizzle

Preheat your oven to 180°C (350°F).
  Place the beetroot in a small roasting dish, add the water and cooking oil, season, then cover with tinfoil and roast in the oven for an hour or more until the beetroot are soft through to the centre. Remove and let cool, then peel off the skins. Cut into pieces of your desired size and refrigerate until required.

To make the basil pesto, place the ingredients in a tall jar or similar. Blitz with a stick blender until smooth. Taste and season accordingly, and refrigerate until required.

For the creamed lentils, place the lentils in a large saucepan and cover with water. Add a little flaky sea salt. Place pan over medium-high heat. Once it boils, turn the heat down to a rolling simmer and cook, stirring occasionally, for 30 minutes. Keep an eye on the water level and add more if the lentils are looking dry. The lentils are cooked when they are soft to the bite but holding their shape. Drain and let cool completely.
  Once the lentils are cold, stir in the yoghurt, spices and lemon juice. Take out about half of the lentils, place in a bowl and blitz using a stick blender so the mixture becomes kind of smooth but whole lentils are still visible. Add the puréed lentils back into the rest. Stir through the olive oil, then taste and season with salt and pepper. Refrigerate until required.

To serve, place the creamed lentils on a platter or individual plates. Top with the roasted beetroot, spoon over some basil pesto, then scatter with the pine nuts. Pour over a little extra-virgin olive oil to finish. Eat now.

Crisp Parmesan-crumbed globe artichokes

Available fresh from October through to January, globe artichokes are considered by most as quite a delicacy. They are such a beautiful-looking vegetable, but are quite a lot of work for a relatively humble result. It you are time-poor, there are quite a few canned or jarred artichokes out there at good delis that would work equally well.

Serves 6 as a pass-around

10 large globe artichokes
4 lemons
1 cup (150 g/5½ oz) plain flour
3 eggs, beaten
1 cup (60 g/2¼ oz) panko breadcrumbs
1 cup (100 g/3½ oz) grated Parmesan cheese
cooking oil, for frying
mayonnaise, to serve

To prepare the artichokes, use a sharp knife to cut off the top half of the bulb and peel the stem to remove the fibrous outer layer. Place the prepared artichokes in a large saucepan and cover with salted cold water. Halve two lemons and add those to the pan. Place a plate over the artichokes to weigh them down and keep them submerged in the water. Place the pan over high heat and bring up to a boil, then simmer for 40 minutes, or until the stems and hearts are tender.

Drain and allow to dry in a colander. Once cool enough to handle, remove the leaves and the inner thistle choke with a spoon or similar, and discard. Using a sharp knife, quarter the artichoke hearts. If not using within a day or two, place the artichokes in a bowl and cover with oil. Refrigerate until required.

Place a cast-iron pan or similar heavy-bottomed pan over medium-low heat. Set up your breading station: flour on a plate, beaten eggs in a bowl and combine the breadcrumbs and grated Parmesan in another bowl. Dip the quartered artichokes in the flour, followed by the eggs, then finally the Parmesan breadcrumb mixture.

When the pan is up to heat, add a little oil, then carefully add the crumbed artichokes, a few at a time. Cook for a minute or two on each side, removing when golden and crisp. Remove and repeat with the remaining breaded artichokes.

Serve with a little mayo on the side for dipping and some lemon wedges for squeezing.

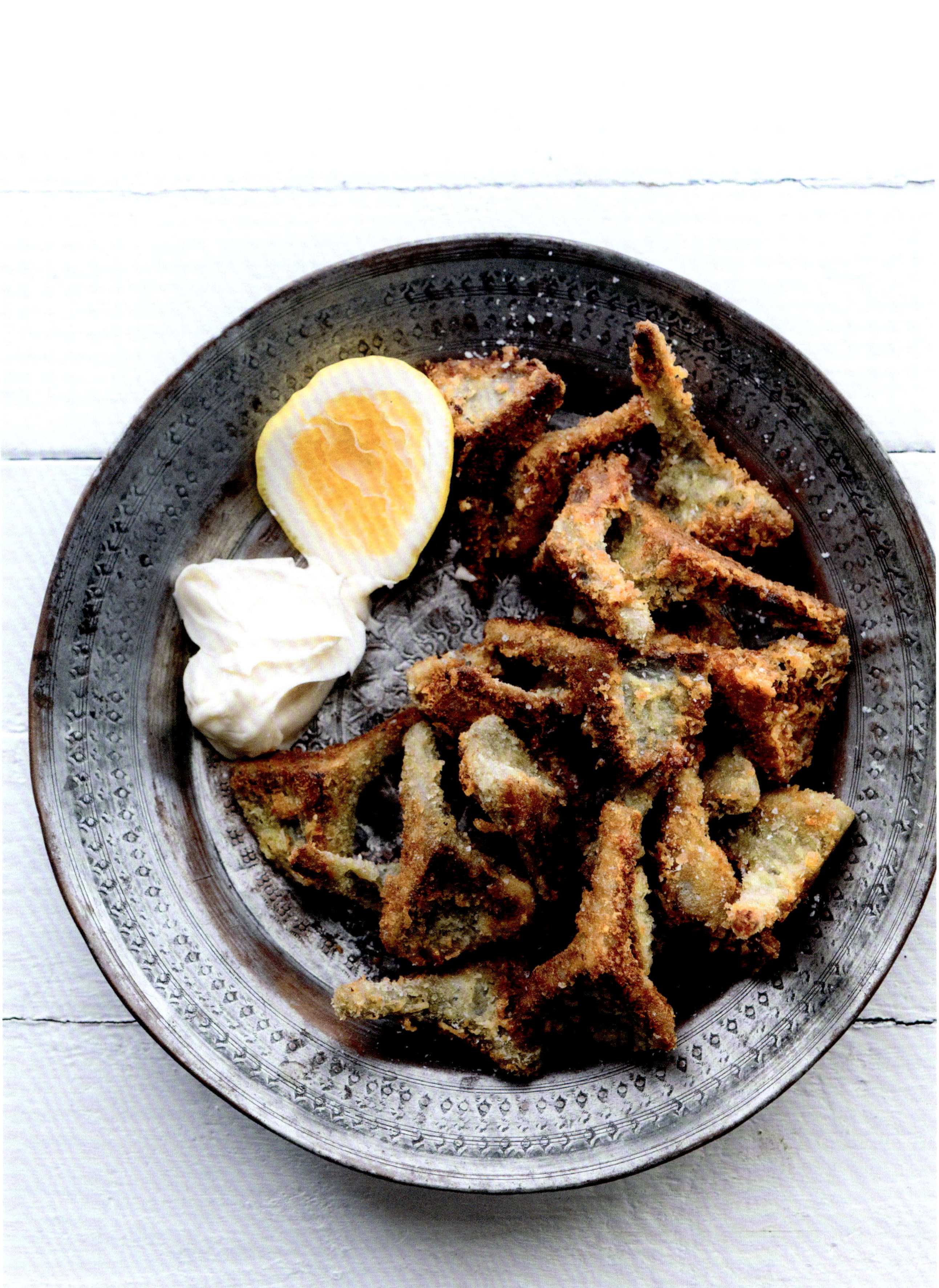

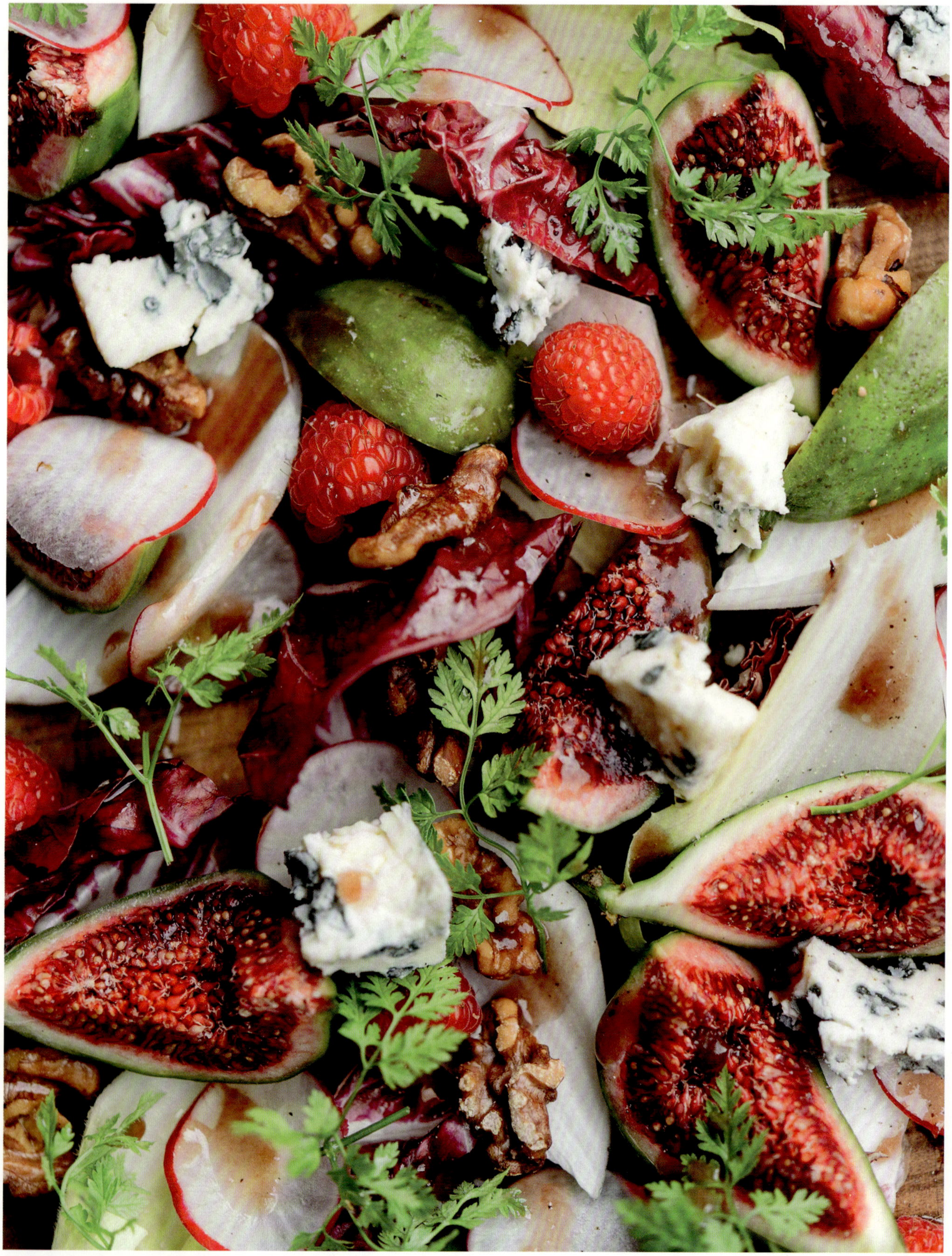

Fig, raspberry and blue cheese salad

I think autumn is probably my favourite season. I'm definitely a cooler season sort of guy. Lighting fires, shorter daylight hours, hunkering down and embracing the slow-cooking times ahead appeals to me. It's also the time of year when the fruit on offer always feels so exotic, with such unique flavours and fragrances. Feijoas, quinces, persimmons and tamarillos are all fruits that signal autumn is upon us. It's also time for figs. What many people don't realise is that autumn also produces a small late flush of beautiful raspberries into the market. It's like the last tangible link to summer before the days shorten and winter takes hold.

Serves 6 as a starter

RED WINE VINAIGRETTE
⅓ cup (80 ml/2½ fl oz) good-quality red wine vinegar
¼ cup (50 g/1¾ oz) finely diced shallots
1½ tablespoons sugar
1 teaspoon Dijon mustard
1 cup (250 ml/9 fl oz) walnut oil
flaky sea salt and freshly ground black pepper

SALAD
8 fresh figs, quartered
1 punnet raspberries (approx. 1 cup/125 g/4½ oz)
1 small radicchio, ripped into pieces
2 witlof, sliced
2 radishes, finely sliced
½ cup (50 g/1¾ oz) toasted walnuts
100 g (3½ oz) crumbled blue cheese
4 stems chervil
walnut oil, to serve

To make the red wine vinaigrette, place the vinegar, shallots, sugar and mustard in a small saucepan over high heat. Bring up to the boil, then remove and pour into a jug-like container. Take a stick blender and blitz the vinegar mixture. With the motor running, slowly drizzle in the walnut oil until combined and emulsified. Season to taste with salt and pepper. Refrigerate until required.

Arrange the figs, raspberries, radicchio, witlof and radish on a platter or individual plates. Top with the walnuts and blue cheese, then spoon over a little red wine vinaigrette and drizzle with a liberal amount of walnut oil. Garnish with picked chervil leaves. Serve the salad with extra red wine vinaigrette on the side. Eat now.

Fresh porcini and Swiss cheese toasties with truffle salt

There is a network of porcini mushroom gatherers out there, mainly in the South Island, and I have been lucky enough to tap into a couple of these secretive clans over the years. If you still like the sound of these decadent toasties, but don't have access to these extraordinary porcini mushrooms, just use store-bought portobello mushrooms, which make a decent substitute. Truffle salt can be purchased at most good delis and food stores.

Makes 6

PORCINI MUSHROOMS
canola oil, for frying
2 garlic cloves, finely diced
1 tablespoon finely chopped thyme leaves
500 g (1 lb 2 oz) fresh porcini mushrooms, thinly sliced
30 g (1 oz) butter
½ cup (15 g/½ oz) roughly chopped flat-leaf parsley
flaky sea salt and freshly ground black pepper

TO COOK AND SERVE
12 slices toast-slice white bread, buttered on one side
12 liberal slices Swiss or Gruyère cheese
truffle salt (optional)

Place a frying pan over medium heat. Once hot, cook the mushrooms in a few batches. Add a small amount of oil, followed by some of the garlic and thyme. Add some of the mushrooms. Cook for a couple of minutes until the mushrooms are golden.

Just prior to removing from the pan, add a knob of butter and some of the chopped parsley and season with salt and pepper. Toss to combine, then with a slotted spoon remove the mushrooms and place on a plate lined with kitchen paper. Wipe out the pan and repeat with the remaining garlic, herbs and mushrooms. Set aside.

Heat up your toastie machine or place a non-stick frying pan over medium heat.

Lay six slices of the buttered bread, buttered side down, on a clean surface or chopping board. Divvy up the mushrooms, then top with a couple of slices of cheese. Sprinkle liberal amounts of the truffle salt over the cheese, then top with the remaining slices of bread, buttered side up.

Toast your toasties until golden brown and crisp on both sides and the cheese is melted. Remove, keep warm and cook the remaining toasties.

Slice in half and serve now.

VEGE 283

284 EAT UP NEW ZEALAND: THE BACH EDITION

Mock eel

This is a crazy-delicious vegetarian dish that was served to me by a dear chef friend at her very hip and cool restaurant, Kings County Imperial in New York. Tracy Jane Young and her business partner, chef Josh Grinker, cook traditional Chinese cuisine but serve it in an uber-cool space down a side street in Williamsburg. Please check it out if you're in that great city; you won't be disappointed. This was the first dish Tracy served up, and it blew my mind. The only association with eel is actually the look. Tracy told me that the Chinese have a tradition of mimicking animal protein with vegetables or vegetable protein. I love this dish. It's savoury, sweet, salty and also a little crunchy.

Serves 6 as a starter

MUSHROOMS
100 g (3½ oz) dried shiitake mushrooms

TO COOK AND SERVE
4–8 cups (1–2 litres/35–68 fl oz) canola oil, plus 1½ tablespoons
1½ teaspoons finely chopped ginger
1½ teaspoons finely chopped garlic
1 red chilli, finely sliced on the diagonal
2 spring onions, sliced on the diagonal
cornflour, for dusting
1 tablespoon soy sauce
1 tablespoon hoisin sauce
1 tablespoon sugar
⅓ cup (80 ml/2½ fl oz) chicken stock
1 teaspoon sesame oil
½ tablespoon toasted sesame seeds, to serve

Place the shiitake mushrooms in a bowl and cover with boiling water. Let sit for 30 minutes to rehydrate. Drain.

Take the rehydrated mushrooms and squeeze out any excess water. With kitchen scissors, start at the outside lip of the mushroom and snip your way inwards in a spiral, creating a long eel-like strip around until you get to the stem. Discard the tough stem. Repeat with all the mushrooms and set aside.

Place a large non-stick frying pan or wok over medium-high heat. Once warm, add the 1½ tablespoons canola oil, followed by the ginger, garlic, chilli and half the spring onions. Sauté for a minute, until the ginger and garlic are golden but don't let them burn. Remove the pan from the heat.

Heat the remaining canola oil in your deep-fryer to 180°C (350°F). Alternatively, heat the oil in a heavy-bottomed saucepan. You can gauge this by adding a piece of bread to the oil; if it's at around 180°C, it will take about a minute for the bread to turn golden and crisp.

Place the thick strands of mushrooms in a bowl. Dust liberally with cornflour, then pat off any excess. Carefully drop into the hot oil and cook for 1–2 minutes, until crisp and golden. Drain on kitchen paper.

While the mushrooms are frying, place the pan with the ginger, garlic and chilli back over high heat and add the soy sauce, hoisin sauce, sugar, stock and sesame oil.

Toss the mushrooms through the sauce to cover. Pour into the centre of a serving plate and finish by garnishing with the remaining sliced spring onion and toasted sesame seeds.

Falafel with tomato kasundi, labneh and feta

My, have things changed regarding the vegetarian scene since I was a lad! I'm not quite ready to commit to veganism just yet, but I can understand why my daughter Connie and a good percentage of the world have dropped a large amount of meat from their diets. There is just so much more on offer these days—the huge variety of vegetables available, plus grains, legumes and nuts. This, coupled with the world's different cuisines, many of which revolve around a vegetarian diet, makes for some compelling eating. I adore well-made falafel. Texturally wonderful when paired with chutneys, relishes and yoghurt, they make for a satisfying side dish or a main meal. Super easy to make as well.

Serves 6–8 as a side dish

FALAFEL
1 kg (2 lb 4 oz) cooked chickpeas
3 eggs
juice of 3 lemons
1½ cups breadcrumbs
¼ cup (40 g/1½ oz) finely diced onion
½ cup (15 g/½ oz) finely chopped flat-leaf parsley
½ cup (20 g/¾ oz) finely chopped mint
1½ tablespoons cumin seeds, toasted and ground
1½ tablespoons coriander seeds, toasted and ground
pinch cayenne pepper
1 teaspoon sugar
flaky sea salt and freshly ground black pepper

TOMATO KASUNDI
1 cup (250 ml/9 fl oz) canola oil
½ cup curry leaves
3 tablespoons mustard seeds
2 teaspoons fenugreek seeds, toasted and ground
2 cups (310 g/11 oz) finely diced onions
⅓ cup finely diced garlic
½ cup finely diced ginger
1 red chilli, finely chopped
10 cardamom pods, toasted seeds only
2 tablespoons cumin seeds, toasted and ground
2 teaspoons ground turmeric
1½ cups (375 ml/13 fl oz) malt vinegar
1½ cups (330 g/11½ oz) sugar
4 x 400 g cans whole peeled tomatoes, crushed
flaky sea salt and freshly ground black pepper

TO SERVE
4–8 cups (1–2 litres/35–68 fl oz) cooking oil
1 cup (250 g/9 oz) labneh or plain natural yoghurt
⅔ cup (100 g/3½ oz) crumbled feta cheese
½ cup (15 g/½ oz) picked coriander leaves
extra-virgin olive oil

First, make the falafels. Place the chickpeas in a saucepan and cover with salted water. Place over medium heat and bring up to the boil. Remove and drain, then let the chickpeas cool for 5 minutes. Transfer to a food processor with the remaining ingredients, except the salt and pepper. Process until smooth and combined. Taste, then season with salt and pepper. If it tastes a little bland, add a bit more lemon juice. Mould your falafel mix into your desired shape and size, then refrigerate until required.

To make the tomato kasundi, place a heavy-bottomed saucepan over medium heat, add the canola oil and, once hot, add the curry leaves, mustard and fenugreek seeds. Stirring with a wooden spoon, cook for 30 seconds or so. Now add the onion, garlic, ginger, chilli, cardamom seeds, cumin and turmeric. Turn down the heat and sweat the vegetables for 10 minutes. Add the vinegar, sugar and crushed tomatoes, and simmer away for an hour or so, stirring occasionally. Once the mixture becomes jammy in consistency, season to taste and refrigerate until required, or pour into preserving jars.

Preheat your oven to 120°C (235°F).

Heat the cooking oil in your deep-fryer to 180°C (350°F). Alternatively, heat 3 cm of oil in a heavy-bottomed saucepan. You can gauge the temperature by adding a piece of bread to the oil; if it's at around 180°C, it will take about a minute for the bread to turn golden and crisp. Carefully add your falafel and fry, in batches, until golden and crisp, keeping the cooked falafel warm in the oven while you finish the rest.

To plate up, put a liberal amount of the tomato kasundi down on each plate and top with the hot crunchy falafel. Add a dollop of the labneh to each plate, then crumble over some feta cheese. Lastly, sprinkle over the coriander leaves and finish with a glug or two of extra-virgin olive oil. Serve now.

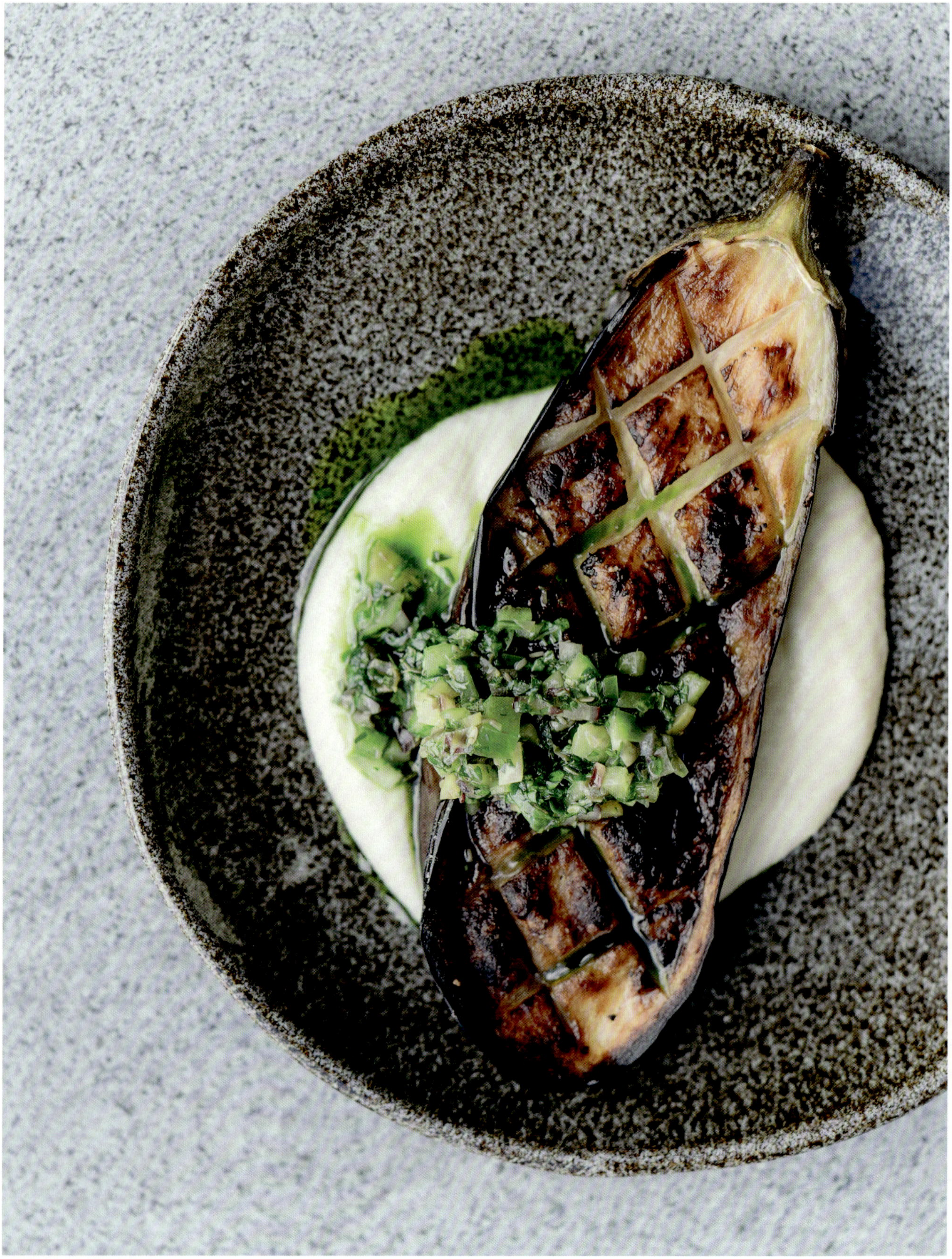

Roasted eggplant with creamed cauliflower and salsa verde

I look at this dish and it feels rustic and elegant at the same time. Serve this as a terrific side with a simple grilled steak or the like. Equally, it would be an impressive and simple dish to begin a meal with.

Serves 6 as a starter or side dish

CAULIFLOWER
½ head cauliflower
1¼ cups (310 ml/10¾ fl oz) cream
flaky sea salt and freshly ground black pepper

SALSA VERDE
1 green capsicum, finely diced
¼ cup (40 g/1½ oz) finely diced shallots
½ tablespoon finely minced garlic
2 tablespoons finely chopped capers
⅓ cup finely diced gherkins
1 tablespoon finely chopped anchovies (optional)
⅓ cup (10 g/¼ oz) finely chopped flat-leaf parsley
¼ cup (15 g/½ oz) finely chopped mint
¼ cup (15 g/½ oz) finely chopped basil
1 tablespoon finely chopped tarragon
finely grated zest of 1 lemon
2 tablespoons lemon juice
½ cup (125 ml/5½ fl oz) Al Brown & Co Lemon Infused Olive Oil or extra-virgin olive oil
½ tablespoon sugar
freshly ground black pepper

EGGPLANT
3 eggplant
extra-virgin olive oil, for brushing
flaky sea salt and freshly ground black pepper

Take the cauliflower and cut into medium-sized florets, complete with the stalk. Place in a saucepan and cover with cold salted water. Place over high heat, bring up to the boil, then simmer for 15 minutes until the cauliflower is soft. Drain, then return the cauliflower to the pan and add the cream. Place back on the heat and cook for another 5 minutes so the cream reduces slightly.

Pour into a blender (or use a stick blender) and process until silky-smooth. If it seems a little thick, add a bit more cream until you are happy with the consistency. Taste and season with salt and pepper. Let cool, then refrigerate until required.

To make the salsa verde, mix all the ingredients together in a bowl. Refrigerate for half a day to let the flavours blend and develop. Check the seasoning and add a little more lemon juice if you think it's required. (You can keep this in the refrigerator for up to a week.)

Preheat your oven to 180°C (350°F).

Take a cast-iron or other heavy-bottomed pan and place over high heat. Cut the eggplant in half, lengthways. Score the flesh in a 5 mm (¼ in) deep criss-cross pattern. Brush the eggplant halves with olive oil and season with salt and pepper. Once the pan is hot, place a couple of the eggplant halves in, flesh side down. Cook for 2 minutes, until the flesh has begun to caramelise.

Place the eggplant on an oven tray and repeat with the remaining eggplant halves. Now place the oven tray in the preheated oven and cook the eggplant for another 20–30 minutes, until super soft.

To serve, heat up the creamed cauliflower on the stovetop or in the microwave, and spoon a liberal amount onto the centre of warm plates. Top this with the caramelised roasted eggplant, then spoon over a generous amount of the salsa verde. Serve now.

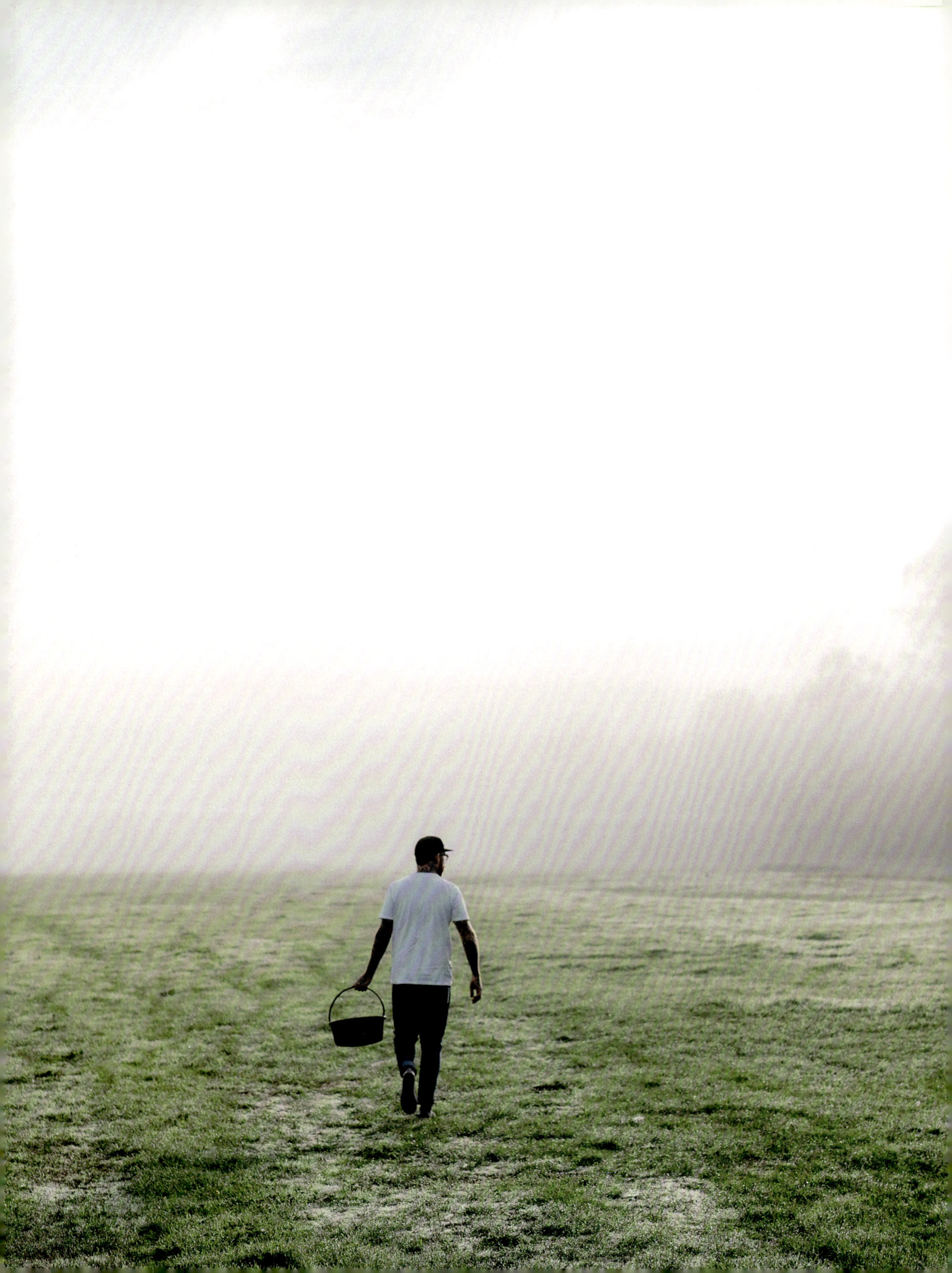

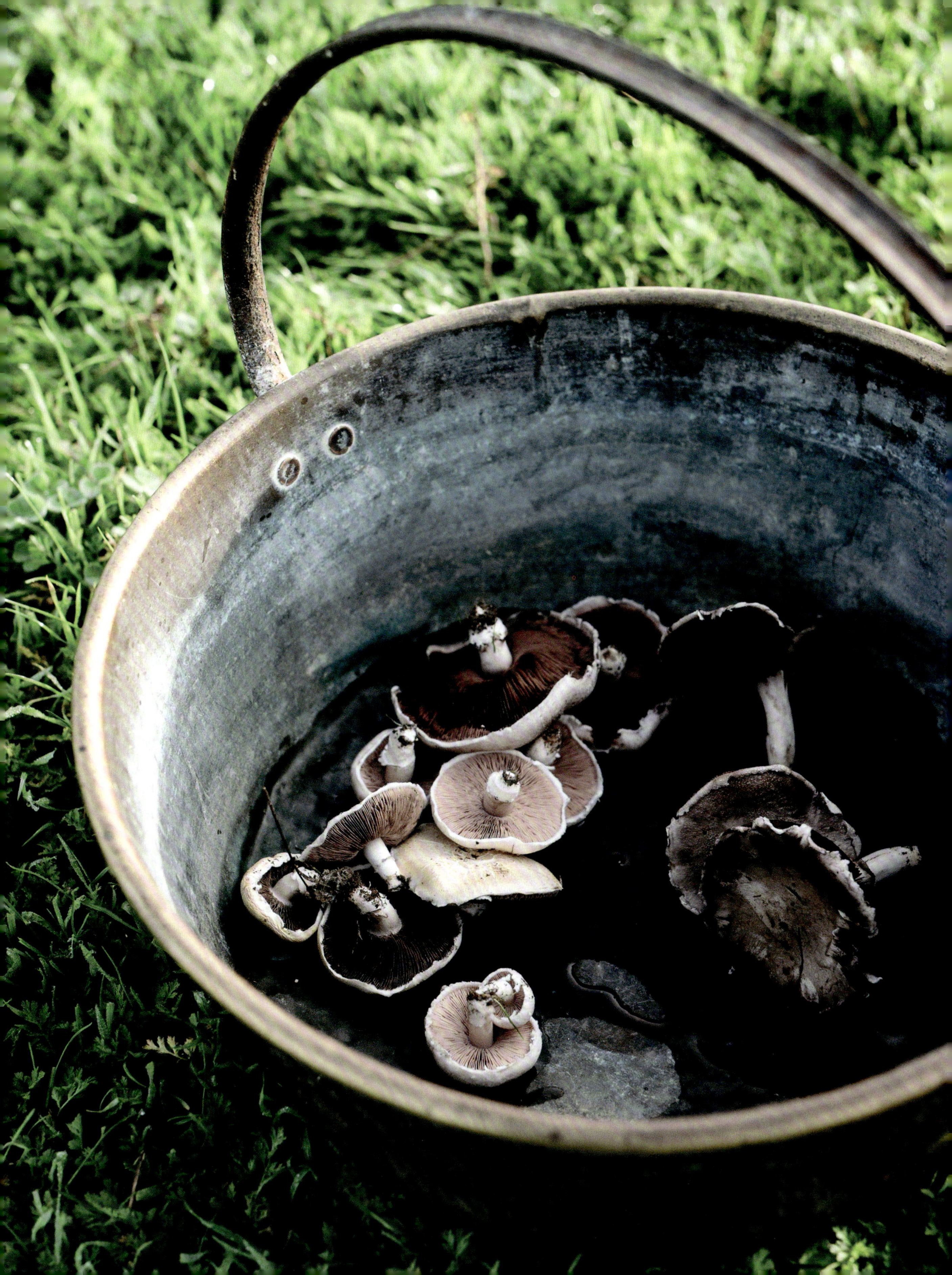

Chargrilled carrots with spiced eggplant and yoghurt

With great chefs like Yotam Ottolenghi writing beautiful books and showing us all how to cook delicious examples of Middle Eastern food, it's not surprising that we are seeing this style becoming popular here in New Zealand. I don't think it's just a passing trend, as this style of cuisine suits our country and climate beautifully. A plentiful supply of seasonal vegetables, every fresh herb imaginable, lashings of olive oil, spices and the use of natural-style yoghurts are all making a big play in the kind of food we are embracing and serving these days. I love pairing the humble with the more exotic, and this carrot and eggplant salad is a perfect example. I have used small, young carrots for this, but by all means use big, bright orange carrots for an equally delicious result.

Serves 8 as a side dish

SPICED EGGPLANT
4 medium eggplant
olive oil, for brushing
flaky sea salt and freshly ground black pepper
2 teaspoons ground sumac
2 teaspoons cumin seeds, toasted and ground
⅓ cup (80 ml/2½ fl oz) extra-virgin olive oil

CHARGRILLED CARROTS
1.5 kg (3 lb 5 oz) baby carrots (or regular carrots)
canola oil, for tossing
flaky sea salt and freshly ground black pepper
½ cup (20 g/¾ oz) roughly chopped mint leaves
½ cup (15 g/½ oz) roughly chopped coriander leaves
¼ cup (60 ml/2 fl oz) Al Brown & Co Orange and Chilli Infused Olive Oil or extra-virgin olive oil

TO COOK AND SERVE
1½ cups (375 g/13 oz) thick natural yoghurt
⅓ cup (30 g/1 oz) almond flakes, toasted
2 tablespoons currants
2 tablespoons fried red chillies (page 445)
1 lemon, halved, for squeezing

Preheat your oven to 180°C (350°F).

Slice the eggplant lengthways, then score in a 1–2 cm (½–¾ in) criss-cross pattern. Brush the scored flesh with liberal amounts of olive oil. Season with salt and pepper.

Place a frying pan over medium-high heat. Once hot, place a few eggplant halves at a time, skin side down, in the pan. Cook for 4–5 minutes, until they begin to turn golden. Remove and place, skin side down, on an oiled oven tray.

Mix the sumac and cumin together, then sprinkle over the golden eggplant flesh. Place the tray in the oven and cook for 30 minutes or so, until the eggplant is super soft. Remove from the oven, let cool for 10 minutes then scrape the flesh away from the skin (discard the skin) and place in a bowl. With a fork, break up the cooked flesh a bit, then stir in the extra-virgin olive oil. Taste to check the seasoning. Cover and refrigerate until required.

To make the chargrilled carrots, preheat your chargrill so it's good and hot. Alternatively, preheat your oven to 180°C (350°F).

If using baby carrots, cut lengthways in half. For regular carrots, cut into batons about the size of your finger. Place in a bowl with a little oil, salt and pepper. Toss to combine.

Cook the carrots on the chargrill over medium-high heat, until golden and charred and softish to the bite. If you're cooking indoors, you will need to give the carrots a bit of oven time—about 5 minutes.

Remove from the heat and let cool to room temperature. Toss the carrots in a bowl along with the mint, coriander and olive oil.

To serve, spread the spiced eggplant out over the base of a platter. Spread the chargrilled carrots on top, randomly dollop spoonfuls of yoghurt over the carrots, then sprinkle over the almond flakes, currants and fried chilli. To finish, give the dish a good, liberal squeeze of lemon juice, just prior to serving.

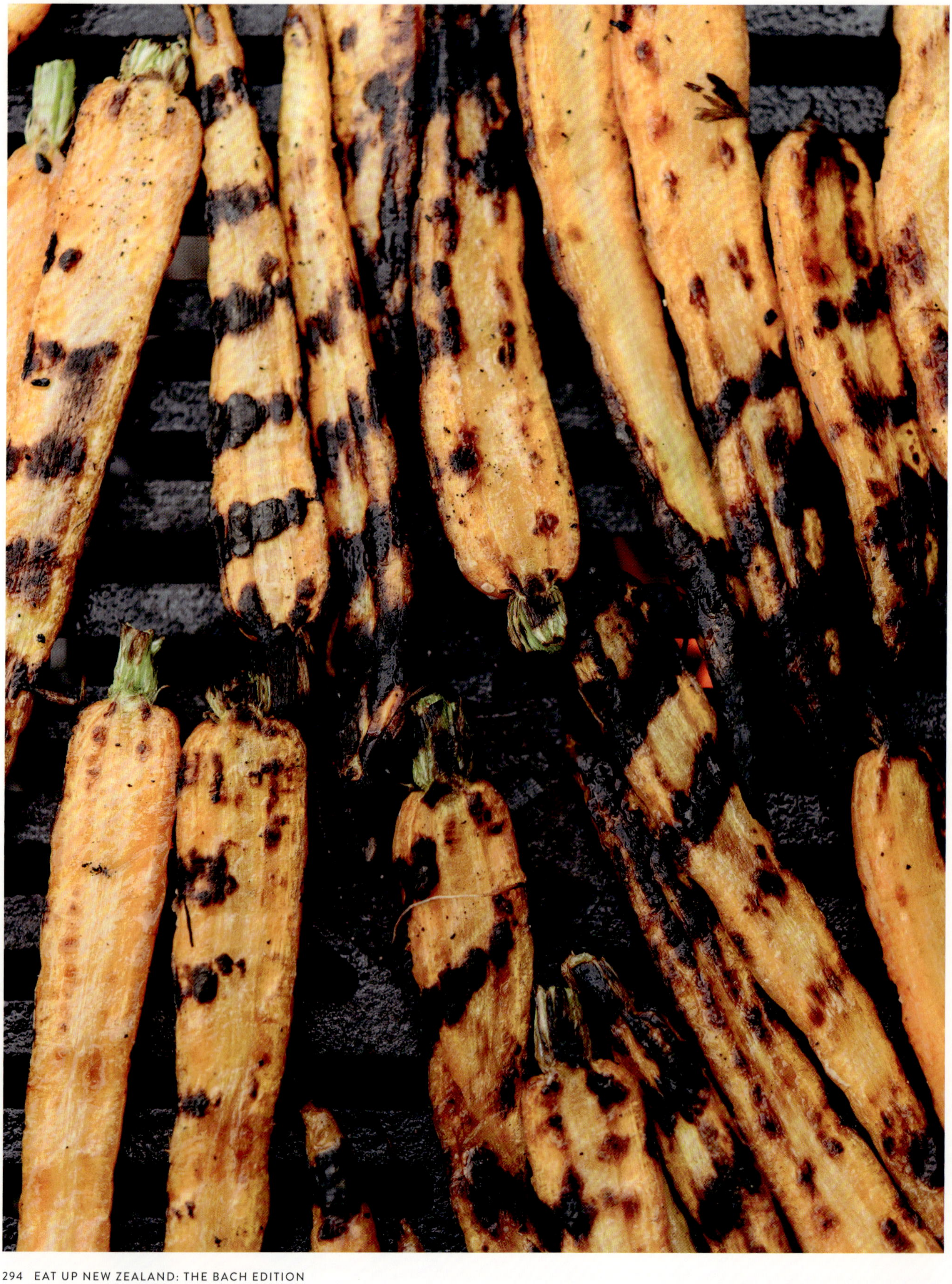

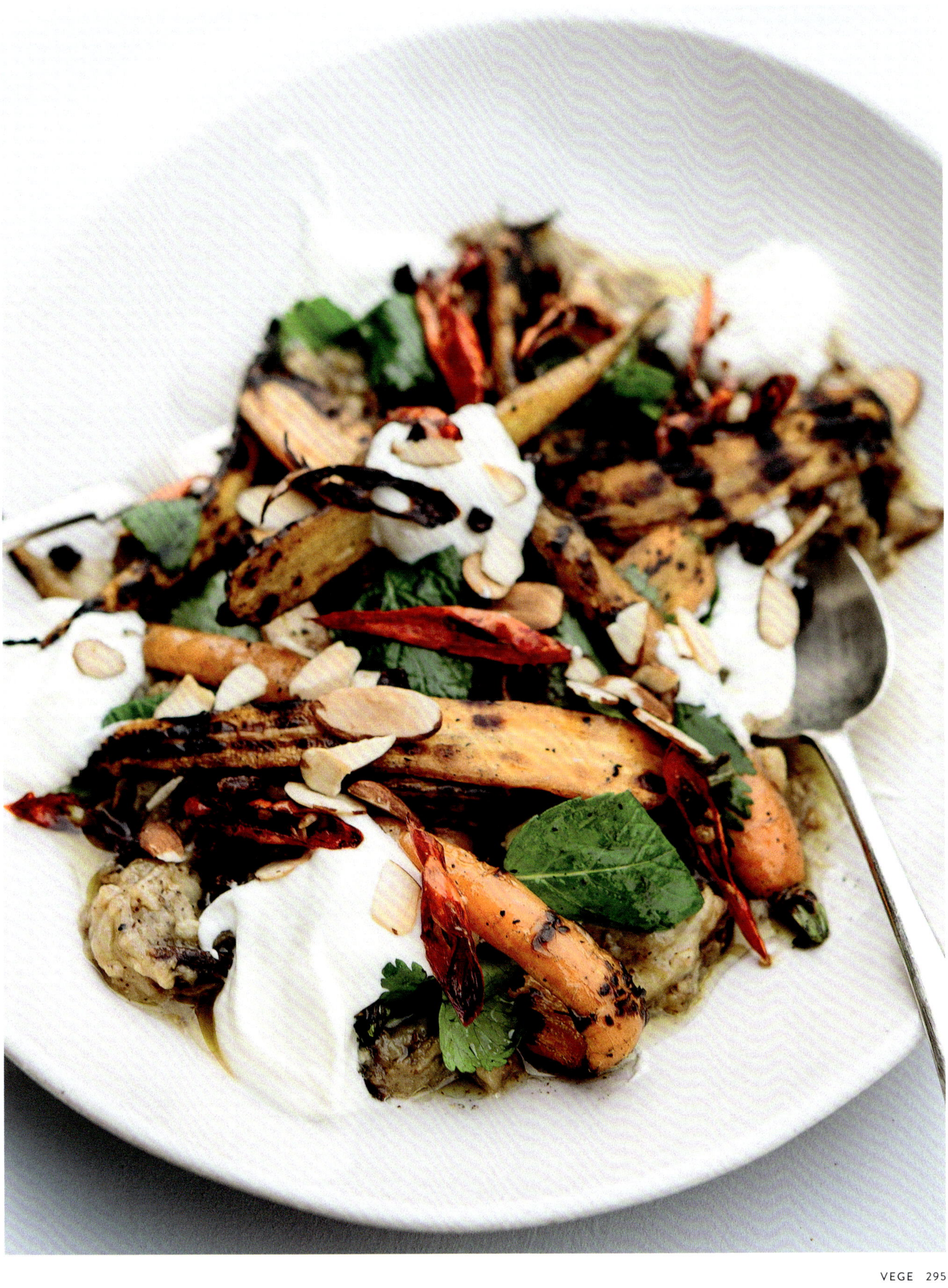

Roasted tomatoes and capsicums

I love the simplicity, ease and impact of putting something like this together. At the height of summer, tomatoes and capsicums are at their best (and cheapest), and by roasting them in a hot oven you intensify the flavour considerably. It's something that you can do a couple of hours prior to eating and just serve them at room temperature.

Serves 8 as a side dish

5 red capsicums
18 ripe tomatoes
handful whole peeled garlic cloves
bunch thyme sprigs
½ cup (125 ml/4 fl oz) olive oil
flaky sea salt and freshly ground black pepper

Preheat your oven to 220°C (425°F).

Cut the ends off the capsicums, remove the cores and seeds, slice into large pieces and place in a large bowl. Add the tomatoes, garlic, thyme sprigs and oil. Toss to combine, then tip into a small-lipped roasting tray. Season liberally with salt and pepper. Place in the oven and blast for 20–30 minutes, until the skins begin to blister. Remove and let cool completely, then serve as a side to anything else you're cooking!

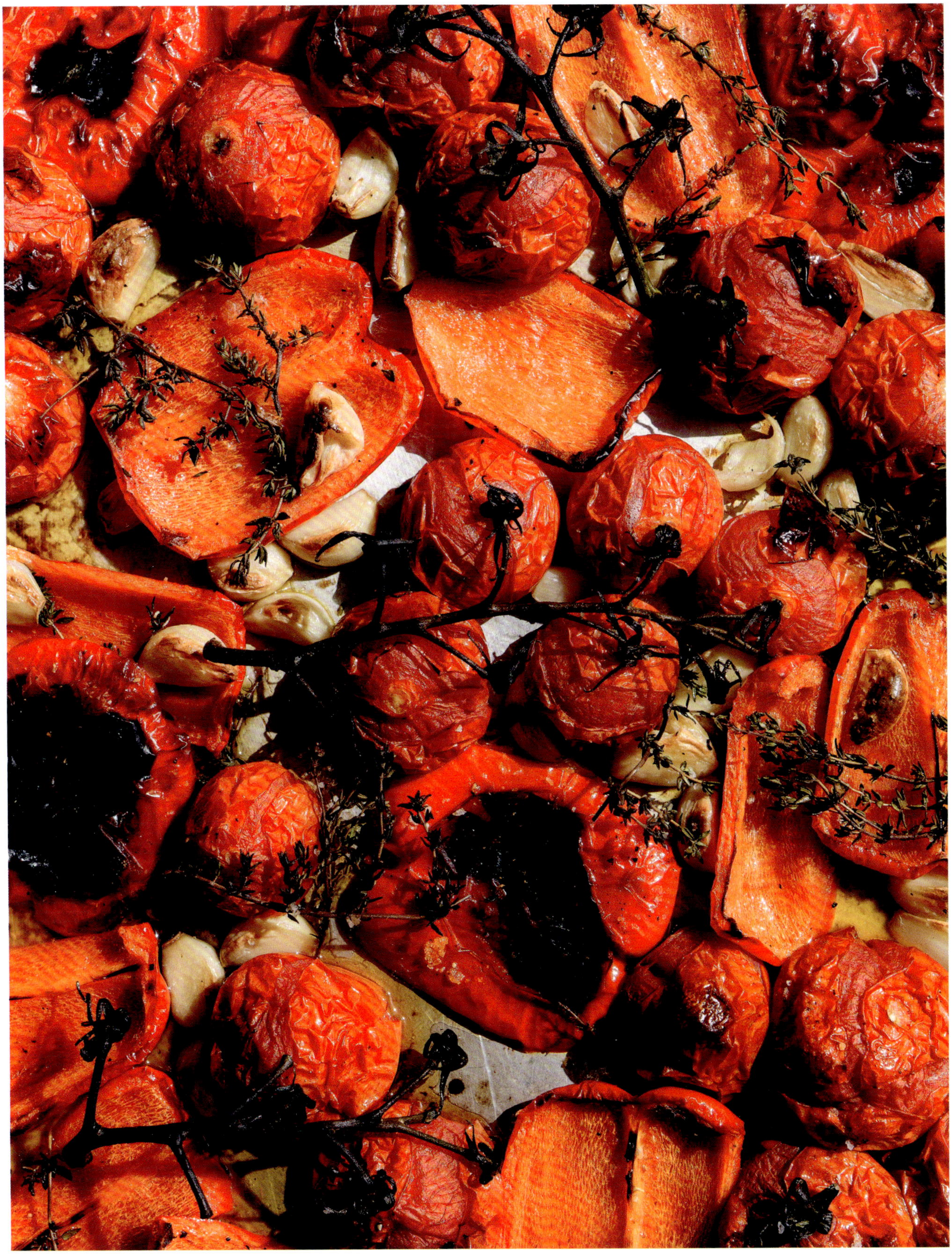

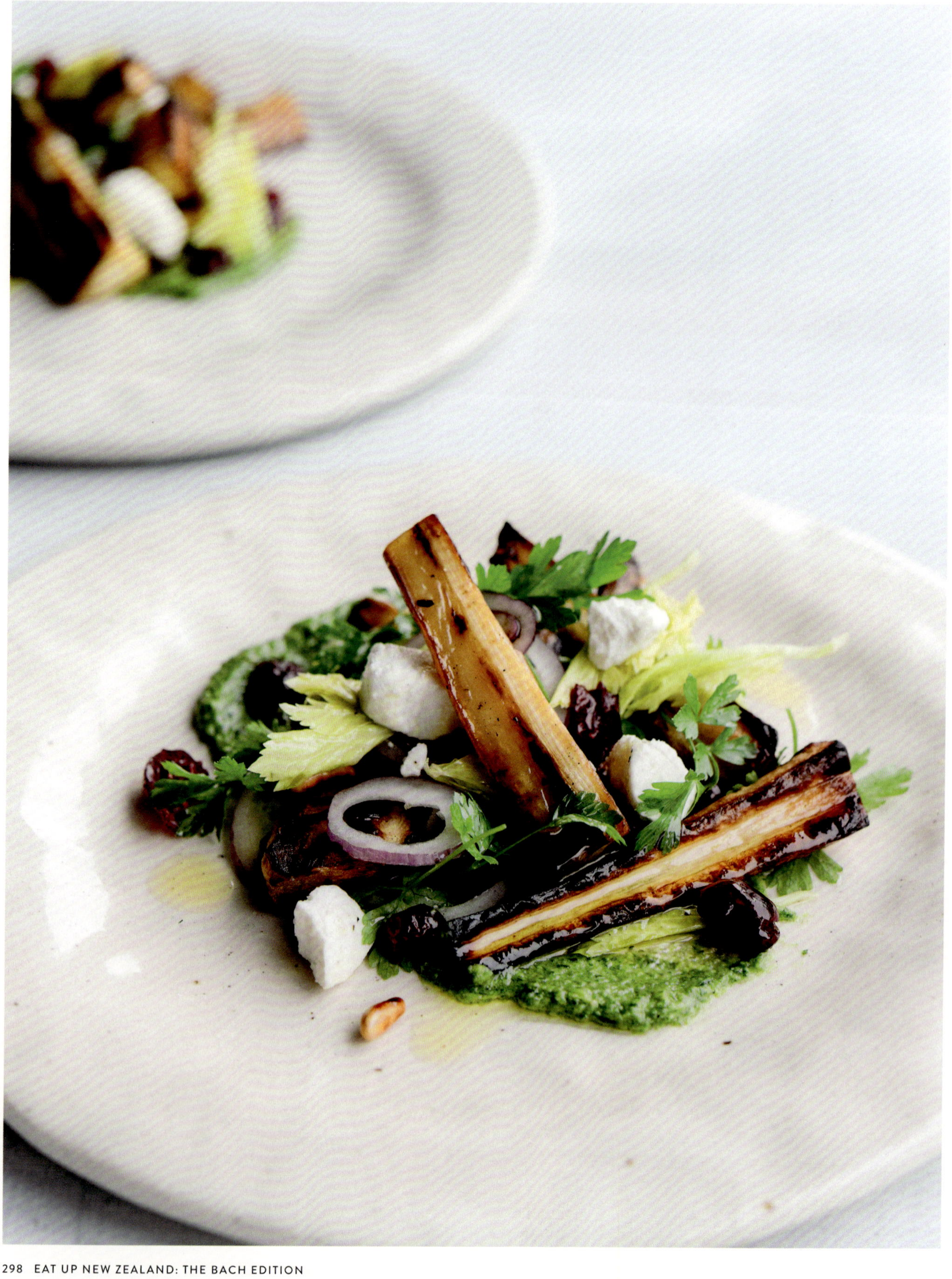

Roasted parsnip salad with goat's cheese, cranberries and rocket pesto

This is a terrific combination for a salad. All the flavours are relatively gutsy but harmonise wonderfully well together. Great textures, sweet, savoury, nutty and peppery, it's got it all going on and eats as good as it looks.

Serves 6 as a side

PARSNIPS
⅓ cup (80 ml/2½ fl oz) canola oil
1 kg (2 lb 4 oz) parsnips, cut into batons

ROCKET PESTO
2 cups tightly packed (70 g/2½ oz) wild rocket leaves
½ cup (50 g/1¾ oz) grated Parmesan cheese
¼ cup (40 g/1½ oz) toasted pine nuts
1 garlic clove, finely chopped
12 basil leaves

1 teaspoon sugar
2 tablespoons lemon juice
½ cup (125 ml/4 fl oz) olive oil

TO SERVE
1 small red onion, finely sliced
1 handful flat-leaf parsley leaves
½ cup yellow inner celery leaves
½ cup dried cranberries
¼ cup (40 g/1½ oz) toasted pine nuts
⅓ cup (80 ml/2½ fl oz) olive oil
100 g (3½ oz) goat's cheese

Preheat your oven to 180°C (350°F).

Place a frying pan over medium heat. Once hot, add the oil, followed by the parsnip in a couple of batches. Cook the parsnip for a couple of minutes on all sides until golden. Remove and place in a roasting pan. Roast for 15–20 minutes, or until soft and cooked through. Remove and let cool.

For the rocket pesto, place all the ingredients in a jug-like container (or food processor). Using a stick blender, blitz until incorporated (or use the food processor). Refrigerate until required.

To a large bowl, add the parsnips, onion, parsley, celery leaves, cranberries, pine nuts and olive oil. Toss gently together to incorporate.

Spoon out some of the rocket pesto onto serving plates. Top with the parsnip salad and finish by crumbling over the goat's cheese. Serve now.

Spiced pumpkin with dal, yoghurt and curry leaves

Recipes like the following one reinforce for me how lucky we are as a country to have such a diverse (and growing) immigrant population. As far as I'm concerned, our culinary landscape would be a much lesser place if we didn't have the multitude of cultures, complete with their delicious and precious cuisines, making New Zealand a far richer and diverse country to eat in. Case in point: the spice mix below is from Kumar, one of our senior chefs at Depot, who was kind enough to flick the recipe through to me.

Serves 6

DAL
½ cup (125 ml/4 fl oz) cooking oil
1 tablespoon brown mustard seeds
50 curry leaves
¾ cup (155 g/5½ oz) finely chopped onion
1½ tablespoons finely chopped ginger
1½ tablespoons finely chopped garlic
1 red chilli, finely chopped
1 teaspoon ground sumac
1 tablespoon ground cumin
1 teaspoon ground turmeric
2¼ cups (500 g/1 lb 2 oz) yellow split peas, rinsed and soaked overnight in water
5 cups (1.25 litres/44 fl oz) chicken stock or water
1–2 lemons
flaky sea salt and freshly ground black pepper

KUMAR'S SPICE MIX
2 tablespoons cumin seeds, roasted and ground
1 tablespoon fenugreek seeds, roasted and ground
1 tablespoon black peppercorns, roasted and ground
3 tablespoons ground turmeric
2 tablespoons ground ginger
2 tablespoons sweet smoked paprika
1 tablespoon ground cinnamon
2 tablespoons flaky sea salt

ROASTED PUMPKIN
1.5 kg (3 lb 5 oz) pumpkin, peeled and cut into chunks
canola oil or other cooking oil

TO SERVE
labneh or thick natural yoghurt
fried curry leaves (page 445)
fried red chillies (page 445)
shallot crunchies (page 445)
coriander leaves
turmeric oil (page 443)
lemon wedges

Take a large heavy-bottomed saucepan and place over medium heat. Once hot, add the oil, then mustard seeds and curry leaves. Cook for 2 minutes, then add the onion, ginger, garlic and chilli. Stir through and turn down the heat to low. Cook for 10 minutes, then add the sumac, cumin and turmeric. Stir. Drain the soaked yellow split peas and add, along with the stock, to the pan. Bring up to the boil then lower the heat to a simmer.

Cook, stirring occasionally, for about an hour, or until the split peas are beginning to break down. If the stock has been absorbed and the split peas are still not quite cooked through, add some more stock or water, a little at a time. (I like my dal quite wet and slightly sloppy.) Remove from the heat, season with a squeeze or two of lemon and add salt and pepper to taste.

To make the spice mix, place all the ingredients in a bowl, combine well, then store in an airtight container.

Preheat your oven to 200°C (400°F).

Brush the pumpkin with the oil, then liberally sprinkle the spice mix all over. Place a roasting dish in the oven for 5 minutes to get super hot. Remove, add a little more oil, then carefully add the spice-covered pumpkin pieces. Place in the oven to roast for 25–30 minutes, until the pumpkin is just soft through. Remove and let cool.

On large plates, spread out some dal, then add a piece of roasted spiced pumpkin on top. Add some liberal dollops of the labneh or yoghurt, then garnish by sprinkling over fried curry leaves, fried chilli, shallot crunchies and some fresh coriander leaves.

Finish with turmeric oil and a fresh squeeze of lemon juice. Eat now.

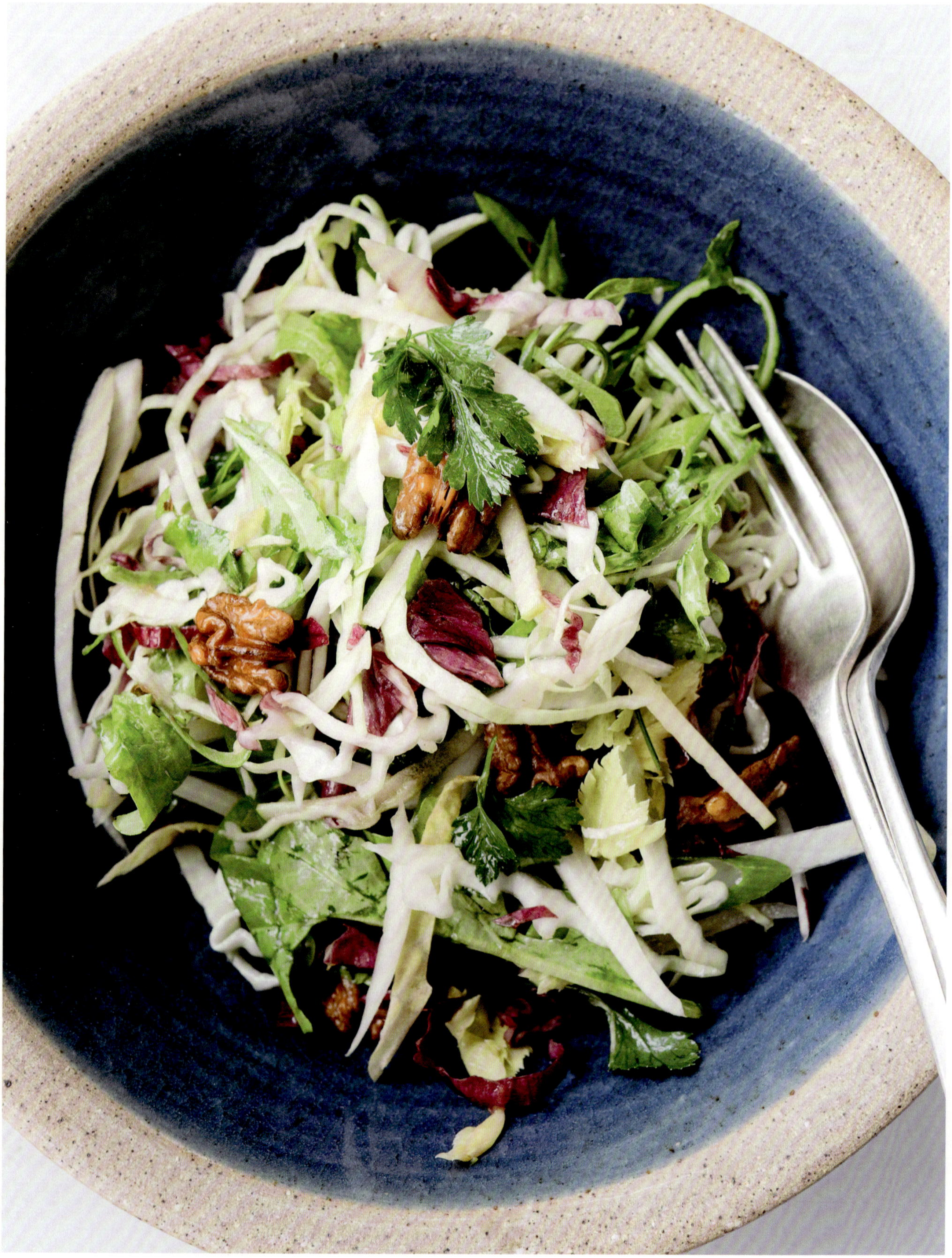

Bitter green apple slaw

I've become a big fan of bitter. It's probably the least-loved flavour profile, but when it's combined and used with other components that bring balance to the table it adds plenty of interest and complexity to any dish. This is a terrific slaw made using a number of greens that offer up delicious bitterness. We dress this with just a little walnut oil and apple syrup to taste. It's super fresh and adds 'cut through' as a side dish to any rich main component. If you like creamy slaw, by all means add a mayo or a ranch dressing to the greens, but eliminate the walnut oil and apple syrup.

Serves 6 as a side dish

1 witloof, finely sliced
½ radicchio, finely sliced
2 handfuls cabbage, finely sliced
1 handful wild rocket
2 spring onions, finely sliced
⅓ cup (7 g/¼ oz) flat-leaf parsley leaves
½ cup yellow inner celery leaves
1½ Granny Smith apples, cut into matchsticks
½ cup (60 g/2¼ oz) toasted walnut pieces
walnut oil, to taste
sweet apple syrup, to taste

Toss all the ingredients except the walnut oil and apple syrup together in a large bowl. Dress to taste with the walnut oil and apple syrup.

Cos lettuce with Depot ranch dressing, hot sauce and sweet spiced sunflower seeds

I have always been a massive fan of cold, crunchy lettuce slathered with liberal amounts of ranch dressing. For a long time our go-to at Depot was iceberg but, recently, when the 'bergs weren't in great shape, we switched to romaine/cos, which is the lettuce used in that famous Caesar Salad (invented in Mexico in 1924). I digress . . . Anyway, it was at Depot that I stumbled upon Vik, one of our managers, having a late-night munch after service, and I noticed that he was eating cos with ranch and had also dribbled hot sauce on top. I tried a bit, and it was a quite a revelation. Along with the fresh crunch of the lettuce, the cold, creamy dressing contrasts with the sting and heat of the hot sauce—bloody brilliant.

I thought about it a bit more and believed I could elevate this humble salad by adding one more layer of texture in the form of some slightly sweet and spicy toasted sunflower seeds.

I still get blown away by the depth of flavour in some of the most uncomplicated dishes. This salad adds so much freshness to any rich protein situation, and is nearly compulsory at any barbecue.

Serves 6

DEPOT RANCH DRESSING
1 cup (235 g/8½ oz) mayonnaise (homemade or Best Foods)
½ cup (125 g/4½ oz) sour cream
2 tablespoons milk
2 teaspoons white vinegar
1 teaspoon finely chopped garlic
¼ cup (15 g/½ oz) finely chopped chives
flaky sea salt and freshly ground black pepper

SWEET SPICED SUNFLOWER SEEDS
1 cup (145 g/5¼ oz) sunflower seeds
2 teaspoons ground cumin
2 teaspoons sweet (dulce) smoked paprika
1 tablespoon brown sugar
pinch flaky sea salt
pinch freshly ground black pepper
1 tablespoon canola oil

TO ASSEMBLE AND SERVE
1½–2 heads medium to large cos or iceberg lettuce
hot sauce (I love using Frank's RedHot Buffalo Wings Sauce)

To make the Depot ranch dressing, take a medium bowl and add all the ingredients except for the salt and pepper. Mix thoroughly, then season to taste. Refrigerate until required.

For the sweet spiced sunflower seeds, place all the ingredients in a suitable-sized bowl and mix thoroughly.

Place a skillet or frying pan over medium heat. Once hot, add the seed mixture and keep moving the seeds around constantly until they start to caramelise. Remove the pan from the heat and spread the seeds out onto a large plate or tray to cool.

Once cooled completely, pour into an airtight jar and secure the lid tightly. Use as you feel, with any ideas you may have.

To serve, cut the cos lengthways into wedges and place them on a platter. Spoon over liberal amounts of ranch dressing and drizzle with hot sauce to your heat requirements. I tend to go lighter on the hot sauce, then just leave the bottle nearby for anyone who wants to turn the heat volume up. Finish by sprinkling over the seeds. Serve now.

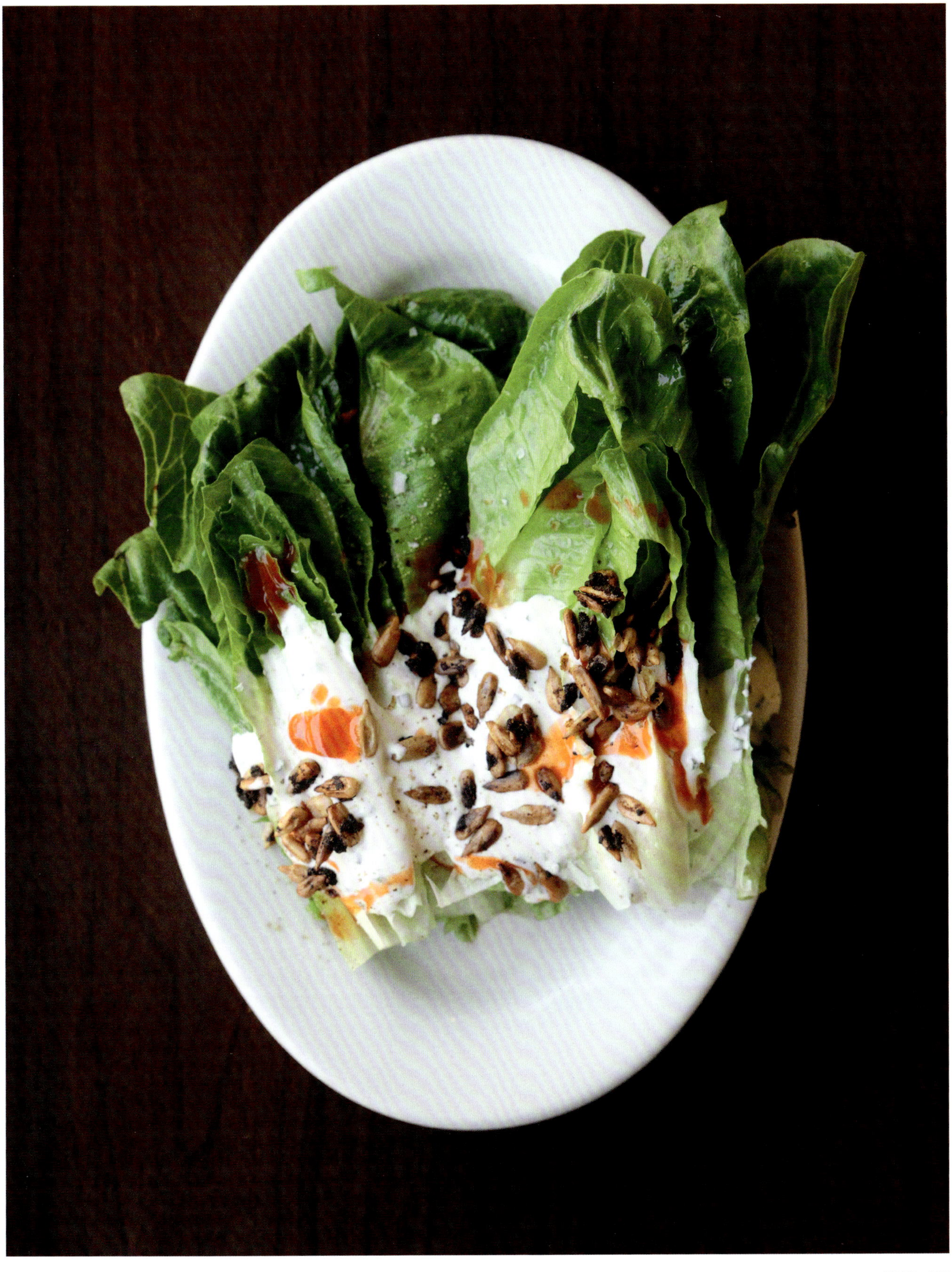

Roasted fennel and red onion salad with white anchovies

Fennel kind of polarises people for some reason. I think many folks believe it is just a weed that grows roadside. Or maybe its shape, with green stalks poking out the top of a weird-looking white bulb, is what puts people off. Its popularity in restaurants these days will soon see it cross the road into domestic kitchens up and down the motu, however. It's delicious sliced thinly and served raw, it roasts and caramelises beautifully, and it makes a lovely purée. It's in the anise family and adds a unique flavour and interest to all meals.

This is a really simple salad and a good example of how less is often more, in the sense that the recipe heroes just three ingredients. While white anchovies are relatively expensive, they are super delicious and add a mildly salty and acid component to the dish.

I use my own Lemon and Fennel Infused Olive Oil, which 'matches the hatch' perfectly for this recipe. Alternatively, just use a good-quality olive oil.

Serves 6

ROASTED FENNEL AND RED ONION
3 fennel bulbs
2 large red onions
¼ cup Al Brown & Co Lemon and Fennel Infused Olive Oil
flaky sea salt and freshly ground black pepper

TO ASSEMBLE AND SERVE
¼ cup (60 ml/2 fl oz) Al Brown & Co Lemon and Fennel Infused Olive Oil
juice of ½ lemon
flaky sea salt and freshly ground black pepper
12 white anchovies

Preheat your oven to 180°C (350°F).

Cut the green stalks from the fennel bulbs. Keep a few of these aside so you can pick some of the fine fronds to use in the salad when you put it together.

Cut the fennel bulbs down the centre, then into quarters. You will see there is a fibrous middle that runs through the centre of the bulb. Use a knife to trim some of that back, but don't go too far because you want the fennel leaves to hold together while roasting. Place in a bowl.

Cut the red onions in half and then in half again, keeping the fibrous ends intact so the quarters will hold together.

Place the red onion in the bowl with the fennel, add the oil, then season with salt and pepper. Place on a baking tray and roast for 30 minutes, until the fennel and onion are nicely caramelised. Remove and cool.

To serve, place the roasted fennel and red onion in a bowl. Roughly rip liberal amounts of the reserved fennel fronds and add them to the bowl. Add the olive oil and lemon juice. Taste, and if you think it needs a little more seasoning then adjust accordingly. Lay the white anchovies over the top and serve in the bowl or on individual plates.

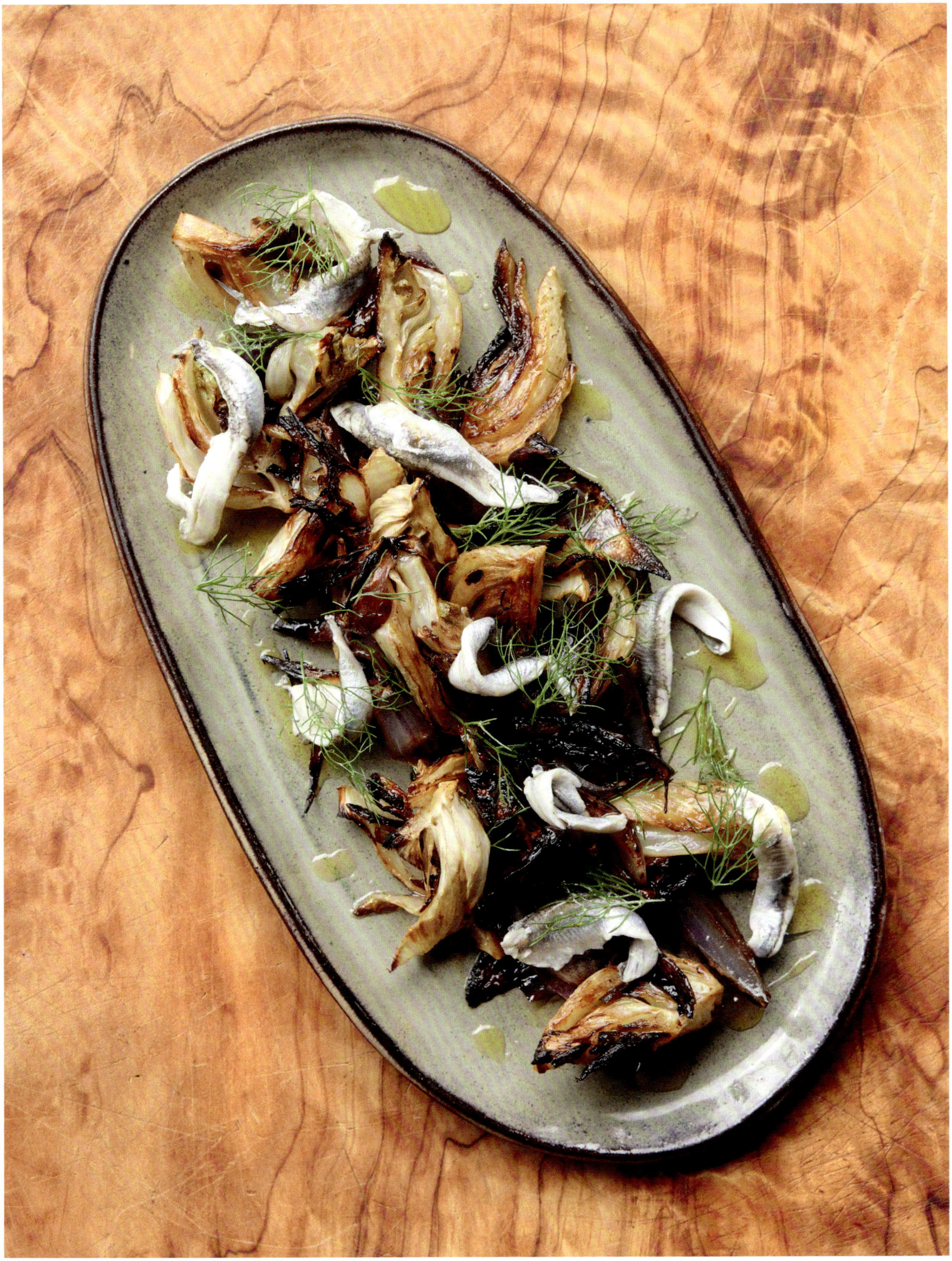

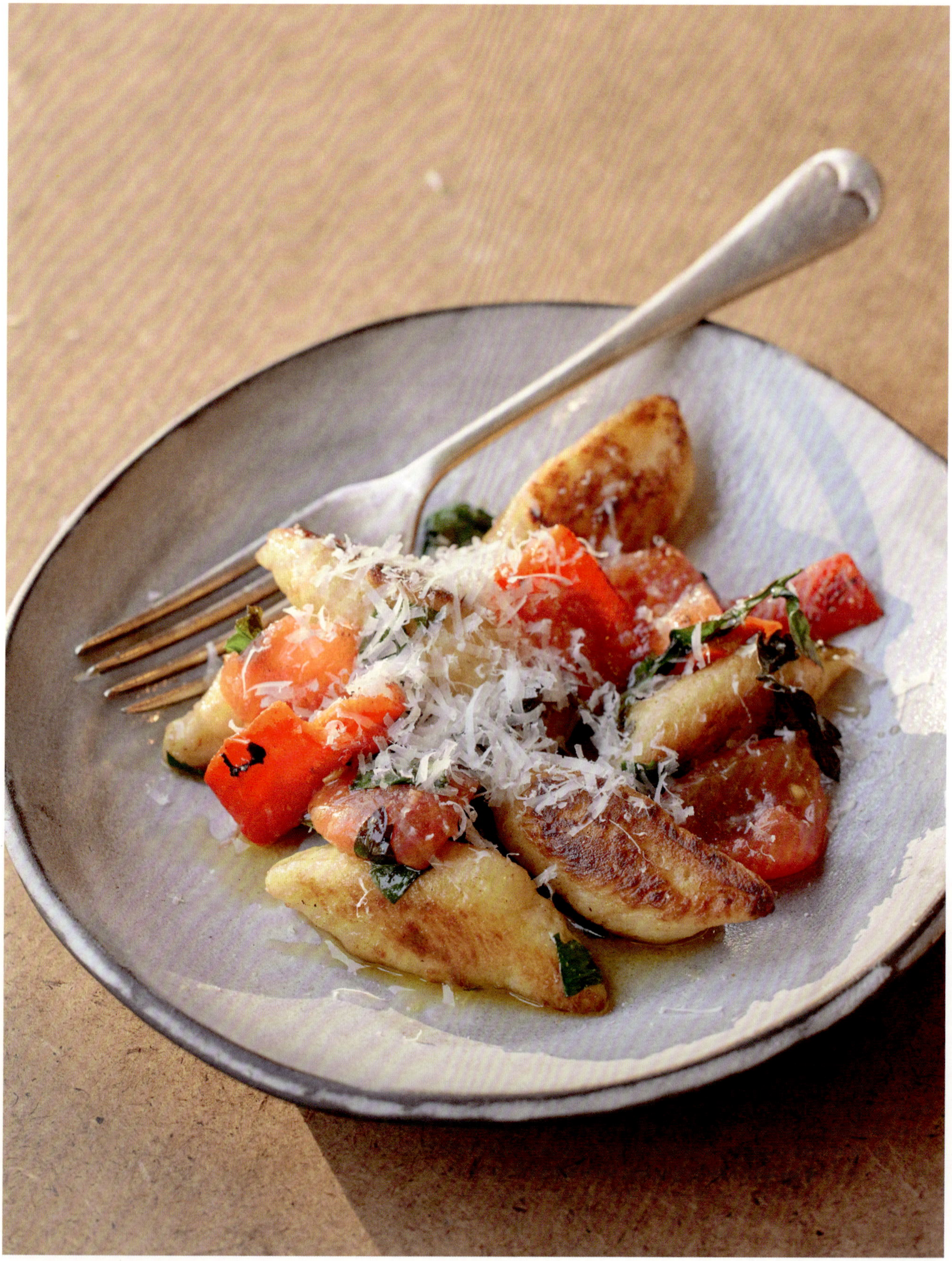

Sautéed gnocchi with roasted red capsicum, tomato and Parmesan

Making gnocchi at home is a bit of a fluff, but the end result always makes it worthwhile. And besides, store-bought is not even close to the real thing. For best results, the potatoes should be relatively old. Your classic and popular Agria works well, but if you come across Yukon, Russet or Idaho, these will garner great results also.

There is a bit of a knack to it, so the following points are good to keep in mind as you make your gnocchi. Pick out the largest potatoes from the variety you have found. Bake the potatoes until they are super soft inside their leathery jackets. Get set up with a good amount of bench space to work on. Work relatively quickly when you are adding the other ingredients to the floury warm potato. Work with a light hand, and try not to overwork the dough.

Serves 6

GNOCCHI
2 kg (4 lb 8 oz) large Agria potatoes, skin on and cleaned
4 egg yolks, stirred
1½ cups (225 g/8 oz) flour, plus extra for the bench and rolling
flaky sea salt and freshly ground black pepper
canola or olive oil, for greasing

ROASTED RED CAPSICUM
3 red capsicums
olive oil

TOMATO PIECES
6 vine-ripened tomatoes

TO COOK AND SERVE
olive oil
small pinch chilli flakes
1 handful basil, roughly torn
1 handful parsley, roughly torn
knob butter
flaky sea salt and freshly ground black pepper
¼ cup (40 g/1½ oz) toasted pine nuts (optional)
fresh Parmesan cheese, for shaving

Preheat your oven to 180°C (350°F) and place your clean large potatoes in to bake for around 1½ hours.

Once the potatoes are very soft through the centre, remove them from the oven and leave to cool for 10 minutes or so.

Place a large saucepan of salted water over high heat and bring up to the boil, then turn down to a simmer. Set up a bowl of iced water. Grease a baking tray with canola oil or similar.

Working with one potato at a time, cut each potato in half lengthways and scoop the cooked floury centre into a large sieve sitting over a suitable-sized bowl. Take a rubber spatula and work the potato through the sieve by forcing it through the mesh with the spatula. Repeat with the remaining potatoes.

Liberally flour your bench, then turn the sieved potato onto the floured bench. Spread it out as best you can, then pour over the stirred egg yolks as evenly as possible. Do the same with about a cup of the flour, and season with salt and pepper. Gently mix with a fork, adding the rest of the flour as you go.

Flour your hands, then carefully bring the dough together with your hands. Turn the dough into a log shape, then cut off a piece and gently roll it into a length that is about

Recipe continued overleaf...

1.5 cm (½ in) thick. Once you've cut half a dozen gnocchi, place them in the simmering water. They should float to the top within a minute. Remove them with a sieve, then plunge them into the iced water for a minute or so to cool down.

Try a couple, and if they are too soft or have fallen apart in the water, you will need to add a bit more flour to the dough. You want them holding together but not too doughy.

When you're happy with the consistency, cut and roll the remaining gnocchi and batch-cook a dozen or so at a time. Plunge each batch into the cold water for a minute, then remove and place them on a clean tea towel to get rid of any excess water. Transfer the cooked, cooled and drained gnocchi onto the prepared tray. Repeat the process with the rest of the dough.

Drizzle with a small amount of oil and gently move the gnocchi about on the tray so they don't stick together. Refrigerate until required. They do freeze pretty well, too.

To make the roasted red capsicum, roast the capsicums (you could use the method on page 296, minus the other ingredients) or char them to remove the skin. Cut into pieces a little larger than the gnocchi, place in a bowl and stir through a little olive oil. Set aside.

For the tomatoes, place a saucepan of salted water over high heat and bring up to the boil. Set up a bowl of iced water.

Score the tomatoes by cutting a cross on the bottom of each one, and remove a circle of flesh where each tomato was attached to the vine.

Plunge the tomatoes into the boiling water for 20 seconds or so, then remove them with a sieve and place into the iced water to arrest the cooking.

Peel and discard the skins, cut the tomatoes into quarters, remove the seeds, then halve each piece. Set aside.

Place a large saucepan over medium-high heat. Once hot, add the oil, chilli flakes and half the gnocchi. Cook the gnocchi for or a minute or so on either side until golden. Remove from the saucepan and set aside. Cook the second batch of gnocchi, then add the first batch of gnocchi back to the saucepan.

Add the capsicum and heat through for a minute, then add the tomato pieces along with the basil, parsley and butter. Season with salt and pepper.

Pour into a large bowl or divide among small single-serve bowls. To finish, top with pine nuts, add another glug of olive oil, and shave a liberal amount of Parmesan on top. Eat now.

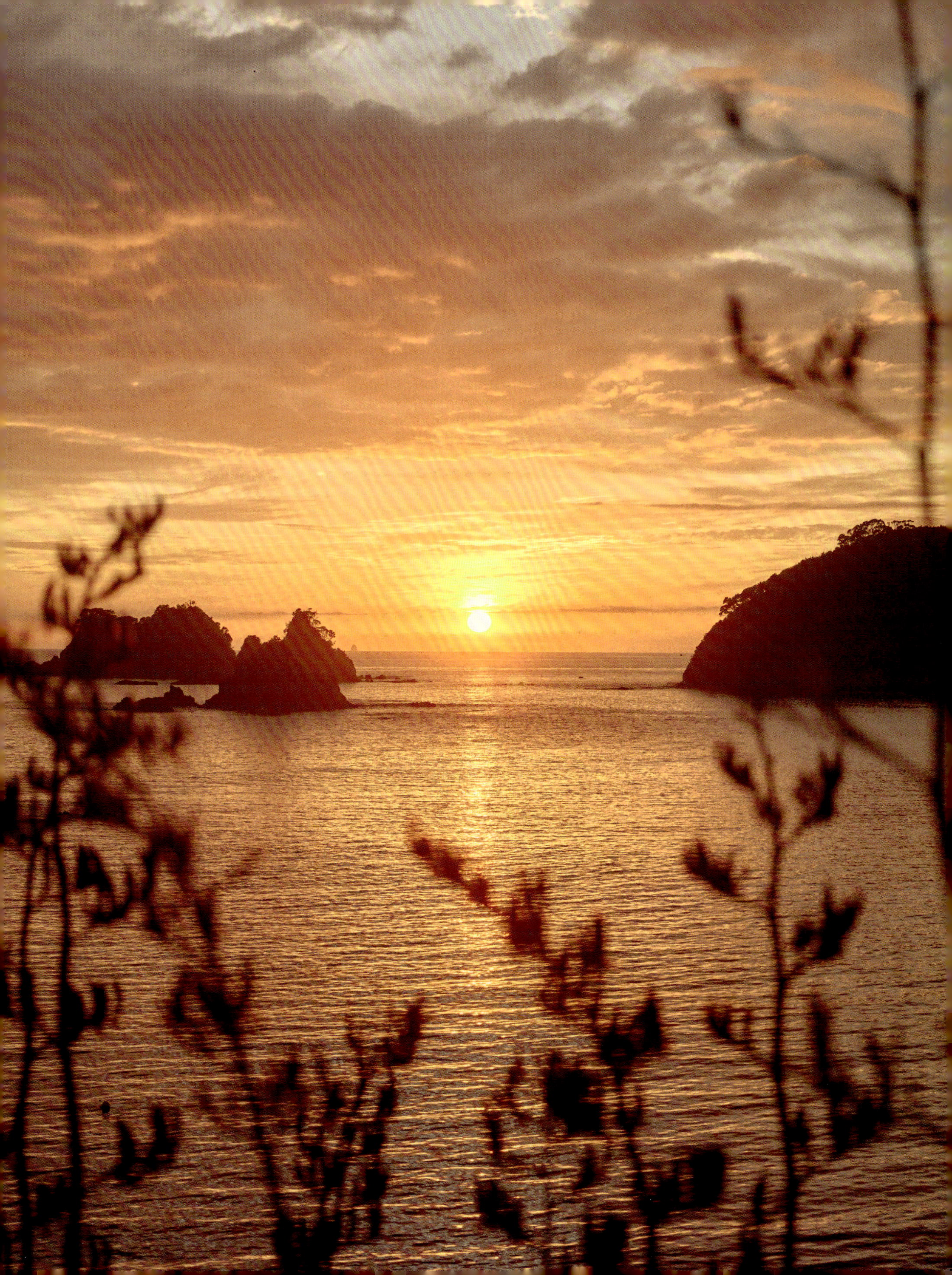

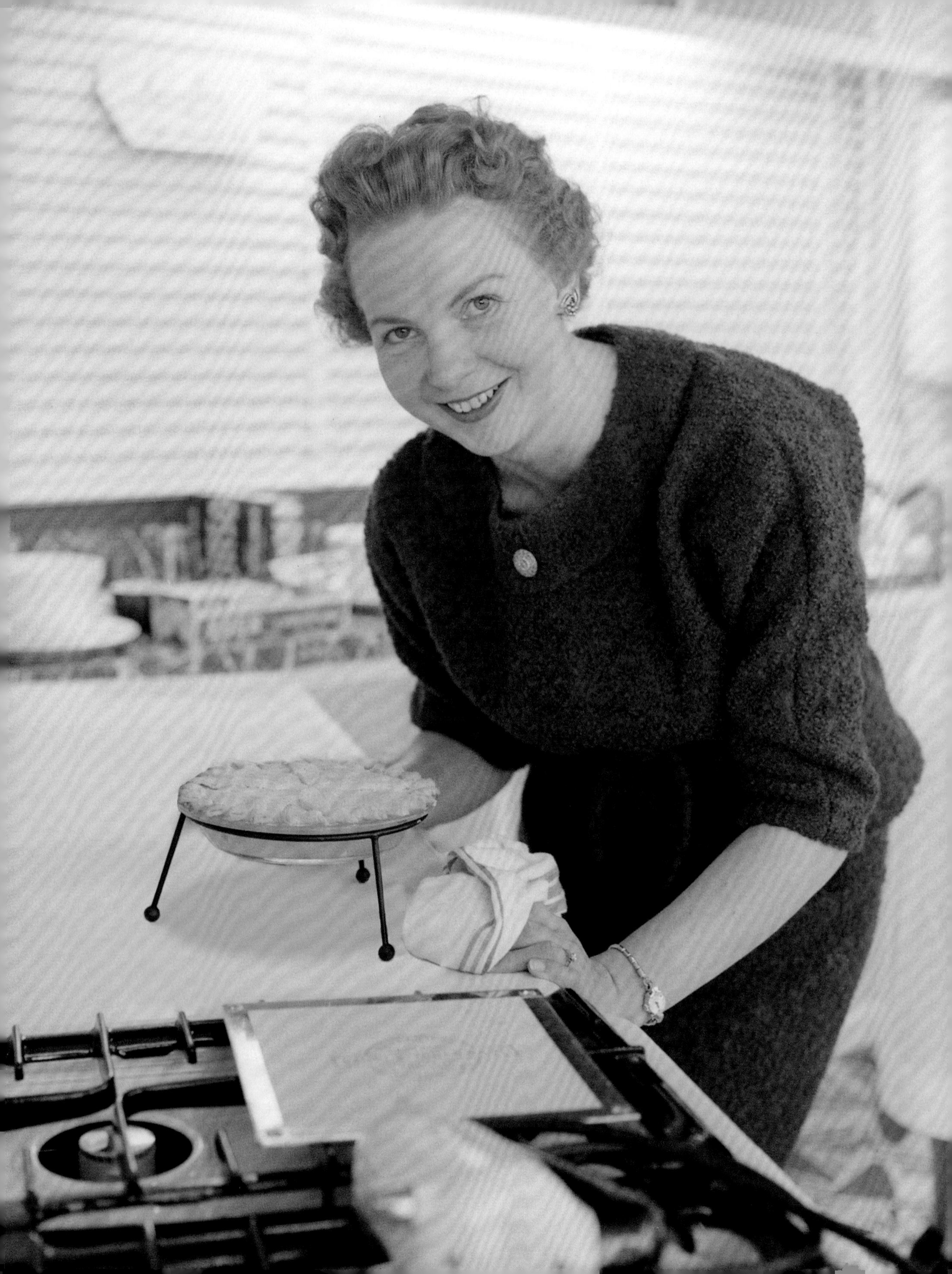

PUDDING
PURINI

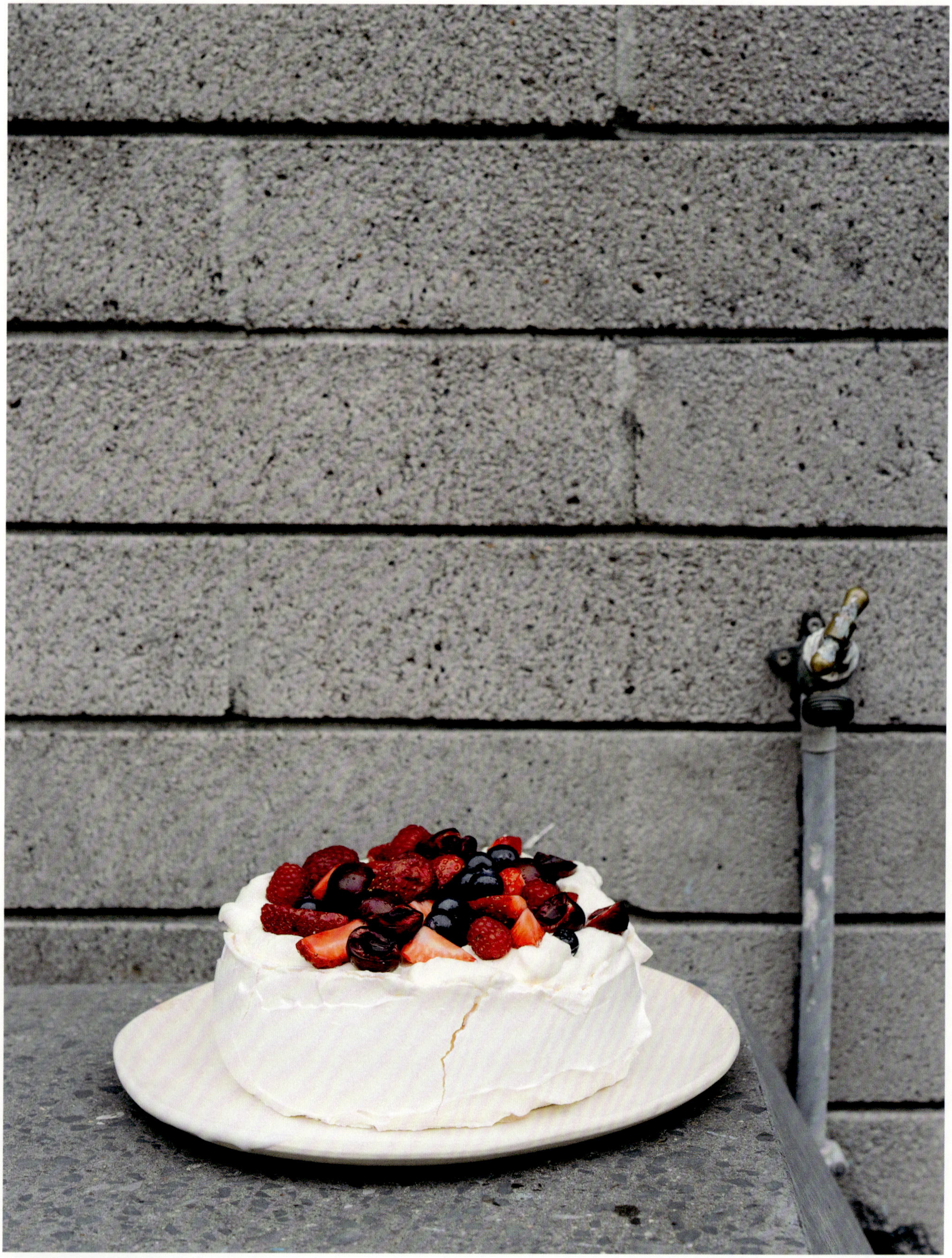

My pav

Firstly, let's get something straight: the pavlova is ours. The Aussies can claim it all they like—they are well practised at doing just that—though how most of them can live with their conscience is beyond me.

I'll admit that this recipe gave Haydo and me a few sleepless nights. Most pav recipes are very similar in their ingredients; however, it's the method and temperature of the oven that we found made the real difference. We think we have worked it out through trial and error, and we have absolute faith that this recipe is a real beauty—and we have both made it a number of times now with excellent results.

I love a pavlova that has a great bark (as in the bark of a tree), with minimal or no cracking, encapsulating a wonderful, soft, marshmallow-like centre. Besides it being our country's most famous (and I'm picking our favourite) dessert, I have always felt the great thing about a pav is that it becomes this sweet vehicle to show off the abundance in our nation's fruit bowl. No matter what time of the year, the pav highlights what's in season.

Serves 8

6 large egg whites, at room temperature
2 cups (460 g/1 lb) caster sugar
2 teaspoons malt vinegar
2 tablespoons cornflour
whipped cream, to serve
fresh seasonal fruit of choice, to serve

Preheat your oven to 120°C (235°F). Line a baking tray with baking paper. If you like, trace a circle onto the paper around something like a cake-tin bottom to give you a guide for when you form the pav. The smaller the circle, the higher the pav. Grease the paper with a little butter.

Set up your stand mixer and fit it with the whisk attachment, or use a handheld electric whisk. Make sure the mixing bowl is super clean. (I like to wipe mine out with a splash of vinegar to remove any possible grease that may be lining the bowl since I last used it.)

Add the egg whites to the bowl and whisk at high speed until frothy, then begin to add the caster sugar, a tablespoon at a time, giving the egg whites time to absorb the sugar—this should take around 10 minutes. The meringue should be beautifully stiff and shiny. Whisk in the vinegar, then remove the bowl from the cake mixer.

Next sift over the cornflour, a little at a time, folding it through the meringue with a rubber spatula until mixed. Carefully spoon out the meringue onto the prepared tray and form your pavlova. Once you are happy with its shape, place it quickly in the oven. Bake for 1½ hours, then turn off the oven. Leave in the oven without opening the oven door to completely cool. It's best if you leave it overnight.

The pavlova is ready for your seasonal fruit touch. Lashings of whipped cream over the top first, then knock yourself out with your personal fruity combination!

Chocolate self-saucing pudding with espresso custard

There are a bunch of self-saucing chocolate puddings out there, and I'm pretty sure I love them all. We developed this recipe a while ago. The cake top of the pudding is quite a bit lighter than many traditional ones, and we upped the ante by folding dark chocolate pieces through the batter. The espresso custard is a dessert in itself, and can be made in individual ramekins and served like a brûlée. Here we just cook it in one large dish, then spoon it out next to the pud with cold pouring cream to finish.

Serves 6

ESPRESSO CUSTARD
3 cups (750 ml/26 fl oz) cream
¼ cup (20 g/¾ oz) freshly ground coffee
¾ cup (165 g/5¾ oz) caster sugar
10 egg yolks

CHOCOLATE PUD
½ cup (125 g/4½ oz) softened butter
¾ cup (165 g/5¾ oz) sugar
1 egg
1 teaspoon vanilla essence
1¼ cups (185 g/6½ oz) plain flour
2 teaspoons baking powder
⅓ cup (40 g/1½ oz) good-quality cocoa, plus 1 tablespoon
1 cup (150 g/5½ oz) roughly chopped dark chocolate
¾ cup (140 g/5 oz) brown sugar
2½ teaspoons cornflour
3 cups (750 ml/26 fl oz) boiling water

TO SERVE
chilled pouring cream, to serve

Preheat your oven to 140°C (275°F).
    To make the espresso custard, pour the cream and coffee into a large saucepan, and bring up to a simmer over medium heat. Remove from the heat and set aside.
    Whisk the caster sugar and egg yolks together in a large bowl until combined. Now slowly pour the hot cream over the egg mixture, whisking continuously, until completely incorporated. Pass through a fine sieve lined with muslin to remove the coffee grounds.
    Pour the custard mixture into a regular loaf tin. Seal tightly with tinfoil. Take a large roasting dish and place the tin with the custard mixture inside it. Pour enough hot water to come halfway up the side of the loaf tin. Cook in the oven for 25 minutes. Check if the custard is set—it should still be slightly nervous in the centre. If not, continue to cook and check at 5-minute intervals until it's set. Remove, let cool and refrigerate until required.

To make the self-saucing pudding, preheat your oven to 180°C (350°F).
    In a stand mixer fitted with the whisk attachment, or using a handheld electric whisk, beat the butter, sugar, egg and vanilla essence until light and fluffy. Sift in the flour, baking powder and ⅓ cup (40 g/1½ oz) cocoa, and fold in with a large spoon until just combined. Lastly, stir through the chopped chocolate.
    Grease a medium-sized ovenproof dish with butter, then spoon in the pudding mixture. In a bowl, combine the brown sugar, cornflour and 1 tablespoon cocoa, and sprinkle over the pudding. Then pour the boiling water over the top. Bake for 35–40 minutes, until the pudding is puffy and springs back when pressed. Remove from the oven and let rest for 10 minutes before serving.
    Divvy up the pudding into bowls. Using a hot, wet spoon, add a generous scoop of espresso custard to each bowl, then finish with a pour of cold fresh cream. Eat now.

PUDDING 317

Black Doris plum, rhubarb and white chocolate trifle

This trifle recipe has been my go-to for some time. It's an absolute beauty, and while there are quite a number of steps, you can do all of them over the course of a few days then bring it all together on the day you want to serve it. If you're strapped for time, skip the sponge below and buy one. The custard in this trifle is actually a white chocolate brûlée recipe, so that's worth remembering if you want to make it as a standalone dessert.

Serves 6

SPONGE
4 eggs
125 g (4½ oz) caster sugar
125 g (4½ oz) plain flour, plus extra for dusting
50 g (1¾ oz) unsalted butter, melted

WHITE CHOCOLATE CUSTARD
2 cups (500 ml/17 fl oz) cream
50 ml (1¾ fl oz) milk
100 g (3½ oz) sugar
½ vanilla bean, split in half lengthways
80 g (3 oz) white chocolate, roughly chopped
5 egg yolks

BLACK DORIS PLUM JELLY
1 x 850 g tin Black Doris plums
100 ml (3½ fl oz) port
2 tablespoons brown sugar
4 cloves
4 dried allspice berries
½ cinnamon stick, broken in half
finely grated zest of ½ orange
3 gelatine leaves

STEWED RHUBARB
400 g rhubarb stalks, roughly chopped
¼ cup (60 ml/2 fl oz) orange juice
¼ cup (55 g/2 oz) sugar

TO ASSEMBLE AND SERVE
2 tablespoons Black Doris plum or raspberry jam
½ cup (125 ml/4 fl oz) port (optional)
300 ml (10½ fl oz) cream, whipped
80 g (3 oz) white chocolate
80 g (3 oz) milk chocolate

To make the sponge, preheat your oven to 180°C (350°F). Grease one springform round (22 cm/8½ in) sponge tin with butter and a dusting of flour.

In a stand mixer fitted with the whisk attachment, or using a handheld electric whisk, beat the eggs with the sugar on medium-high speed for at least 10 minutes, until the mixture is light and airy and forms a thick ribbon when the whisk is lifted. Scrape out into your largest bowl, then sift in the flour and gently but quickly fold through to combine. Follow with the melted butter, folding through in the same manner.

Pour the batter into the prepared cake tin. Place in the oven and bake for 30–40 minutes. Test the sponge by pressing it lightly in the centre—it should gently spring back. Remove from the oven and let cool in the tins for 10 minutes before turning out on a wire rack. Keep in an airtight container until required.

Preheat your oven to 130°C (250°F).

To make the white chocolate custard, pour the cream and milk into a saucepan. Add the sugar and vanilla bean and place over medium heat. Bring up to the boil, then reduce to a simmer. Stir occasionally, until the sugar is dissolved. Remove from the heat, scrape the seeds from the vanilla bean and add these along with the white chocolate to the hot cream. Stir until combined and smooth.

Add the yolks to a large bowl. Take a whisk and very slowly combine the hot cream into the yolks, beating continuously, until incorporated. Pour the custard through a fine sieve into a couple of suitable ovenproof dishes that will fit inside a high-sided roasting pan. Pour hot water into the pan until it comes three-quarters of the way up the side of the custard dishes. Cover with tinfoil and place in the centre of your oven.

Check after 20 minutes, then at 10-minute intervals until set. The custard is ready when it is still a little nervous in the centre. Remove from the water bath and let cool at room temperature before placing in the fridge until required.

To make the Black Doris plum jelly, drain the plums over a bowl to catch the juice. Keep the plums for later in the recipe. Measure out 2½ cups (625 ml/21½ fl oz) of the plum juice and pour into a saucepan. Add the port, brown sugar, cloves, allspice, cinnamon stick and orange zest. Bring up to the boil, then simmer for 15 minutes. Strain off and discard the solids and keep the hot liquid.

Bloom the gelatine leaves in a bowl of cold water for 5 minutes. Drain and squeeze out the water from the gelatine, then stir into the hot liquid. Pour into a dish and place in the refrigerator to set.

For the stewed rhubarb, place all the ingredients in a heavy-bottomed saucepan over medium-low heat. Cook down, stirring occasionally, for 20–30 minutes until nicely stewed. Remove from the heat and let cool, then refrigerate until required.

To put the trifle together, cut the sponge cakes into 3.5 cm (1½ in) strips. Take a large trifle bowl and line the bottom of each with the sponge strips.

Pour the jam and port into a bowl and mix until combined. Brush the jam and port mix onto the sponge. Cut the reserved plums into quarters and discard any pips. Arrange the plums and rhubarb over the top of the sponge, then top with plum jelly.

Now carefully spread the white chocolate custard over the fruit and jelly. Follow with the whipped cream. Place the trifle in the refrigerator.

To garnish, melt the white chocolate in a heatproof bowl set over a saucepan of simmering water (making sure the bowl does not touch the water). Pour onto an oven tray and spread out with a spatula until thinly covered. Do the same with the milk chocolate, spreading it out on a separate oven tray. Refrigerate and let set for 10 minutes. Remove and take a large knife and scrape it towards you over the chocolate to create thin rolls of delicate white and milk chocolate. Sprinkle over the trifle.

To serve, take a large spoon and scoop out portions of the trifle, making sure you dig down to the bottom of the trifle dish so each portion has all the components of the pudding.

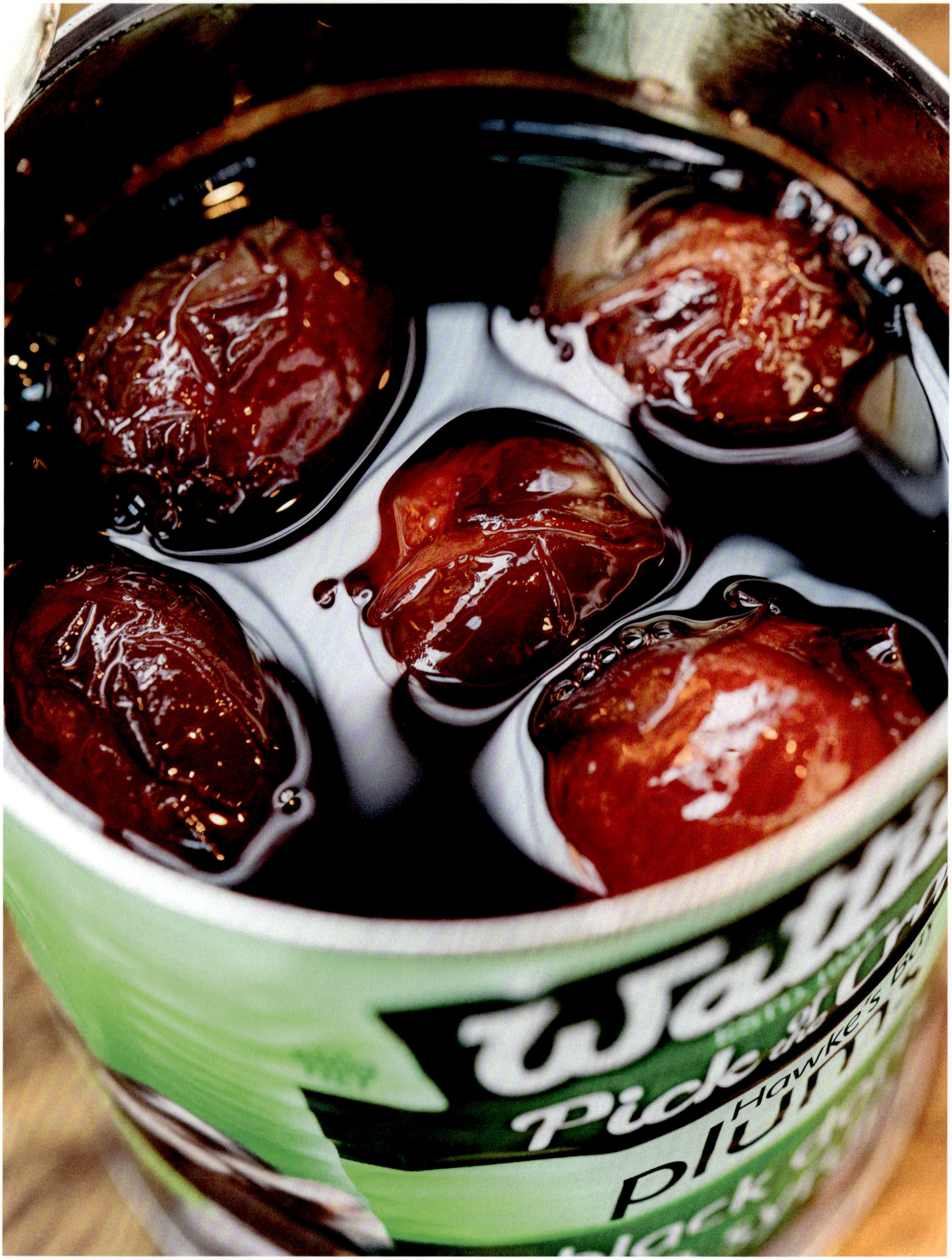
Hawke's

PUDDING 321

Coconut rice pudding with passion fruit, mango and meringue

Having attended boarding school from the age of nine, on a daily basis for many years I was subjected to a large amount of very average institutionalised food. It was simply fodder that I presume ticked a couple of nutrition boxes. The only meagre highlight I recall from the rotating menu was that we were served Tip Top vanilla ice cream every Sunday lunchtime. One of the most vivid of the many disgusting food memories I endured was the vile rice pudding that they used to serve up most weeks, which could be described as 'pale brown gloopy slop'. It was studded with the odd raisin that was plump and bitter due to hours of bathing in the bain-marie with the lid on. I made a pact with myself there and then that rice pudding would never again pass my lips . . . so obviously the recipe below is me reneging on this. I now see it as a challenge to turn each bad food memory from my past (cue Brussels sprouts, tripe and swede) into something wonderful and delicious. Putting bias to one side, I'm adamant you can make any product or dish taste wonderful with a little thought, care and attention.

By all means swap out different fruits in this recipe. I really like the combination of local passion fruit and good-quality imported mangoes; it's both tropical and sharp.

Serves 6

COCONUT RICE PUDDING
¾ cup (165 g/5¾ oz) medium- or short-grain rice
3 cups (750 ml/26 fl oz) milk
½ cup (125 ml/4 fl oz) coconut cream
⅓ cup (75 g/2¾ oz) sugar
½ vanilla bean, split in half lengthways

COCONUT MERINGUES
4 egg whites
4 tablespoons boiling water, slightly cooled
2 tablespoons white wine vinegar
2 cups (460 g/1 lb) caster sugar
1 cup (90 g/3¼ oz) desiccated coconut, toasted

LIME SYRUP
1½ cups (350 g/12 oz) caster sugar
200 g (7 oz) palm sugar, chopped
350 ml (12 fl oz) water
3 tablespoons lime zest
150 ml (5 fl oz) lime juice

TO ASSEMBLE
2 mangoes, cut into small dice
6 ripe passion fruit

Place the rice, milk, coconut cream, sugar and vanilla bean into a saucepan over medium heat. Stir occasionally and bring up to a simmer. Cook low and slow for 30–35 minutes, stirring often to prevent the rice from catching on the bottom of the pan. Check after 20 minutes, and remove from the heat once the rice is plump and cooked. The rice pudding should still have a runny consistency, which will thicken as it chills. Remove from the heat, let cool, remove and discard the vanilla bean and refrigerate until required.

Preheat the oven to 100°C (200°F). Line two baking trays with baking paper.
To make the meringues, whip the egg whites, boiling water and vinegar together in a stand mixer until foamy. Add the sugar, a spoonful at a time, while continuously mixing at medium speed. The meringue is ready when it is stiff and glossy. Fold in the toasted coconut. Spoon heaped teaspoon-sized blobs onto the prepared trays, making sure to leave a little space between them.

Bake for 1½ hours, rotating trays halfway through baking. When the time is up, turn off the oven and leave the meringues in the oven without opening the door until completely cooled, preferably overnight. Keep half a dozen meringues for this dish and freeze the rest for another day.

For the lime syrup, to a saucepan add both sugars and the water. Place over medium heat and simmer for 10 minutes, until the sugars are completely dissolved. Remove from the heat and then stir in the lime zest and juice. Let cool, then refrigerate until required.

I like serving this in glass tumblers or similar so you get to see the layering of the goodies. Start by spooning in some rice pudding, followed by some mango and passion-fruit pulp and then some crushed coconut meringue. Repeat with another layer, then finish with a liberal teaspoon or two of the lime syrup. Chill for an hour or two in the fridge prior to serving, or eat now!

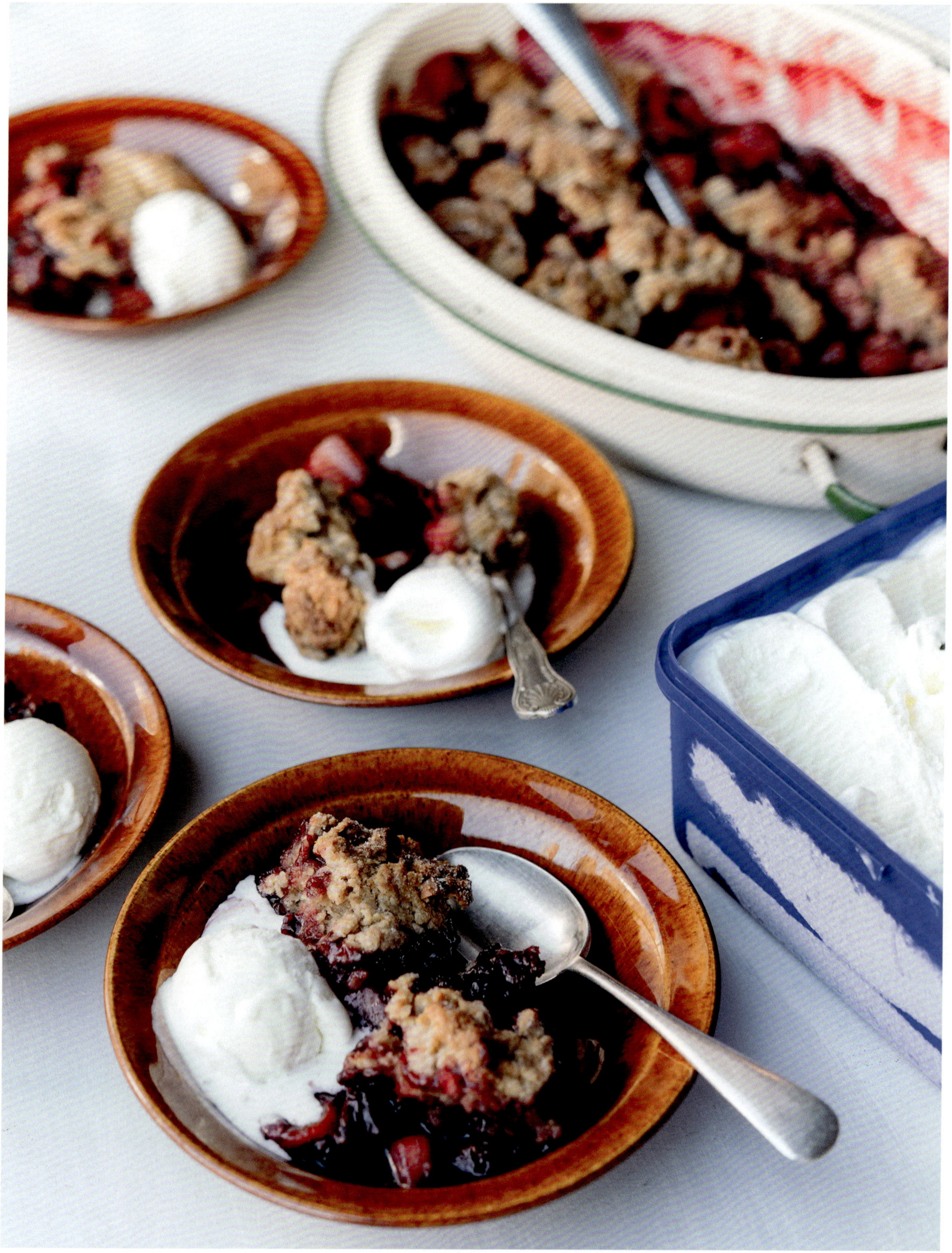

Tamarillo and pear macadamia nut cobbler

I came across the term 'cobbler' while attending culinary school in the US more than 30 years ago. The word actually originates from the UK and refers to a savoury or fruit filling cooked in a baking dish with a cake, biscuit or dumpling topping. I kind of see a cobbler as being the posh cousin of our humble crumble. These styles of puddings, I feel, fit our country's personality perfectly: warm, generous, informal and comforting, with almost infinite possible flavour combinations. Bed partners for warm cobbler? Vanilla ice cream will always be a Kiwi favourite, fresh custard is another go-to, pouring cream always works for me, and of course the last resort to ride shotgun is plain old blue-top milk.

Serves 6

COBBLER DOUGH
2 cups (300 g/10½ oz) plain flour
1 tablespoon baking powder
1 teaspoon ground cinnamon
⅓ cup (75 g/2¾ oz) sugar
pinch salt
75 g (2¾ oz) cold butter, diced
1 cup (160 g (5½ oz) roasted macadamia nuts, roughly chopped

finely grated zest of 1 orange
finely grated zest of 1 lemon
1 cup (250 ml/9 fl oz) cream

TAMARILLOS
1 kg (2 lb 4 oz) ripe tamarillos
1⅓ cups (245 g/8½ oz) brown sugar

TO COOK AND SERVE
1 kg (2 lb 4 oz) pears, peeled, cored and diced
2 tablespoons plain flour
2 tablespoons white sugar

Start by making the cobbler dough. Sift the flour, baking powder and cinnamon into a bowl. Add the sugar, salt and butter. With clean hands, rub the butter into the dry ingredients until the mix resembles coarse breadcrumbs. Now add the macadamia nuts and both zests. Mix through. Finally, as gently as possible, fold through the cream to make a soft dough, being careful not to overwork the mixture. Cover the bowl with clingfilm.

To prepare the tamarillos, place a large saucepan of water over high heat and bring up to a boil. Take a sharp paring knife and score an 'x' on the bottom of each tamarillo and cut the small core at the top away also. Blanch the tamarillos in the boiling water for approximately a minute, until the skins start to split. Remove with a slotted spoon and plunge directly into iced water. Leave for a minute or two to cool, then peel and discard the tamarillo skin. Slice the tamarillos into rounds, and place in a bowl with the brown sugar. Refrigerate for at least a couple of hours, preferably overnight.

Preheat your oven to 180°C (350°F).

Place the pears in a saucepan over medium heat, and cook for 5 minutes or so, until they soften up a little and start letting go of some of their juice. Remove from the heat, sprinkle over the flour and stir through. Mix the pears with the tamarillos and tip into the bottom of an ovenproof dish. Take the cobbler dough and break off largish pieces to top the fruit. Press down slightly. A few gaps are all good, as the juices from the fruit will seep through and stain the dough beautifully.

Sprinkle the dough with the white sugar, then place in the oven to bake for about 40 minutes. Keep an eye on it from the 30-minute mark. It's ready when the cobbler topping is golden and cooked through. Remove from the oven and let it sit for 10 minutes or so before serving with a dollop of your favourite ice cream on the side. Eat now.

Feijoa and ginger parfait

While I do enjoy vegetables a lot, I am a massive fan of nearly all fruit. Somewhere near the top of my favourites list will always be the feijoa. I have always thought of the feijoa as one of our most exotic fruits that grow well in this country. Known in other parts of the world as 'pineapple guava', it's a fruit that signals autumn is upon us. A perfectly ripe feijoa is a real treat to eat, and I also love the perfume that permeates throughout the house from a bowl of them sitting on the bench. And, finally, I guess the reason I feel this beautiful fruit is so inherently New Zealand is that the flowers look like little replicas of our special pōhutukawa blooms.

Serves 6–8

FEIJOAS
1 kg (2 lb 4 oz) peeled ripe feijoas
¾ cup (165 g/5¾ oz) sugar
1 vanilla pod, split in half lengthways

PARFAIT
400 ml (14 fl oz) cream
150 g (5½ oz) sugar
⅓ cup (80 ml/2 fl oz) water
6 egg yolks
4 teaspoons ground ginger

TO SERVE
few ginger biscuits, such as Gingernuts (optional), crushed, to serve

Firstly, cut the peeled feijoas into 5 mm (¼ in) rounds and place them, along with the sugar and the split vanilla pod, in a saucepan. Place over medium-low heat and bring up to a simmer. Cook for 10–15 minutes, stirring occasionally, until the feijoas soften and the liquid begins to thicken slightly. Remove from the heat, let cool, then set a small amount (with the vanilla pods) aside for serving. Purée the remainder with a stick blender and refrigerate.

Line a regular loaf tin with clingfilm and set aside.
In a bowl, whip the cream until soft peaks form. Keep in the refrigerator.
Next, place the 150 g (5½ oz) sugar and the water in a small saucepan and place over medium heat. Simmer for 5–7 minutes, until the sugar has dissolved and the syrup begins to thicken. The mixture needs to reach 115°C (225°F) on a sugar thermometer, or what we call 'soft ball stage'. You can test this without a thermometer by dropping a little of the sugar syrup into a small bowl of cold water. Once the sugar is cold, it should feel soft and pliable when rubbed between your fingers. Set the hot sugar aside while you deal with the yolks.
In a stand mixer fitted with the whisk attachment, beat the egg yolks for 5 minutes or so until pale and thick. Whisk in the ground ginger. With the whisk running, slowly add the hot sugar syrup a little at a time, until incorporated. Whisk for another 5–7 minutes, until the side of the mixing bowl is no longer warm.
With a rubber spatula, turn the egg and sugar mix out into a large bowl. Take the whipped cream, and give it a couple of whisks to get it back to soft peaks.

Fold the cream into the egg and sugar mix. Now gently fold through 2 cups of the feijoa purée, until combined. Keep the remaining puree for serving.

Pour the parfait mixture into the prepared loaf tin and freeze for at least 4 hours or overnight.

If the parfait has been in the freezer overnight, let it sit on the bench for 30 minutes before turning out onto a serving dish.

Either serve the parfait as is with the stewed feijoa poured over the top, or slice individual slices and serve on cold plates with the stewed feijoa on the side. If you have a packet of Gingernuts lying around, crush up a few and add on top. Eat now.

Quince sticky date pudding with orange cinnamon mascarpone and runny custard

I doubt there are many people out there who don't like a bit of sticky date pudding now and then. It's one of those rare dishes that kind of radiates happiness and pleasure when you see it on a menu. Many people love to smother this pudding in butterscotch sauce; however, I find it rich enough as it is. I prefer to add a cold, runny custard and, in this case, some mascarpone flavoured with orange and cinnamon. What takes this sticky date offering into the stratosphere is the introduction of poached quince. The flavour profile is near perfect.

Serves 6–8

POACHED QUINCE
1 kg (2 lb 4 oz) peeled quinces
2 cups (440 g/15½ oz) white sugar
2 cups (500 ml/17 fl oz) water
2 cinnamon sticks

PUDDING
2¼ cups (400 g/14 oz) dates
1 cup (250 ml/9 fl oz) water
1 teaspoon baking soda
250 g (9 oz) butter, at room temperature, plus extra for greasing
1 cup (230 g/8 oz) brown sugar
1 egg
1½ cups (225 g/8 oz) plain flour
1 teaspoon ground mixed spice
1 teaspoon baking powder

ORANGE CINNAMON MASCARPONE
1½ cups (330 g/11½ oz) mascarpone
finely grated zest of 1 orange
½ teaspoon ground cinnamon
1 tablespoon icing sugar

CUSTARD
2 cups (500 ml/17 fl oz) cream
¼ teaspoon vanilla bean paste
3 egg yolks
½ cup (110 g/3¾ oz) sugar

Preheat your oven to 180°C (350°F).

Take the peeled quinces and cut into quarters, cut out the pips and core, then cut the quarters in half again. Set aside.

In a small saucepan, dissolve the sugar in the water over low heat.

Arrange the quince in an ovenproof dish so the pieces sit relatively tightly together. Pour over the sugar water and add the cinnamon sticks. Place in the oven and cook for about an hour, until the quinces are soft through, golden and lightly caramelised on top. Remove from the oven, and let cool. Leave the oven on for the pudding.

Next, take the dates and roughly chop with a sharp knife. Place in a saucepan, cover with the water, then place over medium-low heat, stirring occasionally for 10 minutes or so, until the dates are soft. Remove from the heat and, with a fork, roughly mash the dates into a wet paste with small chunks of dates remaining. Add the baking soda and stir in. Set aside.

In a stand mixer fitted with the paddle attachment, or using a handheld electric whisk, beat the butter and brown sugar until creamy and light. Break in the egg, beating to incorporate. Now stir in the date paste, and sift in the flour, mixed spice and baking powder. Mix thoroughly to create a batter.

Grease a pudding dish or other suitable ovenproof dish (or individual ramekins) with butter. Line the bottom of the dish with the poached quince pieces.

Pour over the sticky date batter. Cover tightly with tinfoil and place in a large, deep oven tray. Fill the tray with enough hot water to come up to about three-quarters of the sticky date dish. Place in the oven and bake for 40–45 minutes, until the sticky date pudding is firm and cooked through but still moist. Remove from the water bath and let cool for 10 minutes.

Meanwhile, place the mascarpone, orange zest, cinnamon and icing sugar in a bowl and combine well. Refrigerate until required.

To make the custard, place the cream and vanilla paste in a saucepan over medium heat. When the cream comes up to a simmer, remove from the heat.

In a bowl, whisk the egg yolks and sugar until creamy and pale. Slowly pour in the hot cream, whisking constantly until completely incorporated. Pour this egg and cream mixture back into the pan and place over low heat. Take a wooden spoon and stir continuously until the custard begins to slightly thicken—just enough to coat the back of the spoon. Remove immediately and strain through a sieve. Serve now or let cool and then store in the fridge until required.

Invert the pudding to highlight and unearth the beautiful poached quince. Portion as you please, spoon on a liberal amount of the mascarpone, then pour over a generous amount of cold runny custard. Eat now!

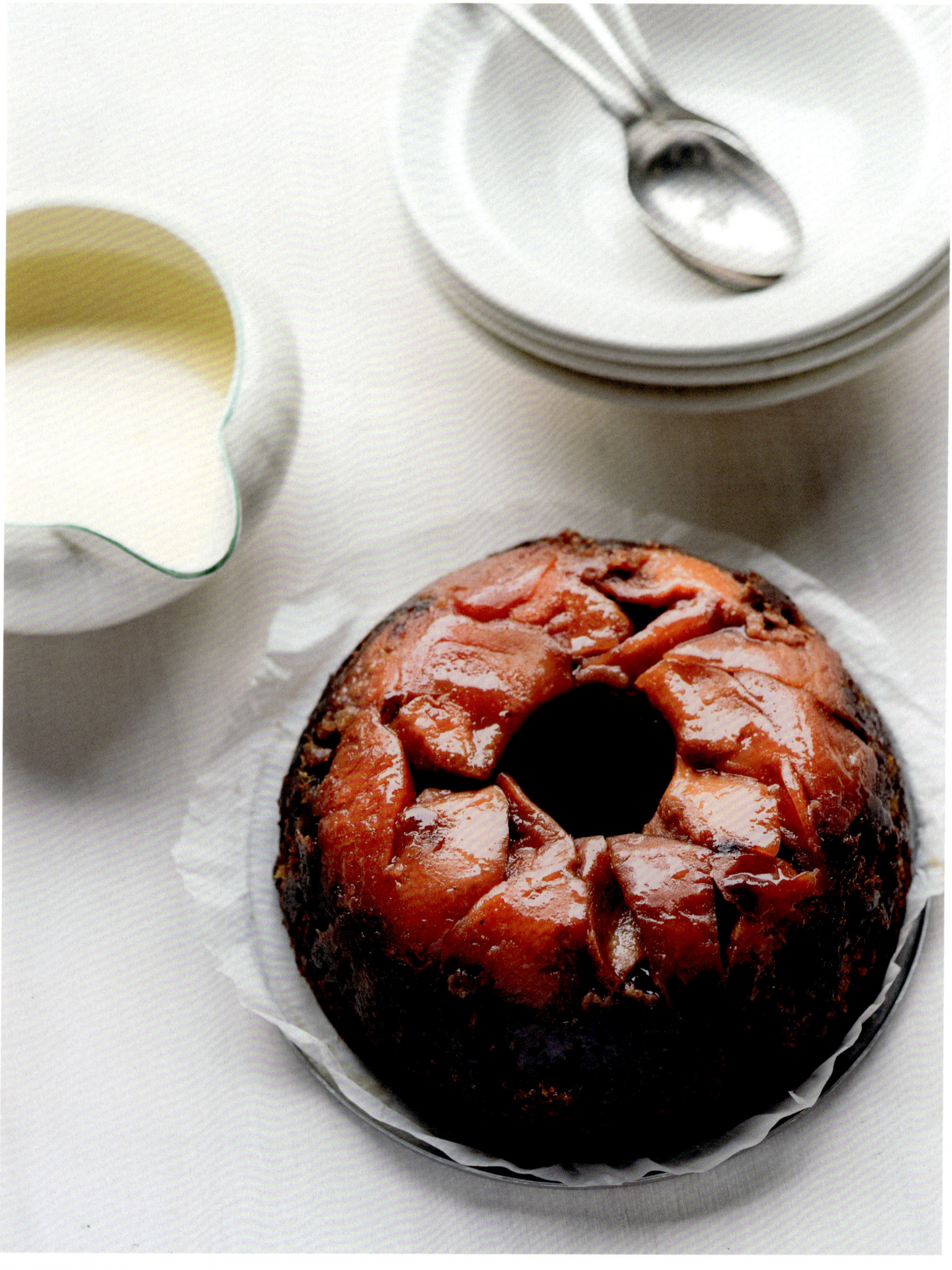

PUDDING 331

Peach and pineapple crumble with coconut custard

It wouldn't surprise me at all if someone told me that, as far as puddings go in this country, apple crumble is made more than any other. Apples are about all year round, and crumble is child's play to put together. In fact, when the word 'crumble' is mentioned, it brings a rush of happy endorphins along with it. So here is a bit of a play on the traditional apple crumble model. I know pineapples aren't grown in New Zealand, but they are among the tropical fruits—along with bananas—that have been around and plentiful since my childhood. Peaches are in season for a good duration of summertime, and perfectly ripe specimens are delicious paired with a super-sweet fresh pineapple. In winter, reach for the tinned versions, but I'd cut back a bit of the sugar.

Serves 6

PEACH AND PINEAPPLE
6 peaches
½ pineapple, peeled
½ cup (110 g/3¾ oz) sugar
1½ teaspoon ground ginger
1 teaspoon vanilla bean paste
¼ cup (60 ml/2 fl oz) orange juice
finely grated zest and juice of 1 lime
2 teaspoons cornflour
1 tablespoon water

CRUMBLE TOPPING
½ cup (75 g/2¾ oz) plain flour
⅓ cup (60 g/2¼ oz) brown sugar
½ cup (45 g/1½ oz) desiccated coconut
½ cup (30 g/1 oz) coconut flakes
½ cup (80 g/2¾ oz) macadamia nuts, roughly chopped
75 g (2¾ oz) cold butter, diced

COCONUT CUSTARD
425 ml (15 fl oz) coconut cream
100 ml (3½ fl oz) cream
½ vanilla bean
3 egg yolks
½ cup (110 g/3¾ oz) sugar

Bring a large saucepan of water up to the boil. Score the peaches with a little cross on the bases, add them to the boiling water for a minute or two, then plunge into iced water to cool. Peel and discard the skins then slice the peaches into eighths, discarding the pits. Place in a bowl.

Take the pineapple and cut into liberal bite-sized pieces. Add to the peaches along with the sugar, ginger, vanilla, orange juice and lime zest and juice. Mix through, then tip into a saucepan and place over medium-low heat. Cook for 15 minutes, until the peaches begin to break down.

Next, combine the cornflour with the water, then stir this through the hot fruit. Allow to thicken slightly, then remove the pan from the heat and let cool to room temperature.

To make the crumble topping, place all the ingredients into a bowl. With clean hands, rub the butter into the dry ingredients until incorporated. Set aside while you make the custard.

For the custard, place the coconut cream, cream and vanilla bean in a saucepan and place over medium heat. Bring to a simmer and remove from the heat.

In a bowl, whisk together the egg yolks and sugar.

Take the vanilla bean out of the pan, use a small sharp knife to split it in half lengthways and scrape the seeds out into the cream. While whisking continuously, slowly add the hot coconut cream mixture into the egg yolks and sugar. Once fully incorporated, pour the entire mixture back into the pan and place over low heat.

Stirring all the time with a wooden spoon, cook gently until the custard begins to thicken—just enough to coat the back of a spoon. As soon as this happens, remove from the heat, pass through a sieve into a bowl and let cool. Refrigerate until required.

Preheat your oven to 160°C (315°F). Pour the stewed peaches and pineapple into an ovenproof dish. Cover with the crumble topping, then place in the oven for 20 minutes, until the crumble topping is golden and crisp. Remove and let cool for 10 minutes prior to serving.

To serve, spoon out liberal amounts of the crumble into pudding bowls, then pour over generous amounts of the coconut custard. Eat now.

334 EAT UP NEW ZEALAND: THE BACH EDITION

Lemon delicious with stewed rhubarb

Some ingredients are just made to go together, and this pud is a case in point. I think it might be something to do with the relationship between the lemon and rhubarb, bringing that sour and tart to the table, then creating the perfect balance by tempering it with just the right amount of sugar. This really is a delicious dessert, and most certainly one of my favourites. The lemon delicious should be served straight from the oven, with the stewed rhubarb and cold runny cream adding a delicious contrast to every mouthful.

Serves 6

STEWED RHUBARB
1 kg (2 lb 4 oz) rhubarb stalks, cut into even-sized pieces
¾ cup (165 g/5¾ oz) sugar
1 star anise
½ vanilla bean, split in half lengthways
1 orange

LEMON DELICIOUS
125 g (4½ oz) butter, plus extra for greasing
finely grated zest and juice of 2 lemons
6 tablespoons self-raising flour
1 cup (250 ml/9 fl oz) full-cream milk
4 eggs, separated
1 cup (220 g/7¾ oz) sugar
icing sugar, for dusting
cream, to serve

To make the stewed rhurbarb, place the rhubarb pieces in a saucepan with the sugar, star anise and vanilla bean. Take the orange and, using a vegetable peeler, peel three or four lengths of orange zest. Add the zest along with the juice of the orange to the pan. Mix everything together with a wooden spoon, then place the pan over medium-low heat. Stirring occasionally, cook for 15–20 minutes or so until the rhubarb is soft and stewed. Remove and let cool. Refrigerate until required.

Preheat your oven to 160°C (315°F). Grease an ovenproof dish with butter.
    In a stand mixer fitted with the paddle attachment, or using a handheld electric whisk, beat the butter and the lemon zest together until creamy. Slowly add the flour, milk and egg yolks until incorporated into the butter. Remove the bowl and stir through the lemon juice. It may curdle a little, but that's okay.
    In a separate and very clean, grease-free bowl, whisk the egg whites until fluffy. Slowly add the sugar, a little at a time, beating until stiff peaks form.
    Now fold a third of the egg whites gently into the lemon-egg yolk mixture. Carefully fold in the next third of the egg whites, followed by the final third. Be careful not to over-mix.
    Pour the lemon delicious batter into an ovenproof dish. Cover tightly with tinfoil and place in a large, deep oven tray. Fill the tray with enough just-boiled water to come about a third of the way up the side of the lemon delicious dish.
    Place in the centre of the oven and bake for 40 minutes, until the pudding is golden on the top and doubled in size.
    Remove and dust the lemon delicious with icing sugar. Spoon the hot pudding into serving bowls, add some stewed rhubarb, then pour over liberal amounts of runny cream. Serve now.

336 EAT UP NEW ZEALAND: THE BACH EDITION

Blueberry and citrus Eton mess

This is going to be my go-to summer dessert. Besides the lemon curd and meringues, which are pretty easy to make, the rest of the ingredients are basically store-bought. You can have a play-around with other citrus juices to make up the curd—try mandarin, grapefruit, orange, etc. This looks killer in a trifle bowl and is a textural symphony.

Serves 6

LEMON CURD
8 egg yolks
⅔ cup (140 g/5 oz) sugar
⅓ cup (80 ml/2½ fl oz) fresh lemon juice
¼ cup (60 g/2¼ oz) butter, roughly chopped
⅓ cup (80 ml/2½ fl oz) cream

MERINGUES
4 egg whites
2 tablespoons white vinegar
2 tablespoons cold water
2 cups (440 g/15½ oz) caster sugar

TO ASSEMBLE AND SERVE
1 x 300 ml (10½ fl oz) bottle cream
limoncello or Grand Marnier (optional)
1 cup (250 g/9 oz) passion-fruit pulp (optional)
3 x punnets blueberries (approx. 375 g/13 oz)
finely grated zest of 1 lemon

To make the lemon curd, put the egg yolks, sugar and lemon juice in a suitable-sized non-reactive saucepan. Whisk until combined.

Place the saucepan over medium heat and stir the mixture continuously with a wooden spoon, or better still a rubber spatula, until it turns into a thick curd—this will be shortly after it comes up to the boil.

Remove from the heat, stir in the butter and let the mixture cool before stirring in the cream. Pour into a jar or similar, then refrigerate until required.

Preheat your oven to 100°C (200°F). Line two baking trays with baking paper.

In a stand mixer fitted with the whisk attachment, or using a handheld electric whisk, beat the egg whites for a minute or so, then add in the vinegar and water. Whisk again for a minute or so until frothy, then slowly start adding the caster sugar, about a tablespoon at a time to begin with, then increasing the amount a little. It should take 10–15 minutes for all the sugar to be incorporated. The meringue batter is ready when it is stiff and shiny with a lovely gloss.

Using a couple of tablespoons, spoon the meringues onto the prepared baking trays.

Bake in the oven for 1½ hours, rotating the baking trays halfway through, then turn off the oven. Leave the meringues in the oven without opening the door until they have cooled to room temperature, or preferably overnight.

Store in a cake tin or airtight container until required. You won't use all the meringues in the Eton Mess so you'll have leftovers—that's a bonus.

Whip the cream until soft peaks form and refrigerate until required.

To assemble, take a glass trifle bowl (preferably one that's high-sided) and start layering. Begin with some slightly broken meringue, followed by a drizzle of booze (if using), some whipped cream, lemon curd and passion-fruit pulp (if using). Repeat the layers, finishing with cream and blueberries, a little passion-fruit pulp and the lemon zest. Refrigerate for an hour or so, then serve in individual bowls. Dream time!

Crêpes with mulled wine poached pears and chocolate sauce

I'm a sucker for fresh, warm, wafer-thin crêpes. When I was growing up crêpes were a bit of a treat, and a Sunday night thing for some reason. They were always served simply, with just lemon juice and white sugar. Eating them is a very textural experience as the crêpes are so soft and light, while the crunch of the sugar contrasts nicely. There is also the sweet-and-sour flavour combination, which everyone seems to love.

We have 'poshed it up' a bit here with the addition of mulled wine poached pears and our go-to chocolate sauce. The three components work beautifully together, or you can use them individually. Of course, you can trade the pears for basically any sort of stewed fruit.

Serves 6

MULLED WINE POACHED PEARS
3 firm, ripe pears
2 cups (500 ml/17 fl oz) red wine
½ cup (95 g/3¼ oz) brown sugar
peeled zest and juice of 1 orange
1 cinnamon stick
2 star anise
6 cloves
6 dried allspice berries

CHOCOLATE SAUCE
1 cup (250 ml/9 fl oz) cream
⅓ cup (40 g/1½ oz) good-quality cocoa
⅔ cup (140 g/5 oz) white sugar

CLASSIC CRÊPES
1 cup (150 g/5½ oz) flour
1 tablespoon sugar
pinch salt
1½ cups (375 ml/13 fl oz) milk
4 large eggs
3 tablespoons butter, melted

TO COOK AND SERVE
1 cup (250 ml/9 fl oz) cream
¼ cup (60 g/2¼ oz) butter, melted

To make the mulled wine poached pears, peel the pears and place them in a suitable-sized saucepan. Pour over the red wine, then add the rest of the goodies and place over medium-low heat. Place a saucer on top of the pears to keep them submerged in the liquid.

Cook ripe pears for 7 minutes or so (a little longer if they're not so ripe), then remove them from the liquid with a slotted spoon so they don't start to fall apart. Reduce the liquid a bit, then remove it from the heat and allow to cool. Place the pears back in the liquid to take on some more flavour and colour. Refrigerate until required.

For the chocolate sauce, place all the ingredients in a small saucepan. Place over medium-low heat and stir until the sugar has dissolved. Refrigerate until required.

To make the classic crêpes, place all the ingredients in a jug. Using a stick blender or similar, blend all the ingredients for a minute or so, until smooth and combined. Refrigerate for at least 30 minutes to let the batter relax.

Whip the cream until soft peaks form and refrigerate until required.

Heat a non-stick frying pan or skillet over medium heat. Brush with a little of the melted butter. Pour in enough crêpe batter to swirl around and cover the bottom of the pan. Cook for a minute or so, then flip and cook the other side for another 20 seconds or so. Repeat until you have used up all the batter, keeping the cooked crêpes warm.

To serve, place a couple of crêpes on each plate with half a poached pear. Add a dollop of cream and a healthy pour of the chocolate sauce to finish. Serve now.

PUDDING 339

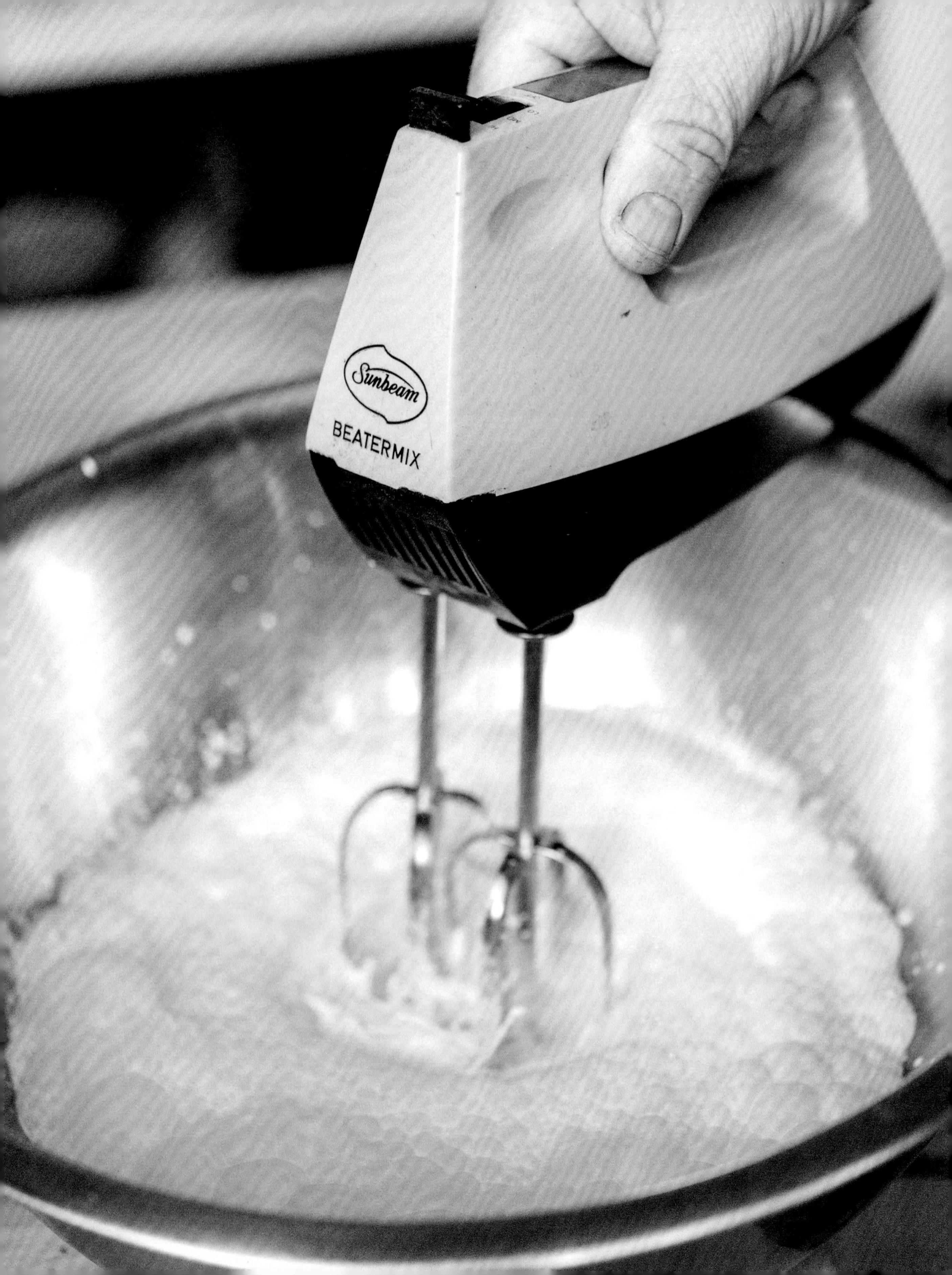
Sunbeam
BEATERMIX

WHIPPED CREAM

KIRĪMI PĀHUKAHUKA

Sponge drops

I adore sponge drops. I was first introduced to them by my good friend Ngaire Callaghan of Lake Tarawera fame some 30 years ago. Ngaire is a wonderfully talented home cook, and sponge drops are just one of her signature go-to treats. She has made them so many times that she could produce them with her eyes closed. Such a generous soul, Ngaire has kindly shared this recipe. Thanks, Ngaire!

Makes 10–12

2 eggs
½ cup (115 g/4 oz) caster sugar
¾ cup (35 g/1¼ oz) plain flour
½ teaspoon baking soda
1 teaspoon cream of tartar
softly whipped cream, to serve
raspberry jelly or jam (optional), to serve
icing sugar, for dusting

Preheat your oven to 200°C (400°F).

In a stand mixer fitted with the whisk attachment, or using a handheld electric whisk, beat the eggs and caster sugar for a good 5–7 minutes until creamy, thick and light. With a rubber spatula, scrape the mixture into a large bowl.

While the eggs and sugar are whipping, sift the flour, baking soda and cream of tartar together in a bowl.

Now sift the dry ingredients, a little at a time, into the beaten egg and sugar mixture, folding in the ingredients as gently as you can.

Line a couple of baking trays with baking paper. Use a regular soup-style spoon to spoon even spoonfuls, trying to keep them as round and as high as possible. Try to leave 2–3 cm (¾–1¼ in) between each sponge drop, to allow for spreading.

Place in the oven and bake for 4–5 minutes. Remove and let cool on the tray before gently extracting by running a thin spatula under each one.

Once the drops are completely cool, fill with whipped cream and, if using, the raspberry jelly or jam.

Refrigerate for a couple of hours prior to serving as this makes the sponge super soft. Dust with icing sugar and watch them disappear.

WHIPPED CREAM 343

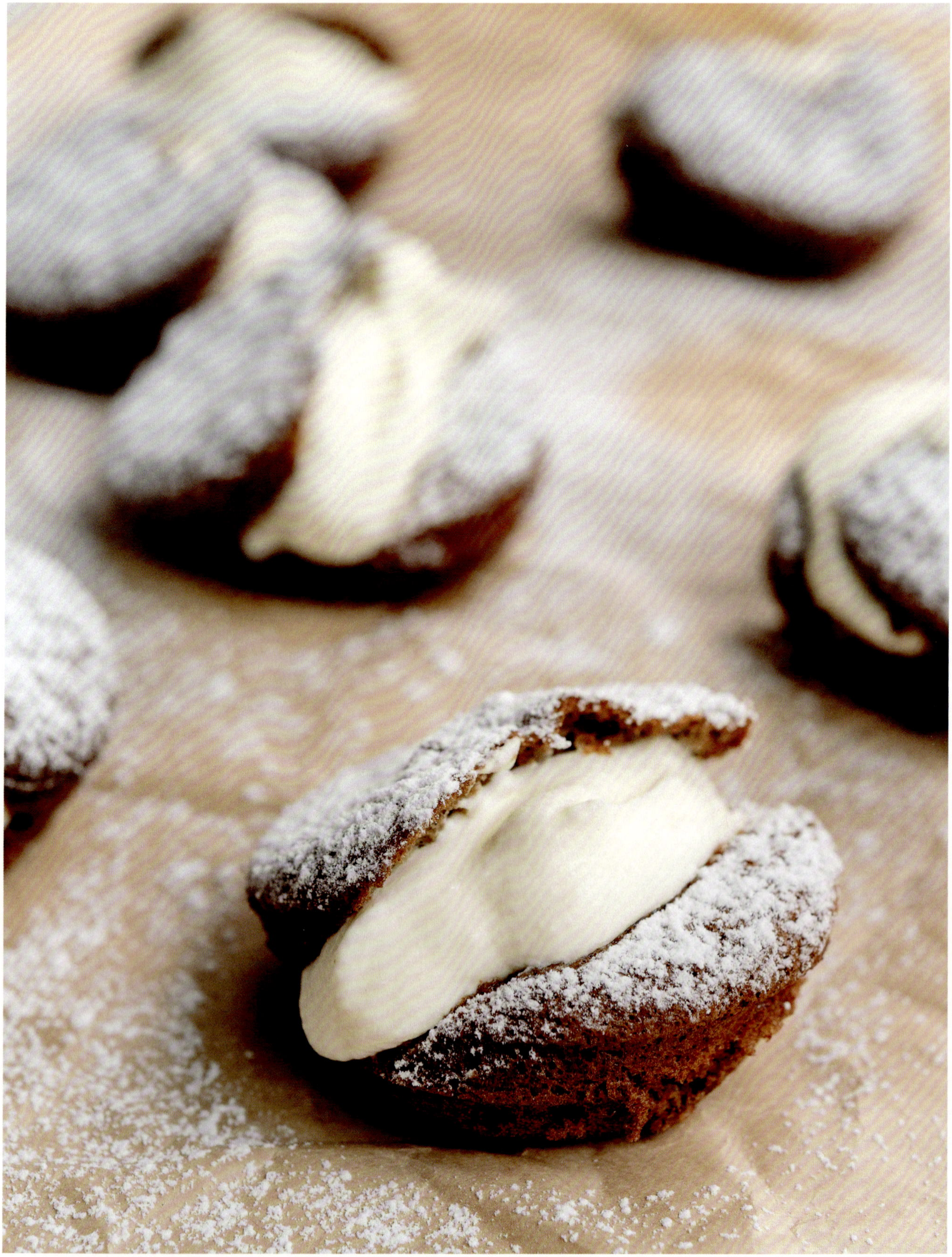

Cinnamon oysters

Haydo worked on this recipe for a couple of weeks, eventually settling on the one below. It was all about getting as delicate and soft a mouthfeel as possible to these delightful little sweet spiced sponges. He came to the conclusion that it was all about three different flours. These are special, too.

Makes 12

2 eggs
¼ cup (55 g/2 oz) caster sugar
2 teaspoons golden syrup
2 tablespoons plain flour
2 tablespoons cornflour
2 tablespoons rice flour
1 teaspoon baking powder
½ teaspoon baking soda
1 teaspoon ground cinnamon
½ teaspoon ginger powder
½ cup (125 ml/4 fl oz) cream
2 tablespoons icing sugar, plus extra for dusting

Preheat your oven to 180°C (350°F). Grease a sponge oyster tin or similar 12-holed tin with butter or oil.

In a stand mixer fitted with the whisk attachment, or using a handheld electric whisk, beat the eggs and caster sugar for at least 5 minutes, until pale and light. Then add the golden syrup and combine.

Sift the dry ingredients in a separate bowl. Now gently fold the dry ingredients into the egg and sugar mixture.

Divvy up the batter by spooning equal amounts into the holes of the greased tin.

Place in the oven and bake for 8–10 minutes, until puffed up and springing back when lightly touched.

Remove from the tin when they begin to cool and transfer to a wire rack.

Meanwhile, whip the cream with the icing sugar to medium-soft peaks.

Once the cinnamon oysters are completely cool, take a sharp knife and cut a slash, nearly all the way through, opening them up, and spoon in the whipped cream. Refrigerate for a couple of hours for ultimate softness, before dusting with icing sugar and serving these light clouds of deliciousness.

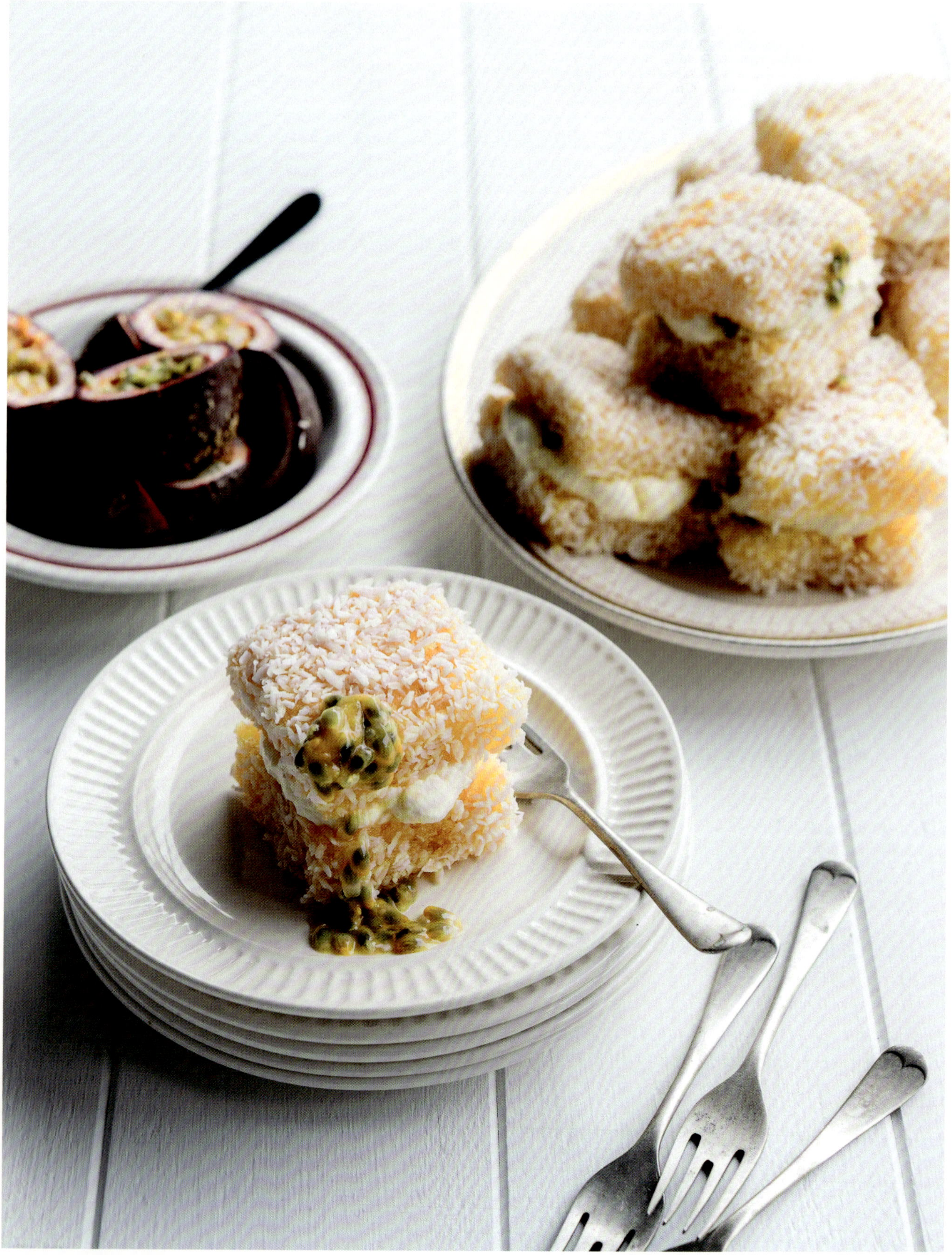

Passion-fruit lamingtons

I do love a fresh cream-filled lamington. They are such a distinctive sweet baking treat. Lamingtons take a bit of effort, but if made as part of a big afternoon tea spread they will inevitably be the first empty plate to be removed. Personally, I've always been a pink lamington guy over the chocolate variety. You'll love this slightly modern idea of using passion fruit, which creates a striking yellow and particularly delicious lamington. If you're short on passion-fruit juice, use half orange juice.

Makes 10–12

SPONGE
4 eggs, at room temperature, separated
1 teaspoon cream of tartar
1 cup (220 g/7¾ oz) sugar
¾ cup (310 g/11 oz) plain flour
1 cup (125 g/4½ oz) cornflour
2 teaspoons baking powder

PASSION-FRUIT SYRUP
2 gelatine leaves
1 cup (250 ml/9 fl oz) passion-fruit juice
1 cup (220 g/7¾ oz) sugar

TO ASSEMBLE
2 cups (180 g/6½ oz) coarse desiccated coconut
1 cup (250 ml/9 fl oz) cream
¼ cup (30 g/1 oz) icing sugar
6 passion fruit (optional), to serve

Preheat your oven to 170°C (325°F). Grease and line a 30 x 24 x 5 cm (12 x 9½ x 2 in) rectangular cake tin with butter or oil.

In a stand mixer fitted with the whisk attachment, or using a handheld electric whisk, beat the egg whites with the cream of tartar until stiff, then slowly incorporate the sugar, beating until the granules are dissolved. Now add the egg yolks, beating in one at a time.

Pour the batter into a large bowl, then, as lightly as possible, sift and fold in the flour, cornflour and baking powder.

Pour the sponge batter into the prepared cake tin. Place in the centre of the oven and bake for 20–25 minutes, until lightly golden and a skewer inserted into the centre of the sponge comes out clean.

Remove from the oven and let the sponge cool completely in the tin.

For the passion-fruit syrup, bloom the gelatine leaves in a small bowl of cold water for 5 minutes, until soft and pliable.

In a small saucepan, combine the passion-fruit juice and sugar. Place over medium-low heat and stir until the sugar has dissolved. Remove and let cool slightly.

While the passion-fruit syrup is still hot, drain and squeeze dry the gelatine leaves, and stir into the syrup. Set aside.

Take a serrated knife and carefully trim and slice a couple of millimetres from the outer layer of the sponge, then cut into lamington squares.

To finish, dip the edges of the sponge squares into the passion-fruit syrup, then press into the coconut. Repeat until complete, then refrigerate.

Split the lamingtons in half and place on a clean tray.

Whip the cream and sugar together to form semi-soft peaks. Top one inner side of a lamington half with cream then top with the other half. Refrigerate until required.

Serve on a small plate with a fork, add extra cream if you like and, if you have fresh passion fruit, I like to serve a little fresh pulp on the side.

348 EAT UP NEW ZEALAND: THE BACH EDITION

Haydo's sponge

There are many classic old-school recipes within these pages, all given a huge amount of respect, but there were certain ones that we felt had to be basically faultless or the best example you could find anywhere. I lost count of how many times we discussed lightness, softness, sweetness, height, colour and the all-important cream-to-sponge ratio. Anyhow, this is 'Haydo's sponge', and if you think you have a better sponge recipe, I'd love to try it. I'm confident that if Haydo entered this in any national A&P show baking competition, he would pick up a rosette every time!

Makes 1 x 22 cm (8½ in) double-layer cake

4 eggs, at room temperature, separated
¾ cup (170 g/6 oz) caster sugar
¾ cup (90 g/3¼ oz) cornflour
1 tablespoon custard powder
1 teaspoon cream of tartar
½ teaspoon baking soda
½ cup (160 g/5½ oz) rhubarb and strawberry jam (page 416)
1½ cups (375 ml/13 fl oz) cream
¼ cup (30 g/1 oz) icing sugar, plus extra for dusting

Preheat your oven to 170°C (325°F). Line the bases of two springform round (22 cm/8½ in) sponge tins with baking paper and grease the sides.

In a stand mixer fitted with the whisk attachment, or using a handheld electric whisk, beat the egg whites until relatively thick. Gradually incorporate the sugar until you have a glossy meringue. Add the egg yolks, one at a time, and beat after each addition. Gently pour the batter into a large bowl.

Sift the cornflour, custard powder, cream of tartar and baking soda into a separate bowl, then repeat a couple of times. Sift once more, this time into the batter, a bit at a time, while lightly folding everything together. Divide the batter between the prepared tins and bake for 20–25 minutes, until lightly golden and a skewer inserted into the centres of the cakes comes out clean. Remove from the oven and let cool in the tins for about 10 minutes, then remove and transfer to a wire rack to cool completely.

Carefully remove the sponges from their tins. Spread the jam over the base sponge. Whip the cream and icing sugar together until stiff and spread over the jam. Place the top sponge on top, then dust with icing sugar to finish.

A classic cream-filled sponge should be light as a feather, hence a big wedge for everyone, served with a cake fork. Eat now.

Chocolate eclairs

I have had a lifelong addiction to chocolate eclairs. They are probably my favourite of all the whipped-cream-filled baked goods produced and loved by Kiwis. I am quite particular, and I'm sure a bunch of people will disagree, but my favourite glaze is and will always be a classic, buttery, bog-standard chocolate icing. Many prefer a real chocolate ganache, but I think that makes them a bit posh and for some reason never as nice to eat. The best (and certainly the biggest) eclairs I have found in my travels are from The Chocolate Eclair Shop, down the southern end of the main street in Ohakune. I've lost count of how many times I've pulled over to get my fix.

Makes 12

ECLAIRS
1 cup (250 ml/9 fl oz) water
125 g (4½ oz) butter
½ teaspoon salt
2 teaspoons sugar
1 cup (150 g/5½ oz) plain flour
4 eggs

CHOCOLATE ICING
1½ cups (185 g/6½ oz) icing sugar
50 g (1¼ oz) unsalted butter, softened
2 tablespoons good-quality cocoa
3 tablespoons boiling water

TO ASSEMBLE
2 cups (500 ml/17 fl oz) cream
2 tablespoons icing sugar
2 drops vanilla essence

Preheat your oven to 180°C (350°F).

To make the eclair pastry, place the water, butter, salt and sugar into a large saucepan over medium heat. Bring up to a simmer, then whisk in the flour. Once a dough starts to form, swap the whisk for a wooden spoon. Cook out the dough for a minute or so, stirring continuously, then remove from the heat.

One by one, beat in the eggs until the dough is smooth and sticky. Place in a piping bag with a large nozzle.

Grease and line a baking tray with baking paper. Pipe out your 12 eclairs, making sure you leave about 2 cm (¾ in) between each. Place in the oven and bake for about 35 minutes, until golden brown and crisp to the touch. Remove from the oven and let cool completely on a wire rack.

To make the chocolate icing, beat the icing sugar and softened butter together, using an electric mixer, until smooth. Slowly add the cocoa and boiling water, a bit at a time, while continuously whisking. Adjust the thickness of the icing using more or less boiling water. It should be quite thick, but still spreadable.

Whisk the cream, icing sugar and vanilla essence in a bowl to semi-stiff peaks. Slice your cooled eclairs lengthways, then ice them, and set aside to allow the icing to set. Fill with lashings of whipped cream. Serve immediately if you like your eclairs crisp or refrigerate for 30 minutes to allow them to soften.

WHIPPED CREAM 351

352 EAT UP NEW ZEALAND: THE BACH EDITION

Macadamia nut brandy snaps

My mother often used to serve brandy snaps as a quick and easy dessert for a dinner party. It was always the first thing I scoured the fridge for the morning after, hoping there may be one or two left. They would have gone a bit soft and sticky after that amount of time in the fridge but, being the store-bought variety, they were relatively thick, and would still have a bit of crunch to them.

There is something wonderful about the contrasts offered up when eating whipped-cream-filled brandy snaps. The textural difference is so extreme, but there's also the contrast of toffee sweetness tempered perfectly by the blandness of the cold cream. The following recipe makes a more delicate and relatively brittle brandy snap. They are best served immediately once filled with whipped cream.

Makes 12–18 (depending on size)

200 g (7 oz) butter, softened
200 g (7 oz) icing sugar
50 g (1¾ oz) liquid glucose
¾ cup (110 g/3¾ oz) plain flour
1 teaspoon ground ginger
1 teaspoon brandy
1 cup (160 g/5½ oz) macadamia nuts, finely ground
1 cup (250 ml/9 fl oz) cream

Preheat your oven to 180°C (350°F).

Place all the ingredients, except the cream, in a stand mixer and beat until well combined.

Create a template for the brandy snaps by cutting a circle in the lid of a plastic ice cream container or similar. Leaving a few centimetres of plastic around the outside of the circle, cut away the bulk of the rest of the plastic lid so essentially you have a ring-shaped template. (Note that the brandy snap batter will spread when cooking and will end up being slightly larger than the template circle itself.)

Line a baking tray with baking paper. Place the plastic template on the prepared tray and, with a palette knife, spread a generous amount of the batter across the circle template. Make two more brandy snap circles on the tray, leaving a little room for spread as they cook.

Place the tray in the oven and bake for approximately 6–8 minutes, until deep golden. Remove from the oven, let cool for 30 seconds or so, then quickly and carefully mould the brandy snap circles around a metal whisk handle (or similar). You have to move quickly as you can only mould these while they are still pretty hot. If the brandy snaps cool too much, place the tray back in the oven for 30 seconds or so until the snaps are pliable again. Repeat, making three at a time, until you have as many brandy snaps as required. Freeze or refrigerate the rest of the batter for another session.

Once the brandy snaps are cold, whip the cream to your desired consistency and use a piping bag (or a plastic bag with the corner snipped out) to fill the brandy snaps. Serve now.

Turkish delight meringues

If memory serves me right, I think I first saw rose water meringues at Queen Sally's Diamond Deli in Wellington's Lyall Bay. Katie Richardson heads up the talent in the kitchen there and at Maranui Cafe, a couple of hundred metres down the road. Both gaffs deserve the iconic reputation they have garnered over the years, serving delicious coffee and fabulous food. Anyway, the rose water touch always intrigued me, and because I love Turkish delight I thought I'd have go at folding little pieces of this sticky sweet into the meringues just prior to putting them in the oven. And I'll be darned, it actually worked! The Turkish delight adds a little chew, and the rose water gives the meringues this delicious kind of sweet floral note. Cream and strawberries complete these treats.

Makes 24–30

2 tablespoons water
2 tablespoons rose water
2 tablespoons white wine vinegar
4 egg whites
2 cups (460 g/1 lb) caster sugar
few drops red food colouring
100 g (3½ oz) rose Turkish delight, cut into small pieces
strawberries, hulled and quartered, to serve
whipped or runny cream, to serve
icing sugar, for dusting (optional)

Preheat your oven to 100°C (200°F). Line two baking trays with baking paper.
To a small saucepan, add the water, rose water and vinegar. Bring up to the boil, then remove from the heat.
    In a stand mixer fitted with the whisk attachment, or using a handheld electric whisk, beat the egg whites on medium speed for a minute or so. Add the rose water and vinegar mixture and continue to beat for a further minute, until the egg whites have become frothy. While beating, start slowly adding the caster sugar, a tablespoon at a time—it should take around 15 minutes to add most of the sugar. When you are about three-quarters of the way through the sugar, add a few drops of the red food colouring to give you the desired pink colour.
    The meringue is ready when it is stiff and glossy. With a rubber spatula, turn the meringue out into a large bowl and fold through the Turkish delight pieces. If you want a bit of a marbled effect, add a few more drops of the red food colouring and gently fold through without mixing it all in.
    Using a couple of tablespoons, spoon the meringues onto the prepared trays. Place in the oven and bake for 1½ hours, rotating trays halfway through the baking time. When the time is up, turn off the oven and leave the meringues in the oven without opening the door until completely cooled, preferably overnight.
    To serve, divvy up the strawberries into bowls. Add a meringue or two and liberal amounts of cream. Dust with icing sugar, if you feel the need. Eat now!

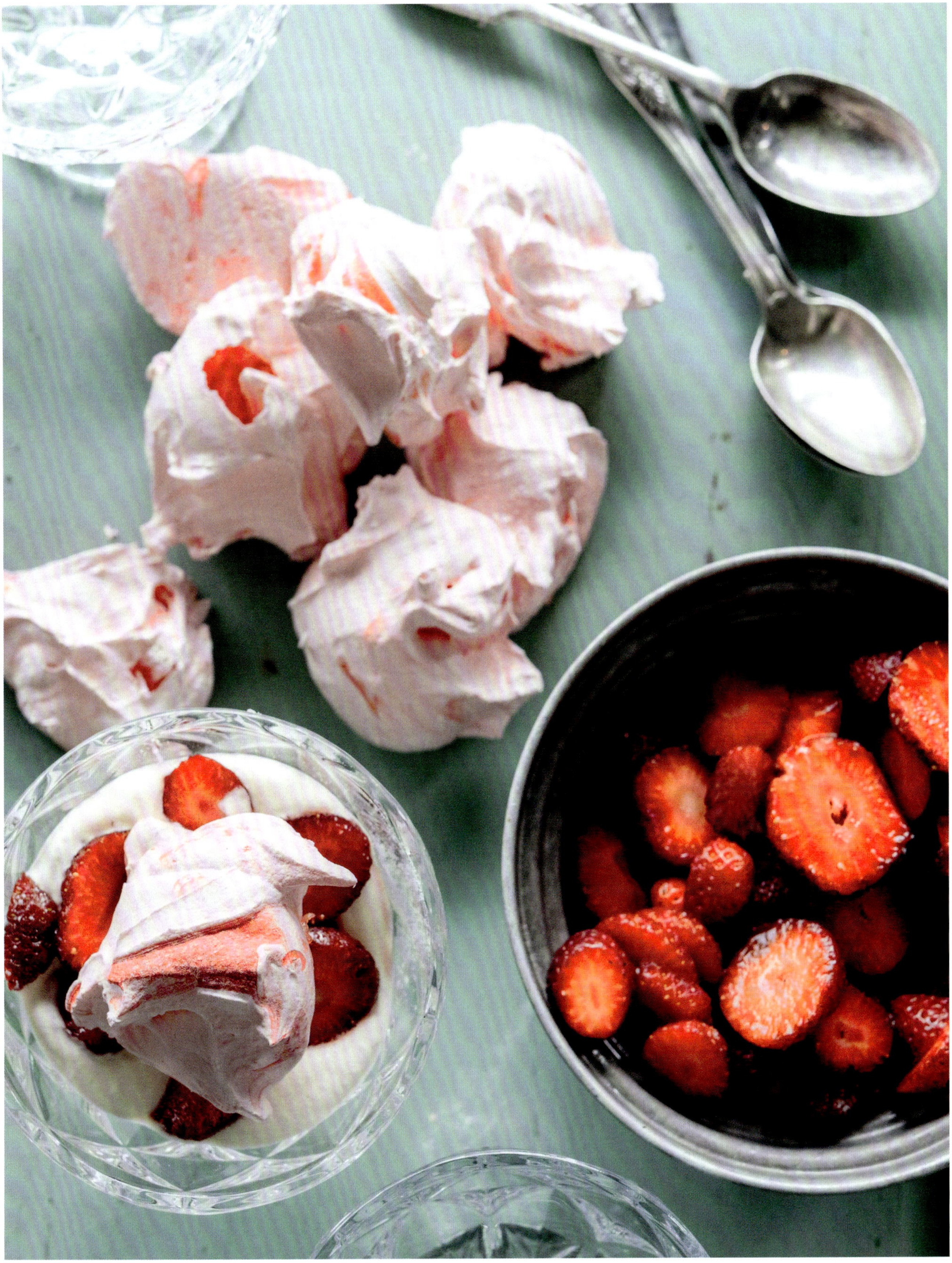

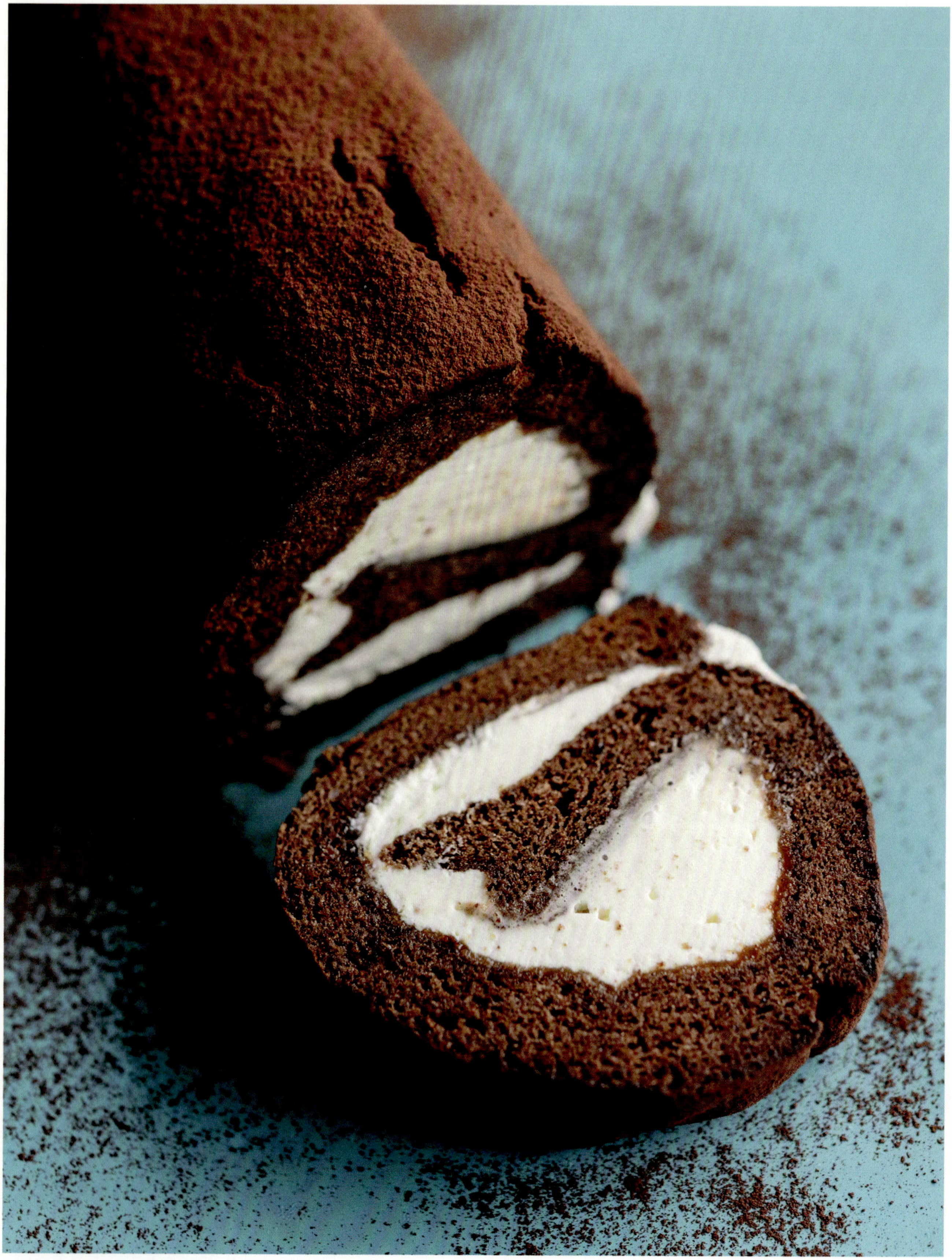

Spiced chocolate Swiss roll with quince jam

I was passed this wonderful recipe by a great pastry-chef friend who I worked with in New York City more than 30 years ago. It's pretty simple to make, with a subtle but interesting combination of cocoa and ground spice—kind of like chocolate sponge meets ginger kiss. I lined this one with quince jam and that worked wonderfully well, but you could use any preserve really, or none at all.

Makes 1 x 26 cm roll; serves 6–8

5 eggs, separated
¾ cup (170 g/6 oz) caster sugar
1 teaspoon ground cinnamon
1 teaspoon ground allspice
1 teaspoon ground cardamom
1½ teaspoons ground ginger
pinch finely ground black pepper
½ teaspoon ground cloves
1 tablespoon Dutch (unsweetened) cocoa, plus extra for dusting
1 tablespoon plain flour
quince jam (page 414) or other jam of your choice (optional)
1 cup (250 ml/9 fl oz) cream
2 tablespoons icing sugar
stewed fruit of choice (optional), to serve

Preheat your oven to 170°C (325°F). Grease and line a 26 x 35 cm (10¼ x 14 in) adjustable sponge roll tin with baking paper.

Place the egg yolks along with ½ cup (115 g/4 oz) of the caster sugar in stand mixer bowl fitted with a whisk attachment (or use a handheld electric whisk). Whisk at high speed for 7 minutes or so, until the mixture is pale and thick. Transfer the batter to a large bowl, then sift in the spices, cocoa and flour. Gently fold through with a spatula. Note the mixture will become quite sticky.

Wash the stand mixer bowl, then add your egg whites with the remaining ¼ cup (55 g/2 oz) caster sugar. Whisk for 4 minutes or so, until the whites form stiff peaks.

Using a large rubber spatula, gently fold the egg whites into the cocoa mixture, until combined. Pour the batter into the prepared tin and level out with the spatula. Place in the oven to bake for 5–7 minutes, until cooked through. Give it the old skewer test; if it comes out clean, it's ready. Leave in the tin, but place on a wire rack to cool completely, then cover with clingfilm if you are baking this the day before using.

Lay a clean tea towel down on your bench, and dust the cocoa liberally through a sieve to cover the tea towel. Turn out the sponge by quickly tipping the tin upside down in one confident movement on top of the cocoa-dusted tea towel. Remove the baking paper. With a palette knife, spread a layer of the quince jam (if using) over the sponge, right to the edges.

Whip the cream with the icing sugar to medium peaks, then slather on top of the quince jam.

Using the tea towel like you would a sushi mat, gently roll the cream-covered sponge into a Swiss roll. Refrigerate in the tea towel until required.

To serve, cut thick slices of the spiced Swiss roll. Serve unadulterated or with stewed fruit on the side.

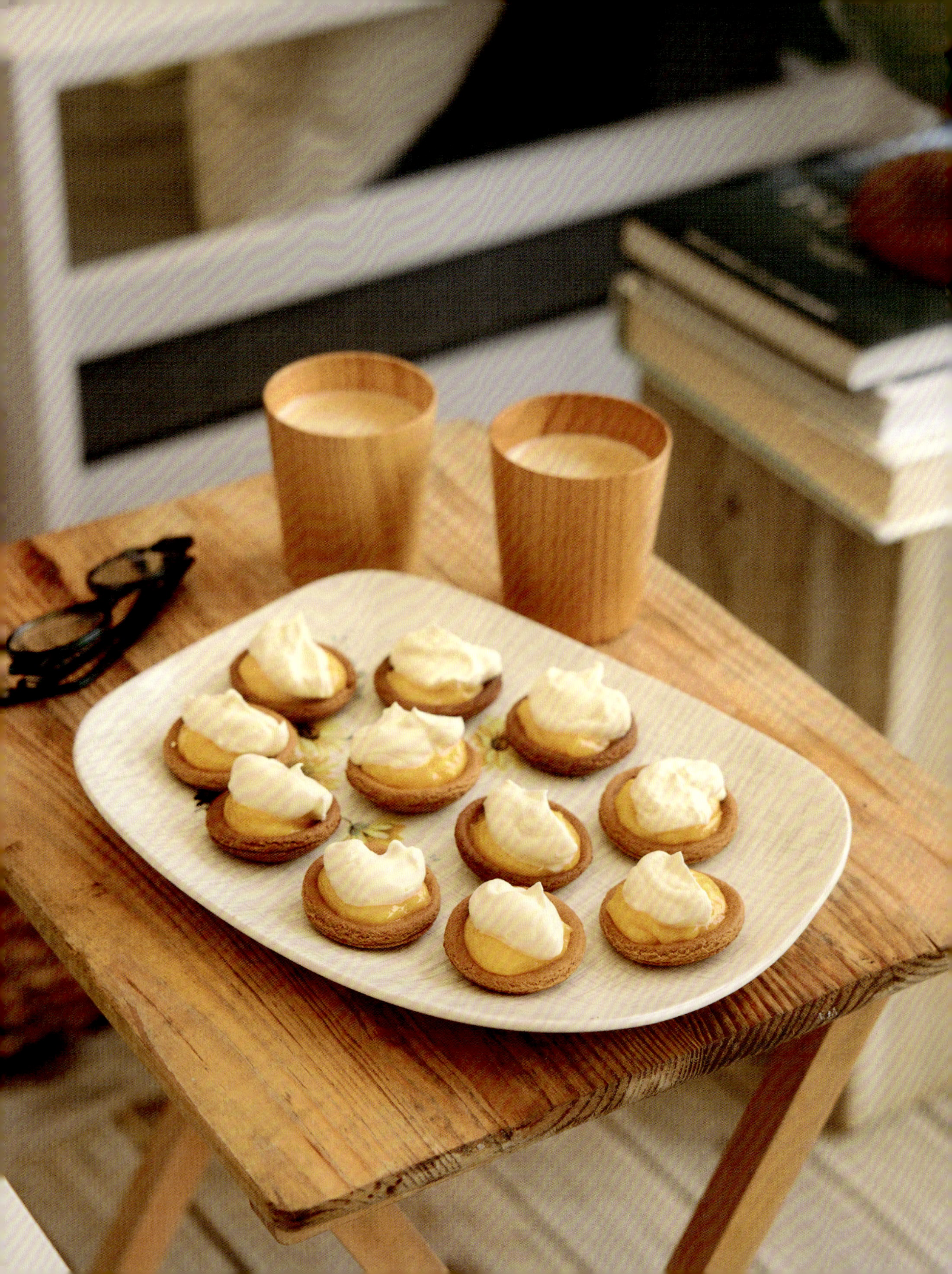

Gingernut lemon curd tarts

My mother used to serve these at dinner parties as a pretty posh offering back in the seventies. As a kid I would always hope there were some left over in the fridge the next morning. The gingernut bases would have softened up a bit by then, but I'd still smash one or two before breakfast. I love Griffin's Gingernuts: quite possibly the best coffee, tea or Milo dunkers in the business.

Makes 20 tarts

GINGERNUT LEMON CURD TARTS
1 x 250 g (9 oz) packet Griffin's Gingernuts
lemon curd (page 337)

TO ASSEMBLE AND SERVE
300 ml (10½ fl oz) cream

Preheat your oven to 180°C (350°F).

Spread the gingernuts out on a baking tray and place in the oven for 3–4 minutes. Remove from the oven and, while they are still hot and pliable, press each one down into the hole of a small muffin tray or similar. (Once they cool, they go back to their crunchy hard selves.) Repeat in batches.

Fill the tart bases with lemon curd. Refrigerate for a couple of hours to slightly soften.

To serve, whip the cream until soft peaks form, and spoon a liberal amount over each tart. Serve now.

Date and dried apricot scones with jam and cream

I say it all the time, but it seems to me I have always garnered more pleasure from simplicity executed well than from contrived and often over-embellished dishes that feed the eyes but not so much the taste buds. Classics are just that—they are tried and true, and have been made time and time again for a simple and very valid reason: they taste great, and often evoke wonderful eating memories and nostalgia.

There is something about a freshly made scone, and I can never pick whether I prefer savoury or sweet. I credit Peter Gordon with making the best cheese scone in the country; the sweet variety I believe is still up for grabs. Here's my latest attempt.

Makes 12 scones

SCONES
3 cups (450 g/1 lb) self-raising flour
2 teaspoons baking powder
150 g (5½ oz) chilled butter, roughly chopped
⅓ cup (75 g/2¾ oz) sugar, plus 1 tablespoon extra for sprinkling
zest of 1 orange
1½ cups (240 g/8½ oz) dates, halved
1½ cups (235 g/8½ oz) dried apricots
1 cup (250 g/9 oz) sour cream
½ cup (125 ml/4 fl oz) pouring cream, plus extra to brush

TO ASSEMBLE AND SERVE
butter (optional)
jam
1 x 300 ml (10½ fl oz) bottle cream, whipped

Preheat your oven to 200°C (400°F). Grease a baking tray.

Take a large bowl and sift in the self-raising flour and baking powder. Add the cold butter and, with clean hands, rub the butter through the flour for a minute or two. Add the sugar, orange zest, dates and dried apricots. Mix through.

Add the sour cream and pouring cream, and mix gently until the scone dough just comes together. Try not to overwork it, as that will make the scones tougher.

Turn the scone dough onto a clean, lightly floured bench. Work into a rough rectangle of about 20 x 30 cm (8 x 12 in). It will be about 4–5 cm (1½–2 in) high. Cut into 12 scones, then brush with a little extra cream and sprinkle over the extra sugar.

Place the scones on the prepared tray, leaving a little room between each one to allow them to expand and rise a little. Bake in the oven for 15–20 minutes, until golden. Remove from the oven and leave to cool on a wire rack.

To serve, cut the scones in half through the middle. Lightly butter them, if desired, then top with a decent schmear of jam and finish with a liberal dollop of the whipped cream. Serve now.

WHIPPED CREAM 361

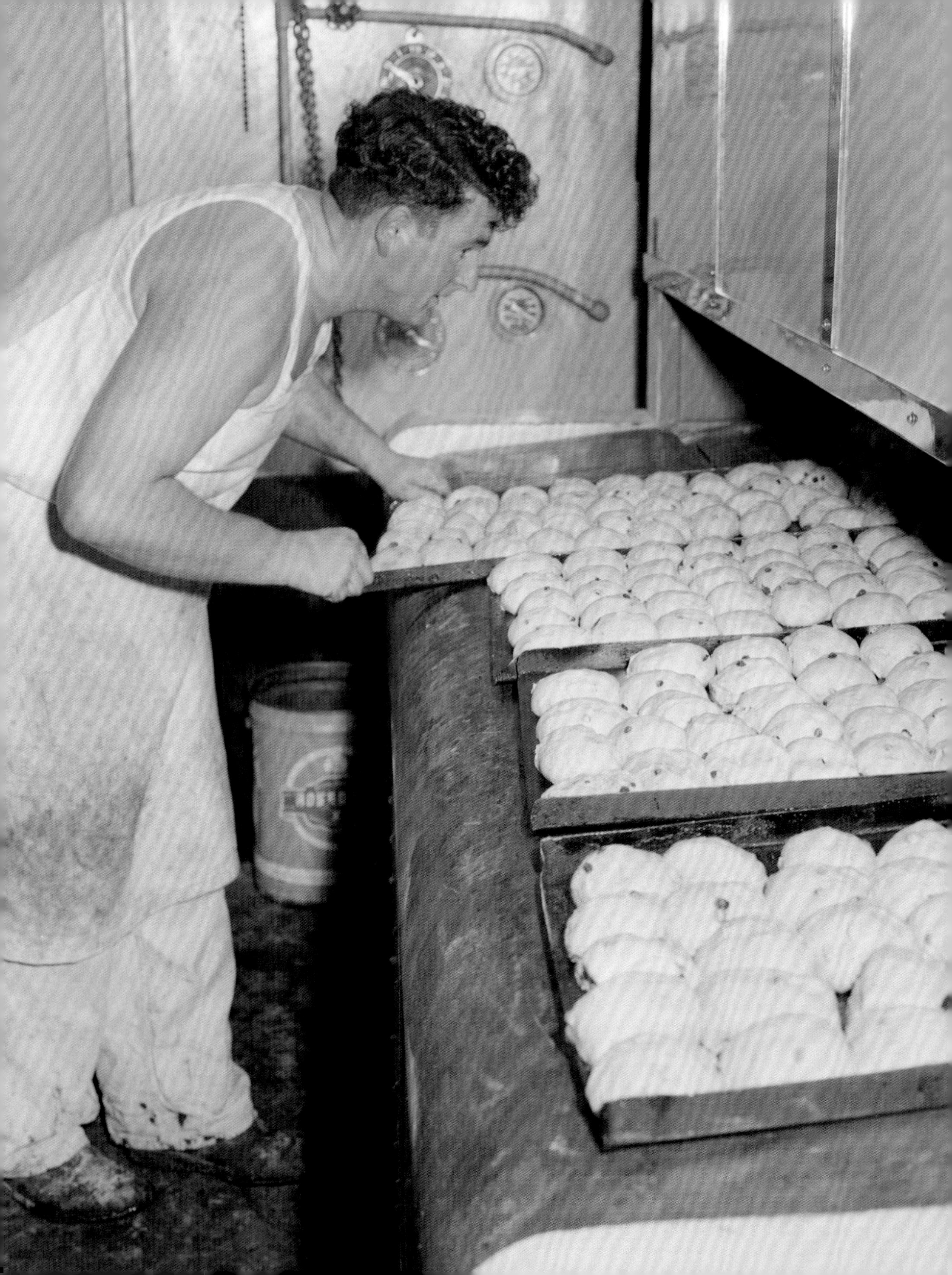

BAKED
Ō TUNU

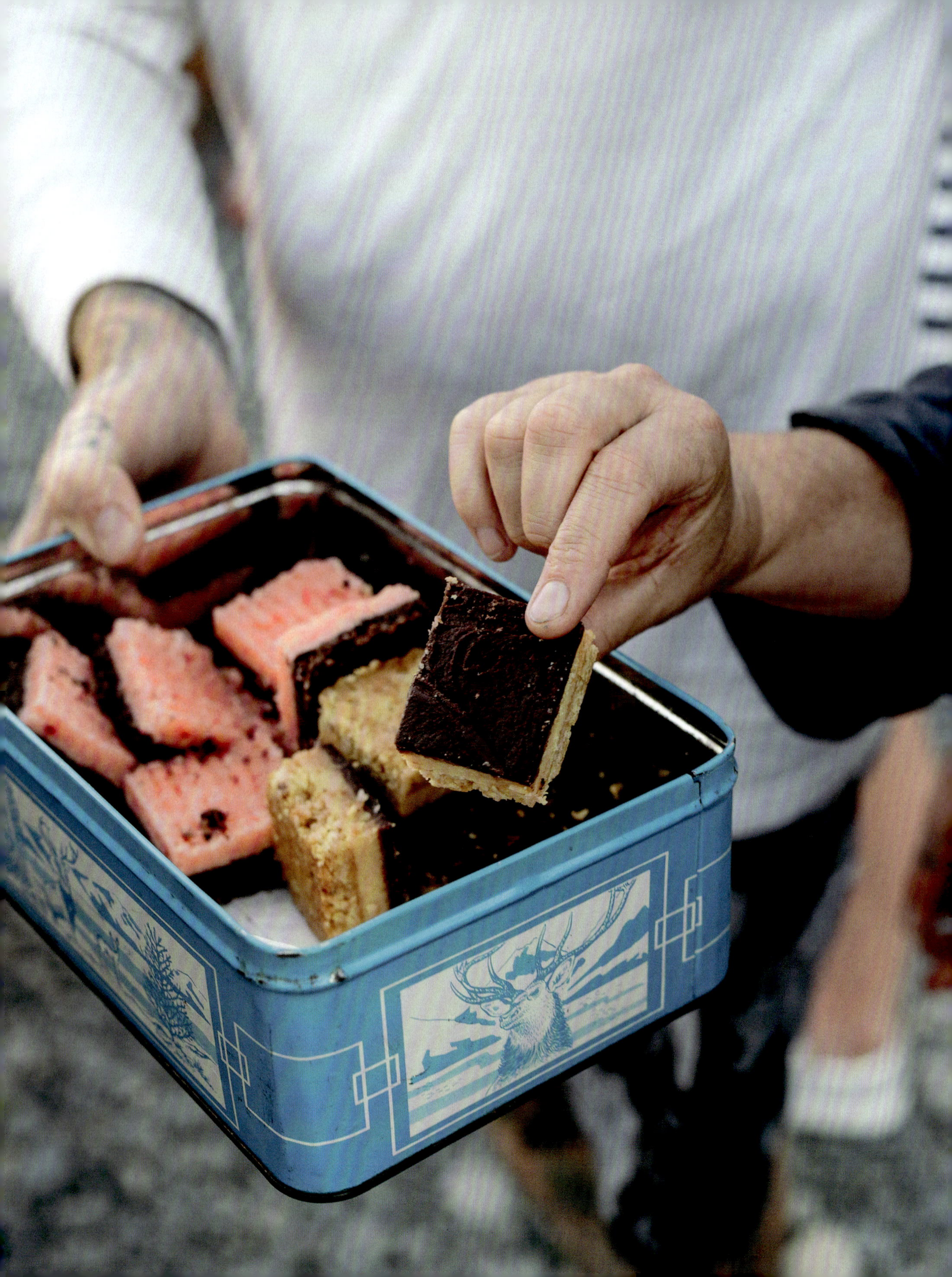

Fill the Tins

I think I can safely say that it is uncommon to bake purely for oneself. When we bake, we are invariably thinking about others—simple biscuits for our kids' lunchboxes, a plate of muffins for the school cake stall, fruit tarts for Christmas presents, baking club at work, or a cake left on the back doorstep for someone going through a tough time. I believe that's why, to most people, baking is never considered a chore.

On the contrary, it is more often than not an act of kindness and generosity.

Throughout our lives we experience many varied eating occasions, and they all offer up a memory of some sort, be it good, bad or indifferent. Personally, I think that home baking offers up more pleasure and goodness than almost any other edible moment. Opening my lunchbox at the age of five, no matter what the savoury option or piece of fruit on offer, it was always the treasure wrapped in waxed paper sitting in the corner that was of the most interest to me. Vivid recollections of late-night card sessions under dim kerosene lights while camping, and hearing the lid of an old cake tin being jimmied open—one of the sweetest of sounds imaginable. Christmas parties at the local rural hall, where, in our traditional New Zealand way, we would celebrate with a generous afternoon tea: long trestle tables laden with icing-sugar-topped cream sponges, hot sausage rolls, chocolate eclairs, lamingtons, pink-and-white coconut ice, mince savouries, and cream scones with fresh raspberry jam. And no trestle table worth its salt would ever be seen without a number of large platters piled high with—though they're not strictly home baking—blaze-pink cheerios circling small pudding plates filled to the brim with our country's red sauce of choice: Mr Wattie's.

These are all terrific food memories from my 50-plus years. I tell you, I can easily recall dozens and dozens of occasions when the passing around of something home-baked has shaped a lasting impression or anchored that single moment in time. What has always interested me is that it's often the combination of the occasion or where you were with what you were eating that creates the cut-through of recollection. One example comes to mind, when some twenty years ago

I was offered a delicate cream- and jelly-filled sponge drop while waiting for the whitebait to run on the Mōkihinui River. I will never forget that moment, or the taste and texture of that extraordinary treat in that equally extraordinary location. Just one instance of the power and reach of sweetness.

As a nation, one of the things we should be proud of is our baking prowess. It's a pillar of our young eating heritage, and is also usually the first thing that enters my mind when I'm asked about the history of our cuisine. I may be a little biased (or more likely just stubbornly loyal), but I truly believe that collectively, over the past hundred years or more, we have created—and, more importantly, passed down—what is principally our nation's DNA in our baking skills. We are amazing bakers, and more than ever there is evidence of this wherever you turn. I'm sure that most urban- and rural-dwelling adults in this country come into contact with wonderful examples of fresh baked goods at least once a day. Take our national obsession with coffee (and let's not forget that we have always had a love affair with a cuppa tea). For city folk, that daily ritual of forking out close to a fiver to patiently wait for a flat white while standing in front of elaborately decorated cakes, colourful iced slices, freshly baked muffins and scones, and tempting jars of crisp-baked biscuits is, I have always felt, like a daily lesson in hunger self-control. Most Kiwis won't even need to read the label to point out the goodie that they'll be justifying purchasing in their mind. Names like Louise cake, melting moments, Afghans, Anzac biscuits, yoyos and ginger crunch are all synonymous with New Zealand upbringings, and add a convivial sweet layer to our country's identity.

For as long as I can remember, I have always had an affection for the word 'sweet'. Besides the culinary meaning of 'containing a lot of sugar', it is a delightful word, with such positive connotations no matter how it is being used. Words like 'happiness', 'goodness', 'kindness', 'pleasure', 'warmth' and 'gratification' all live close to our beloved 'sweet'. And, of all of the five tastes, sweet is surely the dream card in the deck! It can stand alone in its purity, but it also plays many roles in all forms of cooking. It's the ultimate balancer, adding depth to savoury, counterbalancing our good friends bitter and sour, and at times taking salty head on.

It should come as no surprise that I understood the meaning of having a 'sweet tooth' from a very early age. Sugar might be the most recent ingredient out there to sit front and centre in the culinary Hall of Shame, but my love affair with sweet remains steadfast. As far as I'm aware, sugar is still a legal substance, and I'm happy to confess that I have been self-medicating on the Devil's Dust for most of my life and am still a regular user. I make no apologies for my mild (and controlled) relationship with sweetness. Like many other 'bads' out there, I dip in and out with regularity. I'm a 'one life, I say' sort of guy, and I'm damned if I'm not going to enjoy every bite of it! I'll hit the kale, carrot sticks and almonds when my conscience gathers momentum, mumbling something in my mind like 'It's time to pull up, Al.' I'll generally obey, punishing myself with a burst of green garden goodness, fizzy water, long walks and just an occasional small treat to break the monotony of my tastebud-deadened, dull life at that time.

To all the naysayers out there, let's talk instead about things like moderation, self-control and balance. I get so tired of individual ingredients getting a public roasting. If it's not sugar, it's fats. If it's not fats, it's salt. If it's not salt, it's carbs . . . There is always one ingredient or product that is fashionable to give a good old shaming to. It's not the particular product's fault, though—it's how much we as consumers gobble it up.

As grown-ups, it's our responsibility to take control of our own consumption, to set boundaries and limits. It's about making the right choices, showing some self-restraint and a little bit of discipline. No one is holding a gun to your head to purchase that 2-litre bottle of Fanta. Yes, it might be on special and is cheaper than milk, but that is no excuse or reason to buy it. I enjoy a glass of ice-cold Coke from time to time. Do I drink it every day? No. Once a week? I doubt it. But when I do I enjoy it, not only because it tastes good but because, the way I look at it, it's a treat. Like ice cream, foie gras, fish and chips, sticky date pudding, mince and cheese pies or fresh cream doughnuts . . . Sure, we could bring in sugar taxes, and remove GST from vegetables, but come on now. Please let common sense prevail when making decisions around food choices.

When I reached the second half of the book, I was faced with some hard decisions: which baking and pudding recipes to include, and which ones to leave out? There are just so many wonderful traditional New Zealand baking and pudding recipes out there.

While delicious in their own way, I find many 'new' baked goods and desserts somehow don't quite offer up the soothing deliciousness that our beautiful old-school recipes do. So much of the pastry presented to us today seems to be designed around the visual aspect, and lacks the comforting and heart-warming appeal that the older, tried-and-true recipes deliver. I have never professed to be a particularly competent pastry chef; I always find the exactness required sort of annoying, which is slightly weird as I'm extremely detail-oriented and know I have a tendency to be a little obsessive compulsive.

So, the baking and pudding recipes that I have chosen are a bunch of personal favourites—they made the cut purely because I am the author. I'm sure the chosen few will be met with some debate, with cooks up and down the country voicing their alternative opinions (and quite rightly so) or even disbelief about how I could possibly have left out this or that recipe for something dear to them. To you all, I apologise, but I also trust you'll understand my dilemma.

Each of the following cakes, slices and biscuits, in one way or another, has a real connection to my childhood memories and to many wonderful and vivid occasions past. You may have noticed in the earlier section that I prefer to call dessert 'pudding'. I love the word pudding, as it conjures up something more comforting, personal and satisfying than I feel dessert does. 'Dessert' seems formal and a little stiff, while 'pudding' to me always feels fun, unpretentious and way more gratifying.

I have mastered all of the 'sweet dreams' that lie in the pages ahead, and nothing would please me more than to know that many of these treats have ended up gracing trestle tables, kitchen benches, boat galleys and tea trolleys up and down the country. So please, bake away!

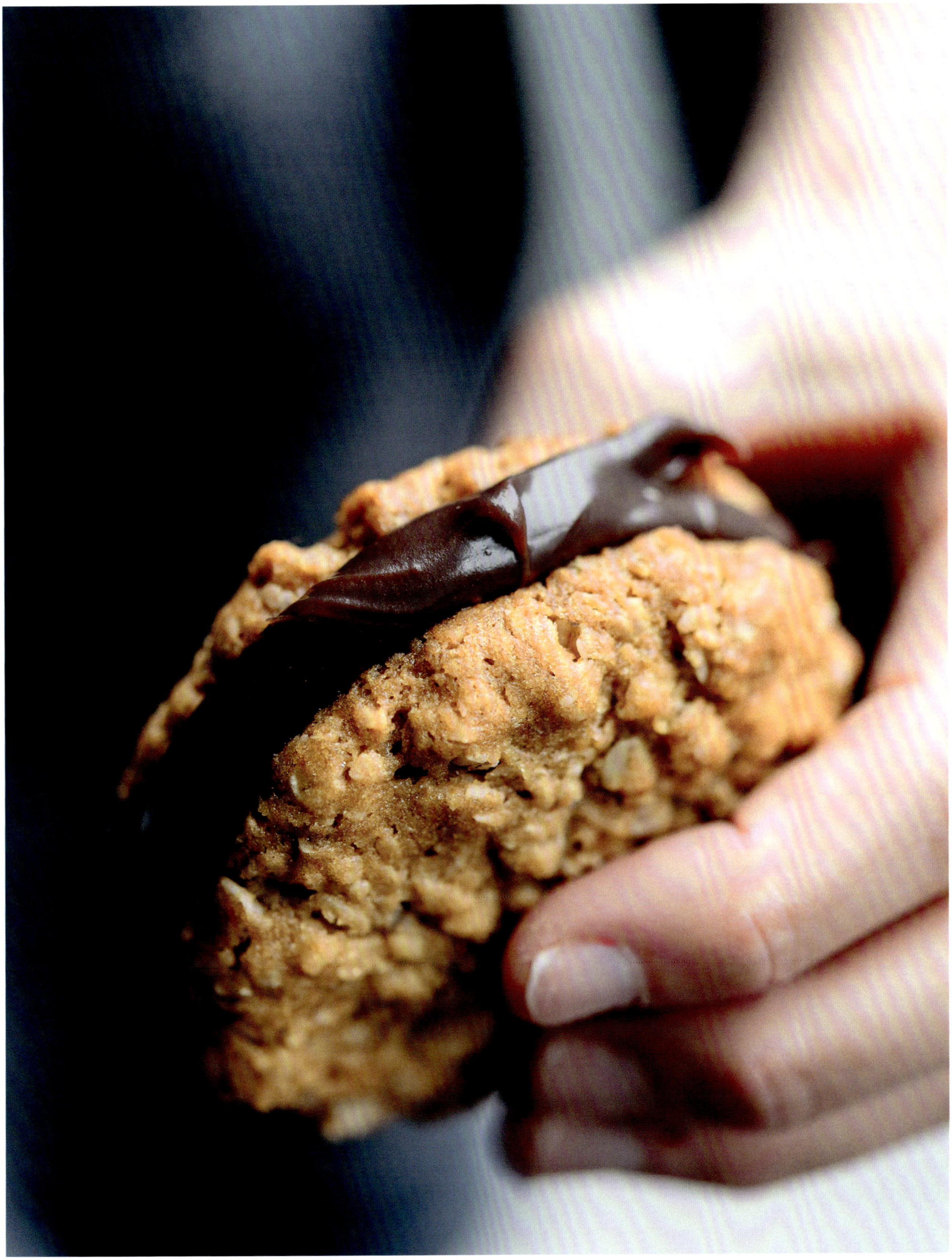

Cranberry and orange scones

I always struggle when standing at a counter, faced with the decision of ordering a savoury or a sweet scone. Things typically work out for the best if I can convince whoever I am with to order the other one. That way, we can share and we both end up with half a sweet and half a savoury. Scones play a big role in New Zealand's morning- and afternoon-tea heritage; I'd be surprised if there was any other product that was served up with more regularity than our humble scones. A date scone will always be a favourite, but we've played around a bit lately and come up with this great example, too.

Makes 12

3 cups (450 g/1 lb) plain flour, plus extra for dusting
2 teaspoons baking powder
½ teaspoon baking soda
⅓ cup (80 g/2¾ oz) caster sugar, plus extra for sprinkling
½ teaspoon salt
150 g (5½ oz) cold butter
1½ cups dried cranberries
finely grated zest of 2 oranges
2 cups (500 ml/17 fl oz) cream
milk, for brushing
salted butter, to serve

Preheat your oven to 190°C (375°F). Grease and lightly flour a baking tray.
    Place the flour, baking powder, baking soda, sugar and salt into a relatively large bowl. Cut in the cold butter, and rub through the dry ingredients with your fingers until the mixture resembles fine breadcrumbs. Add the cranberries and the fine orange zest and mix through.
    Make a well in the centre and slowly add the cream. Mix gently to form a soft dough. Do not knead the dough—in fact, handle it as little as possible.
    Place on a lightly floured surface and form a round about 20 cm (8 in) across. Brush with milk and sprinkle with the extra sugar.
    Place the round on the prepared baking tray, and cut into 12 triangular scones but keep the pieces together as a whole. Place in the oven and bake for 20–25 minutes, until golden. Serve warm with liberal amounts of butter.

BAKED 373

Cheese scones with Parmesan and blue cheese butter

I'm a massive scone fan, and find it very hard to overlook them in a cafe or coffee situation. I kind of judge cafes on the prowess of their scone baking, because a well-made scone is not an easy thing to achieve. It's mostly about how you handle the dough, being very careful not to overwork it. Haydo and I worked tirelessly on this scone recipe, playing around with different flour combinations until we were satisfied we had a cheese scone we were proud of. Once we nailed the recipe, it was a case of taking it up a notch or two with the ridiculously delicious Parmesan and blue cheese butter. You'll enjoy these.

Makes 8–12

PARMESAN AND BLUE CHEESE BUTTER
200 g (7 oz) butter, at room temperature
10 g (¼ oz) finely grated Parmesan cheese
100 g (3½ oz) blue cheese

SCONES
2 cups (300 g/10½ oz) plain flour, plus extra for dusting
⅓ cup (40 g/1½ oz) cornflour
2 teaspoons baking powder
½ teaspoon salt
100 g (3½ oz) cold salted butter, diced
2 cups (250 g/9 oz) grated tasty cheese
½ cup (50 g/1¾ oz) grated Parmesan cheese
2 cups (90 g/3¼ oz) roughly chopped rocket leaves
1 cup (250 ml/9 fl oz) milk

To make the Parmesan and blue cheese butter, place the butter and Parmesan in a bowl. Crumble in the blue cheese and, with clean hands, mix until just combined. Keep at room temperature, then refrigerate what is left (it's also great on vegetables like broccoli, or stirred through pasta).

Preheat your oven to 200°C (400°F). Line a baking tray with baking paper.
    Sift the flour, cornflour, baking powder and salt into a large bowl. With clean hands, rub the cold butter into the dry ingredients until it resembles coarse breadcrumbs.
    Add 1½ cups (185 g/6½ oz) of the tasty cheese, the Parmesan and the rocket, and mix through. Make a well in centre of the mix, pour in the milk and use a knife to gently stir until the dough just comes together.
    Turn the dough out onto a floured bench, and shape into a 2 cm (¾ in) thick slab. Try not to overwork the dough. Cut out 5-cm (2-in) round scones, then reshape the excess dough and repeat.
    Place the scones on the prepared tray, with a bit of space in between each one. Top with the remaining ½ cup (60 g/2¼ oz) of tasty cheese. Bake for 14 minutes, until the scones are golden and lightly puffed. Remove and let the scones cool slightly.
    Once cool enough to handle, split them and spread liberal amounts of the Parmesan and blue cheese butter on each half, let it melt for a minute . . . then go for it!

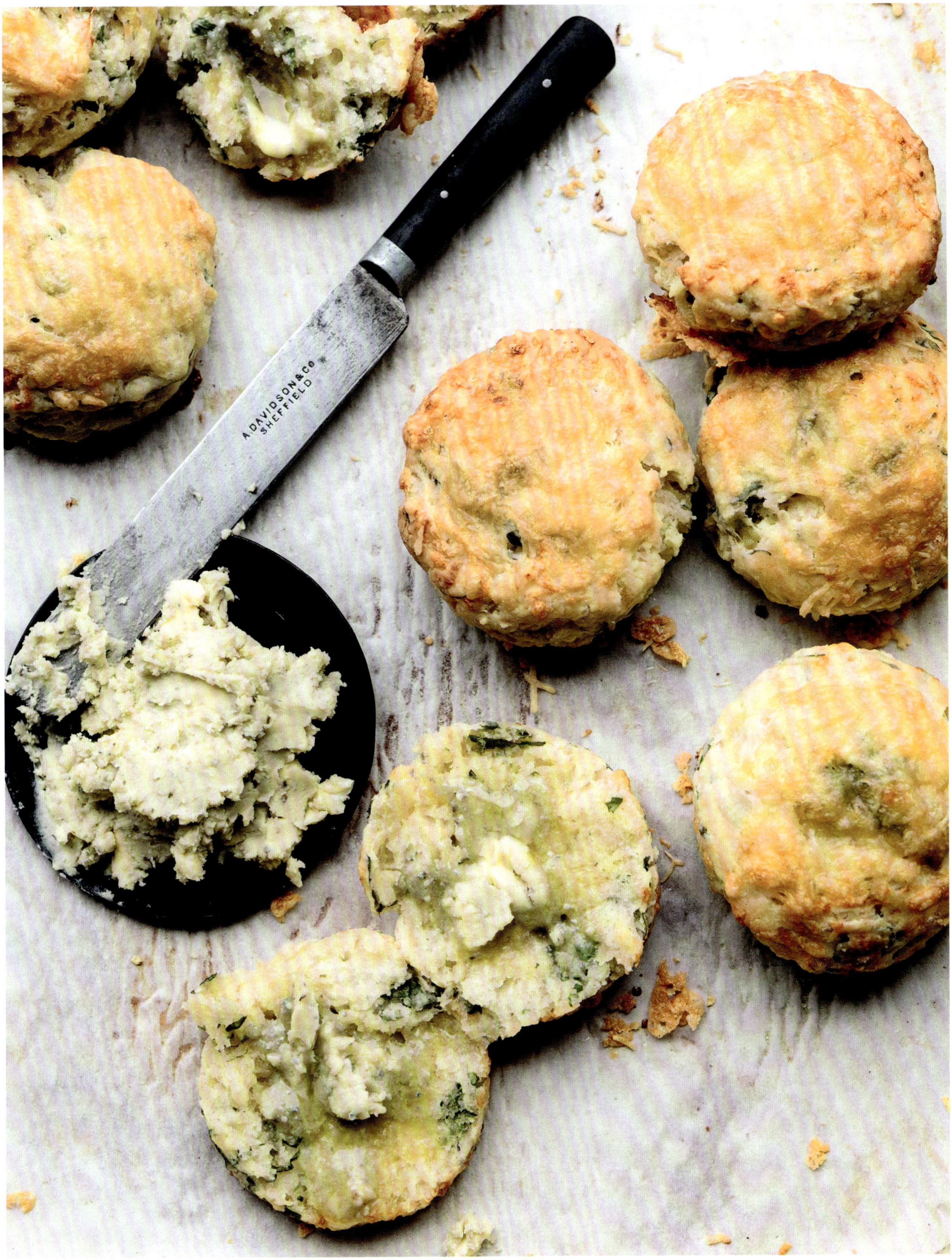
A.DAVIDSON&CO
SHEFFIELD

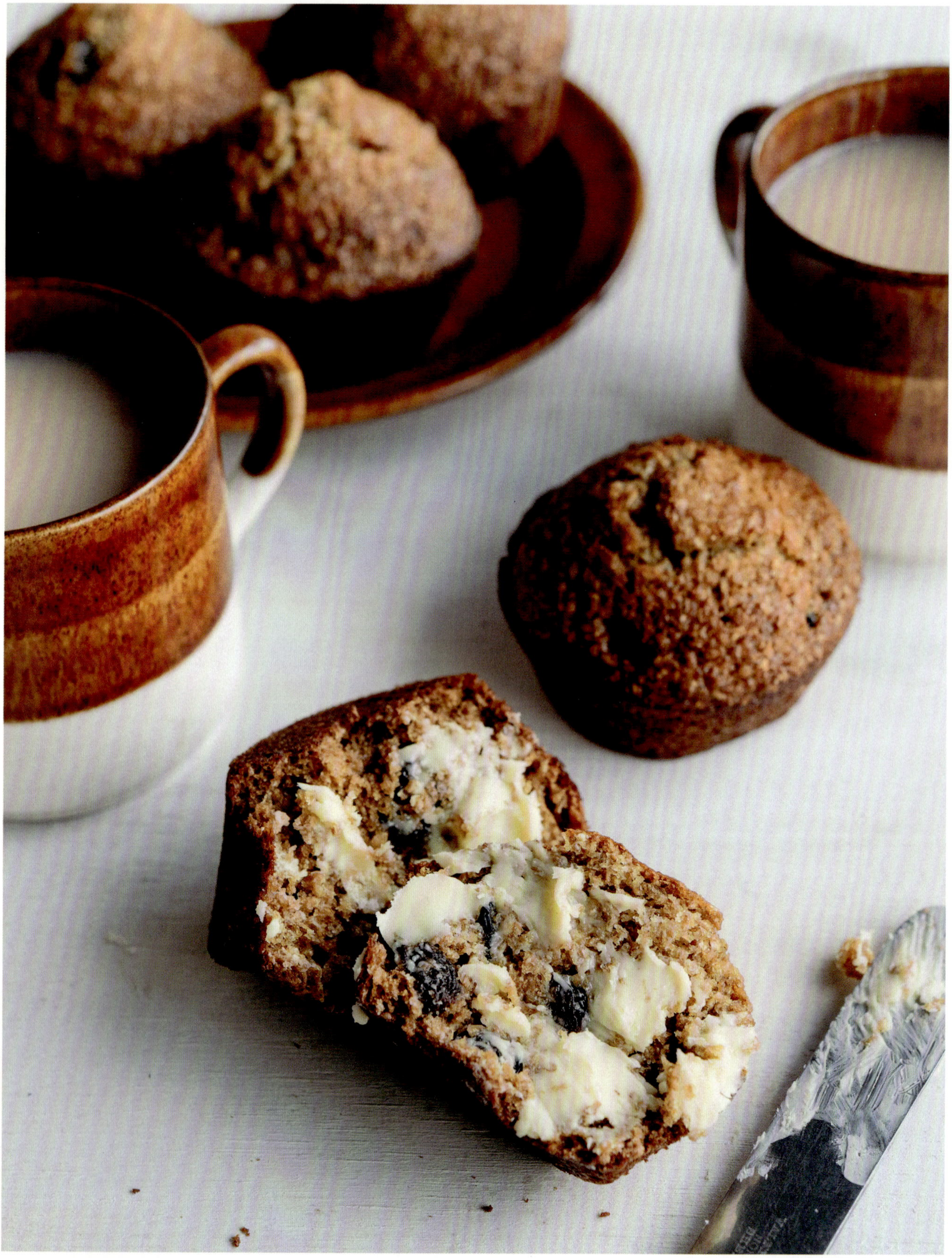

Aunty Edna's bran muffins

As far as I'm concerned, there is but one muffin in the world and that is the humble bran muffin. I hate to be the bearer of bad news but, while you may have always felt that anything that finished with the word 'muffin' somehow wasn't too bad for you, I can assure you that the raspberry, banana and white chocolate number you have a steady relationship with is, in fact, a cake! It is one of my pet annoyances how the traditional names of products morph into something that has little or no resemblance to the original.

Anyway, I love a great bran muffin, and I have for some unknown reason always viewed them as a bit of a New Zealand classic. There are a bunch of bran muffin recipes floating about out there, but I believe the following is the best around. They are delicious to eat the day you bake them, but I have always thought they actually get better in the days that follow, as they take on a more moist and slightly sticky texture. Thanks to Claire Hunter for sharing this recipe.

Makes 12

1 cup (150 g/5½ oz) plain flour
2 cups (150 g/5½ oz) bran
½ cup (110 g/3¾ oz) sugar
¾ cup (60 g/2¼ oz) sultanas
1 egg
1 cup (250 ml/9 fl oz) milk
½ cup (175 g/6 oz) golden syrup
2 tablespoons butter, plus extra for greasing and serving
1 teaspoon baking soda

Preheat your oven to 210°C (410°F). Grease a 12-hole muffin tin with butter.

In a suitable-sized bowl, add the flour, bran, sugar and sultanas. Break in the egg. (Don't mix it yet.)

Grab a small saucepan and add the milk, golden syrup and butter. Place on medium-low heat. Stir until the syrup has incorporated into the milk and the butter is melted. Remove from the stove and immediately mix through the baking soda.

Pour this warm mixture into the bowl of dry ingredients, and mix with a wooden spoon until just combined. Divide between the greased holes in the muffin tin and place in the oven to bake for 10 minutes. Check with a toothpick or skewer—if it comes out clean, you know the deal! Remove from the oven and let the muffins sit for 15 minutes before carefully extracting from the tin. Serve with generous licks of butter.

Lemon shortbread

I have always had a soft spot for shortbread. Buttery and dry, I enjoy the way it melts away in your mouth. Shortbread is also one of those really terrific combos when served with a cuppa tea. Definitely give this shortbread a go. The lemon zest adds a lovely layer of mild citrus and, if you want to make it even more special, dip one end of the cooled shortbread in melted white chocolate.

Makes about 30

250 g (9 oz) butter, softened
1 cup (125 g/4½ oz) icing sugar
finely grated zest of 2 lemons
2 cups (300 g/10½ oz) plain flour, plus extra for dusting
1 cup (125 g/4½ oz) cornflour
¼ cup (55 g/2 oz) sugar

Preheat your oven to 150°C (300°F). Line a baking tray with baking paper.
    In a stand mixer fitted with the paddle attachment, or using a handheld electric whisk, beat the butter, icing sugar and lemon zest for 5 minutes, until light and fluffy. Sift the flour and cornflour into a bowl, then add to the creamed butter and mix well to form a smooth dough.
    Lightly dust your bench with flour, then roll out the dough to a 5 mm (¼ in) thick rectangle, measuring approximately 25 x 35 cm (10 x 13 in). Cut the shortbread into rectangles, and carefully place on the prepared baking tray. Sprinkle the shortbread with sugar, then bake for 25 minutes until lightly golden around the edges. Remove from the oven and let cool. Store in an airtight container until consumed! It also freezes well.

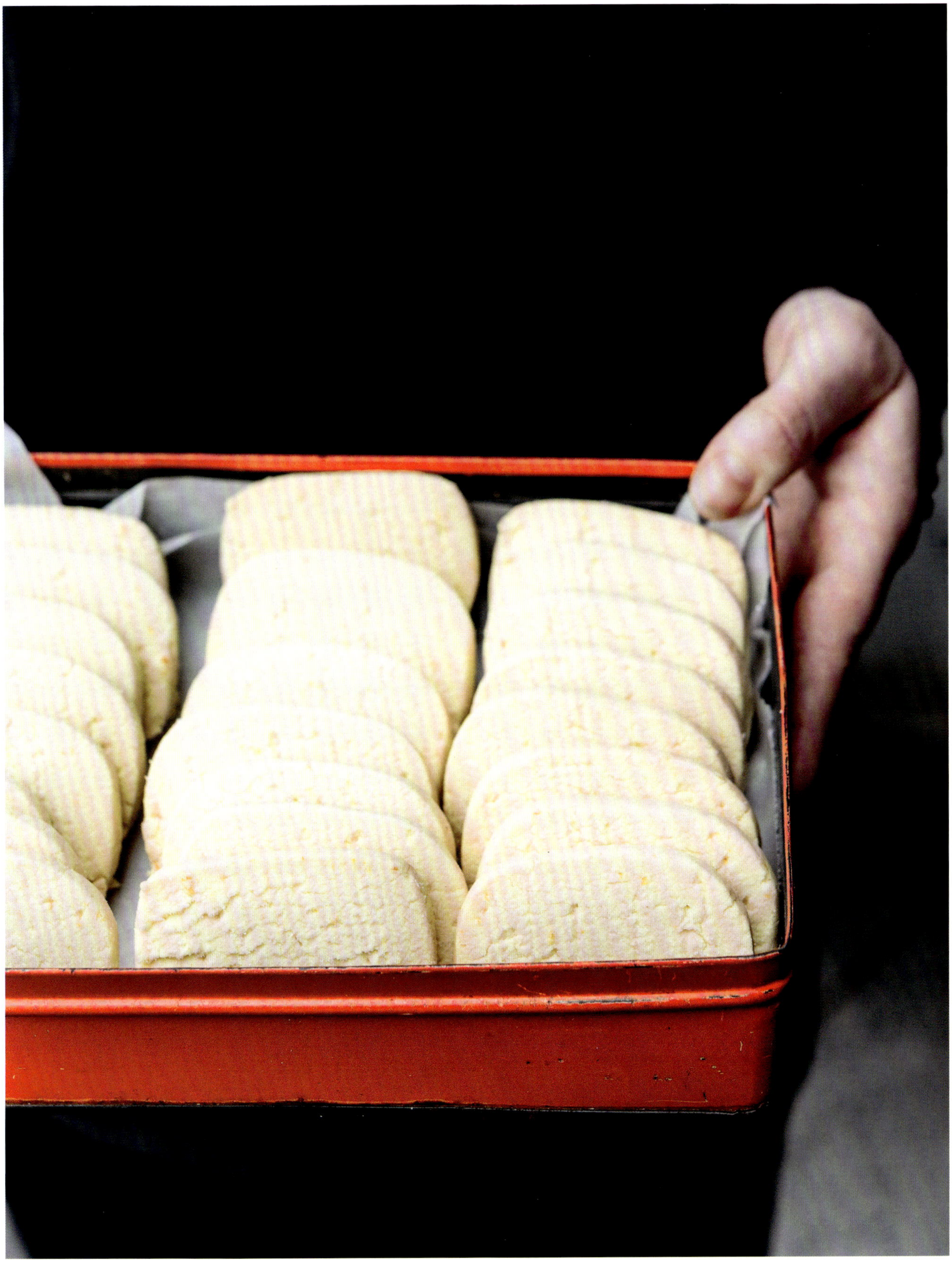

Anzac chocolate ganache biscuits

Anzac biscuits play such an important part in New Zealand's baking tradition. For such a humble baked good, the Anzac biscuit not only offers up a chewy and satisfying eat but also—on another, far more important level—reminds us in a very small way of the brave Kiwis and Aussies who fought and the many who lost their lives on foreign battlefields far from home all those decades ago. These biscuits are terrific by themselves, but become a bit more of a posh affair with the addition of the chocolate ganache.

Makes 8–10 sandwiched biscuits

ANZAC BISCUITS
1¼ cups (125 g/4½ oz) rolled oats
1 cup (90 g/3¼ oz) desiccated coconut
1 cup (150 g/5½ oz) plain flour
½ cup (95 g/3¼ oz) brown sugar
¼ cup (55 g/2 oz) caster sugar
pinch salt
125 g (4½ oz) butter
3 tablespoons golden syrup
1 teaspoon baking soda
2 tablespoons boiling water

CHOCOLATE GANACHE
250 g (9 oz) semi-sweet chocolate, broken up into pieces
300 ml (10½ fl oz) cream

Preheat your oven to 160°C (315°F). Line two baking trays with baking paper.
    In a bowl, combine the oats, coconut, flour, sugars and salt.
    Place the butter and golden syrup in a small saucepan and melt together over low heat. In a small bowl, add the baking soda and boiling water. Mix until dissolved, then add this to the butter and syrup mixture.
    Pour the wet ingredients into the dry, and mix until combined. Shape the dough into balls about half the size of a golfball, and place on the prepared trays. Leave some space between them all, as they will spread during baking. Press to slightly flatten. Place in the oven and bake for 10–12 minutes until the biscuits are golden around the edges, but still soft to the touch. Remove from the oven and let cool completely.

For the chocolate ganache, melt the chocolate and cream together in a saucepan over low heat. Once melted and combined, let cool and allow to thicken to a spreadable consistency. Spread a layer of ganache on the flat side of a biscuit, then sandwich with a second on top. Repeat with the other biscuits. Allow the chocolate ganache to set before tucking in.

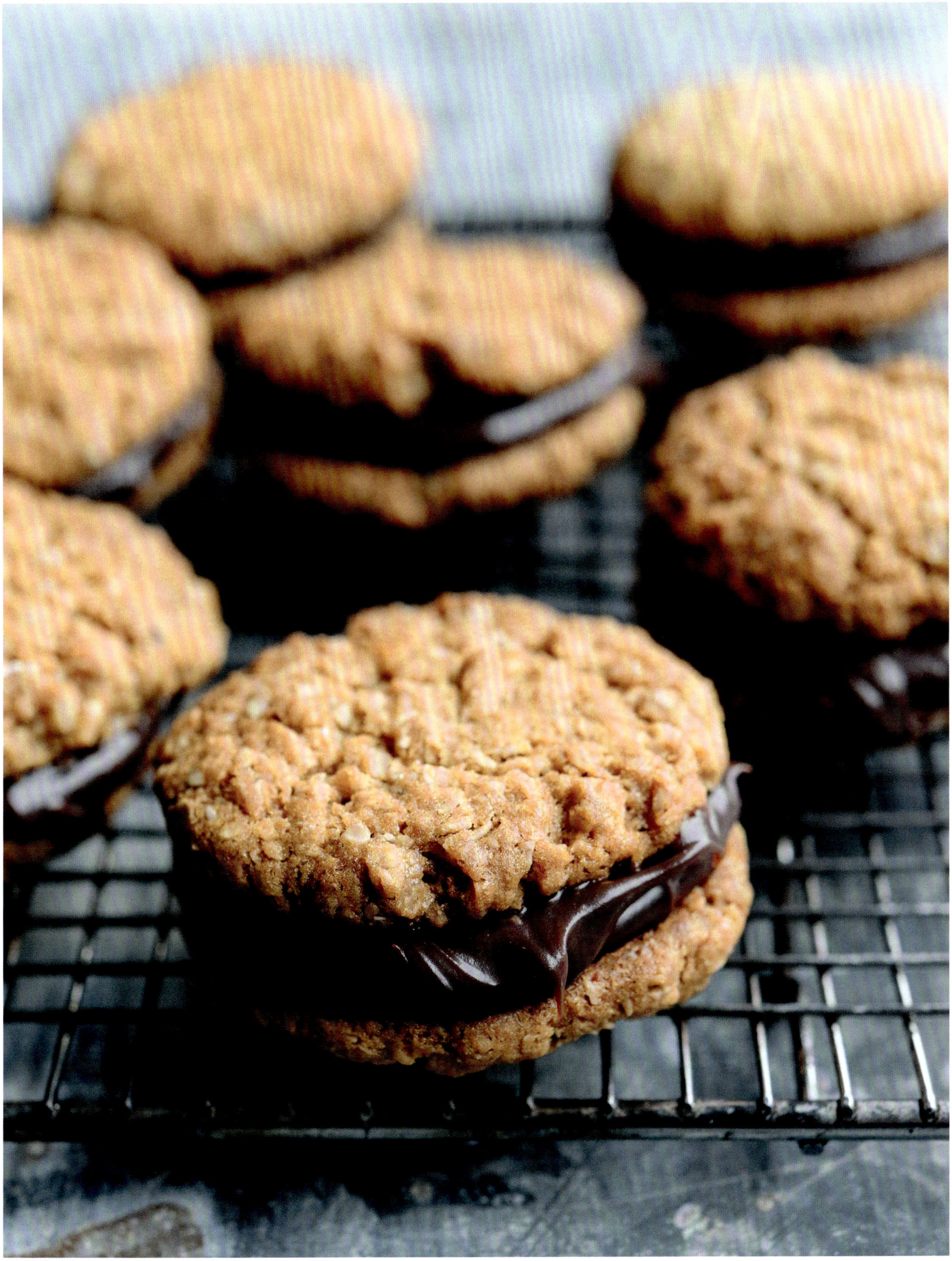

CAKES AND BISCUITS

BIRTHDAY CAKE

¾ lb. Butter
½ lb. Brown Sugar
2 tablespoons Golden Syrup
7 Eggs
½ teaspoon *Edmonds* Baking Powder
1 lb. Flour

12 ozs. Sultanas
12 ozs. Currants
8 ozs. Mixed Peel
1 teaspoon Mixed Spice
4 ozs. Chopped Almonds

Beat butter and sugar to a cream, add syrup, then eggs one by one (unbeaten). Mix dry ingredients together, add fruit and mix all together. Bake 3 to 4 hours at 250-275°F. Ice with Royal Icing.

BOURNVITA BISCUITS

4 ozs. Butter
2 ozs. Sugar
3 heaped teaspoons
   Sweetened Condensed Milk

6 ozs. Flour
1 teaspoon
   Edmonds Baking Powder
2 tablespoons Bournvita

Cream butter, sugar and condensed milk together. Add flour, baking powder and Bournvita. Roll into balls. Place on cold greased trays, flatten with fork. Bake 15 to 20 minutes at 375°F.

BRAN BISCUITS

4 ozs. Butter
3 ozs. Sugar
1 Egg
¾ breakfastcup Flour
Pinch of Salt

1 raised teaspoon
   Edmonds Baking Powder
1 breakfastcup Bran
¾ breakfastcup Wholemeal

Cream butter and sugar, add egg and beat well. Sift flour, baking powder and salt, and add wholemeal and bran. Knead well. Roll out on a floured board, cut and bake 20 minutes at 375°F.

BUTTERFLY CAKES

4 ozs. Butter
4 ozs. Sugar
2 Eggs
6 ozs. Flour

1 teaspoon
   Edmonds Baking Powder
1 tablespoon Milk

Beat butter and sugar to a cream, add eggs well beaten, then flour and baking powder mixed, and lastly milk. Half fill paper cases with mixture, place on cold oven shelf and bake about 10 to 15 minutes at 400°F. When cool, cut a small piece off the top of each, put a heaped teaspoon of whipped cream on, cut piece in half and stand these on edge on whipped cream. If desired, decorate with small pieces of jelly made with *Edmonds* Jelly Crystals.

Before breaking preserved eggs intended for cakes or puddings, stand eggs in warm water for a few minutes and they will beat as lightly as fresh ones.

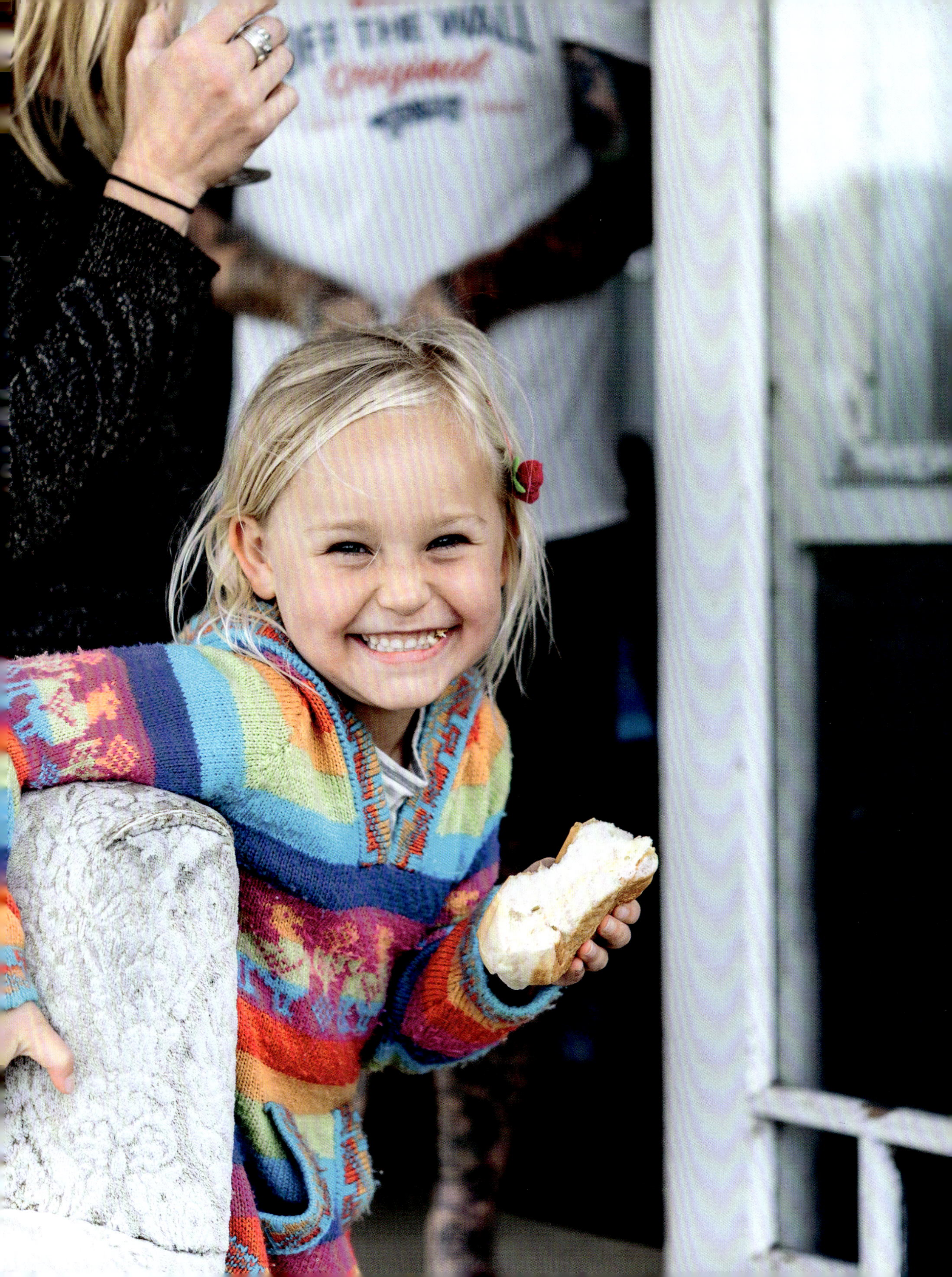

Sally Lun Bun $3.00

Raspberry Bun $2.50

Our Bakery Love Affair

One of life's most pleasurable experiences is walking into a bakery first thing in the morning. At that time of the day, if you're like me, your senses are still in a sort of slumber cruise control, and what happens when you enter these unmitigated sensory pleasure zones is nothing short of nirvana. Your senses are assaulted by a blast of pure delight.

The first thing to hit you as you step over the threshold of a bakery is warmth. It's a unique warmth that has an almost physical weight to it. Large ovens that never really get a chance to cool radiate a constant heat that permeates the entire shop. Leaning against a warm concrete pillar while you wait to place your order is soothing and comforting. And bakeries have another kind of warmth, too, which is almost tactile in a whole other way: it's the sentiment of nourishment, the feeling of familiarity, with a generous helping of goodness.

Once that warmth has washed over you, you are completely ambushed by smell. I struggle to think of a more delightful scent than that emitted from a bakery. It's a complex, multilayered richness, where the aromas of savoury and sweet battle it out. It doesn't matter whether it's a tray of golden-crusted sausage rolls or of apple shortcakes—whatever has just been taken out of the oven, the aroma is the culinary perfume of joy.

When you see shelf after shelf of familiar shapes, textures and colours laid out before you, it's always difficult to focus due to the sheer variety, and it takes a fair degree of concentration to pick out each goodie. You have to weigh up selection, memories, desire, greed and, in my case, a short-lived smidgen of guilt.

Baked goods hardly ever come with garnishes. They are complete in their singular natural beauty. They don't need anything else besides being slipped into very basic packaging. The contrast of a simple brown paper bag or plain cardboard box with something so delicious and appealing is never lost on me. It frames the treat in such an honest and humble way.

I'm a firm believer that you should eat fresh baked goods shortly after you leave a bakery. It's similar to what I think about eating produce close to where it was grown. The further away you get from the hallowed bakery, I believe, the less integrity and flavour the baked goods retain.

Once you remove your precious purchase from its wrapper, you check out the weight and texture. Both are of equal importance. A true bakery junkie will immediately be able to get a pretty good gauge on the baker's expertise. If the steak and kidney pie is heavy with the weight of the filling and the pastry is layered and flaky, you are in good shape. Mind you, it could well be the opposite. You don't want things like sponge drops or eclairs to be heavy—unless, of course, that weight comes from a generous lick of whipped cream or vanilla custard sandwiching the two feather-weights together.

You can't take texture for granted, either. People seem to forget how much joy texture brings to the eating of anything, be it a soft bread roll housing something crunchy and fresh, or the layers in a well-made apple pie. I think about texture a lot when I'm developing a recipe or when I'm bringing together individual components to create a single dish.

And then, of course, the most wonderful sense is taste! Like all food, baked goods offer six layers of possible interest: sweet, savoury, salty, sour, bitter and umami. It's not often that they all align—and nor should they, as that's the point. Cooking is all about bringing just a few of them together, depending on what you are trying to achieve. It's about harmony, balance and often restraint. From the simplest of recipes to the more complicated, these things are all equally important.

When I was growing up on a farm 30 minutes or so from Masterton, my parents used to play bridge in town most Wednesday nights. On those nights I would be dropped off at Granny's just after six, to spend the night. I only really had one grandparent of significance growing up, and that was

Granny Brown. She died years ago, but I still have extremely fond memories of this special person in my life. Granny Brown was kind, very unassuming and generous to a fault. She wasn't by any means a culinary goddess, but she was pretty capable nevertheless. I remember she was a dab hand at two things: one was her sweet butter shortbread, and the other was her savoury mince.

There was a bunch of great things about staying in town for the night. First of all, I could sleep in because I didn't need to catch the old rural bus that took close to 40 minutes to get to school. But the one thing above all else that made my mid-week stay so wonderful and memorable was Granny's Thursday-morning before-school treat. We would hop in her old metallic-blue Avenger and head out. She might have been a proficient cook, but her driving sent shivers down my spine, even as a seven- or eight-year-old. Anyway, it was a short drive to 180 Queen Street, where the Ten O'Clock Cookie Bakery still stands today. I would run in with what I guess was something like a ten-cent coin and patiently wait to be served. I didn't mind if there was a queue, as it gave me more time to concentrate on the two or three rows of fresh cream buns that, at my young age, were squarely at eye level. I would survey the glorious scene laid out in front of me, weighing up things like the size of individual buns, cream-to-bun ratio and the dusting of icing sugar before pointing out the exact one I wanted.

I think Granny always presumed that I would eat my cream bun at playtime for morning tea. I don't believe I ever let on that, as soon as that Avenger made a left at the end of Hadlow School's long driveway, I would find an out-of-the-way spot with no people around where I could take my time to slowly and purposefully indulge in this wonderfully decadent fresh-baked goodie before the bell rang for class!

Now there is so much more variety and selection on offer in bakeries, and I figure they are all equally delicious—but, to this day, a fresh cream bun is still my go-to bakery treat. I presume there is some sentimental significance rolling around in my subconscious that plays a part in my devotion to these humble buns of sweet goodness, but I truly believe a beautifully made, slightly chilled fresh cream bun is something special. The super-soft white roll that is just ever so slightly chewy, the generous pillow of perfectly whipped cream that brings a texture contrast and acts like a foil by lightening up the bread, and then a liberal dusting of powdered sugar that brings just enough sweetness without it being sickly. Compared with cream doughnuts, which I often feel are bit full-on with too much sugar, a well-made cream bun has balance, finesse and modest refinement.

That's the wonderful thing about food and eating memories: they are so diverse and varied. Some memories are of grand feasts of epic proportions, while others are a trip down memory lane to buy a simple cream bun once a week with Granny Brown in her metallic-blue Avenger. One memory is no better than any other; they are all special in one way or another and I treasure them all.

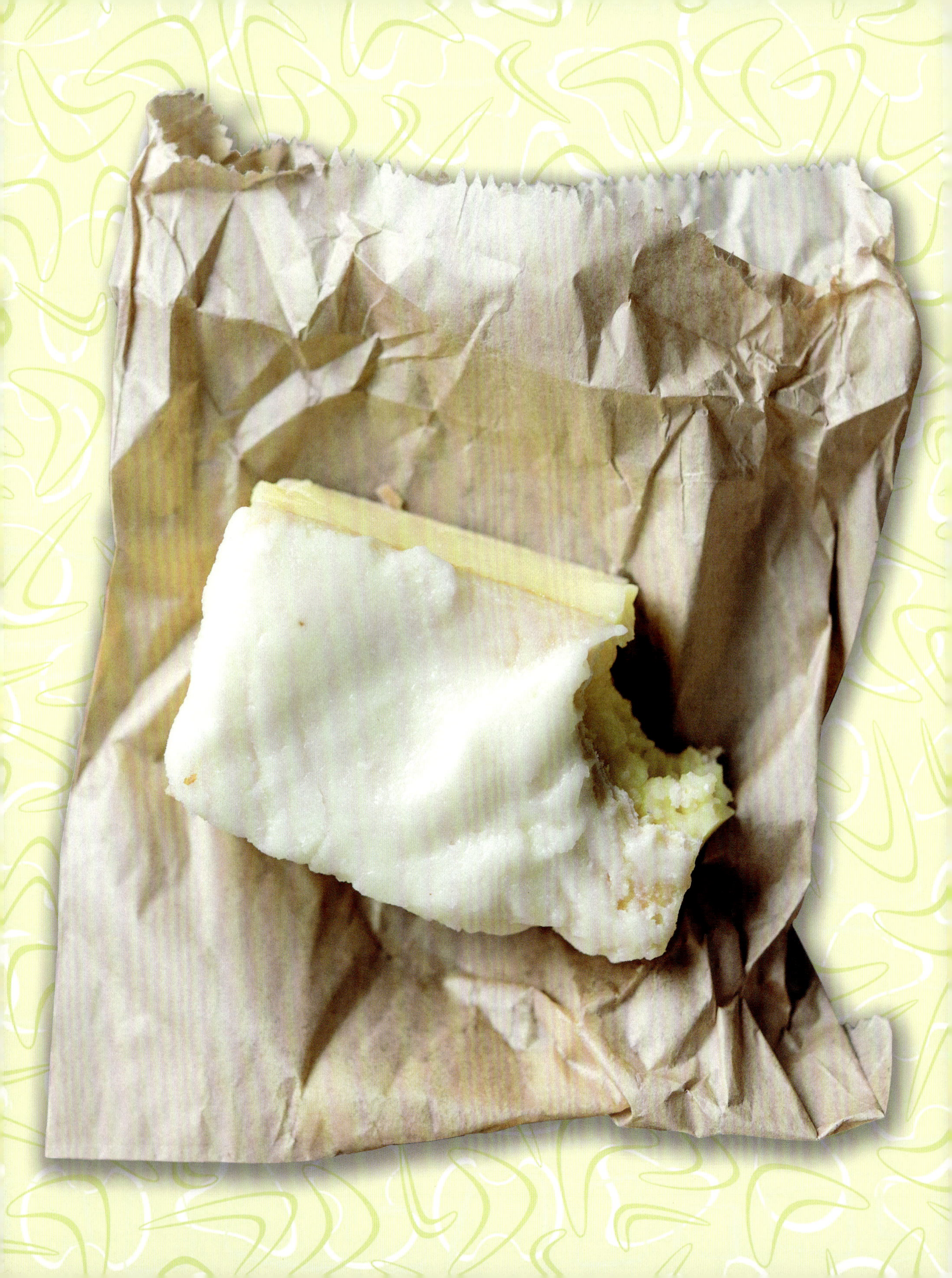

Bakery
HAND MADE DAILY
THE OLD BAKEHOUSE LTD
Est.2013
Open 4am - 2pm
Phone 06 377 5472
Bread • Pies • Sandwiches • Coffee • Cakes • Rolls
OPEN HOURS
Monday to Friday
4am - 2pm
Open
OPEN HOURS
Monday to Friday
4am - 2pm
Bread
Pies
Coffee
Sandwiches
Cakes
Rolls

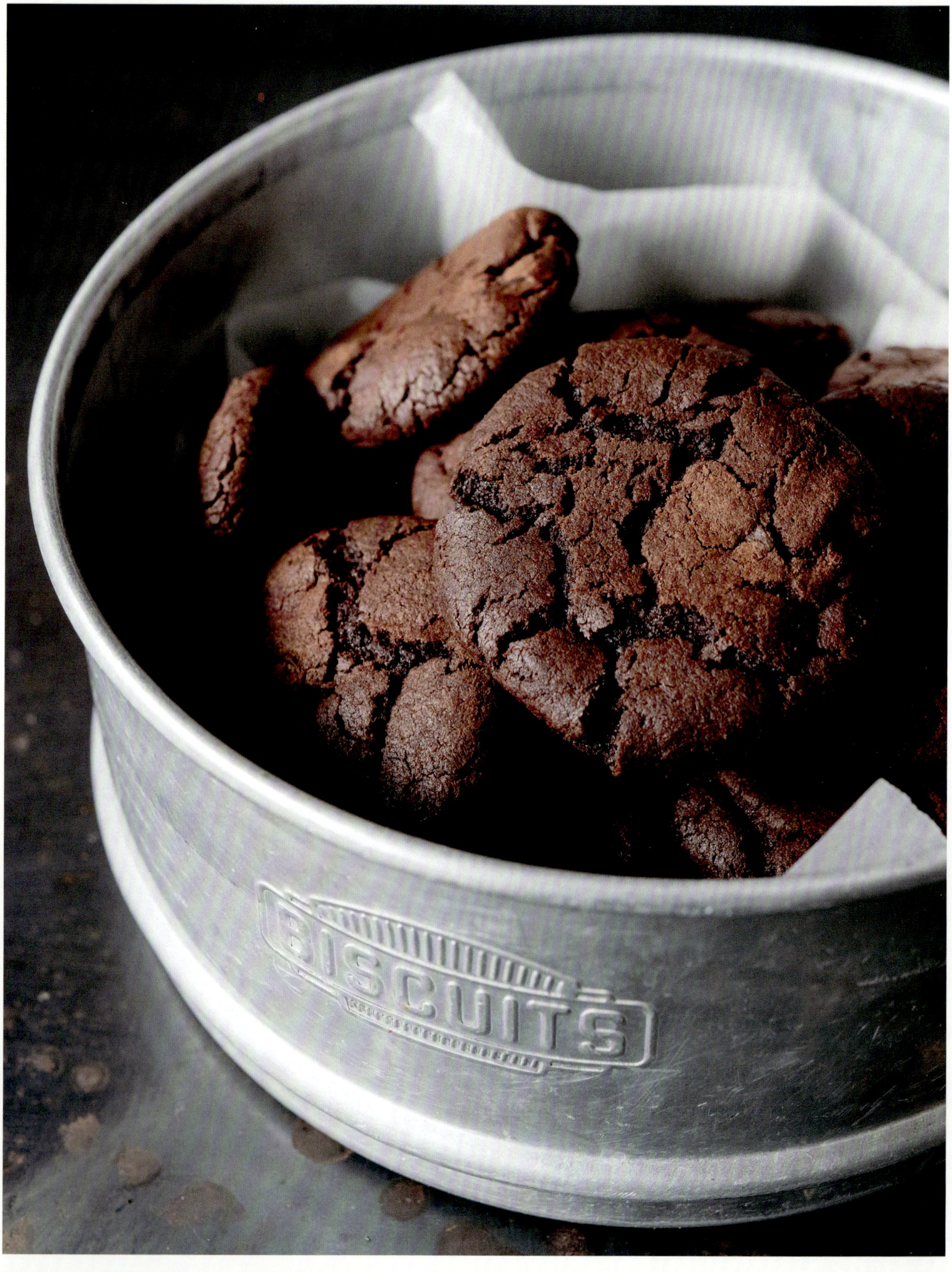
BISCUITS

Choco block biscuits

This biscuit recipe comes from our great friends at Poronui Lodge in Taupō, where I am fortunate enough to host one or two events a year. These guys always have jars of home-baked treats dotted about the lodge, and these biscuits are one of the latest in the Poronui repertoire. I've named them 'choco block' as it's the best way to describe them. They are truly delicious and decadent, with the chocolate dial turned up to max!

Makes 24–28

200 g (7 oz) butter
1½ cups (330 g/11½ oz) sugar
½ teaspoon vanilla essence
2 eggs
2 cups (300 g/10½ oz) self-raising flour
1 teaspoon baking powder
¾ cup (90 g/3¼ oz) Dutch (unsweetened) cocoa
250 g (9 oz) dark chocolate (preferably 72% cocoa solids), chopped into chunks

Preheat your oven to 180°C (350°F). Line two baking trays with baking paper.
    In a stand mixer fitted with the paddle attachment, or using a handheld electric whisk, beat the butter and sugar together for 5 minutes, until pale. Add the vanilla, followed by the eggs, one at a time, until mixed in. Now mix through the flour, cocoa and chocolate chunks to form a dough.
    With clean hands, roll your dough into ping-pong-sized balls. Place on the prepared trays, leaving room between each ball to allow for spreading during baking. Place in the oven and bake for 8 minutes, or until the biscuits have spread out flat and are cracked on top but still soft to the touch. Remove from the oven and let cool completely before putting into tins. These won't last long . . .

Sultana cake

A cuppa tea and piece of sultana cake offer, for me, one of life's more simple and pleasurable moments. This one is super easy to make and doesn't require icing, which is a little bonus. However, being a bit of a butter fiend, I generally add a lick on my piece of cake just for good measure.

Makes 1 x 21 cm cake

2 cups (250 g/9 oz) sultanas
250 g (9 oz) butter, diced
2 cups (440 g/15½ oz) sugar
3 eggs
1 teaspoon vanilla bean paste or vanilla essence
finely grated zest of 1 lemon
2½ cups (375 g/13 oz) plain flour
½ cup (60 g/2¼ oz) custard powder
1½ teaspoons baking powder
½ teaspoon salt

Preheat your oven to 160°C (315°F). Grease and line a 21 cm (8¼ in) cake tin with baking paper.

Place the sultanas in a saucepan and cover with water. Set over medium-high heat and bring up to the boil, then lower the heat and simmer the sultanas for 15 minutes, until plump. Strain the water from the sultanas, then stir through the butter, allowing it to melt.

In a stand mixer fitted with the whisk attachment, or using a handheld electric whisk, beat the sugar and the eggs together until pale, light and creamy. Stir in the sultana and butter mixture, along with the vanilla and lemon zest.

In a separate bowl, sift in the flour, custard powder, baking powder and salt. Add to the sultana and egg batter and mix through.

Spoon the batter into the prepared tin, then bake in the centre of the oven for 1–1¼ hours. Check the cake is cooked by inserting a skewer or toothpick, and if it comes out clean, you're in good shape!

Remove from the oven and cool on a wire rack. Store in a lined, clean cake tin, where it will eat well for 4–5 days.

BAKED 395

Feijoa friands

I reckon friands kick muffins' butt! I love their buttery, soft richness, and they still eat well a few days after baking. As an optional extra, I like to brush my friands with a nice fruit syrup when they come out of the oven. For these ones I use Six Barrel Soda feijoa syrup, which is outstanding (like all their other soda syrups). Elderflower syrup would work beautifully also, or even just make up a little lemon syrup by heating lemon juice, sugar and a dash of water together.

Makes 12

12 feijoas
½ cup (75 g/2¾ oz) plain flour
1½ cups (185 g/6½ oz) icing sugar
1½ cups (155 g/5½ oz) ground almonds
6 egg whites
200 g (7 oz) butter, melted and cooled, plus extra for greasing
feijoa syrup or elderflower syrup (optional)
icing sugar, for dusting

Preheat your oven to 180°C (350°F). Grease a 12-hole friand tin (or a small muffin tin) lightly with butter.

Peel or cut away the feijoa skins and discard. Cut 12 rounds from four of the feijoas and set aside. Chop the rest of the peeled feijoas into small dice and set aside.

In a medium-large bowl, sift together the flour and icing sugar, then mix in the ground almonds. Make a well in the centre of the dry ingredients.

Whisk the egg whites until just foamy. Pour the whisked egg whites and cooled melted butter, along with diced feijoas, into the well of the dry ingredients and gently mix together.

Evenly divide the batter into the moulds in the prepared tin. Top each with the reserved feijoa rounds. Place in the oven and bake for 15–20 minutes, until the friands are firm to the touch and golden brown. Remove from the oven.

While the friands are still warm, brush the top of each one with feijoa or elderflower syrup as a nice flavour boost. Take out of the moulds and, once cool, dust with icing sugar and help yourself.

BAKED 397

Crumpets with date and orange butter, treacle and cinnamon almond crunch

Growing up in our household, Golden brand crumpets were regarded as a treat. Mum would buy them with the week's groceries only every so often. We would toast them, spread them with lashings of butter and liberal amounts of golden syrup, then eat them as a quick and delicious dessert. You can of course still purchase the original store-bought crumpets; however, as you'll see below they are actually quite simple to make. These crumpets will stay super soft for a few days if you want to make them ahead. Serve them with these delicious add-ons for a wicked and slightly sinful brunch dish.

Makes 10 to 12

CRUMPETS
1 cup (250 ml/9 fl oz) water
½ cup (125 ml/4 fl oz) milk
2 teaspoons caster sugar
2 teaspoons dry active yeast
1½ cups (225 g/8 oz) plain flour
½ teaspoon salt
½ teaspoon baking soda
butter, for frying
treacle or golden syrup, to serve

DATE AND ORANGE BUTTER
250 g (9 oz) salted butter, at room temperature
finely grated zest of 1 orange, plus 2 tablespoons juice
1 cup (180 g/6½ oz) pitted dates, chopped

CINNAMON ALMOND CRUNCH
1 cup (155 g/5½ oz) blanched almonds
75 g (2¾ oz) butter, at room temperature
½ cup (75 g/2¾ oz) plain flour
½ cup (115 g/4 oz) caster sugar
1 teaspoon ground cinnamon

To make the crumpets, pour ½ cup (125 ml/4 fl oz) of the water and the milk into a small saucepan, and place over low heat for about 2 minutes, just until lukewarm. Take off the heat, stir in the sugar and the yeast, and set aside, until the yeast has become creamy and bubbled up at the surface.

Take a medium-sized mixing bowl, and sift in the flour and salt. Make a well in the centre. Pour the yeast liquid into the well of dry ingredients, and stir together to form a wet dough. Cover the bowl with a tea towel or clingfilm, and set aside in a warm place for 30 minutes, until the dough has doubled in size.

Take a small bowl and mix the baking soda and remaining ½ cup (125 ml/4 fl oz) water, then mix into the wet dough until fully incorporated.

Place a large frying pan over medium-low heat. Grease some egg rings or similar, then place in the pan. Add a small knob of butter to each ring, then pour in enough batter to come three-quarters of the way up the sides of the rings. Cook slowly on one side, until bubbles form and burst on the top. Once the batter is nearly cooked all the way through, remove the ring and flip the crumpet. Cook the remaining side for 1 minute or so, or until golden. Remove and let cool on a wire rack. Repeat until you have used up all the batter. Once cooled, wrap the crumpets in clingfilm and refrigerate until required.

To make the date and orange butter, place the butter in a stand mixer fitted with the paddle attachment and beat until creamy and light. With the motor running, slowly incorporate the orange zest and juice. Remove the butter from the mixer, place in a bowl, then, using a wooden spoon, work the chopped dates into the butter, until incorporated. Lay out a sheet of clingfilm on your bench, then form the butter into a sausage shape and firmly wrap. Refrigerate until required.

Preheat your oven to 170°C (325°F). Line a baking tray with baking paper.

For the cinnamon almond crunch, place the almonds in a food processor and blitz to a relatively fine meal. Place in a bowl, then add the butter, flour, sugar and cinnamon. Use clean hands to rub the mixture together for a minute or two, until combined.

Tip onto the prepared tray and break up the mixture, crumbling it into clusters on the tray. Bake for 10–15 minutes, until golden. Remove from the oven and let cool completely before storing in an airtight container.

To serve, toast the crumpets until golden and crisp. Top with lashings of the date and orange butter, then drizzle over the treacle or golden syrup and sprinkle with the almond cinnamon crunch. Serve now.

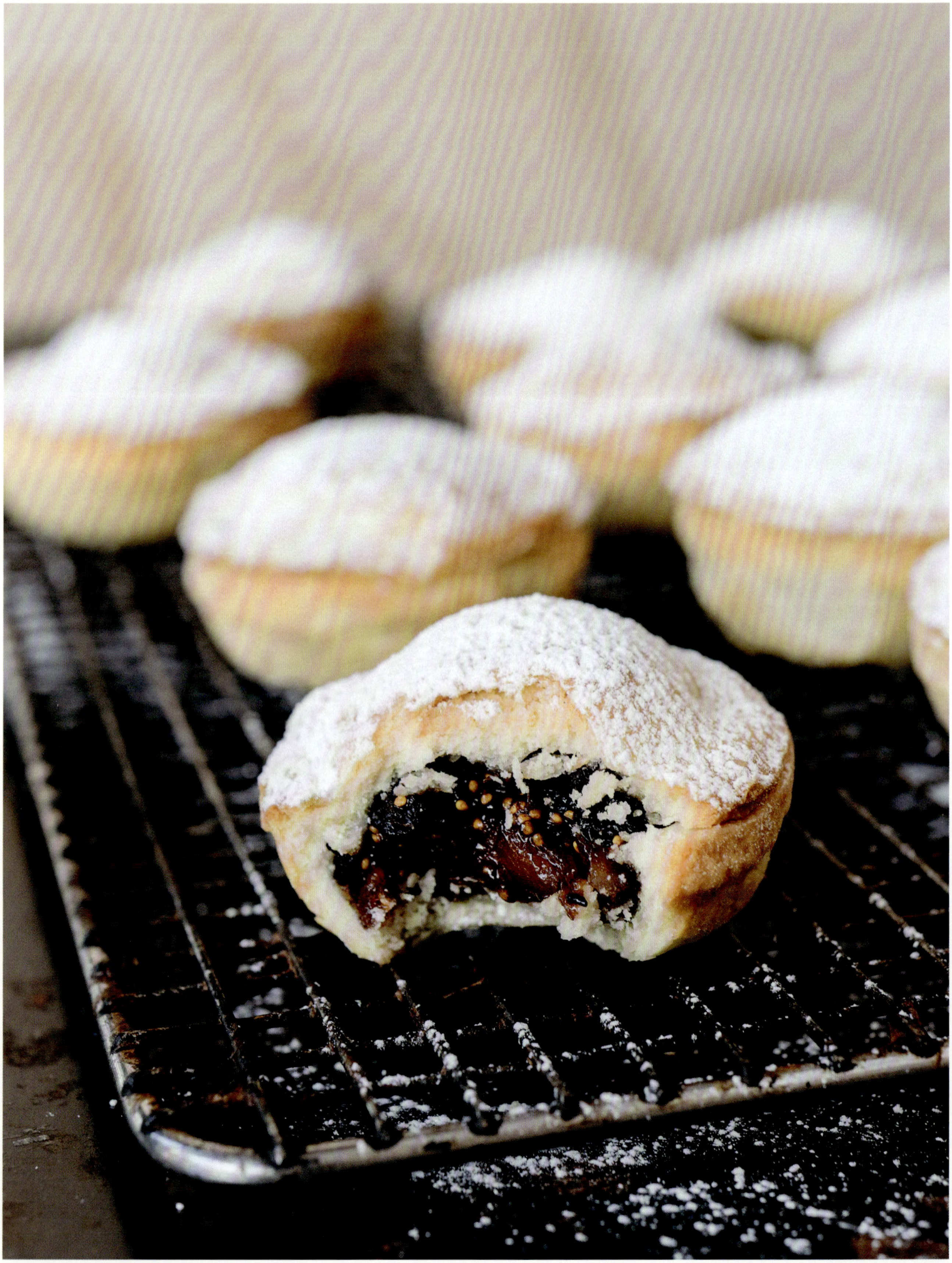

Fig and cranberry Christmas pies

Haydo knocked this recipe up when we were asked to come up with a Christmas mince pie recipe for a charity thingy. I have never been a huge fan of this sort of pie, so when we were discussing what we should do we both agreed that dried fig and cranberry could be a good place to start. The following is the result—and yes, I think they are delicious. Cheers to Haydo.

Makes 12

PASTRY
240 g (8½ oz) plain flour, plus extra for dusting
120 g (4¼ oz) cold butter, diced
½ cup (60 g/2¼ oz) icing sugar, plus extra for dusting
2 tablespoons orange juice
pinch salt
1 egg, beaten

FIG AND CRANBERRY FILLING
¼ cup (60 ml/2 fl oz) port
¼ cup (60 ml/2 fl oz) brandy
½ cup (95 g/3¼ oz) brown sugar
2 cups (370 g/13 oz) roughly chopped dried figs
1 cup (150 g/5½ oz) dried cranberries
1 cup (125 g/4½ oz) raisins
½ cup (75 g/2¾ oz) currants
1 cup (250 ml/9 fl oz) orange juice
1 teaspoon ground cinnamon
1 teaspoon ground ginger
¼ teaspoon ground cloves
2 tablespoons honey

To make the pastry, place the flour, butter, icing sugar, orange juice and salt in a food processor, and blitz until it comes together to form a dough. Work by hand on the bench quickly, until smooth, then cover with clingfilm and refrigerate until required.

For the filling, place all the ingredients into a saucepan, and simmer on a medium-low heat for 15 minutes, until the mixture starts to thicken and become jammy. Remove from the heat and let cool, then store in airtight container at room temperature until required.

Preheat your oven to 180°C (350°F).

On a lightly floured bench, roll out the pastry to around 3 mm (¹⁄₁₂ in) thick. Cut the rounds of the pastry for the bases. (These will obviously be bigger that the actual circumference of the pie to allow for the depth.)

Gently press the bases into a greased 12-hole muffin tin. Fill the bases to the top with the fruit filling, then lightly brush the top edges of the pastry bases with the beaten egg. Cut the pastry lids out of the remaining pastry and place on top. Lightly pinch together the pastry to seal.

Bake in the oven for 20 minutes, until golden. Remove from the oven, then let the pies sit for 10 minutes before extracting from the moulds and transferring to a wire rack to cool completely. Store in an airtight container and dust with icing sugar prior to serving.

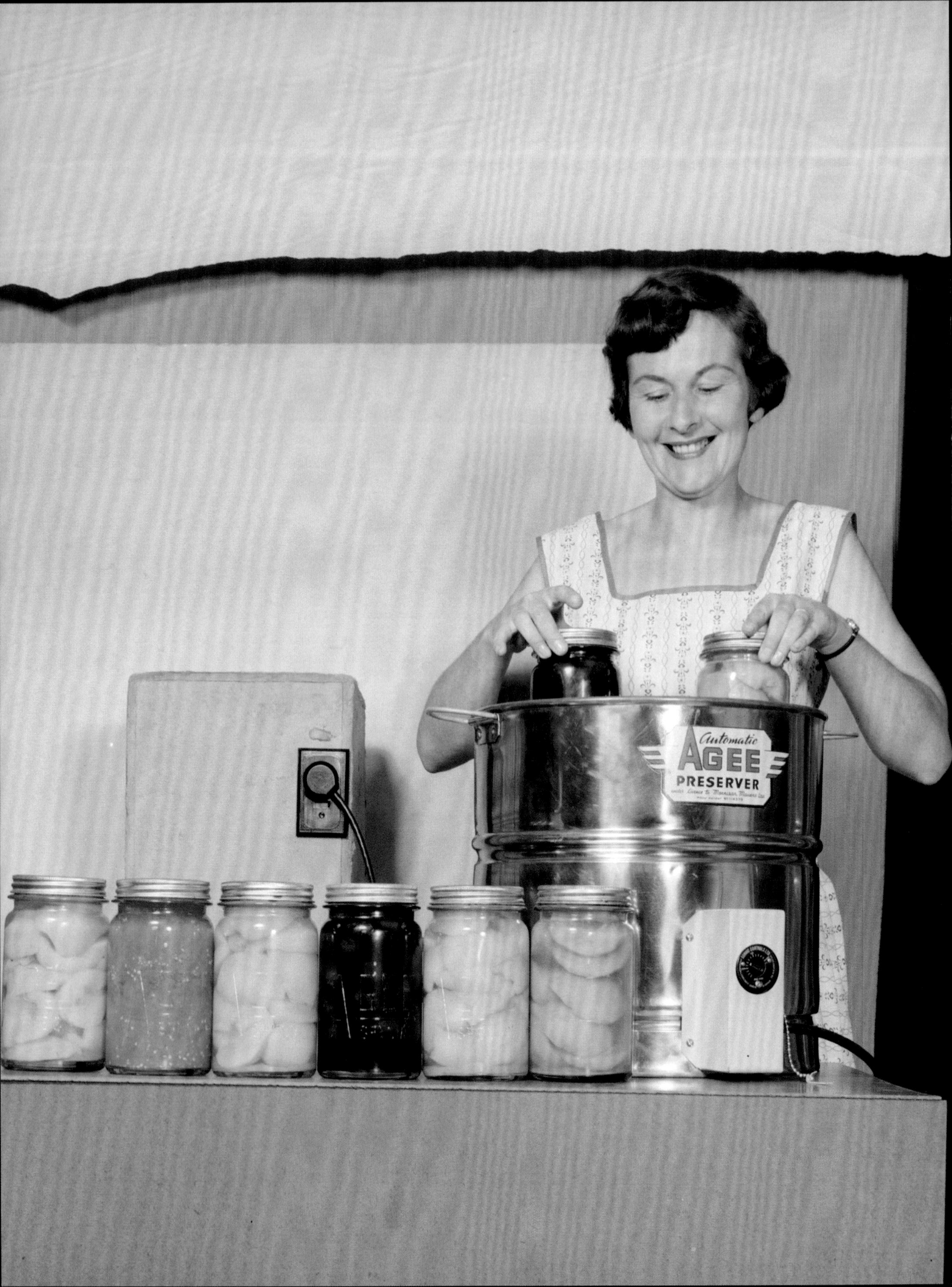
Automatic
AGEE
PRESERVER

PRESERVES
KAI WHAKAPOUNAMU

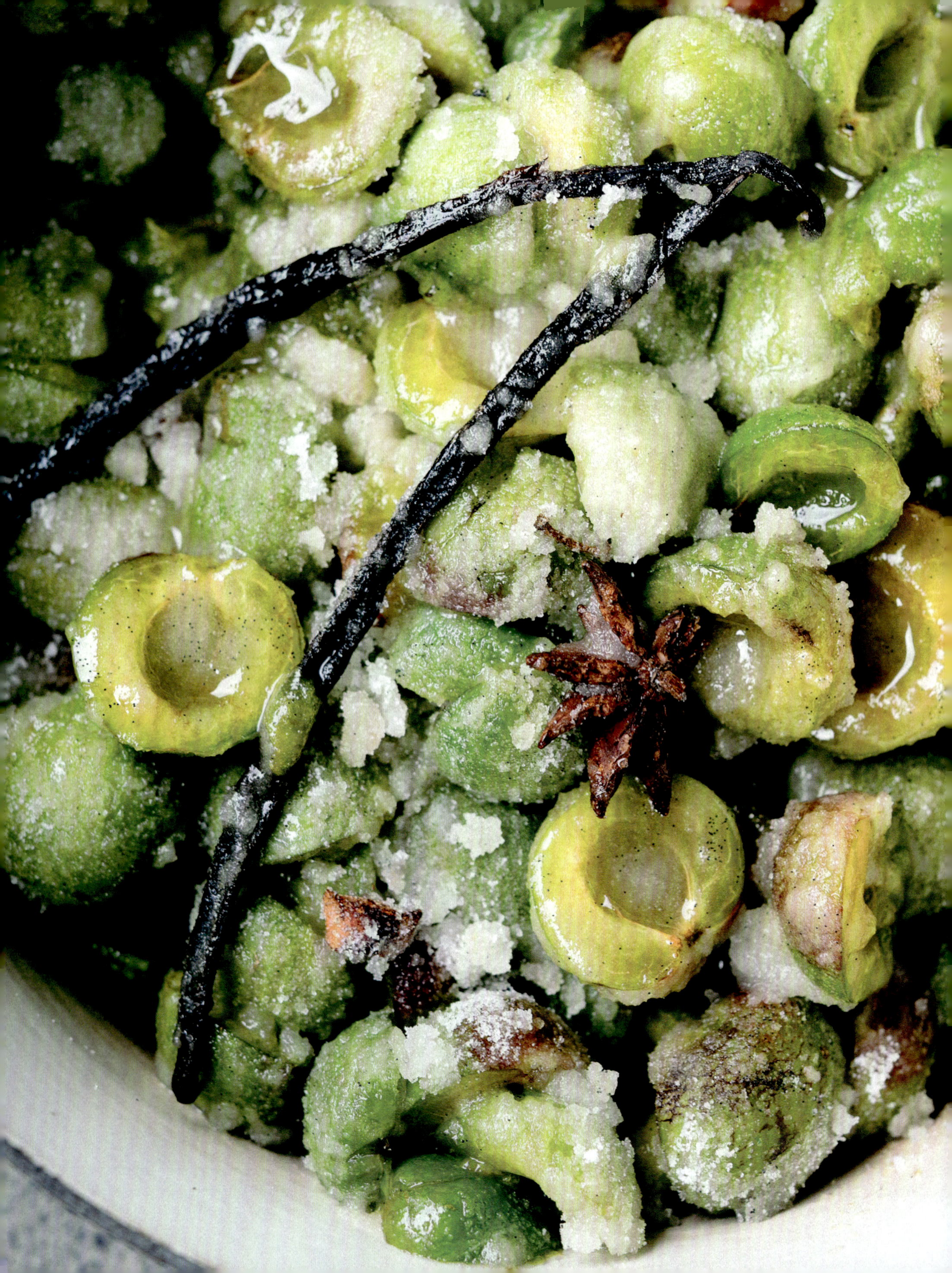

Let Us Preserve

Out of all of the senses, I have always been particularly enamoured with our sense of smell. Most would argue that when it comes to cooking and eating, our most important sense is taste. And, yes, I would have to agree with that—however, smell comes in a very close second for me, mainly because it hits you first and is so evocative, often rekindling memories or igniting those reassuring endorphins.

It's like the sweet aroma of your grandmother's shortbread cooling on a wire rack in the kitchen when you go to visit, instantly recognisable, adding a special layer to an already warm welcome. The smell of a roasting leg of lamb, for me, is one of life's most delightful culinary scents. I believe I can even tell what stage the roast is at by the strength of the aroma in the kitchen. Whenever I get a whiff of the savoury, slightly sweet, rich scent created by the skin of the lamb caramelising, I'm immediately taken back to my childhood.

There is something else I enjoy about the sense of smell, and that is the scale and perspective of contrast that exists within the sense. Smell can be such an extraordinarily pleasurable moment, a feeling that excites and stimulates. For me, it's things like the smell of bacon cooking, the scent of expensive perfume, fresh-cut grass . . . even the scent of av gas or the smell of discharged gunpowder can be extremely gratifying. Of course, at the other end of the scale, an odour can also be so heinously vile it makes your face contort like a bent old sandshoe!

One particular smell from my childhood that I think sits somewhere in the middle of the pleasurable and repugnant spectrum is that of vinegar and sugar cooking. I find it sort of hard to categorise. It's not actually the smell itself (which I would describe as aggressive and slightly abrasive) that I love, but its familiarity.

When I was growing up, near the end of the summer Mum would make a cracker peach chutney. It was the only chutney that she would produce each year; the one condiment that graced our kitchen table on a regular basis. Like a lot of simple fruit chutneys back in the fifties and sixties, Mum's was made with a combination of fresh fruit—in this case Golden Queen peaches—dried fruit, a few spices, salt and a large amount of malt vinegar and sugar.

As with many foods you relate to growing up, I enjoyed it quite simply because that was all there was. It was a versatile condiment, providing the flavour point in the cold mutton sandwiches we consumed with great regularity throughout the year. It would also weave its magic in dollops on top of cheddar cheese and crackers—the go-to canapé when people dropped by unexpectedly for a cuppa or a cold beverage.

I can recall Mum scribbling out the recipe on more than one occasion for those who asked. Back then there was nothing even close to the proliferation of cookbooks that fill large sections of bookshops today, so the sharing of recipes was commonplace. Most families had what we would call these days 'signature recipes', which they would swap and share, scribbled down on whatever paper was at hand. I have always made a habit of scouring second-hand bookshops or garage sales for old cookbooks. I enjoy reading the published recipes from back then, but of much more value to me is stumbling across beautifully handwritten and often very soiled ingredient measures and cooking instructions. These handwritten recipes feel so incredibly personal, as if you are privy to something very special.

I used to subscribe to *Lucky Peach*, a kind of 'rock-and-roll'-style food magazine that sadly ceased publishing in 2017. It was a unique and terrific read, with contributions from the likes of famous chefs David Chang, Anthony Bourdain and co. What was refreshing about it was reading so many terrific stories and articles that celebrated down-to-earth, traditional styles of cooking and eating. I especially loved the way they often paid homage to simple and what could be described as 'down and dirty' food, which of course could not be further from the truth. I look at these foods with the same awe and respect with which Michelin-star chefs might look at plates of food put together with tweezers in kitchens resembling science labs.

I don't like snobbery around food. Just because it's new and hasn't been seen or eaten before doesn't necessarily mean it's good. I concede that much of it is wonderful and very often extraordinarily creative, but most of the time I find this sort of food soulless and somehow lacking the gratification that simple, time-honoured dishes always offer up.

Anyway, I read one particular piece in *Lucky Peach* where the writer was in New Zealand researching one thing or another, and was hosted by a farming family. On his first night, he was offered some classic homemade plum sauce with his evening meal. To say it was a complete epiphany for this guy is an understatement; he was by all accounts euphoric. At that moment he believed he had discovered the most glorious ketchup in the world! He poured it on his eggs in the morning—something I'm sure many of us can relate to—then continued to have a puddle of it sitting next to almost everything he ate for the rest of his trip.

The point I make here is that many of the traditional foods or tastes that have become everyday to us here in New Zealand are seen by the rest of the world as completely unique. And that's what it is all about: treasuring and celebrating what we often fail to realise is unique about our country and our cuisine.

We have been a country of picklers, preservers and fermenters from day dot. Early Māori preserved large quantities of food, and understood the importance of having food on hand for leaner times of the year while also using it as an important commodity for trading with other tribes. Much of the food gathered or caught was preserved by drying the products. This technique was used for fish, shellfish, fruit and also seeds. Tītī (muttonbirds) were cooked then preserved in their own fat (still practised today) and often stored in inflated bull kelp. Māori also practised 'mara kai', a fermentation process to preserve fish and crayfish, and later corn that the European settlers brought with them to New Zealand. The European settlers were also a frugal bunch and waste was frowned upon—a lesson that sadly seems lost in this day and age.

Chutneys, relishes, stewed fruits, jams, preserved sauces and pickles have played a major role in what has been our cuisine of sorts over the past hundred years, and these preserves are still firmly entrenched in our cooking and eating DNA today. For as long as I've been cooking, I have been a been massive fan of preserving, incorporating chutneys, relishes and, in more recent times, pickles into my culinary repertoire. I love the intensity and wake-up call they bring to the eating experience—playing around with sweet, sour and salt, then introducing spice and heat to the mix often produces some pretty heady outcomes. I have a bunch of chutneys and relishes that have been gracing my menus for decades, and they are all in this book. Hand on heart, I never tire of them; in fact, in a weird sort of a way, I look at them like old friends that I bring out to impress with from time to time.

When it comes to cooking activities, preserving, much like baking, is one of those feel-good, cheerful pursuits. It often seems like a bit of an occasion or a big cooking adventure. The thing about preserving is that it's generally done in large batches, so having a propensity towards being completely organised before beginning will serve you well. Locating and dusting off your big old saucepan or cauldron from the dark depths of the pot cupboard. Digging out your big old wooden spoon that, like your cauldron, only gets an outing once or twice a year for these sorts of occasions. Kilos of sugar, litres of vinegar, onions, ginger, whole spices, fresh chillies, pickling salt all at the ready . . .

If you're lucky enough to have a selection of Agee jars with their old screw rings and a pile of fresh, shiny lids, all the better. If you don't, there are plenty of second-hand stores up and down the country where you can pick them up, and Agee and Perfit still manufacture the metalware. I enjoy using Agee jars because they look so beautiful and always bring a kind of comforting nostalgia to the kitchen and pantry. Also, with so many food products reaching our kitchens in jars of all shapes and sizes, it does seem wasteful not to put them to good use once they're empty.

I like having a bunch of different-sized jars, as it gives you great options—preservers are nearly always gifters, too, and different-sized jars fit different giving occasions. With preserving comes sharing. A glass jar complete with a handwritten label is a gift that just keeps on giving—such a personal offering, a special treat that brings joy to not only the recipient but also just as much (if not more) to the maker.

One of the other great and obvious things about preserving is that it is generally a job done at the height or the end of the season, when there is an overabundance of wonderful ripe fruit or produce on offer. It always blows my mind how inexpensive produce can be at these times when the fruit is super plentiful. Farmers' markets, roadside stands and 'pick your own' orchards are the sorts of places to score large amounts of produce for ridiculously small amounts of money. Or you might be lucky enough to have kind neighbours who hate the thought of waste and have more produce than they know what to do with, so they simply give it away.

Having been in decline for a number of decades, preserving is now making quite a significant comeback. I believe this is due to the fact that there is definitely a real concern these days around food wastage, coupled with the backlash against mass-produced and over-processed foods flooding our supermarkets. Preserving just makes good sense.

As clichéd as it might sound, the simple pleasure of spreading your toast with delicious homemade strawberry jam on a cold winter morning is a serious little ray of sunshine, bringing a taste of summer to a gloomy outlook. And it can, of course, go the other way too, like a jar of piccalilli made from cauliflower in the winter served at the height of summer next to a plate of chargrilled lamb chops. Yes please!

With our love of travel and eating, we are now also beginning to embrace the special and traditional preserving methods and tastes of other cultures and cuisines. The sort of exposure we get every minute of the day to the rest of the now very small world, courtesy of Mr Google, is simply extraordinary. With every possible flavour combination and recipe from every corner of the globe at our fingertips, it's difficult for our young country to create a distinct New Zealand cuisine. I don't think that's a bad thing, as volume of flavour matched with the ridiculous amount of different produce available here will always hold us in good stead and keep us highly regarded on the world's culinary stage.

I simply love preserves. They have played a major role in all of my cooking and eating since I was a boy. The sweetness and acid, along with salt, heat and spice, all bring, in a humble way, the 'wow' to so many eating occasions. If the recipes within this book seem daunting (and I hope they don't), I urge you to at least make a few of the following preserves. That way you can bring some delicious flavour points to any meal that otherwise may feel a little flat or ordinary.

Go on, jar up! Get jammin'!

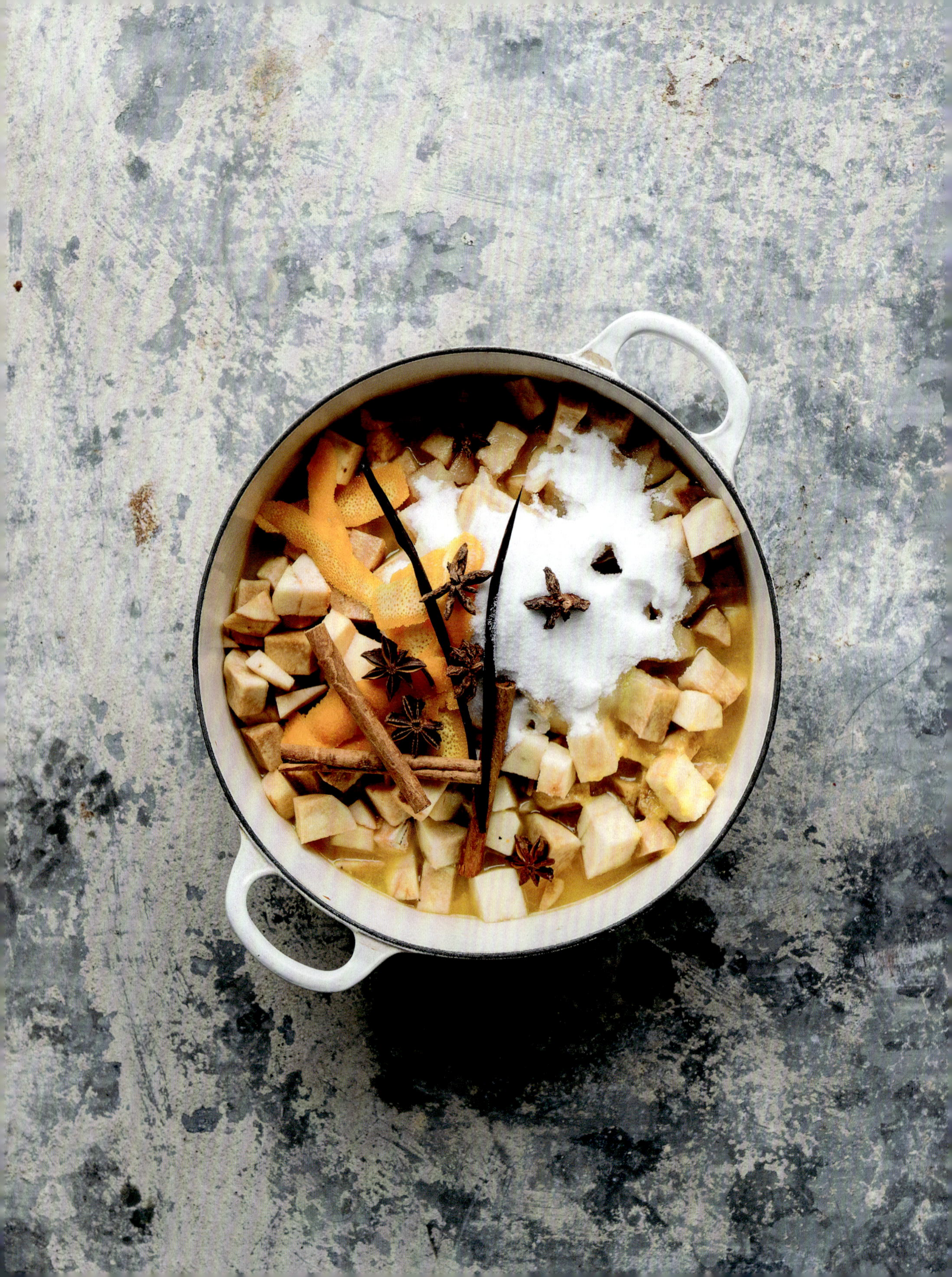

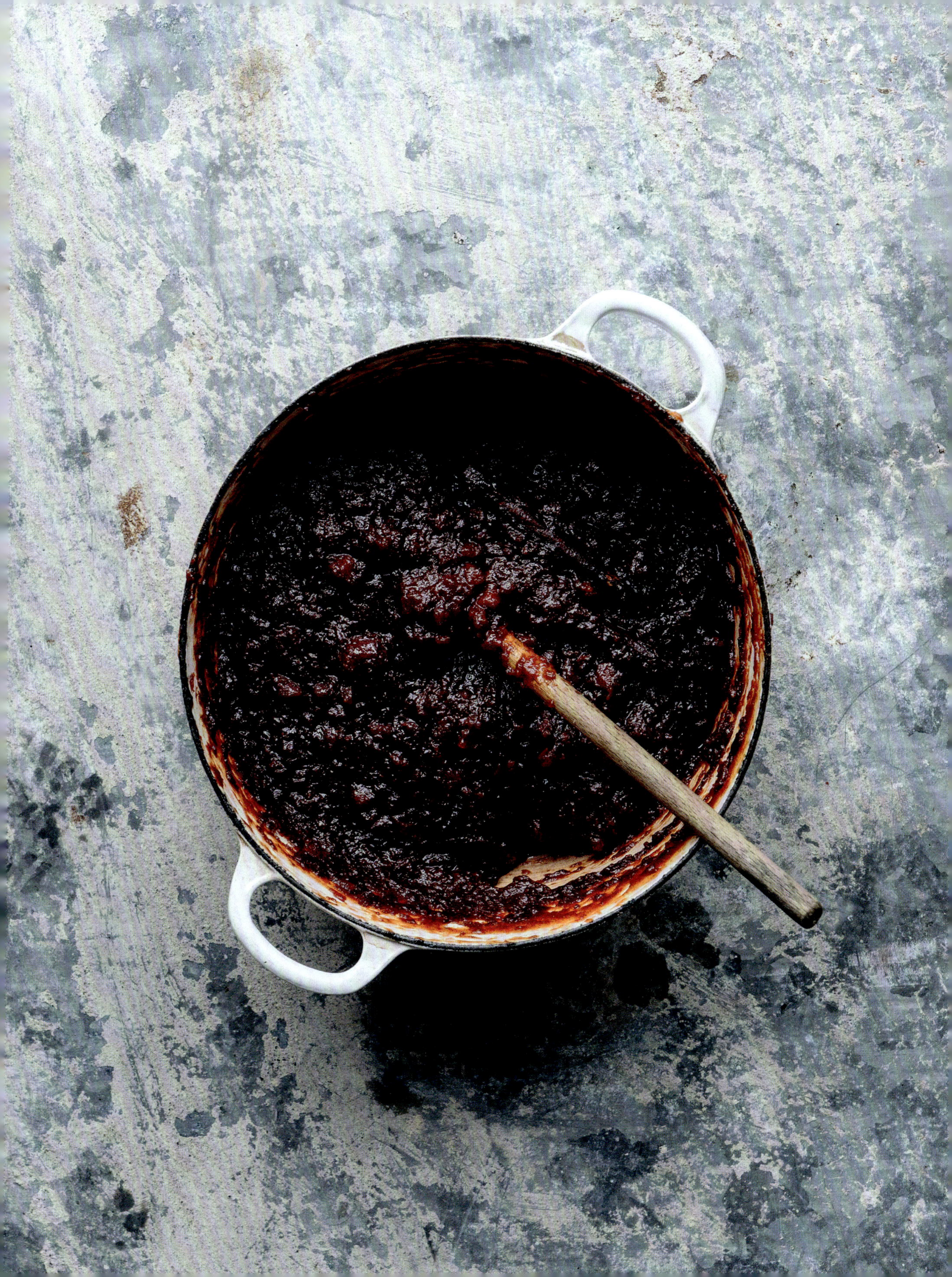

Quince jam/paste

I make a batch of quince jam or paste most years, embracing the long, slow process of making this wonderful preserve. Watching the colour develop from pale yellow to deep red is a thing of beauty, and the sweet perfume that the slow cooking produces permeates throughout the house and signals that autumn is upon us and winter is just around the corner.

Makes 4–6 medium jars

2 kg (4 lb 8 oz) quince, peeled and diced
700 g (1 lb 9 oz) sugar
1 vanilla bean, split in half lengthways
4 star anise
3 cinnamon sticks
pared zest of 1 orange
8 cups (2 litres/68 fl oz) orange juice

Take a heavy cast-iron saucepan and add the quince, sugar, vanilla bean, star anise, cinnamon sticks and orange zest. Pour over 1 litre (35 fl oz) of the orange juice.

Place the pan over medium-high heat and bring up to the boil. Reduce the heat to low and cook at a bubbling simmer, stirring occasionally, for about 4 hours.

If you are making jam, it is ready when the quince has turned a bright orange-red, is soft through and there is practically no liquid left in the pan. Remove from the heat. Dig out the vanilla bean and use a small knife to scrape out the seeds, adding them back into the quince. Discard the vanilla bean along with the star anise and cinnamon sticks. Use a stick blender to purée the quince, then pour into hot sterilised jars and seal.

To make a quince paste, add the remaining orange juice in intervals while cooking out the quince for a further 3–4 hours. Near the end of the process, when the quince has turned a deep burgundy red, it is important to stir regularly to prevent it from sticking. Once again remove the solids, purée, then divide into hot sterilised jars, as with the jam.

Preserved lemons

I find I reach for preserved lemons more and more these days, especially when a dish is a little flat and just needs a bit of oomph. Preserved lemon brings salty and sour flavours and a slight bitterness to any dish.

Makes 2 x 1 litre (35 fl oz) jars

lemons (look for thin-skinned lemons such as the Meyer variety)
plenty of sea salt
lemon juice, if needed

Wash the lemons to remove any sprays or chemicals.

Take a sharp knife and cut down the length of the lemon in slices about 5 mm thick, while keeping both ends intact. The cuts should go right through the heart of the lemon so if you squeeze both ends it opens up, a bit like a lantern.

Take a clean sterilised jar and sprinkle 2 tablespoons of salt in the bottom.

Over a bowl, to catch any juice, slightly squeeze the lemons to open the cuts, then force a heaped teaspoon of salt into each cut. Place each lemon in the jar and repeat the process. Sprinkle a few tablespoons of salt between each layer as you go. Pack the lemons in tightly to the top, then add a final layer of salt before screwing on the lid. Leave to sit at room temperature for a few days, keeping an eye on them and monitoring the juice level. After the third day, if the lemons are not completely submerged in liquid, top up with fresh lemon juice.

The preserved lemons should be ready in 2–3 weeks and will last up to a year.

To use, remove a preserved lemon from the jar with a wooden spoon. Open up and discard the pith and flesh of the lemon. Lightly rinse off the skin, then finely dice and use as you so choose.

PRESERVES 415

Grapefruit and orange marmalade

Without question, my favourite preserve to spread on toast in the morning is marmalade. There's something about that sweet and bitter thing going on that feels like it's putting a bit of zing in your morning. Sometimes I think we forget to realise what a wonderful country this is when it comes to growing varieties of citrus. I am a massive fan of all of it, and not just to eat in its natural state; I find that so many dishes that I cook are enhanced by a burst of one citrus or another. I added some kaffir lime leaves to this recipe, and I love the floral note they bring to the table—subtle but quite intriguing.

Makes 2 x 1 litre (35 fl oz) jars

2 grapefruit
4 oranges
8 cups (2 litres/68 fl oz) water
caster sugar (¾ cup for every 1 cup fruit pulp)
4 kaffir lime leaves

Roughly cut and mince up the grapefruit and oranges (skin and pith, but remove the pips) into pretty small, fine dice, then place in a bowl and cover with the water. Leave on the bench overnight to soak.

In the morning, tip the soaked fruit and the water into a large heavy-bottomed saucepan. Place over medium-high heat and bring up to the boil. Simmer for 45 minutes, until the fruit is soft and pulpy. Take off the heat and let cool, then measure out how many cups of citrus pulp you have. For every 1 cup of fruit pulp, add ¾ cup sugar into the pan, along with the kaffir lime leaves.

Place a plate in the freezer or refrigerator.

Place the pan back over medium heat and simmer for 45 minutes, until thickened and the setting point is reached. Test by spooning a little of the marmalade onto a fridge-cold plate—if it wrinkles when pushed with your finger, it is set.

Pour into warm sterilised jars, then seal.

Rhubarb and strawberry jam

Rhubarb and strawberry is one of those classic combos that will never go out of fashion. This jam is a little ripper and, while it will always be appreciated with toast and butter, it really deserves a fresh scone and a little cream action!

Makes 2 x 300 ml (10½ fl oz) jars

1 kg (2 lb 4 oz) rhubarb, washed and cut into large dice
500 g (1 lb 2 oz) strawberries, hulled and quartered
2 cups (440 g/15½ oz) sugar
½ vanilla bean
finely grated zest of 1 lemon
1 tablespoon lemon juice

Place all the ingredients in a suitable-sized saucepan over medium-low heat. Simmer for 25 minutes, stirring occasionally until both fruits have begun to break down and the jam has a thick consistency.

Pour into hot sterilised jars and seal accordingly.

Greengage plum jam

Most definitely my favourite plum, greengages arrive late at the end of summer with the last of the stone fruit. It's a cracker jam, this one!

Makes 3 x 500 ml (17 fl oz) jars

2 kg (4 lb 8 oz) greengage plums
2¼ cups (500 g/1 lb 2 oz) sugar
finely grated zest and juice of 1 lemon
1 vanilla bean
2 star anise

Cut the plums in half and discard the stones.

In a large mixing bowl, toss together the plums, sugar, lemon zest and juice. Split the vanilla bean in half lengthways, scrape out the seeds and add both the bean and seeds to the bowl, along with the star anise.

Allow to macerate for 30 minutes to let the juices draw out of the fruit slightly.

Transfer the ingredients to a large saucepan and place on medium-high heat. Bring up to the boil, then reduce to a low simmer and cook for 1 hour, stirring occasionally. Pour the jam into sterilised jars and tightly fasten the lids.

Star anise and vanilla poached pears

The spice combination with these pears works a treat. They taste like pears for grown-ups, and are wonderful as a side dish or foil for a steamed-pudding-like dessert in winter.

Makes enough for 3 x large Agee jars

2 kg (4 lb 8 oz) firm, ripe pears
6 cups (1.5 litres/52 fl oz) water
4½ cups (1 kg/2 lb 4 oz) caster sugar
2–3 star anise
1½ cinnamon sticks
1 vanilla bean, split in half lengthways and seeds scraped

Peel the pears, then cut in half. Using a teaspoon, scoop the core out of each half, and remove any visible fibrous stalk.

Place the water, sugar, spices and vanilla seeds into a large saucepan over medium heat. Bring up to a gentle boil to dissolve the sugar, then add your pears. Cover with a plate, to keep the pears submerged in liquid, and poach for approximately 10 minutes, or until the pears feel tender. You can test them by inserting a skewer into them, and if there is little to no resistance they are ready. Remove the pan from the heat and use a slotted spoon to scoop the pears out of the hot liquid.

Place the poached pears in sterilised jars, then pour the hot liquid into the jars to fill to 1 cm (½ in) from the top. Seal tightly with sterilised lids, and allow to cool completely before storing.

Poached apricots with saffron and cinnamon

I always think of Central Otago when I eat these. I guess it's the aridness of the environment there that produces such intense flavours, be it in cherries, Pinot Noir or, in this case, apricots and saffron. The saffron and cinnamon add a wonderful floral note to the fruit.

Makes 2 x 1 litre (35 fl oz) jars

1 kg (2 lb 4 oz) ripe apricots
3 cups (750 ml/26 fl oz) water
2 cups (440 g/15½ oz) sugar
½ cup (115 g/4 oz) brown sugar
1 cinnamon stick
12 saffron threads

Wash the apricots and remove the stones, leaving them in halves.

To a suitable-sized saucepan add the water, both sugars, cinnamon stick and saffron. Place over medium-low heat, bring up to the boil, then lower to a simmer. Stir occasionally until the sugars have dissolved.

Now add the apricot halves. Poach gently for 5–10 minutes, until the fruit is tender but still intact.

Carefully layer the poached apricot halves in sterilised preserving jars. Pour over the syrup, up to the top, then seal.

Honey and thyme poached peaches

The honey and fresh thyme give these poached peaches an interesting and distinctive floral note. By all means play around with different varieties of honey, different herbs and, of course, other varieties of fruit.

Makes 16 peach halves

8 firm, ripe peaches
3 cups (750 ml/26 fl oz) water
2 cups (460 g/1 lb) caster sugar
½ cup (175 g/6 oz) mānuka honey
4 thyme sprigs
1 cinnamon stick
pinch flaky sea salt

Wash the peaches in cold water, cut in half then remove the stones if they come out easily. If not, leave them and remove after poaching.

To a large, suitable-sized saucepan, add the water, sugar, honey, thyme, cinnamon stick and salt. Bring up to the boil, then reduce to a simmer. Stir to help dissolve the sugar.

Now add the peach halves. Poach for around 6 minutes on each side, depending on how ripe the peaches are. Check their doneness with a skewer or the tip of a sharp knife. They should be just soft through.

Remove from the heat. Take a slotted spoon and remove the peaches from the cooking syrup. Once cold, peel the skins from the peaches and remove any remaining stones. Gently place the peach halves in clean sterilised jars, then pour over the syrup and seal.

PRESERVES 419

Bread and butter pickles

The name 'bread and butter pickles' comes from a pair of cucumber farmers, Omar and Cora Fanning from Illinois, who started selling their sweet and sour pickles in the 1920s. The story goes that the Fannings survived the rough years by making these particular pickles with their surplus of undersized cucumbers, bartering them with their grocer for staples such as bread and butter. These pickles are still a favourite of my mum's, always making an appearance when cheese and crackers are being served.

Makes 2 large jars

600 g (1 lb 5 oz) baby cucumbers, sliced into 2 mm (1/12 in) rounds
1 cup (155 g/5½ oz) thinly sliced onions
¼ cup (35 g/1¼ oz) flaky sea salt
3 cups (750 ml/26 fl oz) white vinegar
1 cup (220 g/7¾ oz) sugar
2 tablespoons yellow mustard seeds
2 teaspoons ground ginger
2 teaspoons black peppercorns
2 tablespoons celery seeds

Toss the sliced cucumbers, onions and salt into a bowl, then mix together. Divide into clean sterilised pickling jars.

In a saucepan, heat the vinegar, sugar, mustard seeds, ginger, peppercorns and celery seeds. Place over high heat, bring up to the boil and stir. Once the sugar has dissolved, pour this brine over the sliced cucumber and onions. Seal the jars, let cool, then store at room temperature until required.

Pickled jalapeño peppers

New Zealanders' palate for taking on and enjoying the heat from fresh chillies and the like has really taken off in the past decade. I have a special friend who grows a bunch of different varieties of chilli in the summer that she enjoys fresh, and then dries the remainder, grinds them up and carries them with her wherever she goes. I love the way she adds a truly homegrown pinch of heat to practically every dish that is put in front of her. These pickled jalapeños will become a staple in your pantry and fridge. I find that more and more these days I am reaching for them, chopping them up finely and adding them to a range of recipes, as they add just another layer of interest to the flavour profile of most dishes.

Makes 3 x 1 litre (35 fl oz) jars

1 kg (2 lb 4 oz) jalapeño peppers
4 cups (1 litre/35 fl oz) white vinegar
2 cups (500 ml/17 fl oz) water
6 garlic cloves, cut into slivers
2 tablespoons sugar
2 tablespoons flaky sea salt
2 tablespoons coriander seeds
6–8 fresh coriander stems

Make sure the jalapeño peppers are clean. Either leave them whole or slice into 5 mm (¼ in) thick rounds.

Pour the vinegar and water into a saucepan and add the garlic, sugar, salt and coriander seeds. Place over high heat, bring up to the boil and stir until the sugar and salt have dissolved.

Divide the jalapeño peppers and coriander stems between sterilised jars. Pour over the pickle brine, seal and store in a cool, dry spot.

PRESERVES 421

Eggplant kasundi

I learned this recipe from a great friend and extraordinarily talented cook, Pippa Lee. It has been on our menu at Depot Eatery since day one—we serve it as a condiment with our wood-roasted hāpuka belly. Everyone loves this relish: it's got a bit of heat, but has terrific depth and a wonderful balance of spice, sweetness and acidity. The recipe seems slightly convoluted in its process, where a number of ingredients are repeated in different stages, but just follow the steps—it's actually child's play.

Makes 1 kg (2 lb 4 oz)

1⅓ cups (330 ml/11¼ fl oz) canola oil
1½ cups (235 g/8½ oz) finely diced onion
½ cup finely diced ginger, plus ½ cup roughly chopped ginger
¼ cup finely diced garlic, plus ½ cup roughly chopped garlic
6 tablespoons cumin seeds
2 teaspoons fenugreek seeds
2 tablespoons yellow mustard seeds
2 tablespoons ground turmeric
1 cup (250 ml/9 fl oz) malt vinegar
1¾ cups (385 g/13½ oz) sugar
2 tablespoons salt
1 kg (2 lb 4 oz) eggplant, cut into 1 cm (½ in) dice
85 g (3 oz) chillies, roughly chopped

Place a medium-large saucepan over medium-low heat. Add ⅓ cup (80 ml/2½ fl oz) of the oil and the onion. Cook for 10–15 minutes, until the onion is soft, then add the finely diced ginger and garlic. Cook down, stirring occasionally, until golden.

In a frying pan, dry roast 3 tablespoons of the cumin seeds, and the fenugreek and mustard seeds. Grind and set aside.

Next, place the roughly chopped ginger, garlic, turmeric and remaining 3 tablespoons of whole cumin seeds, along with a splash of the vinegar, into a food processor and blitz to a paste. Set aside.

Once the diced onion, ginger and garlic are golden, add the dry-roasted ground spices, along with the wet spice paste. Cook out over medium heat for 5 minutes, stirring to prevent sticking.

Now add the remaining vinegar, the sugar and the salt, and mix through to combine. Add the eggplant and chillies and cook down, stirring occasionally, and adding the remaining 1 cup (250 ml/9 fl oz) of oil as you go. (You may not need all of the oil.) The cooking down should take about 40 minutes. The kasundi is ready when it has a soft, jam-like consistency.

Remove from the heat and let cool before refrigerating until required, or preserve in hot sterilised jars.

Eggplant Kasundi 08/16
Eggplant Kasundi 08/16
Eggplant Kasundi 08/16
Eggplant Kasundi 08/16

Tomato table sauce

This is the basic tomato sauce that many of us grew up with. It's a condiment that rarely left the end of our kitchen table. A morning, noon and night sauce, it's great with bacon and eggs, smeared on cold mutton or lamb sandwiches for lunch, and at night a sausage steps up to another level of enjoyment with a lick of tomato sauce on the way through.

Makes 1.5 litres (52 fl oz)

2 cups (310 g/11 oz) finely diced onion
2 cups peeled and finely diced Granny Smith apples
2 cups (500 ml/17 oz) malt vinegar
1 cup (220 g/7¾ oz) sugar
3 x 400 g tins whole peeled tomatoes
½ teaspoon ground allspice
¼ teaspoon ground cloves
¼ teaspoon ground black pepper
1 tablespoon flaky sea salt

Place all the ingredients in a large heavy-bottomed saucepan over medium heat and bring up to the boil, then turn the heat down to a gentle simmer. Cover with a lid and cook for 2 hours, stirring occasionally to prevent sticking.

Blitz with a stick blender to your desired consistency, then store in sterilised bottles or jars.

Haydo's nana's plum sauce

This is a terrific plum sauce that Haydo's mum has always made and that has been standard issue in their family's pantry for years. It's always been called 'Nana's plum sauce', although Haydo has no recollection of ever meeting Nana. I love the way recipes like this were personalised decades ago, and how even though the original creators have passed on their memory is inherently linked with the recipe forever.

Makes 8 cups (2 litres/68 fl oz)

2 kg (4 lb 8 oz) red plums, halved and stones removed
700 ml (24 fl oz) malt vinegar
1⅓ cups (400 g/14 oz) caster sugar
1⅓ cups (250 g/9 oz) brown sugar
1 tablespoon finely chopped ginger
1 teaspoon cayenne pepper
1 teaspoon ground allspice
1 teaspoon cloves
3 tablespoons flaky sea salt

Place all the ingredients in a large heavy-bottomed saucepan over high heat and bring up to the boil. Reduce the heat to low and simmer, stirring occasionally, for approximately 1 hour, until the plums have broken down.

Remove from the heat and place in a food processor or blender. Blitz for a minute before passing through a sieve. Discard the solids.

Pour back into the pan, bring up to a simmer and cook for another 5 minutes. Store in sterilised bottles or jars.

PRESERVES 425

Granny Brown's peach chutney

My mother would make a batch of this chutney most summers. It was a staple in our pantry. It's not a particularly refined preserve, but it does pack a real punch. My favourite application for this rich condiment is in a cold mutton sandwich, which was a regular occurrence while growing up on a farm, where we consumed a leg roast of lamb hogget or mutton once or twice a week.

Makes about 2 kg (4 lb 8 oz)

1 kg (2 lb 4 oz) Golden Queen peaches, stones removed and cut into large dice
700 ml (24 fl oz) malt vinegar
½ cup (120 g/4¼ oz) crystalised ginger, finely chopped
2½ cups (450 g/1 lb) pitted dates, roughly chopped
50 g (1¾ oz) flaky sea salt
1 teaspoon cayenne pepper
900 g (2 lb) brown sugar
30 g (1 oz) garlic cloves, finely diced
½ cup (45 g/1½ oz) almond flakes, toasted

Place all the ingredients except the almonds in a large heavy-bottomed saucepan over medium-high heat and bring up to the boil. Lower the heat to a gentle simmer and cook for an hour or so, stirring occasionally, until reduced and starting to take on a wet, jam-like consistency. The chutney will thicken as it cools. Remove from the heat, then stir in the toasted almonds. Divvy up into warm, sterilised preserving jars and seal.

Condensed milk mayonnaise

This is the mayonnaise that so many of us New Zealanders grew up with. It's sweet and tangy, with just the right amount of heat from the mustard powder and cayenne pepper. I'm sure it doesn't meet too many of the health guidelines, but that will never stop me from spreading a generous lick here and there, be it with cold meat, chilled poached crayfish, boiled new potatoes or with good old iceberg lettuce.

Makes 2 x 500 ml (17 fl oz) jars

1 x 395 g can Highlander sweetened condensed milk
½ cup (125 ml/4 fl oz) canola oil
2 egg yolks
½ cup (125 ml/4 fl oz) malt vinegar
2 tsp dry mustard powder
pinch of cayenne pepper
1 teaspoon salt

Place the sweetened condensed milk in a bowl. Add the remaining ingredients and whisk together until blended. Taste and adjust the seasoning accordingly. Place in the fridge to chill and thicken.

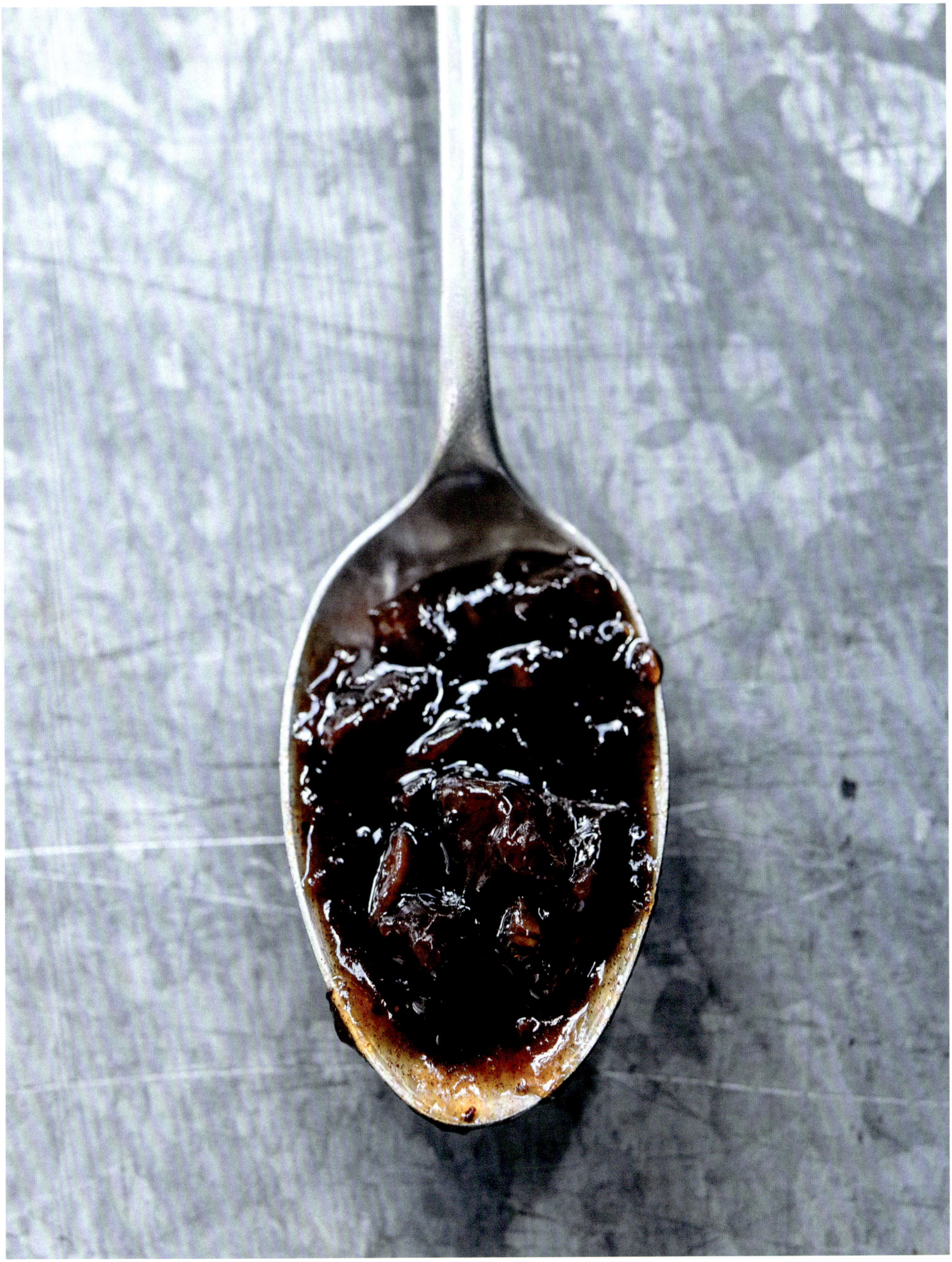

Piccalilli

Piccalilli and chow chow are pretty much the same thing. Like all recipes, it has a habit of changing from person to person or region to region. Of Indian and English descent, the distinctive yellow appearance of the relish comes from the addition of turmeric and yellow mustard powder. I think piccalilli is a terrific condiment and can be served on the side of a plethora of different dishes. I have always loved it with cold corned-beef sandwiches. The recipe I'm sharing is adapted from a great chef-friend of mine, Brad Farmerie, who owns a bunch of super restaurants in the United States and Russia. A while ago, we were cooking together at an event in San Francisco, where he served piccalilli with a salmon dish. Like all of Brad's food, it was simply delicious.

Makes 2 x 1 litre (35 fl oz) jars

1 head cauliflower, broken into small florets
3 cups (465 g/1 lb) diced onion
1 cup (155 g/5½ oz) diced shallots
2 tablespoons salt
1 cucumber, peeled, deseeded and finely diced
600 ml (21 fl oz) white wine vinegar
300 ml (10½ fl oz) cider vinegar
¼ teaspoon cayenne pepper
1 teaspoon paprika
50 g (1¾ oz) yellow mustard powder
25 g (1 oz) ground turmeric
300 g (10½ oz) caster sugar
3 tablespoons cornflour
¼ cup (60 ml/2 fl oz) water

Place the cauliflower florets, onion and shallots into a large bowl. Mix through the salt. Cover and refrigerate overnight.

The next day, place the vegetables in a colander and rinse under cold water. Place in a bowl, then add the cucumber. Set aside.

Combine the vinegars, spices and sugar in a large saucepan. Place over medium heat and bring up to a simmer. Once the sugar is dissolved, mix the cornflour with the water to form a smooth paste, then whisk into the hot spiced liquid.

To finish, add the vegetables to the spice liquid, mix through, then remove from the heat. Divide between hot sterilised preserving jars and seal with lids.

Beetroot relish

This relish is another signature of mine. I came up with the recipe about 30 years ago, and I remember the dish clearly: it was lamb fillets with eggplant fritters, beetroot relish and a mint and basil aioli. The most versatile relish I make, this just seems to go with anything. If you try it, I bet you'll make it again and again. By the way, try to find large beetroot that are really dark in colour. They are easier to handle and make a beautiful, deep, rich-coloured relish.

Makes 2–3 cups (500–750 ml/17–26 fl oz)

1 kg (2 lb 3 oz) beetroot, peeled
400 g (14 oz) onions
2 tablespoons thyme leaves
pinch dried chilli flakes
1 cup (220 g/7¾ oz) sugar
¾ cup (185 ml/6 fl oz) balsamic vinegar
½ cup (125 ml/4 fl oz) orange juice
⅓ cup (80 ml/2½ fl oz) olive oil
flaky sea salt and freshly ground black pepper

You need to julienne the beetroot, so if you have a mandoline, well and good. If not, slice the beetroot into matchsticks as long and thin as possible. For the onions, again you want a julienne cut, so halve the onions and slice with the grain as thinly as possible.

Take a large heavy-bottomed saucepan and add the beetroot and onion. Top with thyme, chilli flakes, sugar, balsamic vinegar and orange juice. Place over medium-low heat and, stirring occasionally, cook for approximately 2 hours, until the beetroot is cooked and the liquid has reduced and become a little syrupy.

Remove from the heat, stir in the oil and season with salt and pepper to taste. Refrigerate or preserve in sterilised sealed jars.

Cherry relish

This cherry relish and my beetroot relish (page 428) are probably my two all-time favourites when it comes to condiments. They have been making appearances on my menus for more than 30 years. This cherry relish has real depth of flavour and partners up well with all red meats, but in particular duck and wild game (as in venison and boar). It also creates a terrific link between the dish and wonderful well-made varieties of red wine.

Makes about 1 kg (2 lb 4 oz)

1 kg (2 lb 4 oz) frozen or fresh pitted cherries
⅔ cup (140 g/5 oz) sugar
½ cup (125 ml/4 fl oz) sherry vinegar
½ teaspoon mixed spice
1 tablespoon finely chopped ginger
½ cup (80 g/2¾ oz) finely chopped shallots
flaky sea salt and freshly ground black pepper

Place all the ingredients except the salt and pepper in a suitable-sized saucepan and place over medium-low heat. Stirring occasionally, reduce over the course of an hour or more, until the relish reaches a jam-like consistency. Remember, it will thicken as it cools. Season with salt and pepper.

Store in sterilised preserving jars or just keep in the fridge.

Capsicum and chilli jam

No need to buy that sugary syrup with a bunch of red flakes suspended in it that is flogged off as 'sweet chilli sauce' any more. This is a doddle. Give it a nudge.

Makes 1 x 500 ml (17 fl oz) jar

4 red capsicums
2 hot red chillies
1 cup (155 g/5½ oz) finely diced shallots
½ cup (125 ml/4 fl oz) red wine vinegar
½ cup (95 g/3¼ oz) brown sugar
1 cup (230 g/8 oz) caster sugar
flaky sea salt and freshly ground black pepper

For best results, blister the skins of the capsicums and chillies directly over a gas flame on the stovetop or barbecue. Alternatively, lightly oil and roast in an oven preheated to 180°C for 15–20 minutes.

Place in a bowl and cover with clingfilm for 10 minutes, until the skins soften. Peel and discard the skins and the seeds of the capsicums, but include the seeds of the chillies. Dice the capsicums and chillies, and place in a saucepan with the shallots, vinegar and both sugars. Place over a medium-low heat and gently simmer for 30–40 minutes, until jam-like in consistency.

Season to taste, then divide between sterilised jars.

Mint jelly/sauce

Please don't shame me, as I sometimes use artificial green food colouring to give this jelly its delightful and super-fake vibrant green. I can assure you it is delicious. If you don't want to make a mint jelly, simply skip straining off the mint and leave out the gelatine leaves.

Makes 1 cup (250 ml/9 fl oz)

1 cup (250 ml/9 fl oz) cider vinegar
½ cup (110 g/3¾ oz) sugar
1½ cups (30 g/1 oz) mint leaves, finely chopped
2 gelatine leaves

Place the vinegar and sugar in a small saucepan over medium-low heat. Once the sugar is dissolved, remove from the heat and add two-thirds of the chopped mint. Let that steep for an hour or two, or preferably overnight. At this stage, you have mint sauce.

To make mint jelly, strain off the mint and heat the vinegar-sugar liquid in a saucepan on the stovetop until just warm through. Take off the heat. Place the gelatine leaves in a small bowl with cold water and leave to bloom for a couple of minutes. Once soft, add and stir through the warm vinegar until dissolved.

Place the warm liquid in a bowl set over an ice bath, then stir until it cools right down before adding the remaining one-third of the mint.

Pour into a jar and place in the fridge. For the next half hour or so, stir the jelly occasionally as it sets, so that the fresh mint is evenly distributed throughout the jelly. Store in the refrigerator until required.

Kimchi paste

There are plenty of kimchi recipes out there, with a bunch of variations. However, the base to all of them is a bright red Korean paste similar to the recipe that follows. You can make kimchi with all sorts of vegetables—our go-to is a mix of Chinese cabbage, thinly sliced lengths of carrot and batons of spring onion all mixed together. The ratio is up to you, but use more cabbage than anything else.

Makes 1½ cups (375 ml/13 fl oz)

½ cup gochugaru (Korean red chilli pepper flakes)
1 cup (110 g/3¾ oz) chopped shallots
½ cup (125 ml/4 fl oz) water
¼ cup garlic, roughly chopped
¼ cup ginger, roughly chopped
¼ cup (55 g/2 oz) sugar
⅓ cup (80 ml/2½ fl oz) fish sauce
2 tablespoons rice wine vinegar
2 tablespoons soy sauce
your choice of vegetables (see note above)

To make the kimchi paste, place all ingredients (except your chosen vegetables) into a food processor or blender. Blitz into a paste, then refrigerate until required.

Place your chosen mixture of vegetables in a bowl, mix together, then season quite aggressively with salt. Cover and leave on the bench for 24 hours to kick-start the fermentation.

Next, rinse off the salt with cold water, drain the vegetables, then add some kimchi paste to your taste—we use about 3 tablespoons for a 1 litre (35 fl oz) jar of vegetables. Seal in a sterilised jar, then leave in the fridge for at least a week, before beginning to consume.

The kimchi will easily last 12 months in the fridge. You can of course make a fresh, crunchy kimchi to eat immediately by just adding the paste to raw vegetables, then letting them sit for 10 minutes before tucking in, Daikon radish, Shanghai cabbage stems and regular cucumber all work really well this way!

Crab-apple jelly

We had a relatively prolific crab-apple tree at home on the farm and Mum made a decent-sized batch of jelly every season to get us through the rest of the year. I can't think of any roast sheep meat that I ate while growing up that didn't have homemade crab-apple jelly and fresh mint sauce (page 430) accompanying it, along with the pan gravy.

Makes 2 x 500 ml (17 fl oz) jars

2 kg (4 lb 8 oz) crab-apples
5 litres (175 fl oz) water
6 cloves
1 tablespoon fennel seeds
3 cups (660 g/1 lb 7 oz) sugar
1 teaspoon flaky salt

Wash the crab-apples and place in a large saucepan along with the water, cloves and fennel seeds. Place over medium-high heat and bring up to the boil. Reduce the heat and simmer for an hour or so, until the liquid has reduced by about two-thirds. Remove from the heat and let cool for 10 minutes.

Line a large sieve with clean muslin and place over a bowl. Tip the cooked crab apples and liquid into the muslin-lined sieve and allow to strain for an hour or more. Don't be tempted to squeeze the muslin, as this will make your jelly cloudy.

Return the crab-apple liquid (approximately 1 litre/35 fl oz) to a saucepan and add the sugar. Return to the heat and simmer for 20 minutes, skimming off and discarding any froth that surfaces to the top and allowing the liquid to slowly reduce. Once it turns a bright red colour, it's ready. Pour into sterilised pickling jars, let cool then seal.

Pickle juice jelly

This is a 'waste not, want not' situation. I got tired of pouring out the pickling liquid left from gherkin jars, so decided to make this simple jelly. I use it as a condiment for antipasto-style platters, in cold corned-beef sandwiches or just to top cheese and crackers. It keeps in the fridge pretty much indefinitely.

Makes 500 ml (17 fl oz)

2 cups (500 ml/17 fl oz) pickle juice
1 tablespoon sugar
5 gelatine leaves

Pour the pickle juice and sugar into a small saucepan and place over medium-low heat, until the sugar has dissolved.

Meanwhile, bloom the gelatine leaves in a bowl of cold water for 5 minutes.

When the sugar has dissolved, pour the hot sweetened pickle juice into a small bowl. Let the liquid cool down for 5 minutes before draining the gelatine leaves and stirring these in.

Pour into a container, then refrigerate. Use as you please.

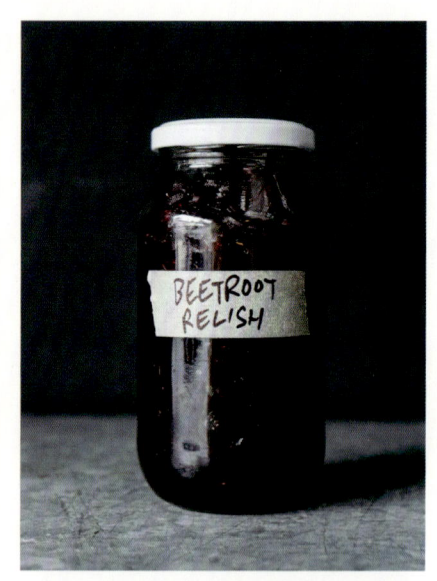

432 EAT UP NEW ZEALAND: THE BACH EDITION

PRESERVES 433

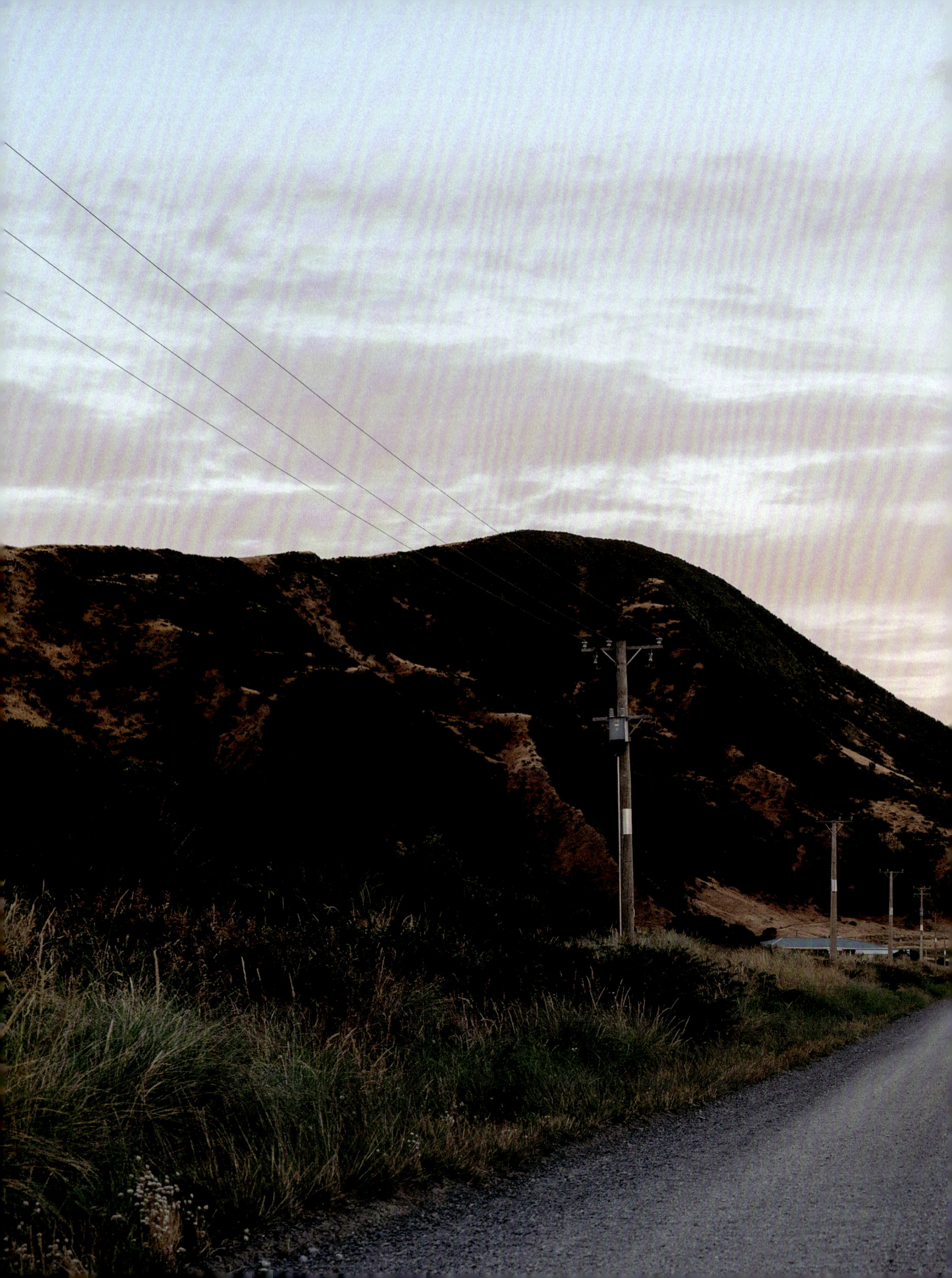

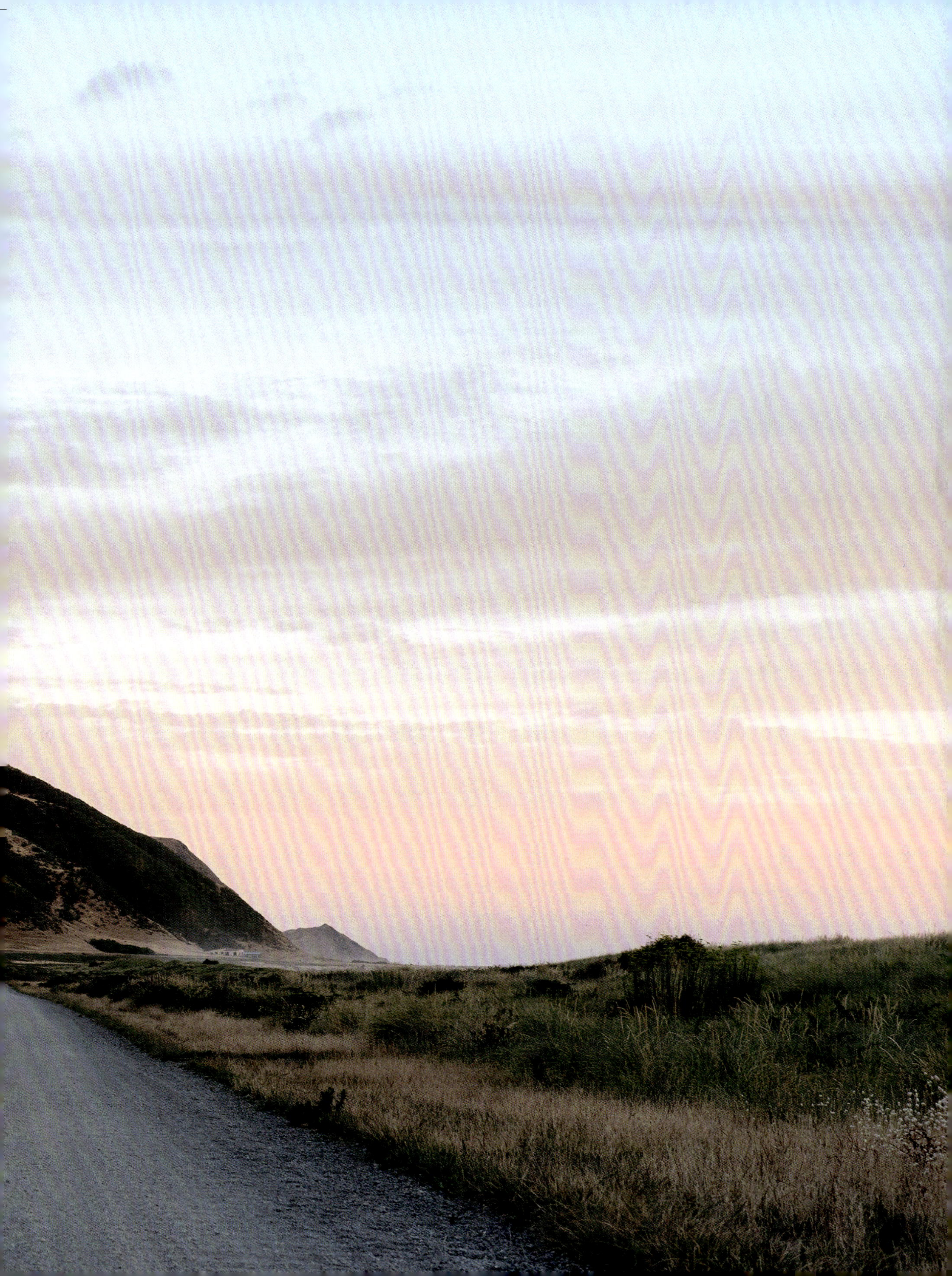

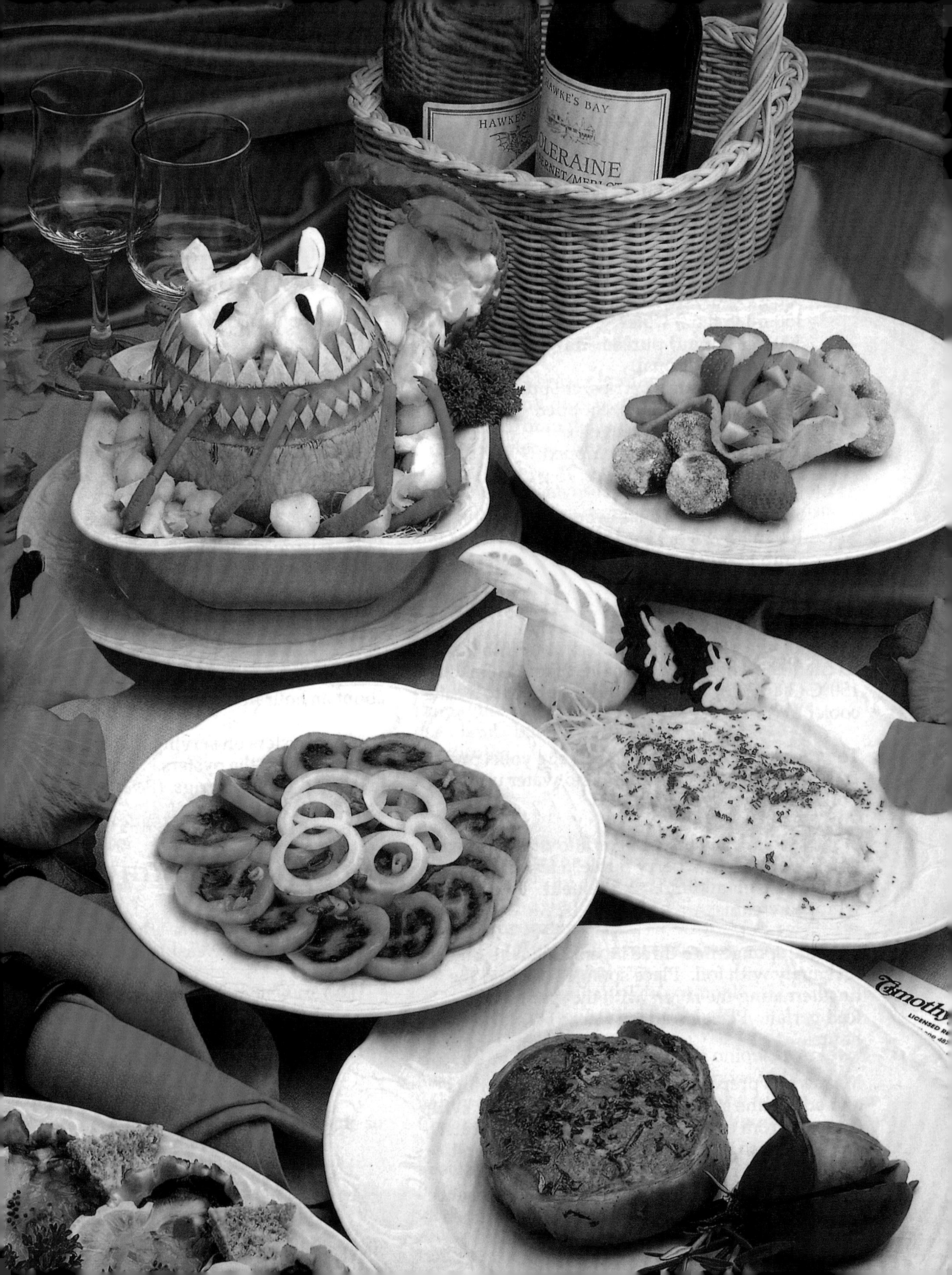
HAWKE'S BAY
HAWKE'S BAY

GO-TOS AND GARNISHES

HOKIHOKINGA ME NGĀ KĪNAKI

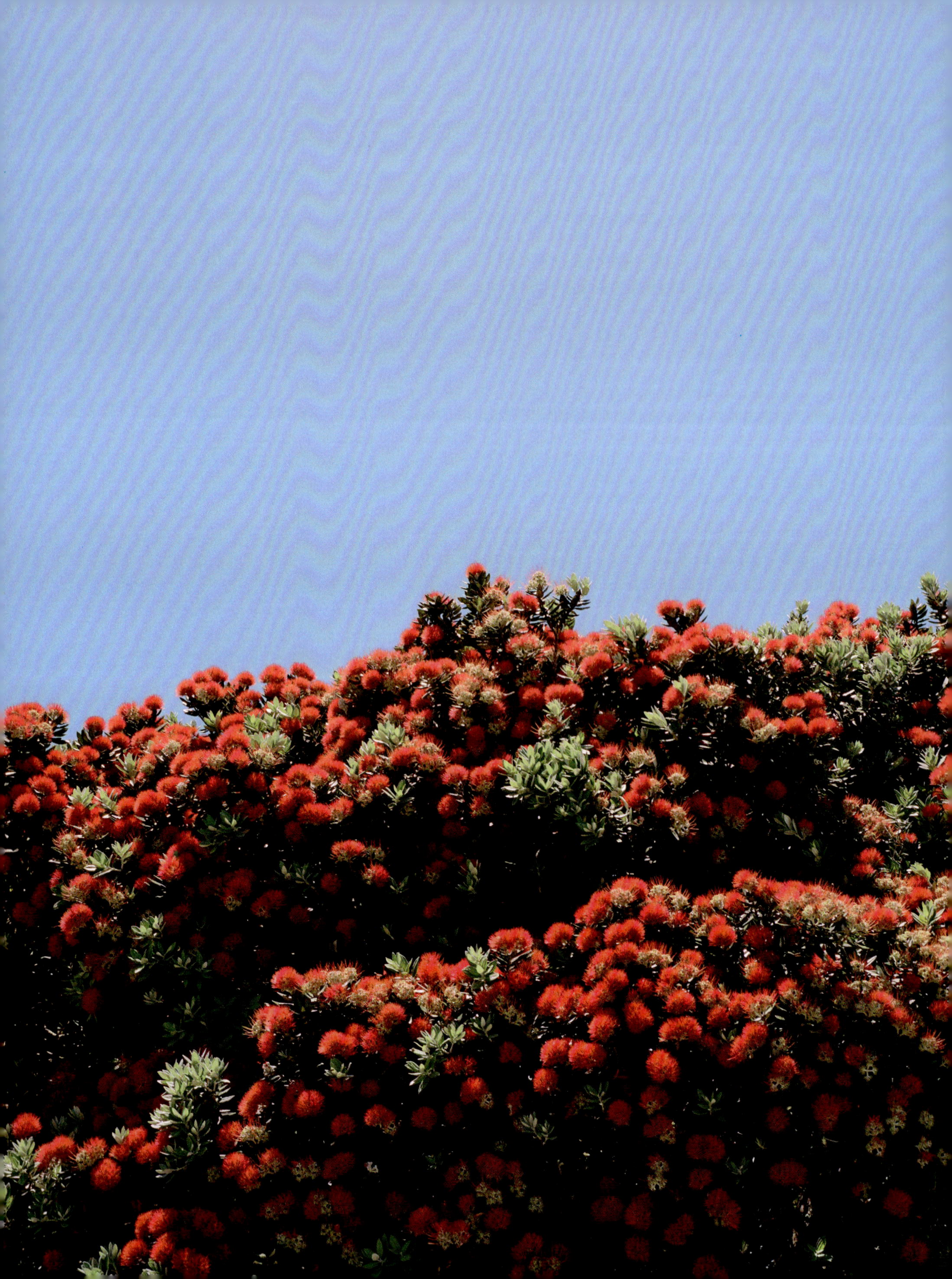

The Art of Garnish

Many people think that a garnish is simply about adding something to the dish that pleases the eye. I get that, but I am not, by any stretch of the imagination, a paid-up member of the edible-flower club. When did the lines become so blurred between kitchens and florists?

Plates of food that look like extraordinarily beautiful works of art: individual micro-herbs placed ever-so-precisely using stainless-steel tweezers, sitting precariously next to paper-thin wafers of colourful raw vegetables, with a few meagre dots of some purée or sauce strategically placed in the gaps, finally finished off with a scattering of petals and pretty flowers to complete the artwork. It really disappoints me that so many chefs these days are going down the 'visual gratification' road as opposed to what I think is the true highway of gastronomy, which may be uneven and rocky in parts but is paved with taste, texture and flavour.

And, while I'm at it, what's with that trend of 'negative space' plating, where only one half or sometimes even less of the plate is actually used? This style of presentation is completely lost on me; it just feels so contrived and miserable. I apologise if I'm offending anyone here, but it is truly how I feel when food like this is placed before me. Plates of food like this offer next to nothing with regard to taste, texture and generosity— surely that should be the main pleasure and point of the eating experience! As Julia Child once said, 'It's so beautifully arranged on the plate, you know someone's fingers have been all over it!'

So, I'm assuming that, given you've just read that rant, you'll now understand my disdain for phrases like 'you eat with your eyes' or 'it looks too good to eat'. Don't get me wrong: I do get a kick out of how plates of food look. But personally I prefer plating to be pared back and natural, without the unnecessary addition of unappetising accessories and pointless bling.

I do garnish food though, in my own way. I look at garnish as an actual ingredient or an important component of the dish, rather than simply something beautiful sitting there but not contributing anything to the eating of the dish. Sprigs of fresh rosemary make no sense resting on a sliced rack of lamb; it's impossible to get actual lemon juice from a sliver of lemon beside a piece of fish; and paprika or finely chopped parsley dusting the edge of a plate is comical at best. In my mind, a garnish must make a significant contribution to the dish that you are about to eat, be truly edible and make perfect sense on the plate.

The following texture and garnish recipes are my kind of 'go-to' collection, which I often draw on to complete a dish. The texture itself is super important, but the individual flavour that most of these crunchy morsels offer up also has a very significant role to play. It is often the case that it's the garnish that gets stealthily picked off and devoured! It is like a barometer of what truly lies below: if it's seasoned, perfectly crisp and offers up a special first mouthful then you know good things are likely to follow.

Play around with the following garnishes. Think about the part they play in adding to and rounding out the dish. Are they salty? Is there a citrus note? Do they bring a hit of heat to the dish?

There are no rules—sometimes I combine a bunch of these garnishes to great effect. Now, go 'eat with your mouth'!

Eve's mum's pastry

If you make this pastry just once I guarantee it will become your go-to pastry recipe from here on in. It works equally well for sweet or savoury fillings, and has the attributes of both short and flaky pastry. This recipe is special to me as it originally hails from Ireland. Eve Reilly is the gorgeous manager of Poronui Lodge, which sits nearly dead centre in the North Island. I have had a wonderful relationship with Poronui for a long, long time. It's a hunting and fishing utopia, where I have cooked many times over the years. I always stay on for an extra night, and it's become a bit of a tradition that we throw together a leftovers mish-mash dinner for the Poronui crew after the guests have left. The only constant to all these dinners past has been fresh apple pie to finish, made, of course, with Eve's mum's pastry. Thanks, Eve.

Makes 600 g (21 oz)

2¼ cups (340 g/11¾ oz) plain flour
225 g (8 oz) cold butter, cut into 1 cm (½ in) dice
pinch sea salt
½ cup (125 ml/4 fl oz) cold water
1 egg yolk

Sift the flour into a large mixing bowl and add the butter, along with the salt. With clean and cold hands, rub the butter into the flour until it resembles chunky breadcrumbs. Do not overwork; there should be plenty of visible chunks of butter.

Place the cold water and egg yolk in a small bowl. Whisk to combine.

Add the liquid ingredients to the dry ingredients, and mix to form a dough. Again, it is paramount that you don't overwork the pastry. It's done when it just comes together.

Wrap in clingfilm and refrigerate for at least 30 minutes before rolling out.

Flour tortillas

You can't beat a freshly made flour tortilla—so much lighter than the store-bought variety. I cut these into perfect circles in the restaurant, but at home you don't need to bother with all of that. Extremely versatile, they can be filled with an infinite number of ingredients for any occasion.

Makes 12 x 18 cm (7 in) or 24 x 9 cm (3½ in) tortillas

1 cup (250 ml/9 fl oz) milk
¼ cup (60 ml/2 fl oz) vegetable oil
3 cups (450 g/1 lb) plain flour, plus extra for dusting
2 teaspoons baking powder
1½ teaspoons table salt

Pour the milk and oil into a saucepan and warm slightly over low heat.

Combine the dry ingredients in a mixing bowl. Pour in the warmed milk mix and bring together with your hands to form a dough. Knead for 2–3 minutes, then cover with clingfilm and rest for 15 minutes. Divide the dough into 12 or 24 balls.

On a lightly floured bench, using a rolling pin, roll out the tortillas as thin as possible. Layer between greaseproof paper with a dusting of flour. Refrigerate until ready to cook.

Cook the tortillas on a hot grill, or in a dry frying pan for 1 minute on each side, until puffed and warm through. Layer between greaseproof paper, cover and refrigerate until required.

Roast chicken gravy

Definitely a bit of effort, but like all good sauces it's the slow cooking and reduction time that delivers something wonderful and delicious. Freezes perfectly well.

Makes 2 cups (500 ml/12 fl oz)

4 chicken frames, roughly chopped
2 onions, roughly chopped
2 carrots, roughly chopped
2 celery sticks, roughly chopped
6 garlic cloves, roughly chopped
2 bay leaves
2 thyme sprigs
2 tablespoons canola oil or similar cooking oil
4 cups (1 litre/35 fl oz) chicken stock
5 tablespoons butter
5 tablespoons plain flour
flaky sea salt and freshly ground black pepper

Preheat your oven to 200°C (400°F).
    Toss the chopped-up chicken frames, vegetables and herbs in oil in a roasting tin and place in the oven for approximately 1½ hours, until golden brown.
    Remove from the oven and, with a metal spatula, transfer all the chicken frames and vegetables to a large saucepan. Pour off any excess rendered chicken fat, then place the roasting tin on medium heat. Deglaze the pan with the chicken stock, scraping up all the caramelised particles off the bottom. Pour this all into a large saucepan and simmer over low heat for 2 hours, until you have about 2 cups (500 ml/17 fl oz) stock remaining. Strain off the reduced stock and discard the bones and roasted vege.
    In a clean saucepan over medium heat, melt the butter with the flour to form a roux. Cook out for 2–3 minutes, until light brown. Slowly whisk in the hot stock to incorporate, a bit at a time. Simmer for 10 minutes or so to cook out the flour, and season to taste with salt and fresh black pepper.

Turmeric oil

Also known in my kitchen as 'high-vis nuclear oil', due to its luminous, bright yellow quality, this turmeric oil has a wonderful depth of character from the fresh ginger and the ground spices that the canola oil is steeped in. It's a wonderful oil to use with all curries, or splashed over thick natural yoghurt as an accompaniment.

Makes 2 cups (500 ml/17 fl oz)

2 cups (500 ml/17 fl oz) canola oil
½ onion, finely diced
2 bay leaves
3 white peppercorns
1 garlic clove, split
knob ginger, grated
3 tablespoons ground turmeric
1 teaspoon curry powder
1 teaspoon cumin seeds, toasted and ground

In a suitable-sized saucepan, heat ⅓ cup (80 ml/2½ fl oz) of oil and sweat the onion, bay leaves, peppercorns and garlic over a low heat, without letting them colour. Add the grated ginger and continue to sweat until the onion is soft. Add the turmeric, curry powder and cumin, and cook out for a couple of minutes.
    Add the rest of the oil and stir through. Pour into a jar, seal with a lid and leave to infuse, giving it a shake every so often over a day or two, then strain off and put into a squeezy bottle. Use as required.

Dukkah

There are hundreds of dukkah recipes out there, and I don't believe there are any that I have tried and haven't liked. It's all about texture and spice, which are two things that will always lift the eating enjoyment of a dish.

1 cup (155 g/5½ oz) blanched almonds
½ cup (70 g/2½ oz) pumpkin seeds
¼ cup (30 g/1 oz) sunflower seeds
¼ cup (40 g/1½ oz) sesame seeds
2 teaspoons ground sumac
1 teaspoon dried oregano
½ teaspoon ground turmeric
½ teaspoon flaky sea salt

Preheat your oven to 160°C (315°F).

Place the almonds, pumpkin, sunflower and sesame seeds in a small roasting dish, and toast in the oven for 10–15 minutes until fragrant and golden brown. Remove from the oven and cool completely.

Now place all the ingredients into a food processor, and blitz into a coarse meal. Store in an airtight container until required.

Tobacco onions

Most people love crunchy fried onion. Tobacco onions are just a variation on that theme. I learned to make these years ago when I was working in a restaurant in New Orleans. They are a terrific side dish for a steak or hamburger, and add a wonderful texture to practically anything that needs a little crunch.

cooking oil, for deep-frying
1 cup (150 g/5½ oz) self-raising flour
1 teaspoon sweet smoked paprika
1 teaspoon table salt
1 teaspoon fine black pepper
2 large onions

Take a largish heavy-bottomed saucepan and place over medium-high heat. Add enough oil so that it comes a quarter of the way up the side of the pan. (Alternatively, use a deep-fryer.) Heat the oil to approximately 180°C (350°F). You can gauge this by adding a piece of bread to the oil; if it's at around 180°C, it will take about a minute for the bread to turn golden and crisp.

To a large mixing bowl, add the flour, paprika, salt and pepper. Whisk to combine.

Now, using a mandoline if you have one, thinly slice the onions and add to the bowl with the flour and paprika. Toss to get plenty of coverage, then dust off any excess.

Deep-fry the onion in batches for 3–4 minutes, until golden. Remove and drain on kitchen paper while you repeat with the rest of the onions. Use then and there.

Fried curry leaves

Fried curry leaves are a doddle to make and I think they are a terrific, unique garnish for any curry situation. Curry leaves can be purchased from most Asian supermarkets year round. They come in relatively large bunches, so just use what you need. The good news is they freeze really well, so you can have some always at hand.

curry leaves
canola oil or similar cooking oil, for shallow-frying

Pick the curry leaves from the stalks. Pour enough oil into a suitable-sized saucepan to shallow-fry. Place over medium-high heat. Once it gets to 170–180°C (325–350°F), or when a cube of bread dropped into the hot oil turns brown in 15–20 seconds, add the curry leaves. As soon as the leaves start turning a dark translucent colour (10–15 seconds), remove immediately with a slotted spoon or sieve and empty onto kitchen paper. Cool completely then store in an airtight container until required.

Shallot crunchies

We use these on practically everything: curries, Thai salads, carpaccio, etc. You can actually buy these pre-made at most Asian supermarkets, but they are quite inferior to homemade. Once cooked, these shallot crunchies will keep really well in an airtight container or even frozen in small containers.

24 shallots
canola oil or similar cooking oil, for shallow-frying

Peel the shallots, discard the skins, then slice as thinly as possible. Place in a container or bowl and cover with cold water. Refrigerate overnight.

In the morning, drain off all the water and place the sliced shallots in a suitable-sized saucepan. Cover with the oil then place over medium-high heat. Bring up to the boil, then lower to a simmer and fry the shallots until golden. Set the timer and keep an eye on them after 15 minutes or so. They will go from uncooked to burnt quite quickly. You want to remove with a slotted spoon and strain off the hot oil as soon as they become a deep golden colour. Drain on kitchen paper and let cool. Store in an airtight container until required.

Fried red chillies

I love these as a garnish, still bright red in parts, but golden brown around the edges. If they are hot chillies, they will still bring plenty of heat to the party!

red chillies
canola oil or similar cooking oil, for deep-frying

With a sharp knife, slice the chillies into rounds as thin as possible. Heat up a moderate amount of oil in a suitable-sized saucepan. Add the chillies, stir and cook until golden and brown around the edges.

Remove with a slotted spoon or sieve, then drain on kitchen paper. Use the same day.

Kūmara shoestring crisps

You will need a mandoline to make these delicious crisps. I use a Benriner Japanese-style mandoline; they're inexpensive and can be purchased from most decent kitchenware shops. A mandoline is super handy, and you'll find you use it all the time . . . just mind your fingers and use the safety guard.

2 large golden or purple kūmara, peeled
canola oil or similar cooking oil, for deep-frying

Using the smallest comb blade, forcefully slide the peeled kūmara down the blade, creating super-thin shoestring fries.

Heat the oil in a suitable-sized saucepan or your deep-fryer to 180°C (350°F). To get a gauge on the temperature of the oil, drop a cube of bread into it when you think it's near 180°C. It should turn golden in around 60 seconds.

Carefully drop a handful of the kūmara fries into the oil and fry for around a minute until golden. Halfway through the process, turn the kūmara fries over to cook on the other side.

Lift out the golden fries with a slotted spoon or sieve and drain on kitchen paper. Repeat in batches until finished. Once cool, store in an airtight container until required.

Lemon and herb croutons

One of my go-to texture garnishes. It's really just a simple crouton, but the addition of fresh herbs and lemon zest and juice definitely takes it up a notch. Toss through salads, top chowders or munch up fine to use as lemony crumb on fish dishes.

½ baguette, crust removed
1 tablespoon finely chopped thyme
2 tablespoons finely chopped parsley
finely grated zest of 1 lemon
¼ cup (60 ml/2 fl oz) lemon juice
2 tablespoons melted butter
1 tablespoon olive oil

Preheat your oven to 180°C (350°F).

Cut the crustless baguette into 1 cm (½ in) squares and place in a suitable-sized bowl. Toss in the thyme and parsley. Add the lemon zest and pour over the juice. Pour over the melted butter and olive oil. With clean hands, gently mix all the ingredients so they are absorbed evenly throughout the uncooked croutons.

Spread out on a small oven tray and bake for 8–12 minutes, until crisp and golden.

Cool, then store in an airtight container until required. They freeze well, too.

Chicken skin crackling

Like a typical pork crackling, crisp chicken skin brings richness, texture and touch of naughty to whatever offering it ends up on.

skin of 1 whole chicken
1–2 teaspoons flaky sea salt

Preheat your oven to 170°C (325°F). Line an oven tray with baking paper.

Spread out the chicken skin on a chopping board, and scrape the fat from the back of the skin using the edge of a sharp knife.

Lay out your chicken skin flat on the prepared tray. Sprinkle with salt, place a sheet of baking paper over the chicken skin, then weigh down with another oven tray on top.

Bake in the oven for 30–40 minutes, until the skin has puffed and crackled. Store in an airtight container until required.

Snapper skin crackling

Most of the time, I cook fish with the skin on. Between the fillet and the skin is a micro-layer of fat that helps baste and keep the fish moist through the cooking process, and the skin also adds another texture contrast to the dish. Snapper skin crackling is really pretty simple to make and can be eaten just as a snack, or served alongside something like a ceviche for an added point of interest.

scaled snapper skin
flaky sea salt and freshly ground black pepper

Preheat your oven to 180°C (350°F).

Take the snapper skin and place, skin side down, on a clean chopping board. With a spoon or the back edge of a knife, scrape away any fat and sinew. Cut the skin into manageable-sized pieces. Note that the skin will shrink to about half its size once cooked.

Line an oven tray or similar with baking paper. Lay out the skin on the paper. Season with salt and pepper. Top with another piece of baking paper, then weigh down with another tray or similar.

Bake in the oven for 10–15 minutes, until the skin begins to turn golden. Remove and cool. Note that the snapper skin will get more brittle and crunchy as it cools. Store in an airtight container until required.

Paprika roasted almonds

These guys are simply delicious as a snack all by themselves. They add a touch of sweet smoke to any manner of dish, or add character and taste to a roasted-nut mix.

2 cups (310 g/11 oz) blanched whole almonds
1 tablespoon olive oil
1 teaspoon sweet smoked paprika
½ teaspoon garlic powder
flaky sea salt and freshly ground black pepper

Preheat your oven to 180°C (350°F).

Place the almonds, oil, paprika and garlic powder in a medium-sized bowl. Toss until combined then liberally season with salt and pepper.

Place in a roasting tray and bake for 15–20 minutes, until toasted. Remove, cool and store in an airtight container until required.

Candied walnuts

These are super simple to make, and roughly chopped and scattered over any salad or coleslaw will add a couple of layers of sweetness and nuttiness.

1 tablespoon flaky sea salt
3 tablespoons sugar
1½ tablespoons boiling water
2 cups (200 g/7 oz) whole walnuts

Preheat your oven to 180°C (350°F). Line a baking tray with baking paper.

Place the salt, sugar and boiling water into a bowl and mix together. Add in the walnuts and toss until evenly coated in the sugar mix.

Transfer the walnuts onto the prepared tray and bake in the oven for 20 minutes, until golden brown, only stirring occasionally. Remove from the oven and cool, then store in an airtight container until required.

Candied hazelnuts

I'm a big fan of any sort of nut that gets the sugar, salt and often spice treatment. I've always looked upon hazelnuts as quite a 'posh' nut, and when you read them on a menu, it often sells the dish.

2 cups (280 g/10 oz) whole hazelnuts (skin on)
1 tablespoon flaky sea salt
3 tablespoons sugar
½ teaspoon ground cinnamon
½ teaspoon ground ginger
½ teaspoon cayenne pepper
1½ tablespoons boiling water

Preheat your oven to 200°C (400°F). Spread the hazelnuts on an oven tray and place in the oven. Roast for about 5 minutes. Remove and place in a clean tea towel or similar. While in the towel, move the hazelnuts between your hands for a couple of minute to remove the skins. Once clean, discard the skins and keep the hazelnuts handy.

In a small bowl, mix the salt, sugar and spices, then add the boiling water. Mix again until incorporated. Pour this over the skinless hazelnuts and toss until covered.

Place the spice-and-sugar-covered hazelnuts on an oven tray lined with baking paper, and roast for approximately 10 minutes, stirring occasionally. Remove from the oven when caramelised and glossy. Let cool, then store in a airtight container until required.

Chocolate curls

These are a great little garnish and texture on anything chocolate. I always garnish the Black Doris plum trifle on page 318 with chocolate curls.

1 cup (250 ml/9 fl oz) water
1–2 cups dark or white chocolate (buttons or chunks)

Pour the water into a saucepan and place over medium heat until simmering. Now add the chocolate pieces to a metal mixing bowl and set on top of the pan, making sure the bowl doesn't touch the water. Stir the chocolate until just melted, smooth and shiny.

Pour the melted chocolate onto a baking sheet, spread out slightly, then place in the refrigerator for about 10 minutes to set.

Remove the chocolate tray from the refrigerator and let the chocolate warm up slightly. Drag a sharp knife, turned to a 45° angle, across the chocolate towards yourself, creating your chocolate curls.

Store the curls in an airtight container and refrigerate until required.

Almond praline

Pretty simple to make, almond praline brings a wonderful texture to nearly any dessert. Even just sprinkled on ice cream, it takes the eating pleasure to a new level.

⅔ cup (100 g/3½ oz) whole blanched almonds
1 cup (220 g/7¾ oz) sugar
2 tablespoons water

Preheat your oven to 180°C (350°F).

Place the almonds on a baking tray and bake in the oven for 12–15 minutes, until golden. Remove and cool.

Add the sugar and water to a small saucepan. Place over low heat to dissolve the sugar, then turn up the heat and cook the sugar out to a golden caramel—this will take 5–7 minutes. Pour immediately over the toasted almonds and let cool. When hard, break up the brittle and blitz in a food processor until it resembles slightly chunky crumbs. Store in an airtight container.

Across from top left: Eve's mum's pastry (page 442), flour tortillas (page 442), roast chicken gravy (page 443), turmeric oil (page 443), dukkah (page 444), tobacco onions (page 444), fried curry leaves (page 445), shallot crunchies (page 445), and fried red chillies (page 445).

Across from top left: kūmara shoestring crisps (page 445), lemon and herb croutons (page 446), chicken skin crackling (page 446), snapper skin crackling (page 446), paprika roasted almonds (page 446), candied walnuts (page 447), candied hazelnuts (page 447), chocolate curls (page 447), and almond praline (page 447).

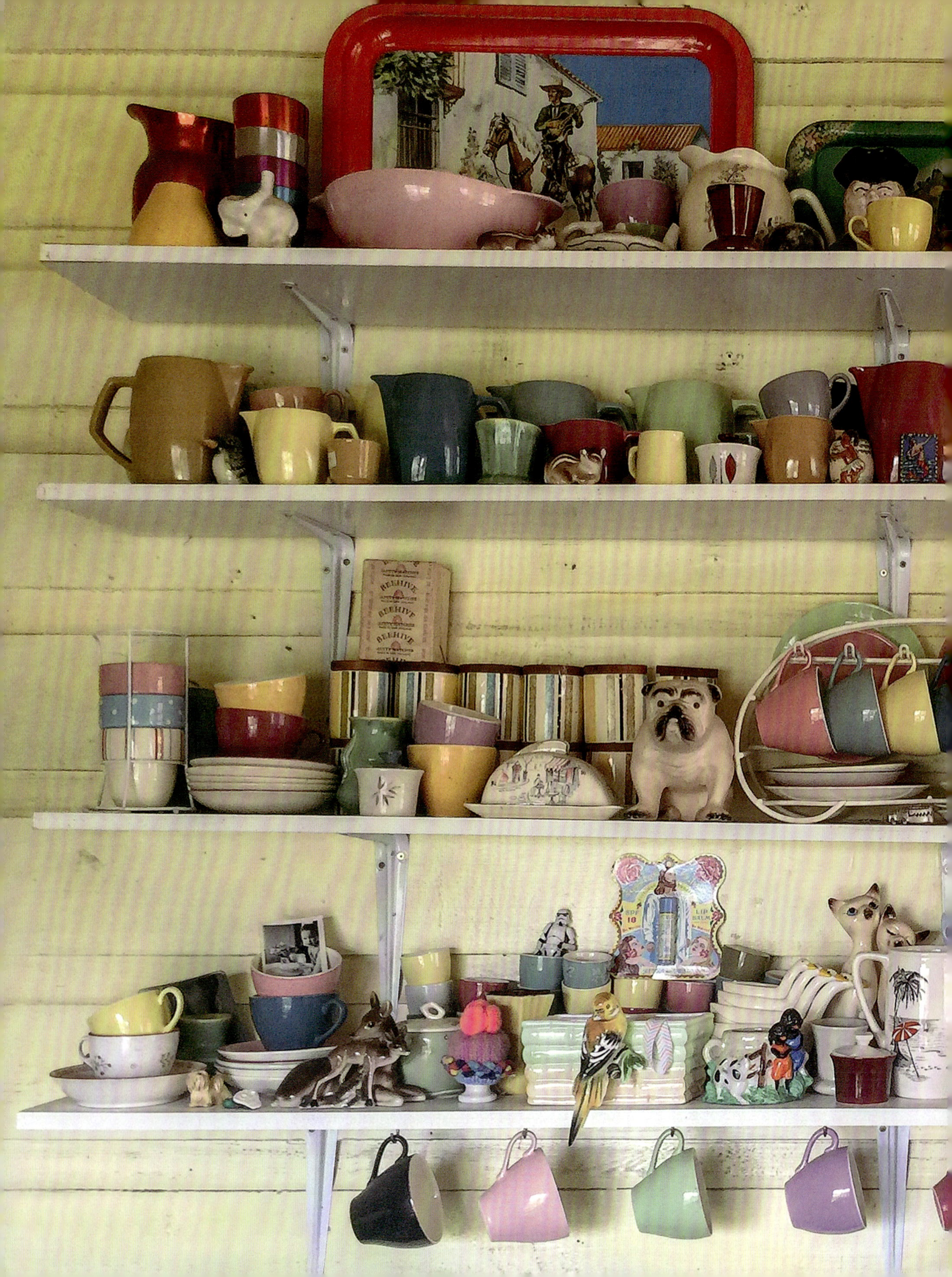
BEEHIVE
BEEHIVE
BEEHIVE
SPF
18
LIP
BALM

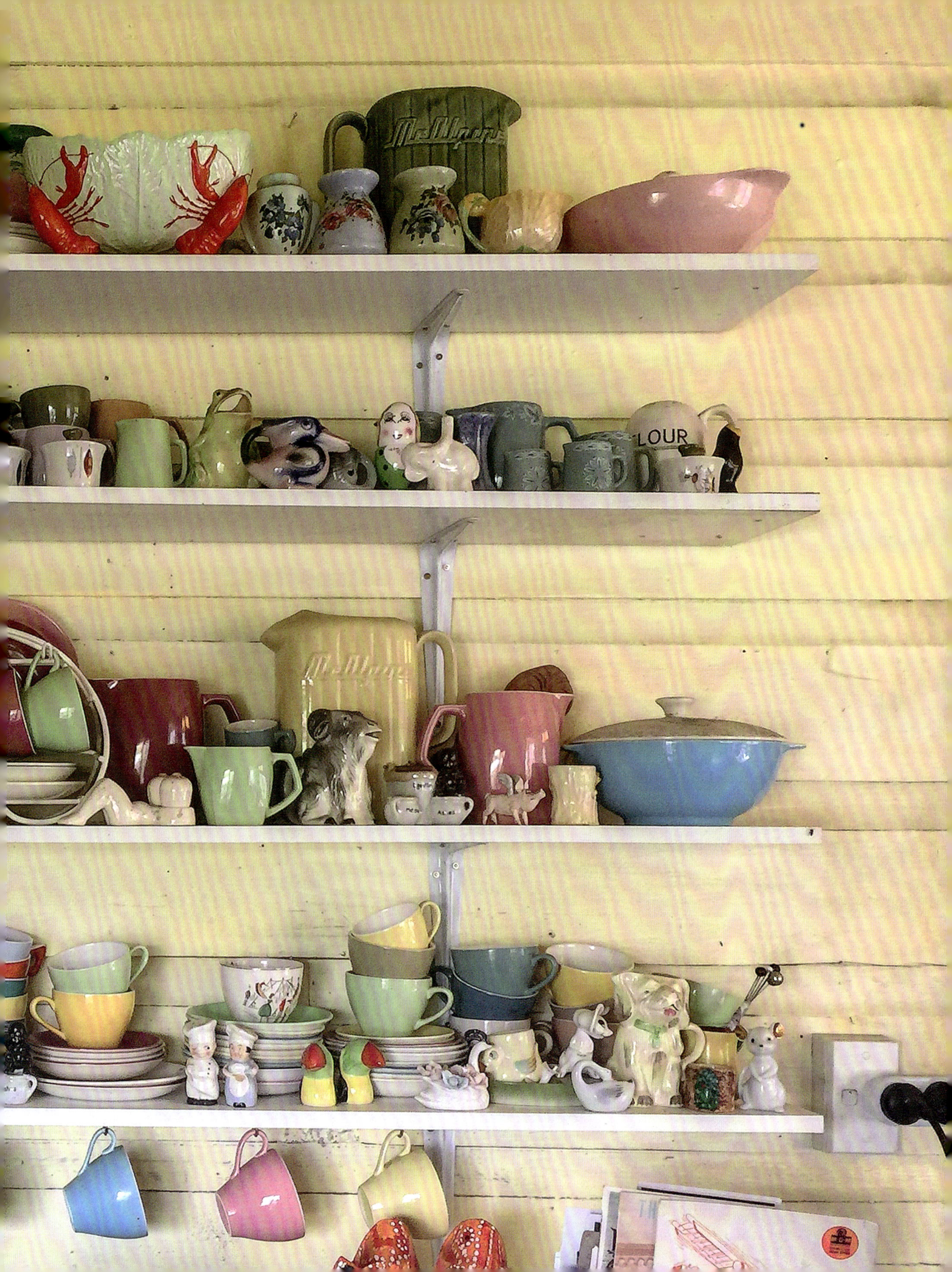

LOUR

Index / Kuputohu

A

almonds
    almond cream 270
    almond praline 447
    cinnamon almond crunch 398
    paprika roasted almonds 446
Anzac chocolate ganache biscuits 380
apple, caramelised 257
apple and caraway salsa 193
apple sauce 273
apple syrup 49
apple slaw, bitter green 303
apricot scones, date and dried 360
apricots, poached, with saffron and cinnamon 417
arrabbiata sauce 118
artichokes, globe, crisp Parmesan-crumbed 278
Aunty Edna's bran muffins 377

B

baba ganoush 67
baking
    Anzac chocolate ganache biscuits 380
    biscuits, Anzac chocolate ganache 380
    biscuits, choco block 393
    bran muffins, Aunty Edna's 377
    brandy snaps, macadamia nut 353
    cake, sultana 394
    choco block biscuits 393
    chocolate eclairs 350
    crumpets with date and orange butter, treacle and cinnamon almond crunch 398
    eclairs, chocolate 350
    lamingtons, passion-fruit 347
    lemon shortbread 378
    muffins, bran, Aunty Edna's 377
    passion-fruit lamingtons 347
    scones, cheese, with Parmesan and blue cheese butter 374
    scones, cranberry and orange 372
    scones, date and dried apricot, with jam and cream 360
    shortbread, lemon 378
    spiced chocolate Swiss roll with quince jam 357
    sponge, Haydo's 349
    sponge drops 342
    sultana cake 394
    Swiss roll, spiced chocolate, with quince jam 357
basil pesto 277
batter, tempura 59, 78
beef
    beef carpaccio, rustic, with tarragon mayo, Parmesan and rocket 197
    beef cheeks with truffled swede 224
    beef short ribs with pumpkin, maple and paprika purée 219
    corned beef with pea and spinach croquettes and mustard sauce 240
    meatballs with spiced tomato lentils 210
    oxtail, pulled, with soft Parmesan polenta 245
    steak and kidney pie 238
    veal schnitzel with creamed celeriac and bitter green apple slaw 237
beetroot and pesto on spiced yoghurt lentils 277
beetroot relish 428
bhaji, fried chicken, with fresh coriander labneh 178
biscuits
    Anzac chocolate ganache biscuits 380
    choco block biscuits 393
black beans, refried 174
Black Doris plum, rhubarb and white chocolate trifle 318
Black Doris plum jelly 318
blue cheese butter, Parmesan and 374
blue cheese salad, fig, raspberry and 281
blue mackerel, grilled, sticky rice and kimchi 129
blueberry and citrus Eton mess 337
bran muffins, Aunty Edna's 377
brandy snaps, macadamia nut 353
brawn, pork, with apple and caraway salsa 193
bread, fried 146
bread and butter pickles 420
breadcrumbs, fried chilli and orange 219
bruschetta, squid ink 116
Brussels sprouts, caramelised 252
buttermilk pancakes 206
butters
    Café de Paris butter 89
    date and orange butter 398
    Parmesan and blue cheese butter 374
    seaweed butter 133
    smoked chipotle butter 206
butties, tempura scallop, with preserved lemon mayo 59

C

cabbage, cream of caraway 257
Café de Paris butter 89
cake, sultana 394
candied hazelnuts 447
candied walnuts 447
caper burnt butter, raisin and 201
capsicum, roasted, and mint 67
capsicum and chilli jam 429
capsicums, roasted tomatoes and 296
caraway salsa, apple and 193
carpaccio, rustic beef, with tarragon mayo, Parmesan and rocket 197
carrot, burnt, feta and date relish 229
carrot hash, parsnip 246
carrot mango chutney 78
carrots, chargrilled, with spiced eggplant and yoghurt 292
cauliflower, creamed 289
cauliflower, tempura, with smoked kahawai cream 90
celeriac, creamed 237
celeriac, crumbed, with witloof, walnuts, blue cheese and apple sauce 273
celeriac purée 223
ceviche, kahawai, with spiced creamed corn 43
cheese
    blue cheese salad, fig, raspberry and 281
    cheese scones with Parmesan and blue cheese butter 374
    mornay sauce 94
    Parmesan-crumbed globe artichokes, crisp 278
    Parmesan polenta 245
    Swiss cheese toasties with truffle salt, fresh porcini and 282
cherry relish 429
chicken
    chicken and chorizo pies 165
    chicken bhaji, fried, with fresh coriander labneh 178
    chicken curry, Puspa's 169
    chicken karaage tacos with fresh daikon kimchi and Kewpie 157
    chicken liver parfait with pear liqueur jelly and fried bread 146
    chicken salad sandwich, 'The Fed' 180
    chicken schnitzel sandwiches, salt and vinegar chip 163
    chicken skin crackling 446
    chicken tacos, charcoal roadside

Mexican, with black beans and tomatillo salsa 174
roast chicken gravy 443
chilli, fried, and orange breadcrumbs 219
chilli cucumber, smashed soy and 269
chilli jam, capsicum and 429
chillies, fried red 445
chimichurri, mint 246
chip, salt and vinegar, chicken schnitzel sandwiches 163
chipotle butter, smoked 206
chocolate
    Anzac chocolate ganache biscuits 380
    choco block biscuits 393
    chocolate curls 447
    chocolate eclairs 350
    chocolate ganache 380
    chocolate icing 350
    chocolate sauce 338
    chocolate self-saucing pudding with espresso custard 316
    spiced chocolate Swiss roll with quince jam 357
    white chocolate custard 318
    white chocolate trifle, Black Doris plum, rhubarb and 318
chops, spiced lamb shoulder, with labneh, honey and dukkah 226
chorizo pies, chicken and 165
Christmas pies, fig and cranberry 401
chutney, carrot mango 78
chutney, Granny Brown's peach 426; *see also* preserves
cinnamon almond crunch 398
cinnamon oysters 345
clam linguine, crayfish and 130
cobbler, tamarillo and pear macadamia nut 325
coconut custard 332
coconut meringues 322
coconut rice pudding with passion fruit, mango and meringue 322
condensed milk mayonnaise 426
cookies *see* biscuits
coriander labneh, fresh 178
corn, spiced creamed 43
corned beef with pea and spinach croquettes and mustard sauce 240
cos lettuce with Depot ranch dressing, hot sauce and sweet spiced sunflower seeds 304
crab, paddle, fish fingers 63
crab-apple jelly 431

crackling, chicken skin 446
crackling, snapper skin 446
cranberry and orange scones 372
cranberry Christmas pies, fig and 401
crayfish
    craydog with wasabi mayo and ginger lime syrup 77
    crayfish and clam linguine 130
    crayfish rolls with thousand island sauce and pickled cucumber 83
cream of caraway cabbage 257
cream of horseradish with fresh dill 49
crêpes with mulled wine poached pears and chocolate sauce 338
crisps, kūmara shoestring 445
crispy-skin snapper with oyster stew 139
croquettes, pea and spinach 240
croutons, lemon and herb 446
croutons, mandarin 41
crumble, peach and pineapple, with coconut custard 332
crumpets with date and orange butter, treacle and cinnamon almond crunch 398
cucumber, smashed soy and chilli 269
cumin sour cream 165
curd, lemon 337
curls, chocolate 447
curried eggs 144
curry, Puspa's chicken 169
curry leaves, fried 445
custard, coconut 332
custard, espresso 316
custard, runny 328
custard, white chocolate 318

D
daikon kimchi 157
dal 300
date and dried apricot scones with jam and cream 360
date relish, burnt carrot, feta and 229
date pudding, quince sticky 328
Depot ranch dressing 304
desserts *see* pudding
dressings *see also* mayos; preserves
    almond cream 270
    cumin sour cream 165
    Depot ranch dressing 304
    horseradish, cream of, with fresh dill 49
    hummus 198
    lemon mayo, preserved 59
    macadamia romesco 151

    ranch dressing, Depot 304
    red wine vinaigrette 281
    romesco, macadamia 151
    rouille 124
    sour cream, cumin 165
    spiced yoghurt 214
    tartare sauce 112
    thousand island sauce 83
    vinaigrette, pickle 262
    vinaigrette, red wine 281
    yoghurt, spiced 214
duck breast and fig salad on macadamia romesco 151
duck shepherd's pie 154
dukkah 444

E
eclairs, chocolate 350
eel, mock 285
egg, gherkin and caper mayo 71
eggplant, roasted 229
eggplant, roasted, with creamed cauliflower and salsa verde 289
eggplant, spiced 292
eggplant kasundi 422
eggs, curried 144
empanadas, lamb shank, with spiced yoghurt 214
espresso custard 316
Eton mess, blueberry and citrus 337
Eve's mum's pastry 442

F
falafel with tomato kasundi, labneh and feta 286
'Fed' chicken salad sandwich, 'The' 180
feijoa and ginger parfait 326
feijoa friands 396
fennel, roasted, and lemon 136
fennel, roasted, and red onion salad with white anchovies 306
feta, green olive and orange 198
feta and date relish, burnt carrot 229
fig, raspberry and blue cheese salad 281
fig and cranberry Christmas pies 401
fig salad on macadamia romesco, duck breast and 151
fish *see also* seafood
    blue mackerel, grilled, sticky rice and kimchi 129
    fish fingers, paddle crab 63
    flounder, pan-fried, with seaweed butter 133

hāpuka, poached, with battered pumpkin, pickled red onion rings and Kalamata olive mayo 108
hāpuka steaks with roasted fennel and lemon 136
kahawai, battered, 'Mumbai tacos' with curry lime mayo and carrot mango chutney 78
kahawai ceviche with spiced creamed corn 43
kahawai cream, smoked, tempura cauliflower with 90
kahawai mishmash, smoked 107
kingfish sashimi with mandarin and dill 41
mackerel, grilled blue, sticky rice and kimchi 129
mullet, raw, with cream of horseradish, apple and dill 49
salmon crudo with apple and fennel 38
sashimi, kingfish, with mandarin and dill 41
sashimi, trevally, with ponzu and truffle oil 37
sashimi, trevally, with soy syrup, wasabi peas and Kewpie mayo 46
smoked fish and curried cauliflower Yorkshire puddings 122
smoked kahawai mishmash 107
snapper, crispy-skin, with oyster stew 139
snapper skin crackling 446
snapper tartare 50
snapper wings, spiced roasted, with ranch dressing 56
trevally, olive oil poached, with baba ganoush, roasted capsicum and mint 67
trevally sashimi with ponzu and truffle oil 37
trevally sashimi with soy syrup, wasabi peas and Kewpie mayo 46
whitebait fritters 114
whitebait on toast with tartare and fried egg 112
flounder, pan-fried, with seaweed butter 133
flour tortillas 442
friands, feijoa 396
fritters, oyster 64
fritters, tuatua and kūmara, with egg, gherkin and caper mayonnaise 71
fritters, whitebait 114

G
ganache, chocolate 380
game
  duck breast and fig salad on macadamia romesco 151
  duck shepherd's pie 154
  rabbit, braised, with fresh pappardelle, broad beans and golden raisins 232
  venison back strap with roasted eggplant and a burnt carrot, feta and date relish 229
garlic, roasted 205
gherkin and caper mayo, egg 71
ginger lime syrup 77
ginger parfait, feijoa and 326
gingernut lemon curd tarts 359
globe artichokes, crisp Parmesan-crumbed 278
gnocchi, sautéed, with roasted red capsicum, tomato and Parmesan 309
Granny Brown's peach chutney 426
grapefruit and orange marmalade 416
gravy, lamb 252
gravy, roast chicken 443
greengage plum jam 416

H
ham hock, smoked, with mustard panna cotta and pickle vinaigrette 262
hāpuka, poached, with battered pumpkin, pickled red onion rings and Kalamata olive mayo 108
hāpuka steaks with roasted fennel and lemon 136
hash, parsnip carrot 246
Haydo's nana's plum sauce 424
Haydo's sponge 349
hazelnuts, candied 447
horseradish, cream of, with fresh dill 49
hot sauce mayo 158
hummus 198

I
icing, chocolate 350

J
jalapeño peppers, pickled 420
jams *see* preserves
jellies *see* preserves

K
kahawai, battered, 'Mumbai tacos' with curry lime mayo and carrot mango chutney 78
kahawai ceviche with spiced creamed corn 43
kahawai cream, smoked 90
kahawai mishmash, smoked 107
kale, oven-roasted, with almond cream and dates 270
kasundi, eggplant 422
kasundi, tomato 286
kimchi, daikon 157
kimchi paste 430
kina, fried, on toast 52
kingfish sashimi with mandarin and dill 41
Kumar's spice mix 300
kūmara cakes, muttonbird and 158
kūmara fritters, tuatua and 71
kūmara mash 154
kūmara shoestring crisps 445

L
labneh, fresh coriander 178
lamb
  lamb gravy 252
  lamb shank empanadas with spiced yoghurt 214
  lamb sweetbreads with silverbeet, raisins and caper burnt butter 201
  lamb's fry with celeriac purée, radicchio and candied hazelnuts 223
  meatballs with spiced tomato lentils 210
  roast leg of lamb with caramelised Brussels sprouts and crab-apple jelly 252
  roasted lamb shoulder with parsnip carrot hash and mint chimichurri 246
  shaved lamb with white anchovies, roasted garlic and mint jelly 205
  spiced lamb shoulder chops with labneh, honey and dukkah 226
  spiced lamb tongue with hummus, feta, green olive and orange 198
lamingtons, passion-fruit 347
leg of lamb, roast, with caramelised Brussels sprouts and crab-apple jelly 252
lemon and herb croutons 446
lemon curd 337
lemon curd tarts, gingernut 359
lemon delicious with stewed rhubarb 335
lemon mayo, preserved 59

lemon shortbread 378
lemons, preserved 414
lentils
    creamed lentils 277
    dal 300
    radicchio lentils 249
    spiced tomato lentils 210
    spiced yoghurt lentils 277
lettuce, cos, with Depot ranch dressing, hot sauce and sweet spiced sunflower seeds 304
lime syrup 322
linguine, crayfish and clam 130

M

macadamia: crumble topping 332
macadamia nut brandy snaps 353
macadamia nut cobbler, tamarillo and pear 325
macadamia romesco 151
mackerel, grilled blue, sticky rice and kimchi 129
mandarin croutons 41
mango chutney, carrot 78
maple and paprika purée, pumpkin 219
marmalade, grapefruit and orange 416
mascarpone, orange cinnamon 328
mash, kūmara 154
mayos *see also* dressings; preserves
    condensed milk mayonnaise 426
    curry lime mayo 78
    egg, gherkin and caper mayo 71
    hot sauce mayo 158
    Kalamata olive mayo 108
    lemon mayo, preserved 59
    malt vinegar mayo 93
    preserved lemon mayo 59
    tarragon mayo 197
    wasabi mayo 77
    white anchovy mayo 205
meatballs with spiced tomato lentils 210
meatloaf, turkey, with whipped potato, gravy and cherry relish 170
meringues (for Eton mess) 337
meringues, coconut 322
meringues, Turkish delight 354
Mexican chicken tacos, charcoal roadside 174
mint chimichurri 246
mint jelly/sauce 430
mishmash, smoked kahawai 107
mock eel 285
mornay, mussels 94

muffins, bran, Aunty Edna's 377
mulled wine poached pears 338
mullet, raw, with cream of horseradish, apple and dill 49
'Mumbai tacos', battered kahawai, with curry lime mayo and carrot mango chutney 78
mushrooms
    fresh porcini and Swiss cheese toasties with truffle salt 282
    mock eel 285
mussels, battered, with malt vinegar mayo 93
mussels, grilled, with Café de Paris butter 89
mussels mornay 94
mustard panna cotta 262
mustard sauce 240
muttonbird and kūmara cakes with hot sauce mayo 158

N

nuts
    almond crunch, cinnamon 398
    almond praline 447
    almonds, paprika roasted 446
    candied hazelnuts 447
    candied walnuts 447
    cinnamon almond crunch 398
    dukkah 444
    hazelnuts, candied 447
    macadamia: crumble topping 332
    macadamia nut brandy snaps 353
    macadamia nut cobbler, tamarillo and pear 325
    macadamia romesco 151
    walnuts, candied 447

O

octopus, grilled, with chorizo, fried potatoes and rouille 124
oil, turmeric 443
olive mayo, Kalamata 108
onion, red, roasted fennel and 306
onion rings, pickled red 108
onions, tobacco 444
orange breadcrumbs, fried chilli and 219
orange butter, date and 398
orange cinnamon mascarpone 328
orange marmalade, grapefruit and 416
orange scones, cranberry and 372
oxtail, pulled, with soft Parmesan polenta 245

oyster fritters 64
oyster stew, crispy-skin snapper with 139
oysters, cinnamon 345

P

paddle crab fish fingers 63
pancakes, buttermilk 206
panna cotta, mustard 262
pappardelle, fresh 232
parfait, chicken liver, with pear liqueur jelly and fried bread 146
parfait, feijoa and ginger 326
Parmesan-crumbed globe artichokes, crisp 278
Parmesan polenta 245
parsnip carrot hash 246
parsnip salad, roasted, with goat's cheese, cranberries and rocket pesto 299
passion-fruit lamingtons 347
passion-fruit syrup 347
pasta
    braised rabbit with fresh pappardelle, broad beans and golden raisins 232
    crayfish and clam linguine 130
    sautéed gnocchi with roasted red capsicum, tomato and Parmesan 309
pastry, Eve's mum's 442
pāua pies 72
pavlova, my 315
pea and spinach croquettes 240
peach and pineapple crumble with coconut custard 332
peach chutney, Granny Brown's 426
peaches, honey and thyme poached 418
pear macadamia nut cobbler, tamarillo and 325
pear liqueur jelly 146
pears, mulled wine poached 338
pears, star anise and vanilla poached 417
pesto, basil 277
pesto, rocket 299
piccalilli 428
pickles *see also* preserves
    bread and butter pickles 420
    cucumber, pickled 83
    jalapeño peppers, pickled 420
    pickle juice jelly 431
    pickle vinaigrette 262
    red onion rings, pickled 108
pies
    chicken and chorizo pies 165
    duck shepherd's pie 154

fig and cranberry Christmas pies 401
lamb shank empanadas with spiced yoghurt 214
pastry, Eve's mum's 442
pāua pies 72
steak and kidney pie 238
pineapple crumble with coconut custard, peach and 332
plum, Black Doris, rhubarb and white chocolate trifle 318
plum jelly, Black Doris 318
plum sauce, Haydo's nana's 424
polenta, Parmesan 245
ponzu sauce 37
porcini, fresh, and Swiss cheese toasties with truffle salt 282
pork
    braised pork shoulder with radicchio lentils, caramelised pear and walnut relish 249
    meatballs with spiced tomato lentils 210
    pork brawn with apple and caraway salsa 193
    roasted pork knuckle with cream of caraway cabbage and caramelised apple 257
    spiced braised pork, buttermilk pancakes, smoked chipotle butter and maple syrup 206
potato, whipped 170
potato purée, citrus 116
praline, almond 447
preserves *see also* pickles
    apricots, poached, with saffron and cinnamon 417
    beetroot relish 428
    capsicum and chilli jam 429
    carrot, feta and date relish, burnt 229
    cherry relish 429
    chilli jam, capsicum and 429
    chutney, carrot mango 78
    chutney, Granny Brown's peach 426
    crab-apple jelly 431
    eggplant kasundi 422
    grapefruit and orange marmalade 416
    jam, capsicum and chilli 429
    jam, greengage plum 416
    jam, rhubarb and strawberry 416
    jam/paste, quince 414
    jelly, Black Doris plum 318
    jelly, crab-apple 431
    jelly, pear liqueur 146
    jelly, pickle juice 431

jelly/sauce, mint 430
kasundi, eggplant 422
kasundi, tomato 286
kimchi paste 430
lemons, preserved 414
marmalade, grapefruit and orange 416
mint jelly/sauce 430
orange marmalade, grapefruit and 416
peach chutney, Granny Brown's 426
peaches, honey and thyme poached 418
pear and walnut relish, caramelised 249
pear liqueur jelly 146
pears, star anise and vanilla poached 417
peppers, pickled jalapeño 420
piccalilli 428
plum jam, greengage 416
plum jelly, Black Doris 318
quince jam/paste 414
relish, beetroot 428
relish, burnt carrot, feta and date 229
relish, caramelised pear and walnut 249
relish, cherry 429
rhubarb and strawberry jam 416
tomato kasundi 286
tomato table sauce 424
pumpkin, battered 108
pumpkin, maple and paprika purée 219
pumpkin, roasted 300
pumpkin, spiced, with dal, yoghurt and curry leaves 300
Puspa's chicken curry 169

Q

quince, poached 328
quince jam/paste 414
quince sticky date pudding with orange cinnamon mascarpone and runny custard 328

R

rabbit, braised, with fresh pappardelle, broad beans and golden raisins 232
radicchio lentils 249
raisin and caper burnt butter 201
ranch dressing, Depot 304
raspberry and blue cheese salad, fig 281
refried black beans 174
relishes *see* preserves
rhubarb, stewed 335
rhubarb and strawberry jam 416

rice, sticky 129
rice pudding, coconut, with passion fruit, mango and meringue 322
roast chicken gravy 443
roast leg of lamb with caramelised Brussels sprouts and crab-apple jelly 252
roast vegetables 252
rocket pesto 299
romesco, macadamia 151
rouille 124

S

salads and slaws
    bitter green apple slaw 303
    cos lettuce with Depot ranch dressing, hot sauce and sweet spiced sunflower seeds 304
    duck breast and fig salad on macadamia romesco 151
    fig, raspberry and blue cheese salad 281
    roasted fennel and red onion salad with white anchovies 306
    roasted parsnip salad with goat's cheese, cranberries and rocket pesto 299
salmon crudo with apple and fennel 38
salsa, apple and caraway 193
salsa, tomatillo 174
salsa verde 289
salt and vinegar chip chicken schnitzel sandwiches 163
sandwiches and rolls
    crayfish rolls with thousand island sauce and pickled cucumber 83
    fresh porcini and Swiss cheese toasties with truffle salt 282
    salt and vinegar chip chicken schnitzel sandwiches 163
    tempura scallop butties with preserved lemon mayo 59
    'The Fed' chicken salad sandwich 180
sashimi, kingfish, with mandarin and dill 41
sashimi, trevally, with ponzu and truffle oil 37
sashimi, trevally, with soy syrup, wasabi peas and Kewpie mayo 46
sauces *see also* mayos and dressings; preserves
    apple sauce 273
    arrabbiata sauce 118
    basil pesto 277
    chimichurri, mint 246
    chocolate sauce 338

mint chimichurri 246
mint jelly/sauce 430
mornay sauce 94
mustard sauce 240
pesto, basil 277
pesto, rocket 299
plum sauce, Haydo's nana's 424
ponzu sauce 37
rocket pesto 299
romesco, macadamia 151
rouille 124
tartare sauce 112
thousand island sauce 83
tomato table sauce 424
scallop butties, tempura, with preserved lemon mayo 59
scallops, seared, with chorizo and citrus potato purée 116
schnitzel, chicken, salt and vinegar chip sandwiches 163
schnitzel, veal, with creamed celeriac and bitter green apple slaw 237
scones, cheese, with Parmesan and blue cheese butter 374
scones, cranberry and orange 372
scones, date and dried apricot, with jam and cream 360
seafood *see also* fish
  crab, paddle, fish fingers 63
  craydog with wasabi mayo and ginger lime syrup 77
  crayfish and clam linguine 130
  crayfish rolls with thousand island sauce and pickled cucumber 83
  kina, fried, on toast 52
  mussels, battered, with malt vinegar mayo 93
  mussels, grilled, with Café de Paris butter 89
  mussels mornay 94
  octopus, grilled, with chorizo, fried potatoes and rouille 124
  oyster fritters 64
  paddle crab fish fingers 63
  pāua pies 72
  scallop butties, tempura, with preserved lemon mayo 59
  scallops, seared, with chorizo and citrus potato purée 116
  seaweed butter 133
  squid, sautéed, with arrabbiata sauce and basil 118
  squid ink bruschetta 116

tuatua and kūmara fritters with egg, gherkin and caper mayonnaise 71
whitebait fritters 114
whitebait on toast with tartare and fried egg 112
seaweed butter 133
seeds, sunflower, sweet spiced 304
self-saucing pudding, chocolate, with espresso custard 316
shallot crunchies 445
shepherd's pie, duck 154
shoestring crisps, kūmara 445
short ribs, beef, with pumpkin, maple and paprika purée 219
shortbread, lemon 378
slaw, bitter green apple 303
smoked fish and curried cauliflower Yorkshire puddings 122
smoked ham hock with mustard panna cotta and pickle vinaigrette 262
smoked kahawai cream 90
smoked kahawai mishmash 107
snapper, crispy-skin, with oyster stew 139
snapper skin crackling 446
snapper tartare 50
snapper wings, spiced roasted, with ranch dressing 56
sour cream, cumin 165
soy and chilli cucumber, smashed 269
soy syrup 46
spice mix, Kumar's 300
spinach croquettes, pea and 240
sponge, Haydo's 349
sponge, lamington 347
sponge, trifle 318
sponge drops 342
squid, sautéed, with arrabbiata sauce and basil 118
squid ink bruschetta 116
steak and kidney pie 238
stewed rhubarb 335
sticky date pudding, quince, with orange cinnamon mascarpone and runny custard 328
sticky rice 129
strawberry jam, rhubarb and 416
sultana cake 394
sunflower seeds, sweet spiced 304
swede, truffled 224
sweetbreads, lamb, with silverbeet, raisins and caper burnt butter 201
Swiss roll, spiced chocolate, with quince jam 357

syrup, apple 49
syrup, ginger lime 77
syrup, lime 322
syrup, passion-fruit 347
syrup, soy 46

T
tacos, charcoal roadside Mexican chicken, with black beans and tomatillo salsa 174
tacos, chicken karaage, with fresh daikon kimchi and Kewpie 157
tacos, battered kahawai 'Mumbai', with curry lime mayo and carrot mango chutney 78
tamarillo and pear macadamia nut cobbler 325
tarragon mayo 197
tartare, snapper 50
tartare sauce 112
tarts, gingernut lemon curd 359
tempura batter 59, 78
tempura cauliflower with smoked kahawai cream 90
tempura scallop butties with preserved lemon mayo 59
thousand island sauce 83
toasties, fresh porcini and Swiss cheese 282
tobacco onions 444
tomatillo salsa 174
tomato kasundi 286
tomato lentils, spiced 210
tomato table sauce 424
tomatoes and capsicums, roasted 296
tongue, spiced lamb, with hummus, feta, green olive and orange 198
tortillas, flour 442
trevally, olive oil poached, with baba ganoush, roasted capsicum and mint 67
trevally sashimi with ponzu and truffle oil 37
trevally sashimi with soy syrup, wasabi peas and Kewpie mayo 46
trifle, Black Doris plum, rhubarb and white chocolate 318
tuatua and kūmara fritters with egg, gherkin and caper mayonnaise 71
turkey meatloaf with whipped potato, gravy and cherry relish 170
Turkish delight meringues 354
turmeric oil 443

V
vanilla poached pears, star anise and 417
veal schnitzel with creamed celeriac and bitter green apple slaw 237
venison back strap with roasted eggplant and a burnt carrot, feta and date relish 229
vinaigrette, pickle 262
vinaigrette, red wine 281

W
walnuts, candied 447
wasabi mayo 77
whipped potato 170
white chocolate custard 318
whitebait fritters 114
whitebait on toast with tartare and fried egg 112

Y
yoghurt
    chargrilled carrots with spiced eggplant and yoghurt 292
    fresh coriander labneh 178
    spiced yoghurt 214
    spiced yoghurt lentils 277
Yorkshire puddings, smoked fish and curried cauliflower 122

Image credits

Inside cover: artwork by Lisa Nicole Moes; **page 2**: artwork by Geoffrey Notman; **pages 30, 450, 460**: photographs © Sara McIntyre (annamilesgallery.com/artists/sara-mcintyre); **page 34**: 'Maori boys holding kina, Awanui district, Northland', Thelma Rene Kent. Alexander Turnbull Library, Wellington, New Zealand (ref: 1/2-010198-F); **page 81**: photograph by Paul Nankivell showing 'Gone Fishing' by artist Steve Trevella at the annual Hokitika Beach Driftwood & Sand event, 2013; **page 85**: Al Brown; **page 96**: artwork by Jenny Sahng; **page 97**: 'Ruatoki North, New Year's Day, 1973' by Ans Westra. Reproduced by permission. Suite Gallery, Wellington; **page 135**: vector art by Anna Zabella (Shutterstock ref 413855575); **page 142**: 'Woman with roast dinner', Crown Studios Ltd. Alexander Turnbull Library, Wellington, New Zealand (ref: 1/2-207979-F); **page 152**: 'Native birds of New Zealand', drawn on stone by W.S.D. Schmidt, printed by the Brett Printing and Publishing Company Ltd. Alexander Turnbull Library, Wellington, New Zealand (ref: C-066-008); background wall image by Shutterstock; **page 161**: 'Muttonbirds/Tītī/Sooty Shearwater', Crown copyright Department of Conservation/Te Papa Atawhai; **page 173**: photograph by Paul Nankivell showing sculpture by artist Donald Buglass at the annual Hokitika Beach Driftwood & Sand event, 2013; **page 190**: 'Sheep walking along a drive, Mangamahu', Robert E. Wells. Alexander Turnbull Library, Wellington, New Zealand (ref: 1/4-110384-F); **page 266**: 'Near Rangitukia, East Coast, 1963' by Ans Westra. Reproduced by permission. Suite Gallery, Wellington; **page 312**: 'Mrs Eunice [Barr?], competitor in an apple pie baking contest', Evening Post. Alexander Turnbull Library, Wellington, New Zealand (ref: EP/1959/2588-F); **page 362**: 'Baking hot cross (Easter) buns', Evening Post. Alexander Turnbull Library, Wellington, New Zealand (ref: EP/1955/0682-F); **page 402**: 'Model demonstrating Agee preserving jars in water bath', K.E. Niven and Co. Alexander Turnbull Library, Wellington, New Zealand (ref: 1/2-209805-F); **page 436**: photograph © Rees Osborne, originally published in A Taste of Kiwi, edited by Jan Bilton (Hospitality Press, 1987). Reproduced by permission of Jan Bilton.

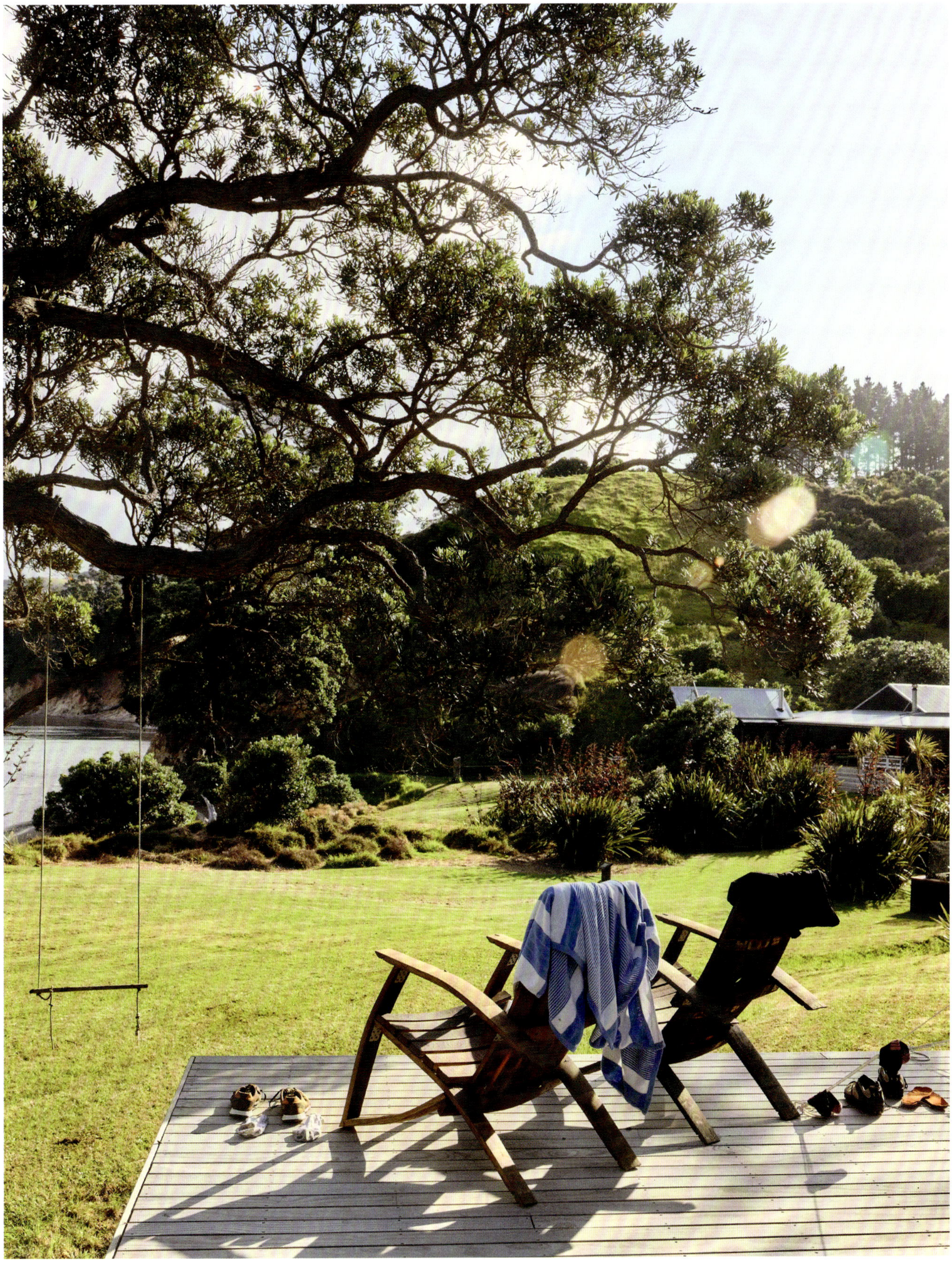

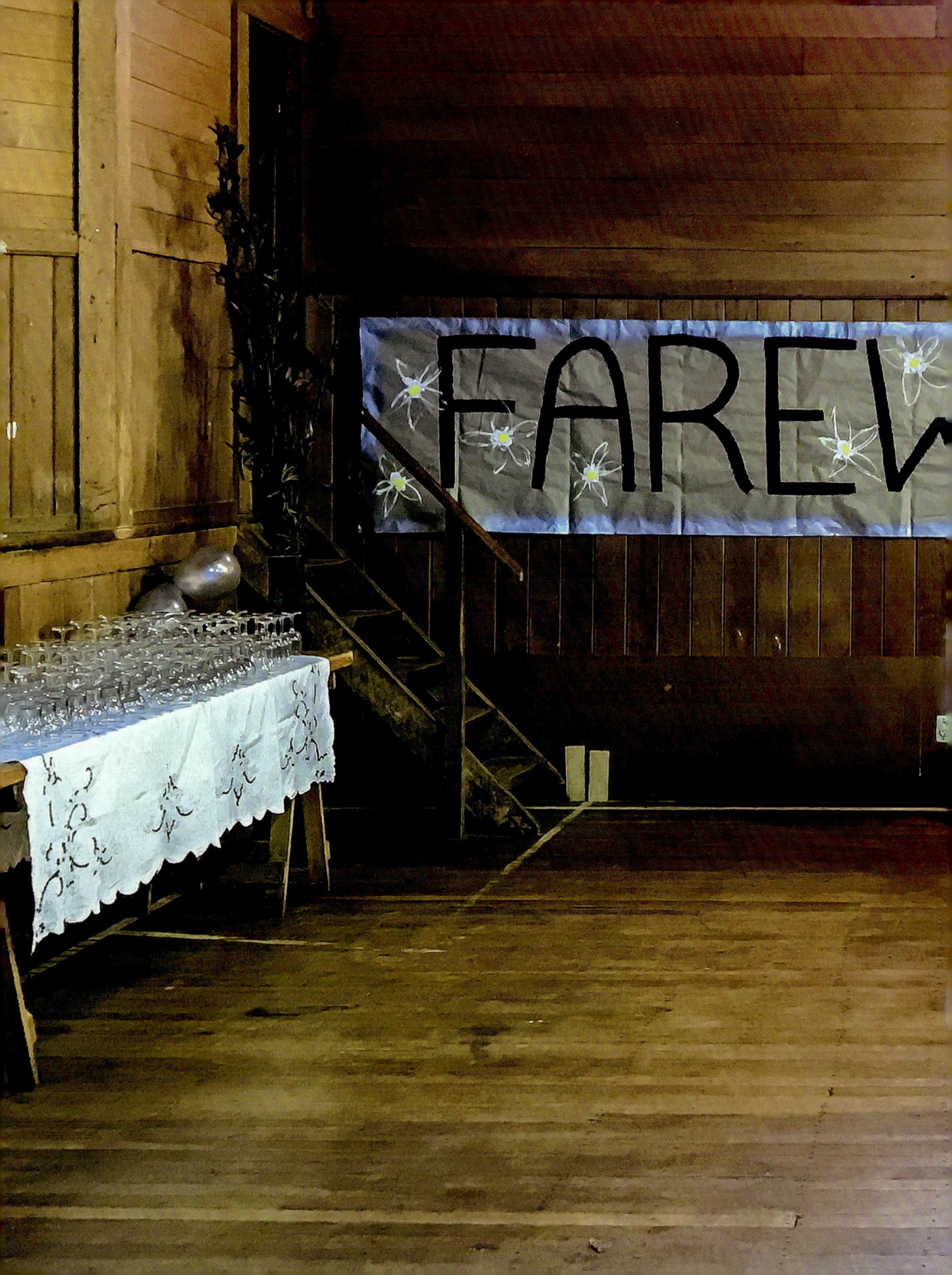
FAREW

Let us give thanks / He mihi

Revisiting and revising *Eat Up New Zealand* into 'The Bach Edition' has been a really fun and rewarding experience. Six years have passed since it originally hit the shelves, and flicking through it still makes me proud, as it feels just as relevant now as it did back then.

It felt very much like that saying 'getting the band back together', and it's super to have the opportunity to thank all the main players once more.

There can only be one person at the top of any list and, as so often is the case, Haydo (Hayden Scott) is always there—or thereabouts. I have had the pleasure and honour of working alongside Haydo for close to fifteen years. Anyone who has had the good fortune of meeting Haydo will attest to the fact that he is an exceptional human being. *Eat Up* is the third book that we have worked on together and I wouldn't mind betting that it's our favourite. Thanks, Haydo, for working so tirelessly. Your 'up-ness' always brings a positive energy to whatever we are grappling with. Thanks also for being such a damn good cook and for putting your personal stamp on this publication. And, more importantly, thanks for being such a wonderful and special friend.

Josh Griggs is the young genius behind the lens of the photos in *Eat Up*. Josh constantly reminds me that, while we all work hard on our individual talents, there are a lucky few who are truly gifted. Thanks, Josh, for putting your heart and soul into this book. You must excuse the pun, but the proof is in the pudding—from the first click of the shutter, you nailed the brief in every aspect. It's been an absolute pleasure to work alongside you on both editions, Josh. Thanks, chum.

Gary Stewart is responsible for the clever collateral around all of the Al Brown & Co businesses—all the postcards, the T-shirts, the menus, the websites, the taglines, all the packaging and all the branding. 'The G' is across every endeavour we take on, creating the personality and breathing the life into each unique enterprise. I can never really thank you enough; it's almost becoming embarrassing. *Eat Up* is the seventh book that we have worked on together. I don't know how you do it, but I'm extremely fortunate that you do. You have an extraordinary eye for detail, a lightning-speed wit and a mind that wanders into places that us other mere mortals didn't know existed. G, I feel very fortunate to call you a close friend, and here I go again. Thanks again, bud, for everything.

A big thank you must also go out to Victoria Bell, who worked tirelessly alongside Josh on the first edition, propping and styling all the recipe shots. It was a fun eighteen months working with you, Vic. Thanks for putting in all that effort to find the textures, plates and backgrounds to make the food look so deliciously edible.

A special mention and thank you must also go out to Dana Johanson. Everyone needs a Dana. Dana worked on the first edition and was responsible for keeping the whole project in order and on track. Dana was all over the communication and relationships at every touchpoint of the book, as well as all the marketing and point-of-sale. A massive thanks to you, Dana, for the way you kept everything behind the scenes ticking over, and for being a great sounding board and part-time editor on the project.

To Jenny Hellen and her team at Allen & Unwin, thank you for being so patient and understanding about the amount of time it took to put this beautiful book together. Jenny has been my publisher for every book I have written, and while there is always plenty of discussion and at times 'push back' I believe there are also equal amounts of passion, respect and admiration for each other. Thanks once again for believing in me and for giving me these opportunities.

To the talented potters and ceramicists whose work appears in this book, thank you all. You have each added another individual, unique layer of goodness to *Eat Up*, with your stunning bowls, plates and platters. A special mention of thanks to:

- Holly at Houston Design Co.
- Peter and Judy at Collis Studio
- Peter at Factory Ceramics
- Janel Scott at OKAY Ceramics
- Katherine Smyth
- Felicity at Wundaire
- Paul Melser
- Tony Sly
- Steiner Ceramics

Also to Lee at Hollywood Props, Cameron at Flotsam & Jetsam, Bernard at Molloy's Mega Antique Centre, Lodge Cast Iron, Citta and Nest for being always willing to let us raid your shelves at a moment's notice.

Also a massive thank you to Kate and Craig from Carve. These special two donated all the beef, lamb and pork products for the development and photos of the recipes. It's been a pleasure working with you both for more than a decade now. I don't know how many lamb ribs, veal schnitzels or pork hocks we have sold in the restaurants over that time, but what I can tell you is that I rest easy at night knowing the quality of product that you supply every day of the week is always top shelf, first class and A+.

A big shout-out and thank you to Neil, Lea and Troy Bramley from Tora in the Wairarapa, as well as to Andy, Kim, Frances and the amazing crew at Black Barn in the Hawke's Bay. Thanks for being so darn generous with your time and organisation around those two very special road-trip photo shoots. And a big thanks to Sara McIntyre for making available some of her gorgeous work to complete the package.

To anyone I have missed, I apologise, and let's just put that down to early signs of Alzheimer's! Thank you all.

—Al